The Library Reference Series

BASIC REFERENCE SOURCES

The Library Reference Series

Lee Ash
General Editor

LOCAL INDEXES
IN
AMERICAN LIBRARIES

A UNION LIST OF UNPUBLISHED INDEXES

Compiled by
Junior Members Round Table
American Library Association

Edited by
Norma Olin Ireland
National Chairman, JMRT, 1938-1939
and
National Editorial Committee of Junior Members

GREGG PRESS
Boston 1972

This is a complete photographic reprint of a work
first published in Boston by the F. W. Faxon Company in 1947.

First Gregg Press edition published 1972.

Copyright 1947 by the F. W. Faxon Company
Reprinted with permission.

Printed on permanent/durable acid-free paper in
The United States of America.

Library of Congress Cataloging in Publication Data

American Library Association. Junior Members Round Table.
   Local indexes in American libraries.

   Reprint of the 1947 ed., which was issued as no. 73 of
Useful reference series.
    1. Indexes--Bibliography. 2. Libraries–United
States. I. Ireland, Norma (Olin) 1907- ed. II. Ti-
tle. III. Series: Useful reference series, no. 73.
Z6293.A5 1972   017'.5   72-6992
ISBN 0-8398-0852-6

Useful Reference Series No. 73

LOCAL INDEXES IN
AMERICAN LIBRARIES

LOCAL INDEXES

IN

AMERICAN LIBRARIES

A UNION LIST OF UNPUBLISHED INDEXES

Compiled by

Junior Members Round Table
American Library Association

Edited by

Norma Olin Ireland
National Chairman, JMRT, 1938-1939
and
National Editorial Committee of Junior Members

The F. W. Faxon Company · *Boston*

1947

Copyright by
THE F. W. FAXON COMPANY
1947

PRINTED IN THE UNITED STATES OF AMERICA
BY THE VAIL-BALLOU PRESS, INC., BINGHAMTON, N. Y.

PREFACE

Begun in 1939 as a project of the Junior Members Round Table of the American Library Association, this work was completed in wartime—which fact has necessarily postponed publication. Time is no factor in its usefulness, however, as most of the indexes are currently in process, except for those historical types which are entirely completed. While the number of entries may, in some instances be changed, the lack of personnel has perhaps halted the continuation of many of the indexes until the postwar period. In most cases, therefore, the status of the indexes has not been changed to any extent from the date when they were orginally recorded.

Size and Scope

Approximately 8000 indexes were submitted for this work, from 950 libraries, not counting separate branches. While editing has reduced both figures, the number of libraries cooperating in this work is still the largest contributing to any union list yet published, with the possible exception of the combined *Gregory's*.[1,2] Over 2500 different subject headings are used, not counting cross-references, the subjects varying from the most popular topics of the day to some of the most specialized and scholarly subjects possible.

Hundreds of individual periodicals and newspapers have been indexed by libraries, as well as a great number of books and other local material. This field of indexing clearly shows the duplication of effort existing in libraries today, the avoidance of which is one of the primary purposes of this latter work.

Compilation and Acknowledgments

Twenty-nine Junior Member state groups took part in the project, including over 100 individual librarians. To them should go most of the credit for this work, and a complete list of acknowledgments is included on pp. xiii-xiv.

I wish to give special acknowledgment and thanks to Dr. Robert Alvarez and Dr. Willard A. Heaps, members of the Editorial committee who assisted in the preliminary editorial work until 1942. I wish to thank also several individuals and organizations who advised and encouraged us in the project: Dr. Joseph Wheeler, whose cooperative indexing ideas encouraged us in the purpose of this work; Miss Althea Warren, who advised us in so many ways; Mr. Everett O. Fontaine, who gave us many helpful editorial tips; The Ameri-

---

1. Gregory, Winifred, ed. Union list of serials in libraries of the U.S. and Canada. N.Y., Wilson, 1927-1933 & Supplements.

2. Gregory, Winifred, ed. American newspapers, 1821-1936; a union list of files available in the United States and Canada. N.Y., Wilson, 1937.

can Library Association, whose provision of funds for committee expenses made the beginning of the project possible; and the Editors of the *American Library Association Bulletin, Wilson Library Bulletin, Special Libraries, Library Journal, College and Research Libraries,* and the many state and local library organs, for their publicity of the project.

No acknowledgment would be complete, however, without mention of the National Committee. The members of this three-year committee canvassed the 19 unorganized states (i.e., states without Junior Member groups), District of Columbia, Hawaiian Islands and Canada, making an average of 2 states per member. The final Editorial Committee functioned from 1941–1942, when the call of war duties made its continuance impossible. This latter committee established policies of form and arrangement, ironed out problems and re-checked libraries for incomplete entries. The Editor has worked alone since that date, so all final inconsistencies, mistakes and omissions must be credited to her alone.

Origin

The idea for this work was based on 3 earlier publications. The first,[3] entitled *Special indexes in American libraries* is only a small pamphlet long since out-of-date, but it was, nevertheless, the basic idea back of this work. The second,[4] *Special indexes in Missouri libraries* was a local, mimeographed work which was a project of the Junior Members of that state. In this was observed the current use of such a list, and the possibility of its expansion on a national basis. The third publication [5] was the Editor's *Index to indexes,* a list of published indexes. *Local indexes* was planned, therefore, as a list of unpublished indexes to make a useful and necessary companion for this work.

After the work was started, it received a further impetus by the article [6] entitled *Needed, a union list of card files* by Robert Alvarez in one of the library periodicals. Dr. Alvarez was then enlisted for help on the project and became a member of the National Committee and the final Editorial Committee.

State Lists

A few copies of state lists, separately issued, may still be available, see pp xv. It must be noted, however, that their arrangement and form differ from this work and such lists are not part of this national union list. They have been issued by the individual state groups and the inclusion of entries has been based on local needs. Inquiries should be addressed to the chairmen of the committees for the states, as named on pp xiii-xiv, or to the editors of the library publications noted.

3. American Library Association. Special indexes in American libraries; a list of subjects separately cataloged or so arranged as to be readily accessible. Chicago, A.L.A., 1917.
4. Special indexes in Missouri libraries. 12p., mim.
5. Ireland, Norma Olin. An index to indexes. Faxon, 1942.
6. Alvarez, Robert S. Needed! A union list of card files. Library journal, 64:395-396, May 15, 1939.

Symbols

A letter-number combination system of symbols is used, for ease and speed in using the index. The system uses *Gregory*[7] as an authority for state symbols, but uses numbers rather than letters for further expansion. The numbers are based on the alphabetical arrangement of libraries within each state. A List of Cooperating Libraries, with Key to Symbols, appears on pp xvi-xxxi. Libraries from all 48 states are represented, as well as the Hawaiian Islands, Puerto Rico and Canada.

In regard to omissions, it must be noted that some libraries did not contribute for various reasons: 1. Lack of staff to compile list, 2. Indexes too small or unimportant, 3. Did not recognize usefulness of such a union list. All large and medium-size libraries were solicited: public, college, university and special, and many smaller libraries including school libraries. Notices appeared in the various library periodicals, both national and state, so that every library must surely have been informed of the project and could have contributed if they cared to do so.

In the few cases where there are gaps in the numbering of the symbols, the reason is that libraries originally assigned these symbols have been withdrawn due to the fact that the indexes submitted were not included. Reassignment of symbols would have necessitated a complete change of all symbols within the state, which would have affected hundreds of indexes. Libraries with numbers plus small letters were added after the main list of symbols was drawn up.

Abbreviations

The authority for abbreviations used is *Webster*.[8] Some exceptions are those commonly used in library practice, for instance *j* for juvenile. A list of Abbreviations Used in This Work is found on pp xxxii-xxxiv. Names of departments and collections (as found in symbols throughout the list) are included in list of abbreviations, except when proper names. In the latter case they are included in the List of Symbols. Since names of branches are proper names, they are indicated only in List of Symbols.

Abbreviations are used for words used most frequently throughout the work, and where the meanings are clearly recognizable. In case of multiple meanings, such abbreviations are used only when subject of index prevents any resulting confusion. Abbreviations for states, since commonly known, are not included in the list of abbreviations.

Subject Headings

The authority for subject headings in twofold: 1. Sears[9] and 2. *A Special list of subject headings prepared for Local Indexes*, unpublished. Subject headings are expressed, as far as possible, in the words of contributing libraries

7. Op. cit.
8. Webster's collegiate dictionary. Merriam, 1938, 5th ed.
9. Sears, Minnie, ed. List of subject headings for small libraries. Fourth ed. rev. by Isabel Stevenson Monro. Wilson, 1941.

with uniformity as the first essential. The headings are simple, but minute when necessary in order to facilitate the use of the work. In view of the fact that headings for indexes are different from those for books, some variation in current practice is allowed, especially in regard to locality. Some questions may be raised concerning our use of subdivisions when only one or two indexes are noted. To justify our practice, we point out that in the case of the Reader's Guide supplements, this fact is also true, and because of this fact they are quickly and easily used.

Both *see* and *see also* references are used. In the case of analytical cross-references, the symbol of the library is given as well as the subject, in order that the index may be quickly located. For specific books and periodicals which are analytical entries, the word *In* is used.

Certain decisions have been made regarding various subjects and subdivisions, which users of the index should understand. They are, as follows:

1. *Two or more subjects*

    When an index contains 2 or more subjects, we have put the main entry under the first or more inclusive subject, with an analytical or partial entry from the others, the latter giving the symbol of the library as well as the subject. Main entry gives full description, thus partial entries save space and unnecessary repetition.

2. *Exhaustive search*

    When exhaustive search is to be made of any subject, it must be remembered to use periodical references in the field, also. For instance if the student is searching for all indexes on Science, he should check names of periodicals on the subject, including publications of colleges, etc.

3. *Locality subdivisions, etc.*

    Locality subdivisions are used for most subjects, with cross-references from locality. Some subjects are put directly under locality, however; we have made variations in library practice when the local usefulness of the index seemed to warrant it. For instance GENEALOGY is subdivided by locality, but the following related subjects are placed directly under locality: CEMETERY RECORDS, CENSUS, DEEDS, NECROLOGY, REGISTERS OF BIRTHS, WILLS, etc.

    No cross-references from states to counties, cities or towns are made. Therefore, those searching for material on MASSACHUSETTS, must remember to check under BOSTON, and other cities and towns in the state.

4. *Bibliographies*

    Bibliographies which are valuable as such, altho not strictly indexes, are located in APPENDIX I, under List of Bibliographies. Cross-references to subjects in this list are included in the main section, in order that the APPENDIX may be easily used altho it is a separate alphabet.

5. *Special Collections*
   Indexes to special collections go under the subject. Cross-reference from the name of library or collection is made only if latter is very well-known. Union lists are placed under the name of subject also, i.e. HAWAII—UNION LISTS, in List of Bibliographies.
6. *Foreign Indexes*
   Foreign indexes are put under the subject, with subdivision FOREIGN LANGUAGES, i.e. PLAYS ONE ACT—FOREIGN LANGUAGES. If one definite language is indicated, then we have subdivided by adjective of nationality, i.e. PLAYS, FRENCH.
7. *Military Service*
   For indexes on military service, we have used names of localities as subdivisions, under names of wars. For instance Virginia's part in the Revolution would be found under the heading U.S.—HISTORY—REVOLUTION—VIRGINIA, with a cross-reference from VIRGINIA—SOLDIERS. The latter heading could be used as a main entry, however, if the index did not specify a certain war.
8. *Fiction*
   We have used the heading FICTION, subdivided by special subject and localities, with appropriate cross-references. Special subjects stories, however, are put under separate headings, i.e. HUMOROUS STORIES, SEA STORIES, etc.
9. *Law; Glossaries; Imprints*
   Law is subdivided by locality and subject. We have used the heading GLOSSARIES for indexes of more than one glossary; for special subject glossaries we have used this term as a subdivision. For imprints we have used BIBLIOGRAPHY—IMPRINTS, as subdivision of locality, i.e. CONNECTICUT—BIBLIOGRAPHY—IMPRINTS.

Arrangement

In any national list, location is of first importance, after subject of course. Indexes are therefore arranged by symbol, under each subject. The size of index, or in the case of periodicals the period covered, comes next. In all main entries, the number of cards or pages is given, except in a few "unestimated" cases. When the number of catalog-drawers was given, we have estimated the number of cards, counting 1320 to a regulation drawer.

Since titles of indexes are mere handles for convenience in reporting, it was decided to omit them. When the indexes cannot be sufficiently described by subject headings, further description is given under the scope. Frequency of additions is the last item indicated. Periodicals and newspapers are the exceptions in the arrangement by subject, see below.

Periodicals and Newspapers

Indexes of individual periodicals are placed under the name of periodical. Indexes of individual newspapers are placed under the name of the city where published, except in the case of a general paper, such as *Christian Science Monitor*.

Indexes of several periodicals or newspapers are put under subjects or locality, according to subject of index, i.e. ART—PERIODICALS; CANADA —PERIODICALS, with cross-references (analytical entries from names of individual periodicals or newspapers, when listed). Dates of runs are not usually included with these indexes.

We have omitted duplicates of published cumulative indexes of periodicals unless years were more inclusive than those issued. *An index to indexes* [10] has been used as an authority for such indexes. In the case of merged or changed periodical runs, entry is by latest title, with *Gregory* [11] as an authority for name.

We have not included short runs, unless of definite historical value, or if magazine has ceased publication after a short life. We include volumes and years for individual periodicals whenever possible, but for individual newspapers, years alone are sufficient. Some periodicals, altho indexed in current periodical indexes, are included because of their special subject indexing.

The abbreviation for newspaper (newsp.) is given in parenthesis after individual entries for newspapers. The abbreviation for periodical (per.) is given only after those individual periodicals whose titles do not indicate that they are periodicals. For instance, all periodicals with magazine, journal, quarterly or review in their titles are self-explanatory.

Books

A great many books and sets of books have been indexed by libraries. Because the subject is usually of primary importance, such as in local historical volumes, the main entry is by subject. Cross-references are made from titles and series. An Author List of Books Indexed is included in Appendix II, pp 218-220. Author, title, publisher and date are given.

Some books with existing indexes and a few books of large scope (encyclopedias) have been included, because of special subject indexing, as in the case of some indexed periodicals.

Ephemeral Material

Pamphlet and picture file indexes, clippings and scrapbooks have been generally omitted, with a few 'exceptions. Those of historical interest and permanent value, as judged from their subject-matter and completeness, have been retained.

Maps are subdivided by subjects and locality, with cross-references from same. Pictures are divided by subject and locality similarly. Paintings, Drawings and Engravings, Photographs and Portraits are all used as separate subjects. The same rule is followed for headings which are cross-references, except in the case of Photographs; the latter is used also as a subdivision of an-

10. Op. cit.
11. Op. cit.

other subject. Pamphlets may also be used as a subdivision under the subject, i.e. ART—PAMPHLETS.

Omissions

Omissions include five different classes of indexes: (1) Indexes to pamphlet and picture files, already mentioned (2) Shelf-lists and library catalogs, unless unusual subject collections (3) Personal libraries (4) Gifts (5) Clippings and scrapbooks, with exceptions noted before (6) Very small indexes of a subject in which the majority of indexes are large, i.e. SHORT STORIES (7) Printed indexes, including those to periodicals (8) College undergraduate magazines and newspapers. (This does not mean extension or scientific publications which *are* included; general indexes to college material and faculty publications are included if extensive).

Weeding out of unimportant indexes was not always easy, because in many cases it was difficult to discern their importance from the titles and description. Perhaps some indexes have been wrongly omitted; then again probably more should have been omitted. Altho some seemingly limited indexes are included, the reason is that they were considered especially helpful to nearby libraries.

Some may voice the question, "Isn't it obvious that a certain library should have such an index?" The answer is "Not always, no." This may be shown by several examples. For instance, genealogical indexes are very spotty and a nearby city may have a much better group of files than the town concerned. A particular library, in our acquaintance, has a very complete index of historical material on all cities and towns in the area—better than the cities and towns themselves, in many cases. Such indexes are of special interest to scholars and will save needless search of many libraries. Some indexes to faculty and alumni publications are likewise included, because of the special subjects included which are not available elsewhere.

Uniformity, Incomplete Indexes

Our committee has striven for uniformity throughout the work, but in the case of some few incomplete indexes, this has not always been possible. As stated earlier, one of the purposes of the Editorial Committee was to recheck with libraries on information lacking in the indexes they submitted. In all cases of such lacks, we have written to the libraries for further information, but of course the response was not 100%. We have, however, done the best we could do under the circumstances. We have included some incomplete indexes because we were convinced of their usefulness. We did not feel justified in omitting indexes just because they did not give the number of entries or frequency of additions.

Filing

We have used the *Cleveland public library Filing Rules* [12] as our authority

12. Filing rules for the arrangement of the dictionary catalogs of the Cleveland public library, 1929.

on filing. But here again, we have made exceptions according to our needs. Our headings do not represent individual books and therefore various problems arose which were necessarily solved according to our best judgment.

Co-operative Indexing

Avoidance of duplication of effort in indexing is one of the primary purposes of this book, as stated above. Another purpose is to promote the idea of co-operative indexing. In *College and research libraries* for December 1944,[13] we have outlined a practical plan for co-operative indexing, based on *Local Indexes*.

We have also stressed the use of *Local Indexes* as a basis for future published indexes. A study of this work will suggest many needs in the library field which are being met locally and which should be expanded into larger publications.

And so, to the librarians, students and scholars of to-morrow, we give this work, *Local Indexes in American Libraries*.

13. Ireland, Norma Olin. Cooperative indexing: a postwar program to-day. College and Research libraries, 6:73–75, Dec., 1944.

COMMITTEE ACKNOWLEDGMENTS

NATIONAL COMMITTEES
1941–42 *Editorial Committee*
Dr. Robert Alvarez
Dr. Willard A. Heaps
1940–41 *National Committee*
Dr. Robert Alvarez
Luis Bejarano
Mary E. Brindley
Mary Frances Focke
Dr. Willard A. Heaps
Mary Worthington Sander
Ruth Yarnell Stern
1939–40 *National Committee*
Mary E. Brindley
Ruth Ferguson
Mary Frances Focke
Dr. Willard A. Heaps
Esther Park
Ruth Yarnell Stern
Mary Eleanor Wright

STATE COMMITTEES

Alabama
Marie Drolet, chmn.

Arkansas
Mrs. Vara Hardcastle Greene, chmn.

California
Yetive Applegate, chmn.
Elizabeth Davison
Mollie Dreizen
E. Ben Evans
Neal Harlow
Armine McKenzie
Ann O'Connor
Flora Elizabeth Reynolds
Doris Stratton
Helen Thornton

Colorado
Jane Gould, chmn.
Leona Galerneau
Elizabeth Knowles
Louise Smith

Connecticut
Mrs. Virginia W. Smith, chmn., 1940–41
Elizabeth Angelo, chmn., 1939–40

Georgia
Agnes Barnes, chmn.
Carolyn Adams
Teresa W. Atkinson
Margaret Lloyd
Margaret Parker
Advisors: Dr. Ralph H. Parker, Hazel Philpatrick

Illinois
Mrs. Martha Banker Stahl, chmn.
Mrs. Margaret Pittman Baird
Elizabeth Burr
Elizabeth Curry
D. Genevieve Dixon
Elinor Johnson
Allan Laursen
Mrs. Melba E. McCoy
Ralph E. McCoy
Albert Rechteger
Harold Teitelbaum
Advisors: Ethel Bond, Amelia Krieg, Rose Phelps

Indiana
Harriet Golay, chmn., 1940–41
Irene Mason, chmn., 1939–40

Iowa
Victoria Hargrave, chmn.
Hazel Conway
Fred Folmer
Virginia Irwin

Kansas
Elizabeth Kellam, chmn.
Maralea Arnett
Teressa R. Fox
Virginia Richard

Kentucky
Caroline Reading, chmn.
Bess Gilbert
Ida Greenleaf
Genevieve Montgomery
Virginia Woodson

Louisiana
Clara Griffon, chmn., 1940–41
Mrs. Lucile Althar Tindol, chmn., 1939–40

Louisiana (ctd.)
  Mrs. Maude Oakland Broussard
  Mrs. Edwarda Parsons Macmurdo
  Mrs. Dorothy Steidman
Maryland
  Barbara Porteus, chmn.
  Agnes Gautreaux
  Forrest L. Mills
Michigan
  Carroll Moreland, chmn.
  John R. Bannister
Minnesota
  Florence Link, chmn.
  Olga Berggren
  Mary Ellsworth
  Mrs. I. Jean Meltzer
  Myra Obershulte
Mississippi
  Mrs. Hobson Houston, chmn.
Missouri
  Carl Dahl, chmn.
  Abigail Holmes
  Katherine McNabb
  Constance Pfaff
  Constance Wellman
  Mary E. Wright
Nebraska
  Eloise Ebert, chmn.
  Adeline Proulx
  Elizabeth Rubendall
New Jersey
  Beatrice Stackhouse, chmn.
New York
  Mildred Woodcock, chmn.
  William Bacon
  Luis Bejarano
  Muriel L. Block
  Helen M. Brown
  Catherine Cardew
  Margaret A. Kateley
  Florence A. Kramer
  Kathryn Leonhard
  Sarah Moore
  Dorothy Morgester
  Violet Myer
  Marian Smith
  Virginia Stockwell
  Helen Winter
  Advisors: John Connor, Florence K. Young

North Carolina
  Evelyn Parks, chmn.
Ohio
  Mildred Stibitz, co-chmn.
  Mary Sommerville, co-chmn.
  Pauline Clemen
  Mrs. Thelma Robinson
  Advisors: Estelle Culp, Mary O'Hare
Oklahoma
  Lee Spencer, chmn.
Pennsylvania
  Elsie M. Kresge, chmn.
  Dorothy A. Adams
  Rebecca K. Bonner
  Sara Louise Elder
  Isabelle Entrikin
  Esther Fox
  Robert Grazier
  Mrs. Robert Hassenplug
  Elizabeth Kane
  Jean May
  B. Elizabeth Ulrich
  Esther Weber
  Mrs. William Yeagley
  Advisors: Gladys R. Cranmer, Dorothy Heiderstadt, Evelyn Hensel, Alfred Decker Keator, Margaret Knoll, W. P. Lewis, Nellie Stevens, Katherine Stokes, Donald Thompson
Puerto Rico (U.S. possession)
  Gretchen Garrison, chmn.
Tennessee
  Estellene Walker, chmn.
Texas
  Mrs. Grace Green Roberts, chmn.
Virginia
  John W. Dudley, chmn.
  Ellen Carlson
  Mae Graham
  Eleanor Lucas
  Elizabeth Vaiden
Washington (state)
  William Tucker, chmn.
Wisconsin
  Gerald Caffrey, chmn.
  Katherine M. Connelly
  Emma Diekroeger
  Evelyn Ann Smith
  Irene E. Varney

STATE LISTS, SEPARATELY ISSUED

COLORADO
Local indexes of Colorado. 8p., typed

GEORGIA
Local indexes in Georgia libraries. 14p., mim.

ILLINOIS
Local indexes in Illinois libraries
In Illinois libraries 23:5–32 Oct. 1941

INDIANA
Subject list of home-made indexes in Indiana
In Library occurrent 13:179–184 April–June 1940
Supplement to Subject list of home-made indexes in Indiana libraries. 7p., typed

IOWA
Local indexes in Iowa libraries
In Iowa library quarterly 14:32 April–May–June 1941; 14:60–64 Oct.–Nov.–Dec. 1941

KANSAS
Kansas local indexes. 10p., typed

KENTUCKY
Local indexes in Kentucky libraries. 39p., mim.

MARYLAND
Union list of indexes in the state of Maryland. 7p., mim.

MINNESOTA
Local indexes and bibliographies in Minnesota libraries. 59p., typed

MISSOURI
Special indexes in Missouri libraries. 12p., mim.

NEW YORK
Local indexes in New York libraries. 42p., mim.

NORTH CAROLINA
Local indexes in the libraries of the state of North Carolina. 7p., typed

OHIO
Local indexes in Ohio libraries. 63p., typed

PENNSYLVANIA
Local indexes in Pennsylvania libraries
In Pa. library and museum notes 17:1–56 Oct. 1940

TENNESSEE
(Local indexes in Tennessee libraries). 17p., typed

TEXAS
Local indexes of Texas. 13p., mim.

WASHINGTON (state)
"Home-made" indexes in Washington libraries. 13 p., mim.
(More complete report, for loan only. 29p. Wash. state lib.)

LIST OF COOPERATING LIBRARIES WITH KEY TO SYMBOLS

(Note: Does not include symbols for general departments of large libraries. *See* LIST OF ABBREVIATIONS).

A	**Alabama**
A1	Montgomery. State dept. of archives & history
Ar	**Arkansas**
Ar2	Fayetteville. University of Arkansas library
Ar3	Fayetteville. High school library
Ar4	Jonesboro. Creighead county library
Ar5	Little Rock. Public library
Ar6	Russelville. High school library
Az	**Arizona**
Az1	Tucson. University of Arizona library
C	**California**
C1	Alameda. Free library
C2	Albany. High school library
C3	Alhambra. Public library
C3a	Altadena. Ireland book & library service
C4	Anaheim. Public library
C5	Azusa. Citrus union high school & junior college library
C6	Bakersfield. Kern county free library
C7	Berkeley. High school library
C8	Berkeley. Public library
C9	Barkeley. U.S. forest service. California forest. & range experiment station library
C10	Burlingame. Public library
C11	Claremont. Claremont colleges library
C12	Claremont. Pomona college library
C13	Daly City. Public library
C15	Eureka. Free library
C16	Eureka. Senior high school library
C17	Fullerton. Public library
C18	Glendale. Public library
C19	Hanford. High school library
C20	Hanford. Kings county free library
C21	Healdsburg. High school library
C22	Hollister. San Benito county free library
C23	Hollywood. Academy of motion picture arts & sciences library
C24	Hollywood. Paramount pictures, Inc. Research dept. library
C25	Hollywood. Twentieth Century-Fox film corporation. Research dept. library
C26	Lodi. Public library
C27	Long Beach. Public library
C28	Los Angeles. Calif. state relief admin. research library
C29	Los Angeles. College of osteopathic physicians & surgeons library
C30	Los Angeles. County health dept. library
C31	Los Angeles. County public library
C32	Los Angeles. Public library
C33	Los Angeles. Sixth district agricultural assoc. library
C34	Los Angeles. University of Southern Calif. Doheny library
C34-Hoose	Hoose library
C35	Los Angeles. White memorial medical library
C36	Los Gatos. Public library
C37	Marysville. City library
C38	Modesto. McHenry public library
C39	Modesto. High school library
C40	Napa. Goodman library
C41	Oakland. Hamilton junior high school library
C42	Oakland. Lockwood junior high school library
C43	Oakland. Free library

C44	Oakland. Safeway stores. Homemakers' bureau library	C81	Santa Monica. Public library
C45	Oakland. Technical high school library	C82	South Pasadena. Public library
		C83	Stockton. Stockton free public & San Joaquin county library
C46	Oakland. Westlake junior high school library	C85	Tulare. High school library
		C86	Ukiah. Public library
C47	Ontario. Public library	C87	Ventura. County free library
C48	Palo Alto. Stanford university libraries	C88	Watsonville. Union high school library
C49	Pasadena. Public library	C89	Whittier. Public library
C50	Petaluma. Public library	C90	Whittier. Union high school library
C51	Pomona. Public library		
C52	Redlands. A. K. Smiley public library	**Ca**	**Canada**
		Ca1	Alberta. Calgary. Public library
C53	Redwood City. San Mateo county free library	Ca2	British Columbia. Vancouver. Public library
C55	Riverside. Riverside public & Riverside county free public library	Ca3	British Columbia. Victoria. Provincial library
		Ca4	Nova Scotia. Wolfville. Acadia university library
C56	Sacramento. California state library	Ca5	Ontario. London. Public library
C57	Sacramento. City free library	Ca6	Ontario. Ottawa. Public library
C58	Sacramento. California state board of equalization library	Ca7	Ontario. Toronto. Toronto daily Star library
C59	Salinas. Monterey county free library	Ca8	Ontario. Toronto. Toronto university library. Library school
C60	Salinas. Union high school library	Ca9	Ontario. Windsor. Willistead library
C61	San Bernardino. County free library		
C62	San Diego. Public library	Ca10	Ontario. Windsor. Public library
C63	San Diego. State college library	Ca11	Quebec. Montreal. Engineering institute of Canada. Library
C64	San Francisco. Ralph H. Cross, Attorney-at-law	Ca12	Quebec. Montreal. Insurance institute of Montreal. Library
C65	San Francisco. Fire underwriters assoc. of the pacific. Library	Ca13	Quebec. Montreal. McGill university library
C66	San Francisco. Mechanics' institute library	Ca14	Saskatchewan. Saskatoon. Public library
C67	San Francisco. Metropolitan life insurance company. Library	**Co**	**Colorado**
		Co1	Alamosa. Adams state teachers college of southern Colo. Library
C68	San Francisco. San Francisco Chronicle library		
C69	San Francisco. Public library	Co2	Boulder. University of Colorado library
C70	San Francisco. Standard oil company of Calf. Library		
		Co3	Colorado Springs. Colorado college. Coburn library
C71	San José. Free public library		
C72	San Leandro. High school library	Co4	Denver. Colorado state library
C73	San Marino. Henry E. Huntington library & art gallery	Co5	Denver. Public library
		Co6	Denver. Public schools. Professional library
C73-Bak.	Mr. Baker's office		
C75	San Rafael. Public library	Co7	Denver. Medical society of the city & county of Denver. Library
C76	Santa Ana. Orange county free library		
C77	Santa Ana. Public library	Co8	Fort Collins. Colorado state college of agriculture. Library
C78	Santa Ana. Senior high school library		
		Co9	Golden. Colorado school of mines. Library
C80	Santa Barbara. State college library		

Co10	Gunnison. Western state college. Library	D15	U.S. bureau of dairy industry library
Co11	Loveland. Public library	D16	U.S. bureau of entomology & plant quarantine library
Ct	**Connecticut**	D17	U.S. bureau of home economics library
Ct1	Ansonia. Public library		
Ct2	Bridgeport. Public library	D18	U.S. bureau of plant industry library
Ct3	Danbury. Library		
Ct4	East Woodstock. May memorial library	D19	U.S. bureau of plant industry—Division of fruit & vegetable crops & diseases. Library
Ct5	Greenwich. Library		
Ct6	Hartford. Hartford seminary foundation. Case memorial library	D20	U.S. Coast & geodetic survey library
		D21	U.S. department of agriculture library
Ct7	Hartford. Connecticut historical society library	D22	U.S. department of justice library
Ct8	Hartford. Connecticut state library	D23	U.S. federal works agency, public roads administration. Library
Ct9	Hartford. Hartford bar library association	D24	U.S. forest service library
Ct10	Hartford. Watkinson library	D25	U.S. naval research laboratory library
Ct11	New Britain. Institute library		
Ct12	New Haven. Free public library	D26	U.S. office of experiment stations & extension service. Library
Ct12-John Dav.	John Davenport branch	D27	U.S. ordnance department library
Ct12-Scr.	Scranton branch	D28	U.S. railroad retirement board library
Ct13	New Haven. Yale university library	D29	U.S. securities & exchange commission library
Ct14	Norfolk. Library		
Ct15	Vernon. Rockville public library	D30	U.S. soil conservation service library
D	**District of Columbia**	D31	U.S. superintendent of documents library
D1	American federation of labor library		
		D32	Washington D.C. public library
D2	Bureau of railway economics library	D33	Washington missionary college library (Columbia junior college)
D3	Daughters of the American revolution library		
D4	Franciscan monastery library	De	**Delaware**
D5	Georgetown university. Riggs memorial library	De1	Newark. University of Delaware Memorial library
D6	Howard university library	De2	Wilmington. E. I. DuPont de Nemours & co. Technical library
D7	National archives		
D8	National resources planning board		
D9	Smithsonian institution. Freer gallery of art	De3	Wilmington. Wilmington institute free library
D10	U.S. bureau of agricultural chemistry and engineering library	F	**Florida**
		F1	Deland. John B. Stetson university library
D11	U.S. bureau of agricultural economics library		
D12	U.S. bureau of agricultural economics—Division of cotton marketing. Library	F2	Jacksonville. Free public library
		F3	Orlando. Albertson public library
		F4	Tallahassee. Florida state college for women library
D13	U.S. bureau of animal industry library		
		F5	Tampa. Public library
D14	U.S. bureau of animal industry—Zoological division. Library	F6	Winter Park. Rollins college library

G	**Georgia**		
G1	Americus. Georgia southwestern college. Wade Lott library		
G2	Athens. University of Georgia library		
G2-DeRen.	DeRenne collection		
G3	Atlanta. Atlanta university library		
G4	Atlanta. Carnegie library of Atlanta		
G5	Atlanta. Federal reserve bank of Atlanta. Research library		
G6	Atlanta. Georgia library commission		
G7	Atlanta. Georgia school of technology library		
G7-D. Gugg.	Daniel Guggenheim school of aeronautics		
G8	Atlanta. Georgia state library		
G9	Atlanta. Insurance library association of Atlanta		
G10	Atlanta. Retail credit company library		
G11	Atlanta. Regional library, U.S. forest service		
G12	Cuthbert. Andrew college library		
G13	Decatur. Agnes Scott college library		
G14	Decatur. Emory university library		
G15	Lawrenceville. Public library		
G16	Macon. Washington memorial library		
G17	Macon. Wesleyan College. Candler memorial library		
G18	Milledgeville. Georgia state college for women		
G19	Oglethorpe. Oglethorpe university library		
G20	Savannah. Public library		
H	**Hawaii**		
H1	Hawaii. Hilo. Hilo library		
H2	Maui. Wailuku. Maui county free library		
H3	Oahu. Honolulu. Library of Hawaii		
H4	Oahu. Honolulu. University of Hawaii library		
I	**Illinois**		
I1	Alton. Shurtleff college library		
I2	Aurora. Public library		
I2-Bra.	Brady branch		
I3	Belleville. Public library		
I4	Berwyn. Public library		
I5	Bloomington. Withers public library		
I6	Brookfield. Free public library		
I7	Carlinville. Blackburn college library		
I8	Champaign. Public library		
I9	Charleston. Eastern Illinois state teachers college library		
I10	Chicago. American osteopathic association. Library		
I11	Chicago. Art institute of Chicago. Library		
I11-Burn.	Burnham library		
I11-Ryer.	Ryerson library		
I12	Chicago. Bureau of placement & unemployment compensation. Reference library		
I13	Chicago. Public library		
I13-Hild	Frederick H. Hild regional branch		
I13-Legler	Henry E. Legler regional branch		
I13-S. Sh.	South shore branch		
I13-Tild.	Tilden high school library		
I13-Wood.	Woodlawn regional library		
I14	Chicago. Chicago tribune		
I14a	Chicago. Cook county school of nursing		
I15	Chicago. University of Chicago		
I16	Chicago. Daprato library of ecclesiastical art		
I17	Chicago. Institute of American genealogy		
I18	Chicago. Joint library of the Jewish charities of Chicago		
I19	Chicago. Joint reference library		
I20	Chicago. Kelvyn Park high school library		
I21	Chicago. Lake View high school library		
I22	Chicago. Library of international relations		
I23	Chicago. Michael Reese hospital. Lillian W. Florsheim memorial library		
I24	Chicago. Municipal reference library		
I25	Chicago. National association of real estate boards. Library		
I26	Chicago. Newberry library		
I26-Ayer	Ayer collection		
I27	Chicago. Portland cement association library		
I28	Chicago. The Rotarian		
I29	Chicago. Sherwood music school library		
I31	Chicago. United States savings & loan league. Library		
I33	Danville. Public library		
I35	Downers Grove. Community high school library		
I36	East St. Louis. Public library		

I38	Elmhurst. Free public library	I73	Urbana. University of Illinois. Library
I39	Evanston. Evanston historical society library	I75	Waukegan. Township secondary schools library
I40	Evanston. Public library	I76	Waukegan. Public library
I41	Evanston. Township high school library	I77	Wheaton. County superintendent's office, DuPage county
I42	Evanston. Garrett Biblical institute. Library	I78	White Hall. Township library
I43	Evanston. Northwestern university library	I79	Winnetka. New Trier high school library
I44	Freeport. Public library	I80	Winnetka. Free public library
I45	Galesburg. Free public library		
I46	Glen Ellyn. Free public library	**Ia**	**Iowa**
I47	Hinsdale. Township high school library	Ia1	Ames. Public library
		Ia2	Ames. Iowa state college library
I48	Jacksonville. Public library	Ia3	Cedar Rapids. Public library
I49	Joliet. College of Saint Francis. Library	Ia4	Council Bluffs. Free public library
		Ia5	Decorah. Luther college library
I51	Kewanee. Township public library	Ia6	Des Moines. Public library
I52	La Grange. Lyons township high school library	Ia7	Des Moines. Iowa state medical library
I53	La Salle. La Salle-Peru township high school & junior college library	Ia8	Des Moines. Meredith publishing company
		Ia9	Des Moines. State traveling library
I54	Macomb. Western Illinois state teachers college library	Ia10	Dubuque. Public library
		Ia11	Fayette. Upper Iowa university library
I55	Marion. Carnegie library		
I56	Maywood. American can company. Research department library	Ia12	Fort Dodge. Public library
		Ia13	Grinnell. Grinnell college library
		Ia14	Iowa City. Iowa university libraries
I57	Moline. Public library		
I58	Monmouth. Monmouth college library	Ia15	Le Mars. Public library
		Ia16	Mason City. Public library
I59	Monmouth. Warren county public library	Ia17	Muscatine. P. M. Musser public library
I60	Mt. Carroll. Frances Shimer junior college. Campbell library	Ia18	Sioux City. Public library
		Ia19	Storm Lake. Public library
I61	Normal. Illinois state normal university. Milner library	Ia20	Waterloo. Public library
		Ia21	Webster City. Kendall Young library
I62	Oak Park. Public library (Scoville institute)		
I63	Ottawa. Township high school library	**Id**	**Idaho**
		Id1	Boise. Carnegie public library
I64	Park Ridge. Maine township high school library	Id2	Moscow. University of Idaho library
I65	Peoria. Public library		
I65-Linc.	Lincoln branch	**In**	**Indiana**
I67	Rock Island. Public library	In1	Bloomington. Indiana university library
I68	Rockford. Public library		
I68a	Silvis. Public library	In2	Brookville. Public library
I69	Springfield. Illinois state department of public health library	In3	Crawfordsville. Public library
		In4	Crawfordsville. Wabash college library
I70	Springfield. Illinois state historical library		
		In5	East Chicago. Public library
I71	Springfield. Illinois state library	In6	Elkhart. Public library
I72	Springfield. Lincoln library	In7	Evansville. Public library
I72-S. Wil.	Susan Wilcox room		

In8	Fort Wayne. Fort Wayne-Allen county public library	K	**Kansas**
In9	Fort Wayne. South side high school library	K1	Atchison. St. Benedict's college library
In10	Garrett. Public library	K2	Concordia. Free public library
In11	Gary. Benjamin Franklin school library	K3	Dodge City. Public library
		K4	El Dorado. Public library
In12	Gary. Horace Mann school. Adult library	K5	Fort Scott. Public library
		K6	Goodland. Carnegie public library
In13	Goshen. Goshen college library	K7	Hiawatha. Morrill free public library
In14	Greencastle. DePauw university library	K8	Hutchinson. Public library
		K9	Kansas City. Public library
In15	Hammond. Public library	K10	Lawrence. Kansas university library
In16	Huntington. Huntington college library	K11	Lawrence. Lawrence public library
In17	Indianapolis. Butler university library	K12	Manhattan. Kansas state college library
In18	Indianapolis. Eli Lilly & company library	K13	Marion City. Library
		K14	Newton. Free library
In19	Indianapolis. Indiana conservation dept.	K15	Ottawa. Carnegie free library
		K16	Ottawa. Ottawa university library
In20	Indianapolis. Indiana historical bureau	K17	Pittsburg. Kansas state teachers college. Porter library
In21	Indianapolis. Indiana legislative bureau	K18	Pratt. Public library
		K19	Wellington. Public library
In22	Indianapolis. Indiana state library	K20	Wichita. City library
		K21	Winfield. Southwestern college library
In22a	Indianapolis. Indianapolis bar association library	K22	Winfield. Public library
In23	Indianapolis. Public library		
In24	Indianapolis. William Henry Smith memorial library	Ky	**Kentucky**
		Ky1	Berea. Berea college library
In24a	Knightstown. Public library	Ky2	Bowling Green. Western Kentucky state teachers college library
In25	Lafayette. Purdue university library	Ky3	Covington. Public library
In26	Marion. Public library	Ky4	Covington. Villa madona academy library
In27	Mt. Vernon. Alexandrian free public library	Ky5	Fort Thomas. Highlands high school library
In28	Muncie. Public library	Ky6	Frankfort. Kentucky dept. of library & archives. Library, extension division
In29	New Harmony. Workingmen's institute		
In30	Notre Dame. University of Notre Dame library	Ky7	Frankfort. Kentucky state historical society
In31	Plymouth. Public library	Ky8	Henderson. Public library
In32	Richmond. Earlham college library	Ky9	Horse Cave. Free library
		Ky10	Lexington. Keeneland race track Club House. Library
In33	South Bend. Public library		
In34	South Whitley. South Whitley-Cleveland township public library	Ky11	Lexington. Kentucky agricultural experiment station library
In35	Terre Haute. Emeline Fairbanks memorial library	Ky12	Lexington. University of Kentucky library
In36	Terre Haute. Indiana state teachers college library	Ky13	London. Sue Bennett college library
In37	Vincennes. Public library	Ky14	Louisville. Filson club library
In38	Whiting. Public library	Ky15	Louisville. Free public library

Ky15-Cresc. Hill	Crescent hill branch
Ky15-E. Col.	Eastern colored branch
Ky15-W. Col.	Western colored branch
Ky16	Louisville. Southern Baptist theological seminary
Ky17	Louisville. University of Louisville library
Ky18	Richmond. Eastern Kentucky state teachers college library
Ky19	Williamsburg. Cumberland college library

L Louisiana

L1	Alexandria. Public library
L2	Baton Rouge. Louisiana state university
L3	Braithwaite. High school library
L4	Crowley. High school library
L5	Hammond. Southeastern Louisiana college library
L6	Iota. High school library
L7	Lake Charles. La Grange high school library
L8	Merryville. High school library
L9	Minden. Harris high school library
L10	Monroe. Northeast junior college library
L11	New Orleans. Howard memorial library
L12	New Orleans. L. E. Rabouin vocational high school library
L13	New Orleans. Loyola university library
L14	New Orleans. Public library
L15	New Orleans. Middle American research institute, Tulane university
L16	Rayne. High school library
L17	Shreveport. Centenary college library
L18	Shreveport. Shreve memorial library

M Massachusetts

M1	Boston. Administration library, Boston school committee
M2	Boston. Boston medical library
M3	Boston. Boston music company
M4	Boston. Public library
M4-Kir.	Kirstein business branch
M5	Boston. Boston society of natural history. Library
M6	Boston. Fieldman's library, New England mutual life insurance company
M7	Boston. Mass. Division of unemployment compensation. Dept. of research & statistics
M8	Boston. Mass. horticultural society
M9	Boston. Mass. state library
M10	Boston. Metcalf & Eddy
M11	Boston. Museum of fine arts
M11-Tolman	Tolman room
M12	Boston. New England historical genealogical society
M13	Brockton. Public library
M14	Brookline. Zion research library
M15	Cambridge. Arthur D. Little, Inc.
M16	Cambridge. Public library
M17	Cambridge. Harvard university library
M18	Fall River. Public library
M19	Haverhill. Public library
M19a	Hopedale. Bancroft memorial library
M20	Lexington. Cary memorial library
M21	Malden. Public library
M22	Melrose. Public library
M23	New Bedford. Free public library
M24	Quincy. Thomas Crane public library
M25	Salem. Essex institute library
M26	South Hadley. Mount Holyoke College. Williston memorial library
M27	Springfield. City library association
M28	Wakefield. Lucius Beebe memorial library
M29	Watertown. Perkins institution library
M30	Wellesley. Wellesley college library
M31	Williamstown. Williams college library
M32	Worcester. Free public library

Md Maryland

Md1	Annapolis. U.S. naval academy library
Md2	Baltimore. Enoch Pratt free library
Md3	Baltimore. Goucher college library
Md4	Baltimore. Maryland historical society
Md5	Baltimore. Mt. St. Agnes college library
Md6	Baltimore. Sealtest, Inc. research laboratories. Library
Md7	Baltimore. University of Maryland library

Md8	Beltsville. Bee culture laboratory library, Bureau of entomology & plant quarantine, national agricultural research center	Mi14	Grand Haven. Public library
		Mi15	Hamtramck. Public library
		Mi16	Hastings. Public library
		Mi17	Holland. Public library
		Mi18	Houghton. Public library
Md9	Cumberland. Free public library	Mi19	Jackson. Jackson county library
Md10	Frostburg. State teachers college library	Mi20	Jackson. Public library
		Mi21	Kalamazoo. Public library
Md11	Towson. State teachers college library	Mi21-Brooks	Mrs. Brooks, D.A.R.
		Mi21-Cen.	Central high branch
Me	Maine	Mi22	Kalamazoo. Western state teachers college library
Me1	Augusta. Maine state library		
Me2	Bangor. Public library	Mi23	Ludington. Public library
Me3	Brunswick. Bowdoin college library	Mi24	Marquette. Peter White public library
Me4	Lewiston. Bates college library	Mi25	Muskegon. Hackley public library
Me5	Orono. University of Maine library		
		Mi26	Pontiac. City library
Me6	Waterville. Colby college library	Mi27	Royal Oak. Public library
Mi	Michigan	Mi28	Saginaw. Butman-Fish library
Mi1	Albion. Albion college library	Mi29	Saginaw. Hoyt public library
Mi2	Ann Arbor. Public library	Mi30	Three Oaks. Township library
Mi3	Ann Arbor. University of Michigan library	Mi31	Wayne. Wayne county library
		Mi31-H. Kief.	Herman Kiefer branch
Mi4	Birmingham. Baldwin public library	Mi31-Mel.	Melvindale branch
		Mi31-Way.	Wayne branch
Mi5	Detroit. Detroit News		
Mi5-Cat.	Catlin library	Mn	Minnesota
Mi6	Detroit. Public library	Mn1	Chisholm. Public library
Mi6-Burt.	Burton historical collection	Mn3	Collegeville. St. Johns university
Mi6-Camp.	Campbell branch	Mn4	Duluth. Public library
Mi6-Chau.	Chauncy Hurlbut branch	Mn5	Duluth. State teachers college library
Mi6-Fenk.	Fenkell branch		
Mi6-H. B.	Herbert Bower branch	Mn8	Fergus Falls. Public library
Mi6-Loth.	Lothrop branch	Mn9	Hibbing. Public library
Mi6-Monn.	Monnier branch	Mn9-S. Hib.	South Hibbing branch
Mi6-Mont.	Monteith branch	Mn10	International Falls. Public library
Mi6-Red.	Redford branch		
Mi6-Rich.	Richard branch	Mn11	Mankato. Free library
Mi6-Sch.	Schoolcraft branch	Mn12	Mankato. State teachers college library
Mi6-Ut.	Utley branch		
Mi6-Walk.	Walker branch	Mn13	Minneapolis. Augsburg college library
Mi7	East Lansing. Public library		
Mi8	East Lansing. Michigan state college of agriculture and applied science	Mn14	Minneapolis. Public library
		Mn14-Cam.	Camden branch
		Mn14-Cen.	Central branch
Mi9	Eaton Rapids. Public library	Mn14-Fran.	Franklin branch
Mi10	Flint. Flint northern high school library	Mn14-Hos.	Hosmer branch
		Mn14-Sum.	Sumner branch
Mi11	Flint. Public library	Mn15	Minneapolis. University of Minnesota
Mi12	Grand Rapids. Creston high school branch library		
		Mn16	Pipestone. Public library
Mi13	Grand Rapids. Public library	Mn17	Rochester. Mayo clinic library
Mi13-Har.	Harrison park branch	Mn18	St. Joseph. St. Benedict College library
Mi13-S. Hi.	South high branch		
Mi13-Un. hi.	Union high branch	Mn19	St. Paul. Hamline university library
Mi13-W. Side	West side branch		

Mn20	St. Paul. Luther theological seminary library	Mt	Montana
Mn21	St. Paul. Minnesota historical society	Mt1	Billings. Parmly Billings memorial library
		Mt2	Helena. Public library
Mn22	St. Paul. St. Catherine college library	Mt3	Missoula. Montana state university library
Mn23	St. Paul. St. Paul public library		
Mn23-Arl.	Arlington Hills branch	N	New York
Mn23-Ham.	Hamline branch	N1	Albany. N.Y. state college for teachers
Mn23-Mer.	Merriam park branch		
Mn23-Riv.	Riverview branch	N2	Auburn. Seymour library
Mn23-St. Anth.	St. Anthony park branch	N3	Bay Shore. Public library
		N4	Binghamton. Public library
Mn24	St. Paul. State social security Board library	N5	Brooklyn. Brooklyn museum reference library of art & ethnology
Mn24a	Two Harbors. Carnegie public library	N6	Brooklyn. Public library
Mn25	Virginia. Virginia junior college library	N7	Brooklyn. Pratt institute library
		N8	Buffalo. Public library
Mn26	Virginia. Public library	N9	Buffalo. Canisius college library
		N10	Buffalo. Grosvenor library
Mo	Missouri	N11	Canastota. Public library
Mo1	Columbia. University of Missouri library	N12	Clinton. Hamilton college library
		N13	Corning. Public library
Mo2	Joplin. Public library	N14	Dunkirk. Free library
Mo3	Kansas City. Public library	N15	Elmira. Elmira college library
Mo3-Linc.	Lincoln branch	N16	Garden City. Adelphi college library
Mo3-Wash.	Washington branch		
Mo3-Wpt.	Westport branch	N17	Green. Moore memorial library
Mo5	Kirksville. Public library	N18	Hamilton. Colgate university library
Mo6	Kirksville. North east Missouri state teachers college library		
		N19	Herkimer. Free library
Mo7	Kirkwood. Public library	N20	Ithaca. Cornell library association
Mo8	Lexington. Public library	N21	Ithaca. Cornell university library
Mo9	Liberty. William Jewell college library	N22	Jamaica. Queens Borough public library
Mo10	Mound City. Public library	N22-L.I.	Long Island collection
Mo11	Poplar Bluff. Public library	N22-Wood.	Woodhaven branch
Mo12	St. Joseph. Public library	N23	Lackawanna. Public library
Mo13	St. Louis. Public library	N24	Lockport. Public library
Mo13-Cab.	Cabanne branch	N25	Locust Valley. Public library
Mo13-Car.	Carondolet branch	N26	Mamaroneck. Free library
Mo13-Grav.	Gravois branch	N27	Monticello. Ethelbert B. Crawford memorial library
Mo13-Soul.	Soulard branch		
Mo13-Stix	Stix branch	N28	New Rochelle. Public library
Mo14	St. Louis. Washington university. Law school library	N28a	New York. Bibliographical society of America
Mo15	Webster Groves. High school library	N29	New York. College of the city of New York
		N30	New York. Columbia university
Ms	Mississippi	N30-Avery	Avery architectural library
Ms1	Blue Mountain. Blue Mountain college library	N30-Low	Seth Low library
		N31	New York. Cooper union library
Ms2	Jackson. Belhaven college library	N32	New York. Council on foreign relations library
Ms3	Jackson. Dept. of archives & history		
		N32a	New York. Fordham university library
Ms4	Laurel. Lauren Rogers' library		

N33	New York. The Lummus company library		N55-Max.	Maxwell school of citizenship branch
N34a	New York. Academy of medicine		N56	Utica. Free academy library
N35	New York. Public library		N57	Utica. Public library
N35-Bronx	Bronx reference center		N58	Walden. Josephine-Louise public library
N35-Cath.	Cathedral branch			
N35-58th	58th Street branch		N59	White Plains. Good counsel college library
N35-Ford.	Fordham branch			
N35-H.P.	Hudson park branch		N60	White Plains. Public library
N35-Hi.B.	High bridge branch		N61	Yonkers. Miss Mary T. Howe
N35-Morr.	Morrisania branch			
N35-Muhl.	Muhlenberg branch		Nb	**Nebraska**
N35-Ott.	Ottendorfer branch		Nb1	Auburn. Public library
N35-Riv.	Riverside branch		Nb2	Broken Bow. Carnegie library
N35-Rivin.	Rivington street branch		Nb3	Falls City. Lydia Bruun Woods memorial library
N35-St. G.	Saint George branch			
N35-Tre.	Tremont branch		Nb4	Lincoln. College view high school library
N35-Wash.	Washington heights-branch			
N35-Web.	Webster branch		Nb5	Lincoln. Nebraska public library commission
N35-Wood.	Woodstock branch			
N36	New York. New York university. Wash. square library		Nb6	Lincoln. Nebraska Wesleyan university library
N37	New York. Rand school of social science. Meyer London labor library		Nb7	Lincoln. Union college library
			Nb8	Lincoln. University of Nebraska library
N38	New York. Simons-Boardman publishing corporation		Nb9	Lincoln. University of Nebraska state historical society library
N39	Newburgh. Free library		Nb10	Oakland. Public library
N40	Niagara Falls. Public library		Nb11	Omaha. Creighton university library
N41	Olean. Public library			
N42	Oneonta. Hartwick college library		Nb12	Omaha. Duchesne college library
N43	Oswego. City library		Nb14	Omaha. Public library
N44	Port Chester. Public library		Nb14-Ben.	Benson branch
N45	Portville. Free library		Nb15	Omaha. Omaha university library
N45a	Poughkeepsie. Adriance memorial library		Nb16	Peru state teachers college library
			Nb17	Scottsbluff. Public library
N45b	Poughkeepsie. Vassar college library			
N46	Rochester. Public library		Nc	**North Carolina**
N47	Rochester. Univ. of Rochester. Rush Rhees library		Nc1	Chapel Hill. University of North Carolina library
N47-Mem.	Memorial art gallery		Nc2	Durham. Duke university library
N48	Saint Bonaventure. Library		Nc3	Greensboro. Public library
N49	Scarsdale. Public library		Nc4	Greensboro. Woman's college of the Univ. of North Carolina. Library
N50	Syracuse. Blodgett vocational high school library			
N51	Syracuse. North high school library		Nc5	Guilford College. Guilford college library
N52	Syracuse. Nottingham high school library		Nc6	Raleigh. North Carolina state library
N53	Syracuse. Onondaga valley academy library			
			Nd	**North Dakota**
N54	Syracuse. Public library		Nd1	Bismarck. Public library
N55	Syracuse. Syracuse university library		Nd2	Grand Forks. Public library
N55-Lym. H.	Lyman Hall branch library		Nd3	Jamestown. Jamestown college library

Nh	**New Hampshire**
Nh1	Durham. University of New Hampshire library
Nh2	Hanover. Dartmouth college library
Nj	**New Jersey**
Nj1	Atlantic City. Free public library
Nj2	Bayonne. Free public library
Nj3	Bloomfield. Bakelite corporation library
Nj4	Bloomfield. Free public library
Nj5	Bound Brook. High school library
Nj7	Camden. Public library
Nj7-Coop.	Cooper branch
Nj7-Fair.	Fairview branch
Nj9	Camden. Woodrow Wilson high school library
Nj10	Clementon. Lower Camden county regional **high school library**
Nj11	East Orange. Free public library
Nj12	East Orange. Panzer college library
Nj13	Edgewater. Free public library
Nj14	Elizabeth. Free public library
Nj15	Englewood. Public library
Nj16	Franklin. High school library
Nj17	Glassboro. State teachers college library
Nj18	Glen Ridge. Public library
Nj19	Glen Rock. Public library
Nj20	Hackensack. High school library
Nj21	Hackensack. Johnson public library
Nj22	Haddon Heights. High school library
Nj23	Haddonfield. Free public library
Nj24	Haddonfield. Memorial high school library
Nj25	Hoboken. Free public library
Nj26	Jersey City. James J. Ferris high school library
Nj27	Jersey City. Free public library
Nj28	Jersey City. Lincoln high school library
Nj29	Kearny. Free public library
Nj30	Keyport. Free public library
Nj31	Lakewood. High school library
Nj32	Madison. Drew university library
Nj33	Montclair. Art museum
Nj34	Montclair. Public library
Nj35	Moorestown. Free library
Nj36	Morristown. Public library
Nj37	New Brunwick. Free public library
Nj38	New Brunswick. New Brunswick theological seminary library
Nj39	New Brunswick. New Jersey college for women library
Nj40	New Brunswick. Rutgers university library
Nj41	Newark. American Insurance company library
Nj42	Newark. Dept. of library & visual aids. Board of education
Nj43	Newark. Prudential insurance Company. Dryden memorial library
Nj44	Newark. Essex county bar association. Law library
Nj46	Newark. New Jersey historical Society
Nj47	Newark. New Jersey state chamber of commerce library
Nj48	Newark. Newark college of engineering
Nj49	Newark. Newark museum library
Nj50	Newark. Public library
Nj51	Newark. Prudential law library
Nj52	Newark. Public service corporation of N.J. Library
Nj53	Newark. New Jersey college of pharmacy library, Rutgers university
Nj54	Newark. Rutstein laboratory & library
Nj55	Nutley. Public library
Nj56	Orange. Free library
Nj57	Paterson. Public library
Nj58	Plainfield. Public library
Nj59	Princeton. Free public library
Nj60	Princeton. Princeton university library
Nj60-Benj. St.	Benjamin Strong collection of foreign public finance
Nj60-Frick	Frick chemical laboratory
Nj60-Guy.	Guyot hall library
Nj60-Obs.	Observatory
Nj60-Pliny	Pliny Fish collection of railroad & corporation finance
Nj61	Princeton. Rockefeller institute for medical research. Dept. of animal & plant pathology
Nj62	Princeton. Theological seminary library
Nj63	South Orange. Public library
Nj64	Springfield. Regional high school library

Nj65	Teaneck. Bergen junior college library	O20-Ch.F.P.L.	Chagrin Falls public library
Nj66	Trenton. Junior four high school library	O20-Clark	Clark branch
Nj67	Trenton. Free public library	O20-Coll.	Collinwood branch
Nj68	Union City. Public library	O20-E. 79th	East 79th street branch
Nj69	Upper Montclair. State teachers college. Visual aids service	O20-E. 131st	East 131st street branch
		O20-Edge.	Edgewater branch
		O20-Euc.-100th	Euclid-100th street branch
Nj70	Verona. Free public library		
Nj71	Westfield. Free public library	O20-F.I.	Friendly Inn branch
Nm	**New Mexico**	O20-Glen.	Glenville branch
Nm1	Las Cruces. New Mexico state college of agriculture & mechanical arts	O20-Hou.	Hough branch
		O20-Jeff.	Jefferson branch
		O20-Mem.	Memorial branch
Nm2	Santa Fe. Library of the Museum of New Mexico	O20-M.P.	Miles Park branch
		O20-Mt. P.	Mount Pleasant branch
Nm3	Silver City. New Mexico state teachers college library	O20-Nott.	Nottingham branch
		O20-Or.T.Sch.	Orange Township school library
Nv	**Nevada**	O20-Quin.	Quincy branch
Nv1	Reno. Washoe county library	O20-Rice	Rice branch
O	**Ohio**	O20-S. Brook.	South Brooklyn branch
		O20-Ster.	Sterling branch
O1	Akron. Public library	O20-Sup.	Superior branch
O1-Ell.	Ellet branch	O20-Tem.	Temple branch
O1-Fires.	Firestone branch	O20-Un.	Union branch
O2	Akron. University of Akron. Bierce library	O20-W. Park	West Park branch
		O20-White	White collection
O5	Akron. John R. Buchtel high school library	O20-Wood.	Woodlawn branch
		O21	Cleveland. Cleveland school of Art library
O6	Akron. North high school library		
O7	Akron. West high school library	O22	Cleveland. John Carroll university
O8	Athens. Ohio university library	O23	Cleveland. John Huntington Polytechnic Institute library
O9	Bay Village. Library of Dover-By-the-Lake		
		O24	Cleveland. The Temple library
O10	Bedford. Maple Heights public library	O25	Cleveland. Western Reserve university
O11	Bexley. High school library	O25-Clev. Coll.	Cleveland college library
O13	Bucyrus. Public library		
O14	Cincinnati. Christ hospital library	O25-Clev. sch. arch	Cleveland school of architecture
O15	Cincinnati. Cincinnati art museum library	O25-F.S.M.	Flora Stone Mather college library
O16	Cincinnati. Public library		
O17	Cincinnati. Historical & philosophical society of Ohio	O26	Cleveland Heights. Public library
		O27	Columbus. Ohio state university library
O18	Cincinnati. Municipal reference Bureau		
		O28	Cuyahoga Falls. Summit county historical bureau
O18a	Cincinnati. University of Cincinnati, Burnham classical library		
		O29	Dayton. Public library
		O29-Day.	Dayton View branch
O19	Circleville. Public library	O29-Elec.	Electra C. Doren branch
O20	Cleveland. Public library	O29-W. Carn.	West Carnegie branch
O20-Alta	Alta branch	O30	Delaware. Ohio Wesleyan university library
O20-Broad.	Broadway branch		
O20-Brook.	Brooklyn branch	O31	East Cleveland. Public library
O20-Carn.	Carnegie West branch	O31-Cal.	Caledonia branch
O20-Cedar	Cedar branch	O32	Elyria. Elyria library

O33	Euclid. Public library	Or5	Portland. Library association of Portland.
O33-Euc. Cen.	Euclid Central branch		
O33-Roose.	Roosevelt branch	Or6	Portland. Lincoln high school library. Library association of Portland.
O34	Granville. Denison university library		
O35	Hamilton. Lane public library	Or7	Salem. Oregon State library
O36	Kent. Kent state university library	Or8	Salem. Willamette University
		P	**Pennsylvania**
O37	Lakewood. Public library	P1	Allentown. Free library
O37-Mad.	Madison branch	P2	Altoona. Public library
O38	Maumee. Lucas county library	P3	Ambridge. Laughlin memorial free library
O40	Medina. Franklin Sylvester library		
		P4	Beaver Falls. Geneva college. McCartney library
O41	Mentor. Public library		
O42	Middletown. Free public library	P5	Bethlehem. Public library
O43	Milan. Public library	P6	California. State teachers college library
O44	Norwalk. City school district public library		
		P7	Chester. American Baptist historical society
O45	Norwalk. Public library		
O46	Oberlin. Oberlin college library	P8	Chester. J. Lewis Crozer library
O47	Oxford. Miami university library	P9	Clarion. Clarion state teachers college library
O47-Scr.	Scripps Foundation		
O49	Piqua. Flesh public library	P10	Danville. Thomas Beaver free library
O50	Rossford. Public library		
O51	Sandusky. Sandusky library association	P11	DuBois. Public library
		P12	East Stroudsburg. State teachers college library
O53	Springfield. Warder public library		
O54	Springfield. Wittenberg college library	P13	Erie. Public library
		P14	Eries. Mercyhurst college library
O55	Toledo. De Sales college library	P15	Greensburg. Library
O56	Toledo. Public library	P16	Harrisburg. Pennsylvania state library
O56-Locke	Locke branch		
O56-Mott	Mott branch library	P17	Haverford. Haverford college library
O57	Troy. Public library		
O58	Van Wert. Brumback library	P18	Honesdale. Honesdale school & public library
O59	Westerville. Otterbein college library		
		P19	Huntington. Juniata college library
O60	Worthington. Public library		
O61	Youngstown. Public library	P20	Indiana. Free library
		P21	Kutztown. Kutztown state teachers college library
Ok	**Oklahoma**		
Ok1	Enid. Senior high school library	P22	Lancaster. Franklin and Marshall college library
Ok2	Oklahoma City. Carnegie library		
Ok3	Sulphur. Oklahoma school for the deaf library	P24	Lewisburg. Bucknell university library
		P25	Lock Haven. Annie Halenbake Ross library
Ok4	Tulsa. Public library		
		P26	Meadville. Allegheny college. Reis library
Or	**Oregon**		
Oro1	Ashland. Southern Oregon college of education library	P27	New Castle. Free public library
		P27a	New Castle. Senior high school library
Or1	Corvallis. Oregon state library		
Or2	Eugene. University of Oregon library	P28	New Kensington. Aluminum research laboratories library
Or3	Pendleton. Umatilla county library		
		P29	New Wilmington. Westminster college. Ralph Gibson McGill memorial library
Or4	Portland. Jefferson high school library		

P30	Philadelphia. Biochemical research foundation of the Franklin Institute		Pr2	Rio Piedras. University of Puerto Rico. Dr. Rafel Pico
P31	Philadelphia. College of physicians of Philadelphia. Library		Pr3	San Juan. Carnegie library
P32	Philadelphia. Drexel institute library		R	**Rhode Island**
			R1	Providence. Public library
P32a	Philadelphia. Philadelphia electric company. Library		R2	Providence. Public library
			Sc	**South Carolina**
P33	Philadelphia. Free library		Sc1	Charleston. The Citadel library
P34	Philadelphia. Temple university. Sullivan memorial library		Sc2	Charleston. College of Charleston library
P35	Philadelphia. United gas improvement library		Sc3	Columbia. University of South Carolina library
P36	Philadelphia. University of Pennsylvania library		Sd	**South Dakota**
			Sd1	Madison. Eastern state normal school library
P36-Lipp.	Lippincott library			
P37	Philadelphia. Women's medical college of Pennsylvania. Library		T	**Tennessee**
			T1	Chattanooga. Public library
			T2	Johnson City. State teachers college library
P38	Pittsburgh. Carnegie institute of technology library		T3	Knoxville. Lawson McGhee library
P39	Pittsburgh. Carnegie library of Pittsburg		T3-Mc.	McClung room
			T4	Knoxville. Tennessee valley authority. Technical library
P39-Wyl.	Wylie branch			
P40	Pittsburgh. Our lady of mercy academy library		T5	Knoxville. University of Tennessee library
P41	Pittsburgh. Pennsylvania college for women library		T6	Memphis. Cossitt library
			T7	Murfreesboro. State teachers college library
P42	Pittsburgh. University of Pittsburgh library		T8	Nashville. Fisk university library
P43	Pottsville. Free public library		T9	Nashville. Public library
P44	Punxsutawney. Free library		T10	Nashville. Vanderbilt library
P45	Reading. Public library		Tx	**Texas**
P46	State College. Pennsylvania state college library		Tx1	Abilene. Hardin-Simmons university library
P47	Swarthmore. Friends historical library of Swarthmore college		Tx2	Austin. Allen Jr. high school library
P48	Swissville. Carnegie free library		Tx3	Austin. University junior high school library
P49	Towanda. Public library			
P50	Upper Darby. Township & Sellers memorial public library		Tx4	Beaumont. Tyrrell public library
			Tx5	Brady. McCulloch county library
P51	Washington. Citizens free library		Tx6	Brownwood. Daniel Baker college library
P52	Waynesboro. Free library			
P53	West Chester. Chester county historical society		Tx7	Cleburne. Cleburne senior high school library
P54	Wilkes Barre. Osterhout free library		Tx8	Commerce. East Texas state teachers college library
P55	Wilkinsburg. Public library		Tx9	Dallas. Dallas news library
P56	Williamsport. James V. Brown library		Tx10	Dallas. Public library
			Tx11	Dallas. Foundren library, Southern Methodist university
P57	York. Historical society of York County			
			Tx12	Edinburg. Edinburg college library
P58	York. Martin memorial library			
Pr	**Puerto Rico**		Tx14	El Paso. Public library
Pr1	Rio Piedras. University of Puerto Rico library		Tx15	Forth Worth. Carnegie public library

Tx16	Fort Worth. Southwestern Baptist theological seminary college library	V8	Richmond. Public library
		V9	Richmond. Virginia state library
Tx17	Galveston. Rosenberg library	**Vt**	**Vermont**
Tx19	Highland Park. Public library	Vt1	Montpelier. Vermont free public library commission
Tx20	Houston. Houston Chronicle library	Vt2	Rutland. Free library
Tx21	Houston. Public library	Vt3	St. Johnsbury. Fairbanks Museum of natural history
Tx21-Col.	Colored branch		
Tx22	Kilgore. Public library	**W**	**Wisconsin**
Tx23	Lubbock. Lubbock county library	W1	Antigo. Public library
		W2	Appleton. Lawrence college library
Tx24	Lubbock. Lubbock senior high school library	W3	Barron. Public library
		W4	Black River Falls. Public library
Tx25	Lubbock. Texas technological College	W5	Eau Claire. State teachers college library
Tx26	Marshall. College of Marshall library	W6	Edgerton. Public library
		W7	Fort Atkinson. Dwight Foster public library
Tx27	Nacogdoches. Stephen F. Austin state teachers college library	W9	Kenosha. Gilbert M. Simmons library
Tx28	Port Arthur. Gates memorial library		
		W10	Madison. State historical society of Wisconsin. Library
Tx29	San Antonio. Public library		
Tx30	San Antonio. Our lady of the lake college	W11	Madison. Traveling library & study club department
Tx31	Sherman. Austin college library	W12	Madison. University of Wisconsin
Tx32	Sherman. Sherman public library		
Tx33	Texarkana. Texarkana college library	W13	Madison. Wisconsin legislative reference library
Tx34	Victoria. Victoria high school & junior college library	W14	Manitowoc. Public library
		W15	Milwaukee. Milwaukee art institute
Tx35	Waco. Public library		
		W16	Milwaukee. Public library
U	**Utah**	W17	Milwaukee. Shorewood high school library
U1	Logan. Utah state agricultural college library	W18	Milwaukee. State teachers college library
U2	Ogden. Carnegie free library		
U3	Provo. Brigham Young university library	W19	Oshkosh. Public library
		W20	Racine. Public library
U4	Salt Lake City. Free public library	W20-Frank.	Franklin branch
U5	Salt Lake City. University of Utah library	W20-Fratt.	Fratt branch
		W20-Horl.	Horlick branch
		W20-McK.	McKinley branch
V	**Virginia**	W20-Wash.	Washington branch
V1	Blacksburg. Virginia Polytechnic institute	W21	Rice Lake. Public library
		W22	Superior. Public library
V2	Charlottesville. Virginia university. Alderman library	W23	Whitewater. State teachers college library
V3	Danville. Public library		
V4	Ettrick. Virginia state college for negroes. Johnston memorial library	**Wa**	**Washington (State)**
		Wa1	Aberdeen. Public library
		Wa2	Bellingham. Public library
		Wa3	Bellingham. Western Washington college of education. Library
V5	Newport News. Mariners' museum library		
		Wa4	Cheney. Eastern Washington college of education. Library
V6	Richmond. Confederate museum		
V7	Richmond. Virginia museum of fine arts	Wa5	Ellensburg. Central Washington college of education. Library

Wa6	Everett. Public library		Wa14	Tacoma. Public library
Wa7	Olympia. Washington state library		Wa15	Walla Walla. Whitman college library
Wa8	Pullman. Washington state college library		Wa16	Yakima. High school library
Wa8a	Pullman. Broadway high school library		**Wv**	**West Virginia**
			Wv1	Buckhannon. West Virginia Wesleyan college library
Wa9	Seattle. Queen Anne high school library		Wv2	Fairmont. Marion county public library
Wa9a	Seattle. Seattle Post-Intelligencer library		Wv3	Huntington. Oley junior high school library
Wa10	Seattle. Public library		Wv4	Morgantown. West Virginia university library
Wa11	Seattle. University of Washington library			
Wa12	Spokane. North central high school library		**Wy**	**Wyoming**
Wa13	Spokane. Public library		Wy1	Laramie. University of Wyoming library

ABBREVIATIONS USED IN THIS WORK

A

abbrev.	abbreviation
abr.	abridged
acc.	according
accred.	accredited
acct.	account, accounting
ad.	adult
add.	addition
admin.	administrative, administration
adv.	advertisement
agric.	agriculture, agricultural
alph.	alphabetical
Amer.	American, Americana
an.	animal
anniv.	anniversary
annot.	annotation, annotated
appt.	appointment
arch.	architecture, architectural, archives, archival
archaeol.	archaeology
arr.	arranged
art.	artist, article
assoc.	association
astron.	astronomy, astronomical
auth.	author
autobiog.	autobiography

B

bd.	board, bound
bibl.	bibliography
Bibl.	Biblical
biog.	biography, biographical
biol.	biology, biological
bk.	book
bldg.	building
bot.	botany, botanical
br.	branch
bul.	bulletin
bur.	bureau
bus.	business

C

C.	Central
cat.	catalog
Cath.	Catholic
cd.	card
cem.	cemetery
cens.	census
cent.	century
cer.	ceramic, ceramics
char.	character
chem.	chemist, chemistry, chemical
chmn.	chairman
chron.	chronological
circ.	circulation, circular
class.	classified, classification, classical
clip.	clipping
co.	company, county
coll.	college, collection, collected
com.	commerce, commercial
comp.	compiler, compiled, compilation, composer, composition
conc.	concerning
cond.	condensed
conf.	conference
cong.	congress
congress.	congressional
const.	constitutional
contemp.	contemporary
contrib.	contribution, contributed
corr.	corrected, correspondence
crit.	critical, criticism
ct.	court
cur.	current

D

dec.	decorative
dent.	dentistry
dept.	department
descrip.	description
dict.	dictionary
diff.	different
dir.	directory
diss.	dissertation
doc.	document
dr.	doctor, doctoral
dup.	duplicate

E

E	East
ea.	each
earl.	early
econ.	economics, economic, economical
ed.	editor, edition, editorial
educ.	education, educational

xxxii

Egypt.	Egyptian	*lib. sch.*	library school
elem.	elementary	*lit.*	literature, literary
ency.	encyclopedia	*loc.*	local, locality, location
eng.	engineering	*loc. hist.*	local history
Eng.	English		

M

ent.	entry
esp.	especially
exec.	executive
exhib.	exhibit, exhibition
exp.	experiment, exposition
ext.	extension

mag.	magazine
manuf.	manufacture, manufacturer
mat.	material
math.	mathematics
med.	medicine, medical
mem.	memorial
mgt.	management
mim.	mimeographed
misc.	miscellaneous
mo.	monthly
mot.	motion
mss.	manuscript
mun.	municipal
mun. ref.	municipal reference
mus.	music, musical

F

f.a.	fine arts
fac.	faculty
fed.	federal
fic.	fiction
for.	foreign
freq.	frequently, frequent

G

gen.	general, genealogy
geog.	geography
geol.	geology, geological
gov.	governor
govt.	government

N

N.	North
n. cur.	not current
natl.	national
necrol.	necrology
newsp.	newspaper
no.	number
non-fic.	non fiction
notebk.	notebook
num.	numerical
nut.	nutrition

H

Haw.	Hawaiian
hi. sch.	high school
hist.	history

I

illus.	illustrator, illustration, illustrated
imp.	important
inc.	including
incomp.	incomplete
ind.	industry, industrial
indiv.	individual
inf.	information
infreq.	infrequent
instit.	institute, institution
instr.	instruction
int.	interlibrary

O

o. p.	out of print
o.s.	open shelf
obit.	obituary
obj.	object
occ.	occasional
occup.	occupation
off.	office, officer, official
orch.	orchestra
ord.	order, ordinance
organiz.	organization
orient.	oriental

J

j	juvenile
Jap.	Japanese
Jew.	Jewish
jl.	journal
journ.	journalism
jt.	joint

P

p.	page
p. t.	parent teacher
pa.	paper
pam.	pamphlet
par.	parent
per.	periodical
perm.	permanent
pers.	person, personal
pert.	pertaining
phar.	pharmacy

L

lands.	landscape
lang.	language
legis.	legislative, legislation, legislature
lib.	library

phil.	philosophy	*shts.*	sheets
phot.	photograph, photostatic	*soc.*	social, sociology
pic.	picture	*soc. serv.*	social service
pol.	politics, political	*spec.*	special
port.	portrait	*specif.*	specifications
prep.	preparations	*st.*	stacks, street
print.	printed, printing	*stat.*	station
proc.	proceeding, process	*stud.*	student
prof.	profession, professional, professor	*subdiv.*	subdivision, subdivided
		subj.	subject
pub.	public, published, publisher, publication	*subseq.*	subsequent, subsequently
		supp.	supplement, supplementary

Q

q.	quarterly, question
q. & a.	questions and answers
quot.	quotation

T

t.	title
t. c.	teacher's college
t. r.	treasure room
tech.	technical, technology
tel.	telephone
terr.	territory, territorial
theat.	theatre
tr.	translator, translation, translated
trans.	transaction
transp.	transportation
tpd.	typed

R

r. a.	reader's aid, reader's assistant, reader's advisor
r. b.	reader's bureau
rare	rare books
read.	reading
recit.	recitation
recreat.	recreation, recreational
ref.	reference
reg.	register, regional
rel.	relations, related, relating, religion
rel. educ.	religious education
reorganiz.	reorganization
repres.	representative
reprod.	reproduction
res.	reserve
rev.	review, revised, revolutionary
rpt.	report

U

unbd.	unbound
unest.	unestimated
univ.	university
unpub.	unpublished

V

v.	volume
v. f.	vertical file
voc.	vocation, vocal

S

S.	South
sch.	school
sci.	science
scrapbk.	scrapbook
sculp.	sculpture, sculptor
sec.	section, sectional
second.	secondary
secy.	secretary
sep.	separate
ser.	series, serials
serv.	service
sess.	session, sessional

W

W.	West
wkly.	weekly
wk.	work
w. s. r.	women's study room

XYZ

y. p.	young people's
yr.	year
yrbk.	yearbook
yrly.	yearly
zoo.	zoology

TABLE OF CONTENTS

	Page
PREFACE	v
COMMITTEE ACKNOWLEDGMENTS	xiii
STATE LISTS, SEPARATELY ISSUED	xv
LIST OF COOPERATING LIBRARIES WITH KEY TO SYMBOLS	xvi
ABBREVIATIONS USED IN THIS WORK	xxxii
LOCAL INDEXES IN AMERICAN LIBRARIES; A UNION LIST OF UNPUBLISHED INDEXES	1
APPENDICES	
I. LIST OF BIBLIOGRAPHIES	198
II. AUTHOR LIST OF BOOKS INDEXED, IN WHOLE OR IN PART, BY LIBRARIES	216

LOCAL INDEXES IN AMERICAN LIBRARIES;
A UNION LIST OF UNPUBLISHED INDEXES

ABBEY THEATRE
Tx19 30 cds. by subj. Abbey players & theat. in per. & bks. Occ. add.

ABBOTT FAMILY (ME.)
Me3 950 cds. by auth. Writings by & about Abbott family inc. Edward, Jacob & Lyman. Occ. add.

ABBREVIATIONS. *See* List of Bibliographies, APPENDIX I

ABERDEEN (WASH.)—HISTORY
Wa1 250 cds. by subj. Loc. hist. mostly in newsp. Occ. add.

ABERDEEN (WASH.)—SOCIETIES AND CLUBS
Wa1 75 cds. by name. Club programs, newsp., etc. Cur. add.

ABILENE (TEX.) REPORTER-NEWS (*newsp.*)
Tx1 1888–1900, 1904–1920, 1925–1940. Tpd. list by subj. Loc. & S.W. items. No add.

ABSTRACT IDEAS
Mo3-ref 500 cds. by subj. Bks., per., pams. Occ. add.

ABSTRACT VIRTUES. *See also* CHARACTER; ETHICS; PERSONALITY
Mi27-ref 150 cds. by subj. Qualities & characteristics, in bks. & per. Yrly. add.
Nd2 230 ent., tpd. list by subj. Bks. Occ. add.

ACCIDENTS—PREVENTION
Nj52 Over 200 cds. by subj. Bks., per., pams. Freq. add.

ACCOUNT BOOKS. *See also* MARION (ILL.) —ACCOUNT BOOKS
M25 800 cds. by pers. & subj. Bks. Occ. add.
Nj40 1200 cds. by tradesman's name, place & type of bus. Acct. bks., ledgers of 18th & 19th cent. bus. enterprises. Occ. add.

ACCOUNTING
C32-sci 900 cds. by subj. Analytical index to acct. bks. Cur. add.
Ca2-sci 200 cds. by subj. Specialized acct. in bks. Mo. add.
Ct12-ind 90 cds. by subj. Bks. Freq. add.
M27-ref 500 cds. by subj. Diff. bus., in bks. Occ. add.
Nj52 Over 200 cds. by subj. Bks., per., pams. Freq. add.
O20-bus 400 cds. by subj. Per. Occ. add.
P39-bus 2300 cds. by subj. Cur. per., pams., bks. Mo. add.
R1-bus 100 cds. by subj. Bks., pams., per. Freq. add.

ACTA ET DICTA (*per.*)
Mn22-sch v. 1, 1909–date. Cds. by auth. & subj. Cur. add.

ACTING EDITION OF PLAYS (*bk.*). *In* PLAYS
L14-ref, N7-circ

ACTIVITIES. *See* UNITS OF WORK

ACTORS AND ACTRESSES *See also* DRAMA—NECROLOGY **C32-lit**
W9 100 cds. by subj. Bks. & per. Freq. add.

ACTORS AND ACTRESSES, SHAKESPEAREAN
W20-ad 100 cds. by play, char. & actor. Modern actors who have played Shakespearean roles, in bks. Occ. add.

ACTUALITÉ ÉCONOMIQUE (*per.*). *In* CANADA —PERIODICALS **Ca13-per**

ADAIR CO. (KY.)—REGISTERS OF BIRTHS, ETC.
Ky7 Unest, cds. by name; also tpd. list. Grooms only, in Adair co. marriages.

ADAMS CO. (PA.)—HISTORY. *See* YORK CO. (PA.)—HISTORY **P57**

ADDRESSES, *See* ORATIONS; SPEECHES

ADULT EDUCATION. *See also* Name of loc., subdiv. ADULT EDUCATION; List of Bibliographies, APPENDIX I
N22-r.a.   2600 cds. by auth., t., subj. Pams. Cur. add.

ADVENTISTS
D33   300,000 cds. by auth., t., subj. Per., Amer. church papers, 1845–date. Cur. add.
N35-ref. read   34,000 cds. by subj. Adventist lit., esp. Pitcairn Island, the "Second coming," and Adventist per. Occ. add.

ADVENTURE—FOREIGN LANGUAGES
Mi6-for   125 cds. by subj. & lang. Bks. Freq. add.

ADVENTURE STORIES. *See* List of Bibliographies, APPENDIX I

ADVERTISEMENTS—BALTIMORE (MD.)
Md2-Md.   2000 cds. by name of firm. Baltimore city dir., 1796–1900. No add.

ADVERTISEMENTS—PHARMACY. *See* PHARMACY—ADVERTISEMENTS

ADVERTISING
P39-tech   380 cds. by state. Infreq. add.

AERONAUTICS
G7-D. Gugg.   7500 cds. by subj. Sci. & eng. jls., trans., & proc. Cur. add.

AERONAUTICS—FOREIGN LANGUAGES
Mi6-for   100 cds. by subj. & lang. Freq. add.

AFRICA
N35-circ. cat   6000 cds. by subj. African tribes, lang. & lit. in bks. & per. Cur. add.

AGGLUTINATION
Nj61   60 cds. by auth. & t. Bks., per., pams. Freq. add.

AGRICULTURAL CHEMISTRY. *See* List of Bibliographies, APPENDIX I

AGRICULTURAL EXPERIMENT STATIONS—PUBLICATIONS. *See also* Names of states, univ. and U.S., subdiv. Agriculture.
D26   22,572 cds. by state & auth. Art. by state exper. stat. workers, in sci. jls., proc. & trans. Cur. add.

O36-v.f.   7500 cds. by subj. All pub. of the stat., 1900–date. Cur. add.

AGRICULTURAL EXTENSION WORK
D26   36,330 cds. by subj. All ext. pub. issued by land-grant coll. previous to and subseq. to passage of Smith-Lever act, 1914. Cur. add.

AGRICULTURAL LAWS AND LEGISLATION
D10   3000 cds. by name of bill. Cur. leg. cat. giving hist. of each bill of interest to Bur. Daily add. when cong. in sess.
D11   3472 cds., num. by bill no. and by subj. Fed. bills, resolutions, repts., etc. Daily add. when cong. in sess.

AGRICULTURAL MACHINERY—PATENTS. *See* PATENTS—MACHINERY, AGRICULTURAL

AGRICULTURALISTS. *See* SCIENTISTS   D21

AGRICULTURE. *See also* names of govt. bureaus & depts. under U.S.; names of state coll. & univ. agric. pub.
C33   2000 cds. by no. of pub. & by subj. Govt. bul. & circ. Freq. add.
D10   16,522 cds. by subj. Bks., pams. & per. Mo. add.
D18   38,000 cds. by auth. Bks., per., ser. with inf. on field crops, soils & fertilizers. Daily add.
D21   20,000 cds. by auth., subj., ser. Pub. of state bds. of agric.: Ala., Calif., Conn., Ill., Ind., Ia., Kans., Me., Mass., Mich., Mo., Neb., N.H., N.Y., Ohio, Pa. (1877–81 only). No add. since 1915.
W3   841 cds. by subj. Pams. Freq. add.

AGRICULTURE—ECONOMIC ASPECTS
D11   90,000 cds. by subj. Per. Cur. add.
D11   15,285 cds. by states & subj. State pub. Cur. add.

AGRICULTURE—ECONOMIC ASPECTS—BOOK REVIEWS
D11   6000 cds. by auth. of bk. Per. Cur. add.

AGRICULTURE—KENTUCKY
Ky11   Unest. cds. by subj., t. & auth. Pub. of Ky. agric. exper. stat. & Univ. of Ky. coll. of agric. Freq. add.

AGRICULTURE—PUERTO RICO. *See* List of Bibliographies, APPENDIX I.

AGRICULTURE—WISCONSIN
W20-ad   325 cds. by subj. Univ. bul., circ., etc. Occ. add.

AIR CONDITIONING
Nj52   Several hundred cds. by subj. Bks., per., pams. on air conditioning, heating & ventilating. Freq. add.

ALABAMA—CENSUS
A1   25,000 cds. by family name. Inf. on Ala. families that can be used as hist. or gen. material. Freq. add.

ALABAMA—LANDS.   See LANDS—ALABAMA

ALABAMA—LAW.   See LAW—ALABAMA

ALABAMA—MUSCLE SHOALS.   See MUSCLE SHOALS—ALABAMA

ALABAMA—MUSIC.   See MUSIC—ALABAMA

ALABAMA—NEWSPAPERS
A1   680p in tpd. shts. by t. and co. where pub. Cur. add.

ALABAMA—OFFICIALS AND EMPLOYEES.   See List of Bibliographies, APPENDIX I

ALABAMA—PERIODICALS
A1   527 cds. by subj. Cur. add.

ALABAMA—SOLDIERS.   See also U.S.—HISTORY—REVOLUTION—ALABAMA; U.S.—HISTORY—WAR WITH MEXICO, 1845–1848—ALABAMA; U.S.—HISTORY—WAR OF 1898—ALABAMA
A1   15,000 cds. by name. Soldiers serving in Indian wars, 1812–1840. Occ. add.
A1   250 cds. by name. Soldiers in Texas war with Mexico. Occ. add.

ALABAMA—TERRITORIAL SERVICE
A1   2500 cds. by name. Men in civil service in 1818. Occ. add.

ALAMEDA (CALIF.)—DOCUMENTS.   See List of Bibliographies, APPENDIX I

ALAMEDA (CALIF.)—HISTORY
C1   9561 cds. by subj. Newsp. Cur. add.

ALAMEDA CO. (CALIF.)—HISTORY
C43-ref   3520 cds. by pers. & place names. Hist. of co., as follows: Joseph Baker, *Past and present of Alameda co.;* William Halley, *Centennial yearbook of Alameda co.;* Frank Merritt, *History of Alameda co.;* Myron Wood, *History of Alameda co.* Later add.

ALGAE.   See List of Bibliographies, APPENDIX I

ALLEGHENY CO. (PA.)—HISTORY
P39-ref. Pa.   600 cds. by subj. of texts, maps & illus. Bk. indexed: *History of Allegheny county, Pennsylvania,* pub. by L. H. Everts & company

ALLIN, J. HAYS.   See CHATTANOOGA (TENN.)—HISTORY   T3-Mc.

ALMANACS
N35-ref. res   3300 cds., alph. & chron. Amer. & a few for., 1474 to present. Cur. add.
Nj40   4300 cds. by auth. or comp., place & t. Occ. add.
Nj40   2900 cds., chron. Occ. add.

ALUMINUM
P28   Unest. cds. by auth. & subj. All phases of ind. in bks., per., pams. Cur. add.

AMBRIDGE (PA.)—HISTORY
P3   240 cds. by subj. Newsp., pams., etc. Freq. add.

AMERICA (per.)
I49   v. 1–53, 1909–1935. Cds. by subj. Lit. sec. Occ. add.

AMERICA IN LITERATURE.   See FICTION, HISTORICAL—U.S.; FICTION, REGIONAL—U.S.

AMERICAN ARCHIVES (Bk.).   *In* U.S.—HISTORY—REVOLUTION   In35-gen(3)

AMERICAN ARTIST (per)
N22-art   v. 3, 1939–date. Cds. by auth. & subj. Supp. to print. index. Cur. add.

AMERICAN ASSOCIATION OF TEACHERS COLLEGES. YEARBOOK
Wa3   v. 9–17, 1930–1938. Cds. by auth., subj., t. No add.

AMERICAN CAN COMPANY—RESEARCH DEPARTMENT LIBRARY. ABSTRACTS
I56   v. 1–7, 1935–1941. Sci. aspects of canning, metallurgy, bacteriology, nutrition, etc. in over 100 per. Mo. add., issued yrly. in mim. bul.

AMERICAN CATHOLIC HISTORICAL RESEARCHES (per.)
In30   v. 1–29, 1884–1912. Alph. & chron. cds. Pers., places & dates. No. add.

AMERICAN CATHOLIC HISTORICAL SOCIETY OF PHILADELPHIA. RECORDS
In30   v. 1-47, 1884–1936. Alph. & chron. cds. Pers., places & dates. No add.

AMERICAN CATHOLIC QUARTERLY REVIEW
In30   v. 1-49, 1876–1924. Cds., by auth. & subj. No add.

AMERICAN CHILDHOOD (per.). *In* CHILDREN'S PLAYS   H2

AMERICAN EXPEDITIONARY FORCE. *See* EUROPEAN WAR, 1914–1918—AMERICAN EXPEDITIONARY FORCE

AMERICAN FEDERATION OF LABOR. LABOR'S MONTHLY SURVEY. *In* LABOR AND LABORING CLASSES—PERIODICALS   O33-Euc. Cen.

AMERICAN FEDERATION OF LABOR. WEEKLY NEWS SERVICE. *In* LABOR AND LABORING CLASSES—PERIODICALS   O33-Euc. Cen.

AMERICAN FORESTS (per.)
O47-ref   v. 38-48, 1932–1942. Cds. by tree name. "Tree ser." Freq. add.

AMERICAN GEOGRAPHICAL SOCIETY BULLETIN. *In* SOUTHWEST   Nm2

AMERICAN HISTORICAL REGISTER AND MONTHLY GAZETTE. *In* GENEALOGY   M19 (1)

AMERICAN HISTORY. *See* U.S.—HISTORY

AMERICAN IMPRINTS. *See* Names of loc., subdiv. BIBLIOGRAPHY—IMPRINTS; List of Bibliographies, APPENDIX I

AMERICAN JOURNAL OF NURSING. *In* NURSES & NURSING   Ia14-med

AMERICAN LITERATURE. *See also* Names of authors; List of Bibliographies, APPENDIX I
N30-ref   12,945 cds. by subj. Per. not indexed elsewhere, dr. diss., masters' essays, etc. Cur. add.

AMERICAN LITERATURE (per.)
P36-ref   v. 1-10, 1929–1939. Cds. chron. & alph. by auth. No add.

AMERICAN MANAGEMENT ASSOCIATION—PUBLICATIONS
Ia8   1929–date, all ser. Cur. add.

AMERICAN MONTHLY MAGAZINE. *In* U.S.—HISTORY—REVOLUTION   In35-gen (1)

AMERICAN MUSEUM JOURNAL. *In* SOUTHWEST   Nm2

AMERICAN MUSEUM OF NATURAL HISTORY. NATURAL HISTORY (per.)
Md11   v. 34-36, 1934–1936. Cds. by subj.

AMERICAN PREFACES (per.). *In* AUTHORS   O36-v.f.

AMERICAN PROCESSION (bk.). *In* U.S.—SOCIAL LIFE AND CUSTOMS—PHOTOGRAPHS   G4-ref

AMERICAN REVOLUTION. *See* U.S.—HISTORY—REVOLUTION

AMERICAN REVOLUTION (bk.) *In* U.S.—HISTORY—REVOLUTION In35-gen (2)

AMERICAN SCANDINAVIAN REVIEW
Nd1   v. 8-19, 1920–1931. Tpd. list by subj. No add.

AMERICANA (per.). *In* GENEALOGY F5, In23-gen; HERALDRY   C49-ref, In23-gen
Me1   v. 14, 1920; v. 21, 1927; v. 22, 1928–date. Cds. Cur. add.
Me2-ref   v. 1, 1906–date. Cds. by auth., t. & subj. Cur. add.
O61-ref   v. 17, 1923, v. 27, 1933–date. Cds. by surname. Cur. add.

AMERICANS ALL (bk.). *In* SHORT STORIES   Tx12

AMES (IA.)—SOCIETIES AND CLUBS
Ia1   147 cds. by name of club. Infreq. add.

AMISH MENNONITES. *See* MENNONITES

AMUSEMENTS. *See* GAMES; PARTIES; SPORTS AND ATHLETIC GAMES

ANATOMY. *See* BONES AND JOINTS; DISSECTION

ANCESTOR (per.). *In* GENEALOGY M19 (1)

ANECDOTAL LINCOLN (bk.). *In* LINCOLN, ABRAHAM   I72

ANIMAL STORIES. *See also* List of Bibliographies, APPENDIX I
Ky15-circ   143 cds. by subj. Bks. Freq. add.
Nj37-circ   186 cds. by kind of animal. Bks. Occ. add.
O56-circ   500 cds. by type of animal. Bks. Occ. add.

ANIMAL STORIES, JUVENILE. *See also* List of Bibliographies, APPENDIX I
 Mn11 Unest, tpd. shts. by groups of animals. Freq. add.

ANIMALS. *See also* PETS; List of bibliographies, APPENDIX I
 C63-j 500 ent. in tpd. list by animal & auth. Bks. Cur. add.
 Nj61 600 cds. by auth. & t. Bks., per., pams. Freq. add.
 V1-agric 15,000 cds. by subj. Bks., per., pams. on wild life. No cur. add.
 W23 1300 cds. by subj. Bks. & per. No add.
 Wa10-j 400 cds. by varieties. Per. Occ. add.
 Wa10-tech 160 cds. by varieties. Bks. & per. on care & feeding of wild and pet animals. Cur. add.

ANIMALS—DISEASES. *See* VETERINARY MEDICINE

ANIMALS—PICTURES. *See* PICTURES—ANIMALS

ANIMALS IN LITERATURE. *See* READERS & PRIMERS O20-Rice-j

ANN ARBOR (MICH.)—SOCIETIES AND CLUBS. *See* WASHTENAW Co. (MICH.)—SOCIETIES AND CLUBS Mi2

ANNALS OF ST. LOUIS (bk.). *In* ST. LOUIS (MO.) Mo13-Soul.

ANNALS OF WYOMING (per.)
 Wy1 v: 3-11, 1925–1940. Mim. list, bd. by subj. & auth.; on cds. since 1935.

ANNOTATIONS. *See* BOOK REVIEWS

ANNUAL BIOGRAPHY AND OBITUARY
 T10 v. 1-2, 1817–1818, v. 4-21, 1820–1836. Tpd. pam. No add.

ANNUAL REGISTER. *In* NECROLOGY N30-ref

ANNUAL REGISTER (OF THE BAPTIST DENOMINATION IN NORTH AMERICA). *In* BAPTISTS P7 (1)

ANSONIA (CONN.)
 Ct1 250 cds. by subj. Bks., Loc. newsp. Loc. hist. & biog. Freq. add.

ANTHEMS. *See also* MUSIC Nc3
 O20-art 1692 cds. by t. Bks. Infreq. add.

ANTHROPOLOGY
 Me3 625 cds. by auth. & t. Jl. reprints & pams. Occ. add.
 U5 800 cds. by subj. Per. Yrly. add.

ANTIGENS AND ANTIBODIES
 Nj61 50 cds. by auth. & t. Bks., per. & pams. Freq. add.

ANTIGO (WISC.) JOURNAL (newsp.)
 W1 1929–1940. Cds. by subj. Freq. add.

ANTIQUES—NEW JERSEY—UNION LISTS
 Nj18 464 ent., mim. list. by auth. & subj. Inc. lib.: Caldwell, Commission, E. Orange, Elizabeth, Glen Ridge, Irvington, Kearny, Madison, Maplewood, Montclair, Morristown, Nutley, Orange, Perth Amboy, So. Orange, State library, Verona. Infreq. add.

ANTIQUES (per.)
 Wa10-art v. 31-37, 1937–1940. Cds. by subj. More detailed than pub. indexes. Cur. add.

ANTITOXINS. *See* TOXINS AND ANTITOXINS

APICULTURE. *See* BEES

APOLLO (per.)
 P39-ref. art v. 1-8, 1925–1928. Tpd. shts., bd. by art. & auth. No. add.

APPLES
 D19 16,000 cds. by variety name. Bks., per., ser., cat., supp. U.S. Bureau plant ind. Bul. 56 on nomenclature of apple. Infreq. add.

APPLETON (WISC.) POST CRESCENT (newsp.). *In* LAWRENCE COLLEGE W2

APPLETON'S ANNUAL CYCLOPEDIA (bk.). *In* NECROLOGY P36-ref

ARABIAN NIGHTS ENTERTAINMENT (bk.)
 C32-lit v. 1-10, v. 10-17 supp. Tpd. list, by t. No add.

ARACHNIDA
 Nj61 125 cds. by auth. & t. Bks., per., pam. Freq. add.

ARCHAEOLOGISTS. *See* ARCHITECTS N30-Avery (1, 2)

ARCHAEOLOGY. *See also* ARCHITECTURE
N30-Avery (2); INDIANS—LEGENDS
N42
Vt3 75 cds. by subj. Bks., per. Cur. add.

ARCHAEOLOGY, BIBLICAL. *See* BIBLE—ANTIQUITIES   N35-ref. Jew.

ARCHITECTS
N30-Avery (1) 7500 cds. by subj. Per., newsp., occ. bks. Obit. of architects, archaeologists & art. Freq. add.
N30-Avery (2) 2600 cds. by subj. Bks., per. Architects of the late 19th, & 20th cent. Freq. add.

ARCHITECTS—PITTSBURGH (PA.)
P39-ref. Pa. 780 cds. by name. Pittsburgh dir. 1815–1900. No add.

ARCHITECTS, ENGLISH
C73-Bak. 1200 cds. by name. Architects of 17th-19th cent. & their wks. Freq. add.

ARCHITECTURAL SCULPTURE. *See* SCULPTURE, ARCHITECTURAL

ARCHITECTURE. *See also* ART   **173-arch**; Art **Mn14-art**; List of Bibliographies, APPENDIX I
C32-art 4000 cds. by subj. Maps, bks. No. add.
Mo13-art 900 cds. by place, name & type of bldg. Coll. of arch. plans. Cur. add.
N30-Avery (1) 1400 cds. by place & bldg. Bks. & per. Freq. add.
N30-Avery (2) 175,000 cds. by subj., occ. auth. & t. Per., pams. Arch., archaeol. & fine arts. Cur. add.
N35-ref. art 37,500 cds. by subj. Bks. & per. Cur. add.
N35-ref. read 600 cds. by place. Pub. of hist. & learned soc. Arch. monuments to about 1800 inc. pic. & floor-plans. Cur. add.
N54-art 800 cds. by subj., styles, etc. Well illus. bks. Occ. add.
Nj60-art 70,000 cds. by subj. & place. Bks., per., pams. Arch. laboratory, for problems of spec. research. Freq. add.

ARCHITECTURE—CHICAGO. *See* List of Bibliographies, APPENDIX I

ARCHITECTURE—CLEVELAND (O.). *See* ART —CLEVELAND (O.)   **O20-art**

ARCHITECTURE—ILLINOIS
15-ref 24 cds. by auth. & architect. Bks. & per. Occ. add.

ARCHITECTURE—LANTERN SLIDES. *See* LANTERN SLIDES   **N30** t.c. art; **Wa15**; LANTERN SLIDES—ART **N55-art**

ARCHITECTURE—PHOTOGRAPHS
N55-art 8765 cds. by Fogg museum class. system. Bks. on art and arch. Infreq. add.
O25-Clev. sch. arch 330 ent., tpd. shts. by subj. Freq. add.

ARCHITECTURE—PITTSBURGH (PA.). *See* ART—PITTSBURGH (PA.)   **P39-ref. art**.

ARCHITECTURE, DOMESTIC. *See* List of Bibliographies, APPENDIX I

ARCHITECTURE, ENGLISH. *See* List of Bibliographies, APPENDIX I

ARCHITECTURE, VIRGINIAN—PHOTOGRAPHS
V7 160 cds. chron. by date acquired. Per. indexed: *Early Virginia architecture, Photographic survey.* Infreq. add.

ARCHIV FÜR DIE ZEICHNENDEN KÜNSTE (per.)
N5 v. 1-16, 1855–date. Tpd. mss. by art. No add.

ARCHIVES
D7-ref 4000 cds. by auth., t; class. by subj. Bks. per., etc. on arch. economy. Freq. add.

ARCTIC REGIONS
Me3 1000 cds. by auth. & t. Freq. add.

ARGENTINA—ARTISTS. *See* ARTISTS—ARGENTINA

ARGONAUT (per.). *See also* BOOK REVIEWS **C8-ord**; CALIFORNIA   **C8-ref**
C69-per v. 2-106, 1878–1929. Cds. by subj. No add.

ARITHMETIC—STUDY AND TEACHING
C11 1000 cds. by auth. & subj. Bks., per., pams. Cur. add.

ARIZONA—MINING AND METALLURGY. *See* MINING AND METALLURGY—SOUTHWEST   **Tx14**

ARIZONA HIGHWAYS (per.)
Az1 v. 1, 1925–date. Tpd. shts. bd. Cur. add.

ARIZONA HISTORICAL REVIEW
Nm2   v. 1, 1928–date.   Cds. by auth., t., subj. Cur. add.

ARKANSAS
Ar5   1500 cds. by auth., t., subj.   Pam. & newsp. Cur. add.

ARKANSAS—BIOGRAPHY
Ar2   7500 cds. by pers.   Bks.   Cur. add.

ARKANSAS—HISTORY
Ar6   75 cds. by auth., t.   Bks., pams., newsp., pic.   Freq. add.

ARKANSAS VALLEY (COL.)—HISTORY
Co3   108p. tpd.   Bk. indexed: M. Florence Harvey, *History of the Arkansas valley, Col.*   No add.

ARMISTICE DAY—POETRY
O56-Locke   200 cds. by auth.   Bks. Infreq. add.

ARMS.   *See* HERALDRY

ART.   *See also* ARCHAEOLOGY; ARCHITECTURE; CHRISTIAN ART AND SYMBOLISM; DRAWINGS AND ENGRAVINGS: JESUS CHRIST IN ART; PAINTINGS; PHOTOGRAPHS; PHYSICIANS AND ART; PICTURES: PORTRAITS: SCULPTURE; List of Bibliographies, APPENDIX I
C24   7500 cds. by art., t. & subj.   Per., newsp.   Freq. add.
De3   3100 cds. by auth. & subj.   Bks. Infreq. add.
I11-Ryer.   Unest. cds. by subj.   Per. & pam. inc. museum pub., exhib. cat. Cur. add.
173-arch   18,000 cds. by subj.   Bks., per., pams. on art & arch.   Freq. add.
Md2-art   Several thousand cds. by subj.   Bks., per.   Cur. add.
Mi6-art   53,000 cds. by subj.   Bks., per.   Cur. add.
Mn14-art (1)   24,000 cds. by subj. Bks., per., pams., pic.   Arch. & art, exclusive of painting, art. lives.   Freq. add.
Mn14-art (2)   4500 cds. by country & art.   Bks., per., pams., pic.   Painting & sculp., inc. biog. of art. & sculp. Infreq. add.
N35-Tre.   500 cds. by subj.   Per. Infreq. add.
N46-art   3800 cds. by subj.   Bks., per.   Cur. add.
N54-art   1200 cds. by subj.   Occ. ad.
Nj27   400 cds. by t.   Bks.   Infreq. add.

O20-art   5320 cds. by name & subj. Freq. add.
W15   478 cds. by subj.   Bks., cats., per.   Freq. add.
Wa3   800 cds. by auth., t., subj.   Bks. Infreq. add.

ART—BIBLIOGRAPHIES.   *See* List of Bibliographies, APPENDIX I

ART—BOOK REVIEWS
Mi6-art   Over 5000 cds. by auth. Per.   Freq. add.

ART—BOSTON (MASS.)
M11-phot   1700 cds. by art. & place. Sculp., paintings, etc. of greater Boston.   Occ. add.

ART—CATALOGS.   *See also* List of Bibliographies, APPENDIX I
I11-Ryer.   11,000 cards, by art. & subj.   Auction sales cat. in fine and dec. arts.   Cur. add.
N45b-art   382v.   Cds. by perm. coll. & temp. exhib.   Cur. add.

ART—CLEVELAND (O.)
O20-art   2273 cds. by name & subj. Per., bks. on arch. & art.   Infreq. add.

ART—EXHIBITIONS.   *See also* ART—PAMPHLETS   **N35-ref. art**
I11-Ryer.   Unest. cds. by name of art. Exhib. cats. except those of Art Inst.   Cur. add.
I11-Ryer.   854 cds. by subj.   Art inst. cats. of exhib.   Cur. add.
N46-art   265 cds. by gallery, art., subj., etc.   Exhib. cats.   Cur. add.

ART—ILLINOIS
I5-ref   70 cds. by auth. & art.   Bks. & per.   Occ. add.

ART—PAMPHLETS
N35-ref. art   1000 cds. by gallery or museum. Pams. Museums & galleries in U.S. and abroad in cats. Cur. add.

ART—PERIODICALS
I11-Ryer.   232,500 cds. by subj.   Per. in fine arts, arch., city planning, land. arch. not indexed by Wilson.   Cur. add.
Nj33   30,000 cds. by subj.   Per. before 1929.   Freq. add.
R2   145,000 cds. by subj.   Per. before 1929.   No add.

ART—PHOTOGRAPHS. *See also* List of Bibliographies, APPENDIX I
Nj49 10,000 cds. by subj. Phot. inc. 800 paintings & 300 pieces of sculp. Freq. add.

ART—PITTSBURGH (PA.)
P39-ref. art 3000 cds. by subj. Per. & bks. on Pittsburgh art & arch. Occ. add.

ART—SOUTH AMERICA. *See* List of Bibliographies, APPENDIX I

ART—SOUTHWEST
Tx27 40 cds. by subj. Unindexed mat. on fine arts in Texas & neighboring states. Cur. add.

ART—STUDY AND TEACHING
Ct3-j 505 cds. by art. & t. of pic. Children's bks. on art appreciation. Cur. add.
I9 2832 cds. by art. & t. Bks. & per. Mat. about pic. Infreq. add.
M20 600 cds. by art. & t. Bks., per. Pic. interpretations. Freq. add.
M27-art 500 cds. by art. Bks. on pic. study, *Perry magazine*, 1898–1906. Infreq. add.
Md10 1100 cds. by art. & t. Bks., *Instructor magazine*. Pic. study. Freq. add.
Mi6-Monn. Unest. ent. tpd. shts., by art. & t. Bk. indexed: Katherine M. Lester, *Great pictures and their stories;* Flora L. Carpenter, *Stories pictures tell.* No add.
Mi6-Walk. 618 cds. by art. & t. Bks. indexed: Mary Bacon, *Pictures that every child should know;* Lorinda Bryant, *Children's book of celebrated pictures;* Flora L. Carpenter, *Stories pictures tell;* Katherine M. Lester, *Great pictures and their stories;* Maude I. G. Oliver, *First steps in the enjoyment of pictures; Turner picture studies.* No add.
Mi-18 67 cds., numerically. Well-known paintings in pic. study. No add.
Nj11-circ 4500 cds. by art. & t. Bks., pams. on pic. study. Infreq. add.
O20-art 2775 cds. by art. & t. Bks. on pic. study. Freq. add.
O20-j 1500 cds. by t. Bks. on pic. study. Infreq. add.
O20-Sup. 1000 cds. by t. Bks. on pic. study. Cur. add.

P39-ref. art 1000 cds. by art. Bks. suitable for children of grade sch. age. Cur. add.
Wa13-j 105 cds. by art. & t. Bk. indexed: Katherine M. Lester, *Great pictures and their stories.* No. add.

ART—TEXAS. *See* ART—SOUTHWEST
Tx27

ART, CANADIAN
Ca5-ref 200 cds. by name & subj. Scrapbks. from newsp. Infreq. add.

ART, JAPANESE
C56-print (1) 300 cds. by name. Bks., per. & prints. Designers of Jap. prints, with signatures. Infreq. add.
C56-print (2) 582 cds. by name. Bks. & per. Designers of Jap. prints, without signatures. Infreq. add.

ART, MEXICAN. *See* List of Bibliographies, APPENDIX I

ART, ORIENTAL. *See also* ART, JAPANESE
D9 11,000 cds. by auth., t. & subj. Ser. devoted to Orient. art & culture: *T'oung pao, Ostasiatische zeitschrift, etc.;* gen. serials such as *Bul. Museum of fine arts, Boston, Illustrated London news.* Cur. add.
P42-art 3000 cds. by art., subj. & t. Bks. indexed: Japan, Imperial Jap. commission to the Panama-Pacific international exposition, *Japanese temples and their treasures;* Shōbi Shiryō; *Materials for art study,* 12v.; Tajima Shiichi, *Selected relics of Japanese art,* 20v.; Tajima Shiichi, *Masterpieces selected from the fine arts of the Far East.* Per indexed: *Kokka.* v. 1–46, 1889–1936.

ART, PERSIAN
N35-ref. Orient. 1500 cds. by subj. Bks. & per. No add.

ART, RELIGIOUS. *See also* CHRISTIAN ART AND SYMBOLISM; JESUS CHRIST IN ART
R2 5200 cds. by subj. & art. Per. indexed: *L'Arte,* 1898–1911; *Bolletino d'Arte,* 1907-1920; Rassegna d'Arte, 1909–1922. No add.

ART, VICTORIAN
N35-ref. art 500 cds. by subj. Bks. & per. on Victorian art, interiors & furniture. Cur. add.

ART AND ARCHAEOLOGY (per.). *In* SOUTH-
WEST **Nm2**
ART JOURNAL
Mn22 v. 16-33, 1864–1881. Cds. by
auth., subj., t. & Art. Illus. & art.
No add.
ART NEWS (per.). *In* PICTURES **I7**
ART OBJECTS. *See* List of Bibliographies,
APPENDIX I
L'ARTE (per.). *In* ART, RELIGIOUS **R2**;
SCULPTURE **R2**
ARTHUR, KING. *See* List of Bibliographies,
APPENDIX I
ARTIFICIAL RADIOACTIVITY. *See* RADIOAC-
TIVITY, ARTIFICIAL
ARTISTS. *See also* DESIGNERS; ILLUSTRA-
TORS; ARCHITECTS **N30-Avery**
(1); ART **Mn14-art** (1), (2);
List of bibliographies, APPENDIX I
C56-print 1500 cds. by form of art.
Bks., per., cats., prints. Early Amer.
engravers, etchers & lithographers.
Infreq. add.
I13-w.s.r. 500 cds. by art. Per.,
newsp. Contemp. biog. Freq. add.
I62 4p tpd. shts., by art. Bk. in-
dexed: *Masters in art* ser., 9v. No
add.
I68-art 400 cds. by art. Bks. & per.
Biog. of painters, mus., sculp. In-
freq. add.
Ia14-art 260 cds. by art. Bk. in-
dexed: Adolfo Venturi, *Storia dell-
'arte Italiana*. 22v. Painters &
sculp. Cur. add. as new v. are pub.
Mi13-W. side 2000 cds. by art.
Biog. of art. & inf. on famous paint-
ings. Freq. add.
N10-ref 16,832 cds. by auth. & subj.
Bks., per. Freq. add.
N35-ref. art 175,000 cds. by art &
subj. Bks. & per. Biog., obit. of
art., reprod. of their wks. Cur. add.
N35-ref. print 27,000 cds. by art.
Separates & bks. Engravers, etchers,
printmakers, lithographers, wood en-
gravers. Cur. add.
Nj21 135 ent., tpd. booklet by subj.
Freq. add.
O56-ref 3200 cds. by art. Biog. &
crit. inf. not indexed. Occ. add.

P31 519 cds. by type of artist. Wks.
of art in coll. & illus. in med. bks.
Caricaturists, engravers, illus., paint-
ers, photographers, pub. of art, sculp-
tors. Cur. add.
T1-ref Tpd. booklet by art. Bk. in-
dexed: *Masters in art*, 9v. No add.
W17 700 ent., tpd. shts. & bd. by art.
under nationality. Freq. add.
ARTISTS—ARGENTINA
V7 300 cds. by art. Contemp. biog.
No add.
ARTISTS—CALIFORNIA
C3 105 cds. by art. Calif. research
W.P.A. project #2874. Infreq. add.
C27-art 675 cds. by art. Bks., per.
Occ. add.
C51 225 cds. by art. Bks., per.,
newsp. Infreq. add.
C69-ref 500 cds. by art. Bks., per.
Occ. add.
ARTISTS—CINCINNATI (O.)
O15 800 cds. by art. Bks., exhib. &
exp. cat., mostly before 1910. Infreq.
add.
ARTISTS—FAIRFIELD Co. (CONN.). *See*
FAIRFIELD CO. (CONN.)—BIOGRAPHY
Ct2-hist.
ARTISTS—IDAHO. *See* AUTHORS—IDAHO
Id2
ARTISTS—ILLINOIS
I11-Ryer. Unest. ent., tpd. shts. by
art. Ill. art. in 1918, 1929; scrapbks.
No add.
ARTISTS—KENTUCKY
Ky15-Ky. 600 cds. by art. Newsp. &
bk. rev. Occ. add.
ARTISTS—MARYLAND
Md2-art 1000 cds. by art. Baltimore
& Md. art. & art teachers. Occ. add.
ARTISTS—OHIO
O16-art 500 cds. by type of art.
Art ency., yrbks., per. Etchers, en-
gravers, etc. Cur. add.
ARTISTS—PITTSBURGH (PA.)
P39-ref. art 14,000 cds. by art. Bks.,
per. & art cat. Emphasis on art. who
have exhibited in Pittsburgh. Cur.
add.
P39-ref. art 1900 cds. by art. Pitts-
burgh dir., 1815–1900 & misc. sources.
Freq. add.

ARTISTS—TEXAS. *See* TEXAS—BIOGRAPHY
Tx27(2)

ARTISTS, AMERICAN
V7 150 ent., letter file by art. Pam., biog., exhib. announcements. Freq. add.

ARTISTS, JAPANESE. *See* ART, JAPANESE
C56-print

THE ARTS (per.)
P39-ref. art v. 1–4, 1925–1928. Tpd. shts., bd. by art. & auth. No add.

ARTWORK (per.)
P39-ref. art v. 1-4, 1925–1928. Tpd. shts., bd. by art. & auth. No add.

ARUNDEL PICTURES. *See* PICTURES—ARUNDEL PRINTS

ASSOCIATION OF AMERICAN COLLEGES. BULLETIN
Wa3 v. 4-14, 1918–1928. Cds. by auth., t., subj. Supp. by later Educ. index. No add.

ASSOCIATION OF PACIFIC COAST GEOGRAPHERS. YEARBOOK
Wa4 1935–1939. Ent. on mim. shts. No add.

ASSOCIATIONS. *See* Names of loc. & subj., subdiv. SOCIETIES AND CLUBS

ASTRONOMY
N61 2500 cds. Bks. Consolidated index of astron. bk. indexes. Occ. add.
Nj60-Obs. 5000 cds. by star positions. All mat. on eclipsing variables. Daily add.

ASTRONOMY—TABLES. *See* MATHEMATICS—TABLES **N35-ref. sci**

ASTROPHYSICAL JOURNAL. *In* PICTURES—ASTROPHYSICS **Ca8-lib. sch**

ATENEO PUERTORRIQUEÑO (per.) *In* PUERTO RICO **Pr1**

ATHENAE OXONIENSES (bk.)
C73-ref 5300 cds. by names of people, bks. 4v., 1813 ed. by Anthony Wood. Cur. add.

ATHLETIC SPORTS AND GAMES. *See* SPORTS AND ATHLETIC GAMES. List of Bibliographies, APPENDIX I.

ATLANTA (GA.)
G4-ref 200 ent., tpd. shts. by subj. Atlanta scrapbks. No add.

ATLANTA (GA.)—ADULT EDUCATION
G4-circ 150 cds. by subj. & name of agency. Dir., newsp. Ad. educ. & recreat. opportunities in Atlanta & Fulton co., Ga. Yrly. add.

ATLANTA (GA.)—BIOGRAPHY. *See* INSURANCE—DIRECTORIES **G9**

ATLANTA (GA.)—CLUB PROGRAMS. *See* CLUB PROGRAMS—ATLANTA (GA.)

ATLANTA (GA.)—SOCIETIES AND CLUBS
G5-circ 42 cds. by type of organiz. Club dir., club programs. Children's organiz. in Atlanta. Yrly. add.

ATLANTA (GA.)—TRANSLATORS. *See* list of Bibliographies, APPENDIX I

ATLANTA (GA.) CONSTITUTION (newsp.)
G2 1941–date. Cds. Mo. add.
G8 1927–date. Cds. by subj. Ga. items. Daily add.

ATLANTA JOURNAL MAGAZINE
G14 1932–date. Cds. by auth. & subj. Cur. add.

ATLANTA UNIVERSITY—PUBLICATIONS
G3 370 cds. by auth. Bks., per. Occ. add.

ATLAS OF LAWRENCE CO., INDIANA (bk.) *In* INDIANA—BIOGRAPHY **In35-gen (1)**

ATOMS. *See* PHYSICS **Nj60-phys (2)**

AUCTION SALES CATALOGS. *See* ART—CATALOGS

AUDIO-VISUAL AIDS. *See also* LANTERN SLIDES; MAPS; MOTION PICTURES IN EDUCATION; PICTURES; List of Bibliographies, APPENDIX I
I77 Unest. cds., by name of film. DuPage co. audio-visual film inf. file; free films from com. co. Cur. add.
Nj69 Several thousand cds. by subj. Charts, exhibits, films, filmslides, graphs, maps, pic., posters, radio in educ., recordings, and pub. (teaching aids). Daily add.

AUDUBON, JOHN JAMES. *See* List of Bibliographies, APPENDIX I

AUDUBON PRINTS. *See* PICTURES—BIRDS **N35-ref. inf**

AUTAUGA CO. (ALA.)—CEMETERY RECORDS
A1 87 ent., tpd. shts. Autaugaville cem.; DeJarnette family cem.; Ivy Creek cem., Mulberry. Freq. add.

AUTHORS. *See also* Names of individual authors; AUTOGRAPHS; ESSAYISTS; LIBRARIANS AS AUTHORS; NECROLOGY; NOVELISTS; POETS; CLASSICAL LITERATURE—**Or8**
C32-lit 22,000 cds. by subj. Bks., per., pams. Freq. add.
C78 400 cds. by auth. Bks., per., newsp. Infreq. add.
C88 200 cds. by auth. Per. indexed: *Scholastic; Wilson library bulletin.* Occ. add.
I13-w.s.r. 3000 cds. by auth. Per., newsp. Freq. add.
I28 2500 cds. by auth. Per. indexed: *The Rotarian.* Freq. add.
Ia20 1000 cds. by auth. *Bks.* indexed: Stanley J. Kunitz, *Authors to-day and yesterday;* Stanley J. Kunitz, *Living authors.* Per. indexed: *Wilson library bulletin.* Cur. add.
In1 5000 cds. by nationality of auth. Bk. indexed: Sander Macclintock, *Sainte Beuve's Critical theory.* Ref. & auth. other than French. In proc.
In5-j 900 cds. by auth. Bks., newsp., per. Cur. add.
In33-j 700 cds. by auth. Bks., newsp. Cur. add.
M14 200 cds. by auth. Bks., per. Biog., necrol., bibl. of wks. Freq. add.
M24 Over 13,000 cds. by auth. Per. indexed: *Wilson library bulletin.* Freq. add.
M32 500 ent., tpd. shts. by auth. Occ. add.
Md2-lit 12,000 cds. by auth. Bks., per., pams. Freq. add.
Md3 150 cds. by subj. Pams., per., etc. Freq. add.
Mi6-Fenk. 403 ent., tpd. shts. by nationality & period. Amer., English, French, Russian, Spanish & Swedish fic. auth. Freq. add.
Mn9 Unest. cds. by auth. Bks., pams. Biog. & crit. Freq. add.
Mn9-S. Hib. 400 cds. by auth. Bks., per. & newsp. Infreq. add.
Mo13-ref 1300 cds. by auth. Bks. Occ. add.
Mt1 1897 ent., tpd. shts. by auth. Bks. indexed: Stanley J. Kunitz, *Authors to-day and yesterday;* Stanley J. Kunitz, *British authors;* Stanley J. Kunitz & Howard Haycraft, *Junior Book of Authors;* Stanley J. Kunitz, *Living authors.* No add. unless new bk. is pub.
N4 1100 cds., by auth. Pam., newsp. Per. indexed: *Book of the month club news; Wilson library bulletin; Wings.* Freq. add.
N23 1935 cds. by auth. Bks., pams. Freq. add.
N54-per 1050 cds. by auth. Per. Freq. add.
N54-ref 7500 cds. by auth. Bks., pams., newsp. Freq. add.
N55 700 cds. by auth. Bks. Lit. crit. Freq. add.
Nd2 2200 cds. by subj. Bks. Freq. add.
Nj11-ref Over 7200 cds. by auth. Bks., pams., newsp. Freq. add.
Nj16 2400 cds. by auth. Bks., ency., per., pams. Wkly. add.
Nj29 300 cds. by auth. Bks., per., pams., newsp. Freq. add.
O1-E. Unest. cds. by auth. Per. indexed: *Wilson library bulletin.* Freq. add.
O7 264 cds. by auth. Per. indexed: *Wilson library bulletin,* 1928–1940. Mo. add.
O20-Euc. 100th Unest. cds. by auth. Per. indexed: *Wilson library bulletin,* 1929–date. Cur. add.
O36-v.f. 1500 ent., tpd. shts. *Per. indexed: American prefaces,* 1935–1939. No add.
O60 500 cds. by auth. Per. indexed: *Wilson library bulletin; Wings.* Cur. add.
Or5-circ 1400 cds. by auth. Bks. Freq. add.
P27a 300 cds. by auth. Per. indexed: *Wilson library bulletin.* Other per. & tpd. mat. secured from auth. & publishers. Freq. add.
P33-ref 2700 cds. by auth. Bks., per., newsp. Freq. add.
P34-ref 2500 cds. by subj. Bks. in Eng. Gen. lit. index to auth. & poets. Occ. add.
P39-j 750 cds. by auth. Bks., pams., per. Occ. add.

P39-Wyl. 555 cds. by auth. Bks., per., pams. Occ. add.
P48 684 cds. by auth. Bks., per., newsp. Occ. add.
Tx4 1250 cds. by auth. Bks. Infreq. add.
Tx23 200 ent., tpd. shts. by subj. Bks., per. Freq. add.
Tx26 334 cds. by subj. Bks., per., newsp. 20th cent. auth. Cur. add.
W16 4000 cds. by auth. Anthologies of lit. Freq. add.
Wa16 4000 ent., tpd. shts. by auth. Author bks. & ency. Freq. add.

AUTHORS—ALAMEDA (CALIF.). *See* List of Bibliographies, APPENDIX I

AUTHORS—ATLANTA (GA.). *See* AUTHORS— GEORGIA G4-ref

AUTHORS—BUFFALO (N.Y.)
N10 120 cds. by auth. Bks. Freq. add.

AUTHORS—CALIFORNIA
C51 255 cds. by auth. Bks., per., newsp. Infreq. add.
C69-ref 650 cds. by subj. Bks., per., newsp. Occ. add.

AUTHORS—CAMBRIDGE (MASS.)
M16-ref 200 cds. by auth. Yrly. add.

AUTHORS—CHICAGO. *See* List of Bibliographies, APPENDIX I

AUTHORS—CLEVELAND (O.)
O20-per 1320 cds. by auth. Per. Cur. add.
O20-ref 12,000 cds. by auth. Freq. add.

AUTHORS—DELAWARE. *See* List of Bibliographies, APPENDIX I

AUTHORS—ELKHART CO. (IND.)
In6 45 cds. by auth. Occ. add.

AUTHORS—FAIRFIELD CO. (CONN.). *See* FAIRFIELD CO. (CONN.)—BIOGRAPHY Ct2-hist.

AUTHORS—GENESEE CO. (MICH.)
Mill-ref 150 cds. by auth. Occ. ref.

AUTHORS—GEORGIA
G2 500 cds. by auth. Freq. add.
G4-ref 1320 cds. by auth. Atlanta newsp. Freq. add.

G14 1700 cds. by auth. Bks. Cur. add.

AUTHORS—IDAHO
Id2 1000 cds. by auth. Bks., per., etc. Auth. & art. who have lived in Idaho or written about Idaho. Infreq. add.

AUTHORS—INDIANA
In24a 32 cds. by subj. Newsp., bks. Freq. add.

AUTHORS—KENTUCKY
Ky2 3700 cds. by auth. Incl. pseudonyms. Freq. add.
Ky6 1400 cds. by auth. Bks. No add.
Ky15-Ky. 850 cds. by auth. Newsp., bk. rev., per. Occ. add.

AUTHORS—LEXINGTON (MASS.)
M20 86 cds. by auth. Bks., pams. Infreq. add.

AUTHORS—LIBRARIANS. *See* LIBRARIANS AS AUTHORS

AUTHORS—LOS ANGELES (CALIF.)
C32-mun. ref 1200 cds. by auth. Bks. & per. Bks. & per. art. written by L.A. city officials & employees. Cur. add.

AUTHORS—MALDEN (MASS.)
M21 425 cds. by auth. Bks., pams. Cur. add.

AUTHORS—MARYLAND
Md2-Md. 900 cds. by auth. Newsp. Freq. add.

AUTHORS—MICHIGAN
Mi13-Mich. Over 3500 cds. by auth. Bks., per., mss. Daily add.

AUTHORS—MINNESOTA. *See also* List of Bibliographies, APPENDIX I
Mn14-clip 1350 cds. by auth. Newsp. Infreq. add.
Mn14-ref 1900 cds. by auth., t., subj. Cur. add.

AUTHORS—MISSOURI
Mo3-cat 1600 cds. by auth. Bks. Freq. add.

AUTHORS—MONTCLAIR (N.J.)
Nj34 75 cds. by auth. Freq. add.

AUTHORS—MYSTERY AND DETECTIVE STORIES
I13-Hild 3 p., tpd. shts. by auth. Bks. Yrly. add.

AUTHORS—NEBRASKA
Nb6 232 ent., tpd. shts. by auth. Bks. & pams. Freq. add.
Nb8 1870 cds. by auth. Bks. & per. Freq. add.

AUTHORS—NEW JERSEY
Nj4 500 ent., tpd. shts. by auth. & by place. Yrly. add.
Nj50-circ 950 cds. by auth. Bks. Freq. add.

AUTHORS—NORTH DAKOTA. *See* List of Bibliographies, APPENDIX I

AUTHORS—OKLAHOMA
Ok4-ref Unest. cds. by subj. Bks., per. In proc.

AUTHORS—OREGON
Or2 500 cds. by auth. Bks., etc. Freq. add.
Wa10-ref 250 cds. by auth. Newsp., per. Occ. add.

AUTHORS—PENNSYLVANIA
P16 2000 cds. by auth. No add.
P27 651 cds. by auth., t. Bks. No add.
P40 1000 cds. by auth. Bks., per. Bibl., biog., crit. & wks. Infreq. add.

AUTHORS—PEORIA (ILL.)
I65 43 p. tpd. booklet by auth. Bks. & pams. Freq. add.

AUTHORS—PHYSICIANS. *See* PHYSICIANS AS AUTHORS

AUTHORS—PITTSBURGH (PA.)
P39-tech 250 cds. by auth. Bks. Auth. of sci. subj. Cur. add.

AUTHORS—PLAINFIELD (N.J.)
Nj58 175 cds. by auth. & t. Bks. & per. Occ. add.

AUTHORS—ROCHESTER (N.Y.)
N46-loc. hist 2500 cds. by auth. Auth. of Rochester & vicinity. Occ. ref.

AUTHORS—RUSSIA
Mi6-for 125 cds. by subj. & auth. Bks. Occ. add.

AUTHORS—ST. PAUL (MINN.)
Mn23-St. Anth. 150 cds. by auth. Bks. Loc. St. Anthony Park auth. Occ. add.

AUTHORS—SHORT STORIES. *See also* AUTHORS—MYSTERY AND DETECTIVE STORIES; AUTHORS—WESTERN STORIES

I49 848 cds. by auth., t. Bks. Cur. add.

AUTHORS—SUMMIT CO. (O.)
O28 Unest. cds. by auth. Freq. add.

AUTHORS—SYRACUSE (N.Y.)
N54 800 cds. by auth. All Syracuse & Onondaga co. mat. & gen. biog. wks. Occ. add.

AUTHORS—TACOMA (WASH.) *See* AUTHORS—WASHINGTON (STATE) **Wa14-ref**

AUTHORS—TENNESSEE
T3 50 cds. by subj. Occ. add.

AUTHORS—TEXAS. *See* TEXAS—BIOGRAPHY **Tx27** (2)

AUTHORS—TOLEDO (O.)
O56-circ 150 cds. by auth. Occ. add.
O56-ref 100 cds. by auth. Occ. add.

AUTHORS—WASHINGTON (STATE)
Wa2 350 cds. by auth. Bks. Infreq. add.
Wa10-ref (1) 1200 cds. by auth. Newsp., per. Freq. add.
Wa10-ref (2) Unest. ent., tpd. shts. Bk. indexed: Lancaster Pollard, *Checklist of Washington authors*. No. add.
Wa14-ref 600 cds. by auth. Emphasis on Tacoma. Freq. add.

AUTHORS—WESTERN STORIES
I13-Hild 3p. tpd. shts. by auth. Bks. Yrly. add.

AUTHORS—WILKES-BARRE (PA.)
P54-ref 104 cds. by auth. Cur. add.

AUTHORS—WORCESTER (MASS.)
M32 350 cds. by auth. Occ. add.

AUTHORS, CATHOLIC. *See also* POETS, CATHOLIC; List of Bibliographies, APPENDIX I
I13-circ 475 cds. by auth. Bks. Freq. add.
I49 2162 cds. by auth. Bks., per. Freq. add.
Md5 140 cds. by auth. Bks. Occ. add.
Mo13-Soul. 290 cds. by auth. Bks. Non-Amer. Cath. auth. Infreq. add.
Mo13-Soul. 250 cds. by auth. Bks. Amer. Cath. auth. Infreq. add.
Mo13-univ 1200 cds. by auth. Bks. & per. Freq. add.

AUTHORS, CHILDREN'S. *See also* ILLUSTRATORS, CHILDREN'S
   Ar5   250 ent., tpd. shts. in notebk. by auth. & illus. Unindexed wks. Freq. add.
   De3   375 cds. by subj. Bks. & per. Infreq. add.
   I65-j   1734 ent., tpd. shts. by auth. Pams., newsp., etc. Occ. add.
   Ia6-j   300 ent., tpd. shts. by auth. Per., newsp., cat., etc. Freq. add.
   In12   13p., tpd. shts. by auth. Per., bks. No add.
   O1-j   500 cds. by t. & subj. Bks., etc. Bk. indexed: Stanley J. Kunitz, *Junior book of authors*. Cur. add.
   O2   45p., tpd. shts. by auth. Bks. & per. Poets, illus. etc. No add.
   O20-j   1000 cds. by auth. Bks., per., pams. Occ. add.
   Wa10-j   250 cds. by auth. Per., bks. Cur. add.

AUTHORS, FOREIGN
   C32-for   8800 cds. by nationality, subdiv. by auth. Crit. bks. & per. Freq. add.
   Mi6-for   50 cds. by subj. & lang. Bks. Infreq. add.

AUTHORS, JUVENILE. *See* AUTHORS, CHILDREN'S

AUTHORS, NEGRO
   Co5-circ   200 cds. by auth. Bks. Amer. negro auth. No add.

AUTHORS, NORWEGIAN-AMERICAN—UNION LISTS
   Ia5   5000 cds. by auth. Bks. & pams. by Amer. of Norwegian descent, as contrib. by following lib: Augsburg college lib., Luther college lib., Luther theological seminary lib., Minn. hist. soc. lib., Red Wing seminary lib., St. Olaf college lib., Univ. of Minn. lib., Private lib. of Waldemar Ager, Eau Claire, Wisc. Comp. in 1926, with supp. add. Cur. add.

AUTHORS TODAY AND YESTERDAY (bk.). *In* AUTHORS **Ia20**; AUTHORS **Mt1**; BIOGRAPHY **C8-ref**

AUTOBIOGRAPHY. *See* BIOGRAPHY

AUTOGRAPHS
   I26-rare   500 cds. by name. Bks. & mss. Freq. add.
   In22-Ind.   600 cds. by name. Autographs of pers. of state & natl. importance. Freq. add.
   Ky1   700 cds. by name. Letters, bks., misc. Freq. add.
   Ky17   200 cds. by auth. Bks. Cur. add.
   Me3   300 cds. by auth. Bks. in Kate Douglas Wiggin autograph coll. No add.
   N10   843 cds. by auth. Bks. Cur. add.
   N34a   2500 cds. by auth. Cur. add.
   N35-ref. prep   13,000 cds. by name. Bks. Cur. add.
   N45b   Unest. cds. for 362 v., by auth. of bk., auth. of autograph. Helen Wright coll. No add.
   N45b   650 cds. by auth. of autograph. Letters, doc., signatures. Freq. add.
   N46-loc. hist   Over 2600 cds. by names of writers & recipients. Mss. letters. Occ. add.
   N47   650 cds. by name. Add. to print. vol., 1940. Cur. add.
   Nj60-treas   10,000 cds. by auth. Letters, deeds, doc. & mss. Freq. add.
   Nj60-treas   1890 cds. by name. Inc. only autographs. Infreq. add.
   O16-ref   700 cds. by subj. & name. Bks. & per. Occ. add.
   O17   1250 cds. by name. Bks., mss., letters, programs, etc. Inc. Whelpley coll. of about 1000 items. Infreq. add.

AUTOMOTIVE ENGINEERING
   Nj52   Several hundred cds. by subj. Bks., per., pams. Freq. add.

AVE MARIA (per.)
   In30   v. 1-n.s. 28, 1865–1928. Cds. by auth. & subj. Cur. add.

AVIATION. *See* AERONAUTICS

AVIATION STORIES, JUVENILE. *See* List of Bibliographies, APPENDIX I

AWARDS. *See* MEDALS AND AWARDS; REWARDS (PRIZES, ETC.)

BACH, JOHANN SEBASTIAN—WORKS
   Mn14-mus (1)   105 cds. by t. Bk. indexed: *Johann Sebastian Bach, Klavierwerke*. No add.
   N35-mus (2)   25 p., tpd. shts. in notebk. by German & Eng. t. & by cantata no. Bach. cantatas. Freq. add.

BACTERIOLOGY
   Nj61   1200 cds. by auth. & t. Bks., per., pams., reprints. Freq. add.

BADGES OF HONOR. *See* MEDALS AND
AWARDS; SEALS (NUMISMATICS)

BAKER, MRS. KARLE WILSON—WORKS
Tx27 30 cds. by auth. & t. Unindexed material, loc. auth. Freq. add.

BAKERSFIELD (CALIF.) CALIFORNIAN (newsp.)
C6-ref 1936–date. Cds. by subj. Daily add.

BALDWIN CO. (ALA.)—CENSUS
A1 700 cds. by name. Heads of families in 1820. No add.

BALLADS
O56-Locke 200 cds. by t. Bks. Infreq. add.
P54-circ 220 cds. by subj. Bks. Infreq. add.

BALLET. *See* DANCING

BALTIMORE (MD.)
Md2-#3 100 cds. by subj. S. Baltimore neighborhood hist. Occ. add.

BALTIMORE (MD.)—ADVERTISEMENTS. *See* ADVERTISEMENTS—BALTIMORE (MD.)

BALTIMORE (MD.)—MUSIC. *See* MUSIC—BALTIMORE (MD.)

BALTIMORE (MD.)—SOCIETIES AND CLUBS
Md2-ref 3500 cds. by name. Per., newsp., letters. Freq. add.

BALTIMORE MAGAZINE
Md2-#14 1938–1940. 36p., tpd. shts. Mo. add.

BALTIMORE MUNICIPAL JOURNAL
Md2-#14 1919–1927. Cds. by subj. No add.

BALTIMORE MUSEUM OF ART NEWS (per)
Md11 1933–1937. Cds. by subj. No add.

BALZAC, HONORÉ DE—WORKS
C32-fic 32p., tpd. shts., by t. Short stories. No add.

BANDITS. *See* BRIGANDS AND ROBBERS; FRONTIER AND PIONEER LIFE

BANKS AND BANKING
I31 6000 cds. by subj. & auth. Bks., per. Daily add.

BANNERS. *See* SEALS (NUMISMATICS)

BAPTISTS. *See also* FLORIDA BAPTIST ASSOCIATION. MINUTES; TEXAS BAPTIST ASSOCIATION. MINUTES
K16 100 cds. by auth., t. & class. no. Bks., per., pams., leaflets. Infreq. add.
Ky7 Unest. tpd. shts. by name. Bk. indexed: John Taylor, *A history of ten Baptist churches*. No add.
Ky16 3000 cds. by area. Baptist minutes. Yrly. add.
Ky16 63 cds. by Dewey class. Minute bks., mss., of Baptist churches & assoc. Occ. add.
P7 (1) 3000 cds. by names, churches, assoc. Per. indexed: Baptist denomination in North America, *Annual register*, 1–6th ed., 1790. No add.
P7 (2) 40,000 cds. by names, churches, assoc., towns, etc. Bk. indexed: David Benedict, *A General history of the Baptist denomination In America*. No add.
P19 Unest. cds. by name. Bk. indexed: Martin G. Brumbaugh, *A History of German Baptist brethren in Europe and America*. In proc.

BARGES. *See* BOATS

BARREN CO. (KY.)—HISTORY
Ky7 35p., tpd. shts., by name. Bk. indexed: Franklin Gorin, *The times of long ago, Barren co., Kentucky*. No add.

BARRY CO. (MICH.)—HISTORY
Mi16 19 ent., typ. shts. Bks. & per. Barry co. or Hastings material. Infreq. add.

BASEBALL PLAYERS. *See also* PORTRAITS—BASEBALL PLAYERS
N35-ref. st 18,660 cds. by names of players & team. Swales coll. No add.

BASIC SONGS FOR MALE VOICES (bk.) *In* MUSIC **Nj15**

BATES COLLEGE—PUBLICATIONS
Me4 32,000 cds. by auth., subj., t., inc. illus. All Bates pub. Freq. add.

BATTLE OF POINT PLEASANT (bk.) *In* KENTUCKY—HISTORY **Ky7** (2)

BEAUCHAMP-SHARP CASE
Ky2 3p., tpd. shts. bd. by auth. Bks. & per. No add.

BEAUMONT (TEXAS)—SOCIETIES AND CLUBS
Tx4   193 cds. by name. Infreq. add.

BEAUMONT (TEXAS) ENTERPRISE (newsp)
Tx4   1926 date. Cds. by subj. Daily add.

BEAVER (per.)
Ca14   1933–1941. Tpd. shts. by subj. Art. & illus. Yrly. add.

BEDINGER, GEORGE M.
Ky7   Unest. tpd. shts. by name. Bk. indexed: Danske Dandridge, *George M. Bedinger.* No add.

BEES
Md8   81,200 cds. by auth. & subj. Bks. & per. Bee culture, all phases inc. diseases. Freq. add.

BELLINGHAM (WASH.)—SOCIETIES AND CLUBS
Wa2   150 cds. by name. Yrly. add.

BENCHLEY, ROBERT CHARLES—WORKS
N46-lit   400 cds. by t. Benchley essays. Occ. add.

BEREA (KY.). See List of Bibliographies, APPENDIX I

BEREA (KY.) THE CITIZEN (newsp)
Ky1   1902–date. Cds. by auth., t. & subj. Freq. add.

BERGEN CO. (N.J.)—HISTORIC HOUSES. See List of Bibliographies, APPENDIX I

BERKELEY (CALIF.). See CALIFORNIA
C8-ref

BERKELEY (CALIF.)—ORDINANCES
C8-ref   414 cds. by subj. Ord. passed since 1928. Occ. add.

BERKELEY (CALIF.)—SOCIETIES AND CLUBS
C8-ref   185 cds. by name. Newsp. Freq. add.

BERKS CO. (CALIF.)—HISTORY
P45-ref   1200 cds. Hist. art. in *Reading eagle* since 1933; *Historical review of Berks co.,* etc. Cur. ref.

BERYLLUM. See List of Bibliographies, APPENDIX I

BEST PLAYS OF (1919–20—DATE) (bk.). *In* PLAYS   **Mi6-Sch., Mi6-Walk., O20-lit (2), O20-Nott., T1-circ**

BETTER HOMES AND GARDENS (per)
Ia8   1928–date. Cds. by auth. & subj. Mo. add.

BEVERAGES
Md2-ind   600 cds. by subj. Bks., per. Recipes, hist., & gen. inf. Infreq. add.

BIBLE
M14   2000 cds. by subj. Bks. & per. Bible & rel. subj.: archaeol., bibl., biog., chron., hist. of Bibl. events, hist. of transmission of Bible, lit., etc. Freq. add.

BIBLE—ANTIQUITIES
N35-ref. Jew   17,500 cds. by subj. Bks. & per. Bibl. archaeol., illus., reprod. of texts, etc. of subj. of Hebrew hist. interest. Cur. add.

BIBLE—OLD TESTAMENT
In16   200 cds. by subj. Bks. Old testament exegesis mat. Infreq. add.

BIBLIOGRAPHIE EGYPTOLOGIQUE. See List of Bibliographies, APPENDIX I

BIBLIOGRAPHIES. See also List of Bibliographies APPENDIX I; Names of subj., subdiv. BIBLIOGRAPHIES
C14   10 p., tpd. shts. by subj. Per. indexed: *Wilson library bulletin,* 1930–1940. No add.
C32-fic   53p., tpd. shts. by subj. Freq. add.
C48-ref   22,000 cds. by subj. Bks., per., diss., doc. Cur. add.
C56   150 ent., tpd. shts. by subj. Freq. add.
C57   200 cds. by subj. Bks., per., pams. Infreq. add.
C76   304 cds. by subj. Bks., per., pams. Freq. add.
C87   200 cds. by auth. Bks., pams. No add.
Ca8-lib. sch   130 cds. by subj. Bibl. by stud. Every 2 yrs.
Ca13-lib. sch   19p., tpd. shts. by subj. Bibl. by stud. to 1939.
Co5   600 cds. by subj. Occ. add.
I45-ref   800 cds. by subj. Infreq. add.
I72   143 ent., tpd. shts. by subj. Freq. add.
K12-ref   800 cds. by subj. & auth. Comp. by govt. depts., lib., museums, etc. Freq. add.
K22   100 cds. by subj. Bks., pers., pams. & pic. Freq. add.
M28   240 cds. by subj. Pams. Freq. add.

Md2-bus 700 cds. by subj. Bks., per., doc., pams. Cur. add.
Mi22-ref 150 cds. by subj. Per., pams., etc. Freq. add.
Mn15-lib. sch 5p., tpd. shts. by subj. Class bibl., 1934–1940.
Mn15-ref 450 cds. by subj. Bks., per., pams. Occ. add.
Mo13-sci 470 cds. by subj. Freq. add.
N7-lib. sch 70 p., tpd. shts. Stud. bibl.
N8-ref 4000 cds. by subj. Bks. & per. Infreq. add.
N22-r.a. 2250 ent. by subj. Freq. add.
N30-t.c. 1200 cds. by subj. Per. indexed: *Saturday review of literature, Reader's guide column.* Cur. add.
Nb7 280 cds. by subj. Bks., per., pams. Freq. add.
O20-ref 5000 cds. by subj. Freq. add.
O20-socy 175 cds. by subj. Pams. Freq. add.
P32-lib. sch 9p., tpd. shts. Stud. bibl.
P34-ref 200 cds. by subj. Bks. Occ. add.
P39-ref 500 cds. by subj. Occ. add.
P56 100 cds. by subj. Bks. Freq. add.
T10 100 cds. by Dewey class. Bks. & per. Freq. add.
W22-ad 150 cds. by subj. Bks., per., pams. Occ. add.
Wa10-tech 1100 cds. by subj. Bks., per., bul. Infreq. add.

BIBLIOGRAPHIES—FIRST EDITIONS. *See* List of Bibliographies, APPENDIX I

BIBLIOGRAPHIES, FOREIGN
Ia14-for 70 cds. by subj. Cur. bibl. in for. lang. per. Freq. add.

BILLS, CONGRESSIONAL. *See* LAW

BINDING OF BOOKS. *See* BOOKBINDING

BINGHAMTON (N.Y.)—SOCIETIES AND CLUBS
N4 277 cds. by name. Newsp. Cur. add.

BIOGRAPHICAL POETRY. *See* POETRY, BIOGRAPHICAL

BIOGRAPHY. *See also* Names of special subj., i.e. ARTISTS; DIARIES; NECROLOGY; List of Bibliographies; APPENDIX I; DRAMA Wa15
C3 1920 cds. by name. Bks. Cur. add.
C4 10p., tpd. shts. Bks. Autobiog. Freq. add.
C8-ref 2640 cds. by subj. Contemp., largely auth. Bks. indexed: David Ewen, *Composers of to-day;* Stanley J. Kunitz, *Authors to-day and yesterday;* Stanley J. Kunitz, *Junior book of authors;* Stanley J. Kunitz, *Living authors;* Per. indexed: *Publisher's weekly; Wilson library bulletin.* Freq. add.
C13 650 cds. by name. Bks., pers., pams. Freq. add.
C17 1200 cds. by subj. Pams., etc. Freq. add.
C24 600 cds. by name. Per. indexed: *New Yorker,* "Profiles," 1930–date. Wkly. add.
C32-hist 19,800 cds. by name & subj. Bks. Cur. add.
C32-per 380 cds. by name. Per. indexed: *New Yorker,* "Profiles," 1928–1940. No add.
C45 500 cds. by subj. Bks. Occ. add.
C49-inf 1152 cds. by name. Bks. Occ. add.
C49-ref 1620 cds. by name. Per. indexed: *Wings.* Newsp., etc. Freq. add.
C57 350 cds. by name & subj. Infreq. add.
C69-j 2200 cds. by name. Bks. Cur. add.
Ca6 1820 cds. by name. Bks. Freq. add.
Ct12-John Dav. 2815 cds. by name. Bks. Cur. add.
Ct12-Scr. 1928 cds. by subj. & t. Bks. Freq. add.
Ct14 2910 cds. by subj. Bks. Freq. add.
D32 5280 cds. by subj. Bks. Freq. add.
De1 2500 cds. by subj. Cur. add.
F4 10,000 cds. by subj. Bks. not indexed in Essay index or Hefling. Bk. indexed: *New international yearbook,* 1910–1938. Freq. add.
I6 Unest. cds. by name. Bks. Freq. add.

I9   800 cds. by name. Bks. No add.
I13-r.b.   680 cds. by name. Bks., per. No add.
I26   2700 cds. by name. Bks. Freq. add.
I60   200 ent., tpd. shts. by subj. Pams. Occ. add.
K8-ref   500 cds. by subj. Bks. Occ. add.
K8-ref   1650 cds. by subj. Newsp., pams. & per. Freq. add.
K17-ref   1986 cds. by name. Pams. & newsp. Freq. add.
Ky3   18p., 900 ent., tpd. shts. by subj. Bks. Freq. add.
L14-ref   2400 cds. by name. Bk. indexed: *Encyclopedia of American biography*, v. 51-54, n.s., v. 1-13. Yrly. add.
M32   600 cds. by name. Occ. add.
Mi4   1320 cds. by name. Bks. Freq. add.
Me2-ref   14,200 cds. by name. Bks. Cur. add.
Mi6-circ   9000 cds. by name. Bks. in class. 100–400, 700–900. Freq. add.
Mi6-circ. o.s.   1350 cds. by subj. Bks. Freq. add.
Mi6-Rich.   1400 cds. by name. Bks. Infreq. add.
Mi12   750 cds. by name. Cur. add.
Mi15   700 cds. by subj. Bks. Freq. add.
Mn4-ref   575 cds. by subj. Bks., per. Freq. add.
Mn14-Cam.   1200 cds. by name. Bks., Per. indexed: *Wilson library bulletin*, 1938–1940.
Mn14-Fran.   2100 cds. by subj. Bks., per., & pams. Freq. add.
Mn14-Fran.-j   300 cds. by name. Bks. & newsp. Freq. add.
Mn14-tech   1980 cds. by name & subj. Tech. books. Cur. add.
Mn23-Arl.   3000 cds. by subj. Bks. Cur. add.
Mn23-Mer.   600 cds. by name. Pams., Per indexed: *Wilson library bulletin*. Mo. add.
Mo3-N.E.   200 cds. by name. Bks. Infreq. add.
Mo3-Wash.   1000 cds. by name. Bks. Freq. add.
Mo6   4500 cds. by name. Bks. & per. Freq. add.

Mo13-Car.   1500 cds. by name. Bks. Cur. add.
Mo13-Soul.   2200 cds. by name. Bks. Occ. add.
Mt1   200 ent., tpd. shts. by name. Pams. Occ. add.
N10-ref   Several hundred cds. by subj. Bks., per. indexed: *New Yorker*, v. 1-15 "Profiles." Freq. add.
N15   59 cds. by name. Bks. indexed: Evert August Duyckinck, *Portrait gallery of eminent men and women of Europe and America*. No add.
N15   369 cds. by name. Freq. add.
N22-ref   900 cds. by name. Bks. not indexed in Hefling. Infreq. add.
N30-jour   1650 cds. by name. Per. indexed: *New Yorker* "Profiles." Weekly add.
N30-Low   10,000 cds. by name. Bks. Infreq. add.
N35-ref. ed   2000 cds. by auth. Amer. writings in bks. & per. Cur. add.
N35-ref. inf (1)   1400 cds. by name & subj. Per. indexed: *New Yorker*, "Profiles," v. 1-date. Cur. add.
N35-ref. inf (2)   500 cds. by region & subj. U.S. & for. in bks. & per. Cur. add.
N35-Tre.   500 cds. by subj. Bks., per., newsp. Infreq. add.
N35-Wood. circ   995 cds. by name. Per., bks. & pams. Freq. add.
N46-biog   12,800 cds. by name. Bks. not indexed in Logasa, Hefling. Cur. add.
N48   200 cds. by subj. Bk. indexed: Elbert Hubbard, *Little journeys to the homes of famous people*, 5v. No add.
N51   878 cds. by name. Bks. Cur. add.
Nb2   912 ent., tpd. shts. by name. Bks. Per. indexed: *Wilson library bulletin*. Cur. add.
Nb8   10,000 cds. by subj. Bks. & per. Freq. add.
Nb10   347 cds. by name. Bks. Freq. add.
Nb10-ref   12,200 cds. by name. Bks., pams. & newsp. Freq. add.
Nc3   1600 cds. by name. Bks. Freq. add.
O1-E.   3300 cds. by subj. Bks. Cur. add.

O18a   Unest. cds. Bks. indexed: *Jahresbericht über die fortschritte der klassischen.* No add.
O20-Broad.   500 cds. by name. Yrly. add.
O20-bus.   4620 cds. by name. Per. & newsp. Freq. add.
O20-Coll.   3000 cds. by name. Bks., pams. Per. indexed: *Wilson library bulletin.* Cur. add.
O20-Edge.   500 cds. by name. Bks. Infreq. add.
O20-Glen.   5280 cds. by subj. Freq. add.
O20-hist   400 cds. by subj. Freq. add.
O20-Hou.   2600 cds. by subj. Bks. Infreq. add.
O20-M.P.   800 cds. by name. Per., newsp. & pams. Freq. add.
O20-Rice   3500 cds. by name. Cur. add.
O20-S. Brook.   1300 cds. by subj. Bks. Freq. add.
O20-W. Park   3000 cds. by name. Bks., pams., newsp. Y.p.'s lit. Freq. add.
O20-y.p.   4000 cds. by subj. Bks., y.p.'s lit. Freq. add.
O50   500 cds. by name. Bks. Cur. add.
O56-circ   5000 cds. by name. Bks. Cur. add.
O56-ref   7100 cds. by name. Newsp. Cur. add.
Ok3   Unest. ent., 15v. Amer. biog. in bks. Infreq. add.
Or1-ref   5292 cds. by subj. Bks. Occ. add.
Or2   20,000 cds. by subj. Per. & bks. Freq. add.
P6   400 cds. by subj. Bks. Infreq. add.
P36-ref   250 cds. by name. Per. indexed: *Wilson library bulletin* & other per. Cur. add.
P40   280 ent., tpd. shts. by subj. Bk. indexed: Charles Francis Horne, *Great man and famous women.* No add.
P55   200 cds. by subj. Pams. & newsp. Freq. add.
T7   1320 cds. by name. Bks. Cur. add.
Tx8   2500 cds. by subj. Bks., per., newsp., & pams. Freq. add.

Tx20   12,000 ent., in folders by name. Pic., cuts, mats & newsp. Daily add.
Tx21-j   126p., 2320 ent., tpd. shts. bd. Bks. not indexed in Logasa. Cur. add.
Tx22   750 cds. by name. Bks. Cur. add.
Tx24   130 cds. by name. Per., etc. Freq. add.
Tx32   5625 ent., tpd. shts., bd. by name. Newsp. indexed: *Sherman (Texas) Democrat,* 1914–1934. Infreq. add.
Tx33   250 cds. by subj. Bks. Occ. add.
U1   105 p., 2300 ent., tpd. shts. in mss. by name. Cur. add.
W12-ref   Unest. cds. by name. Ser. & sep. wks. In proc.
Wa3   2000 cds. by subj. Bks. Infreq. add.
Wa11-ref   400 cds. by subj. Bks. Occ. add.
Wa12   225 ent., tpd. shts. by name. Bks. Yrly. add.
Wv2   Unest. cds. by subj. Per. indexed: *Wilson library bulletin,* 1930–date. Freq. add.

BIOGRAPHY, FRENCH
C26   495 cds. by name. Bks. Freq. add.
O20-hist   1320 cds. by subj. & chron. Coll. of Fr. memoirs. Freq. add.

BIOGRAPHY, HISTORICAL
F2-r.a.   100 cds. by epoch in hist. Bks. Cur. add.
O26   1250 ent., tpd. shts. Ency. Outstanding people by cent. & countries. No add.

BIOGRAPHY, HISTORICAL—U.S.
F2-r.a.   75 cds. by subj. Bks. Famous people in Amer. hist. Cur. add.

BIOGRAPHY, VOCATIONAL. See also Names of vocations
C14   3960 cds. by subj. Bks. Cur. add.
D32-tech   1100 cds. by name. Tech. bks. Freq. add.
I68   1500 ent., tpd. shts. by subj. Bks. of indiv. biog. Freq. add.
I68   13,000 ent., tpd. shts. by subj. Bks. of coll. biog. Freq. add.

Ia18-ad 1500 ent., tpd. shts. by subj. Bks., per., & pams. Cur. add.
Md2-#13 225 cds. by subj. Bks., per., pams. & newsp. Infreq. add.
Md2-hist 21,600 cds. by subj. & name. Bks., per., pams. Cur. add.
Mi6-circ 250 cds. by subj. Bks. Freq. add.
Mi6-Rich. 150 cds. by subj. Infreq. add.
Mi6-Walk. 325 cds. by subj. Bks. & per. Freq. add.
Mi26 500 ent., tpd. shts. by class. Bks. Occ. add.
N50 170 cds. by name & class. Occ. add.
O1-E. 300 cds. by subj. Cur. add.
O1-r.a. 6000 cds. by subj. Bks. Cur. add.
Or2 4000 cds. by subj. Bks., per., etc. Freq. add.
W20-ad 175 cds. by subj. Bks. Infreq. add.
W20-McK. 474 cds. by subj. Bks., per., pams. & newsp. Freq. add.

BIOLOGY. *See also* BACTERIOLOGY; CELLS
C90 400 cds. by subj. Pams., state & govt. doc. Freq. add.
Ca4 800 cds. by auth. Bks. & per. Freq. add.
Ia14-med 800 cds. by auth. Bk. indexed: Emil Abderhalden, *Handbuch der biologischen arbeitsmethoden.* Cur. add.
L17 300 cds. by subj. Bks., per. & pams. Infreq. add.
Nj61 250 cds. by auth. & t. Bks., pers., & pams. Freq. add.
Wa11-ref 4500 cds. by auth. Bks. & per. Infreq. add.

BIRDS
Nj61 65 cds. by auth. & t. Bks., per. & reprints. Freq. add.
Vt3 600 cds. by subj. Bks., per., pams., & docs. Occ. add.
Wa10-j 300 cds. by variety. Bks. & per. Cur. add.

BIRDS—DUBUQUE (IOWA)
Ia10-ref 130 cds. by subj. Bks., per. & newsp. No add.

BIRDS—PICTURES. *See* PICTURES—BIRDS

BIRDS AND NATURE (per.) *In* PICTURES—NATURE **P54-j**

BIRTHDAYS
K22 150 cds., num. by mo. Bks., pams., pic. & per. Freq. add.

BLANDING, DON—WORKS
C32-lit 60 p., tpd. shts. by t., 1st line. All wks. to date. Occ. add.

BLIND. *See also* BRAILLE
M29 Over 8000 cds. & ent. in 3 cat. by auth., subj. & t. Bks., per., news., mss. Freq. add.

BLIND—APPARATUS
M29 100 cds. by subj. Tangible apparatus in museum. Infreq. add.

BLOOMFIELD (N.J.)
Nj4 1320 cds. by subj. Bks., per., pams., newsp., mss. Cur. add.

BLOOMFIELD (N.J.) INDEPENDENT PRESS (newsp.)
Nj4 1929–date. Cds. by subj. All items of hist. interest: biog., educ., organiz., ord., town council, etc. Cur. add.

BLOOMINGTON (IND.)—NEWSPAPERS
In1 5000 cds. by name & subj. Newsp. indexed: *Bloomington republican,* & others being added. Cur. add.

BLOOMINGTON (IND.) REPUBLICAN (newsp.). *In* BLOOMINGTON (IND.)—NEWSPAPERS **In1**

BOATS
Mn14-tech 1000 cds. by type & size. Bks. & newsp. In proc.
Wa10-tech 1350 cds. by type. Per. Freq. add.

BOATS—PHOTOGRAPHS
V5 28 cds. by type. Barges & misc. types of flat boats. Freq. add.
V5 151 cds. by type. Small boats. Freq. add.

BOISE (IDAHO)—SOCIETIES AND CLUBS
Id1 125 cds. by name. Occ. add.

BOISE (IDAHO) DAILY STATESMAN (newsp.)
Id1 1924–date. Cds. Loc. or state hist. & biog., soc., econ. & pol. developments of city, co. & state. Cur. add.

BOLLETINO D'ARTE (per.). *In* ART, RELIGIOUS **R2**; SCULPTURE **R2**

BONES AND JOINTS
Nj61   90 cds. by auth. & t. Bks., per., reprints. Infreq. add.

BOOK BINDING. *See* BOOKBINDING

BOOK CLUBS
In23-ord   300 cds. by auth. 12 tpd. shts. by club name. Selections. Wkly. & mo. add.
N8-ref   100 cds. by t. Per. Freq. add.
N46-fic   300 cds. by name. Amer. bk. clubs. Mo. add.

BOOK END-PAPERS
O21   25 cds. by auth. & t. Bks. Occ. add.

BOOK MENDING. *See* BOOKBINDING

BOOK OF CONTEMPORARY SHORT STORIES (bk.). *In* SHORT STORIES   Tx12

BOOK OF THE MONTH CLUB NEWS (per.) *In* AUTHORS   N4

BOOK PLATES. *See* BOOKPLATES

BOOK RARITIES (Subdiv. BOTANY, SCIENCE, ENGLISH). *See* list of Bibliographies, APPENDIX I

BOOK REVIEWS. *See also* Names of spec. subj., subdiv. BOOK REVIEWS
C8-ord   1320 cds. by auth. Per. indexed: *Argonaut, New York herald tribune. Books, New York times Book review, New republic, Saturday review of literature, Survey, Survey graphic.* Cur. add.
C18-ref   6650 cds. by auth. Per. Freq. add.
C32-ad. educ   3960 cds. by auth. 6 leading bk. rev. per. Wkly. add.
C32-ord   60,000 cds. by auth. & t. Wkly. bk. rev. per. & newsp. Wkly. add.
C32-phil   15,840 cds. by auth. Per. Cur. add.
C51   28,380 cds. by auth. Bks. in lib. Cur. add.
Ct12-ord   4811 cds. by auth. Per. indexed: *New York times book review, Virginia Kirkus bookshop service.* Wkly. add.
In23-ord   Several thousand cds. by auth. Per. indexed: *Saturday review of literature, London Times.* Wkly. add.

Ky15-j   Several thousand cds. by auth. & t. Per. & news. Wkly. add.
M27-ref   4500 cds. by auth. Per. Cur. add.
M32   600 cds. by t. Bks. Cur. add.
Mi6-per   900 cds. by auth. Per. Freq. add.
Mi6-ref   36,000 cds. by auth. Bks., per. for bks. not listed in Book review digest. Freq. add.
Mi13-W. side   Over 500 cds. by auth. Bks. Cur. add.
Mn18   5000 cds. by auth. Per. indexed: *Commonweal.* Cur. add.
Mn23-per   141,000 cds. by t. Per., 1922-to present. Daily add.
Mo3-ord   700 cds. by auth. Per. indexed: *Boston evening transcript book reviews, New York herald tribune. Books, New York times book review. Saturday review of literature.* Cur. add.
N54-per   5200 cds. by t. & subj. Per. Daily add.
Nb14-ref   3000 cds. by auth. Per. Daily add.
O20-E.131st   500 cds. by auth. Wkly. add.
O20-Mem.   1000 cds. by auth. Cur. add.
O20-M.P.   1000 cds. by t. Pub. advance notices. Freq. add.
O20-per   13,200 cds. by auth. 9 bk. rev. per. Cur. add.
O20-ref   500,000 cds. by auth. Per., 1913-date. Supp. Bk. review digest. Freq. add.
O20-Tem.   Unest. cds. by t. Per. indexed: *New York herald tribune. Books, New York times book review.* Freq. add.
O20-Wood.   600 cds. by auth. Bks. in lib. Freq. add.
O31   850 cds. by auth. Per. Freq. add.
O56-ref   470 cds. by auth. Infreq. add.
P39-ref   13,000 cds. by auth. & t. Stud. supp. reading. Bks. & per. Occ. add.
P39-ref   247,500 cds. by auth. & t. Per., 1899-1932. No add.
W16   1000 cds. by auth. & subj. Stud. aids. Occ. add.

BOOK REVIEWS—FOREIGN LANGUAGES
Mi6-for   3600 cds. by subj., lang. & auth. Freq. add.

BOOK REVIEWS—SOURCES
Mi6-ref   150 cds. by subj. Bk. rev. subj. in per., esp. before pub. of Bk. review digest. Infreq. add.

BOOK REVIEWS, JUVENILE. *See* CHILDREN'S LITERATURE—BOOK REVIEWS

BOOK STORES. *See* List of Bibliographies, APPENDIX I

BOOK TITLES. *See* TITLES OF BOOKS

BOOKBINDING
C73-rare   1500 cds. by binder & period. 18th-20th cent. bindings in lib. Cur. add.
I26-rare   1200 cds. by binder. Bks. Freq. add.
N35-ref. res   900 cds. by binder & owner. Bindings of known binders & marks of ownership or armorial emblazons. Cur. add.
Tx5   50 ent. Bks., pams., bul., etc. Bk. mending. Freq. add.

BOOKPLATES
C73-ref   10,000 cds. Burnham coll., rare bks., ref. bks. Freq. add.
De1   63 cds. Occ. add.
Me2-ref   1800 cds. by owner & designer. Freq. add.
Mn15-ref   1279 cds. by owner, subj. & designer. Freq. add.
N10   361 cds. by auth. & subj. Bks. Cur. add.
N35-ref. print   5000 cds. by owner. Bks. Cur. add.
N45b   4760 cds. by owner, designer & engraver. Freq. add.
N46-art   90 cds. by designer. Freq. add.
N47   5000 cds. by designer & engraver. In proc.
Nb8   440 cds. by owner. Bks. Infreq. add.
Nj60-treas   675 cds. by owner. Bookplates. Infreq. add.
O20-art   845 cds. by name. Bks. Infreq. add.
O27   300 cds. by designer & owner. Bookplates. Occ. add.

BOOKPLATES, MEDICAL
Ia7   5v., tpd. shts. in note-bks., by dr. names & instit. 400 plates in med. biog. & hist. Occ. add.
P31   570 cds. by owner. Bks. & scrapbks. Infreq. add.

BOOKS. *See also* TEXTBOOKS
Ia18-ad   Inest. cds. by subj. Bks. without indexes. Cur. add.

BOOKS—REPRINTS
In23-ord   Several thousand cds. by auth. Bks. issued by reprint houses, also cheaper reprints by original pub. Freq. add.

BOOKS, FILMED. *See* List of Bibliographies, APPENDIX I

BOOKS, JUVENILE. *See* CHILDREN'S LITERATURE

BOOKS, PICTORIAL. *See also* List of Bibliographies, APPENDIX I
M11-print   1000 cds. chron. by country. 15th-18th cent. bks. in coll. Freq. add.

BOOKS AND READING. (Subdiv. COLLEGES, FOREIGN-BORN READING, HIGH SCHOOLS, HOSPITAL READING, INSPIRATIONAL READING, INTERNATIONAL MIND ALCOVE, LENTEN READING, MISSIONARY READING, OUT-OF-PRINT BOOKS, READABLE BOOKS, READING COURSES, SIGHT-SAVING BOOKS, SIGHT-SAVING BOOKS, JUVENILE, UNUSUAL SUBJECTS). *See* List of Bibliographies, APPENDIX I

BOOKS IN SERIES. *See* SERIES, BOOKS IN

BOOKSELLERS AND BOOKSELLING—NEW YORK (CITY)
N35-ref. inf   680 cds. by subj. Specialties of regular & 2d-hand booksellers in N.Y. city. Cur. add.

BOONE, DANIEL
Ky2   182 cds. by auth. Bks. & per. Freq. add.

BORDEN, GAIL, JR.
Tx17   4 tpd. shts. by t. Bks., newsp., per. & mag. Occ. add.

BOSTON (MASS.) ART. *See* ART—BOSTON (MASS.)

BOSTON (MASS.)—SCHOOLS
M1   175 cds. by name of sch. Off. records of Boston sch. committee & any other sources. Occ. add.

BOSTON (MASS.) EVENING TRANSCRIPT (newsp.). *In* BOOK REVIEWS **Mo3-ord**; GENEALOGY **F3**, **In22-gen** (3), **M27-ref** (2), **N10-gen** (1), **N20** (1), **U3**, **W10-ref**, **Wa7**, **Wa10-ref** (1); POETRY **M4-ref**

Boston (Mass.) Sunday Globe (*newsp.*).
    In Poetry   **M4-ref**
Boston Museum of Fine Arts. Bulletin.
    In Art, Oriental   **D9**
Boston Symphony Orchestra Programs.
    See also Symphony   **C32-art, Nb14-ref, O16-art, O20-art, O29-ref, O56-ref**
Mn23-art   2085 cds. by comp. & t. Freq. add.
Mo1   1320 cds. by comp. Programs, 1915–1934. No add.
N10-mus   Several thousand cds. by comp. & t. Yrly. add.
N57   2640 cds. by comp. Programs, 1909–date. Yrly. add.
Wa10-art   3000 cds. by comp. & t. Cur. add.

Boston Teachers News Letter (per.)
M1   v.14, 1925–date. Cds. by auth. & t. Cur. add.

Botanical Abstracts
Wa11-ref   v.11-14, 1922–1925. Cds. by auth. In proc.

Botany. *See also* Flowers; Nature
D18   250,000 cds. by subj. Bks., per., & ser. Daily add.
D18   303,000 cds. by auth. Bks., per., & ser. Daily add.
Nj61   650 cds. by auth. & subj. Bks., per., pams., exp. stat. repts. Freq. add.
Vt3   1450 cds. by subj. Bks., per., & pams. Cur. add.

Botany—Pathology
D18   83,000 cds. alph. & by class. Bks., per., ser. Daily add.
Nj61   700 cds. by auth. & t. Bks., per., pams., repts., reprints, exp. stat. repts. Freq. add.

Botany—Physiology
Nj61   90 cds. by auth. & t. Bks., per., pams. Infreq. add.

Botany—Pictures. *See* Pictures—Botany

Botany—Union Lists. *See* List of Bibliographies, Appendix I

Boulder Camera (per.). *In* Colorado—History   **Co2-ref**

Boulder County News (per.) *In* Colorado—History   **Co2-ref**

Bowdoin College—Publications, Alumni
Me3   1300 cds. by auth. Alumni writings. Occ. add.

Bowling Green (Ky.)
Ky2   66 cds. by auth. Bks., & per. Freq. add.
Ky2   20p., tpd. shts. bd. by subj. & name. Minutes of trustees, 1823–1839. No add.
Ky2   25p., tpd. shts. bd. by subj. & name. Minutes of trustees, 1850–1860. No add.

Bowling Green (Ky.)—Cemetery Records
Ky2   90p., tpd. shts. bd. by name. Mss. Pioneer & Fairview. Names & dates of all born before 1900 & dead before 1938. No add.

Bowling Green (Ky.)—History
Ky2   10p., tpd. shts., bd. by name & place. Mss. No add.

Bowling Green (Ky.)—Law. *See* Law—Kentucky   **Ky2**

Boy Scout Merit Badge Pamphlets
W19   100 cds. by auth., t. & subj. Occ. add.

Boy Scouts
Tx5   350 cds. by subj. Bks., per. & pams. Activities. Cur. add.

Boy Scouts—Stories. *See* List of Bibliographies, Appendix I

Bradford Porter and Reporter (per.) *In* Registers of Births, etc.   **P49**

Braille. *See also* List of Bibliographies, Appendix I
M29   2000 cds. by auth. & subj. Principally non-fic. Occ. add.

Brethren Church. *See* Pennsylvania—History   **P19** (1), (2), (3)

Bridgeport (Conn.)—Documents
Ct2-hist   1320 cds. by subj. Charters, ordinances & mun. registers, 1906–1914. No add.

Bridges, Robert—Works
I13-ref   700 cds. by t. & first line. Bks. & per. Infreq. add.

Bridges
C3a   225 cds. by type & loc. Bridges in art, hist., lit. Bks. & per. No add.
N35-ref. sci (1)   1v. scrapbk. by region. Newsp. & illus., 1859–1930. No add.
N35-ref. sci (2)   2v. scrapbk. by type. Newsp. & illus., 1833–1929. No. add.

BRIDGES—NEW YORK (STATE)
N35-ref. sci   2v. scrapbk., chron. Newsp. Bridges, 1890–1891, 1893–1895. No add.

BRIDGES—NORTHWEST
Wa10-tech   160 cds. by loc. & type. Per. Occ. add.

BRIDGES, COVERED—INDIANA.
In24   Unest. tpd. shts. by co. Freq. add.

BRIEF REPORT OF THE MEETING. . . . (bk.). *In* ST. LOUIS (MO.)   **Mo13-Soul.**

BRIGANDS AND ROBBERS.   *See also* FRONTIER AND PIONEER LIFE   **N35-ref.** Amer. hist.
C32-hist.   200 cds. by subj. Bks. & per. Amer. hist. Occ. add.

BRITISH AUTHORS OF THE NINETEENTH CENTURY (bk.).   *In* AUTHORS   **Mt1**

BRITISH COLUMBIA (CAN.).   *See* SHIPWRECKS   **Wa10-ref**

BRITISH COLUMBIA (CAN.)—DOCUMENTS
Ca3   4000 cds. by subj. & auth. British Columbia sess. pa., 1872–date. Yrly. add.

BRITISH COLUMBIA (CAN.)—NEWSPAPERS
Ca3   180,000 cds. by subj. Newsp. indexed: *The Daily colonist*, 1858–1887, 1901–1902, 1915–date; *The Daily province*, 1924–date; *The News-herald*, 1933–date; *The Sun*, 1924–date; *Vancouver evening-sun*, 1924–1934; *Vancouver star*, 1926–1932; *Victoria Daily times*, 1915–date; *Victoria gazette*, 1858–1859.

BRITISH COLUMBIA HISTORICAL QUARTERLY. *In* CANADA—PERIODICALS   **Ca13-per**

BROADSIDES
I26-rare   1500 cds. by state & date. Amer. rev. period broadsides, mostly photostatic reprod. Freq. add.
N35-ref. res   9000 cds., chron. by date of imprint. Originals & facsimiles. Cur. add.

BROCKTON (MASS.)
M13-ref   28 ent. tpd. pam. by auth. & subj. Bks. & pams. Occ. add.

BROOKE, RUPERT—WORKS
I13-ref   200 cds. by t., 1st line, & subj. Bks. & per. Infreq. add.

BROOKLYN MUSEUM QUARTERLY
N5   v. 1-26, 1914–1939. 25,000 cds. by auth., t. & subj. Cur. add.

BROWN CO. (KANS.)—REGISTERS OF BIRTHS, ETC.
K7   Thousands of cds. by surname. Newsp. in courthouse & lib., 1864–present. Bi-mo. add.

BROWNSON'S QUARTERLY REVIEW
N48   v. 3, no. 2 v. 15, 1882–1890. Cds. by auth. & subj. No add.

BRUMBAUGH, MARTIN GROVE
P19   65 ent., tpd. shts. Bks., per., pams. No add.

BUCHNER, SIMON BOLIVAR
Ky2   68 cds. by auth. Bks. & per. No add.

BUCKS CO. (PA.) HISTORICAL SOCIETY. COLLECTION OF PAPERS READ
P5   v. 1-6, 1908–1913. Cds. by auth. & subj. In proc.

BUFFALO (N.Y.)—AUTHORS.   *See* AUTHORS —BUFFALO (N.Y.)

BUFFALO (N.Y.)—BIBLIOGRAPHY—IMPRINTS
N10   706 cds. by auth. Bks., pams. & per. Bks. Occ. add.

BUFFALO (N.Y.)—CENSUS
N10-gen   Several thousand ent., tpd. shts. in bk. by name. Five wards of city as existed in 1850. No add.

BUFFALO (N.Y.)—HISTORY
N10-ref   6490 cds. by subj. Bks., per. Freq. add.
N10-ref   56,260 cds. by subj. Newsp. Freq. add.

BUFFALO (N.Y.)—PICTURES.   *See* PICTURES —BUFFALO (N.Y.)

BUFFALO (N.Y.)—SONGS.   *See* SONGS— BUFFALO (N.Y.)

BUFFALO (N.Y.)—THEATRE.   *See* THEATRE —BUFFALO (N.Y.)

BUFFALO HISTORICAL SOCIETY—PUBLICATIONS
N8-ref   v. 1-33, 1879–1941. Cds. by auth., subj. & t. Infreq. add.
N10-ref   Unest. tpd. shts. by subj., Illus., port. & maps.

BUFFALO MUNICIPAL RESEARCH BUREAU, INC. MUNICIPAL RESEARCH BULLETIN
N8-ref   v. 1, 1931–date (incomp.). Tpd. shts. Freq. add.

BUILDING
Nj52   Several hundred cds. by subj. Bks., per. & pams. Freq. add.

BUILDINGS. See PHOTOGRAPHS, EUROPEAN N45b

BUILDINGS, HISTORIC. See LITERARY LANDMARKS

BULBS
Tx5   Unest. cds. by t. Bks., per. & bul. Freq. add.

BULLETIN D. RECHERCHES HISTORIQUES. In CANADA—PERIODICALS Ca13-per

BULLETIN INTERNATIONALE DES DOUANES
N35-ref. econ   1923/24–1939/40. Cds. by country. No add.

BULLETIN OF BIBLIOGRAPHY AND DRAMATIC INDEX. In PERIODICALS—BIRTHS AND DEATHS C32-per, G4-per

BULLOCK CO. (ALA.)—CEMETERY RECORDS
A1   49 ent., tpd. shts. Perote cem. Occ. add.

BURIALS. See Name of loc., subdiv. CEMETERY RECORDS

BURLINGTON CO. (N.J.)
Nj35   73 cds. by subj. Bks., per. & pams. Occ. add.

BURLINGTON MAGAZINE FOR CONNOISSEURS. See also TEXTILES M11-tex
M11-Tolman   v. 1, 1903–date. Cds. by auth., t. & subj. Mo. add.

BURR, AARON
Ky2   138 cds. by auth. Bks. & per. Freq. add.

BUSES. See MOTOR BUSES

BUSINESS. See also Name of loc., subdiv. BUSINESS
C69-bus   7000 cds. by subj. & auth. Per. & pams. Daily add.
I65-bus   2288 cds. by subj. Bks., per. & pams. Freq. add.
In33-bus   Unest. cds. by subj. Occ. add.
Md2-bus   4000 cds. by subj. Bks., per., govt. doc., pams., addresses, etc. Freq. add.
O20-bus   15,840 cds. by subj. Ser. inc. govt. doc., releases & hearings, per. & pams. Freq. add.
P36-Lipp.   3000 cds. by subj. Per. Freq. add.

BUSINESS—BIBLIOGRAPHIES
Mi6-bus   400 cds. by subj. Bks., per. etc. Freq. add.

BUSINESS—BOOK REVIEWS
M6   1000 cds. by t. Insurance, salesmanship, bus., finance, mgt., pub. speaking, psychology & self-development. Per. Freq. add.
Nj50-bus   4000 cds. by auth. Per. indexed: *New York times book review*, and bus. per. Freq. add.

BUSINESS—DIRECTORIES. See TRADE CATALOGS AND DIRECTORIES

BUSINESS—FICTION. See FICTION, VOCATIONAL

BUSINESS—HISTORY. See ACCOUNT BOOKS Nj40

BUSINESS—PERIODICALS
In33-bus   600 cds. by subj. Per. Freq. add.

BUSINESS CONDITIONS
Nj52   Several hundred cds. by subj. Bks., per. & pams. Freq. add.
P36-Lipp.   300 cds. (yrly.) by subj. Per. indexed: *Journal of commerce, New York times; Wall street journal*. Daily add.

BUSINESS EDUCATION. See Names of individual subjects

BUSINESS INFORMATION SERVICE. See U.S. BUREAU OF FOREIGN AND DOMESTIC COMMERCE. BUSINESS INFORMATION SERVICE

BUSINESS LETTERS. See COMMERCIAL CORRESPONDENCE

BUSINESS MACHINES
R1-bus   150 cds. by subj. Bks., pams. & per. Freq. add.

BUSINESS MANAGEMENT
Nj52   Unest. cds. by subj. Bks., per. & pams. Freq. add.

BUSINESS MEN AND WOMEN
Ky15-circ   70 ent., tpd. shts. by subj. Bks. Occ. add.
M4-Kir.   180 cds. by subj. Bks., per. & pams. Freq. add.
Nj9   56 ent., tpd. shts. by subj. Bks. Freq. add.
P36-Lipp.   2000 cds. by name. Bks., per. & newsp. Freq. add.

BUSINESS NAMES. *See* TRADE NAMES
BUTLER CO. (ALA.)—CEMETERY RECORDS
A1 250 ent., tpd. shts. by name. Magnolia cem., Ebenezer church & Craig cem., Old cem. Greenville. Occ. add.
BUYERS' GUIDES. *See* TRADE CATALOGS AND DIRECTORIES
BUYING HABITS. *See* CONSUMERS' GOODS
C.C.C. CAMPS—WASHINGTON (STATE). *See* WASHINGTON (STATE)—DIRECTORIES **Wa10-tech**
C.I.O. NEWS (per.). *In* LABOR AND LABORING CLASSES—PERIODICALS **O33-Euc. Cen.**
CALDICOTT PRIZES. *See* REWARDS, (PRIZES, ETC.) **In5-j**
CALIFORNIA. *See also* List of Bibliographies, APPENDIX I
C1 138,106 cds. by subj. Bks. & pams. Cur. add.
C8-ref 5280 cds. by subj. & auth. Per. indexed: *Argonaut, California historical society quarterly, Commonwealth club transactions, Grizzly bear, Motor land, Out west, Outing, Overland, Pony express courier, Sierra club bulletin, Sunset, and Westways.* Calif. & Berkeley. Freq. add.
C31-ref 500 cds. by subj. Newsp. & pam. Occ. add.
C31-ref 1500 cds. by subj. Bks. & per. Occ. add.
C51 Unest. cds. by subj. Per. indexed: *Los Angeles times* Magazine section, 1932–1939. Calif. & the Southwest. Freq. add.
C56-Calif. Several million cds. by auth. & subj. Bks. & newsp. San Francisco newsp., 1846–date. Cur. add.
C57 3600 cds. by auth., t. & subj. Bks. Infreq. add.
C69-ref 1200 cds. by subj. Bks., per. & newsp. Freq. add.
C73-Amer. 10,560 cds. by subj. Bks., coll. of phot. of Los Angeles & vicinity, 1850–1938.
CALIFORNIA—ADULT EDUCATION
C43-ref 1600 cds. by subj. of classes. Announcements & cats. Freq. add.
CALIFORNIA—ARTISTS. *See* ARTISTS—CALIFORNIA

CALIFORNIA—AUTHORS. *See* AUTHORS—CALIFORNIA
CALIFORNIA—BIBLIOGRAPHY—PRICES
C31-ord 700 cds. by auth. 2d-hand dealers' cat. Occ. add.
CALIFORNIA—BIOGRAPHY
C32-hist 28,380 cds. by subj. Bks. Freq. add.
C69-ref 2700 cds. by name. Bks., per. & newsp. Freq. add.
CALIFORNIA—COOKERY. *See* COOKERY—CALIFORNIA
CALIFORNIA. DEPARTMENT OF AGRICULTURE—PUBLICATIONS
C32-sci 550 cds. by subj. Doc. Cur. add.
CALIFORNIA. DEPARTMENT OF EDUCATION. BULLETIN
C80 1932–date. Cds. by subj. & t. Freq. add.
CALIFORNIA. DEPARTMENT OF EDUCATION. SCIENCE GUIDE FOR ELEMENTARY SCHOOLS. *See* SCIENCE GUIDE FOR ELEMENTARY SCHOOLS (per.)
CALIFORNIA. DEPARTMENT OF NATURAL RESOURCES. DIVISION OF FISH AND GAMES—PUBLICATIONS
C32-sci 400 cds. by subj. Doc. Cur. add.
CALIFORNIA. DEPARTMENT OF PUBLIC HEALTH—PUBLICATIONS. *In* PUBLIC HEALTH—DOCUMENTS **C32-sci**
CALIFORNIA—DOCUMENTS
C57 6300 cds. Selective indexing since 1930, exclusive of those indexed in Agric. index. Cur. add.
C87 300 cds. by name of bur. Freq. add.
CALIFORNIA—HISTORY. *See also* List of Bibliographies, APPENDIX I
C43-ref 60,000 cds. by subj. & auth. Bks. & per. Per. indexed: *California historical society quarterly, Grizzly bear, Historical society of southern California quarterly, Commonwealth club transactions, Land of sunshine, Out west, Overland monthly.* Freq. add.
CALIFORNIA — HISTORY — PORTRAITS. *See* PORTRAITS—WEST **C57**

CALIFORNIA—INNS
C64   Unest. cds. by subj. Bks., per. & newsp. Freq. add.

CALIFORNIA—LAW. See LAW—CALIFORNIA

CALIFORNIA—NEWSPAPERS. See also List of Bibliographies, APPENDIX I
C32-hist   3960 cds. by subj. W.P.A. project, newsp. from 1850–1900. Per. indexed: Los Angeles:—*El clamor publico*, 1855–1859, *Daily news*, 1860–1873, *Los Angeles express*, 1871–1931, *Los Angeles herald*, 1873–1931, *Semi-weekly news*, 1863–1869, *Southern vineyard*, 1858–1860, *Los Angeles star*, 1851–1864, 1868–1879, *Los Angeles times*, 1881, *Tri-weekly news*, 1865; San Francisco:—*San Francisco bulletin*, 1855–1929, *San Francisco call*, 1856–1914, 1927–1929, *San Francisco chronicle*, 1865; Ventura—*Ventura democrat*, 1883–1915. Incomplete indexing & files. In proc.

CALIFORNIA—OFFICIALS AND EMPLOYEES
C32-mun. ref   Unest. ent. tpd. shts. by name of city. 300 cities. Daily add.

CALIFORNIA—PETROLEUM. See PETROLEUM —CALIFORNIA

CALIFORNIA—PICTURES. See PICTURES—CALIFORNIA

CALIFORNIA—PORTRAITS. See PORTRAITS—CALIFORNIA; PORTRAITS—WEST
C57

CALIFORNIA—SOCIETIES AND CLUBS
C49-ref   1152 cds. by name. Newsp. Freq. add.

CALIFORNIA. STATE MINING BUREAU. REPORTS
C27-ref   25,500 cds. by co., district & name of mine. Q. add.
C32-sci   19,280 cds. by name of mine, mineral & place. Cur. add.
C62-bus   6000 cds. by name of mine & co. Cur. add.

CALIFORNIA—THEATRE. See THEATRE—CALIFORNIA

CALIFORNIA. UNIVERSITY—COLLEGE OF AGRICULTURE—EXPERIMENT STATION. BULLETIN
C37   600 cds. by subj. Occ. add.
C71-ref   685 cds. by subj. Freq. add.
C89   Unest. cds., #116–657, 1897–1941, by subj. Cur. add.

C50   Unest. cds., #256–date, by subj. Cur. add.

CALIFORNIA. UNIVERSITY—COLLEGE OF AGRICULTURE—EXPERIMENT STATION. CIRCULAR
C50   Unest. cds., #135–date by subj. Cur. add.
C89   Unest. cds., #41–348, 1908–1939 by subj. Cur. add.

CALIFORNIA. UNIVERSITY—COLLEGE OF AGRICULTURE—EXPERIMENT STATION —PUBLICATIONS
C8-ref   2640 cds. by auth. & subj. Freq. add.
C17   1400 cds. by subj. Cur. add.
C26   713 ent., tpd. shts. by subj. Freq. add.
C31-ref   1000 cds. by subj. Freq. add.
C52   375 cds. by subj. Yrly. add.
C77-ref   412 cds. by subj. Cur. add.
C86   200 cds. by subj. Infreq. add.

CALIFORNIA. UNIVERSITY—COLLEGE OF AGRICULTURE—EXTENSION SERVICE. CIRCULARS
C50   Unest. cds., #3–date. Cur. add.
C89   Unest. cds., #1, 1926–date. Cur. add.

CALIFORNIA HIGHWAYS AND PUBLIC WORKS (per.)
C71-ref   v. 9, 1931–date. Freq. add.

CALIFORNIA HISTORICAL SOCIETY. QUARTERLY. *In* CALIFORNIA   C73-Amer.; CALIFORNIA—HISTORY   C43-ref

CALIFORNIA HISTORY NUGGET (per.)
C6-ref   1937–date. Cds. by subj. Cur. add.
C46   1937–1940. Cds. by subj. Cur. add.

CALIFORNIA JOURNAL OF MINES AND GEOLOGY
C61-br   v. 18–37, 1922–1941. Cds. by subj. Cur. add.

CALIFORNIA MAGAZINE OF THE PACIFIC
C6-ref   1938–date. Cds. by subj. Cur. add.
C69-per   1930–date. Cds. by auth., subj. & t. Mo. add.
C71-ref   1937–1940, 1942–date. Cds. by subj. Infreq. add.

CALIFORNIA, SOUTHERN—WATER
C11   2000 cds. by auth. & subj. Bks., pams., maps, newsp., phot. Cur. add.

CAMBRIDGE (MASS.)—AUTHORS. *See* AUTHORS—CAMBRIDGE (MASS.)

CAMBRIDGE (MASS.)—HISTORY
M16-ref 12,000 cds. by subj. No add.

CAMP LEWIS (WASH.)—HISTORY
Wa14-ref 46 ent., tpd. shts. Bks. & per. Infreq. add.

CAMPS. *See* U.S. ARMY—CAMPS

CANADA
C24 2000 cds. by auth., subj. & t. Bks., per., pam. & mss. Infreq. add.

CANADA—ART. *See* ART, CANADIAN

CANADA. BUREAU OF MINES—PUBLICATIONS
Wa10-tech 680 cds. by place & subj. Cur. add.

CANADA—DOCUMENTS
Ca2-sci 7007 cds. by subj. Daily add.
Ca5-ref 500 cds. by subj. Yrly. add.
Ca10 5400 cds. by auth. & subj. Freq. add.

CANADA—HISTORY
Ca2-j 117p., tpd. shts. by subj. Canadian history readers. No add.
Ca3 3500 cds. by subj. Newsp. indexed: *The Daily colonist, The Daily province, The News-herald, The Times, the Vancouver sun.* Daily add.
Ca4 930 cds. Bks. mss., newsp. in Baptist hist. coll. of the maritime provinces of Canada. Cur. add.
Ca7 2640 cds. by subj. Bks. & scrapbks. on Toronto & Canada. Occ. add.

CANADA—HOLIDAYS
C27 2640 cds. by subj. Occ. add.

CANADA—MAPS. *See* MAPS—CANADA

CANADA—MURDERS. *See* MURDERS—CANADA

CANADA—PERIODICALS
Ca2-ref 25,850 cds. by subj. Freq. add.
Ca5-ref Unest. Supp. to Canadian per. index. Mo. add.
Ca13-per Unest. cds. Cur. indexing of per., later pub. as Canadian per. index. Per. indexed: *Actualité economique, British Columbia hist. q., Bul. de Recherches historiques, Canada Français, Canada's weekly, Canadian airways Ltd. bul., Canadian antiquarian jl., Canadian bank of comm. mo. letter, Canadian banker, Canadian chartered accountant, Canadian congress jl., C.E.S.A. bul., Canadian geog. jl., Canadian jl. econ. & pol. sci., (Canadian) military gazette, C.N.R. mag., Canadian purchasor, Canadian taxation, Canadian unionist, Civil service review, Crucible, Dalhousie review, Econ. annalist, Educ. record of P.Q., Educ. Review (Moncton), Industrial Canada, Interdependence, Jl. of educ. (Nova Scotia), L. of N. soc. in Can. monthly news, Mental health, McGill news, McMaster univ. q., Maritimer, Mun. review of Canada, Prof. inst. civil service jl., Quebec, Research review C.C.F., Review de l'université d'Ottawa, Review Trimestrielle Canadienne, R.M.C. review, Saturday night, Teachers' magazine, Univ. of Toronto q., World wide.* Cur. add.

CANADA FRANÇAIS (per.). *In* CANADA—PERIODICALS **Ca13-per**

CANADA'S WEEKLY (per.). *In* CANADA—PERIODICALS **Ca13-per**

CANADIAN AIRWAYS LTD. BULLETIN. *In* CANADA—PERIODICALS **Ca13-per**

CANADIAN ANTIQUARIAN & NUMISMATIC JOURNAL. *In* CANADA—PERIODICALS **Ca13-per**

CANADIAN BANK OF COMMERCE. MONTHLY COMMERCIAL LETTER (per.). *In* CANADA—PERIODICALS **Ca13-per**

CANADIAN BANKER (per.) *In* CANADA—PERIODICALS **Ca13-per**

CANADIAN CHARTERED ACCOUNTANT (per.). —*In* CANADA—PERIODICALS **Ca13-per**

CANADIAN CONGRESS JOURNAL. *In* CANADA—PERIODICALS **Ca13-per**

CANADIAN ENGINEERING STANDARDS ASSOCIATION. QUARTERLY BULLETIN. *In* CANADA—PERIODICALS **Ca13-per**

CANADIAN GEOGRAPHICAL JOURNAL. *In* CANADA—PERIODICALS **Ca13-per**

CANADIAN JOURNAL OF ECONOMIC AND POLITICAL SCIENCE. *In* CANADA—PERIODICALS **Ca13-per**

Canadian National Magazine. *In* Canada
—Periodicals Ca13-per

Canadian Purchasor (per.) *In* Canada—
Periodicals Ca13-per

Canadian Taxation (per.). *In* Canada—
Periodicals Ca13-per

Canadian Unionist (per.). *In* Canada—
Periodicals Ca13-per

Canastota (N.Y.)—History
N11 75 ent., tpd. shts. in notebk. 50 scrapbks. in Thomas Barlow coll. No add.

Cancer
C30 75 cds. Bks., per. & pams. Occ. add.
P30 2500 cds. by subj. & auth. Per. & reprints. Freq. add.

Canning and Preserving. *See* American Can Company Research Department Library. Abstracts

Cantatas. *See* Bach, Johann Sebastian—Works N35-mus

Cards, Greeting. *See* Greeting Cards

Careers. *See* Vocations

Caricatures and Cartoons
C73-rare 200 cds. chron. Amer. hist., 1750–1920. Occ. add.
C73-rare 450 cds. by art. Modern original cartoons. Occ. add.
N35-ref. print 1000 cds. by country. Separates. Cur. add.

Carillons. *See* Chimes and Chiming

Carlyle, Thomas
Me3 875 ent., tpd. shts. in bk. Occ. add.

Carman, Bliss—Works. *See* List of Bibliographies, Appendix I

Carnegie, Andrew
P39-ref 225 cds. Per. Infreq. add.

Carnegie Pictures. *See* Pictures—Carnegie Pictures

Cartography—North America
C12 525 cds., chron. Maps. Northwest coast of America to 1800. Infreq. add.

Cartoons. *See* Caricatures and Cartoons

Cartularies. *See* Charters

Casein
D15 2255 cds. chron. Bks., per., etc. Yrly. add.

Catalogs, College. *See also* List of Bibliographies, Appendix I
Ct12-ref 800 cds. by auth. & subj. Freq. add.
Md2-phil 450 cds. by subj. of course. Occ. add.
Mi6-ref 800 cds. by subj. Freq. add.
N28-y.p. 500 cds. by t. & subj. Freq. add.
O20-soc 7260 cds. by name of course. Freq. add.

Catalogs, Union—Nashville (Tenn.)
T10 250,000 cds. by auth. & t. Bks. & ser. Freq. add.

Catholic Authors. *See* Authors, Catholic; Poets, Catholic

Catholic Book Club. Newsletter (per.)
Mn22-sch v. 9, 1933-date. Cds. by auth., t. & subj. Daily add.

Catholic Church—Liturgies
Mn3 1000 cds. by country & city. For. & loc. liturgical per. Occ. add.

Catholic Literature. *See also* Authors, Catholic; Fiction, Catholic; Plays, Catholic; List of Bibliographies, Appendix I
C36 67 cds. by auth. & subj. Bks. Infreq. add.
O56-circ 2000 cds. by auth. & subj. Freq. add.

Catholic Literature, Juvenile. *See* List of Bibliographies, Appendix I

Catholic Mind (per.)
O22 v. 2, 1904, v. 4, 1906, v. 13-20, 1915–1922, v. 22-30, 1924–1932. Cds. by auth., t. & subj. Occ. add.

Catholic Missions—Minnesota. *See* Missions, Catholic—Minnesota

Catholic Pamphlets. *See* Pamphlets, Catholic

Catholic World (per.)
N48 v. 1-49, 1865–1889. Cds. by auth. & subj. No add.

Catholics. *See also* Franciscans; Priests, Missionary
Tx30 84 cds. by auth. Bks. & per. Aspects of Cath. action. No add.

CATHOLICS—PERIODICALS
Mn3 300p. tpd. shts., alph. & chron. For. & loc. pub., chiefly of Cath. church. No add.
Tx30 197 ent., tpd. shts. by auth. Per. Cath. per. combat communism. No add.

CATS. *See* PETS **Co8-biol**

CATTARAUGUS COUNTY (N.Y.)
N41 Unest. cds. by auth. & t. Bks. & pams. In proc.

CAWEIN, MADISON—WORKS
Ky15-ref 650 cds. by t. of poem. Bks. & per. No add.

CAYUGA Co. (N.Y.)
N2 150 ent., tpd. shts. by subj. Bks. Freq. add.

CELEBRITIES—DISEASES
Ia7 400 cds. by disease & person. Med. hist. & biog. Occ. add.

CELLS
Nj61 150 cds. by auth. & t. Bks., per., pams. & repts. Freq. add.

CELLULOSE ACETATE
Nj54 10,000 cds. by subj. Spec. rpts. Freq. add.

CEMENT. *See also* TRADE CATALOGS AND DIRECTORIES **I27**
I27 1500 cds. by subj. Newsp. & corresp. Daily add.

CEMENT—PHOTOGRAPHS
I27 30,351 cds. by subj. or loc. Phot. prints & negatives. Daily add.

CENSUS. *See* Names of loc., subdiv. CENSUS

CENTENNIAL YEARBOOK OF ALAMEDA CO. CALIFORNIA (bk.). *In* ALAMEDA CO. (CALIF.)—HISTORY **C43-ref**

CENTINEL OF THE NORTHWESTERN TERRITORY (newsp.). *In* GENEALOGY **O17**

CENTURY, A POPULAR QUARTERLY
N35-ref. inf v. 1, 1870–indefinite date. Cds. by auth., t. & subj. No add.

CERAMICS
G7-cer. eng 15,000 cds. by subj. Per. Infreq. add.
Wa14-ref 100 cds. by topic. Bks., pams. & per. Pottery & porcelain. Infreq. add.

CEREALS, PREPARED. *See* List of Bibliographies, APPENDIX I

CHARACTER
In5-j 75 cds. by subj. Bks. Infreq. add.
Mi6-Walk. 155 cds. by subj. Bks. & per. Infreq. add.
P19 33 ent., tpd. shts. by auth. Bks. & per. No add.
P39-Wyl. 524 cds. by subj. Bks., pams. & per. Freq. add.

CHARACTER SKETCHES. *See* List of Bibliographies, APPENDIX I

CHARACTERS IN FICTION. *See* HEROES AND HEROINES (IN LITERATURE)

CHARLESTON (S.C.)—EDUCATION. *See* EDUCATION—CHARLESTON (S.C.)

CHARTERS
N35-ref. read 600 cds. by class. no. Bks., per. & learned soc. pub. Cartularies; French & Belgian charters & deeds. Cur. add.

CHARTERS—MARYLAND
Md2-Md. 2800 cds. by subj. Charters granted to Md. organiz. by legis. act, 1692–1937. Freq. add.

CHARTS. *See* MAPS

CHARTS—GLOSSARIES
N35-ref. econ 350 cds. by subj. Bks. & per. Cur. add.

CHATHAM, WILLIAM PITT, 1ST EARL OF—DRAWINGS AND ENGRAVINGS
P39-ref art 75 cds. by art. Gift coll. of prints: groups & memorials, port. & caricatures. No add.

CHATTANOOGA (TENN.)—HISTORY
T3-Mc. 396p., 4000 ent., tpd. shts., chron. Calendar of J. Hays Allen papers. No add.

CHECKER PLAYERS—NECROLOGY
O20-White 1500 cds. by name. Occ. add.

CHECKERS
O20-White 2000 cds. by subj. Bks., per., newsp., etc. Occ. add.

CHECKLIST OF WASHINGTON AUTHORS (bk.). *In* AUTHORS—WASHINGTON (STATE) **Wa10-ref** (2)

CHEMICAL AND METALLURGICAL ENGINEERING (per.). *In* CHEMISTRY **L17**

CHEMICAL INDUSTRY
N30-chem   175 cds. by subj. Repts. Plant design and proc. development. Freq. add.

CHEMICAL WARFARE
Nj54   Unest. cds. by subj. Spec. repts. Freq. add.

CHEMICALS—PRICES
N35-ref. sci   7200 cds. by subj. 50 per. In proc.

CHEMISTRY
L17   1500 cds. Bks., Per. indexed: *Chemical and metallurgical engineering, Jl. chemical educ., Jl. ind. and engineering chemistry.* Cur. add.
Nj61   60 cds. by auth. & t. Bks., per. & pams. Freq. add.

CHEMISTRY—PATENTS. *See* PATENTS—SCIENCE **In18**

CHEMISTRY, ORGANIC
Nj61   40 cds. by auth. & t. Bks., per. & pams. Infreq. add.

CHEMISTRY, PHYSICAL AND THEORETICAL
Nj61   30 cds. by auth. & t. Bks., per. & pams. Infreq. add.

CHEMISTRY, PHYSIOLOGICAL
Nj61   70 cds. by auth. & t. Bks., per. & pams. Infreq. add.

CHEMISTS. *See* SCIENTISTS   **N8-tech**

CHEMOTHERAPY
Nj61   45 cds. by auth. & t. Bks., per. reprints & repts. Infreq. add.

CHEMURGY
Tx19   21 cds. Bks. & per. Freq. add.

CHENANGO AMERICAN (newsp.)
N17   v. 1, 1855–date. Cds. by subj. Cur. add.

CHEROKEE INDIANS. *See* INDIANS   **G2-DeRen.**

CHESS
O20-White   2000 cds. by subj. Occ. add.

CHESS IN LITERATURE
O20-White   1500 cds. by auth. Per. Occ. add.

CHESS PLAYERS—NECROLOGY
O20-White   2640 cds. by name. Per. Cur. add.

CHESTER CO. (PA.)—HISTORY
P53   60,000 cds. by subj., loc., auth., etc. Bks., newsp., mss., pams., etc. Daily add.

CHESTERTON, GILBERT KEITH—WORKS. *See* List of Bibliographies, APPENDIX I

CHICAGO
I13-doc   2640 cds. by subj. Per. Infreq. add.
I13-ref   1600 cds. by subj. Bks. & per. Occ. add.

CHICAGO—ARCHITECTURE. *See* List of Bibliographies, APPENDIX I

CHICAGO. ART INSTITUTE. BULLETIN
I11-Ryer.   Unest. cds. by subj. Cur. add.

CHICAGO. ART INSTITUTE—HISTORY
I11-Ryer.   16,200 ent., tpd. shts. in scrapbk. 1878–date. Cur. add.

CHICAGO—BIOGRAPHY
I13-ref   5000 cds. by subj. Bks., per. & newsp. Freq. add.

CHICAGO—BUILDINGS
I24   200 ent., 4p. tpd. shts. Bk. indexed: *Chicago daily news almanac, 1891–1898.* No add.

CHICAGO—BUSINESS. *See* List of Bibliographies, APPENDIX I

CHICAGO—DESCRIPTION & TRAVEL. *See* List of Bibliographies, APPENDIX I

CHICAGO—HISTORY
I13-Hild   2500 cds. by subj. Bks., pam., newsp., sch. & church dir. maps, etc. Freq. add.
I13-Legler   3500 cds. by auth., t. & subj. Inc. phot., etc. Cur. add.

CHICAGO—HOUSE ORGANS. *See* HOUSE ORGANS—CHICAGO

CHICAGO—INTELLECTUAL LIFE. *See* List of Bibliographies, APPENDIX I

CHICAGO—MUSIC. *See* MUSIC—CHICAGO

CHICAGO—NECROLOGY
I24   12,800 ent., tpd. shts. by name. Bk. indexed: *Chicago daily news almanac,* 1885–1937. No add.

CHICAGO—OFFICIALS AND EMPLOYEES
I24   1500 ent., tpd. shts., bd. by name. Council proc. Centennial list, 1837–1937. No add.

CHICAGO—PHOTOGRAPHS. *See* CHICAGO—HISTORY **I13-Legler**

CHICAGO—PICTURES. *See* PICTURES—CHICAGO

CHICAGO—PLAYS. *See* PLAYS—CHICAGO

CHICAGO—POETRY. *See* POETRY—CHICAGO

CHICAGO—SCULPTURE. *See* SCULPTURE—CHICAGO

CHICAGO—SOCIAL CONDITIONS. *See* List of Bibliographies, APPENDIX I

CHICAGO—SOCIETIES AND CLUBS
I13-doc 2640 cds. by name of club. Newsp. Freq. add.

CHICAGO—STREETS
I13-ref 1400 cds. by subj. Newsp. & pams. Occ. add.
I24 1300 cds. by name of st. City dirs., 1869–1928. No add.

CHICAGO—THEATRE. *See* THEATRE—CHICAGO

CHICAGO. UNIVERSITY — DISSERTATIONS, ACADEMIC. *See* List of Bibliographies, APPENDIX I

CHICAGO. UNIVERSITY—ROUND TABLE. *In* PAMPHLETS **I62**

CHICAGO—VOCATIONAL COUNSELING AGENCIES. *See* List of Bibliographies, APPENDIX I

CHICAGO—WOMEN'S CLUBS
I13-r.b. 925 cds. by name of club. Infreq. add.

CHICAGO—WORLD'S COLUMBIAN EXPOSITION, 1893
I13-ref 1400 cds. by subj. & country. Bks., per. & pams. Infreq. add.

CHICAGO—YOUTH ORGANIZATIONS
I13-r.b. 475 cds. by name of club. Infreq. add.

CHICAGO DAILY NEWS ALMANAC (bk.). *In* CHICAGO—BUILDINGS **I24**; CHICAGO—NECROLOGY **I24**

CHICAGO SYMPHONY ORCHESTRA PROGRAMS. *See* SYMPHONY **C32-art, O16-art, O29-ref, O56-ref**

CHILD LIFE (per.). *In* CHILDREN'S PLAYS **Mn14-j**

CHILD STUDY. *See also* INFANTS—CARE AND HYGIENE; List of Bibliographies, APPENDIX I

Ia14-med 80 cds. by subj. Bk. indexed: *White house conference on child health and protection.* All v. No add.
Mn11 Unest. ent., tpd. shts. by subj. Bks. & per. Freq. add.
N43-j 463 cds. by class. Bks. Freq. add.
P58 Unest. cds. by subj. Bks. Freq. add.
Wa10-par 200 cds. by subj. Pams., bks. & per. Cur. add.

CHILDREN
Nb14-N. 339 ent., tpd. shts. by countries & auth. Bks. Children around the world. Infreq. add.

CHILDREN, HANDICAPPED. *See* List of Bibliographies, APPENDIX I

CHILDREN IN LITERATURE. *See* READERS AND PRIMERS **O20-Rice-j**

CHILDREN'S BOOK OF CELEBRATED PICTURES (bk.). *In* ART—STUDY & TEACHING **Mi6-Walk.**

CHILDREN'S LITERATURE. *See also* ANIMAL STORIES; JUVENILE; AUTHORS, CHILDREN'S; CHRISTMAS STORIES, JUVENILE; DOG STORIES, JUVENILE; FAIRY TALES; HISTORY, JUVENILE; ILLUSTRATORS, CHILDREN'S; NEGRO LITERATURE, JUVENILE; PIRATE STORIES, JUVENILE; READERS AND PRIMERS; SCHOOL STORIES, JUVENILE; SERIES, BOOKS IN—JUVENILE; VOCATIONS—STORIES, JUVENILE: YOUNG PEOPLE'S LITERATURE; List of Bibliographies, APPENDIX I
C43-j 8400 cds. by subj. Fic. Freq. add.
C49-j 1152 cds. by subj. Pop. subj. Freq. add.
Ct3 1038 cds. by subj. Fic. Freq. add.
De1 700 cds. by auth. & subj. Cur. add.
I59 500 cds. by subj. Freq. add.
Ia6-j 7260 cds. by t. Bks. Occ. add.
In8-j 2500 cds. by t. Bks. for 5th grade & up, not indexed in Firkins. Cur. add.
In12 Unest. ent., tpd. shts. by grades. Illus. mat. for classics, grades 4–8.
K5-j 400 cds. by t. Bks. Short stories. Cur. add.

M21-j 2500 cds. by t. & subj. Bks. Short stories. Freq. add.
Mi9 126 cds. by subj. Bks. Freq. add.
Mi31-Mel. 600 ent., tpd. shts., in booklets. Fic. & short stories. Cur. add.
N28-j 3600 cds. by subj. Fic. Infreq. add.
N44-j 35p., tpd. shts. by t. Bks. Yrly. add.
N45b 1100 cds. by auth., t. & country. Uncat. coll. Freq. add.
N45b 621 cds. by auth., t. & country. Clarence Lown coll., late 18th & early 19th cent., chiefly English & Amer. Freq. add.
Nj14 7260 cds. by t. Short stories inc. readers & primers. Freq. add.
Nb14-j 5050 cds. by subj. & t. Bks. & pams. Freq. add.
Nj21-j 1600 cds. by subj. Fic., 1935–date. Freq. add.
Nj50-educ. 900 cds. by auth., t. & ser. Bks. in Stone coll., 1700 to present. Infreq. add.
Nj67-j 3800 cds. by subj. & t. Occ. add.
O20-class 2640 cds. by subj. Fic. Freq. add.
O20-class 1320 cds. by subj. Gen. bks. Freq. add.
O20-j 6300 cds. by t. Short stories. Occ. add.
O20-M.P. 600 cds. Bks. Freq. add.
O29-j 37,800 cds. by subj. & t. Bks. not indexed. Cur. add.
O31-N. 400 cds. by subj. Bks. about places. Freq. add.
O36 32,000 cds. by t. Short stories. Supp. to Eastman & Firkins. Freq. add.
P2 2000 cds. by auth., t. & subj. Short stories. No add.
P39-j 6000 cds. by t. Bks. Cur. add.
P54-j 2080 cds. by subj. & t. Short stories. Freq. add.

CHILDREN'S LITERATURE—BIOGRAPHY. See also AUTHORS, CHILDREN'S; ILLUSTRATORS, CHILDREN'S
C32-j 5280 cds. by subj. Bks. & per. Occ. add.
De3 1320 cds. by subj. Bks. & per. Infreq. add.

Mi13-Har. 2238 cds. by subj. Bks. Infreq. add.
Mi13-W. side 200 cds. by subj. Bks. & per. Occ. add.
Mn14-j 1500 cds. by subj. Bks. Freq. add.
Mo3-Wash. 1000 cds. by subj. Bks. Freq. add.
Mo13-Cab. 750 cds. by subj. Bks. Per. indexed: *Wilson library bulletin.* Freq. add.
Mo13-Stix 1050 cds. by subj. Bks. Freq. add.
N24-j Unest. cds. by subj. Bks. In proc.
O1-Ell. 1320 cds. by subj. Bks. Cur. add.
Wa6 900 cds. by subj. Bks., per. & pams. Freq. add.

CHILDREN'S LITERATURE—BOOK REVIEWS
Nb10-j 6500 cds. by auth. Freq. add.
O37 4500 cds. by auth. & t. Mo. add.
P5-j 700 cds. by auth. Cur. add.
P39-j. off 4125 cds. by auth. & t. Per. indexed: *New York herald tribune. Books,* 1928–date. Wkly. add.

CHILDREN'S LITERATURE—CHRISTMAS
C62-j 180 ent., tpd. shts. by country. Bks. Freq. add.
M21-j 1500 cds. by type. Bks. & per. Cur. add.
Mi31-Way. 350 ent., tpd. shts. by subj. Bks. Freq. add.
Tx29-j 48 cds. by country. Fic. & travel bks. Occ. add.
Tx35 85 ent., tpd. shts. by country. Bks. & per. Infreq. add.

CHILDREN'S LITERATURE—COUNTRY LIFE. See List of Bibliographies, APPENDIX I

CHILDREN'S LITERATURE—EASY BOOKS. See READERS AND PRIMERS

CHILDREN'S LITERATURE—EDITIONS. See List of Bibliographies, APPENDIX I

CHILDREN'S LITERATURE—EDITORS
In12 2p., tpd. shts. by editor. Per. indexed: *Publisher's Weekly;* Bk. indexed: Stanley J. Kunitz and Howard Haycraft, *Junior book of authors.*

CHILDREN'S LITERATURE—ETHICS
K20-j 1000 cds. by subj. Bks. & per. In proc.
P39-j 1250 cds. by subj. Short stories & poetry. Cur. add.

CHILDREN'S LITERATURE—FOREIGN LANGUAGES
Mi6-for 600 cds. by subj. & lang. Bks. Freq. add.

CHILDREN'S LITERATURE—GRADED BOOKS. See List of Bibliographies, APPENDIX I

CHILDREN'S LITERATURE—HISTORICAL FICTION
C62-j Unest. cds., hist. & chron. Fic. with Amer. hist. background. Cur. add.
Tx29-j 315 cds., chron. Fic., from prehistoric period to date. Cur. add.

CHILDREN'S LITERATURE—HOLIDAYS. See also CHILDREN'S LITERATURE—CHRISTMAS; CHILDREN'S POETRY—HOLIDAYS; List of Bibliographies, APPENDIX I
C49-j 2256 cds. by holiday. Bks. Freq. add.
D32-j 1200 cds. by subj. Bks., exclusive of poetry & plays. Freq. add.
I3 1200 cds. by subj. Bks. Freq. add.
165-Linc.-j 420 cds. by auth. Bks. Infreq. add.
Ia19-j 100 cds. by subj. Bks. & per. Freq. add.
In5-j 300 cds. by subj. Bks. & newsp. Yrly. add.
Mi27-j 725 cds. by holiday. Bks. & per. Occ. add.
N44-j 400 cds. by subj. Bks. Cur. add.
Nj27-j 450 cds. by t. Bks. Dramatized stories & recit. Infreq. add.
O20-Quin. 300 cds. by holiday. Prose, poetry & drama. Infreq. add.
O29-Elec. 1000 cds. by class. under each holiday. Poems, stories, plays, art. in bks. Freq. add.
P5-j 900 cds. by holiday & type of mat. Bks. Yrly. add.
P39-j 625 cds. by t. Bks. Christmas & Thanksgiving. Cur. add.
Wa10-j 2500 cds., chron. & by subj. Bks. & per. Cur. add.

CHILDREN'S LITERATURE—HUMOR
Wa10-j 200 cds. by auth. Humorous stories in bks. Cur. add.

CHILDREN'S LITERATURE—INDIANS
C49-j 384 cds. by tribe. Bks. Freq. add.
K14-j 55 cds. by auth. Bks. Freq. add.
Md2-j 350 cds. by tribe. Bks. Infreq. add.
Mi6-Rich. 150 ent., tpd. shts. by auth. Fic. & non.-fic. Freq. add.
Nj19-j 75 ent., tpd. shts. by auth. Fic., 4th grade up. Occ. add.

CHILDREN'S LITERATURE — INEXPENSIVE BOOKS. See List of Bibliographies, APPENDIX I

CHILDREN'S LITERATURE—INSECTS
O20-Tem. 100 cds. by name of insect. Infreq. add.

CHILDREN'S LITERATURE—LANGUAGE AND LANGUAGES
Mi6-Red. 100 cds. by subj. Bks. Cur. add.

CHILDREN'S LITERATURE—MYSTERY AND DETECTIVE STORIES. See also List of Bibliographies, APPENDIX I
C20 123 cds. by auth. Bks. Occ. add.
K14-j 133 cds. by auth. Bks. Freq. add.
Mn11 Unest. ent., tpd. shts. by auth. Bks. Freq. add.
Nj19-j 80 ent., tpd. shts. by auth. Fic., 4th grade up. Occ. add.
P45-j 130 ent., tpd. shts. by auth. Bks. Cur. add.

CHILDREN'S LITERATURE—NATURE. See also CHILDREN'S POETRY—NATURE
O20-j 2600 cds. by subj. Bks. Cur. add.
O20-Quin.-j 75 cds. by subj. Bk. indexed: John Bradford Craig, *Nature study*, v. 1-4. No add.
O20-Sup. 1650 cds. by subj. Bks. Cur. add.

CHILDREN'S LITERATURE—PAMPHLETS
O20-Carn. 50 cds. by subj. & t. Cur. add.

CHILDREN'S LITERATURE—PENNSYLVANIA
P21 30 cds. by auth. Bks. Freq. add.

CHILDREN'S LITERATURE—READERS. See READERS AND PRIMERS

CHILDREN'S LITERATURE—ROCKS
O20-Tem. 25 cds. by name of rock or mineral. Bks. Infreq. add.

CHILDREN'S LITERATURE—SCANDINAVIA
Nj71 64 ent., tpd. shts. by type of bk. Mythology, travel, stories; inc. Vikings. Occ. add.

CHILDREN'S LITERATURE—SCIENCE
O20-class 1320 cds. Bks. Freq. add.
O20-Glen. 1200 cds. by subj. Bks. Cur. add.

CHILDREN'S LITERATURE—SUBNORMAL READING
Mi29-ext 50 ent., tpd. shts. Bks. Infreq. add.

CHILDREN'S LITERATURE—THANKSGIVING DAY. See CHILDREN'S LITERATURE—HOLIDAYS; List of Bibliographies, APPENDIX I

CHILDREN'S LITERATURE—TRAVEL. See List of Bibliographies, APPENDIX I

CHILDREN'S LITERATURE—VOCATIONAL FICTION
Tx29-j 52 cds. by subj. Fic., 1931–date. Freq. add.

CHILDREN'S LITERATURE, REGIONAL. See also CHILDREN'S LITERATURE, subdiv. Names of countries and states; List of Bibliographies, APPENDIX I
C3-j 360 cds. by auth. Fic. about U.S. by states. Cur. add.
C49-j 1152 cds. by name of country. Bks. Plays, poems, songs. Freq. add.
C62-j 3000 ent., tpd. shts. by name of country. Bks. Cur. add.
In8-j 806 cds. by name of country. Bks. Inc. costumes, dances, plays, poetry, short stories & songs. Freq. add.
Nj7-Coop.-j 415 ent., tpd. shts. by name of country. Fic. & non-fic. No add.
Nj23 900 ent., tpd. shts. by name of country & auth. Bks. Freq. add.
Nj50-educ 2600 cds. by auth. under country. Bks. on 54 countries. Freq. add.
O20-class 1320 cds. by name of country. Bks. Freq. add.
O50 350 cds. by name of country & state of U.S. Cur. add.

CHILDREN'S PLAYS
C32-j 5280 cds. by auth., subj. & t. Bks. & per. Occ. add.
C43-j 6300 cds. by auth., subj. & t. Bks. Freq. add.
C49-j 1408 cds. by no. of char. Bks. Freq. add.
C62-j 800 cds. by subj. Bks. Infreq. add.
C69-j 3000 cds. by auth., subj. & t. Bks. Cur. add.
Ca2-j 3410 cds. by auth., subj. & t. Bks. Cur. add.
Co5-j 990 cds. by subj. Bks. Cur. add.
Ct12-j 2380 cds. by subj. & t. Bks. Freq. add.
De3 2700 cds. by subj. & t. Freq. add.
G15-j 5280 cds. by subj. & t. Cur. add.
H2 50 cds. by subj. Per. indexed: *American childhood, Grade teacher, Instructor, Junior arts and activities.* Freq. add.
Ia6-j 300 cds. by auth. & t. Bks. Infreq. add.
M21-j 1000 cds. by subj. & t. Bks. & per. Freq. add.
M27-j 2194 cds. by subj. & t. Bks. Freq. add.
M32 1000 cds. by subj. Per. & bks. Occ. add.
Mi4 390 cds. by auth. & t. Bks. Freq. add.
Mn14-j 6000 cds. by subj. & t. Bks., Per. indexed: *Child life.* Freq. add.
Mn14-Fran.-j 1000 cds. by subj. & t. Bks. Cur. add.
N8-j 900 cds. by subj. Bks. Freq. add.
N28-j 2250 cds. by subj. & t. Supp. A.L.A. index. Freq. add.
Nb14-Ben. 350 cds. by subj. Bks. Freq. add.
Nb14-j 1500 cds. by subj. & t. Bks. & pams. Freq. add.
Nb14-S. 1050 cds. by subj. & t. Bks & pams. Freq. add.
Nj27-j 2250 cds. by t. Bks. Freq. add.
O1-j 4500 cds. by subj. & t. Bks. Cur. add.
O20-j 7000 cds. by subj. & t. Bks., per. & pams. Cur. add.
O20-Sup. 1980 cds. by t. Bks. Cur. add.

O31 750 cds. by subj. & t. Bks. Freq. add.
O38 2500 cds. by auth. t. & subj. Bks. Cur. add.
O50 500 cds. by subj. Bks. Cur. add.
O58-j 150 cds. by subj. Bks. Cur. add.
P39-j 2900 cds. by t. & subj. Bks. & pams. Cur. add.
P54-j 2000 cds. by t. Bks. & per. Freq. add.
W16 800 cds. by subj. Bks. Freq. add.
W19-j 677 cds. by subj. Bks. Freq. add.
Wa10-j 1200 cds. by subj. & t. Bks. & per. Cur. add.
Wa13-j 2500 cds. by subj. & t. Bks., pams. & per. Cur. add.

CHILDREN'S POETRY. *See also* NURSERY RHYMES
C27-j 9000 cds. by auth., subj. & t. Bks. Occ. add.
Ca2-j Unest. cds. by auth., subj. & t. Supp. to Granger's index and McPherson. Cur. add.
Co5-j 1320 cds. by subj. Bks. Occ. add.
D32-j 500 cds. by subj. Supp. to McPherson. Infreq. add.
Ia6-j 640 cds. by subj. Bks. Cur. add.
K5 1500 cds. by t. Bks. Cur. add.
Md2-j 13,690 cds. by auth. & t. Bks. Freq. add.
Mn14-Fran.-j 800 cds. by subj. & t. Bks. Cur. add.
Mo13-j 800 cds. by subj. Bks. Animals, country life, transp., voc., games & sports.
Mo13-Stix Unest. cds. by auth., subj. & t. Poems, readings & recit.
N8-j 13,200 cds. by auth., t. & first line. Bks. Freq. add.
Nj14 5280 cds. by t. Bks. Occ. add.
Nj17 1700 cds. by subj. Bks. Freq. add.
O20-j 525 cds. by subj. Bks. Occ. add.
O26 10,000 cds. by t. Bks. Freq. add.
O31 11,750 cds. by t. Bks. Freq. add.
Or01 4699 cds. by auth. & subj. Supp. to McPherson.

P1-j 2500 cds. by t. Bks. Freq. add.
P39-j 16,800 cds. by subj. & t. Bks. Supp. to Granger. Cur. add.
Tx35 7000 cds. by auth. & t. Bks. Cur. add.
Wa10-j 900 cds. by subj. Bks. Cur. add.

CHILDREN'S POETRY—DOGS
In5-j 50 cds. by t. Bks. Infreq. add.

CHILDREN'S POETRY—HOLIDAYS
O36 250 cds. by t. Bks. Freq. add.

CHILDREN'S POETRY—NATURE
O20-Sup.-j 20p. 200 ent. tpd. shts. by subj. Infreq. add.

CHILDREN'S SONGS
Ca2-j 5520 cds. by subj. & t. Bks. Supp. to Cushing's index. Cur. add.
In8-j 7600 cds. by t. Bks. & pams. Supp. to Cushing's index. No add.
M3 600 cds. by comp. & t. Song coll., kindergarten bks. & pams. Freq. add.
Nj67-j 800 cds. by t. Bks. & pams. Freq. add.
O20-j 25,000 cds. by subj., t. & first line. Bks. Occ. add.
O20-soc 2640 cds. by t. Kindergarten song bks. No add.
O31 1150 cds. by t. Song coll., bks. Infreq. add.
P39-j 3800 cds. by t. Bks. Supp. to Cushing's index. Freq. add.
Wa14-j 1400 cds. by t. Bks. Freq. add.

CHIMES AND CHIMING
Tx19 12 cds. Per. Occ. add.

CHINESE LITERATURE. *See* ORIENTAL LITERATURE M11-Jap.

CHISHOLM (MINN.)—ACCIDENTS. *See* List of Bibliographies, APPENDIX I

CHISHOLM (MINN.)—HISTORY
Mn1 60 cds. by subj. Bks., per. & newsp. Infreq. add.

CHORAL MUSIC. *See also* CHURCH MUSIC
M28 250 ent., tpd. shts. by t. Scores. Occ. add.
O16-art 700 cds. by comp. & subj. Cur. add.

CHRISTIAN ART AND SYMBOLISM. *See also* JESUS CHRIST IN ART
I16   35,000 cds. by subj., t. & art. Bks., pic., & newsp. Ecclesiastical art, christian symbolism, church arch. Freq. add.
Nj60-art   250,000 cds. by subj. All subj. represented on monuments & obj. of Christian art up to the year 1400. 47,000 add. yrly. Phot. copies of index also in Dumbarton Oaks research lib., Wash. D.C. & Metropolitan museum of art, N.Y. City.

CHRISTIAN MONITOR. *In* MENNONITES—HISTORY   In13

CHRISTIAN NAMES. *See* NAMES, PERSONAL

CHRISTIAN SCIENCE MONITOR (newsp.). *In* PRONUNCIATION   Mo12

CHRISTIAN SCIENCE MONITOR MAGAZINE
C32-per   1933–1936. Cds. by subj. No add.

CHRISTMAS. *See also* List of Bibliographies, APPENDIX I; CHILDREN'S LITERATURE—CHRISTMAS
C62-circ   200 cds. by country. Bks. & newsp. Occ. add.
C82   222 ent., tpd. shts. by subj. Bks., pams., per. & newsp. Yrly. add.
Ct5   125 cds. by type of lit. Bks. Occ. add.
Ct11-ref   223 ent., tpd. shts. by subj. Bks. & per. Freq. add.
I13-circ   131 ent., tpd. shts. by country. Freq. add.
I13-ref   1700 cds. by country & subj. Bks. & per. Freq. add.
I51   25 ent., tpd. shts. by subj. Bks., per. & pams. Sci. contribution to Christmas. Yrly. add.
I68-ref   200 cds. by subj. Bks. & per. Freq. add.
Ia3   100 cds. by subj. Bks. & per. Occ. add.
Ia18-ad   1000 ent., tpd. shts. by subj. Bks., per. & pams. Cur. add.
In24a   42 cds. by subj. Bks. Poems & stories. Freq. add.
In26   220 cds. by auth. & subj. Bks. & pams. Occ. add.
Mi25   1400 cds. by subj. Bks. Plays, customs & stories. Cur. add.
Mi29   75 cds. by subj. Bks., per., pams. & newsp. Infreq. add.
Mn11   Unest. ent., tpd. shts. by subj. Bks. & per. Freq. add.
Mn14-ref   950 ent., tpd. shts. by country. Bks. & per. For. customs. Occ. add.
Mn14-ref   550 ent., tpd. shts. auth. & t. Bks. & per. Hist., origin, essays, legends, sermons, prayers, carols. Freq. add.
N4   97 cds. by t. Pams. Plays, poetry & songs. Infreq. add.
N13   162 cds. by subj. Bks. & per. Occ. add.
N22-ref   500 cds. by subj. Bks., per. & pams. Christmas & New Year customs. No add.
N46-lit   1400 cds. by subj., t. & type of mat. Bks. & pams. Freq. add.
Nb2   83 ent., tpd. shts., bd. by type of mat. Bks. & per. Occ. add.
Nj17   180 ent., tpd. shts. by country. Bks. & per. Freq. add.
Nj34   1080 cds. by subj. Bks., per. & pams. Freq. add.
Nj50-educ   588 cds. by auth. subj. & t. Bks. in McEwen coll. Occ. add.
Nj58   385 ent., tpd. shts. by subj. & auth. Bks., pams. & music. Freq. add.
Nj66   300 cds. by subj. Bks. & pams. Freq. add.
O20-lit   5280 cds. by t. Poetry, plays, stories, readings, essays, exercises, etc. Cur. add.
O37-Mad.   100 cds. by country. Bks., pams. & pic. Christmas in other lands. Occ. add.
P14   100 cds. by subj. Bks., per. & yrbks. Freq. add.
P39-circ   660 cds. by class. Plays, poetry, stories. Cur. add.
T1-circ   600 ent., tpd. shts. by subj. Bks. Freq. add.
W6   50 cds. by auth. Bks. & per. Occ. add.

CHRISTMAS CARDS. *See* GREETING CARDS

CHRISTMAS CAROLS. *See* CHRISTMAS MUSIC

CHRISTMAS MUSIC
Ia6-art   100 ent., tpd. shts. by type of mus. Carols, piano & instrumental mus. Occ. add.
Mn14-mus   91p., tpd. shts. by t. nationality & comp. Songs & carols. Occ. add.
Wa14-ref   250 cds. by t. Bks. & per. Freq. add.

CHRISTMAS PLAYS
   Mn14-clip   650 cds. by auth. & t.
      Pams. & newsp. Infreq. add.
   P5   227 cds. by t. Bks., per. & pams.
      Occ. add.
   P6   100 ent., tpd. shts. by source.
      Bks. & per. Infreq. add.

CHRISTMAS STORIES
   I13-circ   60 ent., tpd. shts. by auth.
      Bks. of short stories. Infreq. add.
   I13-circ   28 ent., tpd. shts. by auth.
      Fic. Occ. add.
   In3   400 cds. by auth. & t. Bks. &
      per. Occ. add.
   In22-ref   500 cds. by auth. & t. Bks.
      & per. In proc.
   Mi21-ref   70 cds. by auth. & t. Bks.
      In proc.
   Mn14-clip   320 cds. by auth. & t.
      Pams. & newsp. Infreq. add.
   Mn14-ref   275 ent., tpd. shts. Bks.
      & per. Cur. add.
   P19   41 ent., tpd. shts. by auth. Bks.
      & per. In proc.

CHRISTMAS STORIES, JUVENILE
   Ia6-j   150 cds. by t. Bks. Occ. add.
   In8-j   428 cds. by t. Bks. Cur. add.
   Wv3-j   32 ent., tpd. shts. by t. Bks.
      & per.

CHRONICLES OF AMERICA (bk.). *In* U.S.—
   HISTORY   Nj56

CHRONOLOGICAL HISTORY OF SEATTLE (bk.).
   In SEATTLE (WASH.)—HISTORY
   Wa10-ref (1)

CHURCH ARCHITECTURE. *See* CHRISTIAN
   ART AND SYMBOLISM   I16

CHURCH HISTORY. *See* Names of denominations, i.e., BAPTISTS

CHURCH MUSIC. *See also* HYMNS
   N35-mus   150p., tpd. shts. in notebk.
      by days of church year & subj. Coll.
      & unbd. sacred music. Freq. add.
   N35-mus   115p., tpd. shts. in notebk.
      by days of church year & subj. Bks.
      & per. Suggestions for organists &
      choirmasters. Freq. add.
   N35-mus   2000 cds. by auth., t. &
      subj. Coll. choruses & unbd. choral
      works. Freq. add.

CHURCH OF SCOTLAND. *See* PRESBYTERIANS

CHURCHES—NEW JERSEY. *See* NEW JERSEY
   —CHURCHES

CICERO, MARCUS TULLIUS—SPEECHES
   N46-lit   100 cds. by t. Bks. Infreq.
      add.

CINCINNATI (O.)—ARTISTS. *See* ARTISTS—
   CINCINNATI (O.)

CINCINNATI (O.)—HISTORY
   O16-ref   40,000 cds. by subj. Bks.
      Cur. add.

CINCINNATI (O.)—NEWSPAPERS
   O16-ref   35,000 cds. by subj. Freq.
      add.

CINCINNATI (O.)—PICTURES. *See* PICTURES
   —CINCINNATI (O.)

CINCINNATI (O.)—POLITICS AND GOVERNMENT
   O18   250 cds. by subj. Per. Freq.
      add.

CINCINNATI (O.)—SOCIETIES AND CLUBS
   O16-ref   1800 cds. by name. Newsp.
      Freq. add.

CINCINNATI SYMPHONY ORCHESTRA PROGRAMS. *See* SYMPHONY   O29-
   ref; O47-ref

CINCINNATI (O.) LIBERTY HALL & CINCINNATI GAZETTE (newsp.). *In*
   GENEALOGY   O17

CIST'S CINCINNATI MISCELLANY (bk.). *In*
   GENEALOGY   O17

CITIES AND TOWNS. *See also* Names of
   states, subdivision CITIES AND TOWNS
   Wa10-mun. ref   12,000 cds. by subj.
      Bks., per., pams., corr. & ordinances.
      Cur. add.

CITIZENSHIP. *See also* List of Bibliographies, APPENDIX I
   K11   34 cds. by subj. Freq. add.
   N55-Max.   8660 cds. by auth., t. &
      subj. Bks. & per. Freq. add.

CITY MANAGER GOVERNMENT. *See* MUNICIPAL GOVERNMENT BY CITY MANAGER

CITY OF DUBOIS (bk.). *In* DUBOIS (PA.)—
   HISTORY   P11

CITY PLANNING—PERIODICALS
   I73-lands.   Unest. cds. by subj.
      Freq. add.

CITY WORTH SEEING (bk.) *In* ST. LOUIS (MO.) **Mo13-Soul.**

CIVIL ENGINEERING
I27 10,000 ent. by subj. Newsp. Daily add.
Nj52 Several hundred cds. by subj. Bks., per. & pams. Freq. add.

CIVIL SERVICE. *See also* List of Bibliographies, APPENDIX I
M27-ref 400 cds. by subj. Bks. & pams. Freq. add.
Mi6-soc 325 cds. by occup. Manuals & per. Cur. add.
Mn14-ref 250 cds. by occup. Bks. Cur. add.
Mn14-tech 450 cds. by subj. Infreq. add.
N8-ref 250 cds. by subj. Bks. Freq. add.
N35-Bronx 2640 cds. by occup. Manuals, newsp., etc. Freq. add.
N35-Morr. 1800 cds. Manuals, bks., & newsp. Freq. add.
N35-Wash. 600 cds. by occup. & test. State, fed. & mun. exams. & manuals. Cur. add.
N35-Wood. 745 cds. by occup. Bks., pams. & multigraph mat. Cur. add.
N46-soc 250 cds. by type of work. Bks., pams. & per. Freq. add.
O1-circ 300 cds. by subj. Bks. Cur. add.
O20-soc 704 cds. by occup. Examinations. No add.
Wa10-ref 250 ent., tpd. shts. Bks. Seattle civil service examination. No add.
Wa10-ref 300 ent. by subj. Bks., per. & govt. doc. Fed. civil service examinations. Cur. add.

CIVIL SERVICE REVIEW. *In* CANADA—PERIODICALS **Ca13-per**

CIVIL WAR. *See* U.S.—HISTORY—CIVIL WAR

CIVILIAN CONSERVATION CORPS. *See* WASHINGTON (STATE)—DIRECTORIES **Wa10-tech**

CLARK, GEORGE ROGERS
Ky2 156 cds. by auth. Bks. & per. Freq. add.

CLARK CO. (KY.)
Ky7 Unest. ent., tpd. shts. by name & place. Newsp.

CLARK CO. (O.)—BIOGRAPHY
O53 10,000 cds. by name. Hist. bks. No add.

CLASSICAL LITERATURE. *See also* List of Bibliographies, APPENDIX I
O20-ref 18,000 cds. by auth. Class. ser. & per., issued by Lib. of Univ. of Utrecht. Infreq. add.
Or8 350 cds. by auth. & class. Auth. & class. in the field of lit.

CLASSROOM TEACHER (bk.) *In* EDUCATION **P4**

CLAY, HENRY
Ky2 220 cds. by auth. Bks. & per. Freq. add.

CLEAR CREEK CO. (COL.)—MINING AND METALLURGY. *See* MINING AND METALLURGY—CLEAR CREEK CO. (COL.)

CLEMENS, SAMUEL LANGHORNE—WORKS
I13-ref 800 cds. by t. Bks. & per. Infreq. add.

CLERGYMEN
I65-educ 240 cds. Clergy & educators. Freq. add.

CLERGYMEN, METHODIST—NECROLOGY
I42 19,800 cds. by surname. Jls. of all conf. Methodist Episcopal church ministers, 1789-1939. Cur. add.
I42 1320 cds. by surname. Jls. of all conf. Methodist church ministers, 1939-date. (Union of Methodist Episcopal, Methodist Episcopal South, and Methodist Protestant). Cur. add.
I42 7260 cds. by surname. Jls. of all conf. Methodist Episcopal Church, South, ministers, 1844-1939. Cur. add.

CLEVELAND (O.)
O20-hist 2640 cds. by subj. Bks. & per. Infreq. add.
O20-per 2640 cds. by subj. Per. Cur. add.
O20-ref 1980 cds. by subj. Per. Freq. add.
O20-ref 1320 cds. by auth., subj. & date. Fugitive loc. interest mat. Occ. add.
O20-sci 1000 cds. by subj. Per. & ser. Cleveland & Ohio tech. subj., i.e. bldgs., bridges, etc. Cur. add.

CLEVELAND (O.)—ADULT EDUCATION
O20-soc   3960 cds. by subj. Educ. opportunities. Freq. add.

CLEVELAND (O.)—ART. See ART—CLEVELAND (O.)

CLEVELAND (O.)—AUTHORS. See AUTHORS—CLEVELAND (O.)

CLEVELAND (O.)—BIBLIOGRAPHY—IMPRINTS
O20-ref   3900 cds. by auth. Bks. & pams. Completed in 1938, now continued by Cleveland Publisher's index. No add.

CLEVELAND (O.)—BIOGRAPHY
O20-per   3960 cds. by subj. Per. Cur. add.
O20-ref   5280 cds. by name. Cleveland & Ohio biog. dict. & hist. Occ. add.

CLEVELAND (O.)—HISTORY
O20-ref   1320 cds. by subj. Newsp. Freq. add.

CLEVELAND (O.)—MUSICIANS. See MUSICIANS—CLEVELAND (O.)

CLEVELAND (O.)—PICTURES. See PICTURES—CLEVELAND (O.)

CLEVELAND (O.)—PLAYS. See PLAYS—CLEVELAND (O.); THEATRE PROGRAMS—CLEVELAND (O.)

CLEVELAND (O.)—PORTRAITS. See PORTRAITS—CLEVELAND (O.)

CLEVELAND (O.)—PUBLISHERS AND PUBLISHING. See PUBLISHERS AND PUBLISHING—CLEVELAND (.O)

CLEVELAND (O.)—SOCIETIES AND CLUBS
O20-Brook.   400 cds. by name & leader. Br. district only. Cur. add.

CLEVELAND (O.) PLAIN DEALER (newsp.). In NECROLOGY   O20-ref

CLEVELAND SYMPHONY ORCHESTRA PROGRAMS. See SYMPHONY   O47-ref

CLIMATOLOGY
N35-ref. sci   800 ent., tpd. shts. by state. Bks. & govt. doc., complete through 1930. No add.

CLOCKS AND WATCHES
N35-ref. sci   2500 cds. by subj. Bks. No add.

CLUB PROGRAMS
Ia9   7000 ent., tpd. shts. Study outlines & Iowa club programs.
Ia18-ad   150 ent., tpd. shts. by subj. Pams. & study outlines. Cur. add.
K11   100 ent., chron. Pams. & programs. Yrly. add.
Ky6   200 cds. by subj. Pams., per. & newsp. Freq. add.
Mi6-ref   300 cds. by subj., pub. & programs. Freq. add.
O20-ref   660 cds. by subj. Study programs, inc. Cleveland. Freq. add.

CLUB PROGRAMS—ATLANTA (GA.)
G4-ref   500 cds. by subj. Atlanta study club yrbks. Yrly. add.

COAST (per.)
C69-per   v. 1, 1937–date. Cds. by subj. Mo. add.

COATS OF ARMS. See HERALDRY

COATSWORTH, ELIZABETH—WORKS
Ia6-j   205 ent., tpd. shts. in bk. form. Poems in bks. & per. No add.

COLBY COLLEGE
Me6   850 cds. by auth. & subj. Per. & newsp. Freq. add.

COLLECTOR (per.)
I71-art   v. 1-8, 1927–1929. Tpd. shts. by subj.

COLLECTORS AND COLLECTING
Me1   Unest. cds. by subj. Per., etc. In proc.

COLLEGE SEALS. See SEALS (NUMISMATICS)

COLLEGE STORIES
Nj37-circ   100 ent., tpd. shts. by auth. Bks. Occ. add.

COLLEGE STUDENTS—RELIGION. See List of Bibliographies, APPENDIX I

COLLEGES. See UNIVERSITIES AND COLLEGES

THE COLONIAL (per.) In GENEALOGY M19 (1)

COLONIAL LIFE AND CUSTOMS. See U.S.—HISTORY—COLONIAL PERIOD

COLONIAL RECORDS OF GEORGIA (bk.). In GEORGIA—HISTORY   G2

COLORADO
Co5-ref   30,360 cds. by subj. State hist., newsp., per. & pams. Cur. add.

COLORADO—DOCUMENTS
Co4   4510 cds. by dept. Off. state doc. Freq. add.
Co5-doc   18,480 cds. by auth., t., & subj. Cur. add.

COLORADO. GEOLOGICAL SURVEY BULLETIN
Co5-doc   No. 18–31. Cds. by subj. Loc., cos., towns, mines & formations. No add.

COLORADO—GEOLOGY. *See* GEOLOGY—COLORADO

COLORADO—HISTORY. *See also* ARKANSAS VALLEY (COL.)—HISTORY
Co2-ref   24,000 cds. by subj. Bks., pams., newsp. Per. indexed: *Boulder camera, Boulder co. news.* Freq. add.
Co4   280 ent. by dept. Newsp. Freq. add.

COLORADO—LIBRARIANS—DIRECTORIES
Co4   870 cds. by name. Librarians, bd. members, Friends of the lib. Freq. add.

COLORADO—MAPS. *See* MAPS—COLORADO

COLORADO—MINING AND METALLURGY. *See* MINING AND METALLURGY—COLORADO

COLORADO—NAMES, GEOGRAPHICAL. *See* NAMES, GEOGRAPHICAL—COLORADO

COLORADO—NEWSPAPERS
Co3   Unest. ent. tpd. shts. Misc. notes on early newsp. & journalists of Col., 1860–1920. No add.
Co5-W. hist   51,990 cds. by subj. Cur. add.

COLORADO UNIVERSITY
Co2-ref   Unest. cds. by subj. Pub. of studs., fac. & admin. members. Hist., traditions, stud. activities, bldgs., pub. of Col. univ. Cur. add.

COLORADO UNIVERSITY—PUBLICATIONS, FACULTY
Co2-ref   Unest. cds. by auth. & subj. Cur. add.

COLORADO MAGAZINE
Co3   v. 1-13, 1923–1936. Tpd. shts. by subj. No add.
Co8   v. 1-15, 1923–1938. Cds. by auth., t. & subj. Cur. add.

COLORADO SPRINGS—NEWSPAPERS
Co3   10,000 cds. by subj. Infreq. add.

COLORED AMERICAN MAGAZINE. *In* NEGROES
Ky15–W. Col. (1)

COLUMBIA CO. (PA.). *See* DANVILLE (PA.)—HISTORY   P10

COLUMBIA UNIVERSITY—DISSERTATIONS, ACADEMIC—CHEMISTRY
N30-chem   700 cds. by auth. Freq. add.

COLUMBIA UNIVERSITY QUARTERLY
N30-Low   1898–date. Cds. by auth. & subj. Yrly. add.

COLUMNISTS
C32-per   2840 cds. by t. of spec. depts., columns & columnists. No add.

COMMENCEMENTS
Tx5   75 cds. by auth., subj. & t. Bks., pams. & mim. sheets. Freq. add.

COMMERCIAL CATALOGS. *See* TRADE CATALOGS AND DIRECTORIES

COMMERCIAL CORRESPONDENCE
N46-bus   600 cds. by subj. Bks. Freq. add.

COMMERCIAL LAW
Ca7   2640 cds. by subj. Inc. criminal law. Daily add.

COMMISSIONED OFFICERS (bk.). *In* U.S.—HISTORY—WAR OF 1812—KENTUCKY
Ky7 (2)

COMMODITIES. *See* INDUSTRIES—HISTORY
Wa10-tech

COMMONWEAL (per.) *In* BOOK REVIEWS
Mn18

COMMONWEALTH CLUB OF CALIFORNIA. TRANSACTIONS. *In* CALIFORNIA
C8-ref; CALIFORNIA—HISTORY
C43-ref
C89   v. 3-33, 1908–1941. Cds. by auth. & subj. Yrly. add.

COMMONWEALTH REVIEW OF THE UNIVERSITY OF OREGON (per.)
Or2   v. 1-3, 1916–1918, ns. v. 1-23, 1919–1941. Cds. by auth. & subj. Q. add.

COMMUNICABLE DISEASES. *See* CONTAGION AND CONTAGIOUS DISEASES

COMMUNICATION. *See also* Names of various types of communication, i.e. RAILROADS
C72   51 ent., tpd. shts. by topic. Bks. & pams.

Communism. *See also* Shakers; Catholics—Periodicals **Tx30**

Comoedia (per.)
 N45b 45 cds. by auth. & t. Infreq. add.

Compass (per.)
 Mn14-soc. serv v. 1, 1921–date. Cur. add.

Complete Book of Games (bk.) *In* Games **N22-art, N46-fic**

Composers. *See* Musicians

Composers of Today (bk.). *In* Biography **C8-ref**

Les Concours (per.)
 I73 1906–1907, 1938–1939. Cds. by subj. & t. Yrly. add.

Concrete Construction. *See* Cement; Trade Catalogs and Directories **I27**

Conduct of Life
 O20-S. 200 cds. by subj., auth. t. & class. Bks. on pers. regimen. Freq. add.

Conecuh Co. (Ala.)—Census
 A1 700 cds. by name. Fed. census of 1820. No add.

Conecuh Co. (Ala.)—Taxpayers
 A1 500 cds. by name. Taxpayers of 1818. No add.

Confederate States of America. *See* Manuscripts, Confederate; Music, Confederate; Ships—Confederate States of America; U.S.—History—Civil War; List of Bibliographies, Appendix I

Confederate Veteran (per.)
 T6-ref v. 1–40, 1893–1932. Cds. by subj. No add.

Confidential Weekly Letter (per.)
 I25 1934–date. Cds. by subj. Wkly. add.

Congressional Digest (per.) *In* Debates **C43-ref, Mn4-ref, N35-Hi.B. P39-Wyl.** (2).

Connecticut—Bibliography—Imprints
 Ct7 55 cds. Bks., cats., corr., etc. Conn. Imprints to 1800. Infreq. add.
 Ct13 6500 cds. by auth. Bks. & per. Conn. imprints except New Haven.

Connecticut—Biography
 Ct8 (1) 2300 cds. by name. Bk. indexed: *Encyclopedia of Conn. biog.*, 10 v. No add.
 Ct8 (2) 5100 cds. by name. Members of Conn. gen. assembly, in *Conn. register & manual*. Cur. add.

Connecticut—Cemetery Records
 Ct8 886,243 cds. by name. Vital statistics, 1644–1934, as given on headstones in 2276 burial places in Conn. No add.

Connecticut—Census
 Ct8 654,864 cds. by name of person & town. Conn. names in U.S. decennial cens. 1790–1850 inc. No add.
 Ct8 503,000 cds. by town & person. 1917 cens. of all men in Conn. 16 yrs. of age or over. No add.

Connecticut—Documents
 Ct8 4440 cds. by auth. & subj. Bd. Conn. pub. doc., 1850–date. Cur. add.
 Ct8 373,000 cds. by name, place & subj. Mss. files of Gen. assembly through 1820. Freq. add.
 Ct8 2600 cds. by subj. Governors' messages, 1812–1836 (scattered), 1837–date. Cur. add.
 Ct8 150,000 cds. by subj., bill no. & introducer. All bills introduced in Gen. assembly, 1913–date. Add. Every 2 yrs.
 Ct8 62,400 cds. by name & subj. Trumbull papers: Conn. off. papers, 1631–1794, in 48 mss. v. Occ. add.
 Ct9 Unest. cds. by subj., file & bill nos. Conn. leg. bills & files. Cur. add.

Connecticut—European War, 1914–1918. *See* European War, 1914–1918—Connecticut

Connecticut—Flowers. *See* Flowers—Connecticut

Connecticut—Genealogy. *See* Genealogy—Connecticut

Connecticut—Law. *See* Law—Connecticut

Connecticut—Maps. *See* Maps—Connecticut

Connecticut—Portraits. *See* Portraits—Connecticut

CONNECTICUT—SOLDIERS. *See also* EURO-
PEAN WAR, 1914–1918—CONNECTICUT
Ct8   60,000 cds. by name. Conn. newsp., 1755–1866 & headstones. Covers period from Pequot war to World War. Freq. add.

CONNECTICUT INDUSTRY (per.)
Ct5   v. 12-20, 1934–1942. Cds. by subj. Mo. add.
Ct12-ref   v. 8, 1930-date. Cds. by subj. Mo. add.

CONNECTICUT MAGAZINE. *In* GENEALOGY **M19** (1)
Ct3   v. 3-12, 1897–1908. Cds. by subj. No add.
Ct9   v. 1-12, 1895–1908. Cds. by auth. & subj. No add.

CONNECTICUT REGISTER AND MANUAL. *In* CONNECTICUT—BIOGRAPHY **Ct8** (2)

CONNOISSEUR (per.)
Ca14   v. 83-90, 1929–1932, v. 102-103, 1938–1939. Tpd. shts. by subj. Inc. illus. & main art. Semi-yrly. add.
I60   v. 88-105, 1933–1940. Cds. by subj. Art mat., art. & reprod. Yrly. add.

CONQUEST OF SOUTHWEST KANSAS (bk.). *In* KANSAS **K3**

CONSERVATION. *See also* NATURAL RESOURCES; SOIL CONSERVATION; WILD LIFE—CONSERVATION
Tx8   380 cds. by subj. & form of mat. Bks., per., pams. & govt. doc. Freq. add.

CONSTITUTIONAL LAW
N29   1450 cds. by citation. Cases in coll. Freq. add.

CONSTITUTIONS, STATE
O20-soc   88 cds. by state. Bks. & pams. Infreq. add.

CONSTRUCTION. *See* BUILDING; CEMENT

CONSUMER EDUCATION
C8-ref   110 cds. by commodity. Per. indexed: *Consumer's digest*, 1938–date. Freq. add.
D32-tech   450 cds. by subj. Per. indexed: *Consumer's digest, Consumer's guide, Consumer's research bulletin, Consumer's union reports.* Cur. add.

I65-bus   75 cds. by subj. Per. indexed: *Consumer's guide.* No add. since 1938.
Mi6-sci   200 cds. by subj. Per. indexed: *Consumer's digest, Consumer's research bulletin,* 1935–date (incomplete). Freq. add.
N22-sci   3100 cds. by subj. Bks., pams., doc. & per. Cur. add.
O20-bus   Unest. cds. by auth. or organiz. issuing. In proc.

CONSUMER'S DIGEST (per.). *In* CONSUMER EDUCATION   **C8-ref, D32-tech, Mi6-sci**; WEST—PERIODICALS **Wa2**
In6   v. 1-8, 1937–1941. Cds. by subj. No add.

CONSUMERS' GOODS
Mn14-tech   800 cds. by subj. Per. Cur. add.
O20-bus   400 cds. by product. Per., etc. Mo. add.
O37   400 cds. by subj. Per. Cur. add.

CONSUMER'S GUIDE (per.). *In* CONSUMER EDUCATION   **D32-tech, I65-bus**

CONSUMER'S RESEARCH BULLETIN. *In* CONSUMER EDUCATION   **D32-tech, Mi6-sci**

CONSUMER'S UNION REPORTS (per.). *In* CONSUMER EDUCATION   **D32-tech**

CONSUMPTION (ECONOMICS)
Mn14-tech   110 cds. by subj. Bks. & per. Per capita consumption. Occ. add.

CONTAGION AND CONTAGIOUS DISEASES. *See also* EPIDEMICS
C30   300 ent. Bks., pams. & per. Freq. add.
Nj61   700 cds. by auth. & t. Bks., per. & pams. Freq. add.

CONTESTS, PUBLISHERS'. *See* REWARDS (PRIZES, ETC.)   **N46-fic**

CONTRIBUTOR (per.)
U3   v. 1-17, 1880–1896. Tpd. shts. by subj. & auth. No add.

CONVENTIONS—PERIODICALS
P39-tech   25 cds. by name of per. Per. carrying announcements of conventions. Infreq. add.

COOKE, EDWIN VANCE—WORKS
    I13-ref   Unest. cds. by t. & 1st line. Bks. & per. Infreq. add.

COOKERY. *See also* FOOD; NUTRITION
    C44 (1)   25,000 cds. by subj. Per. indexed: *Family circle*. Recipes. Wkly. add.
    C44 (2)   50 cds. by name & loc. Cook bk. coll. in U.S., both public & private. Infreq. add.
    C62-bus   400 cds. by name of dish. Bks. & per. Recipes, unusual. Freq. add.
    I13-ref   950 cds. by country & subj. Bks. & per. Cookery & foods. Freq. add.
    Tx5   150 cds. by subj. Bks., pams. & newsp. Recipes. Freq. add.

COOKERY—BIBLIOGRAPHIES
    C44   25 cds. by auth. Bks., pams. & per. Cookery bks. Infreq. add.

COOKERY—CALIFORNIA
    C44   100 cds. by auth. Cookery bks. pub. in Calif. Infreq. add.

COOKERY, FOREIGN
    C57   600 cds. by country. Per. Infreq. add.
    Mi6-circ   35 cds. by country. Bks. Occ. add.
    O37   100 cds. by country. Bks. Occ. add.
    Wa10-tech   110 cds. by country. Per. Occ. add.

COOPER, JAMES FENIMORE—WORKS
    N42   330 ent., tpd. shts. by class. Bks., letters, mss., per., pic., etc. Infreq. add.

COOSA CO. (ALA.)—CEMETERY RECORDS
    A1   26 ent., tpd. shts. by name. Rockford cem. Occ. add.

CORNELL EXTENSION BULLETIN
    N35-Morr.   1928–1941. Tpd. shts. by subj. Freq. add.

CORNELL UNIVERSITY—PUBLICATIONS
    N14   400 cds. by subj. Cur. add.
    N21   5000 cds. by t. No add.
    N46-sci   350 cds. by subj. Cur. add.

CORNHILL MAGAZINE. *In* WOOD ENGRAVINGS   P39-ref. art

CORONADO AND QUIVIRA (bk.). *In* KANSAS   K3

CORONADO'S QUEST (bk.). *In* KANSAS   K3

CORONET (per.)
    Wa10-per   v. 2-6, 1937–1939. Cds. by subj. No add.

CORPORATION FINANCE. *See* RAILROADS—FINANCE   Nj60-Pliny

CORPORATIONS
    C32-soc   400 cds. by name. Bus. services. Occ. add.
    M4-Kir.   250 cds. by name. Bks., per. & pams. Cur. add.
    N35-ref. prep   1700 cds. by region. Bks. & per. Cur. add.
    Nj60-Pliny   66,000 cds. by name. Per. indexed: *Commercial and financial chronicle*, v. 1-151, 1865–1940. No add.
    O20-bus   300 cds. by name. Per. & newsp. Occ. add.

CORPORATIONS — INDIANA — HISTORY. *See* INDIANA—BIOGRAPHY   In22

CORPORATIONS—RHODE ISLAND
    R1-bus   3960 cds. by name. Loc. & for. corp. indexed: *Providence record and guide*. Wkly. add.

CORRECT ENGLISH, HOW TO USE IT (per.)
    Mo13-ref   1911–1932 (incomp.). Cds. by subj. Points of grammatical usage. Occ. add.

CORRESPONDENCE SCHOOLS AND COURSES
    Wa10-par   350 cds. by subj. Coll. & univ. Occ. add.

COST AND STANDARD OF LIVING
    Nj52   Unest. cds. by subj. Bks., per. & pams. Freq. add.

COSTUME. *See also* DRAMA   Wa15
    C32-art   1500 cds. by country & subj. Bks. No add.
    C49-ref   2680 cds. by subj. Bks. Per. indexed: *Illustrated London news, L'illustration*. Freq. add.
    De1   300 ent., tpd. shts. by region. Carnegie pic. coll. No add.
    G4-ref   500 cds. by subj., place & period. Per. indexed: *Harper's bazaar*, v. 55-56, *Theatre*, v. 20-47. Freq. add.
    I80   2p., tpd. shts. by country & plate no. Bk. indexed: A. C. A. Racinet, *Le Costume historique*. No add.

Ky15-j Several hundred ent. by country & subj. Pic. Occ. add.
Ky15-ref 800 cds. by name & nationality. Bks., per. & newsp. Occ. add.
M27-art 900 cds. by country & type. Bks. Infreq. add.
Mn14-Fran. 550 cds. by subj. Bks. Cur. add.
Mo3-ref 1500 cds. by subj. Per., newsp. & bks. Bk. indexed: A. C. A. Racinet, *Le Costume historique*. Infreq. add.
N6-ref 64p., tpd. shts. by subj. Bks. Occ. add.
N8-ref 22,440 cds. by subj. Pic. in per. & newsp. Freq. add.
N10 11,963 cds. by auth. & t. Bks., per. & pams. Freq. add.
Nj15 7p., tpd. shts. by subj. Bk. indexed: A. C. A. Racinet, *Le Costume historique*. No add.
Nj25-ref 305 ent. by subj. Pic. in bks. & per. Freq. add.
O20-art 1492 cds. by country & subj. Bks. Infreq. add.
O29-W. Carn. 600 cds. by subj. Per. & bks. Occ. add.
P39-ref 5000 cds. by subj. Bks. (Altho indexed in Munro, spec. ref. are not dup.). No add.
Wa10-art (1) 1000 cds. by subj. Bk. indexed: Paul Louis de marquis Giafferi, *History of the feminine costume of the world*. No add.
Wa10-art (2) 1200 cds. by subj. Bks. indexed: A.C.A. Racinet, *Le Costume historique*. No add.
Wa10-j 300 cds. by country. Per. Occ. add.

COSTUME—LATIN AMERICA
P19 14 ent., tpd. shts. by t. Per. No add.

COSTUME, FOREIGN
C32-for 215 cds. by country & sec. Bks., per. & newsp. Costume, customs, dancing. Freq. add.

COSTUME, MEXICAN. *See* PICTURES **Nm2**

COSTUME, SPANISH. *See* PICTURES **Nm2**

COSTUME, THEATRICAL
I58 200 cds. by name of play. Pic. Infreq. add.
O21 34 cds. by auth. of play. Stage costume in bks. Occ. add.

LE COSTUME HISTORIQUE (bk.) *In* COSTUME **I80, Mo3-ref, Nj15, Wa10-art (2)**

COTACO CO. (ALA.)—LAW. *See* LAW-COTACO CO. (ALA.).

COTTMAN, GEORGE. *See* INDIANA—HISTORY **In22-Ind (2)**

COTTON
D12 31,680 cds. by auth., t. & subj. Bks., pams. etc. Occ. add.

COTTON—SOCIETIES AND CLUBS
D12 300 cds. by name. Yrly. add.

COTTON LITERATURE (per.)
D12 2640 cds. by auth. & subj. Mo. add.

COUNCIL BLUFFS (IA.)
Ia4 1000 cds. by subj. Bks., per. & pams. Cur. add.

COUNTIES OF CLAY AND OWEN, INDIANA (bk.). *In* INDIANA—BIOGRAPHY **In35 (3)**

COUNTRY LIFE—STORIES
Mn11 Unest. ent., tpd. shts. by auth. Bks. Freq. add.

COURSES OF STUDY. *See also* CATALOGS, COLLEGE; UNITS OF WORK; List of Bibliographies, APPENDIX I
C31-ref 1000 cds. by subj. & issuing bodies. Units of work, Los Angeles co. pub. & those of imp. educ. depts. of several states & cities. Freq. add.
C34-educ 1700 cds. by subj. & loc. Freq. add.
I9 2350 cds. by auth. & t. Bks. & per. Infreq. add.
Id2 300 cds. by subj. & state. Freq. add.
In12 5p., tpd. shts. by grades, 4–8. Classroom units of instruction. Occ. add.
In36 700 cds. by place. Out-of-state courses of study. Infreq. add.
K17-ref 225 cds. by subj., city & state. Course of study pams. & bks. Occ. add.
Md2-phil 2000 cds. by subj. & pub. Bks., courses of study & pams. Freq. add.
N30-t.c. 9200 cds. by auth. & subj. Courses of study used in elem. & second. sch. in U.S., cur. & hist. Freq. add.

O36   3000 cds. by subj. Bks. & courses of study. Freq. add.
T2   350 cds. by state. Bul. & pams. Freq. add.

COURTS. *See also* List of Bibliographies, APPENDIX I

COVENANTERS. *See* PRESBYTERIANS

COWBOY SONGS. *See* SONGS, COWBOY

THE CRAFTSMAN (per.)
Mo10   v. 1–31. 1906–1916 (incomp.), by subj. & auth. No add.

CRAWFORD CO. (O.)—REGISTERS OF BIRTHS, ETC.
O13   Unest., tpd. shts., 2v. Marriage records, 1831–1864. No add.

CRENSHAW CO. (ALA.)—CEMETERY RECORDS
A1   600 ent., tpd. shts. by name. Beasley cem., Honoraville cem., Mt. Zion Methodist church cem., Routon cem., Rockie Mt. cem., Rutledge cem. Occ. add.

CRENSHAW CO. (ALA.)—REGISTERS OF BIRTHS, ETC.
A1   3000 cds. by name. 1867–1880 marriage records. No add.

CREOLES
Tx30   110 ent., tpd. shts. by subj. Bks. & per. Creoles in La. insofar as they affect southern lit. No add.

CRIME AND CRIMINALS. *See also* List of Bibliographies, APPENDIX I
C32-soc   3960 cds. by subj. Bks., per. & soc. pub. Freq. add.
D22   96 ent., tpd. shts. by auth. Bks., congress. repts., per. etc. Infreq. add.
O20-soc   2640 cds. by name of pers. involved. Bks. Criminals & trials. Freq. add.

CRISIS (per.). *In* NEGROES   Ky15-E. Col. (1), Ky15-W. Col., (2), P39-Wyl., V4; NEGROES—PERIODICALS   D6
D6   1910-date. Cds. by auth., t. & subj. Negro life. Mo. add.

CROCHETING. *See* HANDICRAFTS

CRUCIBLE (per.) *In* CANADA—PERIODICALS   Ca13-per

CRUSADER'S ALMANAC (per.)
D4   1886–1940. Cds. by subj. Yrly. add.

CURRENT (per.). *In* POETRY   I26

CURTIS'S BOTANICAL MAGAZINE. *In* PICTURES—FLOWERS   C32-sci

CYTOLOGY. *See* CELLS

CZECHOSLOVAKIA. *See* List of Bibliographies, APPENDIX I

DAGO RED (bk.). *In* SHORT STORIES   Tx12

DAIRY PRODUCTS. *See* List of Bibliographies, APPENDIX I

DAIRYING. *See also* CASEIN
D15   18,400 cds. by subj. Bks. & per. Dairy cattle feeding & mgt., with abstracts. Freq. add.
D15   35,600 cds. by auth. & subj. Bks., per. etc. Dairy lit. Freq. add.

DALE CO. (ALA.)—CEMETERY RECORDS
A1   150 ent., tpd. shts. by name. Claybank church cem. Occ. add.

DALE CO. (ALA.)—REGISTERS OF BIRTHS, ETC.
A1   3000 cds. by name. 3v., 1884–1923. Cur. add.

DALHOUSIE REVIEW. *In* CANADA—PERIODICALS   Ca13-per

DALLAS (TEXAS) NEWS (newsp.). *In* TEXAS—HISTORY   Tx9
Tx9   1901–1911, 1913–1914, 1918–1935. Cds. by subj. Cur. add.

DALLAS CO. (ALA.)—CEMETERY RECORDS
A1   200 ent., tpd. shts. by name. Cahaba cem., Valley Creek church cem. Occ. add.

DALLAS CO. (ALA.)—CENSUS
A1   700 cds. by name. 1820 & 1870 fed. cens. No add.

DALY, THOMAS AUGUSTINE—WORKS
I13-ref   600 cds. by t. & 1st. line. Bks. & per. Infreq. add.

DAMS. *See also* GRAND COULÉE
C32-sci   750 cds. by name of dam. Per. Occ. add.
Mo3-N.E.   50 cds. by name of dam. Bks. & per.
Wa10-tech   1200 cds. by name of dam. Per. U.S. dams, esp. W. Cur. add.

DANCE MUSIC
M27-art 150 ent., tpd. shts. by form & country. Coll. of dance mus. Mus. with instruct. Infreq. add.
Or2 800 cds. by name of dance & country. Dance forms in mus. Infreq. add.
P41 275 cds. by comp. & t. Bks. Freq. add.

DANCE MUSIC—U.S.
M27-art 75 ent., tpd. shts., chron. Bks. Dance mus. in U.S., 1625–1930. Infreq. add.

DANCERS
I13-w.s.r. 50 cds. by name. Per. & newsp. Freq. add.

DANCING
Md2-art 2000 cds. by t. Bks. Supp. A.L.A. dance index. Freq. add.
N8-ref 600 cds. by subj. Bks. Freq. add.
N35-mus 1200 cds. by subj. Bks., per., etc. Freq. add.
N46-art 600 cds. by t. & subj. Bks. not indexed in other sources. Occ. add.
Nj67-ref 4100 cds. by t. & subj. Bks., per. & pams. Freq. add.
P54-circ 1080 cds. by subj. & t. Bks. Freq. add.
Wa10-art 1500 cds. by choreographer, t. & dancer. Bks. Freq. add.

DANCING—FOLK AND NATIONAL DANCES. See also COSTUME, FOREIGN **C32-for**; FOLK SONGS **Mn23-art**
C27-art 800 cds. by dance & country. Bks. & mus. Cur. add.
C56 2500 cds. by dance, country & type of dance. Bks. No add. since 1934.
Ca2-art 798 cds. by t. & country. Coll. of folk dances. Cur. add.
Ca2-j 400 cds. by t. & subj. Bks., supp. to A.L.A. dance index. Cur. add.
Mi6-par 273 cds. by country & t. Bks. supp. to A.L.A. index. Cur. add.
Mn14-mus Unest. ent. Bks., add. to A.L.A. dance index. Cur. add.
N22-art 300 cds. by t. Bks., supp. to A.L.A. dance index. Cur. add.
N35-mus 3000 cds. by t., form & country. Bks. Freq. add.
O20-art 5537 cds. by country & name of dance. Bks. Freq. add.
O20-j 3000 cds. by t. & subj. J. bks. Occ. add.
O20-Un. 225 cds. by country. Bks. Cur. add.
O26 279 cds. by nationality & t. Bks. Cur. add.
P39-circ 1320 cds. by country & t. Coll. of bks. Cur. add.
P39-j 225 cds. by country & t. Bks. Cur. add.

DANCING—HISTORY—UNION LISTS
N35-mus 103,000 cds. by subj., auth. & lib. Bks., rpts., per. & pams. located in major N.Y. lib. Cur. add.

DANCING—NEW YORK (CITY)
N35-mus 3000 cds. by performer of group, chron. for ea. performer. Newsp. Dance performances in N.Y. city. Wkly. add.

DANCING—OPERAS
N35-mus 650 cds. by t., form & subj. Operas. Dances & ballets in operas. Infreq. add.

DANCING—PICTURES. See PICTURES—DANCING

DANCING, FOREIGN. See DANCING—FOLK AND NATIONAL DANCES

DANVILLE (PA.)—HISTORY
P10 250 cds. by subj. Bks., pams., mss., & newsp. Inc. Montour & Columbia co. history. Freq. add.

DANVILLE (VA.)—HISTORY
V3 251 cds. by subj. Bks., bul. newsp. & pams. Occ. add.

DANVILLE (VA.) BEE (newsp.). *In* VIRGINIA **V3** (2)

DANVILLE (VA.) REGISTER (newsp.). *In* VIRGINIA **V3** (2)

DAUGHTERS OF THE AMERICAN REVOLUTION. See also NATIONAL HISTORICAL MAGAZINE
Ky7 Unest. cds. by family name. Records sent in by state chapters.

DAUGHTERS OF THE AMERICAN REVOLUTION. LINEAGE BOOKS. *In* U.S.—HISTORY—REVOLUTION—INDIANA **In35-gen**
N10-gen v. 81-160. 2v., 278p. ea. by name of patriot. No add.

DAVIDSON CO. (TENN.)—NEWSPAPERS
T9-newsp   60,000 cds. by subj. & name of pers. Inf. on Nashville & Davidson co., W.P.A. project. Cur. add.

DAVIESS, JOSEPH HAMILTON
Ky2   37 cds. by auth. Bks. & per. No add.

DAVIS, JEFFERSON
Ky2   99 cds. by auth. Bks. & per. Freq. add.

DAYS OF . . . (bk.). *In* MUSIC   **Nj15**

DAYTON (O.)
O29-ref   1500 cds. by subj. Hist., per. & newsp. Occ. add.

DEALERS' CATALOGS. See TRADE CATALOGS AND DIRECTORIES

DEATHS. See GENEALOGY; NECROLOGY, and subdiv. under subj. & loc.; REGISTERS OF BIRTHS, ETC., and subdiv. under loc.

DEBATER'S DIGEST (per.) *In* DEBATES **C8-ref, C43-ref, C49-ref, Md2-ref, N7, P39-Wy1** (2)

DEBATERS' MANUAL (bk.). *In* DEBATES **N35-Hi.B.**

DEBATES
C3   500 cds. by subj. Bks. Freq. add.
C8-ref   1320 cds. by auth., subj. & t. Bk. indexed: *Reference shelf;* Per. indexed: *Debater's digest.* Freq. add.
C18-ref   375 cds. by subj. Bks. Cur. add.
C32-soc   1320 cds. by subj. Bks. & per. Freq. add.
C43-ref   1900 cds. by subj. Bk. indexed: *Reference shelf;* Per. indexed: *Congressional digest, Debater's digest.* Freq. add.
C49-ref   2816 cds. by subj. Bk. Per. indexed: *Debater's digest.* Cur. add.
C69-j   300 cds. by subj. Bks. Cur. add.
Co5-ref   1320 cds. by subj. Bks. Freq. add.
G4-ref   2000 cds. by subj. Bks., brief bks. & per. Cur. add.
I8   1000 cds. by subj. Bks. Freq. add.
I13-ref   1200 cds. by subj. Bks. & per. Freq. add.
Ia3   500 cds. by subj. Bks. & per. Freq. add.
Ia14-ref   600 cds. by subj. Bks. Freq. add.
Ia18-ad   Unest. ent., tpd. shts. by auth. & type of debate. Bks., per., doc. & pams. Cur. add.
In8-ref   1029 cds. by subj. Bks. & per. Freq. add.
In9   680 cds. by subj. Bks., pams. & newsp. Freq. add.
In33-ad   851 cds. by subj. Bks. Cur. add.
L14-ref   925 cds. by subj. Bks. Freq. add.
M28   1000 cds. by subj. Bks. Freq. add.
M32   500 cds. by subj. Bks. Infreq. add.
Md2-ref   3100 cds. by subj. Bks., pams. Per. indexed: *Debater's digest.* Freq. add.
Mi6-Rich.   350 cds. by subj. Bks. Infreq. add.
Mi6-soc   750 cds. by subj. Bks., pams. & per. Freq. add.
Mi6-Walk.   332 cds. by subj. Bks., per. & pams. Freq. add.
Mi8-ref   400 cds. by subj. Bks. indexed: *Intercollegiate debates, University debater's annual.* Yrly. add.
Mi13-S. Hi.   411 cds. by subj. Bks. Occ. add.
Mn4-ref   800 cds. by subj. Bks., Per. indexed: *Congressional digest.* Freq. add.
Mn14-Fran.   700 cds. by subj. Bks., per., etc. Freq. add.
Mo3-Wash.   Unest. cds. by subj. Bks. Occ. add.
Mo13-Car.   800 cds. by subj. Bks. Cur. add.
N6-ref   144p., tpd. shts. by subj. Debate manuals. Cur. add.
N7   400 cds. by subj. Bks. indexed: *Handbook series; Intercollegiate debates, Reference shelf, University debater's annual;* Per. indexed: *Congressional digest, Debater's digest.* Freq. add.
N8-ref   1000 cds. by subj. Bks. & per. Freq. add.
N22-ref   1525 cds., by subj. & chron. 98 ent., tpd. shts. in notebk. Bks., per. & pams. Freq. add.

N29 1250 cds. by subj. Bks. & serials. Cur. add.
N35-Hi.B. 500 cds. by subj. Bks. indexed: Edith Phelps, *Debaters' manual; Reference shelf*. Per. indexed: *Congressional digest*. Mo. add.
N35-Tre. 600 cds. by subj. Bks. & per. Freq. add.
N36 1400 cds. by auth. & t. Bks. & ser. Cur. add.
N54-ref 300 cds. by subj. Bks. Freq. add.
Nb8 3600 cds. by subj. Bks. & per. Freq. add.
Nb11 500 cds. by subj. Bks. Freq. add.
Nb14-ref 700 cds. by subj. Bks. & per. Freq. add.
Nc4 900 cds. by subj. Bks. Freq. add.
Nd2 650 cds. by subj. Bks. & per. Freq. add.
Nj11 660 cds. by subj. Bks., per. & pams. Freq. add.
Nj14 1320 cds. by subj. Bks., pams. & per. Freq. add.
Nj56 395p., tpd. shts. in notebk. Bks. indexed: *Intercollegiate debates, Reference shelf, University debater's annual*. Freq. add.
O16-ref 1500 cds. by subj. Bks. & newsp. Mo. add.
O20-E. 131st 300 cds. by subj. Bks. Yrly. add.
O20-Jeff. 1600 cds. by subj. Bks. No add.
O20-ref 2640 cds. by subj. Bks., supp. Wilson co. indexes. Occ. add.
O20-Rice 350 cds. by subj. Bks. Cur. add.
O20-y.p. 1200 cds. by subj. Bks., per., & pams. Freq. add.
O29-h.s. 500 cds. by subj. Bks. & per. Cur. add.
O29-ref 1200 cds. by subj. Per., Bk. indexed: *University debater's annual*. Freq. add.
O31 215 cds. by subj. Bks. & per. Freq. add.
O37 800 cds. by subj. Bks., per. & pams. Cur. add.
O56-ref 1300 cds. by subj. Bks. & per. Occ. add.
O61-ref 1000 cds. by subj. Bks. & per. Cur. add.

P33-ref 700 cds. by subj. Bks. indexed: *Intercollegiate debates*, Edith Phelps, *Debater's manual, University debater's annual*. Freq. add.
P39-ref 800 cds. by subj. Bks. & per. Complete debates. Cur. add.
P39-ref 5100 cds. by subj. Bks. & per. Art, on subj. used for debates. Freq. add.
P39-Wy1. (1) 338 cds. by subj. Bks. Cur. add.
P39-Wy1. (2) 461 cds. by subj. Per. indexed: *Congressional digest, Debater's digest*. Mo. add.
P45-ref 500 cds. by t. & subj. Bks. indexed: *Intercollegiate debates, Reference shelf, University debater's annual*. Cur. add.
P54-ref 640 cds. by subj. Bks. & per. Freq. add.
T5-ref 400 cds. by subj. Bks. Freq. add.
Wa11-ref 900 cds. by subj. Bks. Freq. add.

DEBOW'S REVIEW
L11 v. 1-n.s. v. 1#4, 1846–1880. Tpd. shts. by auth. & subj. No add.

DECLAMATIONS. See ORATIONS

DEEDS. See CHARTERS; Name of loc., subdiv. DEEDS

DEFENSES, NATIONAL. See U.S.—DEFENSES

DELAWARE
De3 30,000 cds. by subj. Bks., per. & newsp. Freq. add.

DELAWARE—DOCUMENTS
De1 Unest. cds. by dept. & pol. div. State, city & co. doc. Occ. add.

DELAWARE—INDIANS. See INDIANS—DELAWARE

DELAWARE—OFFICIALS AND EMPLOYEES
De3 5280 cds. by gen. headings. Newsp. Freq. add.

DELINQUENCY. See CRIME AND CRIMINALS

DEMOCRACY. See List of Bibliographies, APPENDIX I

DENISON UNIVERSITY
O34 794 cds. by auth., t. & subj. Bks. & pams. Mat. about Denison, by and about Denisonians. Freq. add.

DENKMÄLER GRIECHISCHER UND RÖMISCHER SCULPTUR (bk.). *In* SCULPTURE
N35-ref. art

DENTISTRY. *See also* List of Bibliographies, APPENDIX I
In1-dent 310 cds. by subj. Bks. & per. Occ. add.
Md7-dent 600 cds. by subj. Per. Freq. add.
O25-dent 8580 cds. by auth., subj. & t. Per. Cur. add.

DES MOINES, THE PIONEER OF MUNICIPAL PROGRESS (bk.). *In* POLK CO. (IA.)
Ia6-ref

DESERET NEWS (per.)
U3 v. 2-6, 1851–1856, v. 38-57. 160p., tpd. shts. by auth. & subj. Cur. add.

DESIGN
Wa10-per 800 cds. by subj. Per. Handwork, blackboard borders, etc. Cur. add.

DESIGN (per.)
P39-art v. 26-33, 1924–1932. Tpd. shts., bd. by subj. No add.

DESIGNERS
M11-print 11,000 cds. by name. Prints in coll. Designers of prints when they are not also the engravers. No add.

DESIGNERS, JAPANESE. *See* ART, JAPANESE
C56-print (1), (2)

DETECTIVE STORIES. *See* MYSTERY AND DETECTIVE STORIES

DETECTIVES (IN FICTION)
C8-circ 60 cds. by name. Occ. add.
Md2-circ 200 cds. by name. Bks. Freq. add.
Mo13-Soul. 215 cds. by auth. & name. Bks. Occ. add.
N25 57 cds. by name. Bks. Occ. add.
Nj37-circ 135 ent., tpd. shts. by name. Bks. Freq. add.
O37 100 cds. by name. Occ. add.

DETROIT (MICH.)—ADULT EDUCATION
Mi6-ref 750 cds. by subj. Newsp. & announcements. Freq. add.

DETROIT (MICH.)—BIOGRAPHY
Mi6-Walk. 102 cds. by subj. Bks. & per. Infreq. add.

DETROIT (MICH.)—HISTORY. *See also* MICHIGAN—HISTORY **Mi6-Burt** (1, 2)
Mi6-Burt. 11,000 cds. by state, co. & city. Bks. & per. Freq. add.

DETROIT (MICH.)—LANTERN SLIDES. *See* LANTERN SLIDES—DETROIT (MICH.)

DETROIT (MICH.)—OFFICIALS AND EMPLOYEES
Mi6-Rich. 21 cds. by place. Freq. add.

DETROIT (MICH.)—SOCIETIES AND CLUBS
Mi6-ref 1000 cds. by name. Per. & newsp. Freq. add.

DETROIT ART INSTITUTE—PUBLICATIONS
Mi6-art 1320 cds. by subj. Inst. bul., bks., per., etc. Cur. add.

DETROIT (MICH.) FREE PRESS (newsp.). *In* GUEST, EDGAR A.—WORKS **Mi11-ref**

DETROIT (MICH.) NEWS (newsp.). *In* PHOTOGRAPHS **Mi5-ref**
Mi5-ref 1873–date. Cds. by subj. Daily add.

DEUTERIUM
Nj60-Frick 1200 cds. by subj. Complete on subj. No add.

DEVOTIONAL EXERCISES
Ct6-rel. educ 300 cds. by subj. Bks. & per. Worship services for the church sch. Mo. add.

DIALECT POETRY. *See* POETRY, DIALECT

DIALECT READINGS
C32-lit 62p., tpd. shts. by dialect & auth. Bks. Freq. add.
C49-inf 1280 cds. by dialect. Bks. Cur. add.
C62-circ 200 cds. by dialect. Bks. Cur. add.
Co5-circ 300 cds. by type of dialect. Coll. of recit., poetry, plays & stories. No add.
I13-circ 491 cds. by auth. Bks. Occ. add.
I68-ref 750 ent., tpd. shts. by subj. Bks. Occ. add.
In14 383 cds. by type of dialect. Bks. Occ. add.
L14-circ 75 cds. by auth. Bks. Occ. add.
Mn14-ref 112p., 1500 ent., tpd. shts. by type of dialect. Bks. Cur. add.
Mo3-W. 50 cds. by type. Monologs, dialogs & recit. Bks.
Mo3-E.
Mo3-Wash. } 800 cds. by type of dialects. Freq. add.
Mo3-Wpt.

Mo13-circ 300 cds. by t. & subj. Bks. indexed: Phineas Garrett, *One hundred choice selections, Werner's readings and recitations*, 58v.
N54-ref 1100 cds. by t. Bks. Infreq. add.
Or7-ref 4500 cds. by auth., subj., t. & 1st line. Bks. Infreq. add.
W16 400 cds. by type of dialect. Poetry, readings, monologues, dialogues & plays. Occ. add.
W20-ad 450 cds. by lang. Bks. Infreq. add.
Wa9 200 cds. by nationality. Bks. Occ. add.

DIALOGUES. *See also* MONOLOGUES O31; PLAYS O37; READINGS AND RECITATIONS G4-circ
W16 500 cds. by subj. Bks. Infreq. add.

DIALOGUES, JUVENILE
Wa13-j 32 cds. by subj. & t. Bks. Occ. add.

DIARIES. *See also* List of Bibliographies, APPENDIX I
C73 Unest. cds. by auth., chron. by date of writing. Diaries, jls. & ship logs. Per., 1694–1938.
N35-ref. ed 1500 cds. by auth. Amer. writings in bks. & per. Cur. add.

DIARIES, WESTERN
U3 70 ent., tpd. shts. by name. Western diaries, mostly Utah. Freq. add.

DICTIONARIES. *See* GLOSSARIES Mo13-sci

DICTIONARIES—FOREIGN LANGUAGES
O20-ref 2640 cds. by lang. For. & dialect dict. Cur. add.

DICTIONARY OF AMERICAN BIOGRAPHY (bk.). *In* PENNSYLVANIA — BIOGRAPHY P16

DIET. *See* COOKERY; FOOD; NUTRITION

DIPHENYLAMIDE
Nj54 Unest. cds. by subj. Spec. rpts. Freq. add.

DIRECTORIES. *See also* PERIODICALS O20-bus; TRADE CATALOGS AND DIRECTORIES; Name of subj., subdiv. DIRECTORIES

C3a 72 cds. by subj. Bks. & per. Occ. add.
C22-ref 8200 cds. by place. City & tel. dir. Cur. add.
C32-soc 500 cds. by subj. Bks. Occ. add.
C49-ref 3700 cds. by city & town. City & tel. dir. Freq. add.
Ca2-ref 8200 cds. by place. City & tel. dir. Cur. add.
I71-ref 254 cds. by town. Princ. cities & majority of Ill. towns. in tel. dir. Semi-yrly. add.
In23-bus 1200 cds. by city & dist. City & tel. dir. Cur. add.
Mi6-bus 12,000 cds. by city & state. City & tel. dir. Infreq. add.
N6-ref 1400 cds. by city. City & tel. dir. Occ. add.
N8-ref 17,160 cds. by state & city. Tel. dir. Freq. add.
N8-ref 200 cds. by city. City dir. Freq. add.
N46-ref 4000 cds. by city & town. Tel. dir. Large cities in U.S. & Canada, some European countries, cities or sec. for which no city dir. is available, W. & C. New York state & sec. in Pa. bordering N.Y. Cur. add.
N46-ref 16p., tpd. shts. by city. City dir. Leading cities of U.S. & Canada, large cities of N.Y. state, small towns of W. & C. New York state. Cur. add.
N54-per 2200 cds. by place. Gen. & tel. dir. Freq. add.
Nj50-bus 1000 cds. by city. City dir. Cur. add.
Nj67-bus 2500 cds. by town. Tel. dir. Infreq. add.
O20-ref 5280 cds. by state & city. Tel. dir. Cur. add.
P45-ref 8580 cds. by place. Pa. tel. dir. Cur. add.
R1-bus 8580 cds. by city & town. U.S., some Canadian, London city & tel. dir. Freq. add.
T9-bus 150 cds. by city or town. Tel. dir. Occ. add.
W22-ad 175 cds. by city. City & tel. dir. Occ. add.

DISEASES. *See* Names of diseases, i.e. TUBERCULOSIS; CELEBRITIES—DISEASES; CONTAGION AND CONTAGIOUS DISEASES; VIRUSES

DISH GARDENS. *See* GARDENS, MINIATURE

DISSECTION
P39-tech   175 cds. by animal. Bks. Infreq. add.

DISSERTATIONS, ACADEMIC. *See also* Name of institution, subdivision DISSERTATIONS, ACADEMIC
O27   10,560 cds. by name of dept. Q. add.

DISSERTATIONS, ACADEMIC—CHEMISTRY
N30-chem   20,000 cds. by auth. Freq. add.

DISSERTATIONS, ACADEMIC—FOREIGN LANGUAGES
Mn15-ref   75,000 cds. by auth. Theses pub. in for. countries & U.S., Minn. excluded. Cur. add.

DISSERTATIONS, ACADEMIC—PERIODICALS
I43-ref   20 headings, tpd. shts. Per. sources of inf. on diss., 1920–date. Freq. add.

DOCUMENTS. *See* GOVERNMENT DOCUMENTS; Name of loc. or subj., subdiv. DOCUMENTS

DODGE CITY, COWBOY CAPITAL (bk.). *In* KANSAS   **K3**

DODGE CITY, KANSAS (bk.). *In* KANSAS **K3**

DOG STORIES. *See* List of Bibliographies, APPENDIX I

DOG STORIES, JUVENILE
K14   52 cds. by auth. Bks. Freq. add.
Nj19-j   50 ent., tpd. shts. by auth. Occ. add.

DOGS. *See* PETS   **Co8-biol**; CHILDREN'S POETRY—DOGS; List of Bibliographies, APPENDIX I

DOLLS
Mn14-tech   100 cds. by type. Bks. & per. Doll houses & furniture. Freq. add.

DOMESTIC SCIENCE. *See* HOME ECONOMICS

DOOLEY, MR.—WORKS
P39-ref   300 cds. by subj. Bks. of humor by Finley P. Dunne (Mr. Dooley). No add.

DRAMA. *See also* PLAYS
I26   3000 cds. by t. Bks. & per. 18th & 19th cent. plays in English. Bks. & per. Freq. add.

I43-ref   800 cds. Bks. Plays written before 1800. Occ. add.
M21-ref   1000 cds. by subj. Bks. & per. Freq. add.
Mi6-mus   52,800 cds. by subj. Bks. & per. Drama, theat., mus., moving pic., puppetry, radio & dance. Cur. add.
N54-per   900 cds. by t. Per. Drama & mus. Freq. add. ,
Nj67-ref   24,700 cds. by t. & subj. Bks., per. & pams. Cur. add.
P14   450 cds. by auth. Bks. & per. Freq. add.
Wa15   677 cds. by auth., subj. & t. Bks. & pams. Theatre, cinema & costume, inc. biog. Freq. add.

DRAMA—FOREIGN LANGUAGES
C32-for   5655 cds. by t. Bks. & per. Freq. add.

DRAMA—NECROLOGY
C32-lit   2300 cds. by name. Newsp. Writers, actors & producers. Freq. add.

DRAMA, EUROPEAN
O54   370 cds. by auth. & t. Bks. Infreq. add.

DRAMATISTS. *See also* DRAMA—NECROLOGY **C32-lit**
I49   405 cds. by auth. & t. Bks. Cur. add.
Mi17   722 cds. by subj. Bks. Freq. add.

DRAWINGS AND ENGRAVINGS. *See also* CHATHAM, WILLIAM PITT, 1st EARL OF—DRAWINGS AND ENGRAVINGS; WALKER, DUGALD STEWART—DRAWINGS AND ENGRAVINGS; DESIGNERS **M11-print**; PAINTINGS **Nj33**; PICTURES **N35-ref. print**; PORTRAITS **C73**
C56-print   15,000 cds. by art., t., form, country & port. Prints. Cur. add.
C73-rare   Unest. ent., tpd. shts. by sitter, subj. etc. Prints. Occ. add.
M11-print   30,000 cds. by subj. Prints. No add.
Mo13-art   650 cds. by art. Prints & plates. Occ. add.
N5-ref   500 ent., tpd. mss. Bk. indexed: Vasari society, *Reproductions of drawings by old and modern masters*, ser. I, pts. 1–10, ser. II, pts. 1–16. No add.

N35-ref. print 8500 cds. by subj. Bks. & separates. Cur. add.

N35-ref. print 3450 cds. by subj. Bks., per. & sep. Proofs, port. of print makers, etc. Cur. add.

Nj50-art 12,300 cds. by art., t. & subj. Original engravings & reprod. of paintings. Freq. add.

O16-art 5000 cds. by art., subj. & t. Prints. Cur. add.

O16-art 4000 cds. by art. & t. Bks. Freq. add.

Wa10-art 3000 cds. by t., painter & engraver. Gift coll. of prints. No add.

DRILL (NOT MILITARY)
Nj67-ref 350 cds. by subj. Bks., per. & pams. Freq. add.

W16 300 cds. by subj. Bks. Occ. add.

DRINKS. *See* BEVERAGES

DUBOIS (PA.)—HISTORY
P11 300 ent. tpd. shts. by subj. Bk. indexed: W. C. Pentz, *City of Dubois*. No add.

DUBOIS (PA.) COURIER (newsp.)
P11 3000 cds. by subj. Daily add.

DUBUQUE (IA.)—BIRDS. *See* BIRDS—DUBUQUE (IA.)

DUBUQUE (IA.)—FLOWERS. *See* FLOWERS—DUBUQUE (IA.)

DUBUQUE (IA.)—HISTORY
Ia10 Unest. cds. by subj. Loc. newsp. Freq. add.

DUBUQUE (IA.)—NECROLOGY
Ia10 Unest. cds. by subj. Loc. newsp. Freq. add.

DULUTH (MINN.)—SOCIETIES AND CLUBS
Mn4-ref 750 cds. by name. Newsp. Freq. add.

DUMAS, ALEXANDRE PÈRE—WORKS
C32-fic 29p., tpd. shts. by t. No add.

DUNNE, FINLEY P. *See* DOOLEY, MR.—WORKS

DUPAGE COUNTY (ILL.)—HISTORY
I38 350 cds. by auth. & subj. Bks., pams., newsp. & pic. Freq. add.

DURHAM (N.C.) HERALD (newsp.)
Nc2 1938–date. Cds. by subj. Durham & Durham co. Freq. add.

DUTCHESS CO. (N.Y.)—HISTORY
N45a 3960 cds. by auth., t. & subj. Bks., pams., mss. & maps. Freq. add.

DYE PLANTS
Nj54 Unest. cds. by subj. Spec. rpts. Freq. add.

EARLHAM COLLEGE—DISSERTATIONS, ACADEMIC
In32 2640 cds. by auth., t. & subj. Bachelor & master theses, 1892–1921. No add.

EARLY HISTORY OF ST. LOUIS AND MISSOURI (bk.). *In* ST. LOUIS (MO.)
Mo13-Soul.

EARLY SETTLER'S ASSOCIATION (CUYAHOGA CO., O.)—ANNUALS
O31 50 cds. by subj. Occ. add.

EARLY TIMES IN MEADE CO., KENTUCKY (bk.). *In* MEADE CO. (KY.)—HISTORY

EARLY VIRGINIAN ARCHITECTURE (per.). *In* ARCHITECTURE, VIRGINIAN—PHOTOGRAPHS **V7**

EARLY WATERFRONT DAYS OF SEATTLE (bk.). *In* SEATTLE (WASH.)—HISTORY
Wa10-ref (2)

EAST AND WEST (bk.). *In* SHORT STORIES
Tx12

EAST CHICAGO (IND.)
In5 250 ent. by subj. Newsp. Freq. add.

EAST CLEVELAND (O.)
O31 2500 ent., tpd. shts. by subj. Pams. Freq. add.

EAST ST. LOUIS (ILL.)—NEWSPAPERS
I36 100,000 cds. by subj. Loc. newsp. Occ. add.

EAST TEXAS STATE TEACHERS COLLEGE—PUBLICATIONS
Tx8 250 cds. by auth. Bks., per., yrbks., pams. etc. Freq. add.

EASTER. *See also* List of Bibliographies, APPENDIX I
Mn11 Unest. ent., tpd. shts. by subj. Bks. & per. Customs, hist., etc. Freq. add.

EASTER—POETRY. *See* POETRY—EASTER

EASTER CARDS. *See* GREETING CARDS
M27-art

ECCLESIASTICAL ART. *See* CHRISTIAN ART AND SYMBOLISM

ECLECTIC MAGAZINE OF FOREIGN LITERATURE. *In* PORTRAITS **In35**

ECONOMIC ANNALIST (per.). *In* CANADA—PERIODICALS **Ca13-per**

ECONOMIC REVIEW. *In* PUERTO RICO **Pr1**

ECONOMICS. *See also* AGRICULTURE—ECONOMIC ASPECTS
Nj16 260 cds., 158 ent., tpd. shts. by subj. Bks., per. & pams. Freq. add.

EDUCATION. *See also* Names of various phases and types of educ.; NEW YORK UNIVERSITY—DISSERTATIONS, ACADEMIC—EDUCATION; List of Bibliographies, APPENDIX I
C61-sch 1000 cds. by subj. Bks. & per. not indexed. Freq. add.
Ky19 160 cds. by subj. Per. Mo. add.
Mi6-par 1080 cds. by subj. Bks. & pams. Freq. add.
Mn14-Fran. 200 cds. by subj. Bks., pams. & govt. doc. Cur. add.
O20-soc. educ 1320 cds. by pers. or organiz. Newsp. Freq. add.
P4 28p. tpd. shts. by auth., subj. & t. Bk. indexed: *Classroom teacher*, 12v.

EDUCATION—BOOK REVIEWS
N30-t.c. 3000 cds. by auth. Per. indexed: *Bulletin of International bureau of education, 1932–date.* Cur. add.
O20-soc. educ 7260 cds. by auth. Per. Freq. add.

EDUCATION—CALIFORNIA. *See* CALIFORNIA. DEPARTMENT OF EDUCATION. BULLETIN

EDUCATION—CHARLESTON (S.C.)
Sc2 6000 ent., tpd. shts. chron. Charleston newsp., 1767–1886. No add.

EDUCATION—MARYLAND. *See* MARYLAND SCHOOL BULLETIN

EDUCATION—PERIODICALS. *See also* List of Bibliographies, APPENDIX I
N30-t.c. ref 240,000 cds. by auth., subj. & t. Per., 1919–1929. Dup. of index comp. in Ohio state univ. Dept. of educ. research. No add.

W23 1300 cds. by subj. Per. No add.

EDUCATION—TENNESSEE
T2 225 cds. by subj. Bul., pams. etc. Freq. add.

EDUCATION, SECONDARY. *See* List of Bibliographies, APPENDIX I

EDUCATIONAL LAWS AND LEGISLATION
Tx27 Unest. cds. by popular name of bill. Unindexed mat. Freq. add.

EDUCATIONAL RECORD OF THE PROVINCE OF QUEBEC (per.). *In* CANADA—PERIODICALS **Ca13-per**

EDUCATIONAL REVIEW (MONCTON). *In* CANADA—PERIODICALS **Ca13-per**

EDUCATIONAL TESTS. *See* TESTS AND MEASUREMENTS

EDUCATIONAL TRENDS (per.)
I43-ref v. 1–7, 1932–1939. Tpd. shts. by auth. & subj. No add.

EDUCATORS. *See* CLERGYMEN **I65-educ**

EDWARD'S GREAT WEST (bk.). *In* ST. LOUIS (Mo.) **Mo13-Soul.**

EGYPT—ANTIQUITIES
N35-ref. orient 14,000 cds. by subj. Bks. & per. Sup. to 1932 printed index. Cur. add.

EL PASO (TEX.)—NEWSPAPERS
Tx14 232,000 cds. by subj. & date. Newsp. indexed: *El Paso herald, El Paso times, El Paso morning tribune, Monday graphic, Thirty-four, El Paso lone star;* 1879–date. Cur. add.

EL PASO (TEX.) HERALD-POST (newsp.). *In* EL PASO (TEX.)—NEWSPAPERS **Tx13**

EL PASO (TEX.) LONE STAR (newsp.). *In* EL PASO (TEX.)—NEWSPAPERS **Tx13**

EL PASO (TEX.) MONDAY GRAPHIC (newsp.). *In* EL PASO (TEX.)—NEWSPAPERS **Tx13**

EL PASO (TEX.) MORNING TRIBUNE (newsp.). *In* EL PASO (TEX.)—NEWSPAPERS **Tx13**

EL PASO (TEX.) TIMES (newsp.). *In* EL PASO (TEX.)—NEWSPAPERS **Tx13**

ELECTRIC APPARATUS AND APPLIANCES. *See also* LIGHTING
Nj52 Several hundred cds. by subj. Bks., per. & pams. Freq. add.

ELECTRIC ENGINEERING
Nj52 Several hundred cds. by subj. Bks., per. & pams. Freq. add.

ELECTRIC INDUSTRIES
Nj52 Several hundred cds. by subj. Bks., per. & pams. Freq. add.

ELEMENTARY EDUCATION
O20-soc. educ 2640 cds. by subj. Courses of study in elem. educ. Freq. add.

ELIZABETH (N.J.) JOURNAL (newsp.)
Nj14 1916–date. Cds. by place & subj. Daily add.

ELIZABETHAN THEATRE. *See* THEATRE, ELIZABETHAN

ELKHART (IND.)—EUROPEAN WAR, 1914–1918. *See* EUROPEAN WAR, 1914–1918—ELKHART (IND.)

ELKHART CO. (IND.)—AUTHORS. *See* AUTHORS—ELKHART CO. (IND.)

ELMORE CO. (ALA.)—CEMETERY RECORDS
A1 500 ent., tpd. shts. by name. Primitive Baptist church near Buyck, Holman cem., Hagerty Hill, Harrogate Springs, Bullard Plot, Spratlen graveyard, Bibb family cem., Lebanon cem., Wetumpka cem., Cem. below Sistrunk place, Old cem. below Brassell home, Old Tallassee Road. Occ. add.

EMBRYOLOGY
Nj61 80 cds. by auth. & t. Bks., per. & pams. Infreq. add.

EMINENT DOMAIN. *See* List of Bibliographies, APPENDIX I

EMORY UNIVERSITY
G14 2500 cds. by auth. Bks., pams., mss., etc. Freq. add.

EMORY UNIVERSITY—PUBLICATIONS, ALUMNI
G14 525 cds. by auth. Freq. add.

EMORY UNIVERSITY—PUBLICATIONS, FACULTY
G14 225 cds. by auth. Freq. add.

EMPLOYEES AND OFFICIALS. *See* Name of loc., subdiv. OFFICIALS AND EMPLOYEES

EMPLOYMENT MANAGEMENT. *See also* JOB ANALYSIS
G11 200 cds. by subj. Bks., per. & pams. Personnel admin. Occ. add.
Nj52 Several hundred cds. by subj. Bks., per. & pams. Ind. rel. Freq. add.

ENCYCLOPEDIA BRITANNICA (bk.). *In* PICTURES **Tx8**

ENCYCLOPEDIA OF AMERICAN BIOGRAPHY (bk.). *In* BIOGRAPHY **L14-ref**

ENCYCLOPEDIA OF AMERICAN QUAKER GENEALOGY (bk.). *In* FRIENDS, SOCIETY OF **Nc5**

ENCYCLOPEDIA OF CONNECTICUT BIOGRAPHY (bk.). *In* CONNECTICUT—BIOGRAPHY **Ct8** (1)

ENCYCLOPEDIA OF THE HISTORY OF ST. LOUIS (bk.). *In* ST. LOUIS (MO.) **Mo13-Soul.**

ENCYCLOPEDIAS AND DICTIONARIES
Nj61 50 cds. by auth. & t. Infreq. add.

END PAPERS. *See* BOOK END-PAPERS

ENGINEERING. *See* List of Bibliographies, APPENDIX I; Names of various types and phases of eng.

ENGINEERING—LANTERN SLIDES. *See* LANTERN SLIDES—ENGINEERING

ENGINEERING—PERIODICALS
P32a 95,000 cds. by subj. Per. Wkly. add.

ENGINEERING—TABLES. *See also* SPECIFICATIONS; SYMBOLS
Wa10-tech 160 cds. by subj. Trade cat. & per. Occ. add.

ENGINEERING AND MINING JOURNAL. *In* WEST—PERIODICALS **Wa2**

ENGINEERING JOURNAL
Ca11 v. 1, 1918–date. Cds. by auth. & subj. Cur. add.

ENGINEERS. *See* TECHNOLOGY—BIOGRAPHY **N35-ref**

ENGLAND—PAMPHLETS, POLITICAL. *See* PAMPHLETS, POLITICAL—ENGLAND

ENGLAND—REGISTERS OF BIRTHS, ETC.
O20-hist 2640 cds. by co. & parish. Eng. parish reg. Infreq. add.

ENGLAND—SOCIAL LIFE AND CUSTOMS
Mn14-ref   3500 cds. by subj. Anglo-Saxon times to present. Infreq. add.

ENGLISH FICTION
Mn15-ref   200 cds. by auth. Bks. & per. Infreq. add.

ENGLISH IMPRINTS. *See* List of Bibliographies, APPENDIX I

ENGLISH LANGUAGE
I49   901 cds. by subj. Bks. & per. Infreq. add.
N46-lit   900 cds. by subj. Bks. Freq. add.

ENGLISH LITERATURE. *See also* Names of various divisions of lit., i.e. ENGLISH POETRY; PICTURES—ENGLISH LITERATURE
C28   4000 cds. by auth. & t. Bks. Plays, short stories & crit. essays. Freq. add.

ENGLISH MADRIGAL SCHOOL (bk.). *In* MUSIC   **Mn14-mus**

ENGLISH POETRY
M30   3194 cds. by auth. Bks. Infreq. add.
Tx30   169 ent., tpd. shts. by periods of lit. Bks. No add.

ENGRAVERS. *See* ARTISTS   **C56-print, N35-ref. print**

ENGRAVINGS. *See* DRAWINGS AND ENGRAVINGS

ENTERTAINING. *See* GAMES; PARTIES

ENTOMOLOGISTS—BIOGRAPHY
D16   2500 cds. by name. Bks. & per. Biog. & obit. Freq. add.

ENTOMOLOGY. *See also* ARACHNIDA
D16   2950 cds. by auth., chron. Doc. Auth. index to entomology in print. pub. of U.S. Dept. of agric. Freq. add.
D16   6238 cds. by auth. & t. Per. Bur. of entomology & plant quarantine auth., non-dept. pub., 1913–date. Freq. add.
D16   750 cds. by auth. Mim. pub. of Bureau of entomology & plant quarantine. Freq. add.
D16   630 cds. by subj. Mim. ser. of Bur. of entomology & plant quarantine. Freq. add.
D16   1350 cds. by common name of insect. Print. pub. of Bureau of entomology & plant quarantine. Freq. add.
D16   50,000 cds. by sci. name of insect. Lit. of continental N. Amer., inc. Canada, Alaska, Mexico, Panama canal zone, Cuba, Guam & Philippines, 1940–44. Daily add.
D16   4700 cds. by subj. & sci. name of insect. Print. pub. of U.S. Dept. of agric.
D16   1520 cds. by ser. & no. Print. pub. of U.S. Dept. of agric. Wkly. add.
Nj16   600 cds. by auth. & t. Bks., per. & pams. Freq. add.
Vt3   450 cds. by subj. Bks., per., pams. & govt. docs. Freq. add.

ENTOMOLOGY—BIBLIOGRAPHIES
D16   700 cds. by subj. Bibl. on entomological subj. in print. pub. of U.S. Dept. of agric. Freq. add.

ENZYMES
P30   2000 cds. by subj. & auth. Reprints, jl. entries. Freq. add.

EPHRATA
P19   14 ent., tpd. shts. by auth. Bks., per. & pams. Ephrata cloisters. No add.

EPIC CENTURY (per.)
Tx8   1936–date. Cds. by subj. Mo. add.
Tx10-ref   v. 1, 1934–date. Cds. by auth., t. & subj. Cur. add.

EPIDEMICS
Nj61   80 cds. by auth. & t. Bks., per., pams. & rpts. Freq. add.

ERIE (PA.)—HISTORY
P13-ref   99 cds. by subj. Bks., pams. newsp. etc. Non-cat. mat. on Erie & vicinity. Cur. add.

ERIE CO. (PA.)—SOLDIERS. *See* U.S.—HISTORY—WAR OF 1812—ERIE CO. (PA.)

ESSAYISTS
I49   702 cds. by auth. & t. Bks. & per. Occ. add.

ESSAYS. *See also* BIOGRAPHY; POETRY   **C43-ref**;   SHORT STORIES   **O25-F.S.M., Or2**
I35   3000 cds. by auth. & t. Bks. Cur. add.

I49 5329 cds. by t. Bks. & per. Occ. add.
I58 700 cds. by auth. & t. Bks. Cur. add.
I63 500 cds. by auth. & t. Bks. Cur. add.
K4 1800 cds. by auth. & t. Bks. Cur. add.
Mi6-circ 550 cds. by auth. Bks. not indexed in Essay index. Occ. add.
Mi13-S. Hi. 938 cds. by auth. & t. Bks. Cur. add.
Mn14-Fran. 1100 cds. by subj. & t. Bks. Cur. add.
Mn14-ref 750 cds. by subj. Bks. Occ. add.
Mn15-ref 500 cds. by subj. Bks. Infreq. add.
Mn23-Ham. 2316 cds. by auth. & t. Bks. Infreq. add.
N45 1000 cds. by auth. & t. Bks. Cur. add.
N51 735 cds. by auth. & t. Bks. Cur. add.
N56 2825 cds. by auth. & t. Bks. Cur. add.
Nb8 17,160 cds. by auth. & t. Bks. Infreq. add.
O20-lit 3960 cds. by auth. & t. Bks. Essay, short stories & speeches. Cur. add.
O40 3500 cds. by t. Bks. Freq. add.
Or1-cat 18,426 cds. by auth. & t. Bks. Cur. add.
Tx11 950 cds. by auth. & t. Bks. No add.
W16 15,000 cds. by t. Bks. Cur. add.
Wa3 700 cds. by auth. & t. Infreq. add.

ESSEX ANTIQUARIAN (per.). *In* GENEALOGY M19 (1)

ESSEX CO. (N.J.)—GENEALOGY. *See* GENEALOGY—NEW JERSEY Nj46 (1)

ESSEX CO. (N.J.)—REGISTERS OF BIRTHS, ETC.
Nj36 49p., tpd. shts. by name. Bk. A., Essex co. records, marriages. No add.

ESSEX CO. HISTORICAL AND GENEALOGICAL REGISTER (per.). *In* GENEALOGY M19 (1)

ESSEX INSTITUTE BULLETIN. *In* GENEALOGY M19 (1)

ESSEX INSTITUTE HISTORICAL COLLECTIONS (per.). *In* GENEALOGY M19 (1)

ETCHERS. *See* ARTISTS C56-print

ETCHINGS. *See* DRAWINGS AND ENGRAVINGS

ETHICS. *See also* CHARACTER; CHILDREN'S LITERATURE—ETHICS
C32-phil 2570 ent., tpd. shts. by subj. Bks. Cur. add.

ETHNOLOGY
Vt3 115 cds. by subj. Bks., per., pams. govt. doc. Occ. add.

ETIQUETTE. *See* List of Bibliographies, APPENDIX I

ETUDE (per.). *See also* MUSIC Mi27-ref; SONGS M22
H3-art 1907–date. Cds. by comp., t. & subj. Freq. add.
W23 v. 33, 1915, v. 47-54, 1929–1936. Cds. by mus. & t. Infreq. add.

EUGENE (ORE.) DAILY EMERALD (newsp.)
Or2 18,000 cds. by subj. Mo. add.

EUGENE (ORE.) STATE JOURNAL (newsp.)
Or2 1902–1908. Tpd. shts. by subj. No add.

EUGENICS
Nj61 150 cds. by auth. & t. Bks., per. & pams. Infreq. add.

EUROPE—HISTORY. *See also* List of Bibliographies, APPENDIX I
N54-treas 20,000 cds. by auth., t. & subj. Bks. & mss., in many lang., Leopold von Ranke coll. No add.

EUROPE—LITERATURE. *See* List of Bibliographies, APPENDIX I

EUROPE, UNITED STATES OF
Tx30 45 ent., tpd. shts. by auth. Bks. & per. No add.

EUROPEAN ARCHITECTURE (per.). *In* PICTURES P39-ref. art

EUROPEAN WAR, 1914–1918
C25 32,200 cds. by subj. Per. Per. indexed: *N.Y. mid-week pictorial*, 1928–date. Cur. add.
Ia12 45 ent., tpd. shts. Bks., fic. & non-fic. Occ. add.
Mn14-Fran. 200 cds. by subj. Bks., ency. & pams. Cur. add.
N4 400 cds. by country. Pams., per. & govt. doc. Infreq. add.

57

O32-hist. 1320 cds. by subj. Bks. Occ. add.

Wa8 10,000 cds. by subj. Bks. & pams. Freq. add.

EUROPEAN WAR, 1914–1918—AMERICAN EXPEDITIONARY FORCE
N46-hist. 1320 cds. by popular name of fighting unit, also numerical acc. to army setup. Bks. & per. Occ. add.

EUROPEAN WAR, 1914–1918—CONNECTICUT
Ct8 4800 cds. by subj. Conn. state council of defense records. War resources of state, 1917–1919. No add.
Ct8 14,000 cds. by name of soldier. Service questionnaires, 1917–1918. Service records of Conn. soldiers. Infreq. add.

EUROPEAN WAR, 1914–1918—ELKHART (IND.)
In6 1500 cds. by name. No add.

EUROPEAN WAR, 1914–1918—HAMILTON CO. (IA.)
Ia21 1100 cds. by name. Service records. Inc. 500 phot. Infreq. add.

EUROPEAN WAR, 1914–1918—LYCOMING CO. (PA.)
P56 2000 cds. by name. World war records. Occ. add.

EUROPEAN WAR, 1914–1918—PAMPHLETS
O20-hist 200 cds. by auth., subj. & t. World war pams. No add.

EUROPEAN WAR, 1914–1918—PICKAWAY CO. (O.)
O19 1500 cds. by name. No add.

EUROPEAN WAR, 1914–1918—POETRY. See POETRY—EUROPEAN WAR, 1914–1918

EUROPEAN WAR, 1914–1918—POSTERS
C56-ref 2000 cds. by name of issuing agency, under country. No add.
N35-ref 4000 cds. by t. & name of issuing offices & organiz. Cur. add.
Nj60-treas 332p., tpd. shts. Photostats. Freq. add.
P39-art 200 cds. by art. French & Amer. war posters. Occ. add.

EUROPEAN WAR, 1914–1918—RIVERSIDE CO. (CALIF.)
C55-ref 1000 ent., class. Phot. letters, off. pa. Infreq. add.

EUROPEAN WAR, 1914–1918—STORIES
P5 150 ent., tpd. shts. by auth. Bks. Cur. add.

EUROPEAN WAR, 1914–1918—WILLIAMSON CO. (ILL.)
I55 4000 cds. by subj. with co. & other data. All sources. Occ. add.

EUROPEAN WAR, 1939–1945
C68 Unest. cds. by subj. Newsp. Daily add.
N35-ref. econ 300 cds. by country & subj. Bks., U.S. & for. docs. Cur. add.

EVANGELINE (bk.). See LONGFELLOW, HENRY WADSWORTH—EVANGELINE

EVANSTON (ILL.)—HISTORY
I39 5000 cds. by subj. Bks., newsp., letters, etc. Freq. add.

EVERYBODY'S FAVORITE SERIES (bk.). In MUSIC Ia20

EWING, GEORGE W. See INDIANA—HISTORY In22-Ind (1)

EXAMINATIONS, COMPREHENSIVE. See List of Bibliographies, APPENDIX I

EXPLORERS. See also List of Bibliographies, APPENDIX I
Ca5-circ 90 ent., tpd. shts. by name. Bks. Infreq. add.

EXPLOSIVES. See also TRINITROLOLUENE
Nj54 Unest. cds. by subj. Spec. rpts. on explosive plants. Freq. add.

FAIRFIELD CO. (CONN.)—BIOGRAPHY
Ct2-hist 1320 cds. by name. Newsp. Auth., art. & mus. Freq. add.

FAIRFIELD CO. (CONN.)—SHIPPING. See SHIPPING—FAIRFIELD CO. (CONN.)

FAIRY TALES
Ca2-j 715 cds. by subj. & t. Bks., supp. to Eastman. Cur. add.
Md2-j 800 cds. by t. Bks., supp. to Eastman. Freq. add.
Mi20 1200 cds. by auth. & t. Freq. add.
Mn12 1466 cds. by t. Bks., supp. to Eastman. Freq. add.
N8-j 3960 cds. by t. Bks. Freq. add.
Nj7-E 700 cds. by t. Bks. Infreq. add.

P8 550 cds. by t. Bks. Cur. add.
P10 1500 cds. by t. Bks. & per. Freq. add.
P39-Wyl. 1557 cds. by t. Bks. Cur. add.

FALCONRY
Ca13-zoo 30p., tpd. shts. by auth. & art. Bks., per. & paintings. Cur. add.

FALL RIVER (MASS.)
M18-ref 31 cds. by subj. Per. Infreq. add.

FALL RIVER (MASS.)—BIOGRAPHY
M18-ref 40 cds. by name. Newsp. Prominent citizens. Freq. add.

FALL RIVER (MASS.)—CEMETERY RECORDS
M18-ref 40 cds. by name. Pams. Infreq. add.

FALL RIVER (MASS.)—HISTORY
M18-ref 42 cds. by subj. Bks. & newsp. Freq. add.

FALL RIVER (MASS.)—SOLDIERS. See U.S. — HISTORY — REVOLUTION — FALL RIVER (MASS.)

FAMILIES. See Subdiv. under loc., CENSUS GENEALOGY; NAMES, PERSONAL

FAMILY
Tx5 Unest. cds. by auth., subj. & t. Freq. add.

FAMILY (per.)
Mn14-soc v. 1, 1920–date. Cds. by auth., subj. & t. Cur. add.

FAMILY CIRCLE (per.). *In* COOKERY C44 (1)

FAMILY HISTORY. See GENEALOGY

FAMILY RECORDS (bk.). *In* GENEALOGY—NEW JERSEY Nj36

FAMOUS COMPOSERS AND THEIR WORKS (bk.). *In* MUSIC Nj15

FARM MACHINERY. See PATENTS—MACHINERY, AGRICULTURAL D10

FARMERS. See SCIENTISTS D21

FATHER MISSISSIPPI (bk.). *In* ST. LOUIS (MO.) Mo13-Soul.

FATHER'S DAY
T1-circ 50 ent., tpd. shts. by subj. Bks. Infreq. add.

FAYETTE CO. (KY.)
Ky7 143p., tpd. shts. by subj. Bk. indexed: Robert Peter, *Fayette county*. No add.

FAYETTE CO. (bk.). *In* FAYETTE CO. (KY.) Ky7

FEDERAL EMPLOYEE (per.) *In* LABOR AND LABORING CLASSES—PERIODICALS O33-Euc. Cen.

FEEBLE-MINDED. See List of Bibliographies, APPENDIX I

FERNS—CONNECTICUT. See FLOWERS—CONNECTICUT

FESTIVALS. See List of Bibliographies, APPENDIX I

FEUDALISM. See List of Bibliographies, APPENDIX I

FICTION. See also CHILDREN'S LITERATURE; DETECTIVES (IN FICTION); INDIANS—STORIES; MYSTERY AND DETECTIVE STORIES; SEA STORIES; SERIES, BOOKS IN; SHORT STORIES; SPORT STORIES; List of Bibliographies, APPENDIX I
C4 85p., tpd. shts. by subj. Bks. Freq. add.
C8-circ 2640 cds. by subj. Bks. Freq. add.
C18-r.a. 5425 cds. by subj. Bks. Freq. add.
C43-circ 4200 cds. by subj. Bks. Freq. add.
C47 600p., tpd. shts. by subj. Bks. Occ. add.
C49-inf 1408 cds. by subj. Bks. Wkly. add.
C63-circ 3500 cds. by subj. Bks. Cur. add.
C86 800 cds. by subj. Bks. Infreq. add.
Ca1 2000 cds. by subj. Bks. Cur. add.
Co5-circ 5400 cds. by subj. Bks. Freq. add.
D32 30,000 cds. by subj. & t. Bks. Cur. add.
De3 73,200 cds. by auth., subj. & t. Bks. Cur. add.
F4 5300 cds. by subj. Bks. Freq. add.
G18 500 cds. by subj. Bks. Freq. add.
I8 1600 cds. by subj. Bks. Freq. add.

I13-circ 2500 cds. by subj. Bks. Freq. add.
I13-r.b. 21,900 cds. by subj. Bks. Freq. add.
I33 670 cds. by subj. Bks. Freq. add.
I62 800 cds. by subj. Bks. Freq. add.
I68 3600 ent., tpd. shts. by subj. Bks. Occ. add.
Ia4 1800 cds. by subj. Bks. Cur. add.
In14 Unest. cds. by auth. & subj. Bks. Cur. add.
In15 700 cds. by subj. Bks., 1935–date. Freq. add.
Ky1 750 cds. by auth. & subj. Bks. Freq. add.
L14-circ 1500 cds. by subj. Bks. Freq. add.
Md2-circ 2500 cds. by subj. Bks. Freq. add.
Mi6-Camp. 1000 cds. by subj. Bks. Freq. add.
Mi6-circ 7600 cds. by subj. Bks. Wkly add.
Mi6-fic 3600 cds. by subj. Bks. Freq. add.
Mi6-H.B. 12,000 cds. by auth., t. & subj. Bks. Cur. add.
Mi6-Monn. 1000 cds. by auth., subj. & t. Freq. add.
Mi6-Mont. 2100 cds. by subj. Bks. Occ. add.
Mi6-par 1000 cds. by subj. Bks. Occ. add.
Mi6-Ut. 1000 cds. by subj. Bks. Freq. add.
Mi20 1100 cds. by subj. Bks. Occ. add.
Mn8 1477 cds. by subj. Bks. Freq. add.
N8-o.s. 15,840 cds. by subj. Bks. Freq. add.
N14 3000 cds. by subj. Bks. Cur. add.
N22-circ Unest. cds. by subj. Bks. Freq. add.
N28-cat 10,000 cds. by subj. Bks. Freq. add.
Nb14-r.a. 5000 cds. by subj. Bks. Freq. add.
Nj14 2960 cds. by auth., subj. & t. Bks. Occ. add.
Nj21 550 cds. by subj. Bks., 1939–date. Freq. add.

O1-circ 1920 cds. by subj. Bks. No add.
O1-Fires. 1300 cds. by subj. Bks. Occ. add.
O1-W. ⎫ 700 cds. by subj. Bks.
O1-y.p. ⎭ Y.p. fic. Cur. add.
O20-Brook. 1980 cds. by subj. Bks. Cur. add.
O20-Euc. 100th 1000 cds. by subj. & type. Bks. Freq. add.
O20-fic 48,840 cds. by subj. Bks. Cur. add.
O20-fic 5280 cds. by subj. Lists & aids: bk. club selections, best-sellers, auth., pseudonyms, pronunciations, translators, detectives in fic., etc. Cur. add.
O20-y.p. 7800 cds. by subj. Y.p.'s bks. Freq. add.
O31 2650 cds. by subj. Bks. Freq. add.
O31-N. 1500 cds. by subj. Bks. Freq. add.
O56-circ 20,000 cds. by subj. Bks. Cur. add.
Or5-circ 1400 cds. by subj. Bks. Occ. add.
P25 1200 ent., tpd. shts. by subj. Bks. Freq. add.
P39-circ 17,160 cds. by subj. Bks. Cur. add.
P54-circ 720 cds. by subj. Bks. Occ. add.
Tx14 4000 cds. by subj. Bks. Freq. add.
W7 1500 cds. by subj. Bks. Occ. add.

FICTION—BOOK REVIEWS
C8-circ 1320 cds. by auth. Bks. Freq. add.
Mi6-circ 4000 cds. by auth. Bks., 1925–date. Wkly. add.
N46-fic 19,800 cds. by subj. Bks. Freq. add.
O1-circ 2000 cds. by auth. Bks., 1935–date. Cur. add.
O20-fic 84,480 cds. by auth. Bks. Wkly. add.

FICTION—BUSINESS. *See* FICTION, VOCATIONAL

FICTION—CALIFORNIA. *See* List of Bibliographies, APPENDIX I

FICTION—CANADA. *See* List of Bibliographies, APPENDIX I

FICTION—CHRISTMAS. See CHRISTMAS STORIES

FICTION—EDITIONS. See List of Bibliographies, APPENDIX I

FICTION—EUROPEAN WAR, 1914–1918. See List of Bibliographies, APPENDIX I

FICTION—FALL RIVER (MASS.). See List of Bibliographies, APPPENDIX I

FICTION—FAMILY LIFE. See List of Bibliographies, APPENDIX I

FICTION—FLORIDA. See List of Bibliographies, APPENDIX I

FICTION—FRIENDS, SOCIETY OF
P17-mss   306 cds. by auth. Bks. & per. Freq. add.

FICTION—INDIANS. See INDIANS—STORIES

FICTION—LAW. See List of Bibliographies, APPENDIX I

FICTION—LOCALITY. See FICTION, REGIONAL

FICTION—MEDICINE. See List of Bibliographies, APPENDIX I

FICTION—MICHIGAN. See List of Bibliographies, APPENDIX I

FICTION—MUSIC. See List of Bibliographies, APPENDIX I

FICTION—MUSICIANS—FOREIGN LANGUAGES
Mi6-for   30 cds. by lang. and name. Bks. Infreq. add.

FICTION—NEW YORK (STATE). See List of Bibliographies, APPENDIX I

FICTION—NORTH CAROLINA. See List of Bibliographies, APPENDIX I

FICTION—NOVELETTES. See List of Bibliographies, APPENDIX I

FICTION—ORIENT. See List of Bibliographies, APPENDIX I

FICTION—PENNSYLVANIA
P39-ref   282 ent., tpd. shts. by auth. & region. Bks. & per. Occ. add.

FICTION—PHYSICIANS. See List of Bibliographies, APPENDIX I

FICTION—TRANSLATIONS. See also List of Bibliographies, APPENDIX I
C32-fic   450p., 3000 ent., tpd. shts. by country & auth. Freq. add.

N22-r.a.   1825-cds. by auth. & original lang. European novelists to 1933. No add.
Nb14-r.a.   1000 cds. by lang. Bks. Infreq. add.
O20-Euc.100th   451 cds. by lang., auth. & t. Cur. add.
O20-fic   5280 cds. by lang. & auth. Cur. add.
P5   620 ent., tpd. shts. by country & auth. Bks. Cur. add.

FICTION—WAR—FOREIGN LANGUAGES
Mi6-for   200 cds. by subj. & lang. Bks. War stories. Occ. add.

FICTION—WAR—U.S.
Nj21   92 ent., tpd. shts. by subj. Bks. U.S. wars in fic. Freq. add.

FICTION, BIOGRAPHICAL. See also List of Bibliographies, APPENDIX I
N44-ad   20p., tpd. shts. Bks. Biog. & hist. novels. Yrly. add.

FICTION, CATHOLIC. See also List of Bibliographies, APPENDIX I
Mo13-univ   225 cds. by subj. Bks. & per. Occ. add.

FICTION, FRENCH. See List of Bibliographies, APPENDIX I

FICTION, GENEALOGICAL. See also List of Bibliographies, APPENDIX I
Ia12   Unest. ent., tpd. shts. by countries. Bks. Freq. add.

FICTION, HISTORICAL. See also FICTION, BIOGRAPHICAL   N44-ad
C51   450 ent., tpd. shts. by auth. Bks. England, 1500–1789, France 1500–1789, Europe 1789–1914. No add.
C75   593 cds. by country, period & auth. Bks. Freq. add.
Ct5   347 cds., chron. Bks. Hist. fic. for y.p. Freq. add.
F2-r.a.   200 cds. by country & period. Bks. Cur. add.
I6   Unest. ent., tpd. shts. by auth., chron. Bks. Freq. add.
I8   700 cds. by country & chron. Bks. Freq. add.
In2   206 ent., chron. Bks. Infreq. add.
K8-circ   534 ent., tpd. shts. by auth. Bks. Yrly. add.
K9-ref   900 cds. by auth., t. & subj. Bks. Freq. add.

K11 292 cds. by auth., t. series, & country. Bks. Infreq. add.
L14-circ 750 cds. by country, chron. Bks. Freq. add.
L16 55 cds. Bks. Yrly. add.
Mi6-Rich. 650 ent. by period. Bks. Freq. add.
Mi10 1000 ent., tpd. shts. by auth. & period. Bks. Yrly. add.
Mn11 Unest. ent., tpd. shts. by auth. Bks. Freq. add.
Nb14-N. 348 ent., tpd. shts. by country & period. Bks. Occ. add.
Nj71 250 ent., tpd. shts. by subj. Ancient, European, Amer. hist. fic. for 8th & 9th grades. Occ. add.
O56-circ 2000 cds. by subj. Bks. Freq. add.
P5 1110 ent., tpd. shts. by country & auth. Bks. Cur. add.
Tx2 600 cds. by country. Junior hi. fic. Freq. add.
Tx30 285 ent., tpd. shts. by topic. Bks. No add.

FICTION, HISTORICAL—ANCIENT HISTORY
I20 21 ent., tpd. shts. chron. & geog. Bks. Freq. add.

FICTION, HISTORICAL—EUROPE
I20 65 ent., tpd. shts. chron. & geog. Bks. Freq. add.

FICTION, HISTORICAL—FOREIGN LANGUAGES
C32-for 400 cds. by lang. & auth. Bks. Freq. add.
Mi6-for 300 cds. by subj. & lang. Bks. Freq. add.

FICTION, HISTORICAL—JUVENILE BOOKS. See CHILDREN'S LITERATURE—HISTORICAL FICTION

FICTION, HISTORICAL—U.S.
I20 122 ent., tpd. shts. chron. Bks. Freq. add.
I35 94 ent., tpd. shts. by auth., subj. & chron. Occ. add.
I51 300 ent., tpd. shts., auth. & chron. Bks. Freq. add.
L4 51 cds. chron., alph. Bks. Yrly. add.
Mi6-Red. 110 ent., auth. & chron. Bks. Mo. add.
Mi21-ref 200 ent., tpd. shts., chron. & by auth. Bks. Infreq. add.
N50 111 ent., tpd. shts. by auth. Bks. Freq. add.

Nb14-N. 219 ent., tpd. shts. by period. Intermediate & j. fic. Infreq. add.
O56-Locke 155 cds. by auth. Bks. Cur. add.

FICTION, JEWISH. See List of Bibliographies, APPENDIX I

FICTION, JUVENILE. See CHILDREN'S LITERATURE

FICTION, PROLETARIAN. See List of Bibliographies, APPENDIX I

FICTION, PSEUDO-SCIENTIFIC. See List of Bibliographies, APPENDIX I

FICTION, PSYCHOLOGICAL. See List of Bibliographies, APPENDIX I

FICTION, REGIONAL. See also CHILDREN'S LITERATURE, REGIONAL; FICTION, HISTORICAL
C39 Unest. cds. by auth., t. & loc. Bks. Occ. add.
Mi6-Fenk. 200 cds. by loc., auth. & state. Bks. Freq. add.
Mi6-par 1200 cds. by loc. Bks. Freq. add.
Or5-circ 1200 cds. by subj. Bks. Freq. add.
P26 53 ent., tpd. shts. by loc. Bks. Infreq. add.

FICTION, REGIONAL—U.S.
I13-S.Sh. Unest. cds. by state. Bks. Cur. add.
I79 127 ent., tpd. shts. by loc. Bks. Freq. add.
Ky15-circ 405 ent., tpd. shts. by state. Bks. Occ. add.
Nb14-N. 149 ent., tpd. shts. by period. Bks. Occ. add.
Nb14-N. 217 ent., tpd. shts. by state. Bks. Occ. add.
Nj9 114 cds. by auth. Bks. Freq. add.

FICTION, RELIGIOUS—FOREIGN LANGUAGES
Mi6-for 75 cds. by subj. & lang. Bks. Freq. add.

FICTION, REPLACEMENT. See List of Bibliographies, APPENDIX I

FICTION, ROMANTIC. See List of Bibliographies, APPENDIX I

FICTION, SOCIOLOGICAL. See also List of Bibliographies, APPENDIX I

FICTION, VOCATIONAL.
C75   41 cds. by auth. Bks. Bus. & voc. stories. Freq. add.
Ca5-circ   130 ent., tpd. shts. by occup. Bks., 1927–1937. No add.
Mi6-Camp.   100 ent., tpd. shts. Bks. Career stories. Freq. add.
N50   77 ent., tpd. shts. by auth. Bks. Freq. add.
Nb14-N.   186 ent., tpd. shts. by occup. Bks. Occ. add.

FICTION, WESTERN.   *See* List of Bibliographies, APPENDIX I

FIELD, EUGENE—WORKS
I13-ref   2000 cds. by t. & 1st line. Bks. & per. Occ. add.

THE FIFTH COLUMN (bk.). *In* SHORT STORIES   Tx12

FIFTY ART SONGS (bk.). *In* MUSIC
Nj15

FIFTY YEARS ON THE MISSISSIPPI (bk.). *In* MISSISSIPPI RIVER   Mo13-ref

FIFTY-TWO SACRED SONGS (bk.). *In* MUSIC
Nj15

FIFTY-SIX SONGS YOU LIKE TO SING (bk.). *In* MUSIC   Nj15

FIFTY-NINE PIANO SOLOS (bk.). *In* MUSIC
Nj15

FIGURES IN A LANDSCAPE (bk.). *In* SHORT STORIES   Tx12

FILMS. *See* LANTERN SLIDES; MOTION PICTURES

FINANCE
Nj52   Several hundred cds. by subj. Bks., per. & pams. Freq. add.
Nj60-Benj. st.   40,000 cds. by subj. Off. doc., for. per. & pams. For. pub. finance. Freq. add.

FIRE PREVENTION
Nj52   Several hundred cds. by subj. Bks., per. & pams. Freq. add.

FIRE PREVENTION—PERIODICALS. *See* INSURANCE—PERIODICALS   C65

FIRES—TACOMA (WASH.)
Wa14-ref   75 cds. Bks. & newsp. Cur. add.

FIRST CENTURY OF PIQUA (O.) (bk.). *In* PIQUA (O.)—HISTORY   O49

FIRST STEPS IN THE ENJOYMENT OF PICTURES (bk.). *In* ART—STUDY & TEACHING
Mi6-Walk

FIRST THINGS OF TORONTO (bk.). *In* TORONTO (CANADA)—HISTORY
Ca8-lib. sch

FISHERIES
Wa10-tech   420 cds. by subj. Bks., per. & govt. doc. Cur. add.

FISHES.   *See also* PICTURES—FISHES
Nj61   75 cds. by auth. & t. Bks., per. & pams. Freq. add.

FLAGS
C24   1500 cds. by country. No add.
O16-ref   1400 cds. by continent, country & state. Bks., per. & newsp. Flags & seals. Occ. add.

FLAT BOATS.   *See* BOATS

FLEMING CO. (KY.)
Ky7   Unest. cds. Newsp. No add.

FLINT (MICH.)—BIOGRAPHY
Mi11-ref   2000 ent. Newsp. Daily add.

FLINT (MICH.)—HISTORY
Mi11-ref   230 cds. by subj. Newsp. Freq. add.

FLOODS. *See* List of Bibliographies, APPENDIX I

FLORIDA—BIOGRAPHY
F2-r.a.   12 ent., tpd. shts. by subj. Bks. Yrly. add.

FLORIDA—DOCUMENTS. *See* FLORIDA—HISTORY   F5

FLORIDA—HISTORY
F3   1150 cds. by subj. Bks., per., pams. & newsp. Freq. add.
F5   1470 cds. by subj. State doc., newsp., per. & bks. Freq. add.

FLORIDA—LAW. *See* LAW—FLORIDA

FLORIDA—MAPS. *See* MAPS—FLORIDA

FLORIDA—PICTURES. *See* PICTURES—FLORIDA

FLORIDA BAPTIST ASSOCIATIONS. MINUTES
F1   Unest. cds. by assoc. 42 assoc., inc. Colgate univ., S. Baptist Theological seminary, State secy., Stetson univ. Freq. add.

FLORIDA GROWER (per.)
F2-ref   v. 1, 1908–1936. Cds. by subj. No add.

FLOWERS. *See also* BULBS; PICTURES—FLOWERS
Wa10-j   200 cds. by variety. Per. Occ. add.

FLOWERS—CONNECTICUT
Ct4   650 cds. by name. Bks. Flowers & ferns of Woodstock & Windham co. Yrly. add.

FLOWERS—DUBUQUE (IA.)
Ia10   300 cds. by name. Bks., per. & newsp. Wild flowers in Dubuque & vicinity. No add.

FLOWERS—MAINE
Me3   950 cds. by name. Paintings of nearly 1000 Me. flowers in Kate Furbish coll. of flora of Me. No add.

FLUSHING (N.Y.)—HISTORY
N22-L.I.   1600 cds. by name. Flushing town records, 1790–. In proc.

FOLK SONGS
Mn23-art   5838 cds. by t. & country. Bks. Occ. add.

FOLK SONGS—KENTUCKY
Ky2   8p., tpd. shts. by t. Bks. & per. Folk songs & ballads. No add.

FOLK SONGS, ITALIAN
O20-White   2640 cds. by t. Bks. Occ. add.

FOLK SONGS, RUSSIAN
N35-mus   700 cds. by t. Bks. Infreq. add.

FOLKLORE. *See also* DANCING—FOLK AND NATIONAL DANCES
C49-j   384 cds. by country. Bks. Freq. add.
Ia16   550 ent., tpd. shts. by country. Bks., per., pams. & newsp. Freq. add.
K12-ref   300 cds. by subj. & country. Per. Occ. add.
N55-lib. sch   1000 cds. by subj. & place. Folklore stories. Cur. add.
O20-White   27,500 cds. by subj. Bks., per. & ser. Folk lore & orient. subj. Occ. add.
Wa14-ref   200 ent., tpd. shts. by country. Bks. & per. Infreq. add.

FOLKLORE—TEXAS. *See* TEXAS FOLK-LORE SOCIETY—PUBLICATIONS

FOOD. *See also* COOKERY; NUTRITION; Names of foods; INDUSTRIES—HISTORY   Wa10-tech
Nj61   150 cds. by auth. & t. Bks., per. & pams. Food, dietetics & nutrition. Freq. add.

FOOD, COST OF. *See* COST AND STANDARD OF LIVING

FOOD FADS. *See* List of Bibliographies, APPENDIX I

FORAMINIFERA
W2   197 ent., tpd. shts., bd., by auth. & t. Bks., pams. & per. in Rufus Mather Bagg coll. No add.

FORDHAM UNIVERSITY — DISSERTATIONS, ACADEMIC. *See* List of Bibliographies, APPENDIX I

FOREIGN AFFAIRS. *See* INTERNATIONAL LAW AND RELATIONS

FOREIGN COUNTRIES
N35-ref. econ   1280 cds. by country. Per. & govt. doc. Exchange rates. No add.
Nj25-ref   294 ent., by name. Bks. & per. Freq. add.

FOREIGN LANGUAGES. *See also* Names of subj., subdiv. FOREIGN LANGUAGES; TRANSLATIONS
C43-circ   4000 cds. by lang. Bks. Freq. add.
K9-ref   1000 cds. by auth., t. & subj. Bks. in German, French & Spanish. Freq. add.
M16-ref   2700 cds. by lang., auth. & t. Bks. in 28 lang. Occ. add.
Mn24a   572 cds. by lang. Bks. Infreq. add.
P42-cat   2000 cds. by auth. Bks. Occ. add.
Vt2   1060 cds. by auth. & t. Bks. Infreq. add.

FOREIGN POLICY REPORTS (per.)
I1   v. 7-11, 1931–1935. Cds. by auth., t. & subj. No add.
N35-Morr.   v. 4-11, 1928–1935. Cds. No add.

FORENAMES. *See* NAMES, PERSONAL

FORESTS AND FORESTRY. *See also* WOOD; List of Bibliographies, APPENDIX I
D24   400 ent., tpd. shts. mim. by subj. Bks., per. etc. Cur. add

G11   300 cds. by subj. Bks., per., pams. etc. Freq. add.

N55-for   52,468 cds. by auth., t. & subj. Bks. Freq. add.

Vt3   200 cds. by subj. Bks., per. govt. doc. & pams. Occ. add.

Wa11-ref   150 cds. by auth. & subj. Bks. & per. Occ. add.

FORESTS AND FORESTRY—SOUTH. See also LUMBERING—SOUTH
G11   50 cds. by t. Per. & pams. Econ. & soc. conditions in S. states, in rel. to forestry. Occ. add.

FORT NISQUALLY (WASH.)
Wa14-ref   36 ent., tpd. shts. Bks. & per. Infreq. add.

FORT WORTH (TEX.)—BIOGRAPHY
Tx15   20,000 cds. by name. Fort Worth newsp., 1873–1907. No add.

FORTIFICATIONS. See U.S. ARMY—CAMPS 016-ref

FOSS, SAMUEL WALTER—WORKS
I13-ref   700 cds. by t. & 1st line. Bks. & per. Occ. add.

FOSTER, STEPHEN COLLINS—WORKS
Ky8   Unest. ent., cat. by auth., t. & 1st line. Songs. No add.

FOUR CENTURIES IN KANSAS (bk.). See KANSAS K3

FOX, GUSTAVUS VASA. See U.S. NAVY Md1 (1)

FOX RIVER VALLEY MAGAZINE (per.). In WISCONSIN—HISTORY W19

FRA (per.)
N8-ref   v. 2, #3, v. 3-13, v. 15-19, 1903, 1909–1914, 1915–1917. Cds. by subj. No add.

FRANCE—BIOGRAPHY. See BIOGRAPHY, FRENCH

FRANCE—HISTORY—REVOLUTION, 1789–1799
M13-ref   60 ent., tpd. shts. by subj. Bks. Infreq. add.

THE FRANCISCAN (per.)
N48   1926–1939. Cds. by auth. No add.

FRANCISCANS
N48   5000 cds. by auth. Bks., per. & pams. Franciscans in Holy Name Province, friars in E. states. Freq. add.

FRANKFORT (KY.)—CEMETERY RECORDS
Ky7   Unest. cds. by name. Bk. indexed: Lewis E. Johnson, History of the Frankfort cemetery.

FRANKFORT (KY.) ARGUS OF WESTERN AMERICA (newsp.)
Ky7   1827–1830. Cds. by subj. No add.

FRANKFORT (KY.) COMMENTATOR (newsp.)
Ky7   1828, 1830–1932. Cds. by subj. No add.

FRANKFORT (KY.) COMMONWEALTH (newsp.)
Ky7   1833–1835, 1839–1841. Cds. by subj. No add.

FRANKFORT (KY.) DAILY SESSION YEOMAN (newsp.)
Ky7   v. 1, 1843. Cds. by subj. No add.

FRANKFORT (KY.) THE PATRIOT (newsp.)
Ky7   1826. Tpd. shts. by name. No add.

FRANKFORT (KY.) SPIRIT OF 76 (newsp.)
Ky7   1826. Tpd. shts. by name. No add.

FRANKFORT (KY.) STATE JOURNAL (newsp.)
Ky7   Sesqui-centennial ed. Tpd. shts. by subj. No add.

FRANKLIN CO. (ALA.)—CENSUS
A1   700 cds. by name. 1820 Fed. cens. No add.

FRANKLIN CO. (KY.)—HISTORY
Ky7   Unest. cds. by subj. Bk. indexed: Lewis E. Johnson, The History of Franklin county. No add.

FREEPORT (ILL.)—GENEALOGY. See GENEALOGY—FREEPORT (ILL.)

FRENCH, SAMUEL—PLAYS. See PLAYS—FRENCH, SAMUEL

FRENCH BIOGRAPHY. See BIOGRAPHY, FRENCH

FRENCH LANGUAGE
Nj58   1300 cds. by auth. & t. Bks. Occ. add.

FRENCH LITERATURE
I52   115 ent., tpd. shts. by subj. & lit. form. Bks. Yrly. add.

FRENCH PLAYS. See PLAYS, FRENCH

FRENCH REVOLUTION. See FRANCE—HISTORY—REVOLUTION, 1789–1799

FRIARS. See FRANCISCANS

THE FRIEND (per.). *In* FRIENDS, SOCIETY OF—NECROLOGY P17; INDIANS G2-DeRen.

FRIENDS, SOCIETY OF
Nc5   1186p., tpd. shts. Bk. indexed: William Wade Hinshaw, *Ency. of Amer. quaker genealogy.* No add.
Nj35   140 cds. by subj. Bks., per. & pams. Occ. add.
P17-mss   18,000 cds. by name & subj. Bks. & per. Freq. add.

FRIENDS, SOCIETY OF—CEMETERY RECORDS
P47   13,200 cds. by name of cem. & person. 96 Quaker burial grounds. Infreq. add.

FRIENDS, SOCIETY OF—LITERATURE. *See also* FICTION—FRIENDS, SOCIETY OF
P17-mss   52 cds. by auth. Quakers & Quaker beliefs in lit. Infreq. add.

FRIENDS, SOCIETY OF—NECROLOGY
P17   66,000 cds. by name. Per. indexed: *The Friend, Friends intelligencer, Friends review.* Cur. add.

FRIENDS INTELLIGENCER (per.). *In* FRIENDS, SOCIETY OF—NECROLOGY   P17

FRIENDS REVIEW (per.). *In* FRIENDS, SOCIETY OF—NECROLOGY   P17

FROM DEATH TO MORNING (bk.). *In* SHORT STORIES   Tx12

FRONTIER (per.)
Mt3   v. 1-10, 1920-1936. Tpd. shts. by auth. & t. No add.

FRONTIER AND PIONEER LIFE. *See also* List of Bibliographies, APPENDIX I
Ky2   279 cds. by auth. Bks. & per. Freq. add.
N35-ref. Amer. hist   2500 cds. by name. Bks. & per. Outlaws & peace officers (sheriffs) of frontier Amer. Cur. add.

FRONTIER AND PIONEER LIFE—MANUSCRIPTS
C56-Calif.   Several thousand cds. by name & date. Original letters & mss. Occ. add.

FRONTIER AND PIONEER LIFE—NEBRASKA
Nb9   10,120 cds. by subj. Bks. Nebraska pioneers. Infreq. add.

FRONTIER AND PIONEER LIFE—STORIES. *See also* List of Bibliographies, APPENDIX I
Ky8-circ   49 cds. by auth. Bks. In proc.

Mn11   Unest. cds. by auth. Bks. Freq. add.

FRONTIER TIMES (per.). *In* TEXAS—PERIODICALS   Tx17
Tx29-ref   v. 1, 1923-date. Cds. by auth., t. & subj. In proc.

FRUIT. *See also* APPLES
D19   4000 cds. by name & variety. Descrip. & hist. esp. Amer. fruit. Freq. add.
D19   2640 ent., tpd. shts. by variety. Nursery trade lists of fruit varieties (70 repres. nurseries). Yrly. add.

FUGITIVES. *See* REFERENCE AIDS

FULLERTON   (CALIF.)   NEWS-TRIBUNE (newsp.)
C17   1893-1919. Cds. by subj. In proc.

FULTON CO. (GA.)—ADULT EDUCATION. *See* ATLANTA (GA.)—ADULT EDUCATION   G4-circ

FUNGI
Nj61   300 cds. by auth. & t. Bks., per., pams. & rpts. Freq. add.

FUNGICIDES. *See* INSECTICIDES   Nj61

FURNITURE. *See also* PICTURES—FURNITURE
Mi13-ref   1400 cds. by name. Bks. & per. Indiv. art. of furniture. Freq. add.
Mi13-ref   1400 cds. by name of period & style. Bks. & per. Furniture periods & styles. Freq. add.
Mi13-ref   100 cds. by auth. & t. Bks., per. & pams. Upholstering in furniture. Occ. add.
Mi13-ref   Several hundred cds. by name. Bks. & per. Infreq. add.
N8-tech   900 cds. by art. Bks. Freq. add.

FURNITURE—DESIGNERS
Mi13-ref   Unest., cds. by name. Bks. & per. Infreq. add.

FURNITURE—MUSEUMS
Mi13-ref   100 cds. by museum. Bks., per. & pams. Occ. add.

FURNITURE, VICTORIAN. *See* ART, VICTORIAN   N35-ref. art

GALESBURG (ILL.)—BIOGRAPHY. *See* List of Bibliographies, APPENDIX I

GALESBURG (ILL.)—HISTORY
I45   622 ent., tpd. shts. by subj. Pams., pic. newsp., etc. Infreq. add.

GALESBURG (ILL.)—SOCIETIES AND CLUBS
I45-ref   179 cds. by name. Freq. add.

GALLOWAY, EWING. See PHOTOGRAPHS—GALLOWAY, EWING

GALVESTON (TEX.). See TEXAS—HISTORY
Tx17

GALVESTON (TEX.)—BIBLIOGRAPHY—IMPRINTS
Tx17   56 ent., tpd. shts., chron. Bks. & pams. Imprints prior to 1871. Occ. add.

GALVESTON (TEX.)—CHARITIES
Tx17   18p., tpd. shts. by subj. Newsp. & per. Notable Galveston benefactions. No add.

GALVESTON (TEX.)—HISTORIC HOUSES, ETC.
Tx17   3p., tpd. shts. by subj. Hist. landmarks in Galveston. No add.

GALVESTON (TEX.)—NEWSPAPERS
Tx17   14,520 cds. by subj. Loc. newsp. Freq. add.

GALVEZ, BERNARDO DE. See List of Bibliographies, APPENDIX I

GAMES. See also DANCING—FOLK AND NATIONAL DANCES; MATHEMATICS—GAMES; SPORTS AND ATHLETIC GAMES; Names of games, i.e. CHECKERS
I68-art   500 ent., tpd. shts. by type of game. Bks. Freq. add.
Mi6-par   200 cds. by t: Bks. Supp. to Minneapolis index. Freq. add.
Mn14-ref   2400 cds. by subj. Bks., etc. Games & parties. Supp. to Silk & Fanning index. Freq. add.
N8-ref   1000 cds. by t. Bks. Freq. add.
N22-art   1496 cds. by t. Bks. Cur. add.
N22-art   22p., tpd. shts. by game. Bk. indexed: Clement Wood and Gloria Goddard, *The complete book of games*. No add.
N46-fic   9p., tpd. shts. by game. Bk. indexed: Clement Wood and Gloria Goddard, *The complete book of games*. No add.
O1-circ   1600 cds. by subj. Bks. & pams. Games & parties. Cur. add.

O20-art   1850 cds. by t. & subj. Bks. Games, parties & stunts. Freq. add.
O20-Tem.   660 cds. by t. of game or party. Bks. No add.
O37   2500 cds. by subj. Bks. Cur. add.

GARDENS, MINIATURE
Tx5   Unest. ent., tpd. shts. Plates, newsp., etc. Dish gardens. Freq. add.

GARDENS AND GARDENING. See also List of Bibliographies, APPENDIX I
Ca5-circ   800 cds. by subj. Inc. furniture, trellises, etc. No add.
Mn14-tech   350 cds. by t., class. Gen. & spec. seed & bulb cat. Cur. add.
Tx5   200p., tpd. shts. by subj. Bul., newsp. Gardens & pools. Freq. add.
V3   305 cds. by subj. Bks. & per. Flowers & gardens. Occ. add.

GAS APPLIANCES
Nj52   Several hundred cds. by subj. Bks., per. & pams. Freq. add.

GAS ENGINEERING
Nj52   Several hundred cds. by subj. Bks., per. & pams. Freq. add.

GAS INDUSTRY
Nj52   Several hundred cds. by subj. Bks., per. & pams. Freq. add.
Nj52   Several hundred cds. by subj. Bks., per. & pams. Gas plants. Freq. add.

GASES, ASPHYXIATING AND POISONOUS
Nj54   Unest. cds. by subj. Spec. rpts. Freq. add.

GAZETTEERS. See NAMES, GEOGRAPHICAL

GENEALOGICAL ADVERTISER (per.). *In* GENEALOGY   M19 (1)

GENEALOGICAL MAGAZINE (per.). *In* GENEALOGY   M19 (1)

GENEALOGICAL QUARTERLY MAGAZINE (per.). *In* GENEALOGY   M19 (1)

GENEALOGY. See also BIOGRAPHY; DAUGHTERS OF THE AMERICAN REVOLUTION; HERALDRY; NAMES, PERSONAL; NECROLOGY; PENSIONS, MILITARY; Name of loc., subdiv. CEMETERY RECORDS; CENSUS; REGISTERS OF BIRTHS, ETC.; Names of gen. per., i.e. AMERICANA
C32-gen   32,000 cds. by family name. Loc. hist., vital records, family hist., war rosters. Freq. add.

Co5-gen 16,800 cds. by indiv. & family name. Bks. & per. Cur. add.
Ct1 3000 cds. by name. Bks. & per. Freq. add.
Ct7 11,880 cds. by name. Per. from Munsell's period to Jacobus. No add.
Ct12-ref 154 cds. by family name. Bks., per. & pams. Indiv. gen. Freq. add.
F2-ref 30,000 cds. by family name. Bks. Cur. add.
F3 12,100 cds. by family name. Newsp. Newsp. indexed: *Boston (Mass.) Evening transcript,* 1923–1939. Daily add.
F5 910 cds. by family name. Bks. Per. indexed: *Americana.* Mo. add.
I17 550,000 cds. by family name. Bks., mss., per., family archives, pedigree questionnaires, charts, etc. Daily add.
I17 Unest. cds. by family name. Bks. & per. Derivation of surnames. Freq. add.
I17 3000 cds. by subj. Bks. & per. Topical index to gen. source material such as parish reg., military lists, geog. source books, methods of research, etc. Cur. add.
I17 75,000 cds. by subj. Bks. & per. Town & co. hist., bks. & mss. Daily add.
I70 7000 cds. by family name. Bks. Cur. add.
In22-gen (1) 5000 ent. by name. Newsp. indexed: *Hartford Times,* 1939–date.
In22-gen (2) 15,000 cds. by family name & loc. Bks., per., gen. & co. hist. Freq. add.
In22-gen (3) 33,000 cds. by surname. Newsp. indexed: *Boston (Mass.) Evening transcript,* 1934–date. Cur. add.
In23-gen 700 cds. by surname. Per. indexed: *Americana.* Occ. add.
In35-gen 4475 ent., tpd. shts. by name. Bks. Per. indexed: *Americana.* Occ. add.
Ky7 Unest. cds. by surname. Bks. Occ. add.
M12 4000 cds. by surname. Mss., etc. Freq. add.
M12 27,000 cds. by surname. Bks. & per. Greenlaw index. Freq. add.
M12 22,500 cds. by place. Bks., per. & pams. State index. Freq. add.
M12 17,500 cds. by surname. Bks., pams., charts, newsp., mss., etc. Cur. add.
M16-ref 1260 cds. by surname & auth. Family hist., esp. New England. Occ. add.
M19 (1) 1350 cds. by state & town. Bks. & per. Vital records index, largely New England. Freq. add. Per. indexed: *American historical record,* v. 1-2, 1872–1873; *American historical register,* v. 1-4, 1894–1896; *Ancestor* (English), v. 1-12, 1902–1905; *Bangor historical magazine,* v. 1-9, 1885–1895; *The Colonial,* v. 1-5, 1913–1917; *Connecticut quarterly,* v. 1-12, 1895–1908; *Essex antiquarian,* v. 1-13, 1897–1909; *Essex co. historical & genealogical register,* v. 1-2, 1894–1895; *Essex institute bulletin,* v. 1-30, 1869–1898; *Essex institute historical collections,* v. 1, 1859–date; *Genealogical advertiser,* v. 1-4, 1898–1901; *Genealogical magazine,* v. 1-4, #2, 1905–1917; *Genealogical quarterly magazine,* v. 1-5, 1900–1905; *Genealogy,* v. 1, 1912–1930; *Grafton magazine,* v. 1-2, 1908–1910; *Granite monthly,* v. 1-6, 1877–1930; *Granite state magazine,* v. 1-7, 1906–1914; *Gulf states historical magazine,* v. 1-2, 1902–1904; *Heraldic journal,* v. 1-4, 1865–1868; *Journal of American history,* v. 1-13, 1907–1919; *Magazine of American history,* v. 1-8, 1877–1892; *Magazine of history,* v. 1-6, 1905–1919; *Magazine of history, extra nos.,* v. 1, 1907–date; *Magazine of New England History,* v. 1-3, 1891–1893; *Maine historical and genealogical recorder,* v. 1-9, 1884–1898; *Massachusetts magazine,* v. 1-10, 1908–1917, v. 11, no. 1, 1918; *Mayflower descendant,* v. 1, 1899–date; *New England family history,* v. 2-4, 1908–1912; *New England historic and genealogical society register,* v. 1, 1847–date; *New England quarterly,* v. 1, 1928–date; *New Hampshire genealogical record,* v. 1-7, 1903–1910; *New York genealogical and biographical record,* v. 35, 1904–date; *Old Eliot,* v. 1-9, 1897–1909; *Old time New England,* v. 11, 1920–date; *Pilgrim notes and queries,* v.

1-5, 1913-1917; *Putnam's historical magazine,* v. 1-7, 1892-1899; *Society for the preservation of New England antiquities Bulletin,* v. 1-10, 1910-1919.

M19 (2) 2800 cds. by name of town Bks., town hist. Freq. add.

M19 (3) 2750 cds. by family. Gen. bks. & per. Freq. add.

M27-ref (1) 5365 cds. by subj. Per., family hist., etc. not indexed by Durrie or Jacobus. Cur. add.

M27-ref (2) 220,000 cds. by name. Newsp. indexed: *Boston (Mass.) Evening transcript.* Cur. add.

Me1 (1) 828p., tpd. shts. by family. Bks. supp. to Munsell's gen. index, 1935. Cur. add.

Me1 (2) 150p., tpd. shts. by family. Gen. Freq. add.

Mi6-hist 176,600 cds. by family name. Bks., per., newsp. mss. & tpd. transcripts. Freq. add.

Mn21-ref 14,000 cds. by family name. Bks. & pams. Q. add.

Mo3-ref 2000 cds. by family name. Bks., per., & newsp. Freq. add.

Mo13-ref 12,000 cds. by name, place & subj. Bks. & per. Freq. add.

Ms4 2640 cds. by subj. Per., pams. & newsp. Freq. add.

N10-gen Several thousand cds. by family name. Newsp. indexed: *Boston (Mass.) Evening transcript,* 1904-date. Wkly. add.

N10-gen Several thousand cds. by family name. Bks., per., & newsp. Freq. add.

N10-gen Several thousand cds. by family name. Newsp. indexed: *Hartford (Conn.) times,* 1909-1911, 1936-date. Wkly. add.

N20 (1) 13,000 cds. by name. Newsp. indexed: *Boston (Mass.) Evening transcript,* 1927-date. Cur. add.

N20 (2) 8580 cds. by name. Loc. newsp. before 1870. Infreq. add.

N54 25,000 cds. by name. Gen., hist., per. & mss. Freq. add.

Nb8 69,500 cds. by subj. Bks. & per. Freq. add.

Nj58 500 cds. by subj. Bks. & per. Occ. add.

O16-ref 350,000 cds. by country, state, co. & family. Bks. & per. Cur. add.

O17 1250 cds. by name. Newsp. indexed: *Centinel of the Northwestern territory,* 1793-1796; *Liberty Hall,* 1804-; *Western Spy,* 1799-. Per. indexed: *Cist's Cincinnati miscellany,* 1845-1846. Cur. add.

O20-hist 9240 cds. by family name. Family pedigrees, per., & newsp. Occ. add.

O29-ref 100,000 cds. by name. Loc., co. & state hist. & biog. Freq. add.

O56-ref 3000 cds. by family name. Bks. & per. Infreq. add.

T1-gen 2200 cds. by state, family, etc. Bks. Freq. add.

T6-ref 1500 cds. by family name. Bks. & per. Gen. & coats of arms. Freq. add.

U3 225p., tpd. shts. Newsp. indexed: *Boston (Mass.) Evening transcript,* 1934-date. Semi-yrly. add.

W10-ref 9240 cds. by name & place. Newsp. indexed: *Boston (Mass.) Evening transcript,* 1911-1915. Occ. add.

Wa7 60,000 cds. by name. Newsp. indexed: *Boston (Mass.) Evening transcript,* 1919-1929. No add.

Wa10-ref (1) 15,000 cds. by family name. Newsp. indexed: *Boston (Mass.) Evening transcript.* Cur. add.

Wa10-ref (2) ˙8500 cds. by family name & place. Bks. & per. Cur. add.

GENEALOGY—CHESTER Co. (PA.). *See* CHESTER Co. (PA.)—HISTORY P53

GENEALOGY—CONNECTICUT

Ct8 300,000 ent., tpd. vol. & cds. by name of town & pers. Vital records of Conn. towns from beginning to 1850 (except for those printed.) No add.

Ct8 22,500 ent., tpd. shts. by name. Vital statistics from original sources —Bibles, acct. bks., diaries, etc. Occ. add.

Ct8 537,500 ent., tpd. shts. by name of pers. & town. Vital statistics from records of churches. Freq. add.

Ct8 974,587 cds. by name. Newsp. Birth, marriage & death notices in Conn. newsp., 1755-1866. Occ. add.

GENEALOGY—FREEPORT (ILL.)
I44-gen   Unest. ent., tpd. shts. Newsp. indexed: *Hartford (Conn.) Times,* 1935–1940. Yrly. add.

GENEALOGY—INDIANA
In35-gen   65 ent., tpd. shts. by name. Ind. territory Acts of assembly, 1810. No add.

GENEALOGY—JAMAICA (N.Y.)
N22-L.I.   31p., tpd. shts. by name. Subscription lists, petitions, lists of members, etc., 1835–1897. Jamaica residents. No add.

GENEALOGY—KENTUCKY. *See also* HARDIN FAMILY (KY.)
Ky14   7260 cds. by name of family, or indiv. Bks., newsp. Occ. add.

GENEALOGY—LOGAN CO. (KY.). *See* LOGAN CO. (KY.) **Ky2**

GENEALOGY—LONG ISLAND (N.Y.)
N22-L.I.   165 notebks. by name of head of family. Records of L.I. families. Occ. add.
N22-L.I.   10,000 cds. by name of place. Bks., newsp. & transcripts. Cur. add.

GENEALOGY—MAHONING VALLEY
O61-ref   Unest. cds. by surname. 76 original notebks. Baldwin mss. records, cem. inscriptions, names of early settlers of Mahoning & neighboring cos. of Ohio & Pa. No add.

GENEALOGY—MARYLAND
Md4   5280 cds. by name of family. Bks., etc. Maryland families. Freq. add.

GENEALOGY—NEW JERSEY
Nj36   282p., tpd. shts. by family name. Bk. indexed: John Littell, *Family records.* No add.
Nj46 (1)   80,000 cds. by name. Morris and Essex co. families.
Nj46 (2)   200p., tpd. shts. by name of person. Bk. indexed: James P. Snell, *History of Hunterdon & Somerset county.* No add.

GENEALOGY—NEW YORK (STATE)
D3   47v., tpd. & bd. by name of place. N.Y. Bible records. Yrly. add.

GENEALOGY—PENNSYLVANIA
In22-gen   300 cds. by subj. & co. Pa. arch. ser. 1-6, 185, 1914. No add.

GENEALOGY—QUEEN'S CO. (N.Y.). *See* QUEENS CO. (N.Y.)—HISTORY
N22-L.I. (2)

GENEALOGY—VINCENNES (IND.)
In22-gen   66p., 4950 ent. by surname. St. Xavier parish records, 1749–1838. Index by Detroit pub. lib., exchange. No add.

GENEALOGY—VIRGINIA. *See also* LEE FAMILY (VA.)
Ky7 (1)   Unest. ent., tpd. shts. by name. Bk. indexed: Louise P. Dubillet, *Some prominent Virginians.* 4v. No add.
Ky7 (2)   Unest. ent., tpd. shts. by name. Bk. indexed: Philip Slaughter, *A History of Bristol parish, Virginia.* No add.
V9   9,576 ent., tpd. shts. by name. Newsp. No add.

GENEALOGY—WILKES-BARRE (PA.)
P54-ref   40 cds. by subj. Bk. indexed: Oscar J. Harvey, *A History of Wilkes-Barre, Luzerne co., Pa.* No add.

GENEALOGY—WILLIAMSON CO. (ILL.)
I55   500 ent., by surname. Bks., etc. Freq. add.

GENEALOGY MAGAZINE. *In* GENEALOGY
M19 (1)

GENERAL HISTORY OF THE BAPTIST DENOMINATION IN AMERICA (bk.). *In* BAPTISTS   **P7 (2)**

GENESEE CO. (MICH.)—AUTHORS. *See* AUTHORS—GENESEE CO. (MICH).
Mi11-ref

GENEVA COLLEGE—PUBLICATIONS
P4   Unest. cds. by auth., subj. & t. Yrly. add.

GENITO-URINARY ORGANS
Nj61   35 cds. by subj. Bks. & per. Infreq. add.

GEOGRAPHICAL NAMES. *See* NAMES, GEOGRAPHICAL

GEOGRAPHICAL REVIEW. *In* SOUTHWEST   **Nm2**

GEOGRAPHY
De1   100 cds. by subj. Travel, com., vegetation & other geog. subj. Occ. add.

Md2-hist 500 cds. by country or loc. Bks. Occ. add.
Vt3 1000 cds. by subj. Per. Occ. add.

Geography—Dictionaries. *See* Names, Geographical

Geography—Study and Teaching
C11 Unest. cds. by auth. & subj. Bks., per. & pams. Cur. add.

Geography—United States
Mi29 7000 cds. by name. Freq. add.

Geography of Missouri (bk.). *In* St. Louis (Mo.) Mo13-Soul.

Geology. *See also* Princeton University—Theses, Senior—Geology
N35-ref. sci 33,315 ent., tpd. shts. by auth. & subj. Pub. of off. geol. surveys of most states. Cur. add.
Vt43 250 cds. by subj. Bks., per., pams. & govt. doc. Cur. add.

Geology—Canada. *See* Canada. Bureau of Mines—Publications

Geology—Colorado. *See also* Colorado. Geological Survey Bulletin
Co9 1764 ent., tpd. shts. by auth. & subj. Bks., per. & maps. Infreq. add.

Geology—Glossaries
N35-ref. sci 5000 cds. by term. Text & ref. bks. In proc.

Geology—Illinois. *See* Illinois. Geological Survey Bulletin

Geology—Indiana. *See* Indiana. Geological Survey

Geology—Maine
Me1 400 cds. by subj. Govt. doc. Daily add.

Geology—Ohio
O56-tech 500 cds. by subj. Gov. doc. Infreq. add.

Geology—Pennsylvania
P39-tech 2500 cds. by auth. & subj. Bks., per. & proc. Freq. add.

Geology—Washington (State)
Wa11-ref 2875 cds. by auth. & subj. Bks., per. & doc. Freq. add.

Geology, Military
Nj60-Guy. 115 ent., tpd. shts. by auth. Bks., per. & pams. Occ. add.

Geology, Petroleum. *See* Petroleum Geology

Georgetown University—Essays
D5 545 cds. by auth. & subj. Senior essays. Yrly. add.

Georgia
G8 2100 cds. by auth. Bks. & pams. Occ. add.
G18 1000 cds. by class. Bks. by Georgians or about Ga. Cur. add.
G18 500 ent. by subj. Newsp. & pams. Freq. add.

Georgia—Authors. *See* Authors—Georgia

Georgia—Bibliography—Imprints
G14 1500 cds. by place of pub. Freq. add.

Georgia—Bibliography—Prices
G17 2000 cds. by auth. Dealers' cat. Freq. add.

Georgia—Biography
G4 15,000 cds. by name. Bks., per. & newsp. Cur. add.
G17 5000 cds. by name. Bks. Infreq. add.

Georgia—Counties—History
G6 40 ent., tpd. shts. by name of co. Co. hist. Infreq. add.

Georgia—Documents
G8 70p., tpd. shts. by auth. State doc. comp. by Ella May Thorton. No add.

Georgia—History
G2 Unest. ent., tpd. shts., bd. Bk. indexed: Allen D. Candler, *Colonial records of Georgia*, v. 1-19, 21-26. No add.

Georgia—Law. *See* Law—Georgia

Georgia—Libraries. *See* Libraries—Georgia; Library Architecture—Georgia

Georgia—Library Boards. *See* Library Boards—Georgia

Georgia—Maps. *See* Maps—Georgia

Georgia—Pictures. *See* Pictures—Georgia

Georgia—Societies and Clubs
G4-circ 20 cds. by name of city. No add.
G4-ref 2000 cds. by subj. & t. Cur. add.

GEORGIA. SUPREME COURT—BIOGRAPHY
G8   100 ent., tpd. shts. by name. Memorials in Ga. and Ga. Appeals repts. Cur. add.

GEORGIA UNIVERSITY—PUBLICATIONS
G2   Unest. cds. by subj. Bks., per., & pams. In proc.

GEORGIA UNIVERSITY—PUBLICATIONS, ALUMNI
G2   Unest. cds. by name. In proc.

GEORGIA BAR ASSOCIATION—SPEECHES, ADDRESSES, ETC.
G8   100 ent., tpd. shts. by subj. Addresses, pa. & memorials, Ga. Bar assoc. Occ. add.

GEORGIA BUILDER (per.)
G14   1931–1937. Cds. by subj. No add.

GEORGIAN STORIES (bk.). *In* SHORT STORIES **Tx12**

GERMAN BAPTISTS. *See* BAPTISTS

GERMAN LANGUAGE. *See* List of Bibliographies, APPENDIX I

GERMAN LITERATURE. *See* List of Bibliographies, APPENDIX I

GERMAN POETRY
O16-ref   28,000 cds. by auth. & t. Bks. No add.
W16   15,000 cds. by t. Bks. Infreq. add.

GHOSTS (bk.). *In* SHORT STORIES **Tx12**

GILPIN CO. (COL.)—MINING AND METALLURGY. *See* MINING AND METALLURGY—GILPIN CO. (COL.)

GLANDS, DUCTLESS. *See* List of Bibliographies, APPENDIX I

GLASS
O56-tech   6000 cds. by subj. Per. not indexed. Occ. add.

GLENDALE (CALIF.)
C18-ref   50 cds. by subj. Cur. add.

GLENDALE (CALIF.)—OFFICIALS AND EMPLOYEES
C18-ref   25 cds. by t. Glendale off. of non-loc. assoc. Cur. add.

GLENDALE (CALIF.)—SOCIETIES AND CLUBS
C18-ref   375 cds. by t. Cur. add.

GLENDALE (CALIF.) NEWSPRESS
C18-per   Newsp., to 1927. Occ. add.

GLOSSARIES. *See also* Names of subj., subdiv. GLOSSARIES
C3a   75 cds. by subj. Bks. & per. Occ. add.
Ct2-tech   997 cds. by subj. Tech., sci. & bus. Cur. add.
Md2-ind   240 cds. by subj. Bks., per., doc. & pams. Occ. add.
Mo13-sci   365 cds. by subj. Bks., per., pams. & doc. Glossaries & dict. on sci. & tech. subj. In proc.
N46-lit   100 cds. by subj. Bks. Occ. add.
N46-sci   100 cds. by subj. Bks. Infreq. add.
P39-tech   280 cds. by subj. Bks. & per. Freq. add.
Wa10-tech   315 cds. by subj. Bks. & per. Occ. add.
Wa11-ref   400 cds. by subj. Bks. & per. Continued by Wayne Campbell, Col. state teacher's coll. Greeley, Col.
Wa14-ref   30 cds. by subj. Bks. & per. Freq. add.

GODEY'S MAGAZINE. *In* SONGS **Mo13-art**

GOLD
Md2-ind   400 ent., tpd. shts. by subj. Bks., per. & doc. Infreq. add.

GOLDEN BOOK MAGAZINE. *In* PLAYS **I43-ref**

GOLDONI, CARLO—WORKS
O20-Alta   1320 cds. by t. Bks. Infreq. add.

GOOD STORIES (bk.). *In* SHORT STORIES **Tx12**

GOSPEL HERALD (per.). *In* MENNONITES—BIOGRAPHY **In13**; MENNONITES—HISTORY **In13**

GOUDY, F. W. *See* PRINTING **N45b**

GOVERNMENT DOCUMENTS. *See also* ENTOMOLOGY; MUSCLE SHOALS—ALABAMA; PENSIONS, MILITARY; SOIL SURVEYS; List of Bibliographies, APPENDIX I; Names of govt. pub., inc. per.
Ar5   5000 cds. by subj. Freq. add.
Co4   2995 cds. by name of dept. Infreq. add.
D10   1099 cds. by cong. Congress. doc., hearings & acts. Occ. add.
D31   2000 cds. by t. Per. & series. Mo. add.

D31 5000 cds. by auth. & subj. for ea. sess. of cong. Doc. & repts. for cong. Daily add.
H3-ref 800 cds. by subj. Agric. doc., chiefly. Occ. add.
Ia18-ad 1500 cds. by govt. division. Cur. add.
In23-ref 19,800 cds. by subj. Freq. add.
M10 Unest. cds. by dept. Freq. add.
Mi13-ref 5600 cds. by subj. Cur. add.
Mi20 1700 cds. by subj. Freq. add.
Mi29 2000 cds. by dept. Freq. add.
N46-hist 1320 cds. by t. Occ. add.
Nb14-ref 1500 cds. by subj. Freq. add.
O20-ref 2640 cds. by ser. no. Cur. add.
O32-ref 8000 cds. by subj. Freq. add.
O36-v.f. 1200 cds. by auth., t. & subj. Cur. add.
O56-ref 4500 cds. by dept. Freq. add.
U1 2575 cds. by dept. & bus. Freq. add.
W2 20,000 cds. by t. Cur. add.

GOVERNMENT DOCUMENTS, MUNICIPAL
M10 Unest. cds. by place. Bks. & pams. Freq. add.

GOVERNMENT DOCUMENTS, STATE. *See also* List of Bibliographies, APPENDIX I
M10 Unest. cds. by state. Freq. add.
Mo3-doc 1000 cds. by subj. Occ. add.

GOVERNMENT INVESTIGATIONS
N35-ref. econ 450 cds. by popular name of committee & name of chmn. N.Y. state & U.S. govt. rpts. Cur. add.

GOVERNMENT OWNERSHIP
Nj5 1000 cds. by subj. Bks., per. & pams. Freq. add.

GRADE TEACHER (per.). *In* CHILDREN'S PLAYS **H2**; PERIODICALS **O20-Jeff.**

GRAFTON MAGAZINE OF HISTORY AND GENEALOGY. *In* GENEALOGY **M19 (1)**

GRAND COULÉE
Wa11-ref 250 cds. by auth. Bks. doc. & per. Occ. add.

GRAND RAPIDS (MICH.)
Mi13-Mich. Unest. ent. Newsp., etc. Mo. add.

GRAND RAPIDS (MICH.)—BIOGRAPHY
Mi13-Mich. 8580 ent. Newsp., etc. Daily add.

GRAND RAPIDS (MICH.)—INDUSTRIES
Mi13-Mich. Unest. ent. Newsp., etc. Mo. add.

GRANITE STATE MAGAZINE. *In* GENEALOGY **M19 (1)**
Nh1 v. 1, 1877–1878—v. 63, 1930. Cds. by auth. & subj. Occ. add.
Nh2 v. 35-63, 1903–1930. Tpd. shts. by auth. & subj. Copied from N.H. hist. soc. index. No add.

GREAT BRITAIN—DOCUMENTS
Ca3 25,000 cds. by auth., subj. & t. Doc. pub. by Canadian provinces, Canada, G.B. (command papers) & selected Australian, New Zealand & U.S. doc. Daily add.

GREAT BRITAIN—HISTORY—ELIZABETH. *See* SHAKESPEARE, WILLIAM—CONTEMPORARY ENGLAND; List of Bibliographies, APPENDIX I

GREAT EVENTS BY FAMOUS HISTORIANS (bk.). *In* HISTORY **N48 (2)**

GREAT LAKES
N8-ref 7260 cds. by subj. Bks., per., speeches, legends, poetry & pic. Freq. add.
O20-ref 1320 cds. by subj. Bks. & per. Infreq. add.

GREAT MEN AND FAMOUS WOMEN (bk.). *In* BIOGRAPHY **P40**

GREAT PICTURES AND THEIR STORIES (bk.). *In* ART—STUDY AND TEACHING **Mi6-Monn., Mi6-Walk., Wa13-j.**

GREATER INDIANAPOLIS (bk.). *In* INDIANAPOLIS (IND.) **In23-ref**

GREECE—CULTURE
N45b 2700 cds. class. & by auth. Bks. & pams. Greek philology & archaeol. No add.

GREEK LITERATURE
Ky16 15,000 cds. by subj. Bks. & per. Freq. add.

GREEN BAY HISTORICAL BULLETIN. *In* WISCONSIN—HISTORY **W19**

GREENSBOROUGH (N.C.) PATRIOT (newsp.) *In* GUILFORD CO. (N.C.)—REGISTERS OF BIRTHS, ETC. **Nc3**

GREENWICH (CONN.) TIME (newsp.) **Ct5** 1877–date. Cds. by subj. Wkly. add.

GREETING CARDS
M27-art 500 cds. by t. & country. Bks. & octavo mus. Christmas & Easter cds. Infreq. add.
O20-lit 2640 cds. by subj. Cds. kept for illus. Christmas, anniv., babies, birthday, misc. Freq. add.

GRIEG, EDVARD HAGERUP—WORKS
Mn15-mus 31 cds. by t. Bk. indexed: Edvard H. Grieg, *Klavierwerke*. No add.

GRINNELL COLLEGE
Ia13 8000 cds. by subj. & auth. Bks., per. & pams. Occ. add.

GRINSTEAD'S GRAPHIC (per.)
Tx29-ref v. 1-5, 1921–1925. Cds. by auth., t. & subj. No add.

GRIZZLY BEAR (per.). *See also* CALIFORNIA —HISTORY **C43-ref**
C7 v. 4–71, 1909–1939. Cds. by subj. Supp. to print. index. Occ. add.
C49-art v. 36, 1924–date. Cds. by subj. Supp. to print. index. Cur. add.

GUEST, EDGAR A.—WORKS
G4-ref 600 ent., tpd. shts., bd. by 1st line. Coll. verse. No add.
I13-ref 1900 cds. by t. & 1st line. Bks. & per. Occ. add.
Ky15-ref 2517 cds. by t. Bks. No add.
Md2-lit 3960 cds. by t., 1st & last lines. Poetry. No add.
Mi6-ref 4500 ent., cds. & tpd. shts. by t. & 1st line. Bks. & newsp. Freq. add.
Mi11-ref 3600 ent., tpd. shts. by t. Newsp. indexed: *Detroit (Mich.) Free press*. Supp. to Granger. Daily add.
N46-lit 1000 cds. by t. Bks. & newsp. No add.
Nj11-ref 1980 cds. by t. Bks., per. & newsp. Freq. add.
O20-lit 108p., tpd. shts. by t. & 1st line. Poetry. Occ. add.
Wa10-ref 1300 ent., tpd. shts. by t. Bks. No add.

GUILFORD CO. (N.C.)—REGISTERS OF BIRTHS, ETC.
Nc3 4000 cds. by name of pers. Newsp. indexed: *Greensborough (N.C.) patriot*, 1826–1899. Infreq. add.

GUINEY, LOUISE IMOGEN—WORKS
I13-ref 300 cds. by t. & 1st line. Bks. & per. Infreq. add.

GULF STATES HISTORICAL MAGAZINE. *In* GENEALOGY **M19 (1)**

GUNNISON CO. (COL.)—NEWSPAPERS
Co10 1650 cds. by subj. Newsp., 1882–1905. No add.

GYMNASTICS. *See* SPORTS AND ATHLETIC GAMES

HACKENSACK (N.J.)—SOCIETIES AND CLUBS
Nj21 165 cds. by name. Freq. add.

HALLOWE'EN
Mn11 Unest. ent., tpd. shts. by subj. Bks. & per. Freq. add.
P6 200 ent., tpd. shts. by topic. Bks. Infreq. add.

HAMILTON CO. (IA.)—EUROPEAN WAR, 1914–1918. *See* EUROPEAN WAR, 1914–1918—HAMILTON CO. (IA.)

HAMILTON COLLEGE—PUBLICATIONS, ALUMNI
N12 1500 cds. by auth. & t. Bks. & pams. Cur. add.

HANDBOOK SERIES. *In* DEBATES **N7**

HANDBUCH DER BIOLOGISCHEN ARBEITSMETHODEN (bk.). *In* BIOLOGY **Ia14-med**

HANDICRAFTS
C27-art 800 cds. by subj. Bks. & per. Cur. add.
Ca5-circ 800 cds. by subj. Bks. Cur. add.
Md2-ind 880 cds. by subj. Bks. & per. Supp. to Lovell & Hall index. Freq. add.
Mi6-art 1320 cds. by subj. Bks. & per. Freq. add.
Mi27-ref 375 cds. by subj. Per. indexed: *Model craftsman, 1938–date; Popular homecraft, 1938–date*. Supp. to Lovell & Hall index. Mo. add.
Mn14-tech 5280 cds. by subj. Bks. & per. Supp. to Lovell & Hall index. Cur. add.

O20-art 862 cds. by subj. Bks. & per. Knitting, crocheting & handicraft. Freq. add.
O20-sci 3200 cds. by subj. Bks., per. & pams. Cur. add.
O29-ref 1870 cds. by subj. Bks. & per. Occ. add.
O56-tech 8000 cds. by subj. Bks. & per. Projects in wood, metal, plastics, etc. Cur. add.

HANDICRAFTS, JUVENILE
O20-j 200 cds. by subj. Bks. & per. Supp. to Lovell & Hall index. Cur. add.
O20-Tem. 300 cds. by subj. Bks. No add.

HARBORS. See also List of Bibliographies, APPENDIX I
C32-soc 300 cds. by name of harbor. Bks., per., etc. Infreq. add.

HARBORS—PHOTOGRAPHS
V5 334 cds. by name. Phot. of ports & harbors. Freq. add.

HARDIN FAMILY (KY.)
Ky7 Unest. ent., tpd. shts. by name. Gen. No add.

HARLOW'S WEEKLY
Ok4-ref v. 13-23, 1917–1940. Cds. by auth., subj. & t. Cur. add.

HARPER'S BAZAAR (per.). In COSTUME G4-ref

HARRISON, WILLIAM HENRY—CORRESPONDENCE, REMINISCENCES, ETC.
In24 325 cds., chron. Letters, not inc. in Esarey ed. Messages and letters, v. 1. Bks., mss., etc. Freq. add.

HART CO. (KY.)—HISTORY
Ky7 Unest. cds. by name. Newsp. No add.

HARTE, FRANCIS BRET—WORKS
In35 218 ent., tpd. shts. by t. Bks. Occ. add.

HARTFORD (CONN.) TIMES (newsp.). In GENEALOGY In22-gen (1), N10-gen (3); GENEALOGY—FREEPORT (ILL.) I44-gen

HARVARD CLASSICS (bk.). In LITERATURE N46-lit (1)

HAVERHILL (MASS.)
M19 15,500 cds. by subj. Bks., per., newsp. & pams. Freq. add.

HAWAII. See List of Bibliographies, APPENDIX I

HAWAII—LAW. See LAW—HAWAII

HAWAII—NEWSPAPERS
H3-Haw. 19,500 cds. by subj. Loc. newsp. Daily add.

HAWAII—PERIODICALS
H3-Haw. 3000 cds. by auth. & subj. Loc. per. Freq. add.

HAWAII—UNION LISTS. See List of Bibraphies, APPENDIX I

HAWAIIAN ANNUAL
H1 1875–date. Cds. by subj. Yrly. add.

HEADLINE BOOKS. In PAMPHLETS O59, U1

HEALTH. See HYGIENE; PUBLIC HEALTH; PERSONALITY C71-circ

HEALTH EDUCATION. See List of Bibliographies, APPENDIX I

HEARST'S INTERNATIONAL COMBINED WITH COSMOPOLITAN (per.). In SHORT STORIES O56-ref
C69-per v. 1, 1886–date. Cds. by auth. & t. Mo. add.

HEART
Ni61 75 cds. by auth. & t. Bks., per. & pams. Infreq. add.

HEART OF OAK BOOKS (bk.). In READERS AND PRIMERS I6 (1)

HEATING. See AIR CONDITIONING Nj52

HELIUM
Nj54 Unest. cds. by subj. Spec. rpts. Freq. add.

HEMOLYSIS AND HEMOLYSINS
Nj61 60 cds. by auth. & t. Bks., per. & pams. Freq. add.

HENNEPIN CO. (MINN.)—PHOTOGRAPHS
Mn14-Mn. 3500 cds. by subj. Phot. of hist. scenes. No add.

HENRY, O. See PORTER, WILLIAM SYDNEY —WORKS

HENRY E. HUNTINGTON LIBRARY—BURNHAM COLLECTION. See BOOKPLATES C73-ref

HERALD OF TRUTH (per.). In MENNONITES —BIOGRAPHY In13; MENNONITES —HISTORY In13

Heraldic Journal. *In* Genealogy
M19 (1)

Heraldry. *See also* Genealogy   T6-ref
C32-gen   11,880 cds. by subj. Bks. & per. Freq. add.
C49-ref   700 cds. by name. Per. indexed: *Americana.* Q. add.
Co5-gen   5600 cds. by family name, country & state. Bks. & per. Freq. add.
Ct7   1320 cds. by name. Bks. & per. Freq. add.
Ct8   13,000 cds. by family name. Gen. & hist. pub. Freq. add.
Ct12-ref   971 cds. by name. Bks. & per. Occ. add.
F2-ref   1800 cds. by family name. Family hist. Cur. add.
I17   12,000 cds. by family name. Bks., mss., per., & coll. of drawings. Daily add.
I26-gen   40,000 cds. by family name. Bks. & per. Freq. add.
I68-loc. hist   800 cds. by name. Bks. & per. Freq. add.
In23-gen   750 cds. by family name. Per. indexed: *Americana.* Cur. add.
In35-gen   590 ent., tpd. shts. by source. Bks. & per. Cur. add.
Ky7   Unest. cds. by family name. Occ. add.
M27-ref   10,000 cds. by name. Bks. other than bks. on heraldry per. Freq. add.
M32   2200 cds. by name. Bks. & per. Infreq. add.
Mi6-Burt.   4500 cds. by family name & country. Bks. & per. Freq. add.
Mn21-ref   5000 cds. by family name. Bks. & per. Occ. add.
Mo3-ref   2000 cds. by name. Bks., per. & newsp. Black & white, color indicated. Infreq. add.
Mo13-ref   30,000 cds. by name. Bks. & per. Freq. add.
N6-ref   84p., tpd. shts. by family name. Bks. & per. Infreq. add.
N10-gen   2000 cds. by family name. Bks. & per. Freq. add.
N35-ref. gen   19,000 cds. by family name. Bks. & per. Colored illus. Cur. add.
N54   20,000 cds. by name. Bks., per. & pams. Freq. add.
N57   3960 cds. by family name. Bks. & per. Freq. add.
O16-ref   3500 cds. by family name. Bks., per. & pams. Mo. add.
O20-hist   49,600 cds. by family name. Bks., per. & newsp. Occ. add.
O56-ref   2000 cds. by family name. Bks. & per. Occ. add.
T3-Mc.   500 cds. by name. Bks. & per. Freq. add.
Wa10-ref   800 cds. by family name. Bks. Infreq. add.

Here Lies (bk.). *In* Short Stories
Tx12

Heredity. *See* Eugenics

Heroes and Heroines (in Literature)
I10-fic   1320 cds. by name of real char. Real char. mentioned in fic. Occ. add.
O20-lit   2640 cds. by name of char. Plays. Char. in old plays. No add.
O56-Locke   73 cds. by subj. Bks. Freq. add.

Heroes and Heroines (in Literature)—Foreign Languages
Mi6-for   15 cds. by lang. & char. Bks. Infreq. add.

Heroes and Heroines (in Literature), Juvenile
O20-Carn.   60 cds. by name. Little children's bks. Cur. add.

Highroads of History (bk.). *In* History, Juvenile   Ca2j

Highways
D23   200,000 cds. by subj. Per., pams., etc. Wkly. add.

Highways—Periodicals
I27   Unest. cds. by t. 50 highway per. Wkly. add.

Hillsborough Co. (Fla.)—History
F5   65 cds. by subj. Per., newsp., etc. Infreq. add.

Histology
Nj61   40 cds. by auth. & t. Bks., per. & pams. Freq. add.

Historic Houses. *See also* Name of loc., subdiv. Historic Houses
N8-tech   900 cds. by name of bldg. Bks. Hist. bldgs. in U.S. Freq. add.

HISTORIC SHEPERDSTOWN (bk.). *In* SHEPERDSTOWN (KY.)—HISTORY **Ky7**

HISTORIC WALKILL AND HUDSON RIVER VALLEYS (bk.). *In* WALKILL RIVER VALLEY (N.Y.) **N58**

HISTORICAL AND INTERESTING PLACES IN ST. LOUIS (bk.). *In* ST. LOUIS (MO.) **Mo13-Soul.**

HISTORICAL AND PHILOSOPHICAL SOCIETY. QUARTERLY
In14 v. 1-18, 1906 1923. Cds. by auth., subj. & t.

HISTORICAL BIOGRAPHY. *See* BIOGRAPHY, HISTORICAL

HISTORICAL COLLECTIONS OF OHIO (bk.). *In* OHIO—HISTORY **O27**

HISTORICAL FICTION. *See* FICTION, HISTORICAL

HISTORICAL MEMOIR OF THE WAR IN WEST AFRICA AND LOUISIANA (bk.). *In* LOUISIANA—HISTORY **L14-ref**

HISTORICAL MEMORIAL PRESBYTERIAN CHURCH, 1765–1895 (bk.). *In* SUCCASUNNA (N.J.)—REGISTERS OF BIRTHS, ETC. **Nj36**

HISTORICAL PORTRAITS. *See* PORTRAITS, HISTORICAL

HISTORICAL REVIEW OF BERKS CO. (per.). *In* BERKS Co. (PA.)—HISTORY **P45-ref**

HISTORICAL SOUVENIR OF WILLIAMSON CO., ILLINOIS (bk.). *In* WILLIAMSON CO. (ILL.)—HISTORY **I55 (3)**

HISTORY. *See also* Names of loc., subdiv. HISTORY
C41 1200 cds. by subj. Bks. Oakland course of study. Freq. add.
Ky3 1196 ent., 23p., tpd. shts. by subj. Bks. Freq. add.
Md2-hist 1500 cds. by subj. Bks., per. & pams. Infreq. add.
N48 (1) 200 cds. by subj. Bk. indexed: Ainsworth Rand Spofford, *Library of historic characters and famous events of all nations and all ages*, 12v. No add.
N48 (2) 500 cds. by subj. Bk. indexed: Charles Francis Horne, *The Great events of famous historians*, 22v. No add.
Nb10 175 cds. by t. & subj. Bks. Freq. add.

HISTORY—BIOGRAPHY. *See* BIOGRAPHY, HISTORICAL

HISTORY—FICTION. *See* FICTION, HISTORICAL

HISTORY, JUVENILE
Ca2-j 17p., tpd. shts. by subj. Bk. Indexed: *Highroads of history*, 12v. No add.
Nj27-j 100 cds. by t. Bks. Supp. hist. stories. Infreq. add.
O20-class 1320 cds., chron. Bks. Freq. add.

HISTORY, UNIVERSAL. *See also* List of Bibliographies, APPENDIX I
Ar3 300 cds. by auth. & unit. Bks. Cur. add.

HISTORY OF ALAMEDA COUNTY, CALIFORNIA (1) MERRITT (2) WOOD (bk.). *In* ALAMEDA CO. (CALIF.)—HISTORY **C43-ref**

HISTORY OF ALLEGHENY COUNTY (bk.). *In* ALLEGHENY CO. (PA.)—HISTORY **P39-ref. Pa.**

HISTORY OF BOURBON, SCOTT, NICHOLAS, AND HARRISON COUNTIES (bk.). *In* KENTUCKY—BIOGRAPHY **Ky7 (1)**

A HISTORY OF BRISTOL PARISH (bk.). *In* GENEALOGY—VIRGINIA **Ky7 (2)**

HISTORY OF FRANKLIN CO., KENTUCKY (bk.). *In* FRANKLIN CO. (KY.)— HISTORY **Ky7**

HISTORY OF GERMAN BAPTIST BRETHREN (bk.). *In* BAPTISTS **P19**

HISTORY OF GREENE AND SULLIVAN COUNTIES, INDIANA (bk.). *In* INDIANA— BIOGRAPHY **In35 (1)**

HISTORY OF HUNTERDON AND SOMERSET COUNTIES, N.J. (bk.). *In* GENEALOGY—NEW JERSEY **Nj46 (2)**

HISTORY OF KENTUCKY (bk.). *In* KENTUCKY—HISTORY **Ky7 (1)**; U.S. — HISTORY — REVOLUTION — KENTUCKY **In35-gen**

HISTORY OF KNOX AND DAVIES COUNTIES, INDIANA (bk.). *In* INDIANA **In37-gen;** INDIANA—BIOGRAPHY **In35 (2)**

HISTORY OF METHODISM (bk.). *In* METHODIST CHURCH **G14**

History of Missouri (bk.). *In* St. Louis (Mo.) **Mo13-Soul.**

History of Missouri for High Schools (bk.). *In* St. Louis (Mo.) **Mo13-Soul.**

History of Newark (bk.). *In* Newark (N.J.)—History **Nj50-circ** (1)

History of St. Louis City and County (bk.). *In* St. Louis (Mo.) **Mo13-Soul.**

History of Shelby County, Kentucky (bk.). *In* Shelby Co. (Ky.)—History **Ky7**

History of Ten Baptist Churches (bk.). *In* Baptists **Ky7**

History of Tennessee (bk.). *In* Tennessee—History **T3-Mc.** (2)

History of the Arkansas Valley (bk.). *In* Arkansas Valley (Col.)—History **Co3**

History of the Church (bk.). *In* Mormons and Mormonism **U3** (1)

History of the Development of Missouri (bk.). *In* St. Louis (Mo.) **Mo13-Soul.**

History of the Feminine Costume of the World (bk.). *In* Costume **Wa10-art** (1)

History of the Frankfort Cemetery (bk.). *In* Frankfort (Ky.)—Cemetery Records **Ky7**

History of the State of Washington (bk.). *In* Washington (State)—History **Wa7**

History of Vigo and Parke Counties (bk.). *In* Indiana—Biography **In35** (2)

History of Wilkes-Barre (bk.). *In* Genealogy—Wilkes-Barre (Pa.) **P54-ref**

History of Williamson Co., Illinois (bk.). *In* Williamson Co. (Ill.)—History **I55** (2)

History Teachers Bulletin
Tx8 v. 4, 9, 10, 12, 13, 14, 1919, 1921, 1922, 1925, 1927. Cds. by auth., t. & subj. No add.

Hobbies. *See also* Names of hobbies, i.e. Handicrafts

Mi6-par 898 ent., tpd. shts. by subj. Bks. & pams. Cur. add.
Mi16 79 ent., tpd. shts. by subj. Bks. Infreq. add.
Nj25-ref 283 ent. Newsp. Occ. add.
Wa8a 439 ent., tpd. shts. by hobby. Bks., per., pams. & newsp. Cur. add.

Hobbies (per.)
C62-ref 500 cds. by subj. Cur. add.

Hobby Horse (per.). *In* Pictures **I43-ref** (2)

Hoboken (N.J.)—History
Nj25-ref 32 cds. by subj. Newsp. Freq. add.

Hoboken (N.J.)—Pictures. *See* Pictures—Hoboken (N.J.)

Hoboken (N.J.) Jersey Observer (newsp.). *In* New Jersey **Nj68**

Holding Companies—Railroads. *See* Railroads—Holding Companies

Holidays. *See also* Birthdays; Children's Literature—Holidays; Plays, Holiday; Poetry, Holiday; Songs, Holiday; Names of individual holidays, i.e. Christmas; Readings and Recitations
C32-for 300 cds. by t. of holiday & country. Bks. & pams. Stories, poems, songs, for. observance. Freq. add.
C32-lit 1900 cds. by holiday & auth. Plays, poetry, recit., etc.
C51 3000 ent., tpd. shts. by auth. & class. Bks. & newsp. Freq. add.
Co5-circ 1000 cds. by subj. Fic., plays, poetry, games, recit., hist. Infreq. add.
Co11 40 cds. by subj. Bks., per. & newsp. Occ. add.
Ct11 612 cds. by subj. Bks. Freq. add.
G4-circ 500 ent., tpd. shts. by subj. Bks. Cur. add.
I33 802 cds. by subj. Bks., per. & pams. Freq. add.
I76 350 cds. by subj. Bks., per. & newsp. Mo. add.
Ia1 335 cds. by subj. Bks. Infreq. add.
In6 1350 cds. by subj. Bks. & per. Freq. add.
L14-circ 500 cds. by subj. Bks. Occ. add.

Md2-#6 Unest. cds. by country. Bks., inc. j. Cur. add.
Mi6-circ.o.s. 1150 cds. by subj. Bks. Read., poems, parties, etc. Occ. add.
Mi6-Mont. 650 cds. by subj. Bks. & per. Infreq. add.
Mi6-par 1638 ent., tpd. shts. by day, chron. Bks. & pams. Cur. add.
Mi13-ref Unest. cds. by subj. Bks., per., poetry, & plays. Infreq. add.
Mi28-ref 450 cds. by subj. Bks. Infreq. add.
Mn1 600 cds. by subj. Bks. & per. Mo. add.
Mo13 1700 cds. by subj. Bks. Freq. add.
N8-circ 400 cds. by subj. Bks.
N40 3960 cds. by auth. & t. Bks. & pams. Freq. add.
N54-ref 560 cds. by subj. Bks. Occ. add.
Nj21 900 cds. by subj. Bks. Occ. add.
Nj27-sch 11,200 cds. by subj. Bks. Occ. add.
Nj32 69 ent., tpd. shts. by subj. Bks., per. & pams. Occ. add.
Nj50-educ 5965 cds. by name of holiday. Bks., per., pams. & newsp. Freq. add.
Nj67-ref 1200 cds. by name of holiday. Bks., per. & pams. Freq. add.
O1-read 2640 cds. by name of holiday & type of mat. Bks., etc. Cur. add.
O29-ref 6500 cds. by holiday & type of mat. Bks. Cur. add.
O35 402 cds. by name of holiday. Bks. Freq. add.
O37 400 cds. by name of holiday. Bks. Cur. add.
O56-circ 4000 cds. by subj. Plays, songs, poetry, etc. Cur. add.
Or3 1700 cds. by name of holiday & type of mat. Bks. & per. Cur. add.
Or5-circ 1300 cds. by subj. Bks. No add.
Tx5 Unest. cds. by subj., auth. & t. Bks., pams. & newsp. Spec. day programs. Freq. add.
Tx8 425 cds. by subj. Bks. & per. Freq. add.
V3 574 cds. by subj. Bks., per. & newsp. Freq. add.
W3 870 cds. by subj. Bks., per. & newsp. Cur. add.
W16 2500 cds. by class. Prose, poetry, drama, essays, speeches, etc. Cur. add.
W20-ad 1650 cds. by subj. Bks. & per. Occ. add.
Wa13-ref 1500 cds. by holiday & subj. under ea. Bks. & per. Freq. add.
Wa14-ref 500 ent., tpd. shts. by name of holiday & type of mat. Bks., pams. & per. Infreq. add.

HOLIDAYS—FOREIGN LANGUAGES
Mi6-for 125 cds. by subj. & lang. Bks., pic. & newsp. Freq. add.

HOLLAND (MICH.)
Mi17 197 cds. by subj. Bks., pams. & newsp. Freq. add.

HOLLAND (MICH.)—TULIP TIME
Mi17 82 cds. by subj. Bks., pams. & newsp. Freq. add.

HOLLAND'S MAGAZINE
Tx10-ref v. 45, 1926–date. Cds. by auth., subj. & t. Cur. add.
Tx28 v. 37-59, 1918–1940. Cds. by subj. Semi-yrly. add.

HOLLYWOOD BOWL ORCHESTRA PROGRAMS. See SYMPHONY C32-art

HOME ECONOMICS. See also List of Bibliographies, APPENDIX I
D17 29,000 cds. by auth. & subj. Bks., per., bul., etc. Freq. add.
Mn14-tech 500 cds. by subj. Bks. & per. Cur. add.
N24 125 ent., tpd. shts. by subj. Pams. Freq. add.

HOMILETICS. See SERMONS

HOOVER, HERBERT
C48-ref 800 cds. by class. Occ. add.

HOPE, LAURENCE (PSEUD)—WORKS
I13-ref 350 cds. by t. & 1st line. Bks. & per. Infreq. add.

HOPEDALE (MASS.)—HISTORY
M19a 217 cds. by subj. Bks., per. & pams. Infreq. add.

HORMONES
Nj61 40 cds. by auth. & t. Bks., per. & pams. Freq. add.
P30 1400 cds. by subj. & auth. Reprints & per. Freq. add.

HORN BOOK MAGAZINE
In8-j   v. 1-17, 1924–1941. Cds. by name. Art. & auth. & their bks. Cur. add.

HORSES. *See* List of Bibliographies, APPENDIX I

HORTICULTURE
D19   18,000 cds. by state, country, firm names & nursery names. Horticultural trade cats. of U.S. & For. countries. Freq. add.
M8   15,000 cds. by subj. Per. Occ. add.

HORTICULTURE—HISTORY
D18   1100p., tpd. shts. by auth. & t. 16th, 17th & 18th cent. wks. on horticulture. Infreq. add.

HOSPITAL SOCIAL SERVICE (per.)
Mn14-soc   1922–1933. Cds. by auth., subj. & t. Cur. add.

HOSPITALS—MANAGEMENT
Mn24   94 ent., tpd. shts. by subj. Bks., pams. & per. No add. since 1935.

HOUSE BEAUTIFUL (per.). *In* SOUTHWEST Nm2

HOUSE DECORATION. *See* INTERIOR DECORATION

HOUSE ORGANS
Mn15-per   600 cds. by t. & co. Wkly. add.
Mo13-sci   780 cds. by subj. & co. name. Cur. add.
P39-tech   4000 cds. by subj., t. & name of co. Amer. & for. Cur. add.

HOUSE ORGANS—CHICAGO
I13-r.b.   42 cds. by name. Infreq. add.

HOUSING. *See* List of Bibliographies, APPENDIX I

HOWARD, OLIVER OTIS—CORRESPONDENCE, REMINISCENCES, ETC.
Me3   350 cds. by t. catch-word. Letters & addresses. No add.

HOWARD UNIVERSITY—MOORLAND FOUNDATION—BIOGRAPHY
D6   2956 cds. by subj. Bks. & per. Freq. add.

HOWARD UNIVERSITY—MOORLAND FOUNDATION—PUBLICATIONS, FACULTY
D6   2126 cds. by auth. Bks., pams. & per. Freq. add.

HUGUENOTS
Me3   1450 cds. by auth. & subj. Infreq. add.

HUMBOLDT CO. (CALIF.)—HISTORY
C15   27 cds. by auth., t. & subj. Bks. & pams. Infreq. add.

HUMOR. *See* HUMOROUS STORIES; Names of authors of humorous works, i.e. DOOLEY, MR.

HUMOR—FOREIGN LANGUAGES
Mi6-for   200 cds. by subj. & lang. Bks. Freq. add.

HUMOROUS STORIES
C75   71 cds. by auth. Bks. Freq. add.
I13-Hild.   4p., tpd. shts. Bks. Yrly. add.
I46   37 cds. by auth. Bks. Infreq. add.
Mi13-Un.Hi.   100 cds. by auth. & t. Bks. Occ. add.
Mn11   Unest. ent., tpd. shts. by auth. Bks. Freq. add.

HUNGARIAN LANGUAGE
Nj58   100 cds. by auth. & t. Bks. Infreq. add.
O20-Carn.   29,040 cds. by auth., t. & subj. Bks. Cur. add.

HUNTINGTON CO. (PA.)—REGISTERS OF BIRTHS, ETC.
P19   Unest. cds. by name. Newsp., 1830–1900. In proc.

HYDRAULIC ENGINEERING
C66   350 cds. by name of co. or project, chron. by no. of project. Mss. & rpts., James D. Schuyler coll. No add.
Nj52   Unest. cds. by subj. Bks., per. & pams. Freq. add.

HYGEIA (per.). *In* MEDICAL JURISPRUDENCE   Ct9
P39-Wyl.   1936–date. Cds. by subj. Mo. add.

HYGIENE. *See also* List of Bibliographies, APPENDIX I; PERSONALITY   C71-circ
Nj61   80 cds. by auth. & t. Bks., per. & pams.

HYMNS
C32-phil   5280 cds. by auth., t. & 1st line. Bks. Cur. add.
Ct6   500 cds. by 1st line & t. Bks. & per. Occ. add.
In23-art   4000 cds. by t. Bks. Infreq. add.
Mn23-art   5004 cds. by comp. & t. Bks. Cur. add.
N46-educ   660 cds. by name of tune. Bks. Cur. add.
N46-educ   1980 cds. by t. Bks. Cur. add.
Nj62   8000 cds. by auth., subj. & t. Bks. & pams. Infreq. add.
O16-art   4500 cds. by t. Bks. Cur. add.
O20-art   31,068 cds. by t. Bks. Infreq. add.
O29-ref   600 cds. by t. Bks. No add.

ICARIANS
Nb15   500 cds. by auth. Bks. No add.

IDAHO
Id1   200 cds. by subj. Bks., per. & newsp. Freq. add.
Id2   1500 cds. by subj. Bks., per., newsp. & doc. Freq. add.

IDAHO—AUTHORS. *See* AUTHORS—IDAHO

IDAHO UNIVERSITY
Id2   300 cds. by subj. Newsp. Stud. & fac. activities. In proc.

ILLINOIS
I13-ref   1500 cds. by subj. Bks. & per. Occ. add.

ILLINOIS—ARCHITECTURE. *See* ARCHITECTURE—ILLINOIS

ILLINOIS—ART. *See* ART—ILLINOIS

ILLINOIS—ARTISTS. *See* ARTISTS—ILLINOIS

ILLINOIS—BIOGRAPHY
I71-arch   300,000 cds. by soundex system. Names in state arch. before 1850. Freq. add.

ILLINOIS—COUNTIES—HISTORY
I45   Unest. ent., tpd. shts. by co. Hist. Freq. add.
I45   39 ent., tpd. shts. by co. Atlases. Infreq. add.

ILLINOIS—DOCUMENTS. *See also* ILLINOIS—BIOGRAPHY I71-arch
I71-arch   Unest. ent., tpd. shts. by subj. Ill. House & Senate jls. 1812–1859. Mss. jls. for terr. period; print. jls. 1818–; index to bills only 1843–. No add.
I71-arch   2000 cds. by general assembly, by whom & to whom reported. Rpts. & doc. of spec. legisl. rpts. & committees. All Ill. gen. assemblies, 1850–. Occ. add.

ILLINOIS GEOLOGICAL SURVEY BULLETIN
Mo13-sci   v. 1-60. Cds. by subj. In proc.

ILLINOIS—HISTORY
I38   200 cds. by subj. & auth. Bks. & per. Freq. add.
I68-loc. hist   600 cds. by subj. Bks. & per. Freq. add.

ILLINOIS—LANDS. *See* LANDS—ILLINOIS

ILLINOIS—LAW. *See* LAW—ILLINOIS

ILLINOIS—MUSIC. *See* MUSIC—ILLINOIS

ILLINOIS—NEWSPAPERS
I70-newsp   3500 cds. by name. Loc. index of Ill. papers, 1935–date. Cur. add.

ILLINOIS—SCULPTURE. *See* SCULPTURE—ILLINOIS

ILLINOIS UNIVERSITY. AGRICULTURAL EXPERIMENT STATION—PUBLICATIONS
I62   600 cds. by subj. Infreq. add.

ILLUMINATION. *See* LIGHTING

ILLUSTRATED LONDON NEWS (per.). *In* ART, ORIENTAL D9; COSTUME C49-ref; PERIODICALS Wa6

L'ILLUSTRATION (per.). *In* COSTUME C49-ref; PICTURES I7
C7   v. 91-93, 1933–1935. Cds. by subj. No add.
H3-art   v. 80-98, 1922–1940. Cds. by subj. & illus.
Nb15   v. 90-91, 1933–1934. Cds. by subj. No add.

ILLUSTRATION THEATRALE (per.). *In* LA PETITE ILLUSTRATION (per.)   N45b

ILLUSTRATORS. *See also* PICTURES Nd3; List of Bibliographies, APPENDIX I
Ca10-ref   302 cds. by name of illus. & type of illus. Bks. Infreq. add.

N6-ref 75p., tpd. shts. by name of illus. Bks. & per. No add.
N35-ref. print 24,000 cds. by name of illus. Bks. Cur. add.
O20-fic 500 cds. by name of illus. Fiction. Mo. add.

ILLUSTRATORS—CLEVELAND (O.). *See* List of Bibliographies, APPENDIX I

ILLUSTRATORS, CHILDREN'S. *See also* AUTHORS, CHILDREN'S **Ar5, O2;** PICTURES **N28-j**
C46 581 cds. by name. Bks. Cur. add.
C49-j 1408 cds. by name. Bks. Freq. add.
I72-j 150 cds. by name. Bks. Cur. add.
Mn12 999 cds. by name. Bks. Cur. add.
Nj34 850 cds. by name. Bks. Freq. add.
O20-j 275 cds. by name. Bks., per. & pams. Occ. add.
O20-j 2000 cds. by name. J. bks. Freq. add.
O36 150 cds. by name. Bks. Occ. add.
P39-j 3975 cds. by name. Freq. add.
Wa13-j 120 cds. by name. Bks. Cur. add.

IMMIGRANTS
Mn14-Fran. 288 cds. by name, country of birth, for. group. Bks., per. & pams. For.-born Amer. Cur. add.
Nj61 200 cds. by auth. & t. Bks., per., pams. & repts. Freq. add.

IMPRINTS. *See* Name of loc., subdiv. BIBLIOGRAPHY—IMPRINTS

IMPROVEMENT ERA (per.)
U1 v. 1-38, 1898–1935. Tpd. shts. by auth. & subj. No add.
U2-ref v. 1-38, 1898–1935; v. 38, 1935–date. Tpd. shts. by auth., t. & subj. Based on index comp. by Newburn I. Butt, B.Y.U. Cur. add.
U3 v. 1-38, 1898–1935. Tpd. shts. by auth. & subj. Add. every 5 yrs.
U4 v. 1-43, 1897–1937. Tpd. shts. by subj. No add.

INCUNABULA. *See also* List of Bibliographies, APPENDIX I
I26 1794 ent., tpd. shts. by country, chron. Bks. No add. since 1933.

N35-ref. res 1500 cds. by name of printer. Printers & specimens of their works, to 1520. Cur. add.

INDENTURES. *See* MORTGAGES

INDIAN STORIES. *See* INDIANS—STORIES

INDIANA. *See also* List of Bibliographies, APPENDIX I
In12 4p., tpd. shts. by subj. Bks., per. & pams. Calumet region, Gary & Lake co. Infreq. add.
In23-ref 197p., tpd. shts. by subj. Bk. indexed: Jacob P. Dunn, *Indiana and Indianans.* No add.
In28 300 cds. by subj. Bks., per., pams. & state doc. Occ. add.
In37-gen Unest. ent., tpd. shts. by name & subj. Bk. indexed: Goodspeed pub. co., *History of Knox and Davies counties, Indiana.* No add.

INDIANA—AUTHORS. *See* AUTHORS—INDIANA

INDIANA—BIOGRAPHY
In22 Unest. ent., tpd. shts. by name of person & firm. Names of pers. & firms in Ind. co. hist. W.P.A. project.
In22-Ind. 20,300 cds. by name. Bks., per. & newsp. Biog. of pers. with an Ind. connection. Freq. add.
In35 (1) 6850 ent., tpd. shts. by co., Mexican & civil war lists. Bk. indexed: Goodspeed pub. co., *History of Greene and Sullivan counties, Indiana.* No add.
In35 (2) 3400 ent., tpd. shts. by name for ea. co. Bks. indexed: Hiram W. Beckwith, *History of Vigo* and *Parke counties.* No add.
In35 (3) 810 ent., tpd. shts. by co. Bk. indexed: Charles Blanchard, *Counties of Clay and Owen, Indiana.* No add.
In35-gen (1) 350 ent., tpd. shts. by name. Bk. indexed: D. L. Lake & co., *Atlas of Lawrence co., Indiana.* No add.
In35-gen (2) 2800 ent., tpd. shts. by name & co. Bk. indexed: Goodspeed pub. co., *History of Knox and Davies counties, Indiana.* No add.

INDIANA—BRIDGES, COVERED. *See* BRIDGES, COVERED—INDIANA

INDIANA—CENSUS
In22-gen   82,000 cds. by name of pers. Ind. cens. rpts. for 1820 and 1830. No add.
In22-gen   65,000 cds. by surname & co. Mortality records for state & co. for 1850, 1860, 1870 & 1880. In proc.

INDIANA—CITIES AND TOWNS
In22-Ind.   50 cds. by name of town. Acts to vacate towns, 1805-1851. No add.
In22-Ind.   350 cds. by name of town. Incorporation acts rel. to towns, 1805-1851. No add.

INDIANA—COUNTIES—HISTORY
In36   250 cds. by co. & subj. Bks. & per. No add. since 1932.

INDIANA—DOCUMENTS
In20   8000 cds. by name & co. Governor's exec. proc., 1816-1823. No add.
In22-Ind.   500 cds. by subj. Doc. jls. of Ind., 1835-1912. No add.

INDIANS—GENEALOGY. See GENEALOGY—INDIANA

INDIANA. GEOLOGICAL SURVEY
In23-tech   v. 28-40, 1903-1915. 5p., tpd. shts. by subj.

INDIANA—HISTORY
In22-Ind. (1)   56,300 cds. chon., by subj. & name of pers. Calendars of John Tipton, Noah Noble, W. G. and G. W. Ewing mss. coll. Separate calendars. No add.
In22-Ind. (2)   1800 cds. by subj. Bks., per. & newsp. George S. Cottman index. No add.
In22-Ind. (3)   98,450 cds. chron. by dept. Calendar of natl. arch. in diff. depts. in Wash., dealing for most part with Ind. No add.
In22-Ind. (4)   800 cds. by subj. Fugitive inf. on Ind. from various sources. Freq. add.
In23-ref   363p., tpd. shts., mim. & bd. by subj. Hist. of Ind. & Indianapolis. No add.
In24   400 cds. by subj., chron. Hist. sources, esp. reprod. of mss. in Paris (French) arch. Calendar of mat. on French period in Ind. hist. Infreq. add.
In24   1000 cds. by subj. & name. Hist. sources. Freq. add.

In24   300 cds., chron. by mo. & day. Ind. hist. anniv. calendar. Occ. add.
In24a   49 ent., tpd. shts. by subj. Bks. Freq. add.
In37   Unest. cds. by class. Bks. Ind. & Vincennes mat. No add.
In38   1300 cds. by subj. Newsp. Occ. add.

INDIANA—LAW. See LAW—INDIANA

INDIANA—LEGISLATION—MEMBERS
In21   1800 cds. by name. Election returns, legisl. rules, jls. Members of Ind. Gen. assembly, 1907-date. Cur. add.
In22-Ind.   130 p., tpd. shts. by name. Ind. House jls. rules. Names of members of House of repres. of Ind., 1816-1913. No add.
In22-Ind.   1100 cds. by name. Ind. house & senate jls. & rules. Members of Ind. legisl., 1907-date. Cur. add.
In22-Ind.   2600 cds. by name. Ind. senate jls., rules. Members of senate of Ind., 1816-1913.

INDIANA—MANUSCRIPTS
In22-Ind.   6500 cds. by subj. & name of coll. Daily add.

INDIANA—MILLS. See MILLS—INDIANA

INDIANA—MUSIC. See MUSIC—INDIANA

INDIANA—NAMES, GEOGRAPHICAL. See NAMES, GEOGRAPHICAL—INDIANA

INDIANA—NEWSPAPERS
In20   Unest. cds. by name & subj. Newsp. indexed: *Lexington (Ind.) Western*, 1813-1815; *Madison (Ind.) Republican*, 1818. No add.

INDIANA—PICTURES. See PICTURES—INDIANA

INDIANA—POETS. See POETS—INDIANA

INDIANA—POST OFFICES
In22-Ind.   4200 cds. by name. U.S. post off. dept. records. Post off. est. in Ind. from beginning to 1920. No add.

INDIANA—ROADS
In22-Ind.   1100 cds., chron. Ind. laws, 1816-1838. Ind. road laws, 1816-1838. No add.

INDIANA—SOLDIERS, REVOLUTIONARY. *See* U.S.—HISTORY — REVOLUTION — INDIANA **In35-gen**

INDIANA STATE TEACHERS COLLEGE—PUBLICATIONS, ALUMNI
In36 8 cds. by auth. Bks. Infreq. add.

INDIANA STATE TEACHERS COLLEGE—PUBLICATIONS, FACULTY
In36 150 cds., chron. & by auth. & yr. of pub. Bks., per., 1921–date. Occ. add.

INDIANA AND INDIANANS (bk.). *In* INDIANA **In23-ref**

INDIANA MAGAZINE OF HISTORY (per.) **In22-Ind.** 1930–date. Cds. by auth. & subj. Q. add.

INDIANAPOLIS (IND.)
In23-ref 116p., tpd. shts. by subj. Bk. indexed: Jacob P. Dunn, *Greater Indianapolis*. No add.

INDIANAPOLIS (IND.)—HISTORY. *See* INDIANA—HISTORY **In23-ref**

INDIANAPOLIS (IND.)—NEWSPAPERS
In22-Ind. 35,000 cds. by subj. Newsp., 1898–date. Daily add.

INDIANAPOLIS (IND.) GAZETTE (newsp.) **In20** 1822–1826. Cds. by name & subj. No add.

INDIANS. *See also* CHILDREN'S LITERATURE —INDIANS; U.S.—HISTORY **N35-ref.-Amer. hist.**; List of Bibliographies, APPENDIX I
C73-Amer. 3960 cds. by states, tribes, wars & captivities.
G2-DeRen. Unest. ent., tpd. shts. Per. indexed: *The Friend*, v. 1-19, 1827–1846. Amer. Indians, with spec. ref. to Cherokees.
I26-Ayer 482 ent., tpd. shts. Bks. & mss. Narratives of captivity among Indians of N. Amer. No add.
Ky2 340 cds. by auth. Bks. & per. Freq. add.
N46-hist 2640 cds. by subj., tribe & geog. loc. Bks. & per. not indexed elsewhere. Occ. add.
Ok4-ref 500 cds. by subj., auth. & t. Cur. add.
Tx5 150 cds. by auth. & t. Bks., pams., bul. & newsp. Freq. add.
Wa10-ref 400 cds. by subj. Per., govt. doc. & newsp. Occ. add.

INDIANS—ARCHAEOLOGY. *See* INDIANS—LEGENDS **N42**

INDIANS—CHEROKEES. *See* INDIANS **G2-DeRen.**

INDIANS—DELAWARE
Del Unest. ent., tpd. shts. by auth. Amer. Indians within present limits of state of Del.

INDIANS—LANGUAGES
C32-lit., hist. 350 cds. by name of tribe. Bks. No add.
Ct10 Unest. cds. by auth. Amer. Indian lang. & lit. No add.
I26-Ayer 1500 ent., tpd. shts. by tribe. Bks. & per. Freq. add.
Mi6-ref 500 cds. by name of tribe, per. & geog. names, numerals. Bks. & per. Vocabularies. Infreq. add.

INDIANS—LEGENDS
Mn14-ref 900 cds. by subj. & t. Misc. coll. of legends, inc. Minn. legends. Infreq. add.
N42 450 cds. by class. Bks., pams., per. & newsp. Indian lore & archaeol. Infreq. add.

INDIANS—MINNESOTA. *See also* INDIANS—LEGENDS **Mn14-ref**
Mn14-ref 1100 cds. by name. Bks. Infreq. add.

INDIANS—NEW YORK (STATE). *See* PARRISH, JASPER **N45b**

INDIANS—OHIO
O47 200 ent., tpd. shts. by name of chief & tribe. Bks. No add.

INDIANS—PICTURES. *See* PICTURES—INDIANS

INDIANS—PORTRAITS. *See* PORTRAITS—INDIANS

INDIANS—STORIES. *See also* INDIANS—LEGENDS; List of Bibliographies, APPENDIX I
Ky9 40 cds. by t. Bks. & per. Occ. add.
Wv3 26 ent., tpd. shts. by auth. & t. Bks.

INDIANS—STORIES, JUVENILE. *See* CHILDREN'S LITERATURE—INDIANS

INDIANS—TRIBES. *See* INDIANS, subdiv. Name of tribe.

INDIANS—VOCABULARIES. *See* INDIANS—LANGUAGES

INDIANS—WASHINGTON (STATE)
Wa14-ref   100 cds. by subj. Bks., pams. & per. Infreq. add.

INDIANS—WINNEBAGO
W4   20 cds. by auth. Bks., per. & mss. Infreq. add.

INDUSTRIAL AND ENGINEERING CHEMISTRY (per.). *In* CHEMISTRY   **L17**

INDUSTRIAL ARTS. *See* TECHNOLOGY

INDUSTRIAL CANADA (per.). *In* CANADA—PERIODICALS   **Ca13-per**

INDUSTRIAL CATALOGS. *See* TRADE CATALOGS AND DIRECTORIES

INDUSTRIAL RELATIONS. *See* EMPLOYMENT MANAGEMENT

INDUSTRIAL REVOLUTION
Nj9   114 ent., tpd. shts. by subj. Bks. Freq. add.

INDUSTRIES—HISTORY. *See also* CORPORATIONS
Ct2-tech   3600 cds. by subj. tech., sci. & bus. bks. Cur. add.
Wa10-tech   1900 cds. by subj. Bks. & per. Hist. of ind., inc. commodities—silk, food, etc. Cur. add.

INDUSTRIES—SEATTLE (WASH.). *See* SEATTLE (WASH.)—INDUSTRIES

INDUSTRIES—TEXAS
Tx27   Unest. cds. by subj. or factory. Cur. add.

INFANTS—CARE AND HYGIENE
C30   150 cds. by subj. & source. Bks., pams. & per. Freq. add.
K11   70 cds. by subj. Pams., govt. doc. Freq. add.

INFECTION AND INFECTIOUS DISEASE. *See* CONTAGION AND CONTAGIOUS DISEASES

INFLUENCE OF ENVIRONMENT ON THE SETTLEMENT OF MISSOURI (bk.). *In* ST. LOUIS (MO.)   **Mo13-Soul.**

INNS—CALIFORNIA. *See* CALIFORNIA—INNS

INSECTICIDES
Nj61   50 cds. by auth. & t. Bks., per. & pams. Insecticides & fungicides. Infreq. add.

INSECTS. *See* ENTOMOLOGY

INSECTS AS FOOD
D16   410 cds. by auth. World lit. Infreq. add.

INSIGNIA. *See also* U.S. ARMY CAMPS
O16-ref
O16-ref   100 cds. by subj. & name of organiz. Bks. & per. No add.

INSTITUTIONS—MANAGEMENT. *See also* HOSPITALS—MANAGEMENT
P32   700 cds. by subj. Per., 1930–1937. No add.

INSTRUCTOR (per.). *In* ART—STUDY AND TEACHING   **Md10**; CHILDREN'S PLAYS   **H2**; PAINTINGS   **Ct12-John Dav.**; PERIODICALS   **O20-Jeff.**
Ca14-j   v. 42-51, 1933–1942. Tpd. shts. by subj. Freq. add.
Ct12-John Dav.   v. 37, 1927–date. Cds. by subj. Cur. add.
Mn10   v. 35, 1925–date. Tpd. shts. by subj. Freq. add.

INSTRUMENTAL MUSIC
C38   600 cds. by comp. & subj. Bks. In proc.
C49-art   7040 cds. by comp. Bks. & sht. mus. Organ, violin, cello, viola mus. Freq. add.
Ca2-art   5000 cds. by comp. & t. Bks. Freq. add.
I65-art   4950 cds. by t. Mus. in coll. Freq. add.
Mi6-circ   500 cds. by comp. Bks. Piano, organ & violin mus. Infreq. add.
Mi6-mus   1320 cds. by comp., t. & subj. Coll. of chamber & small orch. mus. Occ. add.
Mi25   3100 cds. by comp. Bks. of scores. Cur. add.
N54-art   1525 cds. by t. & subj. Mus. coll. Violin, organ & other instr. Cur. add.
Nj67-ref   2700 cds. by t. & comp. Bks. & sht. mus. Freq. add.
O20-art   5536 cds. by comp. & t. Bks. Freq. add.

INSURANCE
Nj41   704 cds. by t. Bks. Cur. add.
Nj43   4224 cds. by subj. Infreq. add.
Nj51   30 cds. by type & auth. Bks. Occ. add.

INSURANCE—DIRECTORIES
G9   30 ent., tpd. shts. by name, chron. Per. & newsp. Atlanta, Ga. biog., insurance. Wkly. add.

INSURANCE—PERIODICALS
C65 1500 cds. by subj. Insurance & fire protection per., 1939–date. Daily & wkly. add.
G9 2000 ent., tpd. shts. by subj., chron. Wkly. add.

INSURANCE—PERIODICALS, CANADIAN
Ca12 1300 cds. by subj. Freq. add.

INSURANCE—SOCIETIES AND CLUBS
G10 150 cds. by name of organiz. Bk. & pams. Proc. of annual meetings of insurance organiz. Occ. add.

INSURANCE, LIFE
C67 3960 cds. by subj. Bks., per. & pams. Freq. add.

INTERCOLLEGIATE DEBATES (bk.). *In* DEBATES **Mi8-ref, N7, Nj56, P33-ref, P45-ref**

INTERDEPENDENCE (per.). *In* CANADA—PERIODICALS **Ca13-per**

INTERIOR DECORATION. *See also* FURNITURE; List of Bibliographies, APPENDIX I
I68 150 ent., tpd. shts. by subj. Bks. Freq. add.
Tx5 Unest. cds. by subj. Bks., pams. & newsp. Freq. add.

INTERNATIONAL BUREAU OF EDUCATION. BULLETIN. *In* EDUCATION—BOOK REVIEWS **N30-t.c.**

INTERNATIONAL CONGRESS OF MENTAL HYGIENE. PROCEEDINGS
Mn14-soc 125 cds. by auth. & t. Infreq. add.

INTERNATIONAL FALLS (MINN.) DAILY JOURNAL (newsp.)
Mn10 v. 8-31, 1939–1942. Cds. by subj. Freq. add.

INTERNATIONAL LAW AND RELATIONS. *See also* List of Bibliographies, APPENDIX I
Ca5-circ 400 ent., tpd. shts. by country. Bks. & pams., 1928–1938. No add.
I22 7260 cds. by class. Per. Daily add.
N29 900 cds. by citation. Int. law cases. Occ. add.

INTERNATIONAL STUDIO (per.). *In* SOUTHWEST **Nm2**

INTESTINES
Nj66 65 cds. by auth. & t. Bks., per. & pams. Infreq. add.

INVENTIONS
C32-sci 650 cds. by auth. & subj. Bks. Cur. add.
N68-sci 73 cds. by subj. Bks. Occ. add.

INVENTORY BOOKS. *See also* JEFFERSON CO. (KY.)—INVENTORY BOOKS

IOWA
Ia3 800 cds. by subj. Bks. & per. Cur. add.
Ia4 3500 cds. by subj. Bks. & per. In proc.
Ia6-ref 2000 cds. by subj. Freq. add.
Ia9 500 cds. by subj. Per. Per. indexed: *Palimpsest magazine*. Occ. add.
Ia12 185 cds. by subj. Iowa per. Occ. add.
Ia16 1600 cds. by subj. Bks. & per. Occ. add.
Ia17 100 cds. by subj. Freq. add.

IOWA. BOARD OF CONTROL OF STATE INSTITUTIONS. BULLETIN
Ia20 150 cds. by subj., through 1928. No add.

IOWA—HISTORY
Ia18-ad 8000 cds. by subj. Bks., per. & newsp. Occ. add.

IOWA STATE COLLEGE—PUBLICATIONS
Ia2 6500 cds. by subj. Yrly add.
Ia17 25 cds. by subj. Infreq. add.

IOWA STATE UNIVERSITY—DISSERTATIONS, ACADEMIC
Ia14-ref 14,400 cds. by auth. & dept. Theses. Occ. add.
Ia17 50 cds. by subj. Pams. & per. Freq. add.

IOWA GRAND LODGE—PROCEEDINGS. *See* POETRY **Ia18-ad**

IOWA MAGAZINE
Ia20 1920–1925. Cds. by subj. No add.

IRELAND. *See* List of Bibliographies, APPENDIX I

IT TAKES ALL KINDS (bk.). *In* SHORT STORIES **Tx12**

ITALIAN FOLK-SONGS. *See* FOLK-SONGS, ITALIAN

ITALIAN LANGUAGE
C71-ref   600 cds. by auth., subj. & t. Bks. Cur. add.
Nj58   250 cds. by auth. & t. Bks. Infreq. add.

ITALIAN PLAYS. *See* PLAYS, ITALIAN

ITALIAN SAINTS. *See* SAINTS, ITALIAN

JACKPOT (bk.). *In* SHORT STORIES   **Tx12**

JACKSON (MICH.)
Mi20   200 cds. by subj. Newsp. Occ. add.

JACKSON (MISS.)—NEWSPAPERS
Ms3   3500 cds. by subj. No add.

JACKSON CO. (MICH.)—HISTORY
Mi19   262p., tpd. shts. by subj., name & place. No add.

JACKSON CO. (MICH.)—MAPS. *See* MAPS —JACKSON CO. (MICH.)

JACKSONVILLE (FLA.)—SOCIETIES AND CLUBS
F2-ref   470 cds. by name. Cur. add.

JACKSONVILLE (FLA.) TIMES-UNION (newsp.)
F2-ref   Unest. cds. by subj. Art. of Fla. & Floridians. Daily add.

JAHRESBERICHTE ÜBER DIE FORTSCHRITTE DER KLASSISCHEN (bk.). *In* BIOGRAPHY   **O18a**

JAMAICA (N.Y.)—GENEALOGY. *See* GENEALOGY—JAMAICA (N.Y.)

JAMAICA (N.Y.)—HISTORY
N22-L.I.   66p., tpd. shts. by name. Records of the town of Jamaica, 1749–1897. No add.

JAMESTOWN COLLEGE—PUBLICATIONS
Nd3   35 cds. by subj. & name. Bks., pams., per., etc. Occ. add.

JAPANESE ART. *See* ART, JAPANESE

JAPANESE LITERATURE. *See* ORIENTAL LITERATURE   **M11-Jap.**

JAPANESE PRINTS. *See* ART, JAPANESE

JAPANESE TEMPLES AND THEIR TREASURES (bk.). *In* ART, ORIENTAL   **P42-art**

JEFFERSON, THOMAS
Ky2   103 cds. by 'auth. Bks. & per. Freq. add.
V2   10,000 cds., chron. Letters & other writings, pub. & unpub. Freq. add.

JEFFERSON CO. (KY.)—DEEDS
Ky7   Unest. ent., by name. Jefferson co. Deed book, no. 1
Ky14   Unest. ent. by grantor & grantee. Abstracts of first 8 deed bks., 1780–1810.

JEFFERSON CO. (KY.)—INVENTORY BOOKS
Ky14   Unest. ent., by name of testator. Abstracted inventory bks., 1–5.

JEFFERSON CO. (KY.)—POWER OF ATTORNEY
Ky14   Unest. ent. by name of pers. giving power of attorney. Power of attorney bks. 1 & 2., abstracted.

JESUS CHRIST IN ART
N10   Several hundred cds. Bks. & per. Freq. add.
N35-ref. art   5000 ent., 100p., tpd. shts. by art. & subj. 20,000 pic. No add.

JEWS
Mn14-Sum.   370 cds. by subj. Per., pams. & newsp. Jew. lang., lit. & customs. Occ. add.
N35-ref. Jew   8000 cds. by auth. & subj. Bks. Life, phil., sci., law & folklore. Cur. add.

JEWS—PERIODICALS. *See* List of Bibliographies, APPENDIX I

JEWS IN LITERATURE
Mi6-Rich.   58 ent., tpd. sht. by auth. Fic. & non-fic. Freq. add.

JOB ANALYSIS
Nj48   37 ent., tpd. shts. by auth. Bks. & per.

JOHN CRERAR LIBRARY, CHICAGO—REFERENCE LISTS. *See* List of Bibliographies, APPENDIX I

JOINT ESTIMATES ON CURRENT MOTION PICTURES (per.). *In* MOTION PICTURES   **I8, O31**

JOURNAL OF AMERICAN HISTORY. *In* GENEALOGY   **M19 (1)**

JOURNAL OF CHEMICAL EDUCATION. *In* CHEMISTRY   **L17**

JOURNAL OF COMMERCE. *In* BUSINESS CONDITIONS   **P36-Lipp.**

JOURNAL OF EDUCATION (NOVA SCOTIA). *In* CANADA—PERIODICALS   **Ca13-per**

JOURNAL OF INDUSTRIAL AND ENGINEERING CHEMISTRY. *In* CHEMISTRY **L17**

JOURNAL OF NEGRO EDUCATION. *In* NEGROES **Ky15-W.Col.** (4)

JOURNAL OF NEGRO HISTORY. *In* NEGROES **Ky15-W.Col.** (5), **P39-Wyl.**; NEGROES—BIOGRAPHY **D6** (1); NEGROES—PERIODICALS **D6**

JOURNALISM. *See also* COLUMNISTS
N30 5050 cds. by auth., subj. & t. Per., 1930–1938. Per. indexed: *Journalism quarterly*. Jour. & journalists. No add.
N36-newsp 4500 cds. by auth. & subj. Newsp. & per. Journ. & the press. Freq. add.
N46-lit 400 cds. by subj. Bks. Cur. add.
N55 960 cds. by auth., t. & subj. Freq. add.

JOURNALISM QUARTERLY. *In* JOURNALISM **N30**

JOURNALS. *See* BIOGRAPHY; DIARIES

JUDGES. *See* LAWYERS **Ct9**

JUNIOR ARTS AND ACTIVITIES (per.). *In* CHILDREN'S PLAYS **H2**

JUNIOR BOOK OF AUTHORS (bk.). *In* AUTHORS **Mt1**; AUTHORS, CHILDREN'S **O1-j**; BIOGRAPHY **C8-ref**

JUNIOR LITERARY GUILD
C71-j 1500 cds. by auth., t. & subj. Bks. No add.

JUNIOR SCHOLASTIC (per.)
Mi27-j 400 cds. by subj. Per. indexed: *Junior scholastic*, 1938–date, *Mechanix illustrated*, v. 19, 1938–date. Wkly. & mo. add.

JUVENILE AIDS. *See* CHILDREN'S LITERATURE

JUVENILE DELINQUENCY. *See* List of Bibliographies, APPENDIX I

JUVENILE LITERATURE. *See* CHILDREN'S LITERATURE

KALAMAZOO (MICH.)—BIOGRAPHY
Mi21-ref 650 cds. by subj. Bks. Occ. add.

KALAMAZOO (MICH.)—HISTORY
Mi21 125 ent., tpd. shts. by subj. Pams. & scrapbks. Freq. add.

KALAMAZOO (MICH.)—REGISTERS OF BIRTHS, ETC.
Mi21-Brooks 30,725 cds. by name. Newsp., cem. records up to 1867. No add.

KALAMAZOO (MICH.)—SOCIETIES AND CLUBS
Mi21-ref (1) 900 cds. by type & name. Newsp. indexed: *Kalamazoo gazette*. Daily add.
Mi21-ref (2) 224 ent., tpd. shts. by name. Infreq. add.

KALAMAZOO (MICH.) GAZETTE (newsp.). *See also* KALAMAZOO (MICH.)—SOCIETIES AND CLUBS **Mi21-ref**
Mi21 800 ent., tpd. shts. by subj. & port. Centennial ed., Jan. 4, 1937. No add.

KANSAS
K3 Unest. ent., tpd. shts. by auth., subj. & t. Bks., per., newsp., etc. Bks. indexed: Leola Howard Blanchard, *Conquest of Southwest Kansas*; A. Grove Day, *Coronado's quest*; Bliss Isley & W. M. Richards, *Four centuries in Kansas*; Paul A. Jones, *Coronado and Quivira*; Charles Lowther, *Dodge City, Kansas*; W.P.A. Federal writers project, *Kansas*; Robert M. Wright, *Dodge City, cowboy capital*. Freq. add.
K8-ref 1900 cds. by auth., subj. & t. Bks. & per. Per. indexed: *Kansas magazine*. Occ. add.
K9-ref 150 cds. by subj. State doc., bul. & pams. Infreq. add.
K10-ord 5000 cds. by auth., t. & subj. Bks., ser. & pams. Inc. Lawrence coll. Cur. add.
K12-ref 200 cds. by subj. Pams., newsp., state organiz. pub., etc. Freq. add.

KANSAS (bk.). *In* KANSAS **K3**

KANSAS STATE COLLEGE
K12-ref 30 cds. by subj. Newsp. etc. Freq. add.

KANSAS UNIVERSITY. SCIENCE BULLETIN
K10-ext v. 1–date. 1100 cds. by subj. Cur. add.

KANSAS CITY (MO.)—SOCIETIES AND CLUBS
Mo3-ref 2000 cds. by name. Newsp. Daily add.

KANSAS MAGAZINE. *In* KANSAS **K8-ref**

KELLEY, H. GILBERT. *See* NEW JERSEY Nj40 (2)

KEN (per.)
Wa10-per   v. 1-3, 1938-1939. Cds. by subj. No add.

KENNERLEY, MITCHELL—WORKS
N45b   618 cds. by auth., chron. Infreq. add.

KENT Co. (MICH.)—CEMETERY RECORDS
Mi13-Mich.   62,520 cds. by name. All cem. in co. Infreq. add.

Mi13-Mich.   9000 ent., tpd. shts. by name of cem. All cem. in co. Infreq. add.

KENT Co. (MICH.)—LANDS. *See* LANDS—KENT Co. (MICH.)

KENT Co. (MICH.)—REGISTERS OF BIRTHS, ETC.
Mi13-Mich.   Unest. ent., tpd. shts. by name of groom & bride. All marriages abstracted from Kent co. clerk's records to 1870. Infreq. add.

KENT Co. (MICH.)—SOLDIERS
Mi13-Mich.   Unest. ent., tpd. shts., 19v., by name. Soldiers' records. Infreq. add.

KENTUCKY
Ky2   153 cds. by auth. Bks. & per. Descrip. & travel. Freq. add.
Ky9   50 cds. by subj. Bks., per. & newsp. Freq. add.
Ky15-Cres. Hill   200 cds. by subj. Newsp., pams. Per. indexed: *Kentucky progress magazine.* Louisville & Ky. Infreq. add.
Ky15-Ky.   30,000 cds. by subj. Newsp., pams., per., state doc. & bks. Cur. add.
Ky15-W. Col.   200 cds. by subj. Per. Freq. add.
Ky18   12,000 cds. by auth., subj. & t. Bks. in Townsend Ky. coll. Freq. add.

KENTUCKY. AGRICULTURAL EXPERIMENT STATION—PUBLICATIONS. *In* AGRICULTURE—KENTUCKY Ky11

KENTUCKY—ARTISTS. *See* ARTISTS—KENTUCKY

KENTUCKY—AUTHORS. *See* AUTHORS—KENTUCKY

KENTUCKY—BIBLIOGRAPHY—IMPRINTS
Ky2   24p., tpd. shts., chron. Bks. & per. Imprints, 1788–1799. No add.
Ky2   31p., tpd. shts., by auth. Bks. & per., Imprints, 1599–1829.

KENTUCKY—BIOGRAPHY
Ky6   600 cds. by name, class. Pams. & newsp. Freq. add.
Ky7 (1)   Unest. ent., tpd. shts. by name. Bk. indexed: William H. Perrin, *History of Bourbon, Scott, Nicholas & Harrison cos.* No add.
Ky7 (2)   Unest. cds. by family name. Bk. indexed: William H. Perrin, *Kentucky, a history of the state.* No add.

KENTUCKY—FOLK SONGS. *See* FOLK SONGS—KENTUCKY

KENTUCKY—GENEALOGY. *See* GENEALOGY—KENTUCKY

KENTUCKY—HISTORY
Ky2   30p., tpd. shts. by subj. Younglove scrapbks. No add.
Ky2   2500 cds. by subj. Rare newsp. Freq. add.
Ky2   337 cds., chron. Bks. & per. Freq. add.
Ky7 (1)   Unest. ent., tpd. shts. by name. Bk. indexed: William B. Allen, *A History of Kentucky.* No add.
Ky7 (2)   Unest. ent., tpd. shts. by subj. Bk. indexed: Mrs. Livia N. Poppenbarger, *Battle of Point Pleasant.* No add.
Ky7 (3)   Unest. ent., tpd. shts. by subj. Bk. indexed: John Magill, *Pioneer to the Kentucky emigrant.* No add.
Ky7 (4)   Unest. ent., tpd. shts. by subj. Bk. indexed: William H. Perrin, *Pioneer press.* No add.
Ky8   172 cds. by subj. Bks. Freq. add.

KENTUCKY—LANDS
Ky7   Unest. ent., tpd. shts. by name & place. Bk. indexed: James Hughes, *A report of the causes determined by the late Supreme court . . .* No add.

KENTUCKY—LAW. *See* LAW—KENTUCKY

KENTUCKY—MUSICIANS. *See* MUSICIANS—KENTUCKY

KENTUCKY—PENSIONS
Ky7 Unest. cds. by name. Occ. add.

KENTUCKY—PHYSICIANS. *See* PHYSICIANS —KENTUCKY

KENTUCKY—REGISTERS OF BIRTHS, ETC.
Ky7 Unest. cds. by name of groom. Marriage indexes. No add.
Ky14 Unest. cds. by name. Bks. & per. Marriage records & wills. No add.

KENTUCKY—SOLDIERS, REVOLUTIONARY. *See* U.S.—HISTORY—REVOLUTION—KENTUCKY **In35-gen**

KENTUCKY—SPECIAL COLLECTIONS. *See* SPECIAL COLLECTIONS—KENTUCKY

KENTUCKY. UNIVERSITY. LETTERS (per.)
Ky12 v. 1, #1, 1927– v. 5, #20, 1932. Cds. by auth. & subj. No add.

KENTUCKY. UNIVERSITY. COLLEGE OF AGRICULTURE. CIRCULARS. *In* AGRICULTURE—KENTUCKY **Ky11**

KENTUCKY—WILLS
Ky7 Unest. ent., by name. No add.

KENTUCKY, A HISTORY OF THE STATE (bk.). *In* KENTUCKY—BIOGRAPHY **Ky7** (2)

KENTUCKY IN THE WAR OF 1812 (bk.). *In* U.S.—HISTORY—WAR OF 1812—KENTUCKY **Ky7** (1)

KENTUCKY PROGRESS MAGAZINE. *In* KENTUCKY **Ky15-Cres. Hill**
Ky2 v. 1-7, 1928–1932. 86p., tpd. shts. by subj. No add.
Ky7 v. 1, 1928–date. Cds. by subj. No add.
Ky12-ref Unest. cds. by auth. & subj. Per. indexed: *Kentucky progress magazine*, v. 1-7, 1928–1932; *In Kentucky*, v. 1, 1937–date. No add.
Ky17 v. 1-2, 1928–1939, v. 5-6, 1933–1935. Cds. by subj. No add.
Ky18 v. 1-6, 1928–1935. Cds. by auth., subj. & t. Art. & poems. No add.

KENTUCKY STATE HISTORICAL SOCIETY REGISTER (per.)
Ky7 1903–1940. Unest. ent., tpd. shts. by subj. Cur. add.

KERAMIC STUDIO (per.)
Nj57 v. 8-37, 1906–1936. Cds. by subj. No add.

KIDNEYS
Nj61 50 cds. by auth. & t. Bks., per. & pams. Freq. add.

KILMER, JOYCE—WORKS
I13-ref 250 cds. by t. & 1st line. Bks. & per. Infreq. add.

KING CO. (WASH.)
Wa10-mun. ref 340 cds. by subj. Repts. & newsp. Occ. add.

KING CO. (WASH.)—OFFICIALS AND EMPLOYEES
Wa10-mun. ref Unest. ent., tpd. shts., chron. Co. records, etc. Occ. add.

KING CO. (WASH.)—SOCIETIES AND CLUBS. *See* WASHINGTON (STATE)—SOCIETIES & CLUBS **Wa10-ref**

KIPLING, RUDYARD—WORKS
I13-ref 2600 cds. by t. & 1st line. Bks. & per. Occ. add.
N8-ref 900 cds. by t. Bks. Freq. add.

KLAVIERWERKE (BACH) (bk.). *In* BACH, JOHANN SEBASTIAN—WORKS **Mn14-mus** (1)

KLAVIERWERKE (GRIEG) (bk.). *In* GRIEG, EDVARD HAGERUP—WORKS **Mn14-mus**

KLAVIERWERKE (SCHUMANN) (bk.). *In* SCHUMANN, ROBERT—WORKS **Mn14-mus** (1)

KNIBBS, HENRY HERBERT—WORKS
I13-ref 300 cds. by t. & 1st line. Bks. & per. Infreq. add.

KNIGHTS OF MALTA
N45b Unest. ent., tpd. shts. by class. Bks., per. & phot. Infreq. add.

KNIGHTSTOWN (IND.)
In24a 31 ent. by subj. Bks. Freq. add.

KNITTING. *See* HANDICRAFTS **O20-art**

KNOX CO. (ILL.)—HISTORY
I45 4000 cds. by subj. In proc.

KNOXVILLE (TENN.)—NECROLOGY
T3 1160 ent., 58p., tpd. shts. by name. Newsp. No add.

KNOXVILLE (TENN.)—REGISTERS OF BIRTHS, ETC.
T3 1800 ent., 91p., tpd. shts. by name. Newsp. No add

KOKKA (per.). *In* ART, ORIENTAL — P42-art

LABOR AND LABORING CLASSES. *See also* MIGRANT PROBLEM; List of Bibliographies, APPENDIX I
C68   Unest. cds. by subj. Newsp. indexed: *San Francisco (Calif.) Chronicle.* Daily add.
M7   700 cds. by auth., subj. & t. Bks., per., govt. doc. & pams. Unemployment compensation & rel. subj.: employment stabilization, labor problems, seasonal employment & merit rating. Cur. add.
N37   300 ent., tpd. shts. by subj. 200 per. Index to labor art. Mo. add.

LABOR AND LABORING CLASSES—PERIODICALS
O33-Euc. Cen.   Unest. cds. by subj. Per. indexed: *A.F.L. monthly business survey, American federation of labor weekly news service, C.I.O. news, The Federal employee, Federation of labor Weekly news service, Labor information bulletin, Machinists' monthly journal, Steel labor, United automobile worker, United mine workers journal.* Cur. add.

LABOR INFORMATION BULLETIN (per.). *In* LABOR AND LABORING CLASSES—PERIODICALS   O33-Euc. Cen.

LACQUERS AND LACQUERING. *See also* PAINTS   Nj3
Nj54   Unest. ent., by subj. Spec. rpts. Freq. add.

LACTOSE
D15   1266 cds., chron. Bks. & per. Yrly add.

LADY OF THE LAKE. *See* SCOTT, SIR WALTER—LADY OF THE LAKE

LAFAYETTE CO. (MO.)—LANDS. *See* LANDS—LAFAYETTE CO. (MO.)

LAFFITE, JEAN. *See* List of Bibliographies, APPENDIX I

LAKES—NEW JERSEY. *See* NEW JERSEY—LAKES

LANCASTER CO. (PA.)—HISTORY
P22   3000 cds. by subj. Bks., per. & co. hist. Occ. add.

LAND OF LAKES (per.)
W9   v. 2-5, 1926–1929. Cds. by subj. & auth. No add.

LAND WE LOVE (per.)
Nc6   1866–1869. Cds. by subj. No add.

LANDS—ALABAMA
A1   1500 cds. St. Stephens, Ala. terr., reg. of transfers private land claims, 1818. No add.

LANDS—HUNTSVILLE (ALA.)
A1   3000 cds. Grants from 1800–1820. No add.

LANDS—ILLINOIS. *See also* LAW—ILLINOIS —LANDS   I71-arch
I71-arch   3500 cds. by tract & name. Mss. land records in Secy. of state exec. dept. arch. Lands sold by Ill. No add.

LANDS—KENT CO. (MICH.)
Mi13-Mich.   Unest. ent., tpd. shts. Transfers registered in Kent co. reg. of deeds office, to 1870. No add.

LANDS—LAFAYETTE CO. (MO.)
Mo8   Unest. cds. by name. Co. records. Holders of 1st land-grants in co. No add.

LANDSCAPE GARDENING—LANTERN SLIDES. *See* LANTERN SLIDES—LANDSCAPE GARDENING

LANGUAGE AND LANGUAGES. *See also* CHILDREN'S LITERATURE—LANGUAGE & LANGUAGES; List of Bibliographies, APPENDIX I
O20-White   5593 cds. by subj. Bks. per., etc. Freq. add.

LANGUAGE AND LANGUAGES—NORTH AMERICA
M30   232 cds. by auth. & subj. Bks. Infreq. add.

LANGUAGE AND LANGUAGES—STUDY AND TEACHING
C11   Unest. cds. by auth. & subj. Bks., per. & pams. Cur. add.

LANTERN SLIDES. *See also* PHOTOGRAPHS I11; List of Bibliographies, APPENDIX I
I39   640 ent., tpd. by subj., chron. Occ. add.
I53   850 cds. by subj. Sci., hist., city planning.
M10   1500 ent., tpd. shts., chron. Freq. add.
N30-t.c. art   2000 cds. by subj., nationality, etc. (Univ. of Minn. class.) Misc. subj., strong on modern arch. & modern painting. Freq. add.

Nb16 500 ent. by class. No add.
Nj42 22,000 cds. by t. & subj. Freq. add.
Nj42 1500 cds. by t. & subj. Filmslides. Freq. add.
Vt43 500 cds. by subj. Occ. add.
W12 Unest. cds. by subj. Bks. & per. Freq. add.
Wa15 1500 cds. by auth., t. & subj. Inc. art, archaeol., & arch. subj. Freq. add.

LANTERN SLIDES—ART. *See also* LANTERN SLIDES N30-t.c.art, Wa15
N55-art 13,928 cds. by class. Inc. arch. Infreq. add.

LANTERN SLIDES—DETROIT (MICH.)
Mi6-Burt. 735 cds. by subj. Infreq. add.

LANTERN SLIDES—ENGINEERING
I73-eng Unest. cds. Occ. add.

LANTERN SLIDES—LANDSCAPE GARDENING
I73-lands Unest. cds. by subj. In. lands. arch. & city planning. Freq. add.

LANTERN SLIDES—SONGS
I53 140 cds. by subj. & t. Occ. add.

LAS CRUCES (N.M.) THIRTY-FOUR (newsp.). *In* EL PASO (TEX.)— NEWSPAPERS Tx13

LATIN AMERICA
Nm3 75p., tpd. shts. by country & subj. Bks. Yrly. add.

LATIN AMERICA—COSTUME. *See* COSTUME—LATIN AMERICA

LATIN AMERICA—MUSIC. *See* MUSIC—LATIN AMERICA

LATIN LANGUAGE. *See* List of Bibliographies, APPENDIX I

LATIN LITERATURE. *See* List of Bibliographies, APPENDIX I

LATTER DAY LUMINARY (per.)
P7 v. 1, 1818. Cds. by subj., name, churches, etc. No add.

LAUDERDALE CO. (ALA.)—CEMETERY RECORDS
A1 50 ent., tpd. shts. by name. Florence cem. Occ. add.

LAW. *See also* AGRICULTURAL LAWS & LEGISLATION; COMMERCIAL LAW; CONSTITUTIONAL LAW; INTERNATIONAL LAW & RELATION; List of Bibliographies, APPENDIX I
Ct9 2200 cds. by subj. Pams., leaflets, mim. data, etc. Legal & semi-legal mat. Occ. add.
N55-law 15,647 cds. by auth., t. & subj. Bks. & per. Freq. add.
Nj51 2000 cds. by auth., subj. & t. Bradley coll. of early law bks. No add.
O20-soc. 528 cds. by auth. Wigmore law coll. Freq. add.

LAW—ALABAMA
A1 31,020 cds. by subj. & person who introduced bill. Bills, 1923–date. Occ. add.

LAW—CALIFORNIA. *See also* LAW—U.S. C43-ref
C56-law 20,000 cds. by subj. Bks. & advance shts. Calif. supreme & appellate ct. decisions, 1928–date. Freq. add.

LAW—CONNECTICUT
Ct8 223,000 cds. by name of estate. Conn. probate files of 81 out of 118 probate districts. Cur. add.
Ct9 200 cds. by name of plaintiff. Conn. cases in U.S. Supreme ct. records. Occ. add.
Ct9 1200 cds. by subj. Conn. practice forms in records & briefs, 1923–date. Occ. add.
Ct9 3500 cds. by name of plaintiff. Conn. supreme ct. cases cited in legal per. Freq. add.
Ct9 10,000 cds. by name of plaintiff & defendant. Conn. supreme ct. records & briefs, 1904–date. Occ. add.
Ct9 1000 cds. by subj. Conn. supp. other than rpts. Wkly. add.

LAW—COTACO CO. (ALA.)
A1 500 cds. by name. Superior ct. records, v. 3, 1817 to 1820. No add.

LAW—FLORIDA
F2-ref 200 cds. by subj. Sess. laws, 1939 Fla. state legisl. No add.

LAW—FRANCE
N35-ref. read 1250 cds. by Fr. dept. Bks. & per. Fr. customary law, list of coutumes & coutumiers. No add.

Law—Georgia
G8   20,000 cds. by legal subj. Ga. legis. bills, 1911 to date. Cur. add.

Law—Hawaii
H3-Haw.   1000 cds. by subj. Bills of ea. biennial legis. Cur. add.

Law—Illinois
I71-arch   Unest. ent., tpd. shts., 102v., chron. by subj. under co. Ill. sess. laws & mss. enrolled laws, 1812–1906. Legis. conc. cos. No add.
I71-arch   Unest. ent., tpd. shts., 11 v., by dept., chron. under function. Ill. sess. laws. Legis. rel. to hist. of Ill. state depts. Cur. add.

Law—Illinois—Lands
I71-arch   100p., tpd. shts., chron. by subj. Ill. sess. laws. Legis. rel. to lands. No add.

Law—Indiana
In21   14,000 cds. by subj. Bills introd. in Gen. assembly, 1905–date. Cur. add.
In22-Ind.   Unest. cds., 95 scrapbks. Loc. laws by co., chron.; gen. laws by subj., chron. Laws of N.W. & Ind. terr. & of Ind. to 1852. Local & gen. laws, 1788–1852. No add.
In22a   4300 cds. by subj. Bks. & per. Freq. add.

Law—Kentucky
Ky2   150p., tpd. shts., chron. Ky. statutes, 1792–date. Bowling Green & Warren co. Cur. add.
Ky12   234 cds. by subj. Ky. legis. doc., 1839–1917. Occ. add.

Law—Maine
Me1   65,440 cds. by subj. Private & special laws & resolves of Me., 1820–date. Cur. add.

Law—Maryland
Md2-Md.   3800 cds., by art. & sec. no. of const., code of pub. gen. laws & code of public loc. laws, subj. Bills introduced in Md. gen. assembly beginning with spec. session, 1933. Cur. add.

Law—Michigan. See Law—U.S.   Mi6-soc

Law—Mississippi
M33   8500 cds. by subj. Miss. sess. acts, 1866–1904.

Law—Missouri
Mo14-law   Unest. cds. by subj. Mo. briefs, 1937–date. Cur. add.

Law—New Jersey
Nj51   200 cds. by auth. & t. N.J. textbks. on law. Occ. add.

Law—New York (City).   See also Law—U.S.   N35-mun. ref
N35-ref. econ   150 cds. by subj. Govt. doc. Legis., loc. N.Y. city laws, 1939–date.
O18   5000 cds. by dept., subj. & name. Law cases rel. to city of N.Y. Daily add.

Law—New York (State).   See Law—U.S.   N46-soc; N35-mun. ref

Law—Pennsylvania.   See Law—U.S.   P56

Law—Texas
Tx5   Unest. ent. by subj. Newsp. Freq. add.

Law—U.S.
C43-ref   1100 cds. by subj. Slip laws & other pam. ed. U.S. & Calif. Freq. add.
D29   3000 cds. per sess. by auth., subj. & bill no. Current legis. of interest to securities. Freq. add.
I73-ref   660 cds., num. by Congress, then by popular name of law. Slip laws too recent to be indexed in Shepard. Freq. add.
Mi6-soc   1750 cds. by U.S. Congress & Mich., using popular name of bill. Newsp., pams., per. & govt. doc. Freq. add.
N22-ref   1825 cds. by case. Off. reports, #295-d & bks. containing digests of cases. Yrly. add.
N35-mun. ref   125 cds. by nickname. Legis. of city, state (N.Y.) & nation. Freq. add.
N35-ref. econ   975 cds., num. by no. of bill. Legis.; progress of cur. bills through cong. Daily add.
N46-soc   125 cds. by popular & off. t., & subj. Slip laws, pams., per. & bks. Recent U.S. & N.Y. state laws. Cur. add.
O20-soc   352 cds. by subj. & name of law. Statutes at large. Freq. add.
P56   500 cds. by no. & subj. Pa. & fed. slip laws. Cur. add.

LAW—U.S.—EXECUTIVE ORDERS AND PROCLAMATIONS
D7-ref   31,450 cds. by no. & date, by subj. Reg. no. series of presidential proclamations & exec. orders, 1789–1941. Freq. add.
D22   6600 cds. by no. & subj. **Exec.** orders & proclamation issued by president of U.S., 1918–date. Cur. add.

LAW—WISCONSIN
W13   5000 cds. by chap. no. Hist. of Wisc. acts. Cur. add.
W13   6500 cds. by bill no. Amendments to Wisc. bills. Cur. add.
W13   35,000 cds. by section no. Wisc. statutes, private & loc. laws beginning with sess. of 1927. Changes in sections. Cur. add.
W13   500 cds. by subj. All acts & more imp. jt. resolutions & resolutions passed by legis. Cur. Wisc. laws. Cur. add.
W13   89,760 cds. by subj. Bills, jt. resolutions & resolutions introduced into Wisc. legis. from 1900 to date. Wisc. bills. Cur. add.
W13   22,440 cds. by subj. Private & loc. laws of Wisc., 1836–1927. Wisc. private & loc. laws. No add.

LAWRENCE (KANS.).
K11   142 ent. by subj. Newsp., maps, pams. Freq. add.

LAWRENCE COLLEGE
W2   8500 cds. by subj. Newsp. indexed: *Appleton (Wisc.) Post crescent*, 1928–date. Lawrence college news. Daily add.

LAWRENCE COLLEGE—PUBLICATIONS
W2   850 cds. by auth. & t. Lawrence coll. auth. Cur. add.

LAWRENCE COLLEGE—TRUSTEES
W2   300 cds. by name. Lawrence coll. trustees. In proc.

LAWYERS
Ct9   350 cds. by surname. Memorials in U.S. & Conn. rpts. Judges & lawyers. Occ. add.

LE GALLIENE, RICHARD—WORKS
I13-ref   800 cds. by t. & 1st line. Bks. & per. Infreq. add.

LEACOCK, STEPHEN BUTLER—WORKS
N46-lit   300 cds. by t. Bks. Essays. Occ. add.

LEAGUE OF NATIONS—PUBLICATIONS
Mn15-per   1200 cds. by auth. & t. All pub., 1927–date. Freq. add.
O20-soc   1320 cds. by auth., t. & subj. Doc. series. Cur. add.
O56-ref   1000 cds. by subj. L. of N. set. No add.

LEAGUE OF NATIONS SOCIETY IN CANADIAN MONTHLY NEWS (per.). *In* CANADA—PERIODICALS   **Ca13-per**

LECTURE FOUNDATIONS. *See* List of Bibliographies, APPENDIX I

LEE CO. (ALA.)—CEMETERY RECORDS
A1   150 ent., tpd. shts. by name. Concord Baptist church cem. Occ. add.

LEE FAMILY (VA.)
V2   3000 cds. by name & chron. Richard, Henry, Arthur Lee, etc. Freq. add.

LEISURE (per.). *In* RECREATION—PERIODICALS   **Nj12**

LETTER WRITING. *See* COMMERCIAL CORRESPONDENCE

LETTERS. *See* DIARIES; Names of persons, subdiv. CORRESPONDENCE, REMINISCENCES, ETC.

LEXINGTON (IND.) WESTERN (newsp.). *In* INDIANA—NEWSPAPERS   **In20**

LEXINGTON (KY.)
Ky2   57 cds. by auth. Bks. & per. Freq. add.

LEXINGTON (MASS.)—AUTHORS. *See* AUTHORS—LEXINGTON (MASS.)

LEXINGTON (MASS.) HISTORICAL SOCIETY
M20   4000 cds. by subj. Letters, diaries, phot., relics, sermons, newsp., deeds, etc. Infreq. add.

LIBERTY (per.)
C32-per   v. 7, 1930–date. Cds. by auth., t. & subj. Wkly. add.

LIBRARIANS—GEORGIA
G6   800 cds. by name. Cur. add.

LIBRARIANS, CERTIFICATION OF. *See* List of Bibliographies, APPENDIX I

LIBRARIANS AS AUTHORS
O20-per   660 cds. by auth. Per. Mag. art. Freq. add.

LIBRARIES
O20-per 1980 cds. by subj. Per. Freq. add.

LIBRARIES—GEORGIA. *See also* LIBRARY ARCHITECTURE—GEORGIA
G6 500 cds. by type of lib. Cur. add.
G6 201 ent., tpd. shts. by co. Pub. lib. & W.P.A. lib. units—statistics. Yrly. add.

LIBRARIES—TEXAS
Tx30 90 ent., tpd. shts. by subj. Bks., per. & newsp. No add.

LIBRARIES—TORONTO (ONT., CAN.)
Ca8-lib. sch Unest., tpd. shts. by name of lib. Spec. lib. resources in Toronto. No add.

LIBRARIES, HOME. *See* List of Bibliographies, APPENDIX I

LIBRARIES, SPECIAL. *See* LIBRARIES—TORONTO (ONT., CAN.) **Ca8-lib. sch**; List of Bibliographies, APPENDIX I

LIBRARY ADMINISTRATION
Tx5 1500 cds. by auth., t. & subj. Organiz. of a lib. Freq. add.

LIBRARY ARCHITECTURE—GEORGIA
G6 60 cds. by place. Pub., coll. & spec. lib. bldgs. Occ. add.

LIBRARY BOARDS—GEORGIA
G6 1100 cds. by name. Public lib. & W.P.A. lib. units. Bd. members & trustees. Cur. add.

LIBRARY OF CONGRESS—BIBLIOGRAPHIES. *See* List of Bibliographies, APPENDIX I

LIBRARY OF HISTORIC CHARACTERS AND FAMOUS EVENTS (bk.). *In* HISTORY **N48** (1)

LIBRARY SCIENCE. *See* Names of rel. subj.; List of Bibliographies, APPENDIX I

LIBRARY SCIENCE—WORK WITH YOUNG PEOPLE
O31 315 cds. by auth. & subj. Occ. add.

LIBRETTOS. *See also* OPERAS—LIBRETTOS
O16-art 150 cds. by comp. & class. Occ. add.

LIEDER UND GESÄNGE (SCHUBERT) (bk.). *In* SCHUBERT, FRANZ PETER—WORKS **Mn14-mus** (1)

LIEDER UND GESÄNGE (SCHUMANN) (bk.). *In* SCHUMANN, ROBERT—WORKS **Mn14-mus** (2)

LIFE INSURANCE. *See* INSURANCE, LIFE

LIGHTHOUSES—PHOTOGRAPHS
V5 347 cds. by name. Freq. add.

LIGHTING
Nj52 1000 cds. by subj. Bks., per. & pams. Freq. add.

LIMESTONE CO. (ALA.)—CENSUS
A1 700 cds. by name. 1820 fed. cen. No add.

LINCOLN, ABRAHAM. *See also* List of Bibliographies, APPENDIX I
I13-ref 1700 cds. by subj. Bks. & per. Occ. add.
I70 10,000 cds., chron. Bks. Occ. add.
I72 400 cds. by subj. Bk. indexed: Paul Selby, *Anecdotal Lincoln,* p45–254. Stories & incidents. No add.
Ky1 700 cds. by auth. Bks., pams. & per. Freq. add.
Ky2 154 cds. by auth. Bks. & per. Freq. add.

LINCOLN, ABRAHAM—WORKS
I70 1000 cds. by name. Mss. Names appearing in Lincoln mss. Occ. add.

LINDSAY, NICHOLAS VACHEL—WORKS
I13-ref 1200 cds. by t. & 1st line. Bks. & per. Infreq. add.
I72 653 ent., tpd. shts. by t. Poetry. No add.

LINEAGE BOOKS. *See* DAUGHTERS OF AMERICAN REVOLUTION. LINEAGE BOOKS

LIST OF MISSOURI'S CELEBRITIES (bk.). *In* MISSOURI—BIOGRAPHY **Mo8**

LITERARY DIGEST AND INTERNATIONAL BOOK REVIEW (per.)
K6 v. 1-4, 1923–1926. Cds. by subj. No add.

LITERARY LANDMARKS
Tx8 17 cds. by subj. Per. Infreq. add.

LITERARY PRIZES. *See* REWARDS (PRIZES, ETC.), Name of individual prizes.

LITERATURE. *See also* AUTHORS; Names of individual authors; CHILDREN'S LITERATURE; CLASSICAL LITERATURE; Names of types of literature, i.e. ESSAYS, FICTION; Names of national literatures, i.e. AMERICAN LITERATURE; PURITAN LITERATURE; ROMANTICISM; List of Bibliographies, APPENDIX I
 Ca6 600 cds. by subj. Bks. Freq. add.
 Co5-ref 15,840 cds. by auth. & t. Bks., pams., per. & newsp. Freq. add.
 I79 800 ent., tpd. shts. by subj. Bks. Infreq. add.
 Ky17 4000 cds. by auth., subj. & t. Bks. & per. Freq. add.
 N22-ref 750 cds. by subj., lit. form & special type of ed. inf. Anthologies not otherwise indexed. No add.
 N46-lit (1) 500 cds. by auth. Bks. indexed: *Harvard classics.* No add.
 N46-lit (2) 650 cds. by auth. Bk. indexed: *Synopsis & outlines of literature.* Occ. add.
 N48 1000 cds. by auth. Bk. indexed: Richard Garnett, *Universal anthology.* No add.
 Nb1 880 cds. by auth., subj. & t. Bk. indexed: Richard Garnett, *Universal anthology.* No add.
 Nb4 7000 ent., tpd. shts. by t. Bks. Freq. add.
 Nj66 (1) 400 cds. by subj. Bks. & pams. Background mat. for study of *Ivanhoe* & *Men of iron.* Infreq. add.
 Nj66 (2) 27 ent., tpd. shts. by auth. & subj. Mat. to supp. read. of *Scarlet pimpernel.* Infreq. add.
 Sc3 700 cds. by auth. & subj. Bks. Lit. crit. Cur. add.

LITHOGRAPHERS. *See* ARTISTS C56-print

LITTLE JOURNEYS TO THE HOMES (bk.). *In* BIOGRAPHY N48

LIVER
 Nj61 80 cds. by auth. & t. Bks., per. & pams. Freq. add.

LIVING AUTHORS (bk.). *In* AUTHORS Ia20, Mt1; BIOGRAPHY C8-ref

LOGAN Co. (KY.)
 Ky2 3p., tpd. shts. by name. George Blakey scrapbk. Gen. & hist. of Logan co., Ky. No add.

LOGGING—SOUTH. *See* LUMBERING—SOUTH

LONDON (ONT., CAN.)—HISTORY
 Ca5-ref 500 cds. by name & subj. Newsp. & pic. Infreq. add.

LONDON, EDINBURGH AND DUBLIN PHILOSOPHICAL MAGAZINE
 N35-ref. sci Ser. 1, v. 1-68, 1796–1825; ser. 4, v. 1-50, 1851–1875. Tpd. shts. by auth. & subj. No add.

LONDON TIMES (newsp.). *In* BOOK REVIEWS In23-ord; NECROLOGY N30-ref

LONG, GENERAL JAMES. *See* List of Bibliographies, APPENDIX I

LONG ISLAND (N.Y.)—BIBLIOGRAPHY—IMPRINTS
 N22-L.I. 1000 cds. by place, chron. Occ. add.

LONG ISLAND (N.Y.)—GENEALOGY. *See* GENEALOGY—LONG ISLAND (N.Y.)

LONG ISLAND (N.Y.)—NAMES, GEOGRAPHICAL. *See* NAMES, GEOGRAPHICAL—LONG ISLAND (N.Y.)

THE LONG VALLEY (bk.). *In* SHORT STORIES Tx12

LONGFELLOW, HENRY WADSWORTH
 Me3 900 cds. by subj. Mat. by & about Longfellow. Occ. add.

LONGFELLOW, HENRY WADSWORTH—EVANGELINE
 In11 6p., tpd. shts. by subj. Per., bks., pams. & lantern slides. Infreq. add.

LONGFELLOW, HENRY WADSWORTH—MUSIC
 Me3 775 cds. by t. of poem. Mus. based on poems of Longfellow. Occ. add.

LOS ANGELES (CALIF.)
 C32-mun. ref 6000 cds. by subj. Bks. & per. Cur. add.

LOS ANGELES (CALIF.)—ADULT EDUCATION
 C32-ad. educ 2640 cds. by subj. of course. Courses of study. Semi-yrly. add.

LOS ANGELES (CALIF.)—AUTHORS. *See* AUTHORS—LOS ANGELES (CALIF.)

LOS ANGELES (CALIF.)—CHURCHES. *See* List of Bibliographies, APPENDIX I

LOS ANGELES (CALIF.). DEPT. OF HEALTH. BULLETIN. *In* PUBLIC HEALTH—DOCUMENTS C32-sci

Los Angeles (Calif.)—Officials and Employees
C32-mun. ref   1800 cds. by name. Bks., per., mss. & off. city files. All off. since 1850. Cur. add.

Los Angeles (Calif.)—Officials and Employees—Portraits
C32-mun. ref   1800 cds. by name. Bks. & per. All off. since 1850. Occ. add.

Los Angeles (Calif.)—Photographs. See California   C73-Amer.

Los Angeles (Calif.)—Schools—Publications
C32-educ   430 ent., tpd. shts. by subj. Pub. of L.A. city sch. Freq. add.

Los Angeles (Calif.)—Societies and Clubs, Foreign
C32-for   365 cds. by nationality. For. clubs in L.A. Freq. add.

Los Angeles (Calif.)—Translators. See List of Bibliographies, Appendix I

Los Angeles (Calif.) Daily News (newsp.). In California—Newspapers   C32-hist

Los Angeles (Calif.) El Clamor Publico (newsp.). In California—Newspapers   C32-hist

Los Angeles (Calif.) Express (newsp.). In California—Newspapers   C32-hist

Los Angeles (Calif.) Herald (newsp.). In California—Newspapers C32-hist

Los Angeles (Calif.) Semi-Weekly News (newsp.). In California—Newspapers   C32-hist

Los Angeles (Calif.) Southern Vineyard (newsp.). In California—Newspapers   C32-hist

Los Angeles (Calif.) Star (newsp.). In California—Newspapers   C32-hist

Los Angeles Symphony Orchestra. See Symphony   C32-art; C49-art

Los Angeles (Calif.) Times (newsp.). See also in California—Newspapers C32-hist
C32-per   1928–date. Tpd. shts., chron. Daily add.

Los Angeles Times Magazine (per.). In California   C51

Los Angeles (Calif.) Tri-Weekly News (newsp.). In California—Newspapers   C32-hist

Los Angeles Co. (Calif.)—Politics and Government
C32-mun. ref   1400 cds. by subj. Bks. & per. Cur. add.

Louisiana
Ky2   62 cds. by auth. Bks. & per. Freq. add.
L2-La.   100,000 cds. by subj. Bks., per., pams., newsp., maps, pic., etc. Cur. add.
L14-circ   500 cds. by subj. Bks. New Orleans & La. mat. Freq. add.
L14-ref   200 cds. by subj. Per. 1802–1932. New Orleans & La. mat. Infreq. add.

Louisiana—Biography
L14-ref   7400 cds. by name. Bks., per. & newsp. Freq. add.

Louisiana—Documents
L14-ref   1100 cds. by auth., t. & subj. Infreq. add.

Louisiana—History
L14-ref   Unest. ent., tpd. shts. by subj. Bk. indexed: Lacarriere A. Latour, *Historical memoir of the war in West Africa and Louisiana in 1814–1815.* No add.

Louisiana—Natural Resources. See Natural Resources—Louisiana

Louisiana—Pictures. See Pictures—Louisiana

Louisiana—Portraits. See Portraits—Louisiana

Louisiana Conservation Review
L9   1930–date. Cds. by subj. Cur. add.

Louisiana Historical Society—Publications
L14-ref   2000 cds. by auth. & subj. Yrly. add.

Louisiana Historical Society. Quarterly
L11   v. 1-21, 1917–1918. Cds. by auth. & t. Occ. add.

Louisville (Ky.)
Ky2   127 cds. by auth. Bks. & per. Freq. add.

LOUISVILLE (KY.)—NAMES, GEOGRAPHICAL.
See NAMES, GEOGRAPHICAL—LOUIS-
VILLE (KY.)

LOUISVILLE (KY.)—SOCIETIES AND CLUBS
Ky15-Ky.   250 cds. by name of club.
Newsp., etc. Occ. add.

LOUISVILLE (KY.) UNIVERSITY—PUBLICA-
TIONS, FACULTY
Ky17   300 cds. by auth. Bks., per.,
& reprints. Occ. add.

LOUISVILLE (KY.) COURIER JOURNAL
(newsp.)
Ky15-Ky.   Over 2000 cds. by name
& subj. *Courier journal* & *Louisville
times*. Ky. & Louisville mat. Daily
add.

LOUISVILLE (KY.) HERALD POST (newsp.)
Ky15-Ky.   30,000 cds. by name &
subj. No add.

LOUISVILLE (KY.) TIMES. *In* LOUISVILLE
(KY.) COURIER JOURNAL (newsp.)
Ky15-Ky.

LOVE—FOREIGN LANGUAGES
Mi6-for   175 cds. by subj. & lang.
Bks. Freq. add.

LOVE STORIES
I4   105 ent. by auth. Bks. Occ. add.
Nj21   79 ent., tpd. shts. by auth.
Bks. Occ. add.

LOWNDES CO. (ALA.)—CEMETERY RECORDS
A1   350 ent., tpd. shts. by name.
Mt. Willing cem.; McQueen cem.;
Letohatchie cem.; Dunklin cem.;
Oak view cem.; Hayneville cem.;
Public cem., Hayneville; Haigler
cem., Rives cem., Willis Brewer
cem.; Brightman cem.; Graves bury-
ing ground; Stone cem. Occ. add.

LUCAS CO. (O.). *See* TOLEDO (O.)
O56-ref

LUMBERING—SOUTH
G11   50 cds. by t. Bks., per., pams.,
etc. Lumbering & logging in the
southern states. Occ. add.

LUNGS
Nj61   150 cds. by auth. & t. Bks.,
per. & pams. Freq. add.

LUTHER THEOLOGICAL SEMINARY—DISSER-
TATIONS, ACADEMIC
Mn20   1000 cds. by auth. & subj.
Theses. Yrly. add.

LYCOMING CO. (PA.) EUROPEAN WAR,
1914-1918. *See* EUROPEAN WAR
1914-1918—LYCOMING CO. (PA.)

LYCOMING CO. (PA.)—NEWSPAPERS
P56   40,000 cds. by name & subj.
Newsp., 1807-1900. No add.

LYON, MARY. *See* MOUNT HOLYOKE COL-
LEGE   M26

LYRIC POETRY. *See* POETRY, LYRIC

McCULLOCH CO. (TEX.)—HISTORY
Tx5   Unest. ent., tpd. shts. by t. of
art. Newsp., etc. Freq. add.

McGILL NEWS (per.). *In* CANADA—PERI-
ODICALS   Ca13-per

McGILL UNIVERSITY—DISSERTATIONS, ACA-
DEMIC. *See* List of Bibliographies,
APPENDIX I

MACHINERY, AGRICULTURAL—PATENTS. *See*
PATENTS—MACHINERY, AGRICULTURAL

MACHINISTS' MONTHLY JOURNAL (per.).
In LABOR AND LABORING CLASSES—
PERIODICALS   O33-Euc. Cen.

MACLEAN, JOHN—WORKS
Nj60-treas   3960 cds. by auth. Mss.
& pa., letters to & from. Infreq. add.

MACLEAN'S MAGAZINE
Ca3   v. 32, 1919-date. Cds. by auth.,
t. & subj. Cur. add.
Ca14   v. 46-51, 1933-1938. Tpd. shts.
by subj. Semi-yrly. add.

MACMASTER UNIVERSITY QUARTERLY. *In*
CANADA—PERIODICALS   Ca13-per

MADISON (IND.) INDIANA BANNER (newsp.).
In INDIANA—NEWSPAPERS   In20

MADONNAS—PICTURES. *See* PICTURES—
MADONNAS

MAGAZINE OF AMERICAN HISTORY. *In*
GENEALOGY   M19 (1); TEXAS—
PERIODICALS   Tx17

MAGAZINE OF ART
P54-ref   v. 8-20, 1916-1929. Cds.
by subj. No add.

MAGAZINE OF HISTORY. *In* GENEALOGY
M19 (1)

MAGAZINE OF NEW ENGLAND HISTORY. *In*
GENEALOGY   M19 (1)

MAGAZINES. *See* PERIODICALS

MAHONING CO. (O.)—HISTORY. *See*
TRUMBULL CO. (O.)—HISTORY
O61-ref

MAHONING VALLEY—GENEALOGY. *See*
GENEALOGY—MAHONING VALLEY

MAHONING VALLEY—HISTORY
O61-ref   3000 ent., tpd. shts. by surname. Name index to hist. coll. No add.

MAINE. *See also* List of Bibliographies, APPENDIX I
Me3   5800 cds. by subj. Freq. add.

MAINE—CITIES AND TOWNS—HISTORY
Me1   62p., tpd. shts. by name of town. Mss. & scrapbks. Freq. add.

MAINE—DOCUMENTS
Me1   50p., tpd. shts. by dept. Supp. to Hasse's index. No add.

MAINE—FLOWERS. *See* FLOWERS—MAINE

MAINE—GEOLOGY. *See* GEOLOGY—MAINE

MAINE—LAW. *See* LAW—MAINE

MAINE—MAPS. *See* MAPS—MAINE

MAINE—NEWSPAPERS. *See* List of Bibliographies, APPENDIX I

MAINE—PERIODICALS
Me2   52p., tpd. shts. by auth., subj. & t. Per. indexed: *Maine highways*, 1932–1933; *Sun-up*, 1926–1927.

MAINE HIGHWAYS (per.). *In* MAINE—PERIODICALS Me2

MAINE HISTORICAL AND GENEALOGICAL RECORDER (per.). *In* GENEALOGY M19 (1)

MAINE HISTORICAL MAGAZINE
Me2   1885–1894. Cds. by name & subj. No add.

MAINE LIBRARY BULLETIN
Me1   v. 1-18, 1911–1933. Tpd. shts. by auth. & subj. No add.

MALDEN (MASS.)—AUTHORS. *See* AUTHORS—MALDEN (MASS.)

MALDEN (MASS.)—NEWSPAPERS
M21   250,000 cds. by subj. Loc. & hist. items, necrol. Cur. add.

MAMARONECK (N.Y.). *See* List of Bibliographies, APPENDIX I

MAMARONECK (N.Y.)—CEMETERY RECORDS
N26   15p., tpd. shts. Early cem. & record of internments. No add.

MAMARONECK (N.Y.)—SOCIETIES AND CLUBS
N26   102 cds. by name. Civic, service, charitable, rel. & educ. Infreq. add.

MAMMOTH CAVE (KY.)
Ky2   137 cds. by auth. Bks. & per. Freq. add.

MANUFACTURERS' CATALOGS. *See* TRADE CATALOGS AND DIRECTORIES

MANUSCRIPTS. *See also* Name of subj. or loc., subdiv. MANUSCRIPTS; List of Bibliographies, APPENDIX I
I26-Ayer   1769 ent., tpd. shts. Mss. in Edward E. Ayer coll. No add.
I70   2000 cds. by writer, to whom written & subj. Amer. hist., biog., gen. Freq. add.
N46-loc. hist.   9240 cds. by name or subj. Rochester hist. coll. No add.
Tx17   480 cds. by t., subj. & donor. No add.
W10-mss   13,200 cds., tpd. shts. by names of writers. Calendars & mss. in lib. Freq. add.

MANUSCRIPTS, CONFEDERATE
V6   21,000 cds. by name, etc. Letters, diaries, log bks. & muster rolls. Occ. add.

MANUSCRIPTS, MEDIEVAL
N45b   1740 cds. by t. Per. indexed: *Société française de réproductions de manuscripts à peintures. Bulletin.* Cur. add.

MAPS. *See also* CARTOGRAPHY—NORTH AMERICA; U.S. GEOLOGICAL SURVEY. TOPOGRAPHIC MAPS; List of Bibliographies, APPENDIX I
C32-hist   10,560 cds. by auth. & subj. Bks., per., govt. doc., & atlases. Freq. add.
C48-ref   2000 cds. by continent & subdiv. Maps, bks., per., doc., etc. Freq. add.
C55-ref   250 cds. by large geog. subdiv. Separate maps. Cur. add.
C57   2200 cds. by loc. Geol. survey pub., etc. Infreq. add.
Ca14   324 ent. by geog. subdiv. Sec. maps, topographical surveys, cities. Freq. add.
Ct2-ref   1200 cds. by name of country & state. Topographical, highway progress maps, transport maps, physical, pol., pic., reg. maps near N.Y. Occ. add.

I14   Unest. cds. by subj. Bks., & per. Occ. add.
I26-Ayer   1000 ent., tpd. shts. by loc., cartographer & date. Bks., mss. & photostats. Freq. add.
I43   200 cds. by subj. Bk. indexed: *New international yearbook,* 1907– date. Yrly. add.
I43-ref   226 cds. by subj. Bk. indexed: *Statesman's yearbook,* v. 1– date. Maps & charts. Yrly. add.
K20-ref   375 cds. by subj. Freq. add.
Ky2   259 cds. by engraver, etc. Freq. add.
Md2-ref   500 cds. by catchword. Bks. & atlases. Occ. add.
Mi6-ref   6000 cds. by place & subj. Maps, bks. & per. Freq. add.
Mi21-ref   1050 cds. by country. Occ. add.
Mn14-Fran.   500 cds. by subj. Bks., pams. & scrapbks. Occ. add.
Mn14-ref   900 cds. by subj. Bks. Occ. add.
Mn23-ref   1500 cds. by no., area & subj. Maps, inc. doc. maps. Freq. add.
Mo11   30 cds. by subj. Maps
N4   800 cds. by country. Posters & maps. Freq. add.
N7   500 cds. by subj. Atlases. Freq. add.
N45b   2700 cds. by loc. & date. Maps in bks., sep. maps. Freq. add.
N45b   Unest. ent., tpd. shts., chron. Atlases & maps, 1572–1926. Lasker coll. No add.
N46-hist   1320 cds. by subj. Bks. & per. Cur. add.
N46-loc. hist   2640 cds. by auth., t. & subj. Flat maps & wall maps. Cur. add.
N55-Lym.H.   7036 cds. by name of place. Maps & charts of all kinds. Freq. add.
Nb8   4400 cds. by cartographer, t. & subj., chron. Bks., per. & single maps. Freq. add.
Nj40   2600 cds. by cartographer, t. & loc. Unbd. maps. In proc.
Nj46   900 cds. by cartographer, place, chron. Cur. add.
Nj50-circ   1900 cds. by loc. & subj. Envelope maps, roller maps & sht. maps. Freq. add.

Nj60-Guy.   2900 cds. by country under continent. Maps in coll. & in other pub. Freq. add.
Nj67-ref   300 cds. by t. & cartographer. Old & new maps, pic. maps & subj. maps. Occ. add.
O18   500 cds. by city & subj. Bks., per. & separates. Freq. add.
P34-ref   4155 cds. by subj. Bks. & road maps. Cur. add.
W12-ext   75 cds. by country. Wall maps, bks. & atlases. Infreq. add.

MAPS—CALIFORNIA
C27-ref   350 cds. by subj. State doc. Cur. add.

MAPS—CANADA
Ca2-ref   3850 cds. by place & auth. Maps of B.C. & Canada. Semiyrly. add.

MAPS—COLORADO
Co9   300 ent. by subj. Q. add.

MAPS—CONNECTICUT
Ct8   650 cds. by place. Bks. to 1926, & mss. No add.

MAPS—FLORIDA
F2-r.a.   228 cds. by date. Hist., topographical, co., precinct, city, geodetic survey, atlases & etc. Cur. add.

MAPS—GEORGIA
G8   Unest. cds. by subj., chron. Bks. & separates. Cur. add.
G17   800 cds. by subj. Bks. Maps & pic. Infreq. add.

MAPS—JACKSON CO. (MICH.)
Mi19   171p., tpd. shts. by name of co. & resident. 1858 maps. No add.

MAPS—MAINE
Me1   Several hundred tpd shts. by subj., chron. Inc. rare maps. Cur. add.

MAPS—NEVADA. See NEVADA—DOCUMENTS
Nv1

MAPS—NEW HAMPSHIRE
Nh2   400 cds. by class. Bks. & maps. Cur. add.

MAPS—NEW YORK (STATE)
N54   600 cds. by place & cartographer. Bks. Infreq. add.

MAPS—OHIO
O56-ref   700 cds. by subj. Hist. maps of Ohio. Infreq. add.

MAPS—SOUTHWEST
Nm2   700 cds. by cartographer, subj. & t. N.M. & S.W. Occ. add.

MAPS, ENGLISH
C73-rare   2000 cds. by loc. "1640" bks. Early English maps. Occ add.

MAPS, GEOLOGICAL
V6   60 cds. by subj. Mss. & printed. Infreq. add.

MAPS, HISTORICAL
Or4   72 cds. by type. Bks. Infreq. add.

MAPS, HISTORICAL—U.S.
N35-ref. Amer. hist   1500 cds. by event & place. Bks. & per. Maps of events & places in Amer. hist. No add.
Nj28   300 cds. by subj. Bks. Occ. add.

MAPS, HISTORICAL—WEST
U3   50p., tpd. shts. by country, state, auth. & t. of maps. Bks. No add.

MAPS, MANUSCRIPT
I26-Ayer   303 ent., tpd., shts., chron. Edward E. Ayer coll. No add.

MAPS, PICTORIAL
N46-ref   50 cds. by subj. & art. Gen. & lit. maps. Freq. add.

MAPS, TOPOGRAPHIC. See U.S. GEOLOGICAL SURVEY. TOPOGRAPHIC MAPS; List of Bibliographies, APPENDIX I

MARINE CASUALTIES. See SHIPWRECKS

MARIOLOGY. See MARY, VIRGIN

MARION (ILL.)—ACCOUNT BOOKS
I55   1000 cds. by subj. Names of art. sold & price 1839–1840. No add.

MARIONETTES
Nj66   55 cds. by subj. & form. No add.

MARITIMER (per.). In CANADA—PERIODICALS   Ca13-per

MARKET SURVEYS. See List of Bibliographies, APPENDIX I

MARQUETTE (MICH.)—HISTORY
Mi24   479 cds. by auth., subj. & t. Bks., per., newsp., etc. Cur. add.

MARRIAGE CUSTOMS AND RITES
P54-circ   40 cds. by country. Bks. & per. Infreq. add.

MARRIAGE RECORDS. See Name of loc., subdiv. REGISTERS OF BIRTHS, etc.; GENEALOGY

MARY, VIRGIN. See also List of Bibliographies, APPENDIX I
I49   446 cds. by subj., auth. & t. Bks. & per. No add.

MARYLAND
Md2-Md.   21,000 cds. by subj. Bks., per., newsp. & doc. Md. places, organiz. & subj. Freq. add.

MARYLAND—ARTISTS. See ARTISTS—MARYLAND

MARYLAND—AUTHORS. See AUTHORS—MARYLAND

MARYLAND—BIBLIOGRAPHY—IMPRINTS
Md2-Md.   400 cds. by auth. Bk. dealers' cat. Prices of Md. items. Occ. add.

MARYLAND—BIOGRAPHY
Md2-Md.   40,000 cds. by name. Bks., per., newsp., doc. & house organs. Freq. add.

MARYLAND—CHARTERS. See CHARTERS—MARYLAND

MARYLAND—DOCUMENTS
Md2-Md.   13,000 cds. by auth. & subj. Freq. add.

MARYLAND—GENEALOGY. See GENEALOGY—MARYLAND

MARYLAND—LAW. See LAW—MARYLAND

MARYLAND—MUSICIANS. See MUSICIANS—MARYLAND

MARYLAND—NATURE. See NATURE—MARYLAND

MARYLAND—PICTURES. See PICTURES—MARYLAND

MARYLAND—SOCIETIES AND CLUBS
Md2-Md.   3900 cds. by name. Newsp. Freq. add.

MARYLAND HISTORICAL MAGAZINE
Md2-Md.   1906–date. Cds. by subj. Yrly. add.

MARYLAND SCHOOL BULLETIN
Md10   Tpd. shts., chron. by v. & no., t. & subj. In proc.

MARYSVILLE (CALIF.) HERALD (newsp.)
C37   1850–1851. Cds. by subj. No add.

MASEFIELD, JOHN—WORKS
I13-ref   500 cds. by t. & 1st line. Bks. & per. Infreq. add.

MASON, CAROLINE ATHERTON (BRIDGES)—WORKS. *See* POETRY   Mo3-ref

MASSACHUSETTS—GENERAL COURT
M9   32,000 cds. by name. Record of pers. who have served in Mass. gen. ct., 1780 to date. Cur. add.

MASSACHUSETTS—HISTORY
M28   400 ent., tpd. shts. by name of co. or town. Infreq. add.

MASSACHUSETTS BAPTIST MISSIONARY MAGAZINE
P7   v. 1-4, 1803–1816. Cds. by name, subj., church etc. No add.

MASSACHUSETTS MAGAZINE. *In* GENEALOGY   M19 (1)

MASTERPIECES SELECTED FROM THE FINE ARTS OF THE FAR EAST (bk.). *In* ART, ORIENTAL   P42-art

MASTERS IN ART (bk.). *In* ARTISTS   I62; T1-ref

MASTERS IN MUSIC (bk.). *In* MUSICIANS   P13-circ

MASTITIS (BOVINE)
Md6   3500 cds. by auth. Bks., per. & govt. doc. Freq. add.

MATERIALS FOR ART STUDY (bk.). *In* ART, ORIENTAL   P42-art

MATERNITY WELFARE. *See* List of Bibliographies, APPENDIX I

MATHEMATICIANS. *See* SCIENTISTS   N8-tech

MATHEMATICS. *See* ACCOUNTING; ARITHMETIC—STUDY AND TEACHING; List of Bibliographies, APPENDIX I

MATHEMATICS—GAMES
Ia14-math   50 ent., tpd. shts. by auth. Bks. & per. Math. recreat. & amusements: puzzles, readings, games, etc. Freq. add.

MATHEMATICS—TABLES
N35-ref. sci   2700 cds. by subj. Bks. Math., astron. & physical tables. No add.

O20-sci   600 cds. by subj. Bks., to 1939. No add.
P39-tech   500 cds. by subj. Bks. Occ. add.

MATHEMATICS—UNION LISTS. *See* List of Bibliographies, APPENDIX I

MAUPASSANT, GUY DE—WORKS
C32-fic   62p., tpd. shts. by t. No add.

MAYAS. *See also* List of Bibliographies, APPENDIX I
Wa8   100 cds. by subj. Bks. & per. Freq. add.

MAYFLOWER DESCENDANT (per.). *In* GENEALOGY   M19 (1)

MAYO FOUNDATION—DISSERTATIONS, ACADEMIC
Mn17   500 cds. by auth. These pub. by fellows in found. Q. add.

MAYO FOUNDATION—PUBLICATIONS
Mn17   17,160 cds. by auth., subj., & chron. Per. Art. pub. by staff of Mayo clinic. Daily add.

MAYO FOUNDATION—PUBLICATIONS—BOOK REVIEWS
Mn17   660 cds. by auth. Per. Mayo clinic bks. Cur. add.

MEADE CO. (KY.)—HISTORY
Ky7   Unest. ent., tpd. shts. Bk. indexed: George L. Ridenour, *Early times in Meade county, Kentucky*. No add.

MECHANICAL ENGINEERING
Nj52   1000 cds. by subj. Bks., per. & pams. Freq. add.

MECHANIX ILLUSTRATED (per.). *See* JUNIOR SCHOLASTIC   Mi27j

MEDALS AND AWARDS
P31   175 cds. by subj. Gold, silver, bronze medals, medallions, "touch pieces," and tokens. Occ. add.
P39-tech   1450 cds. by name of medal, subj., donor & recipients of more than one award. Per. Medals & awards, with spec. file of pic. of medals. Freq. add.

MEDICAL ECONOMICS. *See* List of Bibliographies, APPENDIX I

MEDICAL FILMS. *See* MOTION PICTURES, MEDICAL

MEDICAL JURISPRUDENCE
Ct9 400 cds. by subj. Per. indexed: *Hygeia*, v. 14, 1936–date. Medico-legal mat. Mo. add.
Ia7 1200 cds. by name of disease & organ. Med. jls. & bks. Medico-legal, workmen's compensation. Cur. add.

MEDICINE. See also BOOKPLATES, MEDICAL; CELEBRITIES—DISEASES; DISEASES; HYGIENE; MOTION PICTURES, MEDICAL; NURSES AND NURSING; PHYSICIANS—PUBLICATIONS; PUBLIC HEALTH; List of Bibliographies, APPENDIX I; Names of diseases, i.e. TUBERCULOSIS; Types of medicine, i.e. VETERINARY MEDICINE; Names of institutions, and colleges of medicine.
C35 3000 cds. by subj. Per. Cur. add.
I14a Unest. cds. by subj. Per. Med. & nursing mat. Daily add.
Ia7 40,000 cds. yrly by anatomical subj. or disease. Bks., 222 per. Cur. med. lit. Daily add.
N10-med Unest. cds. by subj. Per. Freq. add.
N55-med 33,320 cds. by auth., t. & subj. Bks., per. & mss. Freq. add.
Nj61 75 cds. by auth. & t. Bks., per., pams. & rpts. Freq. add.
O25-nurs 200 cds. by subj. Bks., per. & pams. Nursing & med. Daily add.
P37 1300 cds. by subj. Per. Cur. add.
W12-med Several hundred cds. by subj. Per. Cur. add.

MEDICINE—BOOK REVIEWS
N10-med Unest. cds. by auth. Per. Freq. add.

MEDICINE—HISTORY
Co7 8580 cds. by subj. Hist. Freq. add.

MEDICINE—PAMPHLETS
Co7 1252 cds. by subj. Addresses, biog., hist. & sci. material. Freq. add.

MEDICINE—PICTURES. See PICTURES—MEDICINE

MEDICINE—PORTRAITS. See PORTRAITS—PHYSICIANS

MEDICINE—POSTAGE STAMPS. See POSTAGE STAMPS, MEDICAL

MEDICINE—REPRINTS
Mn17 Several thousand cds. by auth. Per. Occ. add.

MEDICINE—SOCIETIES AND CLUBS
Mn17 700 cds. by name. Per. Proc. & trans. of soc. Freq. add.

MEDICINE, LEGAL. See MEDICAL JURISPRUDENCE

MEDINA Co. (O.)—REGISTERS OF BIRTHS, ETC.
O40 2v., tpd. shts. by name. Names of all persons married in Medina co. from 1818–1865. No add.

MELODRAMAS. See PLAYS—MELODRAMAS

MEMORIAL DAY
Mn11 Unest. ent., tpd. shts. by subj. Bks. & per. Freq. add.

MEMPHIS (TENN.)—CEMETERY RECORDS
T6-ref 1560 ent., tpd. shts. by name. Burials in Elmwood cem., 1853–1865. No add.

MENKEN, ADAH ISAACS. See List of Bibliographies, APPENDIX I

MENNONITE FAMILY ALMANAC. *In* MENNONITES—HISTORY **In13**

MENNONITE YEARBOOK AND DIRECTORY. *In* MENNONITES—HISTORY **In13**

MENNONITE QUARTERLY REVIEW
In13 1927–1938. Cds., tpd. shts. by auth. In proc.

MENNONITES
In13 Unest. cds. by auth. & t. Per. Art. about Mennonites not pub. in Mennonite pub. Occ. add.
P29 22 cds. by auth. Bks., per. & pams. Amish Mennonites. Occ. add.

MENNONITES—BIOGRAPHY
In13 15,000 cds. by name. Per. indexed: *Herald of truth*, 1864–1908, *Gospel herald*, 1908–1915. Obit. In proc.

MENNONITES—HISTORY
In13 1099 ent., tpd. shts., chron. Per. indexed: *Christian monitor, Gospel herald, Herald of truth, Mennonite family almanac, Mennonite yearbook and directory.* No add. since 1934.

MENTAL HEALTH (per.). *In* CANADA—PERIODICALS **Ca13-per**

MENTAL HYGIENE (per.)
Mn14-soc   v. 1, 1917–date. Cds. by auth., subj. & t. Cur. add.

MERCER CO. (N.J.)—BIOGRAPHY
Nj67   700 cds. by subj. Daily add.

MERCHANT MARINE—FAIRFIELD CO. (CONN.). See SHIPPING—FAIRFIELD CO. (CONN.)

MERCHANTS' MAGAZINE AND COMMERCIAL REVIEW
N30-bus   1839–1870 No add.

METABOLISM
Nj61   80 cds. by auth. & t. Bks., per. & pams. Freq. add.

METEOROLOGY
N35-ref. sci   2200 cds. by auth. & subj. Astron., magnetic & meteorlogical observations made at U.S. Naval observatory, 1845–1892. No add.

METHODIST CHURCH
G14   48p., tpd. shts. by subj. Bk. indexed: George Gilman Smith, Jr., *History of Methodism in Georgia and Florida from 1785 to 1865.* No add.
N55   3000 cds. by auth., t. & subj. Bks., per. & mss. Freq. add.
O30   5500 cds. by auth., subj. & t. Bks. Freq. add.

METHODIST EPISCOPAL CHURCH ANNUAL CONFERENCE. MINUTES. *In* METHODISTS—BIOGRAPHY   Mi1

METHODIST REVIEW
G14   1847–1917. Cds. by auth. & subj. Infreq. add.

METHODISTS—BIOGRAPHY
Mi1   3300 cds. by subj. Per. indexed: *Minutes of the annual conference of the Methodist Episcopal church, 1773–1883.* Occ. add.

METROPOLITAN MUSEUM OF ART. See N.Y. METROPOLITAN MUSEUM OF ART. BULLETIN

MEXICAN WAR, 1845–1848. See U.S.—HISTORY—WAR WITH MEXICO, 1845–1848

MEXICO—MINING AND METALLURGY. See MINING AND METALLURGY—SOUTHWEST   Tx14

MEYNELL, ALICE CHRISTIANA—WORKS
I13-ref   350 cds. by t. & 1st line. Bks. & per. Infreq. add.

MICHAEL REESE HOSPITAL—PUBLICATIONS
I23   Several thousand cds. by auth. Bks. & per., from 1920. Semi-yrly. add.

MICHIGAN
Mi3-govt   300 cds. by subj. Bks., pams., per. & mss. Occ. add.
Mi13-Mich.   13,728 ent. by subj. Newsp., etc. Daily add.
Mi17   Unest. ent. by subj. Pams. & newsp. Per. indexed: *Michigan history magazine*, Autumn 1928–date. Freq. add.
Mi20   230 cds. by subj. Bks., newsp. & per. Freq. add.
Mi29   1000 cds. by subj. Bks., per. & newsp. Per. indexed: *Michigan history magazine* to 1926. Freq. add.

MICHIGAN—AUTHORS. See AUTHORS—MICHIGAN

MICHIGAN—BIOGRAPHY
Mi6-Burt.   96,000 cds. by name. Bks., per. & newsp. Freq. add.
Mi6-ref.   50,000 cds. by name. Bks. & per. Freq. add.
Mi13-Mich.   7392 ent. by name. Newsp., etc. Daily add.

MICHIGAN—CITIES AND TOWNS
Mi13-Mich.   3960 ent. by town or co. Newsp., etc. Daily add.

MICHIGAN—HISTORY
Mi6-Burt. (1)   46,000 cds., chron. Newsp. & mss. letters. Detroit & Mich. Freq. add.
Mi6-Burt. (2)   15,000 cds. by subj. Bks. & per. Detroit & Mich. Freq. add.

MICHIGAN—LOCAL GOVERNMENT—STATISTICS
Mi3-govt   75 ent., tpd. shts. by issuing agency. Sources of statistical inf. on local govt. units in Mich. Infreq. add.

MICHIGAN—PORTRAITS. See PORTRAITS—MICHIGAN

MICHIGAN. PUBLIC HEALTH DEPARTMENT
—PUBLICATIONS
Mi21-ref   350 cds. by subj. Mo. add.

MICHIGAN—SOLDIERS
Mi13-Mich.   5280 cds. by name of Mich. cem. Mich. soldiers' records. All soldiers of all wars, buried in Mich. Freq. add.

MICHIGAN STATE COLLEGE—PUBLICATIONS
Mi29   500 cds. by t., subj. & no. All pub. Freq. add.

MICHIGAN STATE COLLEGE. AGRICULTURAL EXPERIMENT STATION—PUBLICATIONS
Mi21-ref   375 cds. by subj. Q. pub. Q. add.
Mi25   450 cds. by subj. Circ., club, ext., spec. and tech. bul. Cur. add.
Mi26   27p., tpd. shts. by t. & subj. Circ., club, ext., regular, spec. & tech. bul. Cur. add.

MICHIGAN HISTORY MAGAZINE. *See also in* MICHIGAN   **Mi17, Mi29**
Mi11-ref   Cds. Q. add.

MICHIGAN MANUFACTURER AND FINANCIAL RECORD (per.)
Mi6-bus   1925–date. Cds. by co. Freq. add.

MICHIGAN PIONEER HISTORICAL COLLECTIONS (per.)
D3   v. 1-39, 1874–1915. Cds. by name. Gen. mat. Infreq. add.

MICHIGAN SECURITY NEWS (per.)
Mi6-bus   1939–date. Cds. by name of co. Freq. add.

MIDDLE AMERICAN RESEARCH INSTITUTE—PUBLICATIONS
L15   300 ent. by auth. Pub. of auth. of inst. Cur. add.

MIGRANT PROBLEM
C28   400 cds. by auth., t. & subj. Bks., per., pams., etc. Freq. add.
C57   65 ent., tpd. shts. by form of pub. Bks., doc., pams. & per. Migrants & migratory labor. Freq. add.

MILITARY ANNALS OF TENNESSEE (bk.). *In* U.S.—HISTORY—CIVIL WAR—TENNESSEE   **T6-ref**

MILITARY GAZETTE. *In* CANADA—PERIODICALS   **Ca13-per**

MILITARY GEOLOGY. *See* GEOLOGY, MILITARY

MILITARY ROSTERS. *See also* Names of wars; Names of states, subdiv. SOLDIERS
Mi6-Burt.   3000 cds., chron. by Colonial & U.S. wars, alph. by state. Bks. & per. Freq. add.
N35-ref. ed   4500 cds. by name of organiz., war & region. Bks. Cur. add.
O20-hist   400 cds. by state. Bks. & ser. Infreq. add.

MILITARY SCIENCE
D27   500 cds. by subj. Per. Freq. add.

MILITARY SERVICE, COMPULSORY
Tx5   Unest. ent., tpd. shts. by subj. Red Cross bul., newsp., etc. Freq. add.

MILK. *See also* List of Bibliographies, APPENDIX I
Nj61   130 cds. by auth. & t. Bks., per., pams. & rpts. Freq. add.

MILLAY, EDNA ST. VINCENT—WORKS
I13-ref   600 cds. by t. & 1st line. Bks. & per. Occ. add.

MILLEDGEVILLE (GA.)—BIBLIOGRAPHY—IMPRINTS
G18   60 cds. by auth. Infreq. add.

MILLENIAL STAR (newsp.). *In* SMITH, JOSEPH   **U3**

MILLINGTON (N.J.)—REGISTERS OF BIRTHS, ETC.
Nj36   9p., tpd. shts. by name. Church records of Millington Baptist church, 1872–1911. Marriages by Peter Gibb, pastor. No add.

MILLS—INDIANA
In24   Unest. ent. by co. Water powered mills in Ind. Freq. add.

MINEOLA (N.Y.)—WILLS
N22-L.I.   1600 cds. by name. Transcribed mat. Infreq. add.

MINES MAGAZINE
Co9   v. 1-17, 1910–1937. Tpd. shts. by subj. Art. on chem., metallurgy, mining petroleum & eng. Q. add.

MINIATURES. *See* PORTRAITS   **C73**

Mining and Metallurgy
N35-ref. sci   5610 ent., tpd. shts. by subj. Pub. of off. mines bur. of following loc.: Ariz., Calif., Idaho, Mont., Nev., New Mexico, Canada, Ont. Cur. add.

Mining and Metallurgy—California. See California. State Mining Bureau. Reports

Mining and Metallurgy—Canada. See Canada. Bureau of Mines—Publications

Mining and Metallurgy—Clear Creek Co. (Col.)
Co9   3600 cds. by name. Mines. Infreq. add.

Mining and Metallurgy—Colorado
Co5-sci   11,906 cds. by mine, co. & auth. of rpt. Unpub. rpts. on mines, eng. & geol. rpts., maps, briefs, logs. Occ. add.

Mining and Metallurgy—Gilpin Co. (Col.)
Co9   200 ent., tpd. shts. by subj. All mines since gold discovery. Infreq. add.

Mining and Metallurgy—Lake Co. (Col.)
Co9   2700 cds. by name. Infreq. add.

Mining and Metallurgy—Montana
Mt2   1500 cds. by mine & district. Doc. indexed: *U.S. geological survey bulletins.* Freq. add.

Mining and Metallurgy—Northwest
Wa10-tech   740 cds. by name of mine, loc. & type of mine. Mines in Oregon & Wash.

Mining and Metallurgy—Park Co. (Col.)
Co9   700 cds. by name. Infreq. add.

Mining and Metallurgy—Southwest
Tx14   4700 cds. by state, co., district & auth. Per., fed. & state pub. Geol., ore deposits, mining, petroleum of Arizona, New Mexico, Texas & Mexico. Cur. add.

Minneapolis—History
Mn14-clip   400 cds. by subj. Newsp. & pams. Freq. add.
Mn14-ref   1000 cds. by subj. Minn. & St. Paul firsts & other fugitive inf. Occ. add.

Minneapolis Symphony Orchestra Programs. See Symphony   C32-art, O20-art

Minnesota. See also List of Bibliographies, Appendix I
Mn11   Unest. ent., tpd. shts. by subj. Bks. & per. Freq. add.
Mn14-clip   725 cds. by subj. Newsp. & pams. Infreq add.
Mn16   16 cds. by subj. Pams., etc. Freq. add.
Mn23-ref   25,876 cds. by subj. Bks., pic., pams., per. & newsp. St. Paul & Minn. Freq. add.

Minnesota—Authors. See Authors—Minnesota

Minnesota — Bibliography — Imprints.
Mn21-cat   500 cds. by place & date. Bks., pams., ser., per. & newsp. up to 1880. Infreq. add.

Minnesota—Biography. *In* Minnesota—History   Mn14-ref
Mn21-ref   30,000 cds. by name. Bks., per. & newsp. Cur. add.

Minnesota—Counties—History
Mn14-ref   200 ent., tpd. shts. by co. Co. hist. Cur. add.

Minnesota—Documents. See also List of Bibliographies, Appendix I
Mn24   630 cds. by state. Bks., pams. & per. Freq. add.

Minnesota—History
Mn14-clip   450 cds. by subj. Pams. & newsp. Freq. add.
Mn14-ref   1200 cds. by subj. Bks. & per. Minn. hist. & biog. Cur. add.
Mn23-Ham.   925 cds. by subj. Bks., pams. & newsp. Cur. add.

Minnesota—Indians. See Indians—Minnesota

Minnesota—Missions, Catholic. See Missions, Catholic—Minnesota

Minnesota—Societies and Clubs
Mn23-ref   4312 cds. by subj. Newsp. & club handbks. St. Paul & Minn. organiz. Infreq. add.

MINNESOTA—SOLDIERS
Mn21-ref   488p., tpd. shts. by surname. Bk. indexed: Minnesota. Board of commissioners . . ., *Minnesota in the Civil and Indian wars.* Minnesotans in Civil & Indian wars. No add.

MINNESOTA CONSERVATIONIST (per.)
Mn14-ref   v. 3-7, 1935–1939. Cds. by auth. & subj. In proc.

MINNESOTA IN THE CIVIL AND INDIAN WAR (bk.). *In* MINNESOTA—SOLDIERS Mn21-ref

MINUTES OF THE ANNUAL CONFERENCES OF THE METHODIST EPISCOPAL CHURCH (bk.). *In* METHODISTS—BIOGRAPHY Mi1

MISSIONARIES—BIOGRAPHY
Mn14-ref   350 ent., tpd. shts. by name. Biog. of 95 miss. most often requested. Occ. add.

MISSIONARY PRIESTS. *See* PRIESTS, MISSIONARY

MISSIONS, CATHOLIC—MINNESOTA
Mn14-ref   200 ent., tpd. shts. by name. Miss., Minn. Cath. missions. Occ. add.

MISSISSIPPI
L11   Unest. ent., tpd. shts. by name. Bk. indexed: John F. H. Claiborne, *Mississippi, as a province, territory and state.* No add.
Ms3   3000 cds. by auth. Bks., pams. & per. Cur. add.
Ms4   2640 cds. by subj. Per., pams. & newsp. Freq. add.

MISSISSIPPI—BIOGRAPHY
Ms3   1100 cds. by name. Bks. & pams. No add.
Ms4   Unest. cds. by subj. Per., pams. & newsp. Freq. add.

MISSISSIPPI—CITIES AND TOWNS
Ms3   131p., tpd. shts. by name. Incorporated towns of Miss. No add.

MISSISSIPPI—CONFEDERATE STATES OF AMERICA. *See* U.S.—HISTORY—CIVIL WAR—MISSISSIPPI

MISSISSIPPI—DOCUMENTS
Ms3   20,000 cds., chron. Mss. in Ser. A, D, & E. No add.

Ms3   1000 cds., chron. All congress. doc. rel. to Miss. Freq. add.
Ms3   Several hundred cds. by agency, chron. Off. pub. of Miss. Freq. add.
Ms3   6000 cds. by subj. All mss. in Ser. E. No add.
Ms3   2000 cds. by subj. All mss. in Ser. E & D. No add.

MISSISSIPPI—GOVERNORS
Ms3   10,800 cds. by name. All mss. in Ser. E. No add.

MISSISSIPPI—HISTORY
Ms3   Several thousand p., tpd. shts. Off. arch. Freq. add.

MISSISSIPPI—HISTORY—MANUSCRIPTS
Ms3   8p., tpd. shts. by name of coll. Private mss. in dept. Freq. add.

MISSISSIPPI—LAW. *See* LAW—MISSISSIPPI

MISSISSIPPI—NEWSPAPERS. *See* List of Bibliographies, APPENDIX I

MISSISSIPPI—SOLDIERS. *See* U.S.—HISTORY—CIVIL WAR—MISSISSIPPI   Ms3

MISSISSIPPI, AS A PROVINCE, TERRITORY AND STATE (bk.). *In* MISSISSIPPI   L11

MISSISSIPPI HISTORICAL SOCIETY—PUBLICATIONS
Ms3   94p., tpd. shts. by name of pers. & subj. 19v. covered. No add.

MISSISSIPPI RIVER. *See also* RIVERS Ky2
Ky2   114 cds. by auth. Bks. & per. Freq. add.
L11   3500 ent., tpd. shts. by name & subj. Bk. indexed: Emerson W. Gould, *Fifty years on the Mississippi.* No add.
Mo13-ref   3360 cds. by name & subj. Bk. indexed: Emerson W. Gould, *Fifty years on the Mississippi.* No add.

MISSOURI
Mo2   200 cds. by subj. Per. indexed: *Missouri magazine, Ozarkian magazine.* Occ. add.

MISSOURI—AUTHORS. *See* AUTHORS—MISSOURI

MISSOURI—BIOGRAPHY
Mo8 Unest. cds. by name. Bk. indexed: *A List of Missouri's celebrities* . . . ; Per. indexed: *Missouri historical review*, 1906–1935

MISSOURI—LAW. *See* LAW—MISSOURI

MISSOURI, A BONE OF CONTENTION (bk.). *In* ST. LOUIS (Mo.) **Mo13-Soul**

MISSOURI HISTORICAL REVIEW. *In* MISSOURI—BIOGRAPHY **Mo8**

MISSOURI MAGAZINE. *In* MISSOURI **Mo2**
Mo3-Wpt. 1929–1934. Cds. by subj. No add.

MISTICK KREWE (bk.)
L11 Unest. ent., tpd. shts. by name. No add.

THE MIXTURE AS BEFORE (bk.). *In* SHORT STORIES **Tx12**

MODEL CRAFTSMAN (per.). *In* HANDICRAFTS **Mi27-ref**
I65-bus v. 2-10, 1934–1942. Cds. by subj. Freq. add.

MODELS. *See also* SHIP MODELS—PHOTOGRAPHS
O20-sci 1785 cds. by subj. Bks. & per. Cur. add.

MODERN SHORT STORIES (ASHMUN; BROWN) (bks.). *In* SHORT STORIES **Tx12**

MOLECULES. *See* PHYSICS **Nj60-phys** (1)

MOLLUSKS. *See* List of Bibliographies, APPENDIX I

MONOLOGUES. *See also* PLAYS **I43-ref**, **O37**; POETRY **C43-ref**; READINGS AND RECITATIONS **G4-circ**, **Mn14-ref**; **O2**; SCHOOLS—EXERCISES AND RECREATIONS **N22-educ**
I13-circ 63 cds. by auth. Bks. Occ. add.
In23-ref 2640 cds. by t. Bks. Cur. add.
N46-lit 350 cds. by t. Bks. Supp. to Silk & Fanning, Ireland indexes. Cur. add.
N46-lit 1000 cds. by subj. Bks. Supp. to Silk & Fanning, Ireland indexes. Cur. add.
O16-circ 75 cds. by subj. Bks. Cur. add.
O31 300 cds. by t. Bks. Supp. to Silk & Fanning, Ireland indexes. Monologs & dialogs. Freq. add.
P39-circ 800 cds. by t. Bks. Cur. add.
W16 2000 cds. by subj. Bks. Cur. add.

MONOLOGUES—FOREIGN LANGUAGES
Mi6-for 35 cds. by lang. & auth. Bks. Occ. add.

MONROE Co. (ALA.)—CEMETERY RECORDS
A1 100 ent., tpd. shts. by name. Jew. cem., Clairborne; Clairborne cem. Occ. add.

MONROE Co. (ALA.)—ORPHANS COURT MINUTES
A1 2000 cds. by name. 1816–1821 minutes. No add.

MONTANA. AGRICULTURAL EXPERIMENT STATION—PUBLICATIONS
Mt1 645 cds. by subj. Bul., circ. & annual rpts. of M.A.E.S. Cur. add.

MONTANA—MINING AND METALLURGY. *See* MINING AND METALLURGY—MONTANA

MONTANA STATE HISTORICAL SOCIETY. CONTRIBUTIONS
Mt3 v. 1-9. Tpd. shts. by name, subj. & t. Cur. add.

MONTCLAIR (N.J.)—AUTHORS. *See* AUTHORS—MONTCLAIR (N.J.)

MONTCLAIR (N.J.)—BIOGRAPHY
Nj34 500 cds. by subj. Montclair residents interested in spec. hobbies. Freq. add.

MONTCLAIR (N.J.)—SOCIETIES AND CLUBS
Nj34 600 cds. by name. Newsp. Freq. add.

MONTEREY Co. (CALIF.)—PICTURES. *See* PICTURES—MONTEREY Co. (CALIF.)

MONTGOMERY Co. (ALA.)—CEMETERY RECORDS
A1 2000 cds. by name. Owners of lots in Oakwood cem., 1810–date. Occ. add.
A1 4580p., tpd. shts. by cem. & name of person. *Montgomery* cem.: Bledsoe, Gilmer, Hood, Harpers, Hickory Grove, Marks, Nicholas Meriwether, Mount Carmel, Perry, Sand Creek, Ware, Memorial, Remount (negro), Underwood, BrownWood, Stokes or Carter, Dillard,

Greenwood, Sharpe, Oakwood; *Cecil* cem.: Cecil; *Sprague Junction* cem.: John Falconer, Walters, Amason (East of S.J.); *Pine Level* cem.: Pine Level Baptist, Pine Level Methodist, Zuber (W. of P.L.), Zuber (W. of P.L.); *Naftel* cem.: Prospect; *Mittylene* cem.: Taylor, Cem. on Thompson place, *Mt. Meigs* cem.: Pinkston, Ray-Nicholson, Freenie, Antioch; *Merry* cem.: Raoul; *Hope Hull* cem.: McGee or Clark cem.; *Sellers* cem.; Bethlehem (W. of S.). Occ. add.

MONTGOMERY CO. (ALA.)—CENSUS
A1   1500 cds. by name. Heads of families from fed. cens. in co., 1830. No add.

MONTGOMERY CO. (ALA.)—REGISTERS OF BIRTHS, ETC.
A1   9000 cds. by bride & groom. Marriage records. Marriages from 1817–1866. No add.

MONTGOMERY CO. (ALA.)—WILLS
A1   2000 cds. by name. Wills made in co., 1818–1924. Cur. add.

MONTHLY WEATHER REVIEW. *See* U.S. WEATHER BUREAU. MONTHLY WEATHER REVIEW

MONTOUR CO. (PA.)—HISTORY. *See* DANVILLE (PA.)—HISTORY   **P10**

MONUMENTS. *See* SCULPTURE; STATUES

MORGAN, JOHN HUNT
Ky2   120 cds. by auth. Bks. & per. Freq. add.

MORGAN, LEWIS HENRY—CORRESPONDENCE, REMINISCENCES, ETC.
N47   2000 cds. by auth. of letter. Anthropology, ethnology, soc., 1840–1881. Infreq. add.

MORMONS AND MORMONISM. *See also* List of Bibliographies, APPENDIX I
U3 (1)   18,000 cds. by name & subj. Bk. indexed: Joseph Smith, Jr., *History of the Church* . . . No add.
U3 (2)   49p., tpd. shts. by auth. & subj. Wk. indexed: *Mormons in Ohio, Illinois, Missouri, Iowa,* v. 1-8, 1831–1847. No add.
U3 (3)   8000 cds. by name & subj. Newsp. Occ. add.
U3 (4)   2500 cds. by subj. Bks., per. & newsp. Freq. add.

MORMONS IN OHIO, ILLINOIS, MISSOURI, IOWA (bk.). *In* MORMONS AND MORMONISM   **U3** (2)

MORRIS CO. (N.J.)—GENEALOGY. *See* GENEALOGY—NEW JERSEY   **Nj46** (1)

MORRISTOWN (N.J.)—REGISTERS OF BIRTHS, ETC.
Nj36   25p., tpd. shts. by name. Baptisms, St. Peter's church, 1826–1894, 1910–1917. No add.
Nj36   90p., tpd. shts. Reg., minutes & hist. of First Presbyterian church, 1742–1891. No add.
Nj36   24p., tpd. shts. Trans. of the Morris township comm., Apr. 12, 1798–Mar. 31, 1855. No add.

MORTGAGES
Nj40   7500 cds. by name, place & form. Indentures. Occ. add.

MOTHER'S DAY
C41   30 cds. by subj. Bks. & pams. Yrly. add.
Mn11   Unest. ent., tpd. shts. by subj. Bks. & per. Freq. add.
Mn14-ref   575 ent., tpd. shts. by auth. or t. Bks. & per. Pic., banquet programs, songs, poems, stories, etc. Cur. add.
T1-circ   80 ent., tpd. shts. by subj. Bks. Infreq. add.

MOTION PICTURE ACTORS. *See* ACTORS AND ACTRESSES

MOTION PICTURE CLASSIC (per.). *In* MOTION PICTURES   **C32-per**

MOTION PICTURE MAGAZINE. *In* MOTION PICTURES   **C32-per**

MOTION PICTURES. *See also* DRAMA **Wa15**; THEATRE **N35-ref.** theat (1), (3)
C18-ref   3475 cds. by t. Per. Infreq. add.
C23   40,000 ent. by t. Per., newsp., etc. Mot. pic. production file. Freq. add.
C32-art   2640 cds. by t. Newsp. rev. No add. since Mot. pic. rev. digest.
C32-educ   2600 cds. by t. Mot. pic. rev. organiz. Evaluations. Cur. add.
C32-per   7096 cds. by subj. Per. indexed: *Motion picture classic,* 1929–1931; *Motion picture magazine,* 1926–date; *Photoplay,* 1925-date; *Screen book,* 1929–1933. Mot. pic. & actors. Occ. add.

C81-j 450 cds. by t. Mot. pic. bul. Freq. add.
I8 1600 cds. by t. Per. indexed: *Joint estimates on cur. mot. pic.* Cur. add.
I65-educ 2300 cds. by t. Rev., 1935–date. Freq. add.
I68-art 600 cds. by t. Per. Freq. add.
Mn23 Unest. cds. by t. Per. indexed: *Variety,·* 1939–date. Cur. add.
Mn23-per Unest. cds. by t. Per., 1927–date. Mot. pic. crit. Daily add.
N46 650 cds. by t. Per. not elsewhere indexed. Mot. pic. rev. & crit. Occ. add.
N54-per 1700 cds. by t. Per. Freq. add.
O20-fic 3960 cds. by auth., movie & bk. t. Bks. made into movies. Cur. add.
O20-lit Unest. ent., tpd. shts. by t. Newsp. Mot. pic. rev. Cur. add.
O31 1575 cds. by t. Per. indexed: *Joint estimates on current motion pictures.* Freq. add.
O56-ref 3000 cds. by t. Not cur., & not inc. in Motion pic. rev. digest & Harrison's reports. Infreq. add.
U2-circ 1000 ent. by subj. or t. Estimates. Wkly. add.

MOTION PICTURES—RESEARCH. *See* PICTURES **C25**

MOTION PICTURES—STILLS
L7 Unest. cds. by t. Cur. add.
N22-art 176 cds. by subj. Countries, hist. char., hist. events, famous bldgs., hist. instruments, etc. Occ. add.
N35-circ. pic 2000 cds. by subj. Pic. No add.
Nj42 500 cds. by subj. & t. Freq. add.
O20-art 3450 cds. by subj. Freq. add.
Tx20 1000 ent., by name. Port. Freq. add.

MOTION PICTURES, MEDICAL
C29 300 cds. by subj. & distributor. Freq. add.

MOTION PICTURES IN EDUCATION
C87 235 ent., tpd. shts. by subj. & t. Visual mat.: films, slides, film strips. Freq. add.
Nj42 1000 cds. by t. & subj. Educ. films. Freq. add.

MOTION STUDY. *See* TIME AND MOTION STUDY

MOTOR BUSES
Nj52 1000 cds. by subj. Bks., per. & pams. Freq. add.

MOTORLAND (per.). *In* CALIFORNIA **C8-ref**
C20 1938–date. Cds. by subj. Cur. add.

MOUNT HOLYOKE COLLEGE
M26 11,000 cds. by auth., subj. & t. Mss. letters, doc., jls., etc. Mary Lyon, hist. of Mt. Holyoke, alumnae, etc. Freq. add.
M26 2300 cds. by auth., subj. & t. print. materials, newsp., phot., etc. Hist. of coll., its founders, presidents, alumnae, et. Freq. add.

MOUNT RAINIER NATIONAL PARK
Wa14-ref 400 ent., tpd. shts. Bks., pams. & per. Infreq. add.

MOUNTAIN LIFE AND WORK (per.)
Ky1 v. 1–15, 1925–1940. Cds. by auth., subj. & t. Freq. add.

MOUNTAIN WHITES—SOUTHERN STATES
Ky1 700 cds. by auth. & class. Bks., per., extracts, pams., etc. Freq. add.
Ky1 300 cds. by state & co. Bks., per. & bul. Freq. add.

MOVING PICTURES. *See* MOTION PICTURES

MUNICIPAL DOCUMENTS. *See* GOVERNMENT DOCUMENTS, MUNICIPAL

MUNICIPAL GOVERNMENT
C43-ref 12,600 cds. by subj. Mun. govt. & admin. Freq. add.
I19 Unest. cds. by subj. Bks., pams. & per. Pub. of state leagues of municipalities. Cur. add.
I24 90 ent., tpd. shts. by subj. Council proc. Ord. of large cities. Mo. add.
Mi6-soc 3666 cds. by subj. Per., mun. rpts., proc., etc. Corporation counsel's off. index of mat. on mun. affairs. Cur. add.
O18 2500 cds. by subj. Per. Freq. add.

MUNICIPAL GOVERNMENT BY CITY MAN-
AGER
Nj48 70 ent., tpd. shts. by subj.
Bks., pams. & per. Occ. add.

MUNICIPAL OWNERSHIP
Nj52 1000 cds. by subj. Bks., per.
& pams. Freq. add.

MUNICIPAL REVIEW OF CANADA. *In* CAN-
ADA—PERIODICALS **Ca13-per**

MUNSELL'S GENEALOGICAL INDEX—SUPPLE-
MENT (bk.). *In* GENEALOGY **Me1**
(1)

MURAL PAINTING AND DECORATION
I71-art 47 cds. by art. Pic. Infreq.
add.
O21 65 cds. by art. Bks. & per.
Colored pic. Occ. add.
P39-art. ref 2000 cds. by art. & subj.
Per. & annuals of Amer. soc. before
1933. No add.

MURDERS—CANADA
Ca7 2640 cds. by name, yr., co.,
place, hangings, unsolved murders.
Ontario, Quebec noted murders.
Freq. add.

MURPHY, JOHN BENJAMIN—WORKS
I43-med Unest. cds. by subj. Per.,
1880–1916. No add.

MUSCATINE (IA.)
Ia17 35 cds. by subj. Newsp., doc.,
letters, papers, etc. Freq. add.

MUSCLE SHOALS—ALABAMA
T4 381 cds., chron. Off. doc. Muscle
Shoals & Tenn. river, 1824–date.
Occ. add.
T5-ref 144 cds. by ser. no. & con-
gress. Pub. & private rpts. & hear-
ings, fed. doc. Muscle Shoals &
Tenn. river. Occ. add.

MUSEUMS
O51 1506 cds. by auth., subj. & t.
Bks., maps, etc. Freq. add.

MUSIC. *See also* ANTHEMS; BALLADS;
CHILDREN'S SONGS; CHORAL MUSIC;
CHRISTMAS MUSIC; CHURCH MUSIC;
DANCE MUSIC; FOLK SONGS; HYMNS;
INSTRUMENTAL MUSIC; LANTERN
SLIDES—SONGS; MUSICIANS; Names
of musicians; NATIONAL SONGS;
OPERAS; ORATORIOS; ORCHESTRA AND
ORCHESTRAL MUSIC; ORGAN MUSIC;
PHONOGRAPH RECORDS; PHYSICIANS
AND MUSIC; PIANO MUSIC; SHAKE-
SPEARE, WILLIAM—MUSIC; SONGS;
SYMPHONY; Names of individual
symphony programs; TRIO MUSIC;
DRAMA **Mi6-mus, N54-per**
C1 12,000 cds. by t. Scores. Freq.
add.
C8-ref 11,880 cds. by comp., t., etc.
Mus. comp. inc. songs. Freq. add.
C17 Unest. cds. by comp., t. & type
of comp. Freq. add.
C18-r.a. 4650 cds. by t. Bks. &
pams. Freq. add.
C27-art 22,000 cds. by comp. & t.
Bks. & sht. mus. Cur. add.
C56 1600 cds. by instrument, comp.
& t. Sht. mus., voc. & instrumental.
Freq. add.
C56 750 cds. by comp. Bks. & per.
Voc. & instrumental mus. Freq.
add.
C57 1500 cds. by comp., t. & subj.
Bks. & mss. mus. Cur. add.
Ca14 1900 cds. by comp. & t. Sht.
mus. Freq. add.
Ct11-ref 3960 cds. by comp., t., &
1st line. Coll. of instrumental mus.
& songs. Cur. add.
I29 1600 cds. by t. Bks., scores &
per. Instr. & study. Freq. add.
I29 1600 cds. by auth. Bks., scores
& per. Instr. & study. Freq. add.
I29 1600 ent., tpd. shts. by subj.
Bks., scores & per. Instr. & study.
Freq. add.
I45 1101 ent., tpd. shts. by no. Sht.
mus., programs, mus. notes. Ken-
dall mus. coll. No add.
Ia3 3280 cds. by comp., t. & subj.
Bks. & piano scores, songs, not in-
dexed. Occ. add.
Ia20 600 cds. by t. & comp. Bk.
indexed: *Everybody's favorite series,*
13v. In proc.
In23-art 3500 cds. by comp. & t.
Bks. Songs, organ, piano, violin &
other instrumental mus. not indexed.
Freq. add.
In23-art 40,000 ent., tpd. shts. by
comp., arrangement & subj. Octavo
mus. Cur. add.
In26 340 cds. by t. & comp. Infreq.
add.
In29 1146 cds. by t., auth. & comp.
Old sht. mus., 1826–1864. No add.

K20-circ 7475 cds. by comp., t. & form. Bks. Freq. add.

M16-ref 2525 cds. by auth. & t. Scores, instrumental, voc. & piano; coll. & indiv. pieces; textbks., hist., biog. Occ. add.

M23-art Several thousand cds. by comp. & t. Instrumental & voc. mus. coll. Cur. add.

M27-art 30,000 cds. by t. Coll. of songs, piano, organ, violin, chamber & orch. mus. Occ. add.

Md2-art 15,000 cds. by comp. & t. Sht. mus. Cur. add.

Md9 300 cds. by comp., instrument & t. Bk. & sht. mus. Occ. add.

Mi21-cat 3825 cds. by comp. & t. Bks. & per. Cur. add.

Mi27-ref 7000 cds. by subj., comp. & t. Bks. & sht. mus. Per. indexed: *Etude*. Mo. add.

Mn14-mus 47 cds. by auth., t. & v. Bk. indexed: Edmund H. Fellowes, *The English madrigal school*, 32v. No add.

Mn23-art 7506 cds. by comp. & t. Mus. coll. Cur. add.

Mo13-art 3600 cds. by subj. & comp. Per. Cur. add.

Mo13-o.s. 460 cds. by subj. Bks. Folk mus., keys & signatures, musicians, radio mus. Occ. add.

Mo13-o.s. 330 cds. Concertos & other spec. lists of comp. not indexed. Occ. add.

N18 4500 cds. by comp. & t. Bks. Occ. add.

N22-art 8800 cds. by instrument. Bks. not indexed in Sears, Cushing or Quigley. Songs, piano, violin, organ, saxaphone. Cur. add.

N35-Ott. 300 cds. by comp. & t. Sht. mus. Voc., instrumental & orch. Occ. add.

N35-ref. mus (1) 18,000 cds. by name of pub. Sht. mus., U.S. & for. Cur. add.

N35-ref. mus (2) 2500 cds. by subj. Sht. mus. & bks. Songs & instrumental mus. Cur. add.

N35-ref. mus (3) 900 cds. by subj. chron. Sht. mus. & bks. Mus. for spec. occasions. Cur. add.

N45b-mus 546 cds. by t. Bk. indexed: Domenico Scarlatti, *Opere complete per clavicenbalo criticamente rivedute*, 11v. No add.

N46-art 1800 cds. by t. & comp. Concert programs. Occ. add.

N60 15,840 cds. by t. & comp. Bk. Voc. & instrumental mus. Cur. add.

Nb7 5586 cds. by comp. & t. Sht. mus. Freq. add.

Nc3 350 cds. by comp., t. & subj. Inc. anthems. Freq. add.

Nj15 2640 cds. by comp., t. of work & t. of indiv. piece. Bks. indexed: William C. Bridgman, *Basic songs for male voices; Famous composers and their works*, 3v.; *50 art songs, 52 sacred songs; 56 songs you like to sing; 59 piano solos; 60 progressive piano pieces; Scribner radio music library*, 8v.; *Waverley collection of rare and beautiful music*, 4v.; Albert E. Wier, *Days of . . .*, 8v. Cur. add.

Nj37-ref 926 cds. by comp., subj. & t. Orch. music, cantatas, librettos, bks. Freq. add.

Nj50-art 11,000 cds. by t., comp. & subj. Mus. scores & phonograph records. Freq. add.

Nj58 8700 cds by comp., subj., voice & mus. instrument. Sht. & bd. mus. Occ. add.

O20-Clark 660 cds. by t. Bks. Songs & other mus. In proc.

O20-Coll. 300 cds. by t. Sht. mus. Popular & semi-classical songs, comp. for piano & violin. Occ. add.

O29-ref 2600 cds. by comp., t. & subj. Bks. Freq. add.

O36 18,000 cds. by comp. & t. Songs, piano mus., dances. Freq. add.

O44 2000 cds. by comp. Sht. mus.: vocal & instrumental, cantatas, operas, choir, coll., choruses, oratorios. Infreq. add.

O59 500 cds. by comp., t. & subj. Occ. add.

P13-circ 800 cds. by comp. & t. Bks. Occ. add.

P39-Wyl. 951 cds. by comp. & subj. Bks. Piano, violin & organ. Cur. add.

P43 12,000 cds. by comp. & t. Bks., pams. & per. Cur. add.

P50 1500 cds. by auth., subj. & t. Bks., records, voc. & instrumental mus. Freq. add.

Tx4 1280 cds. by comp. Infreq. add.

Wa10-art 14,500 cds. by comp. & t. Bks. Freq. add.

Wa11-ref 14,000 cds. by comp. & comp. Coll. Occ. add.

Wa11-ref 1100 cds. by comp. Bks. & symphony programs. Occ. add.

Wa15 940 cds. by auth., subj. & t. Bks., pams. Inc. biog. Freq. add.

MUSIC—ALABAMA
A1 3500 cds. by comp., auth. of words & t. Daily add.

MUSIC—ANALYSIS, INTERPRETATION, APPRECIATION
N35-mus 1000 cds. by comp. & type. Freq. add.
Sd1 250 cds. by t., auth., comp. & type of mus. Bks., per. & pams. Freq. add.
T6-ref 3200 cds. by t. & comp. Bks. & per. Freq. add.

MUSIC—BALTIMORE (MD.)
Md4 5000 cds. by pub., chron. Sht. mus. Baltimore pub., comp. or loc. pers. to whom songs were dedicated, 1790–1865 (incomplete), 1865–date. Freq. add.

MUSIC—CHICAGO
I13-circ 19 ent., tpd. shts. by auth. Bks. Occ. add.

MUSIC—ILLINOIS
I5-ref 69 cds. by auth. & musicians. Bks. & per. Occ. add.

MUSIC—INDIANA
In22-Ind. 300 cds. by comp., t., subj. & type. Voc. & instrumental mus. by Ind. comp., & songs by Ind. writers. Occ. add.

MUSIC—ITALY. See FOLK-SONGS, ITALIAN

MUSIC—LATIN AMERICA
I5-ref 128 ent., tpd. shts. by auth. & musician. Bks. & per. Occ. add.

MUSIC—LONGFELLOW, HENRY WADSWORTH. See LONGFELLOW, HENRY WADSWORTH—MUSIC

MUSIC—PERIODICALS
I26 398,000 cds. by auth. & subj. Per. No add.
N35-mus 4500 cds. by subj. 300 per. Cur. add.
N47-mus 7920 cds. by subj. For. & Amer. per., 1923–date. Cur. add.
Or5-mus 3700 cds. by subj. Per. & pams. Cur. add.

P54-ref 674 cds. by name of comp. Per. indexed: *Etude*, v. 12-27, 1894–1909; *Musician*, v. 10-15, 1905–1910. No add.

MUSIC—POETS
M27-art 58 ent., tpd. shts. by name. Bks. Infreq. add.

MUSIC—PORTLAND (ORE.)
Or5-mus 650 cds. by subj. Musicians & soc. organiz., etc. Occ. add.

MUSIC—SAN FRANCISCO (CALIF.)
C69-mus Unest. eds. by art & event. Programs of mus. events in S.F., 1870–date. Cur. add.

MUSIC—THEORY. See List of Bibliographies, APPENDIX I

MUSIC, CONFEDERATE
V6 Unest. ent. tpd. shts. Instrumental & voc. mus. Infreq. add.

MUSIC, GEOGRAPHICAL
C27-art 500 cds. by country & period. Bks. Mus. by country. Occ. add.

MUSIC, POPULAR
N8-ref 9240 cds. by t. Bks. Freq. add.

MUSIC, RADIO
I62 25p., tpd. shts. by comp. & t. Bk. indexed: Albert E. Wier, *Scribner radio music library*, 8v. No add.

MUSIC, THEATRICAL. See SONGS—RADIO THEME **M3**

MUSIC, WEDDING
Mn14-mus 230 ent., tpd. shts. by class & auth. Bks. & sht. mus. Piano, organ, songs, etc. Infreq. add.
Mn23-art 250 cds. by comp. & t. Sht. mus. & bks. Occ. add.

MUSIC LITERATURE
C27-art 500 cds. by subj. Bks. Music. hist. & appreciation. Occ. add.
C69-mus 2000 cds. by subj. Bks. of essays, per. & pams. Freq. add.
M3 3500 cds. by auth., subj. & t. Mus. lit. out of print, sold only on definite order & tr. of for. ed. seldom called for. Occ. add.
M3 6800 cds. by auth., subj. & t. Mus. lit. & pams. Cur. add.
N10-mus Hundreds of cards. by comp. & t. Bks. & per. Notes on mus. comp. Freq. add.

N54-art 1100 cds. by subj. Bks. & per. Occ. add.

O20-art 3876 cds. by name & subj. Subj. aids on mus. questions. Freq. add.

MUSICAL AMERICA (per.)
C60 v. 57, 1937–date. Cds. by auth., subj. & t. Occ. add.

MUSICAL COMEDIES
C32-art 135p., tpd. shts by comp., t., song t., date. Coll. to 1933. No add.

MUSICAL INSTRUMENTS
C27-art 1000 cds. by name. Bks. Cur. add.

MUSICIAN (per.). *In* MUSIC—PERIODICALS
P54-ref

MUSICIANS. *See also* ARTISTS. **I68-art**; List of Bibliographies, APPENDIX I
Ca6 250 cds. by name. Bks. Freq. add.
I13-w.s.r. 300 cds. by name. Per., newsp. & programs. Freq. add.
N35-ref. mus 70,000 cds. by name. Bks., per. & newsp. Cur. add.
P13-circ 44 cds. by comp. Bk. indexed: *Masters in music*, 6v. No add.

MUSICIANS—CLEVELAND (O.)
O20-ref 47 cds. by comp. Mus. comp. by Clevelanders. Infreq. add.

MUSICIANS—FAIRFIELD CO. (CONN.). *See* FAIRFIELD CO. (CONN.)—BIOGRAPHY
Ct2-hist

MUSICIANS—KENTUCKY
Ky2 6p., tpd. shts. by name. Ky. comp. & their wks. Occ. add.

MUSICIANS—MARYLAND
Md2-art 500 cds. by name. Baltimore & Md. musicians & mus. Occ. add.

MUSICIANS—NECROLOGY
N35-mus 1000 cds. by name, chron. 1935–date. Freq. add.

MUSICIANS—PORTLAND (ORE.). *In* MUSIC —PORTLAND (ORE.) **Or5-mus**

MUSICIANS—TEXAS. *In* TEXAS—BIOGRAPHY
Tx27 (2)

MUSKEGON (MICH.)
Mi25 26,475 cds. by subj. Newsp., co. hist., etc. Cur. add.

MUSKEGON (MICH.)—SOCIETIES AND CLUBS
Mi25 75 cds. by name. Cur. add.

MY OKLAHOMA (per.)
Ok4-ref v. 1-2, 1927–1928. Cds. by auth., subj. & t. In proc.

MYSTERIES, HISTORICAL. *See* List of Bibliographies, APPENDIX I

MYSTERY AND DETECTIVE STORIES. *See also* DETECTIVES (IN FICTION); List of Bibliographies, APPENDIX I
I13-circ 800 cds. by auth. Bks. Freq. add.
K8-circ 701 ent., tpd. shts. by auth. Bks. Yrly. add.
Mi6-Red. 300 ent., tpd. shts. by auth. Bks. Mo. add.
Mi13-Un. Hi. 100 cds. by auth. & t. Bks. Occ. add.
N44-ad 24p., tpd. shts. Bks. Yrly. add.
Nd2 350 cds. by auth. Bks. Freq. add.
Nj21 840 ent., tpd. shts. by auth. Bks. Freq. add.
Nj58 385 cds. by auth. Bks. Freq. add.
O31 127 cds. by subj. Bks. Freq. add.
P29 40 cds. by auth. Bks. Freq. add.

MYSTERY AND DETECTIVE STORIES—FOREIGN LANGUAGES
Mi6-for 125 cds. by subj. & lang. Bks. Freq. add.

MYSTERY AND DETECTIVE STORIES, JUVENILE. *See* CHILDREN'S LITERATURE—MYSTERY AND DETECTIVE STORIES

MYTHOLOGY
C32-phil 600 ent., tpd. shts. by subj. Bks. Freq. add.
I13-ref 600 cds. by name & subj. Myth. char. Occ. add.
In23-ref 750 ent., tpd. shts. by subj. Personifications & symbols of mythology of all races.

MYTHOLOGY—PICTURES. *See* PICTURES— MYTHOLOGY

NACOGDOCHES (TEX.)
Tx27 400 cds. by subj. Unindexed mat. Cur. add.

NAMES. *See also* PRONUNCIATION
Mi29 500 cds. by name. Pronunciation, spelling & origins of names. Freq. add.

NAMES, GEOGRAPHICAL
Ct1   900 cds. by town & state. Bks. & per. Freq. add.
D10   1408 cds. by subj. & auth. Bks. & per. No add.
N54   5000 cds. by place. Gen., hist., per. & mss. Cur. add.

NAMES, GEOGRAPHICAL—COLORADO
Co5-W. hist   1500 cds. by name. Infreq. add.

NAMES, GEOGRAPHICAL—INDIANA
In24   1320 cds. by name. Bks. & maps. Streams, towns, cos., etc., existing & former inc. inf. conc. origins, loc., etc. Freq. add.

NAMES, GEOGRAPHICAL—LONG ISLAND (N.Y.)
N22-L.I.   3500 cds. by place. Atlases, bks. & maps. In proc.

NAMES, GEOGRAPHICAL—LOUISVILLE (KY.)
Ky15-Ky.   30 cds. by name of st. Bks. & newsp. Hist. & origin of st. names. Infreq. add.

NAMES, GEOGRAPHICAL—PENNSYLVANIA
P57   1000 cds. by name. Names & nicknames in York & Adams cos. Occ. add.

NAMES, GEOGRAPHICAL—SAN DIEGO CO. (CALIF.)
C62   500 cds. by name. Cur. add.

NAMES, PERSONAL
O9   4100 cds. by surname. Freq. add.

NAMES, PERSONAL—FOREIGN LANGUAGES
N46-ref   48p., tpd. shts. by lang. Dict. Occ. add.

NARRATIVE POETRY. *See* POETRY, NARRATIVE

NASHVILLE (TENN.)
T9-ref   800 cds. by subj. Pams. & newsp. Infreq. add.

NASHVILLE (TENN.)—CATALOGS, UNION. *See* CATALOGS, UNION—NASHVILLE (TENN.)

NASHVILLE (TENN.)—SPECIAL COLLECTIONS. *See* SPECIAL COLLECTIONS—NASHVILLE (TENN.)

NATIONAL ADVISORY COMMITTEE OF AERONAUTICS. BULLETIN
Mn14-tech   1320 cds. by subj. Cur. add.

NATIONAL ASSOCIATION OF REAL ESTATE BOARDS. NEWS SERVICE
I25   200 cds. by subj. Wkly. add.

NATIONAL BOARD OF FIRE UNDERWRITERS—PUBLICATIONS
P39-tech   1925 cds. by state & city. Rpts. of several hundred cities, bul., etc. Cur. add.

NATIONAL DEFENSE ADVISORY COMMISSION. RELEASES
N32   400 cds. by subj., addresses & name of speaker. Daily add.

NATIONAL HISTORICAL MAGAZINE. *In* U.S.—HISTORY—REVOLUTION   In35-gen (2); WASHINGTON, GEORGE P39-ref
D3   v. 1-79, 1892-1932. Cds. by name. Gen. Freq. add.
F2-ref   v. 31, 1907-date. Cds. by subj. Mo. add.

NATIONAL MAGAZINE OF AMERICAN HISTORY. *In* OHIO—PERIODICALS   O56-ref

NATIONAL OFFICE MANAGEMENT ASSOCIATION—PUBLICATIONS
P32   14p., tpd. shts. by subj. Per. indexed: *N.O.M.A. Proceedings*, v. 20-21, 1939-1940; *N.O.M.A. Forum*, v. 14-16, 1938-1940. No add.

NATIONAL OFFICE MANAGEMENT ASSOCIATION. PROCEEDINGS. *In* NATIONAL OFFICE MANAGEMENT ASSOCIATION—PUBLICATIONS   P32

NATIONAL SOCIETY FOR STUDY OF EDUCATION. YEARBOOK
Wa3   550 cds. by auth., t. & subj. Yrly. add.

NATIONAL SONGS
I70   150 cds. by t. Sht. mus. of Civil war period, etc. Campaign & patriotic songs, Lincoln songs. Occ. add.

NATURAL RESOURCES. *See also* SOIL CONSERVATION; WILD LIFE—CONSERVATION; List of Bibliographies, APPENDIX I
D8   2000 cds. by state & t. Bks., per., etc. State planning bd. rpts. Freq. add.
D30   11,416 cds. by subj. Bks., per., etc. Daily add.
W20-Fratt.   Unest. cds. by subj. Per. indexed: *Nature mag.*, 1935-date. Cur. add.

NATURAL RESOURCES—LOUISIANA
L3 300 cds. by subj. State doc. & per. Cur. add.

NATURALISTS—PORTRAITS. See PORTRAITS —NATURALISTS

NATURE. See also List of Bibliographies, APPENDIX I
Ca2-sci 350 cds. by subj. Per. Mo. add.
Ca13-zoo 2500 cds. by auth. Per. & soc. pub. Cur. add.
Mi16 91 ent., tpd. shts. by subj. Bks. Infreq. add.
N10-ref 562 cds. by subj. Bks. & per. Freq. add.
N55-Lym. H. 1043 cds. by auth., t. & subj. Bks. & per. Freq. add.

NATURE—ILLINOIS
I73-lands Unest. cds. by bot. name. Trees & shrubs in Champaign, Urbana. Occ. add.

NATURE—MARYLAND
Md2-ind 215 cds. by class. Per. & doc. Md. fauna & flora. Occ. add.

NATURE—NEW ROCHELLE (N.Y.)
N28-loc. hist 1200 cds. by name of obj. Plants, shrubs, trees, etc. Freq. add.

NATURE—PICTURES. See PICTURES—NATURE

NATURE—STUDY AND TEACHING
O37-Mad. 100 cds. by subj. Bks., pams. & pic. Cur. add.
Vt4 475 cds. by subj. Bks., per., govt. doc. & pams. Cur. add.

NATURE IN POETRY. See CHILDREN'S POETRY—NATURE **O20-Sup.-j**

NATURE MAGAZINE. In NATURAL RESOURCES **W20-Fratt.**

NAVAL SCIENCE. See List of Bibliographies, APPENDIX I

NAVAL STORES
G11 50 cds. by t. Bks., per. & pams. Occ. add.

NEBRASKA
Nb8 1000 cds. by subj. Bks. & per. Freq. add.

NEBRASKA—AUTHORS. See AUTHORS—NEBRASKA

NEBRASKA—BIOGRAPHY
Nb14-ref 4200 cds. by subj. Bks., per. & newsp. Omaha & Neb. hist. & biog. Occ. add.
Nb14-S. 864 cds. by name. Bks., pams. & newsp. Freq. add.

NEBRASKA—FRONTIER AND PIONEER LIFE. See FRONTIER AND PIONEER LIFE—NEBRASKA

NEBRASKA—HISTORY. See also NEBRASKA—BIOGRAPHY **Nb14-ref**; List of Bibliographies, APPENDIX I
Nb14-j 350 cds. by subj. & t. Bks., pams. & per. Freq. add.

NEBRASKA — PHYSICIANS — PUBLICATIONS. See PHYSICIANS—NEBRASKA—PUBLICATIONS

NEBRASKA. UNIVERSITY — PUBLICATIONS, ALUMNI
Nb8 1600 cds. by auth. & subj. Per. Occ. add.

NEBRASKA. UNIVERSITY — PUBLICATIONS, FACULTY
Nb8 800 cds. by auth. Bks. & per. Freq. add.

NEBRASKA, UNIVERSITY. COLLEGE OF AGRICULTURE—PUBLICATIONS
Nb14-S. 240 cds. by subj. Bul., circ., rpts., 1930–date. Freq. add.

NEBRASKA. UNIVERSITY. COLLEGE OF MEDICINE—THESES, SENIOR
Nb8-med 1000 cds. by auth. & subj. Theses, 1931–date. Cur. add.

NECROLOGY. See also Names of loc., occup., etc., subdiv. NECROLOGY
M11 Unest. ent. by subj. Newsp. & per. Freq. add.
Mo3-ref 1000 cds. by name. Auth. & other prominent people, not loc. Wkly. add.
N30-ref 40,735 cds. by subj. Per. indexed: *Annual register, London times*—19th & 20th cent. Cur. add.
O20-ref 238,920 cds. by name. Newsp. indexed: *Cleveland plain dealer*. Freq. add.
O56-ref 45,000 cds. by name. Newsp. indexed: *Toledo blade*, 1837–date. Daily add.
P36-ref 6000 cds. by name. Bk. indexed: *Appleton's annual cyclopedia*, 1861–1875. No add.

NEGRO LITERATURE. *See also* AUTHORS, NEGRO; NEGRO STORIES; List of Bibliographies, APPENDIX I
G3   860 cds. by subj. Bks. & per. Freq. add.

NEGRO LITERATURE—BOOK REVIEWS
O20-Ster.   500 cds. by auth. Bks. Cur. add.

NEGRO LITERATURE, JUVENILE
O20-Cedar   40 cds. by class. Bks. Cur. add.

NEGRO SONGS
O20-art   159p., tpd. shts. by t. Bks. Negro spirituals. No add.
O20-Ster.   1250 ent., tpd. shts., by t. Bks. No add.

NEGRO STORIES
K8-circ   7 cds. by auth. Bks. In proc.
Mn11   Unest. ent., tpd. shts. by auth. Bks. Freq. add.

NEGROES. *See also* SLAVERY IN THE U.S.; List of Bibliographies, APPENDIX I
I44   111 ent., tpd. shts. by auth. Bks. & pams. Mus., poetry, plays, novels, pol. Freq. add.
Ky15-E. Col. (1)   216 cds. by subj. Per. indexed: *The crisis.* Freq. add.
Ky15-E. Col. (2)   84 cds. by subj. Per. indexed: *Opportunity.* Freq. add.
Ky15-W. Col. (1)   75 cds. by subj. Per. indexed: *Colored American.* Freq. add.
Ky15-W. Col. (2)   500 cds. by subj. Per. indexed: *The crisis.* Freq. add.
Ky15-W. Col. (3)   350 cds. by subj. Per. indexed: *Opportunity.* Freq. add.
Ky15-W. Col. (4)   100 cds. by subj. Per. indexed: *Journal of negro education.* Freq. add.
Ky15-W. Col. (5)   450 cds. by subj. Per. indexed: *Journal of negro history.* Freq. add.
Ky15-W. Col. (6)   200 cds. by subj. Per. indexed: *Southern workman.* Freq. add.
Mo3-Linc.   150 cds. by subj. Freq. add.
Ms3   517p., tpd. shts. by subj. Pams. & per. Alfred H. Stone index. No add.

N35-circ. cat   54,000 cds. by auth. & subj. Bks. Lit., hist. & art, Schomberg coll. Cur. add.
Nj7-ad   86 cds. by subj. Bks. Freq. add.
O20-F.I.   300 cds. by auth., t. & subj. Bks. & per. Cur. add.
O20-Wood.   600 cds. by class. Per., per. & bk. reviews. Freq. add.
O29-W. Carn.   800 cds. by subj. Bks. & per. Cur. add.
P39-Wyl.   365 cds. by subj. Per. indexed: *Crisis, Journal of negro history, Opportunity.* Mo. add.
Tx21-Col.   750 cds. by auth. Bks. Freq. add.
V4   1500 cds. by subj. Per. indexed: *Crisis, Opportunity, Southern workman.* Cur. add.

NEGROES—BIOGRAPHY
D6 (1)   900 cds. by name. Per. indexed: *Journal of negro history.* Mo. add.
D6 (2)   3000 cds. by auth. Bks. Freq. add.
D6 (3)   2700 cds. by name. Bks. Infreq. add.

NEGROES—MANUSCRIPTS
D6   150 cds. by auth. & subj. Letters of negro leaders & those interested in negroes. Infreq. add.

NEGROES—PERIODICALS
D6   11,400 cds. by auth., subj. & t. Per. indexed: *Crisis, Journal of negro history, Opportunity,* & *Voice of the negro.* Freq. add.

NEGROES—PORTRAITS. *See* PORTRAITS—NEGROES

NELSON, T.A.R. *See* U.S.—HISTORY—CIVIL WAR—TENNESSEE   **T3-Mc.**

NELSON Co. (KY.)—MINUTE BOOKS
Ky7   Unest. cds. by name. Minute bks., 1785–1788. No add.

NERVOUS SYSTEM
Nj61   150 cds. by auth. & t. Bks., per. pams. & rpts. Freq. add.

NEVADA—DOCUMENTS
Nv1   300 cds. by subj. Pams. & maps, state doc. Freq. add.

NEW BEDFORD (MASS.)—NEWSPAPERS
M23-gen   Several thousand cds. by subj. Daily add.

NEW BRUNSWICK (N.J.)—CHURCHES. *See*
List of Bibliographies, APPENDIX I

NEW BRUNSWICK (N.J.) HISTORICAL CLUB
—PAPERS AND ADDRESSES
Nj40   368 ent., tpd. shts., chron.
Mss. & bks. No add.

NEW BRUNSWICK (N.J.)—HISTORY
Nj38   18 cds. by auth. Bks., per. &
pams. Infreq. add.

NEW BRUNSWICK (N.J.)—REGISTERS OF
BIRTHS, ETC.
Nj40   1375 ent., tpd. shts. by name.
Newsp., 1792–1816. No add.

NEW BRUNSWICK (N.J.)—SOCIETIES AND
CLUBS
Nj37-ref   51 cds. by name. Freq.
add.

NEW BRUNSWICK (N.J.) HOME NEWS
(newsp.)
Nj37-ref   995 cds. by subj. Cur.
add.

NEW BRUNSWICK THEOLOGICAL SEMINARY
Nj38   29 cds. by auth. Bks., per. &
pams. Infreq. add.

NEW ENGLAND FAMILY HISTORY (per.).
In GENEALOGY   M19 (1)

NEW ENGLAND HISTORICAL AND GENEALOGICAL REGISTER (per.). *In* GENEALOGY   M19 (1)

NEW ENGLAND QUARTERLY. *See also in*
GENEALOGY   M19 (1)
Ct3   v. 2-4, 1929–1932. Cds. by subj.
No add.

NEW FRIENDS OF MUSIC SYMPHONY (ORCHESTRA) PROGRAMS. *See* SYMPHONY   O16-art

NEW HAMPSHIRE—MAPS. *See* MAPS—
NEW HAMPSHIRE

NEW HAMPSHIRE GENEALOGICAL RECORD
(per.). *In* GENEALOGY   M19 (1)

NEW HARMONY (IND.)—HISTORY
In29   Unest. ent., tpd. shts. by subj.
& t. Bks. & mss. Occ. add.
In29   19,800 cds. by subj. Bks.,
newsp., etc. Cur. add.

NEW HARMONY (IND.) GAZETTE (newsp.)
In1; In29   v. 1-3, 1825–1829. Cds. by
subj. No add.

NEW HAVEN (CONN.)—BIBLIOGRAPHY—
IMPRINTS
Ct13   4000 cds. by date, printer, pub.,
chron. Bks. & per. Imprints up to
& inc. 1850. No add.

NEW INTERNATIONAL YEARBOOK (bk.). *In*
BIOGRAPHY   F4; MAPS   I43

NEW JERSEY. *See also* PRINCETON (N.J.)
Nj59; List of Bibliographies,
APPENDIX I
Nj27-N.J.   5680 cds. by auth., subj.
& t. Misc. inf. Occ. add.
Nj27-N.J.   9925 cds. by auth., subj.
& t. Cur. add.
Nj38   31 cds. by auth. Bks., per. &
pams. Infreq. add.
Nj40 (1)   11,000 cds. by auth. & subj.
Pams., mss., newsp. & pic. Cur.
add.
Nj40 (2)   457 ent., tpd. shts., chron.
Bks. T. rel. to but not printed in
N.J., 1641–1783, by H. Gilbert
Kelley. No add.
Nj58   6000 cds. by auth., subj. & t.
Bks., pams., per. & newsp. Freq.
add.
Nj63   1360 ent., tpd. shts., by subj.
Life, ind. & resources. No add.
Nj68   Unest. cds. by community &.
subj. Newsp. indexed: *Jersey journal, Jersey observer, Hudson dispatch*, 1916–date. Cur. add.

NEW JERSEY—ADULT EDUCATION
Nj18   200 cds. by subj. Ad. educ.
courses. Semi-yrly. add.

NEW JERSEY—ANTIQUES—UNION LISTS.
See ANTIQUES—NEW JERSEY—UNION
LISTS

NEW JERSEY—AUTHORS. *See* AUTHORS—
NEW JERSEY

NEW JERSEY—BIBLIOGRAPHY—IMPRINTS
Nj40   2400 cds. by place & date.
Bks. & pams. In proc.
Nj50-circ   250 cds. by auth. Occ.
add.
Nj67-ref   2500 cds. by subj. Bks.,
per. & pams. Freq. add.

NEW JERSEY—CHURCHES
Nj38   30 cds. by auth. Bks., per. &
pams. Churches & church hist.
Infreq. add.

NEW JERSEY—DOCUMENTS
Nj18   417 cds. by dept. State pub.
Occ. add.

NEW JERSEY—GENEALOGY. *See* GENEALOGY
—NEW JERSEY

NEW JERSEY—HISTORY
Nj38   100 cds. by auth. Bks., per. & pams. Infreq. add.

NEW JERSEY—LAKES
Nj30-circ   1100 cds. by name. Inc. name, nearest post off., co., latitude & longitude. Infreq. add.

NEW JERSEY—LAW. *See* LAW—NEW JERSEY

NEW JERSEY—MANUSCRIPTS
Nj46   900 cds. by subj., name, chron. Cur. add.

NEW JERSEY—NEWSPAPERS. *See* List of Bibliographies, APPENDIX I

NEW JERSEY—PICTURES. *See* PICTURES—NEW JERSEY

NEW JERSEY—PRESBYTERIAN CHURCH—COUNCILS AND SYNODS. *See* PRESBYTERIAN CHURCH—NEW JERSEY—COUNCILS AND SYNODS

NEW JERSEY—REGISTERS OF BIRTHS, ETC.
Nj46   Unest. ent., tpd. shts. by surname. Bible & other records. Occ. add.
Nj46   Unest. cds. by name of bride & groom. Newsp. Vital statistics through 1850. In proc.

NEW JERSEY—SOCIETIES AND CLUBS
Nj14   2640 cds. by subj. Freq. add.

NEW JERSEY HISTORICAL SOCIETY. PROCEEDINGS
Nj37-ref   7 cds. by subj. Freq. add.

NEW JERSEY IN LITERATURE
Nj50-circ   250 cds. by auth. Bks. & per. Occ. add.

NEW MEXICO—MAPS. *See* MAPS—SOUTHWEST **Nm2**

NEW MEXICO—MINING AND METALLURGY. *See* MINING AND METALLURGY—SOUTHWEST **Tx14**

NEW MEXICO—SOLDIERS
Nm2   6400 cds. by name. N.M. soldiers in Spanish & Indian wars, natl. militia. No add.

NEW MEXICO HISTORICAL REVIEW
Nm2   v. 1, 1926–date. Cds. by auth., subj. & t. Cur. add.

NEW ORLEANS. *See* LOUISIANA **L14-circ, L14-ref**

NEW ORLEANS (LA.)—OFFICIALS AND EMPLOYEES
L14-ref   400 cds. by name of off. & dept. Cur. add.

NEW ORLEANS (LA.)—SOCIETIES AND CLUBS
L14-ref   6500 cds. by name, type, mo. of election, name of off. Freq. add.

NEW ORLEANS (LA.) LOUISIANA DEMOCRAT (newsp.)
L1   143 cds. by t. Infreq. add.

NEW REPUBLIC (per.). *In* BOOK REVIEWS **C8-ord**

NEW ROCHELLE (N.Y.)—HISTORY
N28-loc. hist   1200 cds. by auth., subj. & t. Loc. hist. Freq. add.

NEW ROCHELLE (N.Y.)—NATURE. *See* NATURE—NEW ROCHELLE (N.Y.)

NEW ROCHELLE (N.Y.)—SOCIETIES AND CLUBS
N28-ref   175 cds. by name. Rel., civic, cultural organiz. Occ. add.

NEW ROCHELLE (N.Y.) STANDARD STAR (newsp.)
N28-loc. hist   1923–1924, incomp. Cds., by subj. No add.

NEW YEAR'S DAY. *See* CHRISTMAS **N22-ref**

NEW YORK (CITY)
N35-H.P.   8580 cds. by auth., subj. & t. Bks. & pams. Cur. add.

NEW YORK (CITY)—ADULT EDUCATION
N22-r.a.   800 cds. by name of organiz. Per. indexed: *New York adult education council. Bulletin.* Freq. add.

NEW YORK (CITY)—BOOKSELLERS AND BOOKSELLING. *See* BOOKSELLERS AND BOOKSELLING—NEW YORK (CITY)

NEW YORK (CITY)—CIVIC ASSOCIATIONS
N35-mun. ref   2900 cds. by borough & name. Wkly. add.

NEW YORK (CITY)—DANCING. *See* DANCING—NEW YORK (CITY)

New York (City)—Documents
N35-mun. ref   Unest. cds. by name of dept. Rpts., minutes, calendars, etc. of all depts., bur. & commissions of N.Y. City. Daily add.

New York (City)—Law. *See* Law—New York (City)

New York (City)—Pictures. *See* Pictures—New York (City)

New York (City)—Plays. *See* Plays—New York (City)

New York (City)—Schools
N35-ref. inf   100 cds. by subj. Voc. & prof. sch. Cur. add.

New York (City)—Social Agencies
N35-Morr.   160 cds. by t. Infreq. add.

New York (City)—Societies and Clubs. *See also* New York (City)—Civic Associations; New York (City)—Social Agencies
N22-r.a.   200 cds. by name. Cultural & educ. clubs in Queensborough. Infreq. add.

New York (State)—Bibliography—Imprints
N10   235 cds. by auth. & subj. Bks. & pams. Cur. add.

New York (State)—Bridges. *See* Bridges—New York (State)

New York (State)—Cemetery Records
D3   Unest. ent., 136v., tpd. shts. by place. N.Y. cem. & church records. Yrly. add.
P57   90,000 cds. by surname. 250,000 inscriptions from the cem. of York & Adams cos. Infreq. add.

New York (State)—Genealogy. *See* Genealogy—New York (State)

New York (State)—History
N10-gen   Thousands of cards by name of town, co. & state. Bks., per. & newsp. Freq. add.
N55-treas   50,000 cds., chron. Letters & pa. in Gerrit Smith Miller coll. Early hist. of C. N.Y. No add.

New York (State)—Maps. *See* Maps—New York (State)

New York (State)—Newspapers
Nj40   930 ent., tpd. shts., chron. Cur. add.

New York (State)—Pictures. *See* Pictures—New York (State)

New York Adult Education Council. Bulletin. *In* New York (City)—Adult Education   **N22-r.a.**

New York Beaux-Arts Institute of Design. Bulletin
I73-arch   5280 cds. by subj. & t. of problem. Mo. add.

New York Genealogical and Biographical Record (per.). *In* Genealogy **M19** (1)

New York Herald Tribune. Weekly Book Review (per.). *In* Book Reviews   **C8-ord**; **Mo3-ord**; **O20-Tem**; Children's Literature—Book Reviews   **P39-j. off**

New York Metropolitan Museum of Art. Bulletin. *In* Southwest **Nm2**
Nj57-ref   v. 19-31, 1924–1936. Cds. by subj. Supp. to print. index. Cur. add.

New York Public Library. Bulletin. *In* Young People's Literature **N35-sch**
N35-ref. inf   v. 41, 1937–date. Cds. by auth. & t. Cur. add.

New York Symphony Orchestra Programs. *See* Symphony **C49-art**

New York Times (newsp.). *In* Business Conditions   **P36-Lipp.**; Plays **L10**; Poetry   **M4-ref**

New York Times Book Review (per.). *In* Book Reviews   **C8-ord, Ct12-ord, Mo3-ord, O20-Tem.**, Business—Book Reviews   **Nj50-bus**; Poetry   **H3-ref, K5** (2); Quotations   **N60, P39-ref**
C50   v. 36, 1931–date. Cds. by auth. Wkly. add.

New York Times Magazine
K18   1800. Cds. by subj. No add.
Wa10-per   1937–1939. Cds. by subj. No add.

New York University—Dissertations, Academic—Education
N36   1565 ent., tpd. shts. by auth. & subj. Cur. add.

NEW YORKER—"PROFILES" (per.). *In* BIOGRAPHY C24, C32-per, N10-ref, N30-jour, N35-ref. inf (1)

NEWARK (N.J.)—BIBLIOGRAPHY—IMPRINTS
Nj50-circ 500 cds. by auth. Bks. Occ. add.

NEWARK (N.J.)—HISTORY
Nj50-circ 163p., tpd. shts. by subj. Bk. indexed: Joseph Atkinson, *History of Newark*. No add.
Nj50-circ 76p., tpd. shts. by subj. Bk. indexed: Peter J. Leary, *Newark, N.J., illustrated*. No add.

NEWARK (N.J.)—RECREATION
Nj50-circ 225 cds. by subj. Occ. add.

NEWARK (N.J.)—SCHOOLS
Nj50-educ. 2300 cds. by name, type of sch., subj. of course. Newark sch. & courses, where tuition is charged. Freq. add.

NEWARK (N.J.)—SOCIETIES AND CLUBS
Nj50-circ 3200 cds. by name & subj. Freq. add.

NEWARK, NEW JERSEY, ILLUSTRATED (bk.). *In* NEWARK (N.J.)—HISTORY
Nj50-circ (2)

NEWBERRY LIBRARY—AYER COLLECTION. *See* INDIANS—LANGUAGES I26-Ayer; MANUSCRIPTS; I26-Ayer; MAPS I26-Ayer; MAPS, MANUSCRIPT I26-Ayer; PORTRAITS—INDIANS I26-Ayer

NEWBERRY MEDAL BOOKS. *See* REWARDS (PRIZES, ETC.) In5-j; List of Bibliographies, APPENDIX I

NEWBURGH (N.Y.)—HISTORY. *See* List of Bibliographies, APPENDIX I
N39 229 cds. by subj. Bks., per., pams., newsp. & mss. Freq. add.

NEWSPAPERS. *See also* Names of individual newsp.; Names of loc., subdiv. NEWSPAPERS; List of Bibliographies, APPENDIX I
I73-newsp 14,000 cds. by date. Gen. & class newsp. Yrly. add.
I73-newsp 3000 cds. by city & state. Gen. & class newsp. Cur. add.
Nh2 1200 cds., chron. Amer. newsp. Cur. add.
Nj40 1900 ent., tpd. shts., chron. Newsp. pub. elsewhere than N.Y., N.J. & Pa. Cur. add.

NEWSPAPERS—FOREIGN LANGUAGES
I73-newsp 500 cds. by lang. Gen. & class newsp. Cur. add.

NEWSPAPERS—SERIES
O20-ref 300 cds. by auth. & t. Infreq. add.

NEWSPAPERS—SPECIAL EDITIONS
C32-per 550 ent., by name of city. Anniv. ed. of city & co. pa. all over world. Cur. add.

NEWSPAPERS, EARLY AMERICAN
N35-ref. res 900 ent., tpd. shts. by place. Cur. add.

NEWTOWN (N.Y.)—COURTS
N22-L.I. 500 cds. by subj. In proc.

NEWTOWN (N.Y.)—HISTORY
N22-L.I. 1300 cds. by subj. Records, 1656–. In proc.

NIARARA FALLS (N.Y.)—HISTORY
N40 5280 cds. by auth., t. & subj. Bks. & pams. Infreq. add.

NICHOLAS Co. (KY.). DEEDS
Ky7 Unest. cds. by name. No add.

NICHOLSON, MRS. MALCOLM. *See* HOPE, LAURENCE (pseud)—WORKS

NILES' NATIONAL REGISTER (per.). *In* TEXAS Tx8; TEXAS—HISTORY Tx27 (2)

NITROCELLULOSE
Nj54 Unest. ent. by subj. Spec. rpts. Freq. add.

NOBEL PRIZES
Nv1 Unest. cds. by subj. Nobel prize winners since 1900. Yrly. add.

NOBLE, NOAH. *See* INDIANA—HISTORY In22-Ind. (1)

NON-ROYALTY PLAYS. *See* PLAYS—NON-ROYALTY; PLAYS—ONE-ACT—NON-ROYALTY

NORFOLK (TENN.) JOURNAL AND GUIDE (newsp.)
T8 1935–1939. Tpd. shts. by auth., subj. & t. To be ctd. by Hist. records survey project, Wash., D.C.

NORTH AMERICA—CARTOGRAPHY. *See* CARTOGRAPHY—NORTH AMERICA

NORTH CAROLINA
Nc3 2800 cds. by auth., t. & subj. Rpts., pams., etc. Freq. add.
Nc6 Unest. cds. by subj. Bks. & per. Freq. add.

North Carolina—Biography
Nc1   255p., tpd. shts. by auth. & subj. Newsp., prior to 1801. No add.

North Carolina—History. *See* List of Bibliographies, Appendix I

North Carolina—Portraits. *See* Portraits—North Carolina

North Carolina Journal of Education Monthly
Nc6   1858–1875, 1897–1900, 1906–1924. Cds. by subj. No add.

North Carolina Teacher (per.)
Nc6   1883–1875. Cds. by subj. No add.

North Dakota
Nd1   220 cds. by subj. Bks. & per. Freq. add.

North Platte Valley (Nebr.). *See* List of Bibliographies, Appendix I

Northern Pacific Railroad
Wa14-ref   75 ent., tpd. shts. Bks., per. & doc. Infreq. add.

Northern Stories. *See also* Western Stories   **K8-circ**; List of Bibliographies, Appendix I
N44-ad   12p., tpd. shts. by t. Bks. Stories of the west & north. Yrly. add.

Northwest. *See also* List of Bibliographies, Appendix I
Wa8   11,929 cds. by auth. & t. Bks. & pams. Freq. add.
Wa11-ref   23,000 cds. by subj. Bks., per., newsp., pams. & doc. Cur. add.
Wa12   125p., tpd. shts. Bks., etc. Pacific N.W.

Northwest—Bibliography—Imprints
Ca3   7000 cds. by auth. or t. Bk. cat. Yrly. add.

Northwest—Biography
Wa10-ref   10,000 cds. by name. Bks., per. & newsp. Freq. add.

Northwest—Bridges. *See* Bridges—Northwest

Northwest—History
Id2   2200 cds. by subj. Idaho newsp., emphasis on Idaho material. Cur. add.
Wa3   800 cds. by auth. Old & rare bks. Occ. add.
Wa15   1872 cds. by auth., subj. & t. Bks., pams., docs. etc. Freq. add.

Northwest—Mining and Metallurgy. *See* Mining and Metallurgy—Northwest

Northwest—Pictures. *See* Pictures—Northwest

Northwest—Portraits. *See* Portraits—Northwest

Northwest Science (per.)
Wa4   v. 11-15, 1937–1941. Tpd. shts. by auth. & subj.

Northwestern University—Publications, Alumni
143-ref   5000 ent., tpd. shts. by auth. & subj. Alumni pub., 1902–date. Cur. add.

Northwestern University. Medical School—Publications, Faculty
I43-med   2250 cds. by auth. Med. & sci. per., 1936–date. Art. by members of fac. Freq. add.
I43-med   1088 ent., tpd. shts. by auth. Bks., monographs, etc. Occ. add.

Norwalk (O.)
O45   Unest. cds. by subj. Bks., per. & newsp. Infreq. add.

Norwegian—American Authors. *See* Authors, Norwegian—American Union Lists

Notes on the State of Virginia (bk.). *In* Virginia **V2**

Novelists
G1   437 cds. by auth. Bks., per. & newsp. Freq. add.

Noyes, Alfred—Works
I13-ref   900 cds. by t. & 1st. line. Bks. & per. Infreq. add.

Nuclear Physics (per.). *In* Physics **Nj60-phys** (2), (3)

Nursery Rhymes
Nj27-j   55 cds. by t. Infreq. add.

Nurses—Biography
Wa11-ref   100 ent., tpd. shts. by name. Bks. & per. Occ. add.

Nurses and Nursing. *See also* Medicine **I14a, O25-nurs**; List of Bibliographies, Appendix I
Ia14-med   300 cds. by subj. Per. indexed: *American journal of nursing; Trained nurse and hospital review.* Cur. add.

Nurses in Literature. *See* Physicians in Literature   M32-circ

Nutley (N.J.)—Societies and Clubs
Nj55   10p., tpd. shts. by subj.

Nutrition. *See also* Cookery; Cost and Standard of Living; Food
I73-an. nut   160,000 cds. by subj. Abstracts of art. in 112 per. Cur. add.

Oak Park (Ill.)—History
I62   11,000 cds. by subj. Loc. newsp., 1883–date.

Oakland (Calif.)—Newspapers
C43-ref   14,500 cds. by subj. Oakland newsp., 1872–1877, 1869, 1870, 1871 incomp. No add.

Oakland (Calif.)—Ordinances
C43-ref   2600 cds. by subj. Ser. ord. & code amendments, beginning with city-mgr. ser. no. 1, Jly. 1931. Freq. add.

Oakland Co. (Mich.)—History
Mi26   14,200 ent., tpd. shts. by name. Co. hist., 1877. No add.

Obituaries. *See* Biography; Necrology

Occupations. *See* Vocations

Office Management
Nj52   1000 cds. by subj. Bks., per. & pams. Freq. add.

Official Register of the Officers and Men of New Jersey (bk.). *In* U.S. — History — Revolution — New Jersey

Officials and Employees. *See* Name of loc., subdiv. Officials and Employees

Ogden (Utah)
U2-ref   300 cds. by subj., auth. & t. Newsp., per., bks., mss. & pams. Ogden & other Utah inf. Cur. add.

Ogden (Utah) Standard—Examiner (newsp.)
U2-ref   Cds. by subj., auth. & t. Occ. add.

Oglethorpe University
G19   100 ent. by subj. Pams., bul., mss., etc. Infreq. add.

O'Henry. *See* Porter, William Sydney—Works

O'Henry Memorial Award Prize Stories (bk.). *In* Short Stories   Tx12

Ohio. *See also* Cleveland (O.)   O20-sci
Ky2   88 cds. by auth. Bks. & per. Freq. add.
O20-per   2640 cds. by subj. Per. Freq. add.

Ohio—Artists. *See* Artists—Ohio

Ohio—Biography
O20-per   1320 cds. by subj. Per. Freq. add.
O56-ref   3500 cds. by name. Hist., pams., etc. Occ. add.

Ohio—Geology. *See* Geology—Ohio

Ohio—History
O20-hist   2640 cds. by subj. Bks., per. & loc. hist. Infreq. add.
O27   6000 cds. by name & subj. Bk. indexed: Henry Howe, *Historical collections of Ohio* . . . Freq. add.
O56-ref   1000 cds. by subj. State doc., co. hist. & per. Per. indexed: *Ohio citizen.* Occ. add.

Ohio—Indians. *See* Indians—Ohio

Ohio—Maps. *See* Maps—Ohio

Ohio—Periodicals
O56-ref   700 cds. by subj. Per. indexed: *Ohio magazine; National magazine of American history.* Occ. add.

Ohio—Portraits. *See* Portraits—Ohio

Ohio—Societies and Clubs. *See* Societies and Clubs   O20-ref

Ohio Archaeological and Historical Society—Publications
O29-ref   10,000 cds. by auth., t. & subj. In proc.

Ohio Archaeological and Historical Society Magazine
O56-ref   v. 1-45, cds. by subj. Infreq. add.

Ohio Citizen (per.). *In* Ohio—History   O56-ref

Ohio Law Reporter (per.)
O25-law   v. 1-40, 1903–1934. Cds. by auth. & t. Freq. add.

Ohio Magazine. *In* Ohio—Periodicals   O56-ref

OHIO RIVER. *See also* RIVERS **Ky2**
Ky2   121 cds. by auth. Bks. & per. Freq. add.

OHIO STATE UNIVERSITY MONTHLY
O27   v. 1, 1909–date. Cds. by auth. & subj. Mo. add.

OIL. *See* PETROLEUM

OKLAHOMA
Ok2-ref   2700 cds. by subj. Per. Freq. add.

OKLAHOMA—AUTHORS. *See* AUTHORS—OKLAHOMA

OKLAHOMA—BIOGRAPHY
Ok3   250 cds. by name. Bks. & pams. Infreq. add.

OLD AND NEW ST. LOUIS (bk.). *In* ST. LOUIS (Mo.) **Mo13-Soul.**

OLD ELIOT (per.). *In* GENEALOGY **M19** (1)

OLD SOUTH LEAFLETS (per.)
Tx8   v. 1-8, 1896–1903. Cds. by subj. & t. No add.

OLD TIME NEW ENGLAND. *See also in* GENEALOGY **M19** (1)
Me1   v. 1-25, 1910–1935. Tpd. shts. by subj. Freq. add.

OLDHAM Co. (KY.)
Ky7   Unest. ent., tpd. shts. by name, place & subj. Newsp. No add.

OLYMPIA (WASH.) WASHINGTON STANDARD (newsp.)
Wa11-ref   1860–1900. Cds. by subj. In proc.

OMAHA (NEB.)
Nb15   85 cds. by subj. Pams. & newsp. Freq. add.

OMAHA (NEB.)—ADULT EDUCATION
Nb14-r.a.   500 cds. by subj. Freq. add.

OMAHA (NEB.)—BIOGRAPHY. *See* NEBRASKA—BIOGRAPHY **Nb14-ref**

OMAHA UNIVERSITY
Nb15   75 cds. by subj. Pams. & newsp. Freq. add.

OMAHA SYMPHONY PROGRAMS. *See* SYMPHONY **Nb14-ref**

ONCE A WEEK (per.). *In* WOOD ENGRAVINGS **P39-ref. art**

ONE-ACT PLAY MAGAZINE AND THEATRE REVIEW. *In* PLAYS **Ia16**

ONE-ACT PLAYS. *See* PLAYS—ONE-ACT

ONE HUNDRED CHOICE SELECTIONS (bk.). *In* READINGS AND RECITATIONS **In16, Mo3-N.E., Mo3-N.E., P4** (1)

ONONDAGA Co. (N.Y.)—BIOGRAPHY
N54   20,000 cds. by name. Bks., pams. & mss. People in co. before 1850; pioneer index. Cur. add.

ONTARIO LIBRARY REVIEW AND CANADIAN PERIODICAL INDEX
Ca8-lib. sch   v. 1-15, 1916–1930. Cds. by auth., subj. & t. No add.

OPEN-AIR SCHOOLS. *See* List of Bibliographies, APPENDIX I

OPERAS
C27-art   3500 cds. by t. Bks. Infreq. add.
I13-ref   1700 cds. by t. & comp. Bks. Occ. add.

OPERAS—ARIAS
Mn14-mus   465 ent., tpd. shts. by t. Loc. of arias in operas. No add.

OPERAS—DANCING. *See* DANCING—OPERAS

OPERAS—LIBRETTOS
Nj34   350 cds. by t. Pams. Infreq. add.

OPERE COMPLETE . . . (bk.). *In* MUSIC **N45b-mus**

OPERETTAS
C32-art   300 cds. by t. 50 light operas. Occ. add.

OPPORTUNITY (per.). *See also in* NEGROES **Ky15-E. Col.** (2), **Ky15-W. Col.** (3), **P39-Wyl., V4**; NEGROES—PERIODICALS **D6**
D6   v. 1, 1923–date. Cds. by auth., t. & subj. Mo. add.

OPTICS, PHYSIOLOGICAL
Nh2   30,000 cds. by auth. & subj. Bks., per., etc. Physics, psychology & physiology of vision. Cur. add.

ORATIONS. *See also* CICERO, MARCUS TULLIUS—SPEECHES; POETRY **C43-ref**
Mi6-Rich.   350 cds. by t. Bks. Infreq. add.
N8-ref   2640 cds. by t. & speaker. Bks. Freq. add.

Nb10   200 cds. by t. Bks. Infreq. add.
Nb17   140 ent., tpd. shts. by t. Bks. & per. Infreq. add.
Nd3   373 cds. by auth. & t. Bks. & pams. Occ. add.
O34   34 ent., tpd. shts. by orator. Amer. & British orators & orations. Infreq. add.
W16   5000 cds. by t. & auth. Orations & speeches. Cur. add.

ORATORIOS
Mn14-mus   456 ent., tpd. shts. by t. Songs from which oratorios are taken. No add.

ORATORS. See ORATIONS   O34

ORCHESTRA AND ORCHESTRAL MUSIC. See also SYMPHONY; Types of orch. mus., i.e. VIOLIN MUSIC
C32-art   1320 cds. by comp. Clark coll. of bks. No add.
Nj67-ref   260 cds. by comp. & t. Full orch. scores for concert use. No add.
P39-ref. mus   7500 cds. by comp. Concert program notes, 1896–date, bks. Cur. add.

OREGON
Or2   17,000 cds. by subj. Pub. not indexed elsewhere. Freq. add.

OREGON. AGRICULTURAL EXPERIMENT STATION—PUBLICATIONS
Or1   1920 cds. by auth., subj. & t. Cur. add.
Or1   624 cds. by no. Cur. add.

OREGON—AUTHORS. See AUTHORS—OREGON

OREGON—BIOGRAPHY
Or1-ref   8068 cds. by subj. Bks. Infreq. add.

OREGON—MINING AND METALLURGY. See MINING AND METALLURGY—NORTHWEST   Wa10-tech

OREGON STATE COLLEGE—PUBLICATIONS, FACULTY
Or1   4352 cds. by auth. Bks. & per. Cur. add.

OREGON. UNIVERSITY—PUBLICATIONS, FACULTY
Or2   5000 ent., tpd. shts.; 500 cds. by auth. Pub. writings of fac. Yrly. add.

OREGON COUNTRYMAN (per.)
Or1-ref   v. 1-22, 1908–1929. Cds. by auth., subj. & t. No add.

OREGON EDUCATION JOURNAL
Or1-ref   v. 1, 1926–date. Cds. by auth., subj. & t. In proc.

OREGON EXTENSION SERIES (per.)
Or1-ref   1918–date. Cds. by no. of bul. Cur. add.
Or1-ref   1918–date. Cds. by auth., subj. & t. Cur. add.

OREGON HISTORICAL QUARTERLY
Wa3   v. 1, 1900–date. Cds. by auth., subj. & t. No add.

OREGON STATE TECHNICAL RECORD (per.)
Or1-ref   Cds. by auth. & subj. Cur. add.

OREGON VOTER (per.)
Or1   v. 1, 1915–date. Cds. by subj. Cur. add.
Or2   v. 1, 1915–date. Cds. by subj. Prepared by Univ. of Ore. lib.; purchased by Ore. state coll. lib. Cur. add.

ORGAN MUSIC. See also CHURCH MUSIC
C43-mus   1400 cds. by t. Coll. Freq. add.
Mi6-mus   3960 cds. by comp. & subj. Coll. Occ. add.
Mn23-art   224 cds. by comp. & t. Bks. Cur. add.
N35-mus   1250 cds. by auth. & t. Coll. & sht. mus. Freq. add.
O16-art   400 cds. by comp. Coll. Cur. add.
O20-art   1922 cds. by comp. Bks. Freq. add.

ORGANISTS' JOURNAL
Ia6-mus   v. 4-15, 1890–1897. Cds. by t. & comp. Occ. add.

ORGANIZATIONS. See SOCIETIES AND CLUBS; Names of loc. and subj., subdiv. SOCIETIES AND CLUBS

ORIENT. See also FOLKLORE   O20-White
C11   4000 cds. by auth. & class. Bks., pams., phonograph records, maps & per. Cur. add.

ORIENT—PICTURES. See PICTURES—ORIENT

ORIENTAL LITERATURE
M11-Jap.   1000 cds. by auth., subj. & t. Bks. & per. written in Chinese & Jap. char. Freq. add.

OSHKOSH (WISC.)—NEWSPAPERS
W19 1320 cds. by subj. Newsp., 1840–1890. In proc.

OSHKOSH (WISC.)—SOCIETIES AND CLUBS
W19 150 cds. by name. Cur. add.

OSTASIATISCHE ZEITSCHRIFT (per.). *In* ART, ORIENTAL **D9**

OSTEOPATHY
I10 1700 cds. by subj. Bks. & per. Freq. add.

OUR LIVING AND OUR DEAD (per.)
Nc6 1874–1876. Cds. by subj. No add.

OUR TIMES (bk.). *In* PICTURES **G4-ref (1)**

OUT WEST (per.). *In* CALIFORNIA **C8-ref**; CALIFORNIA—HISTORY **C43-ref**

OUTDOOR INDIANA (per.)
In19 v. 1, 1934–date. Cds. by subj. Mo. add.

OUTING (per.). *In* CALIFORNIA **C8-ref**

OUTLAWS. *See* BRIGANDS AND ROBBERS; FRONTIER AND PIONEER LIFE

OVERLAND MONTHLY AND OUT WEST MAGAZINE. *In* CALIFORNIA **C8-ref**; CALIFORNIA—HISTORY **C43-ref**

OWEN, ROBERT
N45b 80 cds. by auth., subj. & t. Bks. & per. Mat. by and about Robert Owen. Occ. add.

OXFORD (O.)—PRINTING. *See* PRINTING—OXFORD (O.)

OZARKIAN MAGAZINE. *In* MISSOURI **Mo2**

PACIFIC BINDERY TALK (per.)
C80 v. 1, 1912–date. Cds. by auth., subj. & t. No add.

PACIFIC MOTOR BOAT (per.). *In* WEST—PERIODICALS **Wa2**

PACIFIC NORTHWEST. *See* NORTHWEST

PAGEANT OF AMERICA (bk.). *In* PICTURES—HISTORY **Nb14-ref**

PAGEANTS
Mn14-clip 530 cds. by auth., t. & subj. Newsp. & pams. Infreq. add.
W16 600 cds. by subj. Bks. Occ. add.

PAINTERS. *See* ARTISTS

PAINTINGS. *See also* MURAL PAINTING AND DECORATION; PICTURES—AUDIGIER PICTURES; PICTURES—CARNEGIE PICTURES; ART **Mn14-art (2)**; ART—PHOTOGRAPHS **Nj49**; ARTISTS **Mi13-W. side**; FALCONRY; **Ca13-zoo (1)**; FLOWERS—MAINE **Me3**; PICTURES **C43-ref**; **In37, W14, N46-art**; **P45-ref**; PORTRAITS **A1, I71-art, M11-paint**

C73 Unest. cds. by sitter. Photo. of paintings, by British & Amer. art.
Ca9 425 cds. by t. & painter. Bks. Colored paintings. Occ. add.
Ct2-j 1650 cds. by art. & t. Bks. Cur. add.
Ce5 2079 cds. by art. & t. Bks. Cur. add.
Ct12-John Dav. 1461 cds. by t. Bks. Per. indexed: *Instructor magazine.* Cur. add.
G15-j Unest. cds. by t. Bks. Paintings listed in Art educ., Pub. sch. of Pittsburgh course of study, parochial pic. studies. No add.
I3 3600 cds. by subj. Art bks. No add.
I68-art 600 cds. by t. Bks. Infreq. add.
Id2 30,800 cds. by painter, t. & subj. Bks. & per. Infreq. add.
In6 5000 cds. by t. & art. Bks. & per. Freq. add.
In22-ref 12,000 cds. by art., subj. & country. Freq. add.
K8-ref 7350 cds. by art. & t. Bks. Infreq. add.
Ky13 Unest. ent., tpd. shts. by art. Bks. Cur. add.
Mi25-j 1320 cds. by art. & t. Children's bks. Art. & paintings. Cur. add.
Mi25 750 cds. by t. Bks. Illus. in color. In proc.
Mt1 1085 cds. by t. Bks. Freq. add.
N22-pic 26,499 cds. by art., t. & subj. Bks. Painters, Europeans & modern. To be pub. as Ency. of painters and paintings. No add.
N45a 1805 cds. by t. Freq. add.
N45b-art 456 cds. by country, sch., art. within ea. Large color prints—English, Flemish-Dutch, French, German, Italian, Spanish, U.S. Occ. add.

N46-art 1400 cds. by t. & art. Bks. Cur. add.

N55-art 344 cds. by art. Occ. add.

Nj33 18,000 cds. by art. Pam. Reprod. of paintings & engravings. Freq. add.

Nj46 800 cds. by art., name of subj. Paintings & port. Occ. add.

O20-Glen. 1200 cds. by t. J. bks. Infreq. add.

O20-Hou. 500 cds. by t. & art. J. bks. Occ. add.

O20-Jeff. 900 cds. by t. & art. Bks. & pic. No add.

O20-M.P. 800 cds. by art. Bks. Infreq. add.

O26 600 cds. by art. Bks. Cur. add.

O56-ref 10,000 cds. by t. Bks. & pic. Freq. add.

P39-ref. art 1200 cds. by art. Bks. & per. Color plates. Cur. add.

P54-ref 940 cds. by nationality of art. Freq. add.

R2 2000 cds. by art. Bks. & per. Colored reprod. Freq. add.

Tx35 1050 cds. by art. & t. Bks. Freq. add.

Wa6 11,880 cds. by art. & t. Bks., per. & art cat.

PAINTINGS, RELIGIOUS

M27-art 700 cds. by subj. Infreq. add.

PAINTS

Nj3 63 cds. by auth. Bks. & pams. Paints, varnishes, lacquers, etc. Occ. add.

EL PALACIO (per.)

Nm2 v. 1, 1913–date. Cds. by auth., subj. & t. Cur. add.

PALEOBOTANY

D18 2800 cds. by auth. Bks., per. & ser. Freq. add.

PALIMPSEST MAGAZINE. *In* IOWA **Ia9**

Ia20 v. 1-22, 1920–1941. Cds. by subj. In proc.

PAMPHLET PLAYS. *See* PLAYS, PAMPHLET

PAMPHLETS. *See also* Name of subject, subdivision PAMPHLETS

Ar4 306 cds. by subj. & t. Freq. add.

Ar5 1900 cds. by subj. & series. Freq. add.

C75 788 cds. by subj. Freq. add.

C87 2775 cds. by subj. Freq. add.

Ca1 2500 cds. by subj. Cur. add.

I12 10,000 cds. by auth. & subj. Cur. add.

I62 300 cds. by subj. Bul. indexed: University of Chicago round table, *America's town meeting of the air.* Freq. add.

I79 1440 cds. by t. & ser. Cur. add.

Ia12 1500 cds. by subj. Infreq. add.

Ia15 450 cds. by subj. Freq. add.

In4 800 cds. by auth. & subj. Freq. add.

In11 300 cds. by subj. Freq. add.

In22a 3500 cds. by subj. Freq. add.

In34 1873 cds. by subj. Freq. add.

K2 700 cds. by subj. Freq. add.

K12-ref 13,000 cds. by subj. Freq. add.

K22 1250 cds. by subj. & t. Cur. add.

Ky18 875 cds. by subj. Freq. add.

L5 757 cds. by subj. Freq. add.

L7 105 cds. by subj. Freq. add.

M22 750 cds. by subj. Freq. add.

Mi13-W. side 500 cds. by subj. Agric. bul., travel guides, etc. Occ. add.

Mn4-ref 2000 cds. by subj. Freq. add.

Mn14-clip 1875 cds. by auth. & t. Freq. add.

N4 4500 cds. by subj. Freq. add.

N24 202 ent., tpd. shts. by subj. Inc. bul. indexed: University of Chicago round table, *Town meeting of the air.* Freq. add.

N25 900 cds. by subj. Semi-mo. add.

N51 198 cds. by auth. & subj. Occ. add.

N59 8000 cds. by subj. Freq. add.

Nb3 613 cds. by subj. Freq. add.

Nb7 3724 cds. by auth. & subj. Semi-yrly. add.

Nb14-S. 350 cds. by subj. Freq. add.

Nj29 1100 cds. by subj. & t. Freq. add.

O20-Euc. 100th 5000 cds. by subj. Inc. travel lit. & maps. Cur. add.

O59 Unest. cds. by auth., subj. & t. Pam. indexed: *Headline books, Public affairs pamphlets, World affairs pamphlets.* Freq. add.

Or4 258 cds. by subj. Freq. add.

U1 250 ent., tpd. shts. by t. Pam. indexed: *Headline books, Public affairs pamphlets,* Wkly. add.
W19-S. 614 cds. by subj. Freq. add.
W22-ad 800 cds. by auth., t. & publisher. Inc. bul. indexed: University of Chicago round table, *Town meeting of the air.* Freq. add.
Wa1 1000 cds. by subj. Freq. add.
Wa13-j 750 cds. by subj. & t. Cur. add.

PAMPHLETS—19TH CENTURY
M31 600 cds. by auth. Sermons or items of educ. chiefly. No add.

PAMPHLETS, CATHOLIC
K1 20,000 cds. by auth., t. & subj. Freq. add.
O55 Unest. ent., tpd. shts. Mo. add.

PAMPHLETS, POLITICAL—ENGLAND
O20-hist 640 cds. by auth., chron. Infreq. add.

PAMPHLETS, STATISTICAL
Nj47 10,560 cds. by subj. Cur. add.

PAN AMERICAN UNION. *See also* LATIN AMERICA
Tx5 20 cds. by subj., auth. & t. Bks., per., newsp. & pams. Freq. add.

PANCREAS
Nj61 30 cds. by auth. & t. Bks., per. & pams. Infreq. add.

PANTOMINES. *See also* PLAYS
W16 160 cds. by subj. Bks. Infreq. add.
O37

PAPER MAKING AND TRADE—SOUTH
G11 250 cds. by t. Per. & pams. Occ. add.

PAPYRI
Ky16 250 cds. by class. Freq. add.

PARASITES
Nj61 550 cds. by auth. & t. Bks., per., pams. & rpts. Freq. add.

PARIS (KY.) WEEKLY ADVERTISER (newsp.)
Ky7 1827–1828. Cds. by subj. No add.

PARK CO. (COLO.)—MINING AND METALLURGY. *See* MINING AND METALLURGY—PARK CO. (COL.).

PARRISH, JASPER
N45b 54 ent., tpd. shts., chron. Letters & doc. rel. to govt. service of Parrish among the Indians of N.Y. state, 1790–1831. No add.

PARSIPANNY (N.J.)—REGISTERS OF BIRTHS, ETC.
Nj36 2p., tpd. shts. by name. Parsippanny First Presbyterian church, inc. list of members, Sept. 28, 1858. No add.

PARTIES. *See also* GAMES; SKITS AND STUNTS
C27-art 8000 cds. by subj. Bks. Parties, games & skits. Cur. add.
C49-inf 1536 cds. by subj. Bks. Cur. add.
C57 1600 cds. by type of party. Per. indexed: (Dennison) *Parties.* Infreq. add.
F5 335 cds. by subj. or type of party. Per. indexed: (Dennison) *Parties.* No add.
Ia6-ref Unest. ent., tpd. shts.; 1600 cds. by subj. Bks. Supp. to Silk & Fanning index. Occ. add.
Md2-soc 700 cds. by type of party. Bks. Supp. to Silk & Fanning index. Infreq. add.
Mi25 1100 cds. by subj. Bks. Cur. add.
Mn14-clip 300 cds. by subj. Newsp. & pams. Freq. add.
Mn14-Fran. 500 cds. by subj. Bks., per., pams., etc. Freq. add.
Mn23-Ham. 1450 cds. by subj. Bks., pams. & newsp. Cur. add.
N8-ref 500 cds. by subj. Bks. Freq. add.
N46-fic 400 cds. by subj. Bks., per. & pams. Cur. add.
O31 675 cds. by subj. Bks. Supp. to Silk & Fanning index. Occ. add.
Or7-circ 400 cds. by subj. Bks. & per. Freq. add.
Tx5 Unest. cds. by auth., subj. & t. Bks., pams. & bul. Freq. add.

PARTIES—PAMPHLETS
Mn14-clip 250 cds. by auth. & t. Freq. add.

PARTIES (per.). *In* PARTIES C57; F5

PASADENA (CALIF.)—HISTORY
C49-art 71p., tpd. shts. by subj. Bk. indexed: John Windell Wood, *Pasadena, historical and personal.* No add.

PASADENA, CALIFORNIA, HISTORICAL AND PERSONAL (bk.). *In* PASADENA (CALIF.)—HISTORY C49-art

PAST AND PRESENT OF ALAMEDA COUNTY, CALIFORNIA (bk.). *In* ALAMEDA CO. (CALIF.)—HISTORY   C43-ref

PATENTS
P39-tech   Unest. ent., tpd. shts. by subj. Chem., metallurgy and rel. subj., 1790–1933. 43 classes of U.S. patents. No add.

PATENTS—CEMENT
I27   1000 cds. by patent class. Patents rel. to portland cement and concrete construction. Freq. add.

PATENTS—CHEMISTRY
Nj54   Unest. cds. by subj. Specific rpts. & comp. of patent & lit. searches & original research. Freq. add.

PATENTS—MACHINERY, AGRICULTURAL
D10   4551 cds. by patent no. Freq. add.

PATENTS—PETROLEUM
N33   6000 cds., chron. by no. U.S., British, French, German & other patents on petroleum refining. Freq. add.

PATENTS—SCIENCE
In18   Unest. cds. by patentee, subj. & assignee. U.S., French, German & English patents per. to chem., phar. & rel. sci. Cur. add.

PATENTS, BRITISH
N35-ref. sci   4370 cds. by no. Amended patents of British patent off. In proc.

PATERSON (N.J.)—NECROLOGY
Nj57-ref   11,500 cds. by name; scrapbk., chron. Newsp., 1907–date. No add.

PATHOLOGY. *See also* BOTANY—PATHOLOGY; VETERINARY MEDICINE—PATHOLOGY
Nj61   50 cds. by auth. & t. Bks., per. & pams. Freq. add.

PATRIOTISM
Nj9   37 ent., tpd. shts. by subj. Bks. Cur. add.

PATRON SAINTS. *See* SAINTS

PEACE. *See* List of Bibliographies, APPENDIX I

PELOUBET'S SELECT NOTES (bk.). *In* SUNDAY SCHOOL LESSONS   O16-ref

PENMANSHIP—STUDY AND TEACHING
C11   Unest. cds. by auth. & subj. Bks., per. & pams. Cur. add.

PENNSYLVANIA
P10   250 cds. by subj. Bks., pams. & newsp. Hist. & ind. Pa. Freq. add.
P45-ref   600 cds. by subj. Per. Occ. add.

PENNSYLVANIA—AUTHORS. *See* AUTHORS—PENNSYLVANIA

PENNSYLVANIA—BIOGRAPHY
P16   1000 ent., tpd. shts. by name. Bk. indexed: *Dictionary of American biography*. No add.
P39-ref.-Pa.   145,600 cds. by name. Bks. & per. State, co. & loc. hist. & biog. Freq. add.

PENNSYLVANIA—DIRECTORIES
P45-ref   8580 cds. by name. Pa. tel. dir. Occ. add.

PENNSYLVANIA—FICTION. *See* CHILDREN'S LITERATURE—PENNSYLVANIA; FICTION—PENNSYLVANIA

PENNSYLVANIA—GENEALOGY. *See* GENEALOGY—PENNSYLVANIA

PENNSYLVANIA—GEOLOGY. *See* GEOLOGY—PENNSYLVANIA

PENNSYLVANIA—HISTORY
P19 (1)   Unest. cds. by auth. Bks. & pam. Cassel coll. on Pa. hist. & Brethren church. No add.
P19 (2)   Unest. cds. by auth. Mss. letters. Cassel coll. on Pa. hist. & Brethren church. No add.
P19 (3)   Unest. cds. by t. Pams. & almanacs. Cassel coll. on Pa. hist. & Brethren church. No add.

PENNSYLVANIA—NAMES, GEOGRAPHICAL. *See* NAMES, GEOGRAPHICAL—PENNSYLVANIA

PENNSYLVANIA—NEWSPAPERS
Nj40   800 ent., tpd. shts., chron. Cur. add.

PENNSYLVANIA—PAMPHLETS
P46   3000 cds. by auth. & subj. Freq. add.

PENNSYLVANIA—PICTURES. *See* PICTURES—PENNSYLVANIA

PENNSYLVANIA—POLITICS AND GOVERNMENT
P46   1700 cds. by auth. & t. Inst. of loc. govt. In proc.

PENNSYLVANIA STATE COLLEGE—DISSERTATIONS, ACADEMIC
P46 2093 ent., tpd. shts. by auth., dept. & subj. Theses, 1865-1937. No add.

PENNSYLVANIA STATE COLLEGE—HISTORY
P46 825 cds. by subj. Coll. per. Freq. add.

PENNSYLVANIA. UNIVERSITY — DISSERTATIONS, ACADEMIC
P36-bot 150 cds., chron. by date of degree. Cur. add.

PENNSYLVANIA. UNIVERSITY—PUBLICATIONS
P36-ref 5000 cds. by subj. Alumni & coll. pub. Cur. add.

PENNSYLVANIA. UNIVERSITY. MUSEUM—PUBLICATIONS
N5 300 cds. by subj. Cur. add.

PENNSYLVANIA, SOUTHWESTERN—HISTORY
P51 100 ent., tpd. shts. by subj. Bks. Cur. add.

PENNSYLVANIA GERMAN MAGAZINE
P46 1900-1914. Tpd. shts. by auth. & subj. No add.

PENNSYLVANIA MAGAZINE OF HISTORY AND BIOGRAPHY
P16 v. 1-40, 1877-1916. 7000 cds. by subj. No add.

PENSIONS, MILITARY
In22-gen 23,000 cds. by name. Secy. of war report, v. 1, 1835. Pensioners in Conn., Del., Ind., Me., Md., Mass., New Hampshire, New Jersey, Penn., R.I., Vt. & Va. In proc.
T5-ref 44 cds. by ser. no., war, state, etc. Bks. in U.S. Congress. set. Cur. add.

PEORIA (ILL.)—AUTHORS. See AUTHORS—PEORIA (ILL.)

PEORIA (ILL.)—BIBLIOGRAPHY—IMPRINTS
I65-cat 500 cds. by date. Infreq. add.

PEORIA (ILL.)—BIOGRAPHY
I65-ref 90 ent., tpd. shts. by subj. or prof. Infreq. add.

PEORIA (ILL.)—HISTORY
I65 1200 cds. by subj. Newsp., 1881-1935. No add.
I65-circ Unest. ent., tpd. shts. in notebks. by subj., yr. & day. Newsp. indexed: *Peoria (Ill.) Daily record.* Freq. add.

PEORIA (ILL.)—NEWSPAPERS
I65 50,000 cds. by subj. Newsp., 1839-1863. Freq. add.

PEORIA (ILL.) DAILY RECORD (newsp.). *In* PEORIA (ILL.)—HISTORY **I65-circ**

PERFUMERY
N30-chem 45 cds. by auth. Bks. Levy coll. on perfume. No add.

PERIODICALS. See also Names of subj. and loc., subdiv. PERIODICALS; Names of indiv. per.; List of Bibliographies, APPENDIX I
C34-per 1770 cds. by t. & subj. Freq. add.
L10 3248 cds. by subj. Per. not indexed in R.G. Freq. add.
M4-sci 7260 cds. by subj. Cur. add.
Mn17 650 cds. by country, t. & lang. Cur. add.
N8-ref 500 cds. by subj. Infreq. add.
N27 200 cds. by subj. Infreq. add.
Nb12 2970 cds. by subj. Infreq. add.
O20-bus 1200 ent., tpd. shts. by t. & subj. Per. of yrbk. & dir. type. Occ. add.
O20-Jeff. 1500 cds. by subj. Per. indexed: *Grade teacher; Instructor, School arts.* Mo. add.
O20-per 7920 cds. by subj. Per. not indexed in Reader's Guide. Cur. add.
O20-ref 31,680 cds. by auth., t. & subj. Infreq. add.
O57 4000 cds. by subj. Freq. add.
Wa6 400 cds. by subj. Per. indexed: *Illustrated London news.* Infreq. add.
Wa14-ref 200 ent., tpd. shts. by subj. Bks. & per. Infreq. add.

PERIODICALS—BIRTHS AND DEATHS
C32-per 15,000 cds. by t. Per. indexed: *Bulletin of bibliography,* 1897-date. Cur. add.
G4-per 800 cds. by t. Per. indexed: *Bulletin of bibliography.* Wilson indexes, etc. Cur. add.

PERIODICALS—19TH CENTURY. See List of Bibliographies, APPENDIX I

PERIODICALS—UNION LISTS. See List of Bibliographies, APPENDIX I

PERIODICALS, DENOMINATIONAL
Ky16 250 cds. by t. Freq. add.
Nb7 5453 cds. by subj. 12 denom. per., 1929–date. Occ. add.

PERIODICALS, EARLY. See List of Bibliographies, APPENDIX I

PERIODICALS, SCHOOL. See List of Bibliographies, APPENDIX I

PERRY, OLIVER H.
P13-ref 27 cds. by auth. Bks., per. & newsp. Freq. add.
P13-ref 533 cds. by name. Govt. doc. Perry honor roll. No add.

PERRY CO. (ALA.)—CEMETERY RECORDS
A1 150 ent., tpd. shts. by name. Marion cem. Occ. add.

PERRY MAGAZINE. *In* ART—STUDY AND TEACHING **M27-art**

PERRY PICTURES. See PICTURES—PERRY PICTURES

PERSIAN ART. See ART, PERSIAN

PERSONALITY
C71-circ 70 ent., tpd. shts. by auth. & subj. Bks. Health, personality & pub. speaking. No add.
O1-r.a. 2000 cds. by subj. Bks. Attributes or pers. qualities. Cur. add.

PERSONNEL MANAGEMENT. See EMPLOYMENT MANAGEMENT

PERSONNEL SERVICE IN EDUCATION. See List of Bibliographies, APPENDIX I

LA PETITE ILLUSTRATION (per.). *In* PLAYS, FRENCH **O25-Clev. coll; O47-ref**
Mi6-for Cds. by auth. & t. Plays & poetry. Freq. add.
N45b Cds. by auth. & t. Inc. *Illustration theatrale.* Cur. add.
Nj28 1936–1940. Cds. by auth. & t. No add.
O25-F.S.M. 1926–1939. Cds. by subj. Freq. add.
Tx11 1919–1939. Cds. by auth. No add.
Tx17 1905–1908. Cds. by auth. & t. No add.

PETROLEUM. See also UNIVERSAL OIL PRODUCTS—PUBLICATIONS; List of Bibliographies, APPENDIX I
C70 41,580 cds. by subj. Per. on petroleum, petroleum ind., eng., bus. mgt. & personnel. Freq. add.

N33 150 cds. by subj., chron. Govt. doc. Freq. add.
N33 200 cds. by name of crude oil. Crude oils all over the world. Freq. add.
Nj52 1000 cds. by subj. Bks., per. & pams. Freq. add.
Ok4-tech 67,500 cds. by subj. Bks., per. & pams. Daily add.
Ok4-tech Unest. cds. by subj. Per. & bks. Cur. add.

PETROLEUM—CALIFORNIA
C32-sci 200 cds. by name of field & district. Oil fields in Calif. Cur. add.

PETROLEUM—PATENTS. See PATENTS—PETROLEUM

PETROLEUM GEOLOGY
Ok4-tech Unest. cds. by subj. Per. & bks. Cur. add.

PETS
Co8-biol 1500 cds. by subj. Bks., per., doc. & pams. Cats & dogs. Yrly. add.
Wa10-j 300 cds. by type. Bks. & per. Cur. add.

PHARMACISTS
Wa11-ref 20 ent., tpd. shts. by name. Bks. & per. Occ. add.

PHARMACY
In18 13,000 cds. by name of remedy. Per. New remedies. Cur. add.
Md7-phar Unest. cds., chron. Bks., per., etc. Hanbury Medalists. Yrly. add.
Md7-phar 600 cds. by subj. Bks. & per. Freq. add.
Nj61 150 cds. by auth. & t. Bks., per. & pams. Inc. therapeutics. Infreq. add.

PHARMACY—ADVERTISEMENTS
In18 Unest. ent., by name of product. Domestic & for. adv., all types, 1910–date. Daily add.

PHARMACY—PATENTS. See PATENTS—SCIENCE **In18**

PHARMACY—REPRINTS
Md7-phar 1800 cds. by auth. & t. Freq. add.
Nj53 660 cds. by subj. Pams. Cur. add.

Philadelphia Symphony Programs. *In*
Symphony   C32-art; Nb14-ref;
O16-art; O20-art; O29-ref
N22-art   Unest. cds. by comp. Programs, 1934–date. Cur. add.

Philharmonic Symphony Programs. *In* Symphony   O16-art

Phonograph Records. *See also* Music Nj50-art
C32-art   2640 cds. by comp., t. & type of mus. Cur. add.
C34   3000 cds. by art., comp., subj. & t. Freq. add.
C49-art   6912 cds. by comp., t. & subj. Infreq. add.
C61-sch   10p., tpd. shts. by subj. Yrly. add.
C87   2775 cds. by subj., auth., t., comp. & singer. Cur. add.
Co1   204 cds. by subj., t. & comp. Freq. add.
H2   500 cds. by subj. & t. Infreq. add.
I47   Unest. cds. by comp., t., orch., conductor, art. & auth. 700 records. Freq. add.
I60   880 cds. by comp. & mus. form. 200 records. Cur. add.
Ia16   1100 cds. by t., comp. & type of mus. Occ. add.
M24   150 cds. by comp., t., auth., subj. & mus. form. In proc.
Mn5   5000 cds. by auth., subj. & t. Cur. add.
N35-ref. mus   20,000 cds. by comp. Amer. & for. records. Cur. add.
N55-art   1822 cds. by auth., t. & subj. Freq. add.
Nj58   175 cds. by comp., composition & mus. instrument. Infreq. add.
Wa15   6000 cds. by comp., t., medium & form. 950 records. Infreq. add.

Photographic Survey (per.). *In* Architecture, Virginian—Photographs V7

Photographs. *See also* Names of subj. and loc., subdiv. Photographs; Pictures; Portraits; List of Bibliographies, Appendix I
I11   Unest. cds. by art., subj. & loc. Fine & dec. arts. Inc. lantern slides. Cur. add.
M10   Unest. ent., tpd. shts. in albums, by place under each class. Freq. add.

Mi5-ref   Unest. ent., tpd. shts. by subj. Newsp. indexed: *Detroit (Mich.) News*, 1925–date. Daily add.
N8-tech   5280 cds. by name. Freq. add.
Nm2   3900 cds. by subj. Hist. & archaeol. sites, bldgs., port. Occ. add.
Wa9a   1,500,000 ent. by subj. & name. Cur. add.
Wa9a   50 cds. by subj. & name. Crossfile. Cur. add.

Photographs—Galloway, Ewing
Ky8   1200 cds. by country. World phot., Ewing Galloway. No add.

Photographs, European
N45b   995 cds. by country, etc. Chiefly bldgs. & monuments. No add.

Photographs, Historical—Foreign Languages
C32-for   225 cds. by people & country. Bks. in for. lang. Freq. add.

Photography
O20-sci   700 cds. by subj. Per. & bks. Cur. add.
O56-circ   200 cds. by subj. Freq. add.

Photography in Crime Detection. *See* List of Bibliographies, Appendix I

Photoplay Magazine. *In* Motion Pictures   C32-per

Physical Education and Training Administration. *See also* List of Bibliographies, Appendix I
De1   1500 cds. by subj. Bks. & per. No add.

Physicians—Biography
Ia14-med   60 cds. by name. Bks. Cur. add.

Physicians—Kentucky
Ky2   25p., tpd. shts. by name. Rare newsp., adv., etc. No add.

Physicians—Nebraska—Publications
Nb8-med   2000 cds. by name, chron. Bks. & per. Freq. add.
Nb8-med   Unest. ent. by auth. Reprint pams. Occ. add.

Physicians—Necrology
M2   10,000 cds. by name. Cur. add.

PHYSICIANS—PORTRAITS. *See* PORTRAITS—
PHYSICIANS

PHYSICIANS—PUBLICATIONS. *See also* PHYSICIANS — NEBRASKA — PUBLICATIONS; Names of instit. and univ.
N34a   5500 cds. by auth. Non-med. bks. by drs. Cur. add.

PHYSICIANS AND ART
Ia7   60 cds. by name. Med. hist. & biog. Occ. add.

PHYSICIANS AND MUSIC
Ia7   175 cds. by name. Med. biog. Occ. add.

PHYSICIANS AS AUTHORS
Ia7   400 ent., tpd. shts. in notebks. Med. biog. Occ. add.

PHYSICIANS IN LITERATURE
K8-circ   42 cds. by auth. Bks. Drs. in fic. & biog. Occ. add.
M32-circ   98 cds. by auth. Bks. Drs. & nurses in fic. & popular non-fic. Occ. add.
N34a   200 cds. by auth. Drs. as char. in bks. Cur. add.

PHYSICISTS. *See* SCIENTISTS   N8-tech

PHYSICS
Nj60-phys (1)   2000 cds. by molecule, chron. Per. Band spectra since 1936. Cur. add.
Nj60-phys (2)   7800 cds. by auth., subj. & atomic no. of ea. atom investigated. Per. indexed. *Nuclear physics*, 1936–1939. No add.
Nj60-phys (3)   1200 cds. by atomic & isotopic no. of nuclei. Per. *Nuclear physics*, 1939–date. Cur. add.

PHYSICS—TABLES. *See* MATHEMATICS—TABLES   N35-ref. sci

PHYSIOLOGICAL CHEMISTRY. *See* CHEMISTRY, PHYSIOLOGICAL

PHYSIOLOGY. *See also* CELLS
Nj61   150 cds. by auth. & t. Bks., per. & pams. Infreq. add.

PIANO MUSIC. *See also* SONGS   M32-circ (1)
C32-art   3960 cds. by t. & comp. Piano coll. Occ. add.
C43-mus   5200 cds. by t. Bks. Freq. add.
C49-art   12,800 cds. by comp., t. & subj. Bks. & sht. mus. Freq. add.
I68-art   3000 cds. by comp. & t. Bks. Infreq. add.

In22-ref   1320 cds. by t. & comp. Anthologies. Infreq. add.
M24   8580 cds. by t., comp. & form. Coll. Occ. add.
M27-art   5000 cds. by comp. Coll. Occ. add.
Mi6-mus   5280 cds. by comp. & subj. Coll. Freq. add.
N35-mus   3200 cds. by auth. & t. Coll. & sht. mus. Inc. pieces for 4 hands, 2 pianos, etc. Freq. add.
N54-art   8900 cds. by t. & subj. Coll. Cur. add.
O16-art   1500 cds. by auth., t. & subj. Coll. containing difficult to find or unusual pieces. Occ. add.
O56-circ   10,000 cds. by comp. & t. Bks. Cur. add.
Or2   100 cds. by form & comp. Mus. for more than 2 hands. Infreq. add.
Or2   55,150 cds. by comp. & t. Coll. cont. mus. for more than 2 hands. Infreq. add.
P5   1200 cds. by comp., t. & subj. Sht. mus., albums, etc. Infreq. add.
P39-ref. mus   3300 cds. by comp. & t. Coll. Cur. add.
U4   8000 cds. by comp. & t. Bks. Freq. add.

PIANOFORTE WERKE (SCHUBERT) (bk.). *In* SCHUBERT, FRANZ PETER—WORKS
Mn14-mus (2)

PICKAWAY CO. (O.)—EUROPEAN WAR, 1914–1918. *See* EUROPEAN WAR, 1914–1918—PICKAWAY CO. (O.)

PICKAWAY CO. (O.)—HISTORY
O19   10,000 cds. by subj. Bks. Infreq. add.

PICTORIAL EDUCATION (per.)
Ca14-j   1933–1940. Cds. by subj. Freq. add.

PICTURE STUDY. *See* ART—STUDY AND TEACHING

PICTURES. *See also* ART—STUDY AND TEACHING; ARTISTS; CARICATURES AND CARTOONS: CONNOISSEUR (per.); COSTUME; DRAWINGS AND ENGRAVINGS; ILLUSTRATORS; MAPS, PICTORIAL; MOTION PICTURES—STILLS; PAINTINGS; PHOTOGRAPHS; PORTRAITS; SCULPTURE; BIOGRAPHY   Tx20; BIRTHDAYS   K22
Ar5   2100 cds. by art., t. & subj. Bks., per. & newsp. Freq. add.

C1 15,300 cds. by subj. Bks. Infreq. add.
C8-j 3960 cds. by subj. 25,000 prints. Occ. add.
C25 257,600 cds. by subj. Per. Pic. of interest to mot. pic. research. Cur. add.
C32-art 33,320 cds. by subj. Per. & bks. Freq. add.
C32-j 520 cds. by subj. J. bks. Illus. Freq. add.
C43-pic 4300 cds. by art. Freq. add.
C43-ref 10,300 cds. by art. & subj. Bks. Paintings & illus. Freq. add.
C69-ref 2200 cds. by class no. Bks., per. & newsp. Freq. add.
C75 3105 cds. by subj. Freq. add.
Ca2-art 1000 cds. by subj. Bks. Mo. add.
Ca2-art 13,500 cds. by art. & t. Bks. Occ. add.
Ca3 3200 cds. by art. & t. Bks. Yrly. add.
Ca10-ref 10,000 cds. by subj., t. & art. Bks. Freq. add.
Ct2-ref 250 cds. by subj. Bks. Per. indexed: *Life*. Freq. add.
Ct13-art 15,000 cds. by subj. & art. Per., bks. & auction sales cat. No add.
De3 1950 cds. by subj. Bks. & per. Freq. add.
F4 8000 cds. by t. Bks. & per. Freq. add.
F5 2975 cds. by art., t. & subj. Bks., etc. Freq. add.
F6 Unest. ent., tpd. shts. by country & art. Bks. & plates. Freq. add.
G4-ref (1) 500 cds. by subj. Per. & bks. Bk. indexed: Mark Sullivan, *Our times*, 5v. Cur. add.
G4-ref (2) 2000 cds. by subj. Per., newsp., etc. Cur. add.
I7 3500 cds. by subj. Per. indexed: *Art news; L'Illustration.* No add.
I8 13,900 cds. by art. & t. Bks., etc. Freq. add.
I14 5000 cds. by subj. Bks., per., etc. Occ. add.
I43-ref (1) 2921 cds. Bks. Port. bldgs. & scenes. Occ. add.
I43-ref (2) 57p., tpd. shts. by art. Per. indexed: *Hobby horse*, v. 1-7, 1886-1892. No add.
I53 600 cds. by art. & t.' 6 Portfolios of Art appreciation co., Akron, O. No add.

I62 850 cds. by art. & t. Bks. Cur. add.
I65-art 950 cds. by art. Coll. Freq. add.
I72-j 150 cds. by subj. Pic. hard to find. No add.
Ia16 10,000 cds. by t. & subj. Bks. & newsp. Freq. add.
In8-j 5000 cds. by t. 20 art cat. Cur. add.
In10 100 cds. by subj. Per., newsp., etc. Freq. add.
In17 500 cds. by art. & t. Per. indexed: *Mentor*, v. 1-4, 1913-1916. No add.
In24 3150 cds. by subj. Bks., per., etc. Freq. add.
In37 Unest. cds. by art., t. & subj. Paintings, hist. pic. & port. No add.
K3 1320 cds. by art. Bks., etc. Freq. add.
K15 500 ent., tpd. shts. by subj. & art. Freq. add.
K22 700 cds. by art., t. & subj. Bks. & pams. Freq. add.
Ky2 250 cds. by art. & t. Portfolios, etc. Cur. add.
Ky15-Cresc. Hill 500 cds. by subj. Per., Perry pic. Infreq. add.
L18-ref 2700 cds. by subj., art. & t. Infreq. add.
M16-ref 35,000 cds. by auth. & t. Paintings, sculp. arch. & views. Infreq. add.
M21 2000 cds. by subj. Bks., per., etc. Cur. add.
M21-j 5000 cds. by art. & subj. Medici, Grafton, Alinari prints, etc. Infreq. add.
M22 6000 cds. by subj. Freq. add.
M23-art 960 cds. by subj. Bks. & per. Cur. add.
Md2-art Over 1000 cds. by art., t. & subj. Bks. No add.
Md2-art 30,000 cds. by subj. Bks. Black & white index. No add.
Mi4 2200 cds. by art., t. & subj. Bks., etc. Freq. add.
Mi5-Cat. 77,880 cds. by subj. Bks. & per. Freq. add.
Mi6-art 32,000 cds. by subj. Bks., per., art museum bul. Cur. add.
Mi6-Burt. 14,000 cds. by subj. Bks., etc. Port. & views. Occ. add.
Mi6-circ 1500 cds. by subj. Bks. & per. Occ. add.

Mi7 500 ent., tpd. shts. by art., subj. & t. Yrly. add.

Mi13-ref 2000 cds. by t. Bks. Freq. add.

Mi24 2773 cds. by t. & subj. Bks., per., sets. Cur. add.

Mi31-Way. 1100 cds. by art. & t. Bks. Occ. add.

Mn4-ref 4900 cds. by subj. Per. indexed: *Mentor.* No add.

Mn11 Unest. ent., tpd. shts. by subj. Freq. add.

Mn14-ref 1000 cds. by subj. Bks. & per. Occ. add.

Mn14-tech 600 cds. by subj. Bks., per. & newsp. Occ. add.

Mn23-art 10,147 cds. by auth. & t. Bks. Freq. add.

Mo3-ref 33,000 cds. by art. & t. Bks. & per. No add.

Mo3-ref 15,000 cds. Continues art index. Freq. add.

Mo13-art 8000 cds. by subj. & t. Bks. & per. Illus. Occ. add.

N5 1000 cds. by auth., t. & subj. Bks. & per. Cur. add.

N6-ref 89p., tpd. shts. Bks. & per. Illus. Occ. add.

N8-ref 22,440 cds. by subj. Per. & newsp. Freq. add.

N18 4500 cds. by art. & t. Bks. Occ. add.

N28-j 2100 cds. by subj. J. bks. Illus. Infreq. add.

N31 1320 cds. by subj. All sources. Form & object index for art students. Occ. add.

N35-circ. pic 8500 cds. by subj. Art cat., etc. Cur. add.

N35-ref. art 7000 cds. by art. Bks. & per. Color plates. Cur. add.

N35-ref. inf 1300 cds. by subj. Bks. & per. Illus., emphasis on nature. No add.

N35-ref. print 22,000 cds. by painter or sculp. Separates & bks. Paintings, sculp. or drawings as prints. Cur. add.

N45a 950 cds. by subj. Freq. add.

N46-art (1) 270 cds. by pub. or firm. Art cat. Reprod. of paintings, sculp., etc. Occ. add.

N46-art (2) 3125 cds. by subj. Bks. & per. Pic., illus., phot., etc.

N46-sci 200 cds. by t. Bks. & per. Infreq. add.

N54-art 8800 cds. by t. Bks., ency., etc. Occ. add.

Nd3 17 cds. by name & subj. Bks. Illus. & illustrators. Cur. add.

Nh2-art 2400 cds. by art. & subj. Bks. Cur. add.

Nh2-art 2000 cds. by subj., loc., etc. Loose plates in vols. Cur. add.

Nj4 3000 cds. by t. Bks. & newsp. Freq. add.

Nj25-ref 9506 ent., by subj. Bks. & per. Freq. add.

Nj67-ref 7500 cds. by t. & art. Bks., per. & coll. of prints. Occ. add.

Nm2 700 cds. by subj. Bks. & per. S.W. hist., archaeol., Pueblo Indians, Spanish, Mexican & terr. costume. Freq. add.

O11 2000 ent. by subj. Per. Freq. add.

O20-art 7830 cds. by t., subj. & name. Bks. & per. Illus. Freq. add.

O20-hist 9240 cds. by subj. Bks. & per. Pic. of hist. & soc. interest. Occ. add.

O20-j 1700 cds. by subj. Bks. Illus. Cur. add.

O20-Quin. 1050 cds. by art., subj. & t. Bks. Infreq. add.

O20-Tem. 1320 cds. by t. & art. Bks. No add.

O21 700 cds. by art. Bks., etc. Occ. add.

O25-Clev. Coll 5000 cds. by art., t. & subj. Art prints. Occ. add.

O19-j 9000 cds. by t. & subj. Bks., etc. Freq. add.

O31 1100 cds. by auth. & t. Bks. Occ. add.

O36 20,000 cds. by art. & t. Bks. Freq. add.

O59 Unest. cds. by art. & t. Bks. & per. No add.

Or1-ref. art 11,591 cds. by auth., subj. & t. Bks., pic., folios, etc. Cur. add.

P39-j 900 cds. by subj. Bks. Infreq. add.

P39-ref 1100 cds. by art. Medici & Arundel prints, Century of progress phot., etc. No add.

P39-ref. art 6000 cds. by subj. Bks. & per. Per. indexed: *European architecture,* v. 1-9, 1892–1900. Inc. abstract subj. Freq. add.

P45-ref 1000 cds. by t. & subj. Bks. & per. Paintings & other pic. No add.
R2 2000 cds. by subj. Bks. & per. Infreq. add.
Tx8 900 cds. by t. & art. Bk. indexed: *Encyclopedia Britannica*, 14th ed. No add.
Tx14 22,000 cds. by art., t. & subj. Bks., etc. Cur. add.
W14 100 cds. by art., t. & subj. Bks. Illus. & paintings. Cur. add.
Wa3 2000 cds. by auth., t. & subj. Occ. add.
Wa10-j 600 cds. by subj. Bks. & per. Cur. add.

PICTURES—ALINARI PRINTS. *See* PICTURES M21-j

PICTURES—ANIMALS
Ca2-sci 160 cds. by name. Bks. Colored pic. Cur. add.
Mi18 90 cds. by subj. Infreq. add.
Mo3-ref 400 cds. by name. Freq. add.

PICTURES—ARCHAEOLOGY. *See* PICTURES Nm2

PICTURES—ARCHITECTURE. *See* ARCHITECTURE—PHOTOGRAPHS **N55-art**; PICTURES—CARNEGIE PICTURES **Ia14-art**

PICTURES—ARUNDEL PRINTS. *See also* PICTURES **P39-ref**
N8-ref 500 cds. by subj. No add.

PICTURES—ASTROPHYSICS
Ca9-lib. sch 53 ent., tpd. shts. by subj. Per. indexed: *Astrophysical journal*, v. 45-84, 1917–1936. No add.

PICTURES—AUDIGIER PICTURES
T5-ref 1690 cds. by art. & Fogg Art museum class. Phot. of paintings, sculp. & places. No add.

PICTURES—AUDUBON PRINTS. *See* PICTURES—BIRDS **N35-ref. inf**

PICTURES—BIRDS
Ca2-sci 960 cds. by name. Bks. Colored pic. Cur. add.
I13-ref 5500 cds. by subj. Bks. & per. Freq. add.
Mi18 200 cds. by subj. Infreq. add.
N35-ref. inf 3500 cds. by name. Bks., Audubon prints. No add.

PICTURES—BOTANY. *See also* PICTURES—NATURE; PICTURES—ZOOLOGY
C32-sci
D18 39,000 cds. by genus & species name. Bks., per. & ser. Daily add.

PICTURES—BRIDGES. *See* BRIDGES **N35-ref. sci** (1), (2)

PICTURES—BUFFALO (N.Y.)
N8-ref 37,280 cds. by subj. Bks. Freq. add.

PICTURES—CALIFORNIA
C32-Calif. 3960 cds. by subj. Bks. & per. Occ. add.
C56-Calif. Several hundred cds. by co. & subj. Places & subj. Freq. add.

PICTURES—CARNEGIE PICTURES
De1 Unest. ent., tpd. shts. by subj. & art. 2000 pic. No add.
I73-ref 880 cds. by t. Carnegie cat. of rel. color reprod. No add.
Ia14-art 1200 cds. by name & subj. 1800 phot. on all of art hist. Painting, arch. & sculp. Cur. add.
In14 2000 cds. by subj. & no. Painting, sculp. & arch. No add.

PICTURES—CHICAGO
I13-ref 2000 cds. by subj. Bks. & per. Freq. add.

PICTURES—CINCINNATI (O.)
O16-ref 950 cds. by subj. Bks., pams., newsp. & per. Freq. add.
O17 1335 cds. by subj. & t. Bks. & sep. No add.

PICTURES—CLEVELAND (O.)
O20-hist 2060 cds. by subj. Pic. & phot., 1830–date. Freq. add.
O20-hist 1320 cds. by subj. Bks., maps, & newsp. Infreq. add.

PICTURES—COSTUME. *See* COSTUME

PICTURES—DANCING
N35-mus 2500 cds. by subj. Bks. & per. Freq. add.

PICTURES—EDUCATION
O20-soc 3960 cds. by name. Cur. add.

PICTURES—ENGLISH LITERATURE
I71-art 175 ent., tpd. shts. by art. Freq. add.

PICTURES—FISHES
I13-ref 3000 cds. by subj. Bks. & per. Fish & game. Occ. add.

PICTURES—FLORIDA
F2-ref   160 cds. by place. Bks. & per. Infreq. add.

PICTURES—FLOWERS. *See also* PICTURES—WILDFLOWERS
C32-sci   8000 cds. by bot. name. Per. indexed: *Curtis's botanical magazine*, v. 1-161. No add.
I13-ref. art   4000 cds. by subj. Bks. & per. Freq. add.
P39-ref   1000 cds. by name. Bks. & per. Colored plates. Occ. add.

PICTURES—FURNITURE
M27-art   1300 cds. by subj. Bks. Infreq. add.

PICTURES—GEORGIA. *See also* MAPS—GEORGIA **G17**
G4-ref   5000 cds. by subj. Bks. & per. Cur. add.
G8   Unest. cds. by subj. Bks., per. & sep. Illus. of Ga. & Georgians. Freq. add.

PICTURES—GRAFTON PRINTS. *See* PICTURES M21-j

PICTURES—HISTORY
Nb14-ref   10,000 cds. by subj. Bks. & per. Bk. indexed: *Pageant of America*, 15v. Occ. add.

PICTURES—HOBOKEN (N.J.)
Nj25-ref   3575 cds. by subj. Per., newsp., etc. Infreq. add.

PICTURES—INDIANA
In22-Ind.   1900 cds. by name & subj. Bks., per., Indianapolis dir., H. E. Armstead coll. of aerial views, Indianapolis coll. made by W. H. Bass co. Freq. add.

PICTURES—INDIANS. *See also* PICTURES Nm2
W3   57 cds. by subj. Bks., etc. Freq. add.

PICTURES—LOUISIANA
L11   1500 cds. by auth. & subj. Bks. & per. Freq. add.

PICTURES—MADONNAS
I71-art   415 ent., tpd. shts. by nationality & art. Freq. add.

PICTURES—MARYLAND
Md2-Md.   7800 cds. by subj. Bks., per., etc. Md. pers., houses, bldgs. & objects. Freq. add.

PICTURES—MEDALS AND AWARDS. *See* MEDALS AND AWARDS **P39-tech**

PICTURES—MEDICI PRINTS. *See* PICTURES M21-j; P39-ref (1)

PICTURES—MEDICINE
C35   2000 cds. by subj. Bks. & per. Colored plates. Cur. add.

PICTURES—MONTEREY Co. (CALIF.)
C59   861 cds. by subj. Occ. add.

PICTURES—MYTHOLOGY
I9   968 cds. by subj. Bks. Infreq. add.

PICTURES—NATURE. *See also* PICTURES, subdivision BIRDS, FLOWERS, PLANTS, TREES, WILDFLOWERS, ETC.; PICTURES **N35-ref. inf**
M5   600 cds. by subj. Bks., per. & pams. Freq. add.
Md2-inf   3560 cds. by popular name of animal or plant. Bks. & per. Freq. add.
Mo3-ref   1500 cds. by subj. Freq. add.
N6-ref   22p., tpd. shts. by subj. Bks. & per. No add.
O56-tech   10,000 cds. by name. Bks. & per. Striking pic. in field of natural hist. Occ. add.
P54-j   200 cds. by subj. Per. indexed: *Birds and nature*. No add.

PICTURES—NEW JERSEY
Nj50-circ   36,000 cds. by subj. Bks., etc. Freq. add.

PICTURES—NEW YORK (CITY)
N35-H.P.   6000 cds. by subj. Freq. add.
N35-ref. gen   3500 cds. by type of bldg. Bks. & per. Cur. add.

PICTURES—NEW YORK (STATE)
N31   94p., tpd. shts. by t. of illus. Loc. hist. No add.

PICTURES—NORTH CAROLINA. *See* PORTRAITS—NORTH CAROLINA **Nc1**

PICTURES—NORTHWEST
Wa13-ref   1000 cds. by subj. Bks. Occ. add.

PICTURES—ORIENT
N35-ref.-Orient   8000 cds. by subj. Bks. & per. Cur. add.

PICTURES—PENNSYLVANIA
P16   20,000 cds. by subj. Bks. Hist. & travel, inc. port. Cur. add.
P39-ref.-Pa.   4900 cds. by subj. Bks. & per. Inc. port. Infreq. add.

PICTURES—PERRY PICTURES. *See also* PICTURES **Ky15-Cresc. Hill**
I35 800 cds. by subj. No add.
I48 Unest. cds. by subj., t. & art. Occ. add.

PICTURES—PLANTS
M8 100,000 cds. by subj. Bks. & per. prior to 1910. No add.

PICTURES—POSTCARDS
Mi13-Mich. 10,000 cds. by subj. & loc. Freq. add.
N10-ref 21,120 cds. by subj. Bks. & per. Freq. add.
N35-ref.-Brown 600 cds. by loc. No add.

PICTURES—SCIENCE. *See* PICTURES—TECHNOLOGY **M4-sci**

PICTURES—SCIENTIFIC APPARATUS AND INSTRUMENTS. *See* SCIENTIFIC APPARATUS AND INSTRUMENTS **N35-ref. sci**

PICTURES—SCULPTURE. *See* SCULPTURE

PICTURES—SEEMANN PRINTS
N35-ref. art 1500 cds. by art. Museum cats., bks., etc. Colored pic. Cur. add.

PICTURES—SHIPS. *See also* SHIPS **C32-soc; Md2-ind;** U.S. NAVY **Md1** (2)
C32-sci 1500 cds. by name of ship, chron. Bks. Cur. add.
I13-ref 30,000 cds. by name of ship. Bks. & per. Freq. add.
N35-St. G. Unest. cds. by subj. Bks. Freq. add.

PICTURES—SHIPS—MAINE
Me1 Unest. cds. by name of ship. Bks., etc. Me. built ships. Freq. add.

PICTURES—SOURCES
In12 28p., tpd. shts. by subj. & co. (source). Infreq. add.
Nj50-art 850 cds. by dealer's name & subj. Infreq. add.

PICTURES—SOUTHWEST. *See* PICTURES **Nm2**

PICTURES—STEAMBOATS
In22-Ind. 1468 ent., tpd. shts. by name & size of pic. Harold Brown Adkinson coll. of Mississippi & Ohio river steamboats. No add.

PICTURES—TECHNOLOGY
M4-sci 15,840 cds. by subj. Bks., per., mss., paintings, prints, etc. Pic. mat. on tech. & sci. hist. Occ. add.

PICTURES—TENNESSEE
T6-ref 1600 cds. by subj. Bks. & per. Freq. add.

PICTURES—TEXAS
Tx17 2898 cds. by subj. Bks. No add.
Tx20 2000 ent. by subj. Freq. add.

PICTURES—TOLEDO (O.)
O56-ref 850 cds. by subj. Loc. hist. bks. Infreq. add.

PICTURES—TREES
Ca2-sci 250 cds. by name. Sci. & ind. bks. Cur. add.
I13-ref 1800 cds. by subj. Bks. & per. Freq. add.

PICTURES—UFFIZI GALLERY
Ia14-art 126 cds. by art. No add.

PICTURES—UNITED STATES
N35-ref. ed 5500 cds. by name of place. Bks. & per. Views of Amer. loc. Cur. add.

PICTURES—WEST
Co5-W. hist 12,060 cds. by subj. Bks. Infreq. add.
U2-ref Unest. cds. by subj. Bks., pams., per., etc. Occ. add.
Wy1 600 cds. by subj. Bks. W. & Wyo. subj. Freq. add.

PICTURES—WILDFLOWERS
Ca2-sci 1000 cds. by common name. Bks. in sci. & ind. Colored pic. Cur. add.

PICTURES—WYOMING. *See* PICTURES—WEST **Wy1**

PICTURES—ZOOLOGY
C32-sci 12,800 cds. by subj. Colored plates. Cur. add.

PICTURES, ENGLISH
O20-Alta 4560 cds. by t. Bks. & per. No add.

PICTURES, RELIGIOUS. *See also* CHRISTIAN ART AND SYMBOLISM
O20-Wood. 300 cds. by t. Bks. Poetry & pic. Infreq. add.

PICTURES THAT EVERY CHILD SHOULD KNOW (bk.). *In* ART—STUDY AND TEACHING **Mi6-Walk.**

PIKE CO. (ALA.)—CEMETERY RECORDS
A1   30 ent., tpd. shts. by name. Orion cem. Occ. add.

PILGRIM NOTES AND QUERIES (per.). *In* GENEALOGY   **M19** (1)

PILGRIM TERCENTENARY, 1920
O16-ref   500 cds. by subj. Bks. & pic. No add.

PIONEER LIFE. *See* FRONTIER AND PIONEER LIFE

PIONEER PRESS OF KENTUCKY (bk.). *In* KENTUCKY—HISTORY   **Ky7** (4)

PIONEER TO THE KENTUCKY IMMIGRANT (bk.). *In* KENTUCKY—HISTORY **Ky7** (3)

PIONEER WOMEN OF THE WEST (bk.). *In* WOMEN, PIONEER   **In35-gen**

PIQUA (O.)—HISTORY
O49   2410 cds. by name. Bk. indexed: John A. Rayner, *The first century of Piqua, Ohio*. No add.

PIRATE STORIES, JUVENILE
K14-j   14 cds. by auth. Bks. Infreq. add.
N44-j   10p., tpd. shts. by t. Bks. Pirates & bks. about the sea. Yrly. add.

PIRATES
F2-r.a.   50 cds. by auth. Fic. & nonfic. Famous pirates. Cur. add.

PITCAIRN ISLAND. *See* ADVENTISTS **N35-ref. read**

PITTSBURGH (PA.)
P39-ref.-Pa.   460 ent., tpd. shts. by auth. & subj. Bk. Indexed: *Pittsburgh survey;* findings: ed. by Paul Underwood Kellogg, 1909–1914. 6v. No add.
P39-Wyl.   1575 cds. by subj. Bks. Cur. add.

PITTSBURGH (PA.)—ARCHITECTS. *See* ARCHITECTS—PITTSBURGH (PA.)

PITTSBURGH (PA.)—ART. *See* ART—PITTSBURGH (PA.)

PITTSBURGH (PA.)—ARTISTS. *See* ARTISTS—PITTSBURGH (PA.)

PITTSBURGH (PA.)—AUTHORS. *See* AUTHORS—PITTSBURGH (PA.)

PITTSBURGH (PA.)—BIBLIOGRAPHY—IMPRINTS
P39-ref.-Pa.   550 cds., chron. Bks. & per. Imprints from founding of Pittsburg to 1860. Infreq. add.

PITTSBURGH (PA.)—CARNEGIE LIBRARY—PHOTOGRAPHS
P39-ref   150 cds. by subj. Off. phot. Infreq. add.

PITTSBURGH (PA.)—CHARTERS
P39-ref.-Pa.   12 ent., tpd. shts., chron. Pa statutes at large, newsp. & per. No add.

PITTSBURGH (PA.)—HISTORY
P39-ref.-Pa.   1000 ent., tpd. shts. by subj. Bk. indexed: Erasmus Wilson, ed., *Standard history of Pittsburg, Penna*. No add.

PITTSBURGH (PA.)—REGISTERS OF BIRTHS, ETC.
P39-ref.-Pa.   127,072 cds. by name. Newsp. indexed: *Pittsburgh gazette,* 1786–1910. Death notices. No add.
P39-ref.-Pa.   21,550 cds. by name. Newsp. indexed: *Pittsburgh gazette,* 1786-1910. Marriage notices. No add.

PITTSBURGH (PA.)—SOCIETIES AND CLUBS
P39-ref   1300 cds. by name of organiz. Cur. add.
P39-tech   1225 cds. by name of organiz. Trade & tech. organiz. Occ. add.
P39-Wyl.   271 cds. by subj. Community file. Qcc. add.

PITTSBURGH. UNIVERSITY—PHOTOGRAPHS
P42-ref   300 cds. by subj. Bks., per. & pams. Freq. add.

PITTSBURGH. UNIVERSITY—PUBLICATIONS
P42-ref   900 cds. by auth. Reprints from per., newsp., mss. Freq. add.

PITTSBURGH (PA.)—VISITORS
P39-ref.-Pa.   400 cds. by name. Bks. & newsp. Cur. add.

PITTSBURGH (PA.) GAZETTE (newsp.). *In* PITTSBURGH (PA.)—REGISTERS OF BIRTHS, ETC.   **P39-ref.-Pa.** (1), (2)

PITTSBURGH SURVEY (bk.). *In* PITTSBURGH (PA.)   **P39-ref.-Pa.**

PLACE NAMES. *See* NAMES, GEOGRAPHICAL

PLAINFIELD (N.J.)
Nj58   300 cds. by auth., t. & subj. Bks., pams. & per. Freq. add.

PLAINFIELD (N.J.)—AUTHORS. *See* AUTHORS—PLAINFIELD (N.J.)

PLANT PATHOLOGY. *See* BOTANY—PATHOLOGY

PLANTATION LIFE. *See* List of Bibliographies, APPENDIX I

PLANTS. *See* BOTANY

PLANTS—PICTURES. *See* PICTURES—PLANTS

PLASTIC MATERIALS. *See also* List of Bibliographies, APPENDIX I
- **Nj54** Unest. cds. by subj. Files, rpts., searches. Freq. add.

PLAY
- **C30** 20 cds. by subj. & source. Pams. & per. Infreq. add.

PLAY PICTORIAL (per.)
- **P39-ref** v. 1-28, 1902–1916. Cds. by auth. & t. No add.

PLAYS. *See also* CHILDREN'S PLAYS; CHRISTMAS PLAYS; List of Bibliographies, APPENDIX I; SHORT STORIES **C43-br, O25-F.S.M., Or2**
- **Ar5** 600 cds. by auth., t. & subj. Occ. add.
- **C13** 300 cds. by auth. & t. Bks. Freq. add.
- **C17** 4500 cds. by auth. & t. Bks. & pams. Inc. holiday mat. Freq. add.
- **C18-r.a.** 3590 cds. by auth. & t. Bks. & pams. Freq. add.
- **C21** 200 cds. by nationality of auth. Bks., per. & pams. Freq. add.
- **C24** 3500 cds. by t. Per. indexed: *Theatre magazine.* No add.
- **C32-lit** 12,000 cds. by subj. Plays pub. since 1928. Freq. add.
- **C43-ref** 8300 cds. by auth., t. & subj. Bks., per. etc. Freq. add.
- **C56** 1000 cds. by subj. & t. Bks. & per. Occ. add.
- **C56** 1000 cds. by auth., subj. & t. Bks. George E. Lask coll. No add.
- **C83** Unest. cds. by t.
- **C85** 500 ent., by auth. Bks. Yrly. add.
- **Ca1** 2000 cds. by t. Bks. & pams. Freq. add.
- **Ca5-circ** 9000 cds. by auth. & t. Bks. Freq. add.
- **Ca6** 810 cds. by subj. Bks. Freq. add.
- **Ca6** 2880 cds. by t. Bks. Freq. add.
- **Ca9** 1600 cds. by t. Bks. No add. since 1936.
- **Ca10-ref** 5531 cds. by auth., subj. & t. Bks. & pams. Freq. add.
- **Ca14** 1500 ent., tpd. shts. by auth. & t. Bks. Infreq. add.
- **Co2-ext** 2500 cds. by subj., class. Freq. add.
- **Co5-circ** 3000 cds. by auth., subj. & t. Freq. add.
- **Ct1** 2000 cds. by auth. & t. Freq. add.
- **Ct6** 4000 cds. by auth., subj. & t. Bks. & per. Freq. add.
- **Ct11-ref** 5280 cds. by auth. & t. Bks. Cur. add.
- **Ct12-Scr.** 639 cds. by subj. & t. Bks. Freq. add.
- **Ct14** 1903 cds. by auth. & t. Bks. Freq. add.
- **De1** Unest. ent., tpd. shts. by t. Cur. add.
- **F2-ref** 700 cds. by subj. or type. Bks. No add.
- **I6** Unest. cds. by t. Bks. Freq. add.
- **I35** 1700 cds. by auth. & t. Bks. Cur. add.
- **I36** 3000 cds. by t. Cur. add.
- **I38** 5775 cds. by auth. & t. Bks. Cur. add.
- **I43-ref** 100 cds. by auth. Per. indexed: *Golden book,* 1925–1935. Plays & dramatic monologs. No add.
- **I46** 1550 cds. by t. Bks. Freq. add.
- **I49** 1132 cds. by t. Bks. Cur. add.
- **I54** 1600 cds. by auth. & t. Bks. not indexed in Firkins or Logasa. Cur. add.
- **I59** 900 cds. by auth. & t. Bks. Infreq. add.
- **I60** 2640 cds. by auth. & t. Bks. Cur. add.
- **I68** 11,000 cds. by auth. & t. Bks. & per. Freq. add.
- **I68** 200 cds. by t. & auth. Bks. Freq. add.
- **I73-ref** 1320 cds. by auth. & t. Bks. Cur. add.
- **I80** Unest. cds. by auth. & t. Bks. Cur. add.
- **Ia11** 850 cds. by t. & lang. Bks. Cur. add.
- **Ia13** 6000 cds. by auth. & t. Bks. & per. Occ. add.
- **Ia14-ref** 15,000 cds. by auth. & t. Bks. Cur. add.
- **Ia16** 1100 cds. by subj. & t. Bks. Per. indexed: *One-act play magazine.* Cur. add.

In22-ref 5280 cds. by auth. & t. Bks. Freq. add.
In23-ref 5280 cds. by subj. Bks. Cur. add.
K3 Unest. ent., tpd. shts. by auth. & t. Bks. Freq. add.
K4 800 cds. by auth. & t. Bks. Cur. add.
K5 1000 cds. Bks. Occ. add.
K8-circ 2375 cds. by t. & subj. Bks. Freq. add.
K12-circ 1000 cds. by t. Bks. not indexed in Firkins. Freq. add.
K16 1300 cds. by auth. & t. Bks. & per. Freq. add.
K18 900 cds. by auth. & t. Bks. Cur. add.
K19 Unest. cds. by auth. & t. Bks. Occ. add.
K20-circ 10,900 cds. by auth., t., subj. & form. Freq. add.
Ky1 4000 cds. by auth. & t. Bks. Freq. add.
L10 106 cds. by auth. Newsp. indexed: *New York times*, Sunday ed., 1935–date. Freq. add.
L14-ref 900 cds. by auth. & t. Bks. Bk. indexed: Samuel French and Thomas H. Lacy, *Acting edition of plays*, 146v. No add.
M4-ref 1600 cds. by auth. & t. Bks. Occ. add.
M13-ref 5000 cds. by auth. & t. Bks. Freq. add.
M16-ref 3100 cds. by auth., t. & holidays. Bks. Freq. add.
M22 603 cds. by auth. & t. Bks. Freq. add.
M23-ref 2200 cds. by t. Bks. Cur. add.
M24 1320 cds. by auth. & t. Bks. Cur. add.
M27-ref 8400 cds. by t. Bks. Freq. add.
M32-circ 1000 cds. by auth. & t. Bks. Cur. add.
Md2-lit 50,000 cds. by auth., subj., t. & type. Bks. & pams. Freq. Freq. add.
Me1 500 cds. by t. Bks. Cur. add.
Me2-ref 11,737 cds. by auth. & t. Bks. Cur. add.
Mi4 1240 cds. by auth. & t. Bks. Cur. add.
Mi6-Mont. 1820 cds. by auth., t. & subj. Bks. Freq. add.

Mi6-par 8040 cds. by t. & subj. Bks. & pams. Freq. add.
Mi6-Sch. 190 cds. by auth. & t. Bk. indexed: Burns Mantle, *Best plays of* . . . Yrly. add.
Mi6-Walk. 260 cds. by auth. & t. Bk. indexed: Burns Mantle, *Best plays of* . . . 1926-date. Yrly. add.
Mi8-ref 1400 cds. by auth. & t. Bks. not indexed in Firkins. Freq. add.
Mi17 683 cds. by t. Bks. Freq. add.
Mi21-cat 3825 cds. by auth. & t. Bks. Cur. add.
Mn4-ref 1680 cds. by subj. Bks. Occ. add.
Mn12 1679 cds. by t. Bks. not indexed in Firkins. Freq. add.
Mn14-Cam. 1500 cds. by subj. & t. Bks. Freq. add.
Mn14-Fran. 700 cds. by subj. & type. Bks. Cur. add.
Mn14-ref 12,500 cds. by subj. & type. Bks. Cur. add.
Mn14-Sum. 240 cds. by subj. Bks. Occ. add.
Mn19 473 cds. by t. Bks. One-act & three-act plays. Freq. add.
Mn23-Ham. 1842 cds. by auth. & t. Bks. Cur. add.
Mn23-Mer. 1000 cds. by auth. & t. Per. & pams. Occ. add.
Mn23-per Unest. cds. by t. Per., 1927–date. Daily add.
Mn23-ref 5500 cds. by t. Bks. not indexed in Firkins. Infreq. add.
Mo5 1800 cds. by auth. & t. Bks., per. & bul. Occ. add.
Mo13-circ 1600 cds. by t. Bk. indexed: Samuel French and Thomas H. Lacy, *Acting edition of plays*, 146v. No add.
Mo13-Stix 782 cds. by t. Bks. Freq. add.
N7-circ 1200 ent., 45 tpd. shts. by t. Bk. indexed: Samuel French and Thomas H. Lacy, *Acting edition of plays*. Incomplete. No add.
N8-o.s. 950 cds. by subj. Bks. Infreq. add.
N10-ref 3500 cds. by auth. & t. Bks. & per. No add.
N14 1200 cds. by auth. & t. Bks. Cur. add.
N15 405 cds. by auth. & t. Occ. add.
N19 300 cds. by class. Freq. add.

N22-ref   20,275 cds. by auth., t., subj. & cast. Bks., pams. & per. Mo. add.
N22-Wood.   4548 cds. by t. Bks. Cur. add.
N35-educ   30,000 cds. by auth., t. & subj. Bks., pams. & per. Cur. add.
N35-Ford.   91 cds. by auth. & t. Cur. add.
N35-Muhl.   800 cds. by t. Bks. Occ. add.
N35-ref. inf   9350 cds. by t. Bks. Chiefly modern Amer. drama. Cur. add.
N40   1320 cds. by auth. & t. Bks. Freq. add.
N46-lit   2700 cds. by subj. Bks. & pams. Freq. add.
N50   Unest. cds. by auth. & t. Bks. Freq. add.
N51   538 cds. by auth. & t. Bks. Cur. add.
N55   900 cds. by auth. & t. Bks. not indexed in Firkins. Freq. add.
N56   1700 cds. by auth. & t. Bks. Cur. add.
Nb5   2300 cds. by auth. & t. Bks. Freq. add.
Nb8   5610 cds. by auth. & t. Bks. & per. Freq. add.
Nb11   4000 cds. by t. Bks. Freq. add.
Nb12   1002 cds. by auth. & t. Infreq. add.
Nb14-ref   3900 cds. by t. Bks., per. & pams. Freq. add.
Nb15   2000 cds. by country. Bks. & per. No add. since 1937.
Nd2   1750 cds. by auth. & t. Bks. Freq. add.
Nd3   1862 cds. by auth. & t. Bks. Cur. add.
Nh2   2850 ent., tpd. shts. by auth. Bks. French, German & Eng. plays, chiefly 19th cent. No add.
Nj7-E.   1000 cds. by t. Bks. Infreq. add.
Nj14   2640 cds. by subj. Bks. Cur. add.
Nj14-ref   10,560 cds. by auth. & t. Bks. & pams. Freq. add.
Nj27-circ   2000 cds. by auth. & t. Bks. Infreq. add.
Nj28   2000 cds. by auth., t. & char. Bks. Freq. add.
Nj34   750 cds. by auth. & t. Pams. Freq. add.

Nj40   2750 cds. by auth. & t. Pams. Infreq. add.
O1-Fire.   1800 cds. by auth. & t. Bks. Cur. add.
O1-read   20,000 cds. by auth. & t. Bks. & pams. Cur. add.
O5   Unest. cds. by cast & type. Bks. Occ. add.
O11   100 ent. by auth. Pa. plays. Infreq. add.
O20-lit (1)   5280 cds. by subj. Bks. Cur. add.
O20-lit (2)   5280 cds. by auth. & t. Bk. indexed: Burns Mantle, Best plays of . . . Cur. add.
O20-M.P.   1000 cds. by auth., t. & cast. Bks. Infreq. add.
O20-Mt.P.   1200 cds. by t. & subj. Bks. & pams. Cur. add.
O20-Nott.   600 cds. by auth. & t. Bks. Bk. indexed: Burns Mantle, Best plays of . . . Cur. add.
O20-Wood.   700 cds. by t. Bks. Infreq. add.
O20-y.p.   10,000 cds. by subj. Bks. Freq. add.
O27   9240 cds. by class. Bks. & per. Freq. add.
O29-ref   1800 cds. by auth. & t. Bks. Infreq. add.
O31   7450 cds. by subj. & type. Bks. Freq. add.
O34   Unest. cds. by comp. & t. Bks. not indexed in Firkins, Logasa & VerNooy, Shay. Freq. add.
O37   300 cds. by auth., subj. & t. Bks. 1, 2, 3 act plays; monologs, pantomimes & dialogs. Cur. add.
O46   5500 cds. by auth. Bks. Cur. add.
O54   3300 cds. by auth. & t. Bks. Freq. add.
O56-circ   700 cds. by subj. Bks. not indexed in Firkins or Logasa. Infreq. add.
O56-ref   6050 cds. by t. Bks. not indexed in Firkins, Logasa or Drama index. Occ. add.
O59   3000 cds. by auth. & t. Bks. & per. Freq. add.
Ok1   656 cds. by auth. & t. Bks. Yrly. add.
Ok4-ref   7000 cds. by auth., t. & subj. Bks. & per. Cur. add.
Or1-cat   9976 cds. by auth. & t. Bks. Cur. add.
Or5-circ   1000 cds. by type. Bks. Infreq. add.

P6 500 cds. by auth. & t. Bks. not indexed in Firkins. Cur. add.
P8 800 cds. by t. Bks. Cur. add.
P24 335 cds. by auth. & t. Bks. Occ. add.
P27 673 cds. by t. Bks. Freq. add.
P34-ref 1250 cds. by auth. & t. Bks. Freq. add.
P38 1100 cds. by t. Bks. Freq. add.
P39-circ 8580 cds. by subj. Bks. Cur. add.
P39-Wyl. 3152 cds. by subj. & t. Bks., pams. & per. Cur. add.
P41 750 cds. by auth. & t. Bks. Freq. add.
P45-ref 1200 cds. by auth., t., subj. & type. Bks. Freq. add.
P48 864 cds. by auth. & t. Bks. Cur. add.
P54-circ 3000 cds. by subj. Bks. & pams. Freq. add.
T1-circ 650 ent., tpd. shts., by auth., t. & date. Bk. indexed: Burns Mantle, *Best plays of* . . . 1920–1939. No add.
T7 2640 cds. by auth. & t. Bks. Cur. add.
Tx11 Unest. cds. by auth. & t. Bks. & pams. Cur. add.
Tx17 1250 cds. by auth. & t. Bks. Freq. add.
Tx21-circ. ref 4000 cds. by auth. & t. Bks. Freq. add.
Tx25 800 cds. by auth. & t. Bks. Plays & short stories. Occ. add.
Tx33 500 cds. by auth. & t. Bks. Cur. add.
U1 1000 cds. by auth. & t. Bks. not indexed in Firkins. Freq. add.
U5 4000 cds. by t. Bks. Plays, poetry & short stories not indexed elsewhere. Cur. add.
W5 1021 cds. by auth. & t. Bks. Freq. add.
W12-ext 600 cds. by t. Bks. Occ. add.
W16 4000 cds. by subj., type & cast. Bks. Cur. add.
W19-S. 709 cds. by t. Bks. Freq. add.
W20-ad 5335 cds. by auth. & t. Bks. Cur. add.
W21 1200 cds. by auth. & t. Bks. Cur. add.
Wa2 2500 cds. by t. Bks. Cur. add.
Wa3 1000 cds. by auth. & t. Bks. Cur. add.
Wa5 2500 cds. by t. Bks. Freq. add.
Wa13-ref 6000 cds. by auth. & t. Bks. Cur. add.
Wa16 Unest. cds. by auth. & t. Bks. Plays and short stories. Freq. add.

PLAYS—CHICAGO
I13-ref 150 cds. by subj., chron. Newsp. since 1938. Freq. add.

PLAYS—CLEVELAND (O.)
O20-lit 1320 cds. by t., main actor & stock co. Cleveland newsp., 1922–1930. Per. indexed: *Town topics*, 1899–1904, in proc. to 1926. Occ. add.

PLAYS—FOREIGN LANGUAGES. *See* PLAYS—ONE-ACT—FOREIGN LANGUAGES; PLAYS subdiv. adjective of nationality; SHORT STORIES—FOREIGN LANGUAGES **O56-circ**

PLAYS—FRENCH, SAMUEL
N45b 570 cds. by auth. & t. Samuel French's standard drama, minor drama, acting editions. No add.

PLAYS—MELODRAMAS
I13-circ 24 cds. by auth. Bks. Occ. add.

PLAYS—MEN CASTS
C32-lit 13p., tpd. shts. by t. Plays for men. Freq. add.

PLAYS—NEW YORK (CITY)
C32-lit Unest. ent., tpd. shts. by t. Plays produced in N.Y., 1900–1935. No add. supp. in 10 yrs.
Mn14-clip 120 cds. by t. Per. Cur. N.Y. stage plays. Wkly. add.

PLAYS—NON-ROYALTY. *See also* PLAYS—ONE-ACT—NON-ROYALTY
C32-lit 16p., tpd. shts. by t. One-act & longer plays. Occ. add.
I13-circ Unest. cds. by auth. Bks. Occ. add.
I40-hi.sch Unest. cds. by subj. Single, pa. bd. plays. Infreq. add.
L14-circ 300 cds. by no. of acts, auth. & t. Bks. Freq. add.

PLAYS—NUMBER CHARACTERS
C32-lit 18p., tpd. shts. by t. Plays for 2 char. Freq. add.

PLAYS—ONE-ACT
C42 Unest. cds. by auth. & t. Bks. Cur. add.

C49-inf   5500 cds. by auth., subj. & t. Bks. Cur. add.
G13   Unest. cds. by t. Bks. Freq. add.
I13-circ   1975 cds. by t. Bks. Freq. add.
I13-r.a.   3425 cds. by auth., subj., no. char., t., class no. Bks. No add.
I63   419 cds. by auth. & t. Bks. Cur. add.
I73-ref   660 cds. by auth. & t. Bks. Occ. add.
I73-ref   660 cds. by auth. & t. Bks. Occ. add.
Ia3   2000 cds. by subj. & t. Bks. & per. Freq. add.
In6   500 cds. by auth. & t. Bks. Cur. add.
K14   466 ent., tpd. shts. by auth. & t. Bks. Freq. add.
K21   812 cds. by t. Per. Infreq. add.
Mn23   Unest. cds. by auth. & t. Per. indexed: *One-act play magazine,* 1931–date. Cur. add.
Mo3-E.   150 cds. by t. Bks. Supp. to Logasa. Occ. add.
Mo3-Wash.   Unest. cds. by t. Bks. Supp. to Logasa. Occ. add.
Mo13-Car.   400 cds. by subj. Bks. Occ. add.
N3   800 cds. by auth. & t. Bks. Mo. add.
N8-per   150 cds. by auth., t. & subj. Per. indexed: *One-act play magazine.* Freq. add.
N10-ref   243 cds. by auth. & t. Per. Freq. add.
N16   350 cds. by auth. Bks. Infreq. add.
N35-ref. inf   1680 cds. by auth. Bks. & per. No add.
N35-Rivin.   550 cds. by t. Bks. Freq. add.
N46-lit   2500 cds. by subj. Bks. & pams. Freq. add.
N52   129 ent., tpd. shts. by t. Bks. Infreq. add.
N57   7920 cds. by subj., t., no. char. Bks. Freq. add.
Nb12   54 cds. by auth. & t. Bks. Infreq. add.
Nb14-r.a.   750 cds. by subj. Bks. Cur. add.
O16-circ   350 cds. by subj. Bks. Cur. add.
O20-F.I.   200 cds. by t. Bks. Infreq. add.
O20-M.P.   2150 cds. by auth., subj. & t. Bks. Freq. add.
O20-Stat.   3960 cds. by t. Occ. add.
O56-Locke   1000 cds. by auth. & t. Bks. Infreq. add.
P9   1886 cds. by auth. & t. Freq. add.
Wa8   2300 cds. by auth. & t. Freq. add.
Wa8a   231 cds. by t. Bks. No add. since 1938

Plays—One-Act—Comedies
C32-lit   Unest. ent. 5 tpd. shts. by auth. Occ. add.
I13-circ   250 cds. by no. of char. Bks. Cur. add.

Plays—One-Act—Foreign Languages
C32-for   420 cds. by lang. & auth. Bks. Freq. add.
Mi6-for   225 cds. by lang. & auth. Bks. Freq. add.

Plays—One-Act—Non-Royalty
C9-ref   3960 cds. by t., auth. & subj. Bks. Freq. add.

Plays—Translations
N9   4200 cds. by t. & auth. Freq. add.

Plays—Women Casts
C32-lit   15p., tpd. shts. by t. Plays for women. Freq. add.

Plays, Amateur
D32   2700 cds. by t. & subj. Bks. & pams. Freq. add.
G4-circ   600 cds. by auth. Bks. Cur. add.
Ia4   50 cds. by subj. Pams., etc. Freq. add.
Mn14-clip   1700 cds. by auth., t. & subj. Pams. & clip. Freq. add.
Nj50-circ   3650 cds. by subj. & t. Bks. No add.
Wa10-circ   1600 cds. by t. & subj. Bks. & pams. Cur. add.

Plays, Catholic
Mo13-univ   75 cds. by subj. Bks. & per. Cur. add.

Plays, Early
I43-ref   1354 cds. by auth. & t. Plays written before 1800. Bks. Cur. add.

PLAYS, FRENCH. *See also* LA PETITE ILLUSTRATION (per.)
Ca6 2240 cds. by t. Bks. Freq. add.
Mn15-ref 4200 cds. by auth. & t. Bks. Infreq. add.
O25-Clev. Coll. 200 cds. by auth. & t. Per. indexed: *La petite illustration.* No add.
O47-ref 2000 cds. by auth. & t. Per. indexed: *La petite illustration, Theatre ser.*, 1904–1937. Occ. add.

PLAYS, HISTORICAL
C3a 5280 cds. by subj. Bks. No add.
Nt3 Unest. cds. by auth. Bks. Cur. add.

PLAYS, HOLIDAY. *See also* CHRISTMAS PLAYS
Mi13-W. side 300 cds. by holiday. Bks. Cur. add.
Mn10 300 ent., tpd. shts. by holiday. Bks. Cur. add.
N10-ref 1600 cds. by subj. Bks. Cur. add.
N22-educ 4000 cds. by subj., auth. & t. Bks., per. & pams. Freq. add.
N23 126 cds. by holiday. Bks. & pams. No add.
P5 45 cds. by subj. & t. Bks. Occ. add.

PLAYS, ITALIAN
O20-Alta 1320 cds. by char. Bks. Cur. add.

PLAYS, JUVENILE. *See* CHILDREN'S PLAYS

PLAYS, MANUSCRIPT
C32-lit 1300 cds. by t. Per. Unpub. plays, produced in N.Y. or London, since 1928. Freq. add.

PLAYS, PAMPHLET
In33-ad 350 cds. by auth., t. & subj. Cur. add.

PLAYS, SCHOOL
C32-lit 27p., tpd. shts. by t. Occ. add.
Nj56 3200 cds. by auth., subj. & t. Bks. & pams. Freq. add.
Wa10-par 2200 cds. by auth. & t. Per. Entertainments. Occ. add.

PLAYS, SPANISH
Mn15-ref 500 cds. by auth. Bks. & mss. Occ. add.
Nh2 15,000 cds. by auth. 19th & 20th cent. Spanish plays. Occ. add.

POE, EDGAR ALLAN
V2 750 cds. by auth. Writings about Poe. Occ. add.

POE, EDGAR ALLAN—WORKS
C8-circ 40 cds. by t. Bks. Occ. add.
C32-fic 16p., tpd. shts. by t. Bks. No add.
V2 550 ent., tpd. shts., chron. Letters to and from, pub. & unpub. Occ. add.

POETRY. *See also* CHILDREN'S POETRY; QUOTATIONS; READINGS AND RECITATIONS; Names of poets and various natl. poetry; LA PETITE ILLUSTRATION (per.). PLAYS **U5**
C32-lit 7000 cds. by subj. Bks. since 1932. Freq. add.
C40 11,880 cds. by auth. & t. Bks. not in Granger. Occ. add.
C41 Several thousand cds. by t. Bks. Cur. add.
C43-ref 43,000 cds. by auth. & t. Bks. & per. Poetry, essays, monologs & orations. Freq. add.
C46 30,000 cds. by auth., subj., t. & 1st line. Bks. Infreq. add.
C69-ref 3700 cds. by t. Bks., per. & newsp. Occ. add.
Co5-ref 22,440 cds. by auth., t. & 1st line. Bks. not in Granger. Freq. add.
De3 8580 cds. by auth., t. & 1st line. Newsp. Bks. not in Granger. Infreq. add.
G4-ref 3000 cds. by t., 1st line & subj. Newsp. Bks. not in Granger. Freq. add.
G20 355p., tpd. shts., by t., auth. & subj. Bks. No add.
H3-ref 1800 cds. by t. & 1st line. Per. indexed: *N.Y. Times book review magazine*, 1921–1929. Occ. add.
H3-Haw. 1500 cds. by auth. & t. Per. & newsp. No add.
I13-ref 1000 cds. by t. Bks. & per. Occ. add.
I26 1800 cds. by auth., 1st line & t. Per. indexed: *The Current*, v. 1-2, 1884; *Current literature*, 1891–1910. No add.
I63 453 cds. by auth. & t. Bks. Freq. add.
I72-S.Wil. 900 cds. by auth. Poetry on hi. sch. reading lists. No add.

Ia6-ref 22,600 cds. by auth., t. & 1st line. Bks. not in Granger. Cur. add.

Ia18-ad 1000 ent., tpd. shts. by t., auth. & subj. Per. indexed: *Grand lodge of Iowa, Proceedings.* Freq. add.

In22-ref 22,440 cds. by auth., t., 1st line & subj. Newsp. Freq. add.

K4 15,000 cds. by auth., t. & subj. Bks. Cur. add.

K5 (1) 2600 cds. by t. Bks. Cur. add.

K5 (2) 1000 ent., by t. Per. & newsp. Per. indexed: *N.Y. Times book review magazine.* Infreq. add.

Ky1 8000 cds. by t. Bks. Occ. add.

L8 Unest. cds. by auth. & t. Bks. Cur. add.

M4-ref 2500 cds. by auth., t., 1st line & subj. Newsp. indexed: *New York times, Boston evening transcript, Boston Sunday globe,* 1939 to date. Wkly. add.

Mi6-circ 500 cds. by t. & 1st line. Bks. Occ. add.

Mi6-circ 1200 cds. by subj. Bks., per. & newsp. Cur. add.

Mi6-ref 6000 cds. by auth., t. & 1st line. Bks., per. & newsp. Freq. add.

Mi11-ref Unest. cds. by auth. & t. Bks. not in Granger. Freq. add.

Mi14 600 cds. by auth. Bks., pams. & newsp. Occ. add.

Mn14-Fran. 500 cds. by subj. & t. Bks., per., pams. & scrapbks. Freq. add.

Mn14-ref 14,500 cds. by t. & 1st line. Bks. Poetry, quot. & proverbs. Freq. add.

Mn14-ref 900 cds. by subj. Bks. Infreq. add.

Mn23-ref 131,300 cds. by auth., t. & 1st line. Bks. not in Granger. Infreq. add.

Mo3-ref Unest. cds. by auth. & t. Newsp. Filkin, Guest & Mason poems. Occ. add.

N7 12,000 cds. by 1st line. Bks. & per. Freq. add.

N7 18,000 cds. by t. Bks. No add. since 1937.

N8-ref 60,220 cds. by auth., t. & 1st line. Bks., newsp. & 1st line. Freq. add.

N10-ref 37,745 cds. by auth., t. & 1st line. Bks. & per. Freq. add.

N22-ref 40,450 cds. by auth., t. & 1st line. Bks. not in Granger. Infreq. add.

N22-ref 750 cds. by subj., lit. form & spec. types of ed. inf. Prose & poetry anthologies. No add.

N23 15,619 cds. by t. Bks. No add.

N35-ref. inf 3750 cds. by t. & 1st line. Bks. Cur. add.

N46-lit 4620 cds. by subj. & t. Bks., per., etc. Cur. add.

N54-ref 7000 cds. by subj. Bks. Infreq. add.

Nj1-ref 26,400 cds. by t. & 1st line. Bks. not in Granger. No add.

Nj25-ref 556 cds. by t. Bks. & per. Freq. add.

Nj27-circ 500 cds. by t. Bks. Infreq. add.

O10 20,000 cds. by t. Bks. Cur. add.

O20-lit 206,580 cds. by auth., t. & 1st line. Bks. not in Granger. Cur. add.

O49 1200 cds. by auth., t. & 1st line. Bks. not in Granger. Freq. add.

O56-circ 1500 cds. by subj. Bks. Freq. add.

O56-ref 30,000 cds. by auth., subj. & t. Bks. not in Granger. Freq. add.

O59 4000 cds. by auth. & t. Bks. & per. Freq. add.

Or2 11,000 cds. by auth. & t. Bks. not in Granger. Freq. add.

P33-ref 3000 cds. by t. Newsp. Freq. add.

P39-ref 7000 cds. by auth., t., subj. & 1st line. Bks. not in Granger. No add.

P39-Wyl. 728 cds. by subj. Bks. Cur. add.

P41 3300 cds. by auth. & t. Bks. Freq. add.

P48 741 cds. by t. Bks. not in Granger. Cur. add.

P56 5000 cds. by auth., t. & subj. Per. & newsp. Freq. add.

U1 2000 cds. by auth. & t. Bks. not in Granger. Infreq. add.

W16 72,000 cds. by t. Bks. Freq. add.

Wa3 450 cds. by auth. & t. Bks. Occ. add.

POETRY—CHICAGO
I13-ref   500 cds. by t. & 1st line. Bks. & per. Occ. add.

POETRY—EASTER
Mo3-Linc.   200 cds. by t. Bks. Occ. add.

POETRY—ENGINEERING. *See* POETRY—TECHNOLOGY   P39-tech

POETRY—EUROPEAN WAR, 1914–1918
I13-ref   3000 ent., tpd. shts. by auth., t. & 1st line. Bks. & per. Occ. add.
In35   1100 ent., tpd. shts. by auth. & t. Occ. add.

POETRY—SCIENCE. *See* POETRY—TECHNOLOGY   P39-tech

POETRY—SEASONS. *See* POETRY, HOLIDAY   I49

POETRY—TECHNOLOGY
P39-tech   700 cds. by auth. & subj. Bks., per. & house organs. Poetry dealing with sci. and eng. Occ. add.

POETRY—TREES
Mo3-Wpt.   400 cds. by t. Bks. Occ. add.

POETRY, BIOGRAPHICAL
N8-ref   2640 cds. by name of pers. Bks. & per. Poems on great people. Freq. add.

POETRY, DIALECT
N50   24 cds. by subj. Bks. Freq. add.

POETRY, HOLIDAY
I49   338 cds. by seasons, holidays, & t. Bks. Poetry on seasons & holidays. Occ. add.

POETRY, LYRIC
Nj27-circ   55 cds. by auth. & t. Bks. Infreq. add.

POETRY, MAGAZINE
P33-ref   Unest. cds. by t. Per. Freq. add.

POETRY, NARRATIVE
Nj27-circ   115 cds. by auth. & t. Bks. Infreq. add.
M13-ref   66 cds. by auth. Bks. Freq. add.

POETRY, RELIGIOUS. *See* PICTURES, RELIGIOUS   O20-Wood.

POETRY (AS A LITERARY FORM)
C27-r.a.   300 cds. by subj. Bks. Poetry types. Cur. add.

POETS. *See also* AUTHORS   P34-ref
Mi6-circ   1850 cds. by name. Bks., per. & newsp. Poets, crit. & biog. Cur. add.
W18   1200 cds. by auth. Bks. & per. Chief modern poets of England & Amer. Freq. add.

POETS—INDIANA
In24a   17 ent. by subj. Bks. Freq. add.

POETS—MUSIC. *See* MUSIC—POETS

POETS, CATHOLIC
Md2-#6   325 cds. by name. Bks. Cath. poets. Cur. add.
Tx30   33 ent., tpd. shts. by auth. Bks. & per. No add.

POETS, CHILDREN'S. *See* AUTHORS, CHILDREN'S   O2

POLAND—BIOGRAPHY
O20-E. 79th   105 cds. by subj. Bks. Cur. add.

POLISH LANGUAGE
K9-ref   250 cds. by auth. & t. Bks. Infreq. add.
Nj58   250 cds. by auth. & t. Bks. Infreq. add.

POLITICAL SCIENCE. *See* List of Bibliographies, APPENDIX I

POLK CO. (IA.)
Ia6-ref   3600 cds. by subj. Bk. indexed: Johnson Brigham, *Des Moines, the pioneer of municipal progress* . . . No add.

POMONA (CALIF.)—ORDINANCES
C51   Unest. ent., tpd. shts. by subj., 1928–1940. Cur. add.

PONY EXPRESS COURIER (per.). *In* CALIFORNIA   C8-ref
C71-ref   v. 5, 1939–date. Cds. by subj. Cur. add.

POOLS. *See* GARDENS AND GARDENING   Tx5

POPULAR ASTRONOMY (per.)
N35-ref. sci   v. 1–20, 1893–1912, v. 1–40, 1913–1932. Tpd. shts. by auth. & subj. No add.

POPULAR HOMECRAFT (per.). *See also* HANDICRAFTS   Mi27-ref
I65   v. 5–12, 1934–1942. Cds. by subj. Freq. add.

POPULARITY
Tx30   112 ent., tpd. shts. by subj. Bks. & per. No add.

POPULATION
O47-Scr.   2500 cds. by auth. & subj. Bks., per. & pams. Freq. add.

PORCELAIN.   See CERAMICS

PORTER, WILLIAM SYDNEY—WORKS
C32-fic   69p., tpd. shts. by t. Pub. wks. of O'Henry. No add.

PORTLAND (ORE.)—HISTORY
Or5-ref   380,160 cds. by subj. Newsp. & hist. Loc. hist. & biog. Cur. add.

PORTLAND (ORE.)—MUSIC. See MUSIC—PORTLAND (ORE.)

PORTLAND CITY CLUB BULLETIN (per.)
Or6   v. 11#37, 1931—v. 22#36, 1942. Repts. Freq. add.

PORTRAIT GALLERY OF EMINENT MEN AND WOMEN (bk.). *In* BIOGRAPHY
N15 (1)

PORTRAITS. See also CARICATURES AND CARTOONS; PHOTOGRAPHS: MOTION PICTURES—STILLS Tx20; PAINTINGS Nj46; PICTURES I43-ref (1), In37
A1   274 cds. by subj. Oil paintings hanging in State capitol. Now in proc. of revision.
C73   Unest. cds. by sitter. Port., drawings & miniatures. Occ. add.
Ca2-art   1500 cds. by subj. of port. Bks. Q. add.
D32-tech   850 cds. by name. Bks. Freq. add.
I13-ref   35,000 cds. by subj. Bks. & per. Infreq. add.
I43-med   4500 cds. by subj. Framed & unframed port. Freq. add.
I71-art   321 cds. by name. Pic. reprod. of paintings. Freq. add.
In35   216 ent., tpd. shts. by name. Per. indexed: *Eclectic magazine.* No add.
Ky15-ref   640 cds. by name. Prints, per. & sep. Infreq. add.
M11-paint   300 cds. by subj. Port. in Boston museum. Paintings. Cur. add.
Mo3-ref   35,000 cds. by name. Bks. & per. No add.

N7   7600 cds. by subj. Bks. & per. Occ. add.
N34a   50,000 cds. by name. Cur. add.
N35-ref. print   29,000 cds. by subj. Bks., per., & sep. Cur. add.
N35-Wood.-circ   1025 cds. by subj. Bks., per. & newsp. Freq. add.
Nb10-pic   7800 cds. by name. Pic. Freq. add.
Nc2   Unest. cds. No add.
Nh2-art   2800 cds. by name. Bks. & per. Cur. add.
O20-hist   17,160 cds. by subj. Bks., per. & newsp. Freq. add.
O21   190 cds. by name of art. Bks. & per. Cur. add.
O29-ref   2365 cds. by subj. Bks. & per. Port. & illus. Occ. add.
O56-ref   2200 cds. by name. Infreq. add.
P31   44,464 cds. by surname. Paintings, engravings, phot., busts & illus. in bks. Daily add.
P34-ref   4800 cds. by name. Bks. Occ. add.
T1-gen   2000 cds. by subj. & name. Bks. & per. Infreq. add.
W12-ext   100 cds. by subj. Bks. Freq. add.

PORTRAITS—BASEBALL PLAYERS
N35-ref. inf   320 cds. by name. Spaulding coll. of sport. No add.

PORTRAITS—CALIFORNIA. See also PORTRAITS—WEST   C57
C56-Calif.   Several thousand cds. by name. Calif. pioneers, auth., art., musicians, state off. Freq. add.

PORTRAITS—CLEVELAND (O.)
O20-hist   500 cds. by name of subj. Standiford coll. of famous Clevelanders. Freq. add.

PORTRAITS—CONNECTICUT
Ct7   2640 cds. by name. Occ. add.

PORTRAITS—ENTOMOLOGISTS
D16   3200 cds. by surname of subj. Phot. of entomologists of world. Cur. add.

PORTRAITS—GEORGIA. See PICTURES—GEORGIA   G8

PORTRAITS—INDIANS
I26-Ayer   2000 cds. by tribe. Bks. & per. Ayer coll. No add.

PORTRAITS—KALAMAZOO (MICH.). *See*
  KALAMAZOO (MICH.) GAZETTE
  (newsp.) **Mi21**
PORTRAITS—LOUISIANA
  L11 8000 cds. by name. Bks. & per. Freq. add.
  L14-ref 4200 cds. by name of subj. Bks., per. & newsp. Freq. add.
PORTRAITS—MICHIGAN
  Mi13-Mich. Unest. ent. by name. Newsp., bks., etc. Mo. add.
PORTRAITS—NATURALISTS
  M5 600 cds. by subj. Bks., per., prints, paintings, etc. Occ. add.
PORTRAITS—NEGROES
  D6 2200 cds. by name. Bks. in Moorland foundation. Freq. add.
  D6 2658 cds. by auth. Per. Infreq. add.
  T8 8414 ent., tpd. shts. by name. Bks. & per. No add.
PORTRAITS—NORTH CAROLINA
  Nc1 404 cds. by subj. Port. & pic. Freq. add.
PORTRAITS—NORTHWEST
  Wa14-ref 1800 cds. by name. Bks. Occ. add.
PORTRAITS—OHIO
  O17 7000 cds. by name. Bks. & per. on hist. of Cincinnati, Hamilton co., O. Cur. add.
PORTRAITS—PENNSYLVANIA. *See* PICTURES —PENNSYLVANIA **P16**
PORTRAITS—PHYSICIANS
  M2 30,000 cds. by name. Bks., per., pams., etc. Cur. add.
  N47-med 900 cds. by name. Bks. & per. since 1938. Freq. add.
  N55 12,000 ent., tpd. shts. by subj. Print. port. in early med., Wolff Leavenworth coll. No add.
PORTRAITS—SAINT LOUIS (MO.)
  Mo13-art 1800 cds. by name. Bks. Occ. add.
PORTRAITS—SCIENTISTS. *See also* SCIENTISTS **P39-tech**
  In18 Unest. cds. by subj. Bks., jls., pams., etc. Cur. add.
  N35-ref. sci 15,000 cds. by name. Bks. & per. Port. & biog. index to sci. In proc.

PORTRAITS—U.S. NAVY. *See* U.S. NAVY **Md1** (2)
PORTRAITS—WEST
  C57 11,000 cds. by subj. Bks. on Calif. & W. travel, hist., etc. before 1936. Infreq. add.
PORTRAITS, HISTORICAL
  C73-ref 26,000 cds. Amer. extra-illus. bks. & coll. of over 6500 sep. prints & drawings. Occ. add.
PORTS. *See* HARBORS
POSEY CO. (IND.)—HISTORY
  In27 186 cds. by auth., subj. & t. Newsp. & per. Cur. add.
POST-OFFICES—INDIANA. *See* INDIANA—POST-OFFICES
POSTAGE STAMPS, MEDICAL
  Ia7 109 ent., tpd. shts. by name of Dr. Stamps of med. interest. Occ. add.
POSTCARDS. *See* PICTURES—POSTCARDS
POSTERS. *See* THEATRE, ENGLISH—POSTERS **N35-ref**; MAPS **N4**
POSTERS, TRAVEL
  Wa18-art 300 cds. by country & t. Cur. add.
POSTERS, WAR. *See also* EUROPEAN WAR, 1914–1918—POSTERS
  Wa10-art 300 cds. by case. Infreq. add.
POTTERY. *See* CERAMICS
POUGHKEEPSIE (N.Y.)—BIBLIOGRAPHY—IMPRINTS
  N45a 315 cds. by auth. & t. Bks. Freq. add.
  N45b 26 ent., tpd. shts., chron. Imprints up to 1876. Occ. add.
POUGHKEEPSIE (N.Y.)—NEWSPAPERS
  N45a 202 cds. by t. Freq. add.
POULTRY
  Nj61 250 cds. by auth. & t. Bks., per., pams. & rpts. Freq. add.
POWER PLANTS
  Nj52 1000 cds. by subj. Bks., per. & pams. Freq. add.
PRATT (KANS.) DAILY TRIBUNE (newsp.)
  K18 175 cds. by subj. Wkly. add.

PRESBYTERIAN CHURCH—NEW JERSEY—
  COUNCILS AND SYNODS
Nj62   900 cds. by auth. Bks., pams. & mss. Occ. add.

PRESBYTERIANS
P4 (1)   1500 cds. by auth., subj. & t. Bk. indexed: John C. Johnston, *Treasury of Scottish covenant.* No add.
P4 (2)   10,560 cds. by auth., subj. & t. Covenanter mat. Cur. add.

PRESIDENTS—U.S. *See* LAW—U.S.—EXECUTIVE ORDERS AND PROCLAMATIONS

PREVENTION OF ACCIDENTS. *See* ACCIDENTS—PREVENTION

PRICE, SARAH FRANCES
Ky2   5p., tpd. shts. by auth. Bks. & per. No add.

PRICES
Wa10-tech   210 cds. by subj. Govt. doc. Occ. add.

PRIESTS, MISSIONARY
N48   500 cds. by subj. Bks. No add.

PRIMERS. *See* READERS AND PRIMERS

PRINCETON (N.J.)
Nj59   43 cds. by auth. Bks. & pams. Princeton, Princeton univ., & N.J. Cur. add.

PRINCETON UNIVERSITY—DISSERTATIONS, ACADEMIC—GEOLOGY. *See* List of Bibliographies, APPENDIX I

PRINCETON UNIVERSITY—PUBLICATIONS, FACULTY—SCIENCE. *See* List of Bibliographies, APPENDIX I

PRINCETON UNIVERSITY—THESES, SENIOR—GEOLOGY
Nj60-Guy.   1000 cds. by auth., yr. & subj. Theses since 1928. Yrly add.

PRINTERS—16TH CENTURY
I26-rare   900 cds. by printer. Bks. Freq. add.

PRINTERS—17TH CENTURY
C73-earl. Eng.   13,300 cds. by printer. Bks. Printers in 1640 bks. Cur. add.

PRINTERS' MARKS. *See also* BOOKBINDING
N35-ref. res
Mn15-ref   1400 cds. by cent., country & printer's name. Bks. Freq. add.

P31   266 cds. by name of firm. All early printers & interesting modern ones. Occ. add.

PRINTING
I43-med   74 cds. by subj. Bks. Specimens from famous presses. Infreq. add.
N45b   250 cds. by auth., class. Bks., pams. & per. Village press coll. & those designed by F. W. Goudy. Freq. add.
Nj50-circ   2090 cds. by printer, press & auth. Bks. & pams. in Richard C. Jenkinson coll. Freq. add.
O20-bus   2640 cds. by date & press. Bks. Occ. add.

PRINTING—OXFORD (O.)
O47-Scr.   500 cds. by auth. & type. Per., bks. & addresses. Infreq. add.

PRINTING—PERIODICALS
I26   100,000 cds. by auth. & subj. Per. No add.

PRINTS. *See* DRAWINGS AND ENGRAVINGS

PRISONS. *See* List of Bibliographies, APPENDIX I

PRIZE BOOKS. *See* REWARDS (PRIZES, ETC.); Names of indiv. awards.

PRO PARVULIS HERALD (per.)
Mn22-sch   v. 1-3, 1937–1940. Cds. by auth. & t. Cur. add.

PROBATION. *See* List of Bibliographies, APPENDIX I

PROFESSION, CHOICE OF. *See* VOCATIONS

PROFESSIONAL INSTITUTE OF THE CIVIL SERVICE INSTITUTE OF CANADA. JOURNAL. *In* CANADA—PERIODICALS **Ca13-per**

PROGRESSIVE ARIZONA AND THE GREAT SOUTHWEST (per.)
Az1   v. 1-13, 1925–1933. Tpd. shts.

PROJECTS. *See* UNITS OF WORK

PRONUNCIATION. *See also* NAMES   **Mi29**
C27-r.a.   1500 cds. by name. Bks. & per. Freq. add.
C32-hist   1320 cds. by name. Per. & bks. Occ. add.
C47   31p., tpd. shts. by name. Per. Freq. add.
C82   272 cds. by name. Bks. & per. Auth. & t. Infreq. add.

Ia4 600 cds. by name. Per. & newsp. Daily add.
M27-ref 700 cds. by name. Per., newsp., etc. People, places, etc. Freq. add.
Md2-ref 900 cds. by name. Names not listed in Funk, Mawson or Mackey. Freq. add.
Mn14-ref 1000 cds. by name. Bks. & per. Geog. & pers. names. Cur. add.
Mo3-ref 500 cds. by name. Freq. add.
Mo12 165 cds. by name. Newsp. indexed: *Christian science monitor,* Monday ed. Cur. add.
N10-ref 999 cds. by subj. Bks. & per. Infreq. add.
N14 300 cds. by name. Auth. & char. Cur. add.
N25 90 cds. by name. Bks. Auth. & char. Infreq. add.
N46-biog 500 cds. by name. Cur. add.
Nv1 100 cds. by name. Names in lit. Freq. add.
O31 200 cds. by name. Occ. add.
O37 200 cds. by name. Auth. Freq. add.
Ok2-ref 1100 cds. by name. Freq. add.
Wa14-ref 850 cds. by name. Freq. add.

PROTESTANTISM. See also Names of various Protestant churches
M14 2000 cds. by subj. Bks. & per. Prot. church hist. & rel. subj. Freq. add.

PROTOZOA
Nj61 240 cds. by auth. & t. Bks., per. & pams. Freq. add.

PROVERBS
F1 336 cds. by auth. Proverbiana. Freq. add.

PROVIDENCE RECORD AND GUIDE (per.). *In* CORPORATIONS—RHODE ISLAND R1-bus

PSYCHOLOGICAL TESTS. *See* TESTS AND MEASUREMENTS

PSYCHOLOGY. *See also* List of Bibliographies, APPENDIX I
N30-t.c.-ref 178p., tpd. shts., chron., auth. & subj. Abstract ref. of v. 26-35, 1919–1928 of Psychological index. No add. since 1940.

PUBLIC ADMINISTRATION
I19 850 cds. by subj. Bks., per. & pams. Admin. reorganiz. of govt. units. Cur. add.
I19 4750 cds. by subj. Daily news releases. Cur. add.
Nj60-govt 86p., tpd. shts. & on cds. Bks., per. & pams. Services & areas in loc. govt. by Wm. S. Carpenter. Freq. add.
Nj60-govt 17p., tpd. shts., chron. under type. Pub. & comp. materials, legis. & chartered laws (Sept. 1–Mar. 1, 1940) issued by Princeton loc. govt. survey. Yrly. add.
Nj60-govt 3000 cds. by auth., subj. & t. Bks., pams., per. & mss. Pub. admin., with emphasis on state & loc. govt. Freq. add.
Nj60-pub. admin 5000 cds. by auth. & subj. Bks., per. & pams. Pub. admin. Freq. add.

PUBLIC ADMINISTRATION—BOOK REVIEWS
Mi3-govt 400 cds. by auth. Freq. add.

PUBLIC AFFAIRS PAMPHLETS. *In* PAMPHLETS O59, U1

PUBLIC ART IN ST. LOUIS (bk.). *In* ST. LOUIS (Mo.) Mo13-Soul

PUBLIC FINANCE. *See* FINANCE Nj60-Benj. St.

PUBLIC HEALTH. *See also* HYGIENE
C67 7260 cds. by subj. Bks., per. & pams. Freq. add.
I69 6000 cds. by subj. Pams. Occ. add.

PUBLIC HEALTH—DOCUMENTS
C32-sci 600 cds. by subj. Doc. indexed: *Calif. Dept. of pub. health Biennial rpts., Special bul., U.S. pub. health service bul., Rpts. & reprints, Los Angeles city health dept. bul.* Cur. add.

PUBLIC OFFICIALS. *See* Name of loc., subdiv. OFFICIALS AND EMPLOYEES

PUBLIC UTILITIES
Nj52 1000 cds. by subj. Bks., per. & pams. Freq. add.

PUBLIC UTILITY HOLDING CO. ACT OF 1935
D29 12,000 cds. by auth. & subj. Congress. debates on act. No add.

PUBLISHERS AND PUBLISHING. *See also* PRINTING
Mi6-per 2000 cds. by name. Ed. & pub. of per. Cur. add.

N35-ref. res 8000 cds. by name of press. Amer. & for. presses. Cur. add.

PUBLISHERS AND PUBLISHING—CLEVELAND (O.)
O20-ref 1320 cds. by pub. Bks., pams. & sht. mus. Cur. add.

PUBLISHERS & PUBLISHING—19TH CENTURY
N28a 2000 ent. by name of firm. Amer. bk. pub. Freq. add.

PUBLISHERS AND PUBLISHING, FOREIGN
C32-for 350 cds. by country. European, Asian, Spanish-Amer., U.S. Infreq. add.

PUBLISHERS' SERIES. *See* SERIES, BOOKS IN

PUBLISHER'S WEEKLY (per.). *In* BIOGRAPHY **C8-ref**; CHILDREN'S LITERATURE—EDITORS **In12**

PUERTO RICO
Pr1 700 cds. by subj., auth. or t. Bks., per., etc. Per. indexed: *Ateneo puertorriqueno,* 1938–1940; *Economic review,* 1939–1941; *Journal of agric. of Univ. of Puerto Rico,* 1940; *Puerto Rico labor news,* 1937–1940; *Revista de agricultura, industria y commercio de Puerto Rico,* 1939–1941; *Revista del Colegio de Ingenieros de Puerto Rico,* 1940–1941; *Summer school review,* 1933–1934, 1938–1940. Freq. add.

Pr2 500 cds. by subj. Bks., per., maps, etc., 1931–date. Geog., econ. & pop. of Puerto Rico. Freq. add.

PUERTO RICO—BIOGRAPHY
Pr1-ref 571 cds. by name. Bks. Freq. add.

PUERTO RICO—HISTORY
Pr3 154,896 cds. by subj. Bks. & per. Freq. add.

PUERTO RICO ILUSTRADO (per.)
Pr1 1934–1937. Cds. by auth. & subj. Infreq. add.

PUERTO RICO LABOR NEWS (per.). *In* PUERTO RICO **Pr1**

PUERTO RICO UNIVERSITY. JOURNAL OF AGRICULTURE. *In* PUERTO RICO **Pr1**

PULITZER PRIZES
Ia12 67 ent., tpd. shts. by subj. Bks. Infreq. add.

K11 Unest. ent., tpd. shts., chron. 1919–date. Yrly. add.

Nv1 130 cds. chron. 1928–date. Yrly. add.

PUNISHMENT—COLONIAL PERIOD. *See* List of Bibliographies, APPENDIX I

PUPPET PLAYS. *See* MARIONETTES

PURITAN LITERATURE. *See also* THEOLOGY **Nj62**
Mo9 Unest. cds. by auth. Chas. Haddon Spurgeon coll.

QUAKERS. *See* FRIENDS, SOCIETY OF

QUALITY AND OTHER STORIES (bk.). *In* SHORT STORIES **Tx12**

QUEBEC (per.). *In* CANADA—PERIODICALS **Ca13-per**

QUEEN'S CO. (N.Y.)—CENSUS
N22-L.I. Unest. ent., tpd. shts. by name. 6v. cens. records, 1850. No add.

QUEEN'S CO. (N.Y.)—DEEDS
N22-L.I. 2800 cds. by name. 4v. Occ. add.

QUEEN'S CO. (N.Y.)—HISTORY
N22-L.I. (1) 179p., tpd. shts. by subj. Admin. of Queen's co. No add.
N22-L.I. (2) 22,440 cds. by name. Hist. coll. of Borough of Queen's. In proc.

QUEEN'S CO. (N.Y.)—WILLS
N22-L.I. 199p., tpd. shts. by name. 6v. wills, 1787–1835. No add.
N22-L.I. 14,520 cds. by name. 1835. In proc.
N22-L.I. 199p., tpd. shts. by testator. 1787–1906. No add.

QUINCY (MASS.)—NEWSPAPERS
M24 7260 cds. by name & subj. 1916–1928, 1932–date. Daily add.

QUOTATIONS. *See also* POETRY
Mn14-Fran.-j 100 cds. by subj. Bks., etc. J. quot. Infreq. add.
Mo3-ref 400 cds. by catchword, first word, or source. Bks., newsp., etc. Quot. not found elsewhere. Infreq. add.
N35-ref. inf 2100 cds. by catchword. Bks. & per. Quot. not found elsewhere. Cur. add.

N46-lit 250 cds. by subj. Quot. not found elsewhere. Infreq. add.
N60 65p., tpd. shts. by auth., t. & subj. Newsp. indexed: *N.Y. Times book review*, queries & answers dept., 1933–1934. No add.
O16-ref 60,000 cds. by auth. & t., & subj. Per. & newsp. Freq. add.
P39-ref 13,500 ent. by subj. Newsp. indexed: *N.Y. Times book review*, q. & a. dept. Cur. add.

RACE PROBLEMS
G3 140 cds. by subj. Bks., per. & pams. Freq. add.

RACES
Wa14-ref 200 ent., tpd. shts. by class., race & nationality. Bks., pams. & per. Freq. add.

RACINE (WISC.)—SOCIETIES AND CLUBS
W20-ad 100 cds. by name. Newsp. Yrly. or semi-yrly. add.

RACINE (WISC.) REVIEW (newsp.)
W20-ad 1928–1930. Cds. by subj. No add.

RADIO
Mn14-tech 300 cds. by type of radio. Per. Cur. add.

RADIO ENGINEERING
Nj5 1000 cds. by subj. Bks., per. & pams. Freq. add.

RADIO STATIONS. *See* WASHINGTON (STATE) —DIRECTORIES Wa10-tech

RADIO THEME SONGS. *See* SONGS—RADIO THEME

RADIOACTIVITY, ARTIFICIAL
P30 200 cds. by subj. & auth. Jls., reprints. Freq. add.

RAFINESQUE, CONSTANTINE SAMUEL
Ky2 63 cds. by auth. Bks. & per. Freq. add.

RAILROADS
D2 250 ent., tpd. shts., chron. by subj. Railway club proc. No add.
D28 200 cds. by subj. Railroad pub. Occ. add.
N38 700 cds. by subj. Bks., per., releases, etc. Railroad transp. Infreq. add.

RAILROADS—FINANCE
Nj60-Pliny 139,260 cds. by subj. Annual rpts., mortgages, prospectuses, etc., 1830–date. Railroad & corporation finance. Freq. add.

RAILROADS—HOLDING COMPANIES
D2 64p., tpd. shts., chron. by subj. Bks., pams. & per. Occ. add.

RASSEGNA D'ARTE ARTICA E MODERNA (per.). *In* ART, RELIGIOUS R2; SCULPTURE R2

RAYON
Nj54 Unest. cds. by subj. Special rpts. & searches. Cur. add.

READERS AND PRIMERS. *See also* CHILDREN'S LITERATURE Nj14; List of Bibliographies, APPENDIX I
C43-j 400 cds. by char. & sub-title. Freq. add.
C46 442 ent., tpd. shts. by t. & auth. Cur. add.
C49-j 1408 cds. by auth. Cur. add.
C61-sch 15 cds. by auth. In proc.
C80 Unest. cds. by subj. & t. Freq. add.
Co6 Unest. cds. by subj. Bks. not indexed in Rue or Hockett. Cur. add.
Ct3 337 cds. by subj. Cur. add.
I6 (1) Unest. ent., tpd. shts. by subj. & t. Bk. indexed: Charles E. Norton, *Heart of oak books*, 7v. No add.
I6 (2) Unest. ent., tpd. shts. by subj. & t. Indexed: Ida Coe and A. J. Dillon, *Story hour readers*, 5v. No add.
Ia6-j 5280 cds. by subj. Bks. not indexed in Rue. Cur. add.
In8-j 1000 cds. by subj. No add.
Mi6-par 1075 cds. by subj. Freq. add.
Mi31-Way. 400 cds. by subj. Cur. add.
N8-sch 1320 cds. by t. Bks. Freq. add.
N13 50 cds. by auth. Freq. add.
O20-class 1320 cds. by subj. Freq. add.
O20-j 1200 cds. by subj. Freq. add.
O20-Rice-j Unest. cds. by name. Names of children & animals in j. readers. Occ. add.
O29-W. Carn. 1100 cds. by t. & subj. Freq. add.
W5 1600 cds. by t. & subj. No add. since 1935.
W20-Wash. 1000 cds. ent., tpd. shts. by subj. Freq. add.

READING
C11 Unest. cds. by auth. & subj. Bks., per. & pams. The read. proc. Cur. add.

READING (PA.)—HISTORY. *See* BERKS CO. (PA.)—HISTORY **P45-ref**

READING (PA.) EAGLE (newsp.). *In* BERKS CO. (PA.)—HISTORY **P45-ref**

READINGS AND RECITATIONS. *See also* DIALECT READINGS; DIALOGUES; MONOLOGUES; ORATIONS; POETRY; SPEECHES
C6-ref 75 cds. by subj. Bk. indexed: *Werner's readings and recitations* (incomplete). No add.
C69-ref 3700 cds. by t. Bks., per. & newsp. Occ. add.
G4-circ 50 cds. by auth. Bks. Monologues, dialogues & read. Cur. add.
Ia4 1800 cds. by t. Bks. not indexed in Granger or Silk. Cur. add.
In16 125p., tpd. shts. by auth. & t. Bks. indexed: Phineas Garrett, *One hundred choice selections,* 40v. No add.
In23-ref Unest. ent., tpd. shts. by subj. Bk. indexed: *Werner's readings and recitations.* Freq. add.
Mn14-clip 1025 cds. by t. Newsp. & pams. Infreq. add.
Mn14-ref 850 cds. by subj. & t. Bks. Read. & monologues. Cur. add.
Mn22 560 cds. by auth. & t. Pams. Poetry & dramatic pieces. No add.
Mo3-N.E. Unest. cds. Bks. indexed: Phineas Garrett, *One hundred choice selections; Werner's readings and recitations.*
Mo3-Wash. Unest. cds. Bks. Bk. indexed: *Werner's readings and recitations.*
N8-ref 7920 cds. by t. & speaker. Bks. Freq. add.
Nb16 55 ent., tpd. shts. by t. Bk. indexed: *Werner's readings and recitations.* Infreq. add.
O2 2000 cds. by t. Bks. Dialogs, monologs & skits. Cur. add.
P4 (1) Unest. cds. by auth., subj. & t. Bk. indexed: Phineas Garrett, *One hundred choice selections,* 40v. No add.
P4 (2) Unest. cds. by auth., subj. & t. Bk. indexed: *Werner's readings and recitations,* v. 19, 29, 34, 37, 39, 44, 51, 53, 56. Occ. add.

REAL ESTATE. *See also* NATIONAL ASSOCIATION OF REAL ESTATE BOARDS. NEWS SERVICE
I25 156 cds. by subj. Newsp. Wkly. add.

RECIPES. *See* COOKERY

RECLAMATION PROJECTS. *See* SOIL SURVEYS

RECORDING. *See* PHONOGRAPH RECORDS

RECORDS (IN BUSINESS AND INDUSTRY). *See* List of Bibliographies, APPENDIX I

RECORDS OF THE TOWN OF JAMAICA, L.I. (bk.). *In* JAMAICA (N.Y.)—HISTORY **N22-L.I.**

RECREATION. *See* List of Bibliographies, APPENDIX I

RECREATION—PERIODICALS
Nj12 1500 cds. by subj. Per. Per. indexed: *Leisure,* Recreat., hobbies, sports, etc. Occ. add.

REEDY'S MIRROR (per.)
Mo13-ref v. 4-6, 8-14, 1894–1912. Cds. by auth., t. & subj. Occ. add.

REFERENCE AIDS
Ar3 700 cds. by subj. Bks., pams., newsp. & per. Inf. file. Cur. add.
C8-ref 2640 cds. by subj. Bks., etc. Ref. notes. Occ. add.
C43-ref 2000 cds. by subj. Bks. & per. Misc. index. Occ. add.
C69-ref 2500 cds. by subj. Bks., per. & newsp. Misc. mat. Freq. add.
C81-ref 325 cds. by subj. Bks. & per. Obscure ref. mat. Freq. add.
Ca1 4800 cds. by subj. Bks., per., pams. & newsp. 'Where to look' file. Cur. add.
Ca5-S. 800 cds. by subj. Bks., newsp. & per. 'Where to look' index. Freq. add.
Ca9 6000 cds. by subj. Pams., newsp. & per. 'Where to look' index. Daily add.
Ca14 2088 cds. by subj. Bks., pams., newsp., pic., per. & govt. doc. 'Where to find it' inf. file. Freq. add.

Co5-ref 7260 cds. by subj. Q. file. Cur. add.
De3 6100 cds. by subj. Bks., newsp. & per. Ref. mat. Freq. add.
F2-r.a. 300 cds. by subj. Fugitive facts. Occ. add.
F2-ref 1200 cds. by key word. Fugitive facts: q., oddities, elusive items. Freq. add.
F5 1810 cds. by subj. Gen. ref. file. Cur. add.
H3-Haw. 1500 cds. by subj. Bks., per., etc. Ready ref. index. Freq. add.
I33 462 cds. by subj. Bks., per. & newsp. Inf. file. Cur. add.
I33 1000 cds. by subj. Bks., per. & newsp. Misc. file. Freq. add.
I43-ref 3000 cds. by subj. Bks., per., doc., etc. Misc. inf. file: ref. to maps, costume, charts, bibl., doc. & 'puzzlers'. Freq. add.
Ia17 500 cds. by subj. Q. freq. asked. Freq. add.
In22-ref 1000 cds. by subj. Snag file, obscure subj. Freq. add.
In27 351 cds. by auth., subj. & t. Bks., per., etc. Misc. file. Freq. add.
In28 5000 cds. by subj. Bks., per., pams., doc., etc. Ref. subj. cat. Cur. add.
In33-doc 960 cds. by subj. Per. Repeat q. & mat. not found in indexes. Freq. add.
K8-ref 3850 cds. by subj. Bks. & per. Inf. index. Freq. add.
Ky15-Cresc. Hill 1000 cds. by subj. Per., newsp. & pams. Occ. add.
Ky15-ref 1300 cds. by subj. & name. Bks., newsp., per. & pams. Ready ref., gen. inf. Freq. add.
L12 100 cds. by subj. Bks. & per. Freq. add.
M32 600 cds. by subj. Subj. difficult to find. Occ. add.
Md2-ref 5000 cds. by subj. & catchword. Bks., per., newsp. & letters. Q. file. Freq. add.
Mi5-q. & a. 23,760 cds. by subj. Daily 'q. & a.' column. Misc. inf. Daily add.
Mi6-ref 20,000 cds. by subj. Ref. subj. Freq. add.
Mi6-Rich. 350 cds. by subj. Bks. Ref. file. Occ. add.
Mi6-Sch. 1200 cds. by subj. Pams., per., bks., etc. Ref. desk index. Occ. add.
Mi6-Walk. 787 cds. by subj. Bks., per., pams. & newsp. Misc. index, quick ready ref. to elusive mat. Freq. add.
Mi20 800 cds. by subj. Bks. & per. Misc. ref. index. Freq. add.
Mi25 2250 cds. by subj. Ready ref., odd bits of inf. Occ. add.
Mi27-ref 5000 cds. by subj. Bks., per., pic., etc. Fugitive facts. Occ. add.
Mi29 7500 cds. by subj. Per., pams., pic., newsp. & bks. Freq. add.
Mn9 Unest. cds. by subj. Bks., pams., newsp. & pic. Ref. q. Occ. add.
Mn14-Fran. 1500 cds. by subj. Misc. subj. Freq. add.
Mn14-tech 1980 cds. by subj. Ref. index. Cur. add.
Mn23-Ham. 494 cds. by subj. Bks., per., newsp. & pams. Useful index. Occ. add.
Mn23-ind. art 42,500 cds. by subj. Bks. & doc. Useful index. Freq. add.
Mn23-Mer. 1500 cds. by subj. Bks., pams., newsp. & per. Per. indexed: *Minnesota historical magazine.* Occ. add.
Mn23-ref 125,000 cds. by subj. Bks., per., etc. Useful index. Freq. add.
Mn23-Riv. 100 cds. by subj. Bks. & per. Occ. add.
Mt1 932 cds. by subj. Per. Bibl. file. Freq. add.
N4 1800 cds. by subj. Bks., per., pams., etc. Ref. file of misc. inf. Freq. add.
N8-ref 1500 cds. by subj. Index rerum. Freq. add.
N22-ref 1000 cds. by subj. Inf. cd. file. Infreq. add.
N29 400 cds. by subj. catchword. Ref. questions. Occ. add.
N35-ref. inf 3000 cds. by subj. Bks. & per. Inf. Cur. add.
N46-hist. 2640 cds. Bks. & per. Ready ref. Cur. add.
N54-ref 300 cds. by subj. Inf. on difficult q. Occ. add.
Nb14-r.a. 1200 cds. by subj. Bks. Index of subj. helps. Freq. add.

Nj1-ref 11,880 cds. by subj. Bks., per. & pams. Index to ref. q. Freq. add.

Nj18 143 cds. by subj. Unusual ref. q. Freq. add.

Nj29 900 cds. by subj. Bks., per., pams. & newsp. Ref. q. Infreq. add.

Nj67-ref 6000 cds. by subj. Index to ref. q. Freq. add.

O1-Fires. 450 cds. by subj. Bks., per., etc. Inf. file. Occ. add.

O1-read 6480 cds. by subj. Gen. index. Cur. add.

O6 Unest. cds. by subj. Bks., per. & newsp. Misc. file. Occ. add.

O16-art 1500 cds. by subj., auth. & t. Snag file. Freq. add.

O20-Ch.F.P.L. 250 cds. by subj. Bks., per. & pams. Freq. add.

O20-hist 30,360 cds. by subj. Bks., per. & newsp. Occ. add.

O20-lit 28,380 cds. by subj. Subj. file of misc. inf. Cur. add.

O20-Or.T. Sch. 250 cds. by subj. Bks., per. & pams. Freq. add.

O31 6175 cds. by subj. Bks. & per. Ref. index. Freq. add.

O56-circ 3000 cds. by subj. Misc. file. Cur. add.

O56-ref 2500 cds. by subj. Q. found. Freq. add.

Or4 1144 cds. by subj. Bks. & per. Special q. Freq. add.

Or6 850 cds. by subj. Bks., per. & pams. Freq. add.

P14 2250 cds. by auth. & subj. Per., etc. Misc. file. Freq. add.

P27a 300 cds. by subj. & t. Bks., per. & newsp. Inf. file. Freq. add.

P54-ref 780 cds. by subj. Bks., per., almanacs, etc. Subj. file for elusive mat. Freq. add.

R1-bus 300 cds. by subj. Elusive mat. Freq. add.

Sc1 139 cds. by subj. Bks., per. & pams. Freq. add.

T9-ref 400 cds. by subj. Q. & a. file. Infreq. add.

W12-ext. Unest. cds. by subj. Bks. & per. Ref. list. Freq. add.

Wa13-ref 24,000 cds. by subj. Per. & bks. Quick ref. file. Freq. add.

Wa14-ref 3000 cds. by subj. Gen. inf. Freq. add.

REFERENCE AIDS, JUVENILE
De3 635 cds. by subj. Bks. & per. Ref. mat. for j. Freq. add.

H2 200 cds. by subj. Obscure mat. Freq. add.

I65-j 13,794 cds. by subj. Inf. file. Wkly. add.

Mn14-Fran. 2200 cds. by subj. Bks. & per. Misc. subj. file. Freq. add.

O8-j 1000 cds. by auth., t. & subj. Misc. mat. Freq. add.

O20-Hou. 100 cds. by subj. Ready ref. Occ. add.

O20-j 1000 cds. by subj. Misc. index. Occ. add.

O20-Rice-j 250 cds. by subj. Unusual q. index. Occ. add.

P54-j 520 cds. by subj. Bks. & per. Subj. often asked for. Freq. add.

Wa6 155 cds. by subj. Bks., per., pams., etc. Subj. index, j. Freq. add.

REFERENCE BOOKS. *See also* List of Bibliographies, APPENDIX I
P34 300 cds. by subj. Ref. bks. Analytics. Occ. add.

REFERENCE SHELF (bk.). *In* DEBATES C8-ref, C43-ref, N7, N35-Hi.B., Nj56, P45-ref; SPEECHES P33-ref

REFORMED PRESBYTERIAN COVENANTER (per.)
P4 v. 1-60, 1837–1859. Cds. by auth., subj. & t. In proc.

REGIONAL LITERATURE—U.S. *See also* FICTION, REGIONAL—U.S.
C3a 5280 cds. by region & auth. Bks. Regionalism in lit., inc. fic., drama, poetry, etc. Occ. add.

C72 125 ent., tpd. shts. by region. Bks. Fic. & non-fic. with reg. background. Occ. add.

REGISTERS OF BIRTHS, ETC.
P49 900 cds. by name. Newsp. indexed: *Bradford Porter and reporter*, v. 1-13, 17-19, 21-29. Marriages & deaths. Occ. add.

RELIEF SOCIETY MAGAZINE
U1 v. 1-19, 1913–1932. Tpd. shts. by auth. & subj. Infreq. add. (Prepared by a neighboring lib.)

U3 v. 1-19, 1913–1932. Tpd. shts. by auth. & subj. Occ. add.

RELIGION. *See also* BIBLE; Names of churches and denominations
I42 162,624 cds. by surname or subj. Bks., church hist., etc. No add. since 1930.

Ky16 238 cds. by auth., subj. & t. Bks. Rel. lit. Occ. add.
M14 1500 cds. by auth. & subj. Bks. & pams. Early Bibles, prayerbks., psalms, liturgical & metrical, early hymnals, biog., bibl., etc. Freq. add.
M14 1500 cds. by auth. & subj. Bks. & pams. Early rel. writings, 1450–c1850. Occ. add.
M14 Unest. ent. by subj., patron & date. Bks. & per., letters. Ref. q. by mail. Freq. add.
M14 Unest. cds. by subj. Bks., letters, newsp., etc. Misc. inf. Freq. add.
O16-circ 425 cds. by subj. Bks. Cur. add.

RELIGION—PERIODICALS. See PERIODICALS, DENOMINATIONAL

RELIGION—SOCIETIES AND CLUBS
Md2-educ., phil. & rel 200 cds. by name. Occ. add.

RELIGIOUS ART. See CHRISTIAN ART AND SYMBOLISM; JESUS CHRIST IN ART; PAINTINGS, RELIGIOUS; PICTURES, RELIGIOUS

RELIGIOUS EDUCATION
I44 140 ent., tpd. shts. by subj. Mat. for Bible sch. workers. No add.

RENAISSANCE
M30 Unest. ent., tpd. shts. Bks. & mss. Frances Taylor Pearsons Plimpton coll. Infreq. add.
P43 500 cds. by subj. Bks., pams. & pic. No add.

RENO (NEV.) EVENING GAZETTE (newsp.)
Nv1 1931–date. Cds. by subj. Daily add.

REPORT OF THE CAUSES DETERMINED ... (bk.). In KENTUCKY—LANDS Ky7

REPPLIER, AGNES—WORKS
I13-ref 150 cds. by t. Bks. & per. Infreq. add.

REPRODUCTION
Nj61 70 cds. by auth. & t. Bks., per. & pams. Infreq. add.

REPRODUCTIONS OF DRAWINGS (bk.). In DRAWINGS AND ENGRAVINGS N5-ref

RESEARCH
C34-ref 900 cds. by sch. or dept., auth. Research rpts. Infreq. add.

RESEARCH REVIEW (CO-OPERATIVE COMMONWEALTH FEDERATION). In CANADA—PERIODICALS Ca13-per

RESPIRATORY SYSTEM
Nj61 50 cds. by auth. & t. Per., pams. & lectures. Infreq. add.

RESTAURANTS, FOREIGN
C32-for 100 cds. by nationality. Restaurants abroad & loc. Infreq. add.

REVERE, PAUL—LEDGERS
M11-dec. art 500 cds. by customer & obj. made. Paul Revere's ledgers. No add.

REVIEWS. See BOOK REVIEWS

REVISTA DE AGRICULTURA, INDUSTRIA Y COMMERCIO DE PUERTO RICO (per.). In PUERTO RICO Pr1

REVISTA DEL COLEGIO DE INGENIEROS DE PUERTO RICO (per.). In PUERTO RICO Pr1

REVOLUTIONARY SOLDIERS. See U.S.—HISTORY—REVOLUTION

REVOLUTIONARY SOLDIERS OF VIRGINIA (bk.). In U.S.—HISTORY—REVOLUTION—VIRGINIA Ky7 (1)

REVOLUTIONARY WAR. See U.S.—HISTORY—REVOLUTION

REVUE DE L'UNIVERSITE D'OTTAWA (per.). In CANADA—PERIODICALS Ca13-per

REVUE TRIMESTRIELLE CANADIENNE (per.). In CANADA—PERIODICALS Ca13-per

REWARDS (PRIZES, ETC.). See also Names of individual rewards
C4 23p., tpd. shts. by name. Bks. Freq. add.
C32-for 600 cds. by lang. & t. Lit. prizes, for. Freq. add.
C43-circ 200 cds. by name. Bks. Freq. add.
I13-Hild. 10p., tpd. shts. by name. Bks. Yrly. add.
I13-r.b. 835 cds. by name & date. Freq. add.

I43-ref   101 ent. by name. Per. Famous lit. prizes. Occ. add.

In5-j   21 ent., chron. Bks., per., newsp., etc. Newberry & Caldicott medal mat. Yrly. add.

Mn23-St. Anth.   300 cds., chron. by auth. & t. Prize selections & bk. club selections. No add.

N35-ref. inf   450 cds. by name & field of writing. Amer. & for. lit. prize recipients. In proc.

N46-fic   400 cds. by name of award. Prize awards & pub. contests. Freq. add.

O20-fic   1320 cds. by auth. Prize novels. Freq. add.

O26   94 cds. by prize. Lit. prizes. Occ. add.

RHODE ISLAND—CORPORATIONS. *See* CORPORATIONS—RHODE ISLAND

RHODE ISLAND—TAXATION. *See* TAXATION—RHODE ISLAND

RICHMOND (VA.). *See* VIRGINIA   **V8-ref**

RICHMOND (VA.).—BIBLIOGRAPHY—IMPRINTS

V8-cat   500 cds. by auth. Bks. & pams. Freq. add.

RILEY, JAMES WHITCOMB—WORKS

I13-ref   2000 cds. by t. & 1st line. Bks. & per. Infreq. add.

N8-ref   900 cds. by t. Bks. Freq. add.

RIVERS. *See also* Names of rivers

Ky2   4p., tpd. shts. by auth. Bks. & per. Travel & transp. on the Mississippi & Ohio rivers. No add.

RIVERSIDE (CALIF.)—HISTORY

C55-ref   2000 ent., class. Phot., newsp., etc. Freq. add.

RIVERSIDE (CALIF.) DAILY PRESS (newsp.)

C55-ref   4400 cds. by people, events, etc. Daily add.

RIVERSIDE Co. (CALIF.)—EUROPEAN WAR. *See* EUROPEAN WAR, 1914–1918—RIVERSIDE Co. (CALIF.)

ROADS—INDIANA. *See* INDIANA—ROADS

ROCHESTER (N.Y.)

N46-loc. hist   7260 cds. by subj. Scrapbks.

N46-ref   65p., tpd. shts. by name & subj. Cur. add.

ROCHESTER (N.Y.)—AUTHORS. *See* AUTHORS—ROCHESTER (N.Y.)

ROCHESTER (N.Y.)—BIOGRAPHY

N46-loc. hist   17,160 cds. by name. Bks., per., newsp., etc.

ROCHESTER (N.Y.)—NEWSPAPERS

N46-ref (1)   350 cds. by name. Features in newsp. Yrly. add.

N46-ref (2)   411,840 cds. by subj. chron. Newsp., 1818–1850; 1851–1897. Newsp. indexed: *Rochester daily advertiser*, 1850–. No add.

ROCHESTER (N.Y.)—SOCIETIES AND CLUBS

N46-loc. hist   9240 cds. by name. Newsp. Cur. add.

ROCHESTER. UNIVERSITY—DISSERTATIONS, ACADEMIC. *See* List of Bibliographies, APPENDIX I

ROCHESTER. UNIVERSITY—PUBLICATIONS, *See* List of Bibliographies, APPENDIX I

ROCHESTER (N.Y.) DAILY ADVERTISER (newsp.). *In* ROCHESTER (N.Y.)—NEWSPAPERS   **N46-ref (2)**

ROCK ISLAND (ILL.)—NEWSPAPERS

I67   1839–date. Cds. by subj., chron. Daily add.

ROCKFORD (ILL.)

I68-loc. hist   3075 cds. by subj. Bks., per. & brochures. Cur. add.

ROCKVILLE (CONN.)—NEWSPAPERS

Ct15   600 cds. by subj. Newsp., 1868–date. Yrly. add.

ROD AND GUN AND AMERICAN SPORTSMAN (per.)

Ca14   v. 34–40, 1933–1938. Tpd. shts. by subj. Yrly. add.

RODA (per.). *In* ROTARIAN (per.)   **I28**

ROMANTICISM

Tx31   500 cds. by subj. Bks. & per. Romantic & Victorian lit. Freq. add.

ROSES

Tx5   150p., tpd. shts., also cds. by t. Bks., per. & bul. Freq. add.

ROSTER OF THE MEXICAN WAR (bk.). *In* U.S. HISTORY—WAR WITH MEXICO, 1845–1848—KENTUCKY   **Ky7**

ROTARIAN (per.). *In* AUTHORS I28
I28   1911–date. Cds. by subj., t., auth., etc. Per. indexed: *Roda*. Mo. add.

ROTARY CLUB
I28   6500 cds. by auth. & subj. Bks. Occ. add.

ROYAL ANTHROPOLOGICAL INSTITUTE OF GREAT BRITAIN AND IRELAND. JOURNAL
N5   v. 8-70, 1899–1942. Cds. by subj. Occ. add.

ROYAL OAK (MICH.) DAILY TRIBUNE (newsp.)
Mi27-ref   Unest. cds. by subj. & loc. Wkly. add.

RUSKIN, JOHN—WORKS
M30   773 cds. by auth. Bks. Infreq. add.

RUSSELL Co. (ALA.)—CEMETERY RECORDS
A1   400 ent., tpd. shts. by name. Hurtsboro, Moreland, Seale, Vilula, Glennville cem. Occ. add.

RUSSELLVILLE (KY.)
Ky7   Unest. ent., tpd. shts. by name. Bk. indexed: Edward Coffman, *The story of Russellville*. No add.

RUSSIA—AUTHORS. *See* AUTHORS—RUSSIA

RUSSIAN FOLK SONGS. *See* FOLK SONGS, RUSSIAN

RUSSIANS IN CALIFORNIA. *See* List of Bibliographies, APPENDIX I

RUTGERS UNIVERSITY
Nj40   11,500 cds. by subj. Bks., pams., newsp., pic., etc. Cur. add.

SACRAMENTO (CALIF.)
C57   3884 cds. by subj. Bks. & per. Freq. add.

SACRAMENTO (CALIF.)—NEWSPAPERS
C57   156,000 cds., by subj. Newsp. indexed: *Sacramento Bee*, 1912–1937, *Sacramento Union*, 1905–1911. No add.

SACRAMENTO (CALIF.) BEE (newsp.). *In* SACRAMENTO (CALIF.)—NEWSPAPERS C57

SACRAMENTO (CALIF.) UNION (newsp.). *In* SACRAMENTO (CALIF.)—NEWSPAPERS C57

SACRED MUSIC. *See* CHURCH MUSIC; HYMNS

SAFETY EDUCATION. *See also* ACCIDENTS—PREVENTION
Ky9   50 cds. by subj. Per. Occ. add.

SAGINAW (MICH.)
Mi28-ref   600 cds. by subj. Bks., per. & pams. Occ. add.
Mi29   800 cds. by subj. Newsp., pams., bks. & per. Freq. add.

SAGINAW (MICH.)—SOCIETIES AND CLUBS
Mi29   50 cds. by name. Infreq. add.

SAILING VESSELS. *See* SHIPS

ST. BONAVENTURE COLLEGE—PUBLICATIONS, FACULTY
N48   2000 cds. by auth. Bks., per. & pams. Freq. add.

ST. BONAVENTURE COLLEGE. SCHOOL OF SCIENCE. SCIENCE STUDIES (per.)
N48   1932–date. Cds. by auth. & subj. Q. add.

ST. CLAIR Co. (ALA.)—CENSUS
A1   700 cds. 1820 fed. cens. No add.

ST. LOUIS (MO.)
Mo13-Soul   Unest. cds. Bks. indexed: Lucien Carr, *Missouri, a bone of contention;* James Cox, *Old and new St. Louis;* Richard Edwards & M. Hopwewell, *Edward's great West;* James F. Ellis, *Influence of environment on the settlement of Missouri;* David Harris, *Brief report of the meeting commemorating the early St. Louis movement;* Idress Head, *Historical and interesting places in St. Louis;* William Hyde, *Encyclopedia of the history of St. Louis;* G. Prather Knapp, *City worth seeing;* I. H. Lionberger, *Annals of St. Louis;* Clarence McClure, *History of Missouri;* C. E. Marston, *Geography of Missouri;* Harry J. Petrequin, *St. Louis as it is today;* *Stories of old St. Genevieve;* *State of Missouri;* Mary Powell, *Public art in St. Louis;* Lyle Saxon, *Father Mississippi;* John Scharf, *History of St. Louis city and county;* Shelley print. & pub. co., *Saint Louis views;* Elihu H. Shepard, *The early history of St. Louis and Missouri;* Philip Skrainka, *St. Louis, its history and ideals;* Marshall Snow,

History of the development of Missouri; Thomas Spencer, *Story of old St. Louis;* Walter Stevens, *St. Louis, the fourth city;* Jonas Viles, *History of Missouri for high schools.*

ST. LOUIS (MO.)—HISTORY
 Mo13-ref; Mo13-Grav. 3800 cds.; 1000 ent., tpd. shts. Bk. indexed: Walter Stevens, *St. Louis, the fourth city, 1764–1909,* v. 1. No add.
 Mo13-ref 1500 cds. by subj. & name. Bks., per. & newsp. Occ. add.

ST. LOUIS (MO.)—PHOTOGRAPHS
 Mo13-ref 800 cds. by subj. (place). Bks. Occ. add.

ST. LOUIS (MO.) PUBLIC LIBRARY. CHILDREN'S BOOK NOTES
 L14-j 549 cds. by auth. Bks. Mo. add.

ST. LOUIS AS IT IS TO-DAY (bk.). *In* ST. LOUIS (MO.) **Mo13-Soul.**

ST. LOUIS, ITS HISTORY AND IDEALS (bk.). *In* ST. LOUIS (MO.) **Mo13-Soul.**

ST. LOUIS, THE FOURTH CITY (bk.). *In* ST. LOUIS (MO.) **Mo13-Soul.**

ST. LOUIS (MO.)—HISTORY
 Mo13-ref; Mo13-Grav.

ST. LOUIS VIEWS (bk.). *In* ST. LOUIS (MO.) **Mo13-Soul.**

ST. PATRICK'S DAY. *See* List of Bibliographies, APPENDIX I

ST. PAUL (MINN.). *See* MINNESOTA **Mn23-ref**

ST. PAUL (MINN.)—AUTHORS. *See* AUTHORS—ST. PAUL (MINN.)

ST. PAUL (MINN.)—HISTORY. *See* MINNEAPOLIS—HISTORY **Mn14-ref**

ST. PAUL (MINN.)—SOCIETIES AND CLUBS. *See* MINNESOTA—SOCIETIES AND CLUBS **Mn23-ref**

SAINTE BEUVE'S CRITICAL THEORY (bk.). *In* AUTHORS **In1**

SAINTS
 I13-ref 300 cds. by subj. Bks. Occ. add.
 M11 100 ent. by name & attribute. Freq. add.
 Mo13-univ 500 cds. by subj. of patronage. Bks.

SAINTS, ITALIAN
 O20-Alta 3960 cds. by name. Bks. & per. Freq. add.

SALEM (MASS.)—HISTORIC HOUSES
 M25 200 ent., tpd. shts. by family name. Freq. add.

SALEM (MASS.)—NEWSPAPERS
 M25 Unest. ent., tpd. shts. by subj. Newsp. indexed: *Salem gazette,* 1768–1892; *Salem register,* 1800–1893. Infreq. add.

SALEM (MASS.) GAZETTE (newsp.). *Ir* SALEM (MASS.)—NEWSPAPERS **M25**

SALEM (MASS.) REGISTER (newsp.). *In* SALEM (MASS.)—NEWSPAPERS **M25**

SALESMEN AND SALESMANSHIP
 Nj52 1000 cds. by subj. Bks., per. & pams. Freq. add.

SALT LAKE CITY (UTAH) DESERET NEWS (newsp.)
 U3 v. 2-6, 1851–1856. v. 38-57, 1888–1907. Tpd. shts. by name & subj. Freq. add.

SAMPLERS. *See* List of Bibliographies, APPENDIX I

SAN DIEGO (CALIF.)
 C62-ref 10,000 cds. by auth., subj. & t. Bks., mss., etc. Freq. add.

SAN DIEGO (CALIF.)—NAMES, GEOGRAPHICAL. *See* NAMES, GEOGRAPHICAL—SAN DIEGO CO. (CALIF.)

SAN DIEGO (CALIF.)—NEWSPAPERS
 C62-ref 100,000 cds. by auth., subj. & t. Newsp. Newsp. indexed: *San Diego herald,* 1851–1860. Cur. add.

SAN DIEGO (CALIF.)—ORDINANCES
 C62-bus 175 cds. by no. & subj. New ord. of city & co. Cur. add.

SAN DIEGO (CALIF.) HERALD (newsp.). *In* SAN DIEGO—NEWSPAPERS **C6-ref**

SAN DIEGO STATE TEACHERS COLLEGE—PUBLICATIONS, FACULTY
 C63 187 cds. by auth. & t. Bks. & per. Infreq. add.

SAN DIEGO (CALIF.) UNION (newsp.)
 C62 1868–date. Cds. by subj., t. & auth. Daily add.

SAN FRANCISCO (CALIF.)
C69-ref 1500 cds. by subj. Bks., per. & newsp. Freq. add.

SAN FRANCISCO (CALIF.)—MUSIC. *See* MUSIC—SAN FRANCISCO (CALIF.); SAN FRANCISCO OPERA ASSOCIATION. PROGRAMS

SAN FRANCISCO—PHOTOGRAPHS
C69-ref 5000 cds. by subj. Occ. add.

SAN FRANCISCO (CALIF.) BULLETIN (newsp.). *In* CALIFORNIA—NEWSPAPERS C32-hist

SAN FRANCISCO BUSINESS (per.)
C69-ref v. 1-23, 1920-1933. Cds. by subj. No add.

SAN FRANCISCO (CALIF.) CALL (newsp.). *In* CALIFORNIA—NEWSPAPERS C32-hist

SAN FRANCISCO (CALIF.) CHRONICLE (newsp.). *In* CALIFORNIA—NEWSPAPERS C32-hist

SAN FRANCISCO OPERA ASSOCIATION. PROGRAMS
C69-mus Unest. ent., tpd. shts., chron. by season, date & by art. 1923-date. Yrly. add.

SAN FRANCISCO SYMPHONY ORCHESTRA PROGRAMS. *See* SYMPHONY C32-art

SANDBURG, CARL—WORKS
I13-ref 850 cds. by t. & 1st line. Bks. & per. Occ. add.

SANITATION. *See* List of Bibliographies, APPENDIX I

SANTA FÉ MAGAZINE. *In* SOUTHWEST Nm2

SANTA FÉ (N.M.) NEW MEXICAN (newsp.)
Nm2 1864-1914. Cds. by subj. In proc.

SANTA MONICA (CALIF.)—SOCIETIES AND CLUBS
C81-r.a. 618 cds. by name. Freq. add.

SARETT, LEW R.—WORKS
I13-ref 200 cds. by t. & 1st line. Bks. & per. Occ. add.

SARGENT, JOHN SINGER—WORKS
M11-Tolman 3500 cds. by subj. Bks., sales cat., etc. No add.

SASKATCHEWAN (CAN.)—DOCUMENTS
Ca14 94 ent., tpd. shts. by dept. & br. Freq. add.

SATURDAY EVENING POST (per.)
C69-per v. 184-192, 1911-1929. Cds. by auth. & t. No add.

SATURDAY NIGHT (per.). *In* CANADA—PERIODICALS Ca13-per

SATURDAY REVIEW OF LITERATURE (per.). *See also in* BIBLIOGRAPHIES N30-t.c.; BOOK REVIEWS C8-ord, In23-ord, Mo3-ord
C50 v. 9, 1932-date. Cds. by auth. Wkly. add.

SAVANNAH (GA.)—CEMETERY RECORDS
G20 Unest. ent., tpd. shts. by name. Keeper's record bk., 1850-1938. No add.
G20 Unest. ent., tpd. shts. by name. Keeper's record bk., 1852-1938. No add.

SAVANNAH (GA.)—NEWSPAPERS
G2 Unest. ent., tpd. shts. by auth. & subj. Newsp., 1763-1825. No add.
G20 Unest. ent., tpd. shts. by period & subj. Newsp., 1763-1825. No add.

SAVANNAH (GA.)—SOCIETIES AND CLUBS
G20 150 cds. by name. Newsp., etc. Cur. add.

SAVANNAH (GA.) NEWS (newsp.)
G20 1850-1869. Cds. & tpd. shts.

SCANDINAVIA
Mn14-Fran. 600 cds. by subj. Bks. & per. Occ. add.

SCANDINAVIAN LITERATURE. *See also* AMERICAN SCANDINAVIAN REVIEW (per.)
Ia5 8000 cds. by auth. Dup. of contrib. of Luther Coll. lib. to cat. of Scandinaviana-Americana, comp. by Harvard coll. lib. for Amer.-Scand. foundation. Cur. add.
Nj71 105 ent., tpd. shts. by country. Bks. Cur. add.

SCENERY (STAGE). *See* THEATER—STAGE SETTINGS AND SCENERY

SCHOLASTIC (per.). *In* AUTHORS C88

SCHOOL ARTS MAGAZINE (per.). *In* PERIODICALS O20-Jeff.

SCHOOL HYGIENE (per.). *See* List of Bibliographies, APPENDIX I

SCHOOL HYGIENE—CHILDREN'S PLAYS. *See* List of Bibliographies, APPENDIX I

SCHOOL HYGIENE—GAMES. *See* List of Bibliographies, APPENDIX I

School Libraries. *See also* List of Bibliographies, Appendix I
Nd3   144 cds. by subj. & auth. Per. Occ. add.

School Plays. *See* Plays, School

School Programs. *See* Schools—Exercises and Recreations

School Reports
Nj4   200 cds. by name of city. Annual rpts. of sch. systems. Freq. add.

School Standards. *See* Standards—Accreditation, etc.

School Stories. *See also* List of Bibliographies, Appendix I
O37-Mad.   50 cds. by auth. Bks. Prep. & boarding sch. stories. Occ. add.

School Stories, Juvenile
Mi6-Rich.   30 ent., tpd. shts. by auth. J. fic. Freq. add.
N44-j   10p., tpd. shts. Yrly. add.

Schools
I13-Wood.   2000 cds. by prof. Sch., prof. & qualifications. Freq. add.

Schools—Boston (Mass.). *See* Boston (Mass.)—Schools

Schools—Exercises and Recitations. *See also* Plays, School
H2   500 cds. by subj. Per. Mo. add.
N22-educ   1100 cds. by type of entertainment. Bks., per. & pams. Monologs, shadows, etc. Freq. add.
Tx5   75 cds. by subj., auth. & t. Bks., pams., etc. Freq. add.
W19-j   184 cds. by subj. Pams. Yrly. add.

Schools, Government
Wa10-par   150 cds. by subj. Govt. bul. & per. Occ. add.

Schubert, Franz Peter—Works
Mn14-mus   1177 cds. by t. & 1st line. Bk. indexed: Franz P. Schubert, *Lieder und gesänge*. 10v. No add.
Mn14-mus   46 cds. by t. Bk. indexed: Franz P. Schubert, *Pianoforte werke*, 3v.

Schumann, Robert—Works
Mn14-mus (1)   489 cds. by t. Bk. indexed: Robert Schumann, *Klavierwerke*, 4v. No add.
Mn14-mus (2)   489 cds. by t. & 1st line. Bk. Indexed: Robert Schumann, *Lieder und gesänge*, 4v. No add.

Schuylkill Co. (Pa.)—Biography
P43   8000 cds. by surname. Hist. bks. Freq. add.

Science. *See also* List of Bibliographies, Appendix I; Names of individual sciences
In18   50,000 cds. by auth. & subj. Per. Daily add.
In18   Unest. cds. by auth., subj. & t. Reprints. Daily add.
Mi6-sci   450 cds. by subj. Bks. Occ. add.

Science—History. *See* Technology—History   P39-tech

Science—Pamphlets
Mi6-sci   2750 cds. by auth. & subj. Pams. Freq. add.

Science—Patents. *See* Patents—Science

Science, Foreign
Wa11-ref   300 ent., tpd. shts. by country. Bks. & per. Occ. add.

Science Abstracts (per.)
M17-eng   1932–1939. Cds. by subj. Cur. add.

Science Guide for Elementary Schools (per.)
C22   v. 1, 1934–date. Cds. by subj. Cur. add.

Science Leaflet (per.)
Mn14-tech   v. 3, 1929–date. Cds. by subj. Occ. add.

Science Museum, London. Bibliographical Series
I43-ref   123 cds. by subj. No add.

Scientific Apparatus and Instruments
N35-ref. sci   900 cds. by name. Bks. & per. Illus. & lit. Cur. add.

Scientists. *See also* Portraits—Scientists; Technology—Biography
N35-ref
D21   2500 cds. by name. Amer. & for. agric. workers & scientists. Occ. add.

N8-tech 900 cds. by name. Bks. Imp. physicists, chem. & mathematicians. Freq. add.

O20-Mem. 215 cds. by name. Bks. Cur. add.

P18 300 cds. by name. Bks. Cur. add.

P39-tech 36,400 cds. by name. Bks. & per. Biog. & port. Freq. add.

Wa11-ref 500 ent., tpd. shts. by name. Bks. & per. Occ. add.

SCIENTISTS—PITTSBURGH (PA.). *See* AUTHORS—PITTSBURGH (PA.) P39-tech

SCOTT, SIR WALTER—LADY OF THE LAKE
Nj66 100 cds. by subj. Bks. & per. Mat. for background read. Infreq. add.

SCREEN LIFE (per.). *See* MOTION PICTURES C32-per

SCRIBNER RADIO MUSIC LIBRARY (bk.). *See* MUSIC, RADIO I62

SCULPTORS. *See* ART Mn14-art (2); ARTISTS I68-art; CHRISTIAN ART AND SYMBOLISM Nj60-art; SILVERSMITHS—PITTSBURGH (PA.) P39-ref

SCULPTURE. *See also* STATUES; ART Mn14-art (2); ART—PHOTOGRAPHS Nj49; CHRISTIAN ART AND SYMBOLISM Nj60-art; PHOTOGRAPHS, EUROPEAN N45b; PICTURES N35-ref. print, N46-art (1); PICTURES—CARNEGIE PICTURES Ia14-art, In 14

I13-ref 4000 cds. by subj. Bks. & per. Freq. add.

I68-art 250 cds. by name of wk. Bks. Infreq. add.

Mo13-art 450 cds. by name of sculp. Portfolios.

N22-art 176 cds. by name of sculp. Pic. Occ. add.

N35-ref-art 1500 cds. by place, subj., sculp. & media. Bk. indexed: Heinrich von Brunn, *Denkmäler griechischer und römischer sculptur*. No add.

N46-art 100 cds. by t. & art. Bks. Cur. add.

R2 2000 cds. by subj. & sculp. Per. indexed: *L'Arte*, 1898–1911; *Bolletino d'Arte*, 1907–1920; *Rassegna d'Arte*, 1909–1922. No add.

SCULPTURE—CHICAGO
I43-ref 78 ent., tpd. shts. by subj. & sculp. Bks. & per. Sculp. in pub. parks & sts. in Chicago. Infreq. add.

SCULPTURE—ILLINOIS
I5-ref 79 cds. by auth. & sculp. Bks. & per. Occ. add.

SCULPTURE, ARCHITECTURAL
G7-arch 500 cds. by sculp., bldg. or architect. Per., 1929–date. Arch. sculp. & all free standing sculp. Yrly. add.

SEA STORIES. *See also* List of Bibliographies, APPENDIX I
C75 36 cds. by auth. Bks. Freq. add.

F2-r.a. 100 ent., tpd. shts. by t. Bks. Yrly. add.

I13-Hild. 5p., tpd. shts. by auth. Bks. Yrly. add.

I13-Tild. 70 ent., tpd. shts. by auth. Bks. Cur. add.

K8-circ 31 cds. by auth. Bks. Cur. add.

Mi6-Rich. 73 ent., tpd. shts. by auth. Bks. Freq. add.

Mn11 Unest. ent., tpd. shts. by auth. Bks. Freq. add.

Nj21 160 ent., tpd. shts. by auth. Bks. Freq. add.

Nj37-circ 125 ent., tpd. shts. by auth. Bks., 1926–date. Occ. add.

SEA STORIES—FOREIGN LANGUAGES
Mi6-for 100 cds. by subj. & lang. Bks. Freq. add.

SEA STORIES, JUVENILE. *See also* PIRATE STORIES, JUVENILE N44-j
Nj19-j 70 ent., tpd. shts. by auth. Bks. 4th grade up. Cur. add.

SEALS (NUMISMATICS). *See also* FLAGS O16-ref
Ct2-ref 200 cds. by name of coll. Coll. cats. Coll. seals. Infreq. add.

N36 500 cds. by name of coll. U.S. coll. seals. No add.

O20-hist 1320 cds. by subj. Bks. Seals, banners & badges. No add.

P33-ref 1000 cds. by subj. Bks. No add.

Wa10-par 800 cds. by name of coll. Coll. cats., per., etc. Coll. seals. Occ. add.

SEATTLE (WASH.)
Wa10-ref (1)   50,000 ent. by subj., chron. Newsp. Newsp. indexed: *Seattle (Wash.) Times*. City, co. & state affairs. Cur. add.
Wa10-ref (2)   900 ent., tpd. shts. by subj. Bk. indexed: James Willis Sayre, *This city of ours*. No add.

SEATTLE (WASH.)—HISTORY
Wa10-ref (1)   735 ent., tpd. shts. by subj. Bk. indexed: Thomas W. Prosch, *Chronological history of Seattle*. No add.
Wa10-ref (2)   Unest. ent., tpd. shts. by subj. Pam. indexed: James Willis Sayre, *Early waterfront days of Seattle*. No add.
Wa10-ref (3)   12,000 cds. by subj. Newsp., per. & bks. Cur. add.

SEATTLE (WASH.)—INDUSTRIES
Wa10-tech   125 cds. by name of co. Per. Cur. add.

SEATTLE (WASH.)—NEWSPAPERS
Wa7   11,000 cds. by subj., name & place. Newsp. indexed: *Pioneer and Democrat*, 1854–1861. No add.
Wa11-ref   3000 cds. by subj. Newsp. indexed: *Pioneer and Democrat*, 1852–1861. No add.

SEATTLE (WASH.)—OFFICIALS AND EMPLOYEES
Wa10-mun. ref   1380 ent., tpd. shts., chron. City records, etc. Cur. add.

SEATTLE (WASH.)—ORDINANCES
Wa10-mun. ref   1330 cds. by subj. Newsp., ord. code & comptroller's records. Cur. add.

SEATTLE (WASH.)—POLITICS AND GOVERNMENT
Wa10-mun. ref   150 cds. by auth. Per. & pams. Loc. auth. on Seattle govt., 1930–date. Cur. add.
Wa10-mun. ref   3500 cds. by subj. Newsp., dept. rpts., pams., bks., per. & ordinances. Seattle mun. affairs. Cur. add.

SEATTLE (WASH.)—SCHOOLS
Wa10-par   1100 cds. by subj. Newsp. In which sch. certain subj. are taught. Occ. add.

SEATTLE (WASH.)—SOCIETIES AND CLUBS. *See also In* WASHINGTON (STATE)—SOCIETIES AND CLUBS   **Wa10-ref**
Wa10-art   100 cds. by name. Newsp., club programs, etc. Cur. add.

SEATTLE (WASH.)—STATISTICS
Wa10-ref   250 cds. by subj. Doc. Loc. statistics. Infreq. add.

SEATTLE (WASH.) DEMOCRAT (newsp.). *In* SEATTLE (WASH.)—NEWSPAPERS **Wa7, Wa11-ref**

SEATTLE (WASH.) PIONEER (newsp.). *In* SEATTLE (WASH.)—NEWSPAPERS **Wa7, Wa11-ref**

SEATTLE (WASH.) POST-INTELLIGENCER (newsp.)
Wa9a   Unest. cds. by subj. Daily add.

SEATTLE SYMPHONY ORCHESTRA PROGRAMS. *See* SYMPHONY   **O16-art**

SEATTLE (WASH.) TIMES. *In* SEATTLE (WASH.)   **Wa10-ref** (1)

SECOND ADVENT. *See* ADVENTISTS

SEED CATALOGS. *See* GARDENS AND GARDENING   **Mn14-tech**

SEEMANN PRINTS. *See* PICTURES—SEEMANN PRINTS

SELECTED RELICS OF JAPANESE ART (bk.). *In* ART, ORIENTAL   **P42-art**

SELF GOVERNMENT (IN EDUCATION)
Tx30   77 ent., tpd. shts. by subj. Per. No add.

SELF IMPROVEMENT. *See* List of Bibliographies, APPENDIX I

SEQUELS. *See* SERIES, BOOKS IN

SERIALS
Ia14-ser   200 ent., tpd. shts. by name. U.S. & for. ser.
K20-ref   800 cds. by pub. Pams. & bks. Cur. add.
O20-soc   3960 cds. by subj. Uncat. ser. Freq. add.

SERIALS—UNION LISTS. *See* List of Bibliographies, APPENDIX I

SERIALS, SCIENTIFIC—UNION LISTS. *See* List of Bibliographies, APPENDIX I

SERIES, BOOKS IN
C3a   202 cds. by t. Ed. & pub. ser. No add.
C32-fic   85p., tpd. shts. by auth. Bks. Sequels. Cur. add.
C47   1500 cds. by auth. Sequels. No add.
Ca10-ref   755 cds. by auth. & t. Bks. Sequels & ser. Freq. add.

Ct15 300 ent., tpd. shts. by auth. Bks. Ser. Infreq. add.
I13-Hild. 18p., tpd. shts. by name. Ser. & sequels. Bks. Yrly. add.
L14-ref 225 cds. by auth. & t. Per., 1939–date. Fic. ser. Freq. add.
Mi6-per 500 cds. by auth. & t. Per. Ser. stories. Cur. add.
N35-ref. inf 1000 cds. by name. Amer. pub. ser. No add.
N46-hist 2640 cds. by name. Bks. & pams. Cur. add.
O1-circ 1000 cds. by auth. & t. Adult sequels, supp. to Aldred. Cur. add.
O1-W. 2026 cds. by auth. Adult sequels. Cur. add.
O20-Coll. 250 cds. by auth. Fic. Cur. add.
O20-E.131st 500 cds. by auth. & t. Bks. Sequels. No add.
O20-per 1320 cds. by auth. & t. Per. Ser. stories. Cur. add.
O20-Rice 600 cds. by auth. Sequels. Cur. add.
O31 380 cds. by auth. Bks. Freq. add.
O37 450 cds. by auth. Ser. & sequels in fic. Cur. add.
P44 100 cds. by auth. Infreq. add.

SERIES, BOOKS IN—FOREIGN LANGUAGES
C32-for 350 cds. by auth. Bks. For. sequels. Freq. add.

SERIES, BOOKS IN, JUVENILE
C3 377 cds. by auth. & t. Bks. Cur. add.
Mn14-Hos.-j 250 cds. by auth. Ser. & sequels. Cur. add.
O1-j 1000 cds. by auth. & t. J. sequels. Cur. add.
O20-fic 1320 cds. by auth. Fic. Ser. & sequels. Freq. add.
O20-Hou. 150 cds. by auth. Sequels. Cur. add.
O20-Rice-j 150 cds. by name. Fic. Ser. & sequels. Cur. add.
O20-Un. 100 cds. by auth. J. fic., ser. & sequels. Infreq. add.
Wa10-j 200 cds. by t. Bks. J. ser. Cur. add.

SERMONS
C32-phil 2700 cds. by Bible order. Bks. Cur. add.
I42 17,324 cds. by Bible order. Bks. to 1930. No add.

Ky16 2800 cds. by Bible order & subj. Bks. Occ. add.
Mn14-ref 950 cds. by Bible order & subj. Occ. add.
Nb7 3192 cds. by preacher & text. Bks. Freq. add.

SEROLOGY
Nj61 150 cds. by auth. & t. Bks., per., pams. & rpts. Freq. add.

SERPENTS
Nj61 35 cds. by auth. & t. Per., pams. & reprints. Infreq. add.

SERVICE, ROBERT WILLIAM—WORKS
I13-ref 350 cds. by t. & 1st line. Bks. & per. Infreq. add.

SEVENTH DAY ADVENTISTS. See ADVENTISTS

SHADOW PANTOMIMES AND PLAYS. See SCHOOLS—EXERCISES AND RECREATIONS N22-educ

SHAKER JOURNAL (per.). In STEAMBOATS Ky2

SHAKERS
Ky2 4p., tpd. shts. by auth. Bks., per. & mss. S. Union shakers. No add.
Ky2 7p., tpd. shts. by auth. Bks., per. & mss. No add.
M31 900 cds. by auth., subj. & t. Bks., pams. & mss. Wight coll. Occ. add.
N10-ref 388 cds. by auth. Bks., pams. & per.

SHAKESPEARE, WILLIAM
Ia14-ref 550 cds. by t. & name of char. Bks. Shak. crit. Cur. add.
Mn14-clip 110 cds. by subj. Newsp. & pams. Infreq. add.
Mn14-Fran. 400 cds. by subj. Bks. Cur. add.
Mn14-ref 3500 cds. by name of play, char. & customs. Criticisms. Occ. add.
N46-lit 1320 cds. by subj. Bks. Cur. add.
Nj66 150 cds. by subj. Bks. & per. Background mat. for study of Shak. & Merchant of Venice. Freq. add.
P39-ref 7700 cds. by subj. Bks. Life, wks. & plays. Freq. add.

SHAKESPEARE, WILLIAM—CONTEMPORARY ENGLAND
Mn14-N. 270 cds. by subj. Bks. Cur. add.

SHAKESPEARE, WILLIAM—MUSIC
N35-ref. mus   3000 cds. by name of play, t. & 1st line. Stage mus.: sonnets, songs, speeches set to mus., operas & mus. approp. to plays. Sht. mus. & bks. Cur. add.

SHAKESPEARE ASSOCIATION OF AMERICA. BULLETIN
O2   12p., tpd. shts. by t. of play. Bks. & per. Plays & crit. Infreq. add.

SHELBY, ISAAC
Ky2   74 cds. by auth. Bks. & per. Freq. add.

SHELBY CO. (ALA.)—CEMETERY RECORDS
A1   100 ent., tpd. shts. by name. Cem.: King family burial ground, Montevallo cem. Cur. add.

SHELBY CO. (ALA.)—CENSUS
A1   700 cds. by name. 1820 cens. Family records. No add.

SHELBY CO. (KY.)—HISTORY
Ky7   Unest. ent., tpd. shts. by name & subj. Bk. indexed: G. Lee Willis, *History of Shelby co., Kentucky.* No add.

SHEPERDSTOWN (KY.)—HISTORY
Ky7   Unest. cds. by name. Bk. indexed: Danske Dandridge, *Historic Sheperdstown.* No add.

SHERIFFS. *See* FRONTIER AND PIONEER LIFE
N35-ref. Amer. hist

SHERMAN (TEXAS) COURIER (newsp.)
Tx32   1916–1921. Tpd. shts. by subj. Infreq. add.

SHERMAN (TEXAS) DEMOCRAT (newsp.). *In* BIOGRAPHY **Tx32**

SHERMAN (TEXAS) REGISTER (newsp.)
Tx32   1885–1906. Tpd. shts. by subj. Infreq. add.

SHERMAN (TEXAS) WHITEWRIGHT SUN (newsp.)
Tx32   1914–1921. Tpd. shts. by subj. Infreq. add.

SHIP LOGS. *See* DIARIES   **C73**

SHIP MODELS—PHOTOGRAPHS
V5   374 cds. by subj. Phot. Freq. add.

SHIPPING—FAIRFIELD CO. (CONN.)
Ct2-hist   Unest. cds. by pers., place & ship. Original U.S. customs office records, mss. Early shipping industry. Freq. add.

SHIPS
C32-soc   2640 cds. by ship. U.S. Naval inst. proc., bks. & per. Ships & ship pic. No add.
Ca2-sci   2000 cds. by name of ship. Bks., per. & newsp. Ships & shipwrecks. Freq. add.
Md2-ind   2430 cds. by name & type of ship. Bks., per., pic. Cur. add.
Md2-Md.   21,000 cds. by name of ship. Newsp., to 1820. No add.
Wa10-ref   750 cds. by name of ship. Newsp., per. & bks. Ships & shipwrecks. Freq. add.

SHIPS—CONFEDERATE STATES OF AMERICA—PHOTOGRAPHS
V5   12 cds. by name. Freq. add.

SHIPS—MAINE—PICTURES. *See* PICTURES—SHIPS—MAINE

SHIPS—ORNAMENTATION
V5   215 cds. by name. Phot. Freq. add.

SHIPS—PHOTOGRAPHS
V5   22 cds. by subj. Motor ships. Freq. add.
V5   322 cds. by subj. Sailing vessels. Freq. add.

SHIPS—U.S.—PHOTOGRAPHS
V5   451 cds. by name. U.S. govt. vessels. Freq. add.

SHIPS, FOREIGN—PHOTOGRAPHS
V5   44 cds. by name. Freq. add.

SHIPS, PRIMITIVE—PHOTOGRAPHS
V5   16 cds. by subj. Freq. add.

SHIPWRECKS. *See also* SHIPS   **Ca2-sci; Wa10-ref**
O20-bus   300 cds. by name. Newsp. Marine casualties. Freq. add.
Wa10-ref   150 ent., tpd. shts. by name of ship. Newsp. indexed: *Victoria daily colonist,* 1936–1939. Shipwrecks along the coast of Columbia. Cur. add.

SHOES
M19   450 cds. by subj. Bks. Freq. add.

SHORT STORIES. *See also* Special types of short stories, i.e. CHRISTMAS STORIES: List of Bibliographies, APPENDIX I; ESSAYS O20-lit; PLAYS Tx25, U5

C13 750 cds. by t. & auth. Bks. Freq. add.
C16 2993 cds. by auth. & t. Bks. Freq. add.
C32-fic 59p., tpd. shts. by t. Nonfic. coll. Freq. add.
C32-fic 50,480 cds. by t. Bks. Freq. add.
C41 Over 2000 cds. by t. Bks. Cur. add.
C42 Unest. cds. by auth. & t. Bks. Cur. add.
C43-br Unest. cds. by t. Bks. Short stories & plays. Freq. add.
C43-ref 8800 cds. by auth. & t. Bks. Supp. print. indexes. Freq. add.
C45 2900 cds. by auth. & t. Bks. Cur. add.
C46 Unest. ent., tpd. shts. by t. & auth. Short stories, plays & speeches. Infreq. add.
C85 720 ent., tpd. shts. by t. Bks. Biennial add.
Co5-j 1320 cds. by subj. Bks. Cur. add.
Ct6 11,880 cds. by subj. & t. Bks., per., etc. Freq. add.
Ct14 6040 cds. by auth. & t. Bks. Freq. add.
G12 256 cds. by auth. Infreq. add.
I6 Unest. ent., tpd. shts. by t. Bks. Cur. add.
I35 3500 cds. by auth. & t. Bks. & per. Cur. add.
I36 8000 cds. by subj. Bks. Cur. add.
I49 2165 cds. by t. Bks. Cur. add.
I54 2300 cds. by auth. & t. Bks. Cur. add.
I59 1700 cds. by auth. & t. Bks. Cur. add.
I60 3960 cds. by auth. & t. Bks. Cur. add.
I61-ref 1000 cds. by auth. & t. Bks. Freq. add.
I80 Unest. cds. by auth. & t. Bks. Cur. add.
Ia14-res 2000 cds. by auth. & t. Bks. Freq. add.
K3 1320 cds. by auth. Bks. Freq. add.

K4 4000 cds. by auth. & t. Bks. Cur. add.
K5 1000 cds. by t. Bks. Cur. add.
K12-circ 950 cds. by t. Bks. not in Firkins. Freq. add.
K13 Unest. ent., tpd. shts. by auth. & subj. Bks. Cur. add.
K16 Unest. cds. by auth., subj. & t. Bks. & per. Freq. add.
K17-ref 1215 cds. by t. Bks. Infreq. add.
K20-circ 7500 cds. by auth., t. & subj. Bks. Infreq. add.
Ky1 2000 cds. by auth. & t. Bks. Freq. add.
L6 140 cds. by auth. & t. Bks. Infreq. add.
L14-circ 9400 cds. by auth. & t. Bks. Freq. add.
M28 600 cds. by auth. Bks. Freq. add.
Mi6-Chau. 2500 cds. by auth. & t. Bks. Freq. add.
Mi6-fic 1700 cds. by auth. Bks. not in Firkins. Occ. add.
Mi6-Rich. 500 cds. by auth. & t. Bks. Infreq. add.
Mi6-Walk. 3131 cds. by auth. & t. Bks. Freq. add.
Mi8-ref 2000 cds. by auth. & t. Bks. Freq. add.
Mi12 850 cds. by auth. & t. Bks. In proc.
Mi13-S. Hi. 1363 cds. by t. & auth. Bks. Freq. add.
Mi13-W. side 1500 cds. by t. Bks. Cur. add.
Mi22-ref 1200 cds. by auth. & t. Bks. not in Firkins. Cur. add.
Mn12 1345 cds. by t. Bks. not in Firkins. Freq. add.
Mn14-Cam. 1600 cds. by auth. & t. Bks. Freq. add.
Mn14-Cen. 1320 cds. by auth. & t. Bks. not in Firkins. Freq. add.
Mn14-ref 500 cds. by subj. Bks. Abstract subj. inc. rel. Occ. add.
Mn23-Arl. 5000 cds. by auth. & t. Bks. Cur. add.
Mn23-Ham. 2990 cds. by auth. & t. Bks. Cur. add.
Mn23-per 1680 cds. by auth. & t. Per, indexed: *Story*, v. 3, 1933–date. Mo. add.
Mn23-ref 5500 cds. by t. Bks. not in Firkins. Infreq. add.

Mn25   1500 cds. by auth. & t.   Bks. Cur. add.
Mn26   5000 cds. by auth. & t.   Bks. Cur. add.
Mo3-Wash.   1200 cds. by t.   Bks. not in Firkins. Freq. add.
Mo5   4000 cds. by auth. & t.   Bks., per. & bul. Occ. add.
N3   1600 cds. by auth. & t.   Bks. Occ. add.
N8-stud   1320 cds. by auth. & t.   Bks. Freq. add.
N15   540 cds. by auth. & t.   Bks. Freq. add.
N18   8750 cds. by auth. & t.   Bks. Cur. add.
N22-Wood.   12,686 cds. by t.   Bks. Cur. add.
N23   872 cds. by auth. & t.   Bks. No add.
N46-fic   1700 cds. by auth. & subj.   Bks. not in Firkins. Cur. add.
N50   1440 cds. by auth. & t.   Bks. Freq. add.
N51   936 cds. by auth. & t.   Bks. Cur. add.
N53   700 cds. by t.   Bks. Cur. add.
N56   4900 cds. by auth. & t.   Bks. Cur. add.
Nb2   1086 ent., tpd. shts. by auth. & t.   Bks. Cur. add.
Nb8   8050 cds. by auth. & t.   Bks. Freq. add.
Nb11   4000 cds. by auth. & t.   Bks. Freq. add.
Nb15   2000 cds. by auth.   Bks. No add.
Nj7-E.   1600 cds. by t.   Bks. Infreq. add.
Nj7-Fair.   950 cds. by subj.   Bks. Freq. add.
Nj11-ref   5280 cds. by auth. & t.   Bks. Freq. add.
Nj14   8580 cds. by auth. & t.   Bks. No add.
Nj27-circ   965 cds. by auth. & t.   Bks. Infreq. add.
Nj28   1500 cds. by auth. & t.   Bks. Freq. add.
Nj67-ref   13,000 cds. by t. & subj.   Bks. & per. Cur. add.
O1-Ell.   Unest. cds. by auth. & t.   Bks. Cur. add.
O9   2000 cds. by auth. & t.   Bks. Freq. add.
O16-circ   10,000 cds. by auth. & t.   Bks. Cur. add.
O20-fic   9240 cds. by subj.   Bks. Cur. add.
O20-fic   121,760 cds. by t.   Bks. Cur. add.
O20-fic   21,120 cds. by auth.   Bks. Cur. add.
O25-F.S.M.   11,000 cds. by t.   Bks. & per. Per. indexed: *Golden book magazine*. Short stories, plays & essays. Infreq. add.
O29-Day.   1200 cds. by t. & auth.   Bks. Cur. add.
O29-Elec.   700 cds. by t.   Bks. No add.
O29-hi. sch   1900 cds. by auth. & t.   Bks.
O29-ref   6000 cds. by auth. & t.   Bks. Occ. add.
O31   1000 cds. by auth. & t.   Bks. not indexed in Firkins. Occ. add.
O31-N.   800 cds. by auth. & t.   Bks. not indexed in Firkins. Freq. add.
O34   Unest. ent., tpd. shts. by t. & comp.   Bks. not indexed in Firkins. Freq. add.
O36   32,000 cds. by t.   Bks. Freq. add.
O41   1124 ent., tpd. shts. by auth. & t.   Bks. Cur. add.
O42   500 cds. by auth. & t.   Bks. not indexed in Firkins. Occ. add.
O56-circ   3000 cds. by auth. & t.   Bks. Cur. add.
O56-Mott.   500 cds. by t.   Bks. Infreq. add.
O56-ref   5200 cds. by t.   Bks. & per. Per. indexed: *Hearst's international cosmopolitan*. Freq. add.
Or1-cat   23,028 cds. by auth. & t.   Bks. Cur. add.
Or2   1600 cds. by auth.   Bks. Short stories, plays, essays & speeches. Freq. add.
P4   312p., tpd. shts. by auth. & t.   Bks. Yrly. add.
P6   500 cds. by auth. & t.   Bks. not indexed in Firkins. Occ. add.
P9   3807 cds. by auth. & t.   Bks. Freq. add.
P14   1500 cds. by auth.   Bks. & per. Freq. add.
P18   2500 cds. by auth. & t.   Bks. Cur. add.
P20   1155 cds. by t.   Bks. Cur. add.
P34-ref   2500 cds. by auth. & t.   Bks. Freq. add.

P41 1700 cds. by auth. & t. Bks. Freq. add.
T7 660 cds. by auth. & t. Bks. Cur. add.
Tx6 Unest. cds. by subj. Bks. Cur. add.
Tx11 17,060 cds. by auth. & t. Bks. & pams. Cur. add.
Tx12 1050 cds. by auth. & t. Bks. indexed: Margaret Ashmun, *Modern short stories; Best short stories of 1936, 1937, 1938;* Dorothy Brewster, *A book of contemporary short stories;* Louis Bromfield, *It takes all kinds;* Leonard Brown, *Modern short stories;* Katherine Brush, *This is on me;* Erskine Caldwell, *Jackpot;* Noel Coward, *To step aside;* Stephen Crane, *Twenty stories;* John Fante, *Dago red;* William Faulkner, *The unvanquished;* John Galsworthy, *Quality and other stories; Georgian stories, 1926, 1927;* Charles Grayson, *Stories for men;* William Hastings, etc., *Short stories;* Ernest Hemingway, *The fifth column;* Benjamin Heydrick, *Americans all;* Paul Horgan, *Figures in a landscape;* W. Somerset Maugham, *East and West;* W. Somerset Maugham, *The mixture as before;* Frank Luther Mott, *Good stories; O. Henry memorial award prize stories, 1923;* Dorothy Parker, *Here lies;* Marjorie Rawlings, *When the whippoorwill;* William Saroyan, *The trouble with tigers;* Wilbur L. Schramm, *The story workshop;* John Steinbeck, *The long valley;* Edith Wharton, *Ghosts;* Thomas Wolfe, *From death to morning.* Per. indexed: *Story,* 1941. Cur. add.
Tx31 500 cds. by auth. & t. Bks. Freq. add.
U1 1700 cds. by t. & auth. Bks. not indexed in Firkins. Freq. add.
W16 4000 cds. by auth. & t. Bks. Cur. add.
W16 1200 cds. by subj. Bks. Infreq. add.
W18 7360 cds. by auth. & t. Bks. Cur. add.
Wa3 900 cds. by auth. & t. Bks. Cur. add.
Wa13-ref 6000 cds. by auth. & t. Bks. Cur. add.

SHORT STORIES—FOREIGN LANGUAGES
C32-for 1100 cds. by lang. & auth. Bks. Freq. add.
C32-for 12,000 cds. by t. Bks. Freq. add.
Mi6-for 1600 cds. by subj. & lang. Bks. Freq. add.
O56-circ 2000 cds. by lang. & subj. Bks. in German, French & Spanish. Stories & plays. Freq. add.

SHORT STORIES—PERIODICALS
Mn14-clip 940 cds. by auth. & t. Per. indexed: *Hearst's international cosmopolitan; Story.* Mo. add.

SHORT STORIES—SURPRISE ENDINGS
Mi13-Un. Hi. 300 cds. by auth. & t. Bks. Cur. add.

SHORT STORIES (HASTINGS) (bk.). *In* SHORT STORIES **Tx12**

SIERRA CLUB BULLETIN. *In* CALIFORNIA **C8-ref**
C49-art v. 1, 1893–1940. Cds. by subj. No add.

SILK. *See* INDUSTRIES—HISTORY **Wa10-tech**

SILVERSMITHS—PITTSBURGH (PA.)
P39-ref 240 cds. by name. Pittsburgh directories, 1815–1900. Silversmiths & sculp. No add.

SILVERSMITHS, AMERICAN
M11-dec. art Unest. ent., tpd. shts. by name. Bks. & pams. Cur. add.

SIXTY PROGRESSIVE PIANO PIECES (bk.). *In* MUSIC **Nj15**

SKITS AND STUNTS. *See also* GAMES **O20-art**; READINGS AND RECITATIONS **O2**
C3a Unest. cds. by subj., auth. & t. Cur. add.
C49-inf 640 cds. by t. Bks. Cur. add.
I13-circ Unest. cds. by auth. Bks. Occ. add.
Mn14-clip 230 cds. by t. Newsp. & pams. Infreq. add.
N46-fic 100 cds. by t. Bks. & pams. Hard-to-find stunts & entertainments. Cur. add.
N46-lit 1700 cds. by t., subj. & no. char. Bks. & pams. Cur. add.
O20-lit 1980 cds. by t. Cur. add.
Or5-circ Unest. cds. by subj. & t. Occ. add.

SLAVERY IN THE U.S.
Ky2   220 cds. by auth. Bks. & per. Freq. add.
Ky8   Unest. cds. by subj. Bks. & newsp. Freq. add.

SLAVS
O20-Jeff.   Unest. cds. by subj. Bks. Polish, Russian, Slovak & Ukrainian culture & achievements. In proc.

SLIDES, LANTERN. *See* LANTERN SLIDES

SMITH, JOSEPH
U3   307p., tpd. shts. by auth. & subj. Bk. & per. Per. indexed: *Millenial star,* v. 14-25. No add.

SMITH COLLEGE STUDIES (per.)
Mn14-soc   v. 1, 1930–date. Cds. by auth. & t. Cur. add.

SNAKES. *See* SERPENTS

SNOWBOUND. *See* WHITTIER, JOHN GREENLEAF—SNOWBOUND

SNOWDEN'S SUNDAY SCHOOL LESSONS (bk.). *In* SUNDAY SCHOOL LESSONS   In6

SOCIAL FORCES (per.)
Nc6   1922–date. Cds. by subj. Freq. add.

SOCIAL LIFE AND CUSTOMS. *See also* COSTUME, FOREIGN   C32-for
C32-hist   7260 cds. by country or period & by subj. Bks. Occ. add.

SOCIAL PROBLEMS
I35   Unest. tpd. shts. by auth. Bks. Life problems. Occ. add.
Tx30   89 ent., tpd. shts. by subj. Bks. No add.

SOCIAL PROBLEMS—PERIODICALS
Mn24   31 cds. by name of per. Per. pertaining to soc. welfare, mental hygiene, med., criminology. Cur. add.

SOCIAL SCIENCES
N36   30 ent., tpd. shts. by auth., t. & subj. Bks. & per. No add.

SOCIAL SECURITY ACT
Mn24   23 ent., tpd. shts. by bks., pams. & per. Bks., pams. & per. No add. since 1939.

SOCIAL SERVICE
I18   1000 cds. by subj. Bks., per., 1937–date. Freq. add.
Mi6-soc   Unest. cds. by subj. Bks. jls. & proc. In proc.
Mn24   59 ent., tpd. shts. by bks., pams. & per. Bks., pams. & per. No add. since 1938.

SOCIAL SERVICE, RURAL
Mn24   39 ent., tpd. shts. Bks., pams. & per. No add. since 1935

SOCIAL WORK. *See* SOCIAL SERVICE

SOCIAL WORK TODAY (per.)
Mn14-soc. serv   v. 1, 1934–date. Cur. add.

SOCIAL WORK YEARBOOK
Mn14-soc. serv   v. 1, 1934–date. Cur. add.

SOCIETÉ FRANÇAISE DE REPRODUCTIONS DE MANUSCRIPTS A PEINTURES. BULLETIN. *In* MANUSCRIPTS, MEDIEVAL   N45b

SOCIETIES AND CLUBS. *See also* Name of subj. or loc., subdiv. SOCIETIES AND CLUBS; Names of individual clubs, i.e. BOOK CLUBS
Mi6-soc   800 cds. by name. Newsp., per., etc. Freq. add.
Mn14-tech   51 cds. by subj. Cur. add.
N46-sci   50 cds. by name. Per. Model clubs. Infreq. add.
O20-ref   5280 cds. by subj. Natl., state & local. Freq. add.
P39-tech   85 cds. by name. Yrbks., per. & proc. Freq. add.

SOCIETIES AND CLUBS—OFFICIALS AND EMPLOYEES
O20-inf   2640 cds. by name. Newsp. & per. Freq. add.

SOCIETY FOR THE PRESERVATION OF NEW ENGLAND ANTIQUITIES. BULLETIN. *In* GENEALOGY   M19 (1)

SOCIETY FOR THE PRESERVATION OF NEW ENGLAND ANTIQUITIES. OLD TIME NEW ENGLAND (per.). *In* GENEALOGY   M19 (1)

SOCIOLOGY. *See also* List of Bibliographies, APPENDIX I
Mn23-soc   3600 cds. by subj. Bks. & govt. doc. Freq. add.
N50   191 ent., tpd. shts. by class. Bks. Freq. add.
O20-soc   2640 cds. by subj. Bks. Freq. add.

SOCIOLOGY—BOOK REVIEWS
O20-soc   11,880 cds. by auth. Bks. Per. Cur. add.

SOIL CONSERVATION
  D30   9160 cds. by auth. Per. & govt.
          doc. Daily add.
  Nj17   82 ent., tpd. shts. by subj.
          Bks., pams. & per. Freq. add.
SOIL SURVEYS. *See also* U.S. BUREAU OF
  CHEMISTRY AND SOILS—PUBLICA-
  TIONS; U.S. BUREAU OF CHEMISTRY
  AND SOILS. SOILS SURVEY
  Co8-biol   1300 cds. by state, co. &
          area. U.S. & state soil surveys.
          Cur. add.
  De3   2640 cds. by state. co. & area.
          U.S. & state soil surveys. Cur. add.
SOIL SURVEYS—TENNESSEE
  T5   Unest. ent., tpd. shts. by co. Co.
          soil surveys. Occ. add.
SOILS
  G11   75 cds. by t. Per., pams., etc.
          Soil & soil eng. Occ. add.
  Nj61   100 cds. by auth. & t. Bks.,
          per., pams. & rpts. Freq. add.
SOLDIERS, CONFEDERATE. *See* U.S.—HIS-
  TORY—CIVIL WAR; Names of loc.,
  subdiv. SOLDIERS
SOLDIERS, REVOLUTIONARY. *See* U.S.—HIS-
  TORY—REVOLUTION; Names of loc.,
  subdiv. SOLDIERS
SOME PROMINENT VIRGINIANS (bk.). *In*
  GENEALOGY—VIRGINIA   Ky7 (1)
SONGS. *See also* ANTHEMS; BALLADS;
  CHILDREN'S SONGS; CHORAL MUSIC;
  CHRISTMAS MUSIC; FOLK SONGS;
  HYMNS; LANTERN SLIDES—SONGS;
  NATIONAL SONGS; ORATORIOS; List of
  Bibliographies, APPENDIX I
  C3   8250 cds. by t. Bks. Cur. add.
  C24   8000 cds. by t. Bks. & newsp.
          Freq. add.
  C27-art   50,000 cds. by t. Bks.
          Cur. add.
  C32-art   7260 cds. by t. Bks. Occ.
          add.
  C43-mus   2400 cds. by t. Bks.
          Freq. add.
  C47   199p., tpd. shts. by t. Bks. No
          add.
  C49-art   21,901 cds. by t. & comp.
          Bks. & sht. mus. Freq. add.
  C51   335p., tpd. shts. by auth., t. &
          1st line. Bks. not indexed in Sears.
          No add.
  C81-r.a.   1200 cds. by comp. & t.
          Bks. not indexed in Sears. Freq.
          add.

  Ca2-art   6000 cds. by t. & comp.
          Bks. Freq. add.
  Ca6   1550 cds. by t. Bks. Freq.
          add.
  Ct12-art   5460 cds. by comp. & t.
          Bks. Freq. add.
  De3   3800 cds. by auth., t. & 1st line.
          Bks. Infreq. add.
  H3-art   25,000 cds. by comp. & t.
          Bks. not indexed in Sears, nor Cush-
          ing.
  I8   2000 cds. by t. Bks. Freq. add.
  I26   2500 cds. by comp. & t. Bks.
          Freq. add.
  I65-art   11,205 cds. by t. Bks.
          Freq. add.
  I68-art   7000 cds. by t. Bks. Freq.
          add.
  Ia4   1300 cds. by t. Bks. Cur. add.
  Ia6-mus   4500 cds. by t. Bks. Cur.
          add.
  Ia6-mus   500 cds. by t. & voice
          range. Sht. mus. Cur. add.
  In7-art   6800 cds. by t. Bks. not
          indexed in Sears. Freq. add.
  In23-art   Several thousand cds. by t.
          Bks. Cur. add.
  M3   4650 cds. by t. Bks. & sht. mus.
          Cur. add.
  M22   870 cds. by t. & comp. Bks. &
          per. Per. indexed: *Etude.* Freq.
          add.
  M24   8580 cds. by comp., auth., t. &
          1st line. Bks. not indexed in Sears.
          Cur. add.
  M27-art   285 ent., tpd. shts. by
          voice. Bks. Infreq. add.
  M32-circ (1)   2800 cds. by comp. & t.
          Sht. mus. Songs & pianoforte sht.
          mus. Cur. add.
  M32-circ (2)   1100 cds. by t. Bks.
          not indexed in Sears. Cur. add.
  Md2-art   50,000 cds. by t., 1st line,
          chorus & subj. Bks. Cur. add.
  Mi6-circ   800 cds. by t. & comp.
          Bks. Infreq. add.
  Mi6-mus   21,120 cds. by t., comp.,
          subj. & 1st line. Bks. Freq. add.
  Mi25   12,225 cds. by t. Bks. not in-
          dexed in Sears. Cur. add.
  Mo13-art   1000 cds. by t. & comp.
          Bks. & per. Per. indexed: *Godey's
          magazine.* No add.
  Mt1   1407 cds. by t. Bks. Occ. add.
  N7   14,000 cds. by t. & comp. Bks.
          No add. since 1935.

N8-ref   23,760 cds. by t. Bks. Freq. add.

N10-mus   Hundred of cds. by comp., t., 1st line, 1st line of chorus, yr., pub., lithographer, early prints. Sht. mus. Freq. add.

N22-art   968 cds. by comp. & t. Sht. mus. Cur. add.

N35-educ   20,000 cds. by t. & 1st line. Bks. Cur. add.

N35-mus   1200 cds. by auth. & t. Bks. Secular choruses. Occ. add.

N35-mus   10,000 cds. by auth. & t. Bks. not indexed in Sears. Freq. add.

N35-mus   550 cds. by auth. & t. Bks. not indexed in Sears. Duets, larger voice combinations, etc. Freq. add.

N35-ref   140,000 cds. by 1st line & t. Sht. mus. & bks. Old songs & poems set to mus. Cur. add.

N35-Riv.   5280 cds. by t. Bks. Cur. add.

N46-art   5500 cds. by t. & type. Bks. not indexed in Sears. Cur. add.

N54-art   27,000 cds. by t. & subj. Bks. not indexed in Sears. Cur. add.

Nb8   1430 cds. by t. & subj. Bks. & per. Occ. add.

Nj14   2640 cds. by t. Bks. not indexed in Sears. Cur. add.

Nj50-art   19,850 cds. by t. & 1st line. Bks. not indexed in Sears. Infreq. add.

Nj67-ref   6500 cds. by t. Bks., sht. mus. & pams. Freq. add.

O16-art   4500 cds. by subj. & t. Bks. not indexed in Sears. Freq. add.

O20-art   19,095 cds. by t. & subj. Bks. Freq. add.

O20-Hou.   1700 cds. by t. Bks. Cur. add.

O25-mus   3200 cds. by comp. & t. Infreq. add.

O26   3000 cds. by t. Bks. Cur. add.

O29-ref   7060 cds. by t. Bks. not indexed in Sears. Freq. add.

O56-circ   8000 cds. by t. Bks. not indexed. Freq. add.

O56-ref   3000 cds. by t. Bks. not indexed in Sears. Occ. add.

Or2   12,500 cds. Bks. not indexed in Sears. Freq. add.

P39-ref   3100 cds. by comp. & t. Bks. not indexed in Sears, or Cushing. Freq. add.

P39-W.   3600 cds. by subj. & t. Bks. Cur. add.

P39-Wyl.   701 cds. by t. Bks. not indexed in Sears or Cushing. Inc. folk-songs. Cur. add.

V8   5300 cds. by t. Bks. & per. Freq. add.

Wa10-art   30,000 cds. by t. Bks. Cur. add.

Songs—Buffalo (N.Y.)

N10-mus   Hundreds of cds. by comp., t., 1st line of chorus, yr., pub., lithographer, early prints. Sht. mus. Freq. add.

Songs, American

N10-mus   Thousands of cds. by comp., t., 1st line of chorus, yr., pub., lithographer, early prints. Sht. mus. Freq. add.

Songs, College—Iowa

Ia6-mus   Unest. ent., tpd. shts. by name. 25 coll. repres. In proc.

Songs, Cowboy

M27-art   150 ent., tpd. shts. by t. Bks. Infreq. add.

Songs, Foreign

C32-for   700 cds. by country, & t. Bks. & pams. Freq. add.

Songs, Holiday

C32-for   700 cds. by country & t. Bks. & pams. Freq. add.

Mn14-mus   21p., tpd. shts. by holiday & t. J. & sch. song bks. chiefly. Cur. add.

Songs, Negro. *See* Negro Songs

Songs, Popular

M27-art   108p., tpd. shts., chron. Bks. Freq. add.

Mi11-ref   89 ent., tpd. shts. by t. Hist. of songs not found in bk. form.

Songs, Radio Theme

M3   1800 cds. by name of production. Radio theme songs & theat. mus. Cur. add.

Sons of the American Revolution. Kentucky Society. Yearbook

Ky7   Unest. ent., tpd. shts. by name.

Ky14   Unest. cds. by name of member.

SOUTH. *See* MOUNTAIN WHITES—SOUTHERN STATES; Names of southern states

SOUTH—FORESTS AND FORESTRY. *See* FORESTS AND FORESTRY—SOUTH; LUMBERING—SOUTH

SOUTH—PAPER MAKING AND TRADE. *See* PAPER MAKING AND TRADE—SOUTH

SOUTH AMERICA
Nj66   200 cds. by subj. Bks. & per. Freq. add.

SOUTH ATLANTIC (per.)
Nc6   1877–1881. Cds. by subj. No add.

SOUTH ATLANTIC QUARTERLY
Nc6   v. 1, 1902–date. Cds. by subj. Freq. add.

SOUTH BEND (IND.)—BIOGRAPHY
In33-hist.   4000 cds. by name. Bks., per., newsp. & pams. Prominent loc. & Ind. biog. Freq. add.

SOUTH BEND (IND.)—HISTORY
In33-hist   7300 cds. by subj. Bks., per., newsp., pams., etc. Loc. & Ind. hist. Freq. add.

SOUTH CAROLINA
Sc3   3200 cds. by name & t. Bks., newsp., etc. Cur. add.

SOUTH CAROLINA—WILLS
Sc3   11,500 ent., tpd. shts. by co. & auth. of will.

SOUTH CAROLINA HISTORICAL AND GENEALOGICAL MAGAZINE
Sc2   v. 1-5, 1900–1940. Tpd. shts. by name.

SOUTH DAKOTA—HISTORY
Sd1   3p., tpd. shts. by auth. & subj. Bks., per. & pams. Yrly. add.

SOUTH HANOVER (N.J.)—REGISTERS OF BIRTHS, ETC.
Nj36   23p., tpd. shts. by name. Baptisms, 1802–1837; marriages, 1813–1840, Madison members of South Hanover church, 1803. No add.

SOUTHERN CALIFORNIA. UNIVERSITY—DISSERTATIONS, ACADEMIC
C34-ref   5800 cds. by sch. or dept. & auth. Theses & diss., 1910–date.

SOUTHERN WORKMAN (per.). *In* NEGROES Ky15-W. Col. (6), V4

SOUTHWEST. *See also* CALIFORNIA C51; TEXAS Tx21-circ., ref. hist, Tx25
C32-hist   18,480 cds. by subj. Bks. & per. Freq. add.
Nm2   7000 cds. by subj. & auth. Per. indexed: *American geographical society bulletin; American museum journal; Art and archaeology; Geographical review; House beautiful; International studio; Metropolitan museum bulletin; Natural history; New Mexico highway journal; Santa Fé magazine; Touring topics.* Freq. add.

SOUTHWEST—ART. *See* ART—SOUTHWEST

SOUTHWEST—MAPS. *See* MAPS—SOUTHWEST

SOUTHWEST—MINING AND METALLURGY. *See* MINING AND METALLURGY—SOUTHWEST

SOUTHWEST—PAMPHLETS
Nm2   1300 cds. by subj. Archaeol. & hist. Freq. add.

SOUTHWESTERN HISTORICAL QUARTERLY. *See also* TEXAS—PERIODICALS
Tx17
Tx29-ref   v. 1-15, 1897–1912. Cds. by auth., t. & subj. Semi-yrly. add.
Tx29-ref   v. 16, 1912–date. Cds. by auth., t. & subj. Semi-yrly. add.

SOVIET AUTHORS. *See* AUTHORS—RUSSIA

SPANISH-AMERICAN WAR, 1898. *See* U.S.—HISTORY—WAR OF 1898

SPANISH LANGUAGE—STUDY AND TEACHING
C72   111 ent., tpd. shts. by auth. & class. Bks. & pams. Cur. add.

SPANISH LITERATURE. *See* List of Bibliographies, APPENDIX I

SPANISH PLAYS. *See* PLAYS, SPANISH

SPECIAL COLLECTIONS. *See also* Names of special subjects
N47-ref   200 cds. by subj. Spec. coll. in Amer. lib., 1940–date. Cur. add.
W12-ref   47 cds. by subj. Bks., per., etc. Cat. & lists of spec. coll. Cur. add.

SPECIAL COLLECTIONS—KENTUCKY
Ky2   62p., tpd. shts. by name of lib. Bks. & per. Occ. add.
Ky2   6p., tpd. shts. by name of coll. Bks. & per. Occ. add.

SPECIAL COLLECTIONS—NASHVILLE (TENN.)
T9-lib   200 cds. by subj. No add. since 1934.

SPECIFICATIONS
M10   Unest. cds. by owner. Pams. Specif., not by M & E. Freq. add.
M10   Unest. cds. by client. Specif. by M & E. Freq. add.
Wa10-tech   160 cds. by specifier & subj. Per. & doc. Cur. add.

SPEECH EDUCATION
P12   98 cds. by course. Bks. Cur. add.

SPEECHES. *See also* ORATIONS; POETRY; TOASTS; ESSAYS O20-lit; PERSONALITY C71-circ; SHORT STORIES Or2
Mi6-circ   375 cds. by auth. Bks. not indexed in Sutton. Freq. add.
Mn14-ref   700 cds. by subj. Bks. Occ. add.
N45b   23 ent., tpd. shts. by state & newsp. Carrier's addresses. Infreq. add.
N46-lit   1000 cds. by subj. & t. Bks. & pam. not indexed in Sutton. Cur. add.
N46-lit   700 cds. by subj. Bks. & pams. Pub. speaking & oratory. Cur. add.
O16-circ   2000 cds. by subj. Bks. Freq. add.
P27a   150 cds. by subj. Bks., per. & newsp. Freq. add.
P33-ref   50 cds. by auth. Bk. indexed: *Reference shelf;* (*Representative American speeches*). Occ. add.
Tx5   75 cds. by subj., auth. & t. Bks., pams., etc. Freq. add.
Tx6   150 cds. by subj. Bks. Cur. add.

SPELLING—STUDY AND TEACHING
C11   Unest. cds. by auth. & subj. Bks., per. & pams. Cur. add.

SPIES. *See* List of Bibliographies, APPENDIX I

SPIRITUALS. *See* NEGRO SONGS

SPOKANE (WASH.)—SOCIETIES AND CLUBS
Wa13-ref   646 cds. by name. Newsp. Daily add.

SPOKANE (WASH.) SPOKESMAN-REVIEW (newsp.)
Wa13-ref   6000 cds. by subj. Wkly. add.

SPORT STORIES
F2-r.a.   63 ent., tpd. shts. by name of sport. Yrly. add.
Ia12   35 ent., tpd. shts. by subj. Fic. & biog. Occ. add.
K8-circ   7 cds. by auth. Bks. Sport & recreat. In proc.
Md2-circ   27 cds. by name of sport. Bks. Cur. add.
Nj37-circ   134 ent., tpd. shts. by subj. Bks. Occ. add.

SPORT STORIES, JUVENILE
Mi6-Rich.   38 ent., tpd. shts. by auth. Fic. Freq. add.
Nj19-j   25 ent., tpd. shts. by auth. Fic., 4th grade up. Cur. add.

SPORTS AND ATHLETIC GAMES
Md2-soc   10,000 cds. by subj. Bks. Cur. add.
Me1   Unest. cds. by name. Freq. add.
N46-fic   1150 cds. by subj. Bks. & pams. Cur. add.
P12   222 cds. by name of sport. Bks. on athletic activities. Cur. add.
Wa10-circ   250 cds. by subj. Bks. Infreq. add.

SPORTS FOR WOMEN. *See* List of Bibliographies, APPENDIX I

SPRAGUE'S JOURNAL OF MAINE HISTORY
Me1   1913–1926. Tpd. shts. by subj. & auth. No add.
Me2   1913–1926. Tpd. shts. by auth., t. & subj. No add.
Me5   500 cds. by auth., subj. & t. (Copy of index at Bangor public lib.) No add.

SPRINGFIELD (ILL.)—CORPORATIONS
I72   125 cds. by name. Larger manuf. & processing firms. Infreq. add.

SPRINGFIELD (ILL.)—NECROLOGY
I72   950 cds. by name. Cur. add.

SPRINGFIELD (ILL.)—SOCIETIES AND CLUBS
I72   560 cds. by name. Clubs (not social) and educ. agencies. Freq. add.

SPRINGFIELD (ILL.)—VISITORS
I72   80 cds. by name. Famous people who have visited Springfield. Freq. add.

SPRINGFIELD (MASS.)—HISTORY
M27-ref   7500 cds. by subj. Bks., pams., maps, etc. Freq. add.

STAGE SETTINGS AND SCENERY. *See* THEATRE—STAGE SETTINGS AND SCENERY

STANDARD HISTORY OF PITTSBURG (bk.). *In* PITTSBURGH (PA.)—HISTORY
P39-ref. Pa.

STANDARD OF LIVING. *See* COST AND STANDARD OF LIVING

STANDARDS—ACCREDITATION, ETC.
Mo3-educ   39 cds. by name of accred. agency. Pams., bul., etc. Infreq. add.

STANFORD UNIVERSITY—DISSERTATIONS, ACADEMIC
C48-ref   14,000 cds. by auth., dept. & degree. Freq. add.

STANFORD UNIVERSITY—HISTORY
C48-ref   2400 cds. by subj. Bks., per., newsp. & phot. Freq. add.

STANFORD UNIVERSITY—PUBLICATIONS, ALUMNI
C48-ref   4200 cds. by auth. & t. Occ. add.

STANFORD UNIVERSITY—PUBLICATIONS, FACULTY
C48-ref   14,000 cds. by auth. & t. Freq. add.

STANISLAUS CO. (CALIF.)
C38   275 cds. by auth. & subj. Bks. Cur. add.

STANTON, FRANK L.—WORKS
G4-ref   632 ent., tpd. shts. by t. No add.

THE STATE; A WEEKLY SURVEY OF NORTH CAROLINA (per.)
Nc6   1933–date. Cds. by subj. Cur. add.

STATE DOCUMENTS. *See* GOVERNMENT DOCUMENTS, STATE; Names of states, subdiv. DOCUMENTS

STATE OF MISSOURI (bk.). *In* ST. LOUIS (MO.)   Mo13-Soul

STATE PLANNING. *See* NATURAL RESOURCES

STATES (U.S.). *See also* Names of states
C47   53p., tpd. shts. by state. Bks., almanac. No add.

STATESMAN'S YEARBOOK. *In* MAPS   I43-ref

STATISTICS. *See also* PAMPHLETS, STATISTICAL; VITAL STATISTICS
C43-ref   1500 cds. by subj. Pams., fed. state & loc. doc., newsp., services. Freq. add.
De2   1320 cds. by subj. Bks., per., govt. releases, pub. of trade & tech. assoc. Cur. add.
M4-Kir.   500 cds. by commodity or subj. Per. Infreq. add.
Mi6-bus   6000 cds. by subj. Bks., per. & services. Infreq. add.
Mi6-soc   1900 cds. by subj. Newsp., per. & doc. Freq. add.
Mo3-ref   300 cds. by subj. Govt. doc., etc.
N8-tech   100 cds. by subj. Bks. Freq. add.
Nj52   1000 cds. by subj. Bks., per. & pams. Freq. add.
P39-tech   200 cds. by subj. Bks. & per. Occ. add.
Wa10-tech   1575 cds. by subj. Bks., per. & bul. Cur. add.

STATISTICS—SOURCES
G5   90 cds. by subj. Bks., per. & services. Freq. add.

STATUES
I13-r.b.   30,285 cds. by name of sculp. & t. of statue or monument. Bks., pams., newsp. & per. Infreq. add.

STEAMBOATS
Ky2   Unest. ent., tpd. shts. by name. Per. indexed: *Shaker journal*, 1831–1832. No add.

STEAMBOATS—MACHINERY—PHOTOGRAPHS
V5   172 cds. by subj. Freq. add.

STEAMBOATS—PHOTOGRAPHS
V5   1185 cds. by subj. Freq. add.

STEAMBOATS—PICTURES. *See* PICTURES—STEAMBOATS

STEEL LABOR (per.). *In* LABOR AND LABORING CLASSES—PERIODICALS
O33-Euc. Cen.

STEPHEN F. AUSTIN STATE TEACHERS COLLEGE
Tx27   65 cds. by auth. Cur. add.

STEPHEN F. AUSTIN STATE TEACHERS COLLEGE—PUBLICATIONS, FACULTY
Tx27 Unest. cds. by subj. Cur. add.

STEREOPTICAN SLIDES. *See* LANTERN SLIDES

STEVENSON, ROBERT LOUIS—WORKS
I13-ref 1500 cds. by t. & 1st line. Bks. & per. Infreq. add.

STEVENSON CO. (ILL.)—HISTORY
I44-gen 12,000 cds. by auth., t. & subj. Bks., pams., newsp. & biog. Loc. & co. hist. & biog. Freq. add.

STILL-FILMS. *See* LANTERN SLIDES; MOTION PICTURES—STILLS

STONE, ALFRED H. *See* NEGROES **Ms3**

STORIA DELL'ARTE ITALIANA (bk.). *In* ARTISTS **Ia14-art**

STORIES. *See* CHILDREN'S LITERATURE; SHORT STORIES; Types of stories, i.e. SPORT STORIES

STORIES FOR MEN (bk.). *In* SHORT STORIES **Tx12**

STORIES OF OLD ST. GENEVIEVE (bk.). *In* ST. LOUIS (MO.) **Mo13-Soul.**

STORIES PICTURES TELL (bk.). *In* ART— STUDY & TEACHING **Mi6-Monn., Mi6-Walk.**

STORY, THE MAGAZINE OF THE SHORT STORY. *In* SHORT STORIES **Mn23-per**

STORY HOUR READERS (bk.). *In* READERS AND PRIMERS **I6** (2)

STORY OF OLD ST. LOUIS (bk.). *In* SAINT LOUIS (MO.) **Mo13-Soul.**

STORY OF RUSSELLVILLE (bk.). *In* RUSSELLVILLE (KY.) **Ky7**

STORY PARADE (per.)
H3-j 1937–date. Cds. by t. of story. Cur. add.

STORY TELLING
M32 450 cds. by subj. & t. J. bks. Occ. add.
N24-j Several hundred cds. by t. Bks. & per. Freq. add.
P4 300p., tpd. shts. by auth., subj. & t. Bks. In proc.
P39-j 215 cds. by t. Bks. Freq. add.

THE STORY WORKSHOP (bk.). *In* SHORT STORIES **Tx12**

STUART, BEN C.—WORKS. *See* List of Bibliographies, APPENDIX I

STUDENT SELF-GOVERNMENT. *See* SELF GOVERNMENT (IN EDUCATION)

STUDENTS' SONGS. *See* SONGS, COLLEGE— IOWA **Ia6-mus**

STUDY, METHOD OF. *See* List of Bibliographies, APPENDIX I

STUDY OUTLINES
Nj27-ref 10,920 cds. by auth., t. & subj. Occ. add.

SUCCASUNNA (N.J.)—REGISTERS OF BIRTHS, ETC.
Nj36 19p., tpd. shts. by name. Bk. indexed: *Historical memorial Presbyterian church*, 1765–1895.

SUCCESSFUL FARMING (per.)
Ia8 v. 33, 1935–date. Cds. by auth. & subj. Mo. add.

SUFFOLK CO. (N.Y.)—CEMETERY RECORDS
N22-L.I. Unest. ent., tpd. shts. by name, 5v. Freq. add.

SUGAR
L2-chem 1500 cds. by class & auth. Bks., jls., rpts., etc. Cane sugar, analysis & manuf., some on beets. Mo. add.

SULLIVAN'S EXPEDITION
N57 23p., tpd. shts. by auth. Bks., map. Sullivan's expedition sesquicentennial.

SUMMER SCHOOL REVIEW (per.). *In* PUERTO RICO **Pr1**

SUMMIT CO. (O.). *See* List of Bibliographies, APPENDIX I

SUMMIT CO. (O.)—AUTHORS. *See* AUTHORS—SUMMIT CO. (O.)

SUMMIT CO. (O.)—BIBLIOGRAPHY—IMPRINTS
O28 Unest. cds., chron. In proc.

SUMMIT CO. (O.)—FAMILY REUNIONS
O28 250 cds. by surname. Newsp. Occ. add.

SUMMIT CO. (O.)—NAMES, GEOGRAPHICAL
O28 Cds. by name. Hist., maps, tax lists, postal guides, etc. Occ. add.

SUMMIT CO. (O.)—NEWSPAPERS. *See* List of Bibliographies, APPENDIX I

SUN BATHS. *See* List of Bibliographies, APPENDIX I

SUNDAY SCHOOL LESSONS
Ct6 3000 cds. by auth., subj. & t. Bks., per., etc. Freq. add.
In6 50 ent., tpd. shts. by subj. Bk. indexed: *Snowden's sunday school lessons*. No add.
N43 225 cds. by auth. & t. Bks. & per. Kirshner coll. Cur. add.
O16-ref 4300 cds. by name of bks. of Bible. Bk. indexed: *Peloubet's select notes*, 1878–date. Yrly. add.

SUNNILAND (per.)
F2-ref v. 1, 1900–date. Cds. by subj. No add.

SUNSET (per.). *In* CALIFORNIA **C8-ref**; WEST—PERIODICALS **Wa2**
C6-ref 1934–date. Cds. by subj. Cur. add.
C32-per 1931–1939. Cds. by subj. No add.
C51 1930–1931, 1935–1937. Cds. by subj. Cur. add.

SUN-UP (per.). *In* MAINE—PERIODICALS **Me2**
Me1 v. 1-4, 1925–1932. Tpd. shts. by subj. No add.

SUPERIOR (WISC.)
W22-ad 388 cds. by subj. Bks., per., pams. & newsp. Yrly. add.

SUPERLATIVES
C3a 1320 cds. by subj. Bks., per., newsp. & pams. Cur. add.
Wa10-tech 260 cds. by subj. Bks., etc. Cur. add.

SUPERSTITION
C32-phil 550 ent., tpd. shts. by subj. Bks. Freq. add.

SURVEY (per.). *In* BOOK REVIEWS **C8-ord**

SURVEY GRAPHIC (per.). *In* BOOK REVIEWS **C8-ord**

SYMBOLS
Wa10-tech 50 cds. by subj. Bks., per. & pams. Symbols used in ind. & eng. Cur. add.

SYMPHONY. *See also* BOSTON SYMPHONY ORCHESTRA PROGRAMS; MUSIC
Wa11-ref (2)
C27-art 3000 cds. by name of comp. Five Amer. symphony orch. programs. Wkly. add.

C32-art 3960 cds. by comp. Programs of Boston, Chicago, Hollywood Bowl, Los Angeles, Minneapolis, Philadelphia, San Francisco. Freq. add.
C49-art 1152 cds. by comp. & t. Los Angeles, 1920–date, & N.Y. programs, 1935–1938. Cur. add.
M3 500 cds. by comp. & symphony. Domestic cat. Mo. add.
Mo3-educ 4300 cds. by orch. & comp. Major symphony programs, 1896–date.
N47-mus 4500 ent., tpd. shts. by comp. U.S. orch., 1929–date. Yrly. add.
Nb14-ref 3000 cds. by comp. Boston, Philadelphia, Omaha & other programs. No add.
O16-art 3000 cds. by comp. Boston, Chicago, Philadelphia, Philharmonic, Seattle, New friends of music notes. Wkly. add.
O20-art 2876 cds. by comp. Boston, Minneapolis & Philadelphia programs. Infreq. add.
O29-ref 5000 cds. by comp. & selection. Boston, Chicago, Cincinnati, & Philadelphia programs. Cur. add.
O47-ref 700 cds. by t. & comp. Cincinnati, 1929–date, Cleveland, 1927–1933. Yrly. add. for Cincinnati.
O56-ref 870 cds. by comp. Boston & Chicago programs. Freq. add.
Or5-mus 3100 cds. by comp. Major symphony orch. programs. Occ. add.

SYNOPSIS AND OUTLINES OF LITERATURE (bk.). *In* LITERATURE **N46-lit** (2)

SYRACUSE (N.Y.)—AUTHORS. *See* AUTHORS—SYRACUSE (N.Y.)

SYRACUSE (N.Y.)—BIOGRAPHY
N54 3000 cds. by name. Bks., pams., biog., etc. Freq. add.

SYRACUSE (N.Y.)—SOCIETIES AND CLUBS
N54 900 cds. by name. Newsp. Cur. add.

SYRACUSE UNIVERSITY—DISSERTATIONS, ACADEMIC
N55 1900 cds. by auth. & subj. Freq. add.

SYRACUSE UNIVERSITY—PUBLICATIONS
N55 13,200 cds. by subj. Cur. add.

SYRACUSE UNIVERSITY—PUBLICATIONS, FAC-
ULTY
N55 5555 cds. by auth. Bks. & per. Freq. add.

TABLE
C57 400 cds. by type of party. Per. before 1930. Freq. add.

TABLES. *See* ENGINEERING—TABLES; MATHEMATICS—TABLES

TACOMA (WASH.)—BIOGRAPHY
Wa14-ref 2300 cds. by name. Bks. & newsp., 1920–date. Freq. add.

TACOMA (WASH.)—FIRES. *See* FIRES—TACOMA (WASH.)

TACOMA (WASH.)—HISTORY. *See* WASHINGTON (STATE)—HISTORY **Wa14-ref**

TALLAHASSEE (FLA.) DEMOCRAT (newsp.)
F4 1935–1938. Cds. by subj. Freq. add.

TAMPA (FLA.)—HISTORY
F5 315 cds. by subj. Bks., per., doc., newsp. & pams. Freq. add.

TAX DIGEST (per.)
C6-ref 1938–date.. Cds. by subj. Cur. add.

TAXATION
C58 250p., tpd. shts. by subj. Provisions, rules, letters & bul. Sales tax and use tax rulings. Yrly. add.
C58 3000 cds. chron. by subj. Taxes admin. by Bd., civil service, property tax matters. Attorney general's opinions affecting State bd. of equalization. Freq. add.
D12 10,500 cds. by auth. & name of state & country. Bks., pams. & per. Taxation & the farmer. Cur. add.
Nj52 1000 cds. by subj. Bks., per. & pams. Freq. add.

TAXATION—RHODE ISLAND
R1-bus 40 cds. by city & town. Freq. add.

TAYLOR, ZACHARY
Ky2 78 cds. by auth. Bks. & per. Freq. add.

TEACHERS' MAGAZINE. *In* CANADA—PERIODICALS **Ca13-per**

TEACHING MATERIALS. *See also* AUDIO-VISUAL AIDS
Nj14-educ 2640 cds. by subj. Bks., pams. & per. Freq. add.

TECHNOLOGY. SCIENCE; Names of other technical subjects. *See also* List of Bibliographies, APPENDIX I
C31-ref 1320 cds. by class & subj. Bks., per., doc., & pams. Daily add.
D25 78,000 cds. by auth. & subj. Per. & pams. Daily add.
Mo13-sci 300 cds. by subj. Bks., per., pams. & docs. Freq. add.
N40 3960 cds. by subj. Bks., per. & pams. Niagara Falls ind. plants (electrochem.) union list. Infreq. add.
N46-sci 1200 cds. by subj. Bks. & per. Freq. add.
Nb14-r.a. 75,000 cds. by subj. Bks. Freq. add.
O56-tech 10,000 cds. by subj. Bks., per., pams., etc. Cur. add.
Or-tech 85,800 cds. by subj. Per. & pams. Cur. add.
P35 360,000 cds. by subj. Per., bul., treatises, rpts., 1859–1929. Believed to be the only file of its kind in the world. Infreq. add.
P39-tech 145,900 cds. by Brussels class. Per., 1906–1911. No add.

TECHNOLOGY—BIBLIOGRAPHIES
P39-tech 1240 cds. by subj. Bks., per., etc. Bibl. on sci. & tech. subj. Freq. add.

TECHNOLOGY—BIOGRAPHY
N35-ref 70,000 cds. by name. Bks. & per. Scientists, engineers, etc. In proc.

TECHNOLOGY—BOOK REVIEWS
N7 10,000 cds. by auth. Per., 1910–1935. No add.

TECHNOLOGY—FOREIGN LANGUAGES
Mn14-tech 150 cds. by class. Infreq. add.

TECHNOLOGY—HISTORY
N35-ref. sci 12,000 cds. by subj. Per., bks. & newsp. Hist. aspects of ind. arts. No add.
P39-tech 1700 cds. by subj. Bks., per. & pams. Hist. of sci. & tech. Freq. add.

TECHNOLOGY—PERIODICALS
D20 124,740 cds. by auth. & subj. Per., 1892–1922. No add.

TECHNOLOGY—PERIODICALS—INDEXES
Wa11-ref 1400 cds. by t. Indexes of sci. & tech. per. Occ. add.

TECHNOLOGY—PICTURES. *See* PICTURES—TECHNOLOGY

TECHNOLOGY—POETRY. *See* POETRY—TECHNOLOGY

TEETH. *See* List of Bibliographies, APPENDIX I

TEMPORARY NATIONAL ECONOMIC COMMITTEE
O20-bus   Unest. cds. by subj. Hearings & releases of T.N.E.C. Freq. add.

TENNESSEE
T9-ref   57,000 cds. by auth., t. & subj. Bks. Cur. add.

TENNESSEE—AUTHORS. *See* AUTHORS—TENNESSEE

TENNESSEE—BIOGRAPHY. *See also* AUTHORS—TENNESSEE; WOMEN, FAMOUS—TENNESSEE
T6-ref   11,850 cds. by name. Bks. Freq. add.

TENNESSEE—DOCUMENTS
T5-circ   57p., tpd. shts. by dept. or instit. Appendix v. of Tenn. house & senate jls. Occ. add.

TENNESSEE—EDUCATION. *See* EDUCATION—TENNESSEE

TENNESSEE—HISTORY
T3-Mc. (1)   25,000 cds. by name. Bk. indexed: Goodspeed, firm, *History of Tennessee: Middle Tennessee and West Tennessee.* No add.
T3-Mc. (2)   16,000 ent., tpd. shts. by name. Bks. indexed: Goodspeed, firm, *History of Tennessee, Knox co.; History of Tennessee, Hamilton co.; History of Tennessee, twenty-five to thirty counties of East Tennessee.* No add.

TENNESSEE—PICTURES. *See* PICTURES—TENNESSEE

TENNESSEE—SOIL SURVEYS. *See* SOIL SURVEYS—TENNESSEE

TENNESSEE—SOLDIERS. *See* U.S.—HISTORY—CIVIL WAR—TENNESSEE

TENNESSEE. UNIVERSITY—DISSERTATIONS, ACADEMIC
T5-circ   1000 cds. by auth. & dept. Masters' theses. Semi-yrly. add.
T5-ref   44 ent., tpd. shts. by auth. Theses rel. to loc. sch. units. Occ. add.

TENNESSEE VALLEY AUTHORITY
T4   125 ent., tpd. shts., chron. by auth. & subj. Congress. bills pert. to TVA. 73d-76th cong. Occ. add.
T4   2174 ent., tpd. shts., chron. by auth. & subj. Per. Semi-yrly. add.

TERMINOLOGY. *See* GLOSSARIES

TERRE HAUTE (IND.)—BIOGRAPHY
In35   700 ent., tpd. shts. by name & yr. Pam. indexed: *Terre Haute sch. children in 1874–1875.*

TERRE HAUTE (IND.)—NECROLOGY
In35   Unest. cds., chron. by newsp. Newsp., 1834–1897.

TESTS AND MEASUREMENTS
C34-educ   1400 cds. by auth. & t. Psych. & educ. tests. Freq. add.
N30-t.c.   2600 cds. by auth. & subj. Standard tests, covering last 5 yrs. Cur. add.
O36   1500 cds. by auth., subj. & t. Tests. Freq. add.

TEXAS. *See also* List of Bibliographies, APPENDIX I
Tx4   1880 cds. by subj. Per. Texas & S. material. Mo. add.
Tx5   Unest. cds. by auth., subj. & t. Bks., newsp., club pa., etc. Beauty spots of Texas. Freq. add.
Tx8   75 cds. by t. Per. indexed: *Niles' national register,* v. 1-14. No add.
Tx9   Unest. ent. by subj. Newsp. indexed: *Dallas News* (newsp.), 1936– date. Daily add.
Tx21-circ. ref. hist   10,000 cds. by auth., t. & subj. Bks., per. & proc. of learned soc. Texas & S.W. material. Cur. add.
Tx25   12,000 cds. by auth. & subj. Per. Texas & the S.W. Cur. add.
Tx27   200 cds. by subj. Cur. add.
Tx29-ref   17,000 cds. by subj., auth. & t. Bks., per. & newsp. Daily add.
Tx35   1150 cds. by subj. Per. Cur. add.

TEXAS—BIOGRAPHY
Tx21-j   800 cds. by name. Bks. & per. Texas heroes. Occ. add.
Tx27 (1)   100 cds. by name. Prominent Texans, living or dead. Cur. add.
Tx27 (2)   70 cds. by name. Texas auth., art., musicians. Cur. add.
Tx30   178 ent., tpd. shts. by auth. & subj. Bks. No add.

TEXAS—HISTORY
Tx9 590 cds. by subj. Newsp. indexed: *Dallas news,* 1901–1934. No add.
Tx17 104p., tpd. shts. by subj. & no. Williams pa. & Morgan papers, mss. coll. Hist. exhib. rel. to early Galveston & Texas. No add.
Tx25 6800 cds. by subj. Bks. & newsp. Cur. add.
Tx27 (1) 75 cds. by subj. Cur. add.
Tx27 (2) 70p., tpd. shts. by no. Per. indexed: *Niles national register,* 1811–1849. No add.

TEXAS—INDUSTRIES. See INDUSTRIES—TEXAS

TEXAS—LAW. See LAW—TEXAS

TEXAS—LIBRARIES. See LIBRARIES—TEXAS

TEXAS—LITERATURE
Tx8 2000 cds. by auth. Bks., per. & pams. Freq. add.

TEXAS—MINING AND METALLURGY. See MINING AND METALLURGY—SOUTHWEST **Tx14**

TEXAS—PERIODICALS
Tx17 Unest. cds. by subj. Per. indexed: *Frontier times, Southwestern historical quarterly, Texas Weekly,* to 1935. No add.

TEXAS—PICTURES. See PICTURES—TEXAS

TEXAS BAPTIST ASSOCIATION. MINUTES
Tx16 200 cds. by name of assoc. Freq. add.

TEXAS BAPTIST STATE CONVENTION. MINUTES
Tx16 50 cds. by name of convention. Freq. add.

TEXAS FOLK-LORE SOCIETY—PUBLICATIONS
Nm1 v. 1-2, 4-15. Cds. Cur. add.

TEXAS HISTORICAL QUARTERLY
Tx10-ref v. 1, 1897–date. Cds. by auth., t. & subj. Cur. add.

TEXAS MAGAZINE
Tx29-ref v. 1, 1909–v. 8, 1913. Cds. by auth., t. & subj. No add.

TEXAS PARADE (per.)
Tx10-ref v. 1, 1926–date. Cds. by auth., t. & subj. Cur. add.

TEXAS WEEKLY (per.). See also in TEXAS—PERIODICALS **Tx17**
Tx8 v. 6-17, 1933–1941. Cds. by subj. Infreq. add.

Tx8 1928–1930. Cds. by auth., t. & subj. (Bunker's monthly). No add.
Tx28 v. 6, 1930–date. Cds. by subj. Semi-yrly. add.
Tx29-ref v. 1, 1928–v. 3, 1929. Cds. by auth., t. & subj. (Bunker's monthly). No add.
Tx29-ref v. 4, 1929–v. 6, 1930. Cds. by auth., t. & subj.

TEXTBOOKS. *See also* READERS AND PRIMERS; List of Bibliographies, APPENDIX I
Ct10 6000 ent., tpd. shts. by auth. Bks. No add.
I53 1540 cds. by auth., t., subj. & pub. Freq. add.
In37 Unest. cds. by class. Bks. No add.
M10 1500 cds. by auth., t. & subj. Bks. & reprints. Mo. add.
Mn13 150 cds. by class. Bks. H.S. texts. Frcq. add.
Mn23-Ham. 1933 cds. by auth. Bks. & lists. Infreq. add.
Nd3 131 cds. by auth. & class. Cur. add.

TEXTILES
M11-tex Unest. ent., tpd. shts. by subj. Per. indexed: *Burlington magazine for connoisseurs.* Mo. add.

THANKSGIVING DAY
Ia18-ad 750 ent., tpd. shts. by subj. Bks., pams. & per. Cur. add.
In24a 33 ent. by subj. Bks. Freq. add.
In26 68 cds. by auth. Bks. & pams. Occ. add.
Mn11 Unest. ent., tpd. shts. by subj. Bks. & per. Freq. add.
Mn14-ref 375 ent., tpd. shts. by t. & auth. Bks. & per. Cur. add.

THEATRE. *See also* DRAMA; PLAYS
C62-ref 500 cds. by char., play, actor, etc. Per. Occ. add.
N22-art Unest. cds. by t. Bks. Theatre hist. & technique. Cur. add.
N35-ref. theat (1) 58,500 cds. by name. British & Amer. stage & cinema productions; names of actors, auth., cameramen, comps., costume designers, lighting designers, lyricists, managers, producers, scene designers & productions. Cur. add.

N35-ref. theat (2)   6600 cds. by place & name of theatre. Theat. giving names of plays & dates produced. Cur. add.

N35-ref. theat (3)   37,000 cds. chron. by date. Amer. & for. per. Theat. productions; chron. index of plays & movies. Cur. add.

N35-ref. theat (4)   880,000 cds. by subj. Bks. & newsp. Theat. & stage. Cur. add.

O1-read   4800 cds. by subj. Cur. add.

O20-art   300 cds. by subj. & name. Bks. & per. Freq. add.

THEATRE—BUFFALO (N.Y.)
N8-ref   18,480 cds. by name of pers. & play. Famous people & plays that have come to Buffalo. Freq. add.

THEATRE—CALIFORNIA
C71-ref   Unest. cds. by subj. Freq. add.

THEATRE—CHICAGO
I13-r.b.   200 cds. by name of organiz. Little theat. No add.
I13-ref   Unest. ent., tpd. shts. by auth. Bks. Chicago drama & theatre. Bks. Freq. add.

THEATRE—STAGE SETTINGS AND SCENERY
C56-ref   500 cds. by t. Bks. No add.
N35-58th   1000 cds. by t. Amer., Eng. & continental bks. Stage sets. Cur. add.
O21   435 cds. by auth. Bks. Stage settings. Cur. add.

THEATRE, ELIZABETHAN
Tx30   33 ent., tpd. shts. by auth. Bks. & per. No add.

THEATRE, ENGLISH—POSTERS
N35-ref   1300 cds. by name of production. Eng. productions. Theatrical posters. No add.

THEATRE (per.). *In* COSTUME   G4-ref; PLAYS   C24

THEATRE PROGRAMS
N10-ref   1468 cds. by t., seven subj. Freq. add.
N46   100 cds. by t., auth., actor & producer. Occ. add.

THEATRE PROGRAMS—CLEVELAND (O.)
O20-lit   1320 cds. by t. Cur. add.

THEATRICAL COSTUME. *See* COSTUME, THEATRICAL

THEME SUBJECTS
De1   Unest. ent., tpd. shts. by class. Biog. & gen. subj. No add.

THEOLOGY
In16   75 cds. by subj. Bks. No add.
Nj62   3000 cds. by auth. Bks. & pams. Puritan & Eng. theological lit. Occ. add.

THERAPEUTICS. *See* PHARMACY   Nj61

THESES. *See* DISSERTATIONS, ACADEMIC

THIS CITY OF OURS (bk.). *In* SEATTLE (WASH.)   Wa10-ref (2)

THIS IS ON ME (bk.). *In* SHORT STORIES Tx12

THIS WEEK IN WORCESTER (per.)
M32   400 cds. by subj. No add.

THORNTON, ELLA MAY. *See* GEORGIA—DOCUMENTS   G8

TIETJENS, EUNICE (HAMMOND)—WORKS
I13-ref   250 cds. by t. & 1st line. Bks. & per. Occ. add.

TIME AND MOTION STUDY
Nj48   275 ent., tpd. shts. by auth. Bks., per. & pams. No add.

THE TIMES OF LONG AGO, BARREN CO., KENTUCKY (bk.). *In* BARREN CO. (KY.)—HISTORY   Ky7

TIPTON, JOHN. *See* INDIANA—HISTORY In22-Ind. (1)

TISSUES
Nj61   75 cds. by auth. & t. Bks., per. & pams. Freq. add.

TITLES OF BOOKS. *See also* TRANSLATIONS C32-for
Ky4   800 cds. by t. Bks., plays, Bible, etc. Occ. add.
M27-ref   250 cds. by t. Bks., etc. Freq. add.
N35-ref. inf   800 cds. by t. Amer. & British bks. Cur. add.

TO STEP ASIDE (bk.). *In* SHORT STORIES Tx12

TOASTS. *See also* List of Bibliographies, APPENDIX I
I13-circ   Unest. cds. by auth. Bks. Occ. add.
W16   2000 cds. by subj. Bks. Toasts & after-dinner speeches.

TOLEDO (O.)
O56-ref 1530 cds. by subj. Toledo & Lucas co. inf. Freq. add.

TOLEDO (O.)—AUTHORS. *See* AUTHORS—TOLEDO (O.)

TOLEDO (O.)—PICTURES. *See* PICTURES—TOLEDO (O.)

TOLEDO (O.) BLADE (newsp.). *In* NECROLOGY **O56-ref**

TOPOGRAPHIC MAPS. *See* U.S. GEOLOGICAL SURVEY—TOPOGRAPHIC MAPS

TORONTO (ONT., CAN.)—ELECTIONS
Ca7 660 cds. by name. Per. indexed: *Toronto Daily Star*. Yrly. add.

TORONTO (ONT., CAN.)—HISTORY. *See also* CANADA—HISTORY **Ca7**
Ca8-lib. sch 136 ent., tpd. shts. by subj., chron. Martha Shepard, *The First Things of Toronto*. No add.

TORONTO (ONT., CAN.)—LIBRARIES. *See* LIBRARIES—TORONTO (ONT., CAN.)

TORONTO (ONT., CAN.) DAILY STAR (newsp.), *In* TORONTO (ONT., CAN.)—ELECTIONS **Ca7**

T'OUNG PAO (per.). *In* ART, ORIENTAL **D9**

TOWN MEETING (per.). *See also in* PAMPHLETS **N24**
I53 1940–date. Cds. by speaker & t. Wkly. add.

TOWN TOPICS (per.). *In* PLAYS—CLEVELAND (O.) **O20-lit**

TOXINS AND ANTITOXINS
Nj61 75 cds. by auth. & t. Bks., per. & pams. Freq. add.

TRADE ASSOCIATIONS—WASHINGTON (state). *See* List of Bibliographies, APPENDIX I

TRADE CATALOGS AND DIRECTORIES. *See also* HOUSE ORGANS
C31-ref 660 cds. by name & subj. Mo. add.
C32-sci 8800 cds. by subj. & name. Cur. add.
Ca2-sci 650 cds. by subj. & name of co. Infreq. add.
I27 500 cds. by name of co. Cement & concrete construction. Occ. add.

I57 249 cds. by name of manuf. Freq. add.
I73-eng 8580 cds. by name of co. & product. Manuf. cat. of interest to engineers. Freq. add.
In23-bus 1056 cds. by subj. Trade & prof. Freq. add.
M15 2640 cds. by name of co. & product. Freq. add.
Md2-bus 900 cds. by ind. Bks., pams., per. Cur. add.
Mi6-ref 300 cds. by subj. Dealers' cat. Freq. add.
Mn14-tech 9240 cds. by name of co. & subj. Cur. add.
Mo13-sci 1750 cds. by subj. Bks., per., pams. & docs. Cur. add.
N35-ref. inf 3750 cds. by subj. Bks. & per., Amer. & for. bus., ind., manuf. assoc., etc. Cur. add.
N46-sci 200 cds. by subj. & name of firm. Pams., etc. Freq. add.
Nj50-bus 3200 cds. by subj. Cur. add.
O20-bus 3960 cds. by subj. Bks., per. & pams. Occ. add.
O20-bus 15,840 cds. by name of co. & product. Inc. Cleveland cos. and cos. with Cleveland repres. Freq. add.
O20-bus 600 cds. by name of co. Prospectueses. Mo. add.
O56-tech 23,000 cds. by subj. & name of manuf. Daily add.
Or5-tech 1350 ent. by subj. & name of manuf. Occ. add.
P39-tech 19,600 cds. by subj. & name of co. Cur. add.

TRADE CATALOGS AND DIRECTORIES—AERONAUTICS
G7-D.Gugg. 500 cds. by subj. Sci. & eng. trade cat., house organs, etc. Freq. add.

TRADE MARKS. *See* U.S. PATENT OFFICE. TRADE MARK DIGEST

TRADE NAMES
Mn14-tech 120 cds. by subj. & organiz. Bks. Cur. add.
P39-tech 4000 cds. by name. Per., bks., etc. Freq. add.
Wa10-tech 50 cds. by subj. Per. & pams. Cur. add.

TRAIL, A MAGAZINE FOR COLORADO
Co8 v. 1-8, 1908–1916. Cds. by auth., t. & subj. No add.

TRAINED NURSE & HOSPITAL REVIEW. *In* NURSES & NURSING **Ia14-med**

TRANSLATIONS
C32-for 620 cds. by t. Bks. For. tr. titles. Freq. add.
I79 98 ent., tpd. shts. by auth. Bks. Infreq. add.
Mi6-for 1850 cds. by lang. & auth. Bks. Freq. add.
O37 300 cds. by auth. & country. Bks. Cur. add.

TRANSLATIONS—FICTION. *See* FICTION—TRANSLATIONS

TRANSLATIONS—PLAYS. *See* PLAYS—TRANSLATIONS

TRANSLATIONS, ITALIAN
O20-Alta 1320 cds. by t. Bks. Infreq. add.

TRANSPORTATION. *See also* AERONAUTICS; MOTOR BUSES; RAILROADS; RIVERS; SHIPS; TRAVEL; WATERWAYS
Nj52 1000 cds. by subj. Bks., per. & pams. Freq. add.

TRAVEL. *See also* PAMPHLETS **Mi13-W.** side, **O20-Euc. 100th**; List of Bibliographies, APPENDIX I
C49-j 1472 cds. by country. Bks. Freq. add.
I45-ref 1000 ent. by subj. Pams., maps, etc. Freq. add.
Nb10 274 cds. by t. & class. Bks., per. & pams. Freq. add.

TRAVEL—FOREIGN LANGUAGES
C32-for 630 cds. by place. Bks. in for. lang. Freq. add.

TRAVEL—POSTERS. *See* POSTERS, TRAVEL

TREASURY OF SCOTTISH COVENANT (bk.). *In* PRESBYTERIANS **P4** (1)

TREES
G11 25 cds. by t. Per. & pams. Infreq. add.

TREES—PICTURES. *See* PICTURES—TREES

TREES—POETRY. *See* POETRY—TREES

TRENTON (N.J.)—HISTORY
Nj67-ref 17,000 cds. by subj. Bks., per., pams., newsp., pic., maps, etc. Cur. add.

TRENTON (N.J.)—MANUSCRIPTS
Nj67-ref 1000 cds. by name of pers., place, subj., etc. Deeds, letters, notes, bills, etc. Infreq. add.

TRENTON (N.J.)—PHOTOGRAPHS
Nj67-ref Unest. ent., tpd. shts. by subj. Occ. add.

TRIALS. *See* CRIME AND CRIMINALS **O20-soc**

TRINITROTOLUENE
Nj54 Unest. ent. by subj. Spec. rpts. on manuf. of TNT. Freq. add.

TRINITY ARCHIVES (per.)
Nc6 1896–date. Cds. by subj. Freq. add.

TRIO MUSIC
C32-art 600 cds. by t. & comp. Bks. Occ. add.

THE TROUBLE WITH TIGERS (bk.). *In* SHORT STORIES **Tx12**

TRUMBLE CO. (O.)—HISTORY
O61-ref 12,000 ent., tpd. shts. by surname. Trumbull & Mahoning co. hist.

TUBERCULOSIS
Nj61 450 cds. by auth. & t. Bks., per., pams. & reprints. Freq. add.
P26 23 ent., tpd. shts. by subj. Bks., govt. doc., pams. & per. Soc. & econ. factors in fight against tuberculosis. Infreq. add.

TULIP TIME. *See* HOLLAND (MICH.)—TULIP TIME

TULLIDGE'S QUARTERLY MAGAZINE
U3 v. 1-3, 1880–1885. Tpd. shts. by auth. & subj. No add.

TUMORS. *See also* CANCER
Nj61 300 cds. by auth. & t. Bks., per., pams. & lectures. Freq. add.

TURGENEV, IVAN—WORKS. *See* List of Bibliographies, APPENDIX I

TURNER PICTURE STUDIES (bk.). *In* ART—STUDY AND TEACHING **Mi6-Walk.**

TUSCALOOSA CO.—CEMETERY RECORDS
A1 250 ent., tpd. shts. by name. Evergreen cem., Greenwood cem. Cur. add.

TWAIN, MARK. *See* CLEMENS, SAMUEL LANGHORNE—WORKS

TWENTY STORIES (bk.). *In* SHORT STORIES **Tx12**

TYPOGRAPHY. *See* List of Bibliographies, APPENDIX I

UFFIZI GALLERY—PICTURES. *See* PICTURES—UFFIZI GALLERY

UNCLE REMUS (per.)
G14 1907–1912. Cds. by auth. & subj. Infreq. add.

UNEMPLOYMENT COMPENSATION. *See* LABOR AND LABORING CLASSES **M7**

UNION CITY (N.J.) HUDSON DISPATCH (newsp.). *In* NEW JERSEY **Nj68**

UNION COLLEGE—TERM PAPERS
Nb7 931 cds. by auth., subj. & t. Stud. papers & themes. Yrly. add.

UNITED AUTOMOBILE WORKER (per.). *In* LABOR AND LABORING CLASSES—PERIODICALS **O33-Euc. Cen.**

UNITED MINE WORKERS JOURNAL. *In* LABOR AND LABORING CLASSES—PERIODICALS **O33-Euc. Cen.**

UNITED STATES. *See also* STATES (U.S.); Names of states
Ia12 382 ent. by subj. Bks. Occ. add.

U.S. ARMY—AMERICAN EXPEDITIONARY FORCE. *See* EUROPEAN WAR, 1914–1918—AMERICAN EXPEDITIONARY FORCE

U.S. ARMY—CAMPS
O16-ref 800 cds. by subj. & name of camp, fort, hospital, place & division. Army and navy camps (1917–18) forts, insignia, etc. No add.

U.S. BUREAU OF CHEMISTRY AND SOILS—PUBLICATIONS
N35-ref. econ 1200 cds. by region. Soil surveys: Field operations, 1899–1922; Soil surveys, 1923–date. Cur. add.

U.S. BUREAU OF CHEMISTRY AND SOILS—REPORTS
I65-bus 75 cds. by state. Freq. add.
Mi25 550 cds. by state & co. Freq. add.

U.S. BUREAU OF CHEMISTRY AND SOILS. SOIL SURVEY
M5 1200 cds. by state & region. Cur. add.
Mo3-doc 2000 cds. by state.

U.S. BUREAU OF ENTOMOLOGY AND PLANT QUARANTINE — PUBLICATIONS. *See* ENTOMOLOGY

U.S. BUREAU OF FOREIGN AND DOMESTIC COMMERCE. BUSINESS INFORMATION SERVICE
O20-bus 2640 cds. by subj. Freq. add.
O20-bus 33,320 cds. by auth. & subj. Freq. add.

U.S. BUREAU OF LABOR STATISTICS. BULLETIN
In33-doc 552 cds. by subj. Cur. add.

U.S. BUREAU OF PLANT INDUSTRY—PUBLICATIONS
D18 12,000 cds. by numbered ser., auth. & subj. Cur. add.

U.S. CHILDREN'S BUREAU—PUBLICATIONS
Mn24 199 cds. by ser. no., auth. & subj. Freq. add.

U.S. COAST AND GEODETIC SURVEY—PUBLICATIONS
N35-ref. sci 600 ent., tpd. shts. by auth. & subj. Spec. pub., bul. & annual rpts., 1844–date. Cur. add.

U.S. CONGRESS. HEARINGS
Mo3-doc 1000 cds. by subj. Cur. add.
N8-ref Unest. cds. by subj. Freq. add.
Nb5 2310 cds. by subj. Freq. add.
Nj14-doc 5280 cds. by subj. & auth. Cur. add.
O20-ref 3960 cds. by bill no. & subj. Freq. add.

U.S.—DEFENSES. *See also* NATIONAL DEFENSE ADVISORY COMMISSION. RELEASES; List of Bibliographies, APPENDIX I
C31-ref 1500 cds. by subj. Doc., pams. & newsp. Victory index: civilian defense, training for armed forces, personnel in loc. & natl. defense activities. Freq. add.
I44 30 ent., tpd. shts. by subj. Bks. Freq. add.
M4-sci 1320 cds. by subj.

U.S. DEPT. OF AGRICULTURE. BULLETIN
Mi30 1628 cds. by subj. Cur. add.

U.S. DEPT. OF AGRICULTURE. LEAFLET
C50 No. 2-75, 101. Cds. by subj. Infreq. add.

U.S. DEPT. OF AGRICULTURE—PUBLICATIONS
C17 400 cds. by subj. Freq. add.
Ia8 7260 cds. by subj. & class. Cur. add.

U.S.—DESCRIPTION AND TRAVEL
C49-j 762 cds. by state. Bks. Freq. add.

U.S. ENGINEER DEPT.—PUBLICATIONS. *See* WATERWAYS **N8-tech**

U.S. FISHERIES BUREAU—PUBLICATIONS
I65-bus 200 cds. by subj. No add.

U.S.—FOREIGN LANGUAGES
Mi6-for 150 cds. by subj. & lang. Amer. by for. writers. Occ. add.

U.S. FOREST SERVICE
G11 50 cds. by t. Per. & pams. Infreq. add.

U.S. GEOLOGICAL SURVEY. BULLETIN. *In* MINING AND METALLURGY—MONTANA **Mt2**

U.S. GEOLOGICAL SURVEY—PUBLICATIONS. *See also* MAPS **C57**
C51 Unest. ent., tpd. shts. by state. No add.

U.S. GEOLOGICAL SURVEY. TOPOGRAPHIC MAPS
C62-bus 700 cds. by state. Freq. add.
De3 5280 cds. by state & name of quadrangle. Cur. add.
Id2 6700 cds. by state, quadrangle & co. Cur. add.
Mo3-doc 5000 cds. by state. Cur. add.
P39-tech 5500 cds. by state & quadrangle. Cur. add.

U.S.—HISTORY
Ar3 200 cds. by auth. & subj. Bks. Cur. add.
C3 169 cds. by auth. Bks. Cur. add.
C72 100 ent., tpd. shts. by auth. Bks. Mat. with Amer. hist. background since Civil war. Freq. add.
C72 100 ent., tpd. shts. by auth. Bks. Mat. with Amer. hist. prior to Civil war. Freq. add.
I13-ref 1800 cds. by subj. Bks. & per. Freq. add.
N6-ref 56p., tpd. shts. by state. Bks. Military & regimental hist. of states in wars, 1775–1898. No add. since 1914.
N35-ref.-Amer. hist 75,000 cds. by subj. & name. Scenes, events & personages, esp. Amer. Indians. Cur. add.

N51 225 cds., chron. Bks. Infreq. add.
Nj16 260 ent., tpd. shts. by subj. Bks. Freq. add.
Nj56 Unest. ent., tpd. shts. by subj. Bk. indexed: *Chronicles of America series*, 50v. In proc.
Tx30 109 ent., tpd. shts. by state. Bks. No add.

U.S.—HISTORY—UNION LISTS
Ky12 2254 cds. by auth. Bks. & per. No add.

U.S.—HISTORY—COLONIAL PERIOD
I35 48 cds. by subj. Bks. Occ. add.

U.S.—HISTORY—REVOLUTION. *See also* SULLIVAN'S EXPEDITION
Co5-gen 650 cds. by state. Bks. & per. Infreq. add.
In35-gen (1) Unest. ent., tpd. shts. by state. Per. indexed: *American monthly magazine and critical review*, v. 14-42; *National historical magazine*, v. 43-71. Rev. war soldiers. Cur. add.
In35-gen (2) 1650 ent., tpd. shts. by name. Bk. indexed: Benson J. Lossing, *The American revolution*. Names of soldiers. No add.
In35-gen (3) 6700 ent., tpd. shts. by name. Bk. indexed: Peter Force, *American archives*. Rev. soldiers. No add.

U.S.—HISTORY—REVOLUTION—ALABAMA
A1 1000 cds. by subj. Rev. soldiers who died in Ala. Occ. add.

U.S.—HISTORY—REVOLUTION—FALL RIVER (MASS.)
M18-ref 10 cds. by name. Hist. of Norton, Rhode Island, Taunton, Dartmouth, Freetown, Rehoboth, New Bedford, Bristol co., Fall River. Fall River res. in rev. war. Infreq. add.

U.S.—HISTORY—REVOLUTION—INDIANA
In35-gen 360 ent., tpd. shts. by name. Per. indexed: Daughters of the Amer. rev., *Lineage books*. Rev. soldiers connected with Ind. No add.

U.S.—HISTORY—REVOLUTION—KENTUCKY
In35-gen Unest. ent., tpd. shts. by name. Bk. indexed: Zachariah F. Smith, *History of Kentucky* . . . Rev. war soldiers in Ky. No add.

U.S.—History—Revolution—New Jersey
Nj36 100p., tpd. shts. by name. Bk. indexed: William S. Stryker, *Official register of the officers and men of New Jersey in the Revolutionary War.* No add.

U.S.—History—Revolution—Pamphlets
I26 633 ent., tpd. shts. by auth. Occ. add.

U.S.—History—Revolution—Virginia
In35-gen 4809 ent., tpd. shts. Per. indexed: *Virginia magazine of history,* v. 6-22. Occ. add.
Ky7 (1) Unest. ent., tpd. shts. by name. Bk. indexed: Louis A. Burgess, *Revolutionary soldiers of Virginia,* 2v. No add.
Ky7 (2) Unest. ent., tpd. shts. by name. Bk. indexed: Louis A. Burgess, *Virginia soldiers of 1776,* 2v. No add.

U.S.—History—War of 1812
Co5-gen 100 cds. by state. Bks. & per. Infreq. add.

U.S.—History—War of 1812—Erie Co. (Pa.)
P13-ref 414 cds. by name. Newsp. Erie soldiers who served in War of 1812.

U.S.—History—War of 1812—Kentucky
Ky7 (1) Unest. ent., tpd. shts. by name. Bk. indexed: Anderson C. Quisenberry, *Kentucky in the War of 1812.* No add.
Ky7 (2) Unest. ent., tpd. shts. by name. Bk. indexed: William E. Railey, *Commissioned officers of the War of 1812.* No add.

U.S.—History—War with Mexico, 1845-1848—Alabama
A1 4500 cds. by name. Alabamians in War with Mexico. Occ. add.

U.S.—History—War with Mexico, 1845-1848—Kentucky
Ky7 Unest. ent. by name. Bk. indexed: William E. Railey, *Roster of the Mexican war.* Occ. add.

U.S.—History—Civil War. *See also* List of Bibliographies, Appendix I
Nj66 99 ent., tpd. shts. by auth. Infreq. add.
V6 6100 cds. by auth., t. & subj. Bks., pams. & per. Infreq. add.

U.S.—History—Civil War—Bibliography—Imprints
G14 1000 cds. by auth., t. & subj. Bks., pams., govt. doc., broadsides, maps, sht. mus., per. Confederate imprints. Infreq. add.

U.S.—History—Civil War—Mississippi
Ms3 2000 cds. by name. Miss. captains in C.S.A. Occ. add.
Ms3 150,000 cds. by name. Print. & mss. mat. Miss. confederate military records. Freq. add.

U.S.—History—Civil War—Tennessee
T3-Mc. 300p., tpd. shts. by name. Calendar of T.A.R. Nelson pa. No add.
T6-ref Unest. ent., tpd. shts. by name. Bk. indexed: John B. Lindsley, *Military annals of Tennessee.* In proc.

U.S.—History—War of 1898
Ky7 Unest. ent., tpd. shts. by name. Bk. indexed: William E. Railey, *Roster of the Spanish-American war.* No add.

U.S.—History—War of 1898—Alabama
A1 5000 cds. by name. Alabamians in Spanish-American war. Occ. add.

U.S. Naval Academy
Md1 1600 cds. by subj. Bks., per. & govt. doc. Infreq. add.

U.S. Navy
Md1 (1) 2200 ent., tpd. shts. by subj. Papers of Gustavus Vasa Fox, 2v. No add.
Md1 (2) 1800 cds. by name. Bks., per. & phot. Pic. of ships & off. Freq. add.
Md1 (3) 600 cds. by subj. Secy. of Navy reports, 1823-1915, omitting Civil War. No add.

U.S. Navy—Camps. *See* U.S. Army—Camps **O16-ref**

U.S. Office of Education—Publications. *See also* Education **Mn14-Fran**
C80 Unest. cds. by subj. & t. Freq. add.
Ct2 900 cds. by subj. Pams., leaflets & circ. Occ. add.
In16 700 cds. by subj. Freq. add.
Nj29 200 cds. by subj. Freq. add.

U.S. Office of Experiment Stations. Bulletin
D26   102,500 cds. by auth. & t. Cur. add.

U.S. Office of Experiment Stations—Publications. *See also* Veterinary Medicine   **V1-agric**
Ct2   91 cds. by state, auth. & subj. Bul., circ., leaflets. Inc. New England, Ohio, N.J., Mich., N.Y., Penn., Calif. Occ. add.

U.S.—Officials and Employees
Mi6-soc   325 cds. by govt. unit. Newsp. & per. Freq. add.
N35-ref. econ   2200 cds. by name of dept., bureau. Newsp. & Per. Cur. add.
P39-Wyl.   61 cds. by name of office under subdiv. fed., state, city & co. Newsp. & rpts. Cur. add.

U.S. Patent Office. Trade Mark Digest
N35-ref. sci   1915–date. Cds. by off. class. In proc.

U.S.—Pictures. *See* Pictures—United States

U.S.—Politics and Government
C19   Several thousand ent., tpd. shts. by dept. Bks. & per. Cur. add.

U.S. Public Health Service—Publications. *See* Public Health—Documents   **C32-sci**

U.S. Recruiting Bureau. Recruiting News (per.)
Wa10-ref   1927–1938. Tpd. shts. by subj. Occ. add.

U.S. Securities and Exchange Commission—Speeches, Staff
D29   2000 cds. by auth., subj. & t. Freq. add.

U.S.—Social Life and Customs
Md2-hist   520 cds. by subj. & period. Bks. Freq. add.

U.S.—Social Life and Customs—Photographs
G4-ref   400 ent., tpd. shts. by subj. Bk. indexed: Agnes Rogers, *The American procession.* No add.

U.S. Superintendent of Documents—Price Lists
G4-ref   750 ent., tpd. shts. by subj. Cur. add.

U.S.—Territories. *See* List of Bibliographies, Appendix I

U.S. War Department—Publications
I65-bus   50 cds. by subj. & t. Mo. add.

U.S. Weather Bureau. Monthly Weather Review
N35-ref. sci   v. 1-63, 1873–1935, supp. 1-35. Tpd. shts. by auth. & subj. No add.

United States News (newsp.)
I62   300 cds. by subj. Freq. add.
Mi13-ref   1408 cds. by auth. & subj. Wkly. add.

Units of Work. *See also* Courses of Study   **C31-ref**
C20   1500 cds. by subj. Bks. No add.
C20   170 cds. by subj. Per. Occ. add.
C31-ref   300 cds. by subj. Per. Occ. add.
C32-educ   2700 cds. by subj. Bks., per. & pams. Cur. add.
C49-j   1152 cds. by subj. Bks. Freq. add.
Co6   50 cds. by subj. Freq. add.
Ky2   300 cds. by subj. Courses of study, curriculum bul. Cur. add.
Md2-educ   3500 cds. by subj. Bks. & pams. Freq. add.
Nj42   2500 cds. by name of unit. Pams. & courses. Cur. add.
Nj50-educ   15,000 cds. by subj. Bks., pams. & per. Freq. add.
O20-j   Unest. cds. by subj. Bks. per. & pams. Infreq. add.
O20-soc   1320 cds. by subj. Bks. & pams. Occ. add.
O33-Roose.   1000 cds. by subj. Bks., per. & pams. Cur. add.
O37   1300 cds. by subj. Bks., per. & pams. Cur. add.
Or7-circ   700 cds. by subj. Bks. & per. Freq. add.

Universal Anthology (bk.). *In* Literature   **N48; Nb1**

Universal Oil Products—Publications
In25-chem   368 cds. by subj. Cur. add.
N33   Unest., cds., chron. Freq. add.

UNIVERSITIES AND COLLEGES. *See also* Names of indiv. univ. and coll.; CATALOGS, COLLEGE; COURSES OF STUDY
N30-Low   1500 cds. by coll. Necrol. & gen. inf. Freq. add.
Wa10-per   2600 cds. by subj. Cat. & pams. Coll. & sch. index—where certain subj. are taught. Freq. add.

UNIVERSITIES AND COLLEGES—INSTITUTES. *See* List of Bibliographies, APPENDIX I

UNIVERSITIES AND COLLEGES—PRESIDENTS
N46-educ   100 cds. by name. Per. & newsp. Cur. add.

UNIVERSITIES AND COLLEGES—PUBLICATIONS. *See also* CATALOGS, COLLEGE
N4   300 cds. by name of coll. Cat. & bul. Yrly. add.
O29-ref   7000 cds. by coll., auth., subj. & t. Studies, cat. & bul. Freq. add.
T2   525 cds. by subj. Cat. & bul. Freq. add.
Wa15   400 cds. by coll., dept. & ser. Off. pub. other than cat. Infreq. add.

UNIVERSITY DEBATER'S ANNUAL (bk.). *See also* DEBATES   Mi8-ref, N7, Nj56, O29-ref, P33-ref, P45-ref
In14   1919–date. 157 cds. by subj. Cur. add.

UNIVERSITY OF TORONTO QUARTERLY. *In* CANADA—PERIODICALS   Ca13-per

THE UNVANQUISHED (bk.). *In* SHORT STORIES   Tx12

UPLIFT (per.)
Nc1   1915–date. Cds. by subj. Freq. add.

UTAH. AGRICULTURAL EXPERIMENT STATION. BULLETIN
U2   Unest. cds. by subj. Occ. add.

UTAH—BIOGRAPHY. *See* DIARIES, WESTERN   U3

UTAH—DOCUMENTS
U1   Unest. ent., tpd. shts. by subj. 1930–1938. Cur. add.
U3   1000 cds. by subj. Biennial add.

UTAH—HISTORY. *See also* OGDEN (UTAH) U2-ref
U3   2000 cds. by subj. Bks., per. & pams. Freq. add.
U5   1500 cds. by auth. & subj. Pams., newsp. & per. Freq. add.

UTAH—PERIODICALS
U5   1200 cds. by auth. & subj. Per. indexed: *Utah academy of science. Proceedings; Utah educational review; Utah monthly magazine.* Cur. add.

UTAH UNIVERSITY—PUBLICATIONS
U5   2000 cds. by auth. Freq. add.

UTAH ACADEMY OF SCIENCE. PROCEEDINGS. *In* UTAH—PERIODICALS   U5

UTAH EDUCATIONAL REVIEW. *In* UTAH—PERIODICALS   U5
U1   v. 1, 1907–1941. Tpd. shts. by subj. & auth. In proc.

UTAH FARMER (per.)
U1   v. 1, 1904–1941. Tpd. shts. by subj. & auth. In proc.

UTAH MONTHLY MAGAZINE. *In* UTAH—PERIODICALS   U5
U3   v. 1-9, 1884–1893 (incomp.) Tpd. shts. by auth. & subj. No add.

UTICA (N.Y.)
N57   237p., tpd. shts. by subj., chron. Bks., pams., maps & per.

VACCINATION
Nj61   75 cds. by auth. & t. Bks., per. & pams. Vaccination & vaccines. Freq. add.

VAN DYKE, HENRY JACKSON—WORKS
I13-ref   700 cds. by t. & 1st line. Bks. & per. Infreq. add.

VANCOUVER (B.C.) DAILY PROVINCE (newsp.). *In* BRITISH COLUMBIA (CAN.)—NEWSPAPERS   Ca3; CANADA—HISTORY   Ca3

VANCOUVER (B.C.) EVENING SUN (newsp.). *In* BRITISH COLUMBIA (CAN.)—NEWSPAPERS   Ca3

VANCOUVER (B.C.) NEWS-HERALD (newsp.). *In* BRITISH COLUMBIA (CAN.)—NEWSPAPERS   Ca3; CANADA—HISTORY   Ca3

VANCOUVER (B.C.) SUN (newsp.). *In* BRITISH COLUMBIA (CAN.)—NEWSPAPERS   Ca3; CANADA—HISTORY   Ca3

VARIETY MAGAZINE. *In* MOTION PICTURES   Mn23

VARNISH AND VARNISHING. *See* PAINTS   Nj3

Vassar College—History
N45b   800 cds. by class. Doc., pa., corr., deeds, etc. Freq. add.

Vassar College—Periodicals
N45b   4500 cds. by auth., t. & subj. Per. & yrbks. Cur. add.
N45b   2700 cds. by class. Justice coll. Freq. add.

Vassar College—Publications
N45b   8000 cds. by auth., chron. Bks., pams. & per. since 1926. Pub. of alumnae, fac. & trustees. Cur. add.
N45b   720 ent., tpd. shts., chron. Off. pub. Cur. add.

Vassar College—Publications, Alumni
N45b   2500 cds..by auth. Bks., per. & pams. Freq. add.

Vassar College—Publications, Faculty
N45b   1500 cds. by auth., chron. Bks., pams. & per. Freq. add.

Vaudeville
C32-lit   5p., tpd. shts. by auth. Occ. add.

Venereal Diseases
Nj61   100 cds. by auth. & t. Bks., per. & pams. Freq. add.

Ventilation. See Air Conditioning   Nj52

Ventura (Calif.)—Newspapers
C87   200 cds. by subj. Freq. add.

Ventura (Calif.) Democrat (newsp.). *In* California—Newspapers   C32-hist

Ventura Co. (Calif.)—Documents
C87   25 cds. by dept. Freq. add.

Vermont
Vt2   375 cds. by auth. & subj. Bks. Freq. add.

Vermont Free Public Library Commission. Bulletin
Vt1   1000 cds. by auth. & subj. Q. add.

Vermonter (per.)
Vt1   v. 1-15, 1895–1912; v. 18-44, 1913–1939; v. 44, 1940. Cds. by auth. & subj. Mo. add.

Verne, Jules—Works
C32-fic   17p., tpd. shts. by t. No add.

Vertebrates. *See* List of Bibliographies, Appendix I

Veterinary Medicine. *See also* Mastitis (Bovine)
Nj61   1100 cds. by auth. & t. Bks., per., pams. & reprints. Freq. add.
V1-agric   1000 ent., tpd. shts. by subj. Exp. stat. rpts. & bul., 1889–1936.

Veterinary Medicine—Pathology
D13   280,000 cds. by auth. & subj. Freq. add.

Victoria (B.C.) Colonist (newsp.). *See also* Canada—History   Ca3; Shipwrecks   Wa10-ref
Ca3   1858–1879. Cds. by subj. Freq. add.

Victoria (B.C.) Gazette (newsp.). *In* British Columbia—Newspapers   Ca3

Victoria (B.C.) Times (newsp.). *In* Canada—History   Ca3; British Columbia—Newspapers   Ca3

Victorian Art. *See* Art, Victorian

Victorian Literature. *See* Romanticism   Tx31

Victrola Records. *See* Phonograph Records

Vigo Co. (Ind.)—Registers of Births, etc.
In35-gen   720 ent., tpd. shts. by subj. St. Mary of the Woods, Ind., village church records. Births, marriages & deaths.
In35-gen   4280 ent., tpd. shts. by name. Marriage records. 1818–1850.

Vincennes (Ind.)—History. *See* Indiana—History   In37

Vincennes (Ind.) Western Sun and General Advertiser (newsp.). *In* Vincennes (Ind.)—Newspapers   In22-Ind.

Vincennes (Ind.)—Newspapers
In22-Ind.   28,000 cds. by subj. Newsp. indexed: *Indiana gazette*, 1804–1806; *Western sun*, 1807–1827. No add.

Vincennes (Ind.) Indiana Gazette (newsp.). *In* Vincennes (Ind.)—Newspapers   In22-Ind.

VIOLIN MUSIC
 C32-art 2640 cds. by t. & comp. Bks. Occ. add.
 C43-mus 900 cds. by t. Bks. Freq. add.
 I68-art 400 cds. by comp. & t. Bks. Infreq. add.
 Mi6-mus 2640 cds. by comp., subj. & t. Bks. Occ. add.
 N35-mus 1000 cds. by auth. & t. Bks. & sht. mus. Freq add.

VIPERS. *See* SERPENTS

VIRGINIA
 Ky2 298 cds. by auth. Bks. & per. Freq. add.
 V2 50 cds., chron. Bk. indexed: Thomas Jefferson, *Notes on Virginia.* Infreq. add.
 V3 (1) 370 cds. by subj. Bks., newsp., pams. & per. Occ. add.
 V3 (2) 2845 cds. by subj. Newsp. indexed: *Danville register; Danville Bee.* Daily add.
 V8-ref 4560 cds. by subj. Bks., per. & newsp. Richmond & Va. Freq. add.

VIRGINIA—BIBLIOGRAPHY—IMPRINTS
 V2 3000 cds. by state, city & yr. Freq. add.

VIRGINIA—BIOGRAPHY
 V2 3000 cds. by name. Occ. add.

VIRGINIA—GENEALOGY. *See* GENEALOGY—VIRGINIA

VIRGINIA—REGISTERS OF BIRTHS, ETC.
 Ky7 Unest. cds. by co. & name. Va. marriages.

VIRGINIA—SOLDIERS. *See* U.S.—HISTORY—REVOLUTION—VIRGINIA

VIRGINIA. UNIVERSITY
 V2 50,000 cds. by subj. Per. & bks. Freq. add.

VIRGINIA EDUCATION ASSOCIATION
 Mn25 300 cds. by subj. Infreq. add.

VIRGINIA MAGAZINE OF HISTORY. *In* U.S.—HISTORY — REVOLUTION — VIRGINIA
 In35-gen

VIRGINIA POLYTECHNIC INSTITUTE—HISTORY
 V1 2400 ent., tpd. shts. by subj. Cur. add.

VIRGINIA SOLDIERS OF 1776 (bk.). *In* U.S. — HISTORY — REVOLUTION — VIRGINIA Ky7 (2)

VIRTUES, ABSTRACT. *See* CHARACTER

VIRUSES
 Nj61 250 cds. by auth. & t. Bks., per., pams. rpts., lectures, reprints. Freq. add.

VISUAL INSTRUCTION. *See* AUDIO—VISUAL AIDS

VITAL STATISTICS. *See* GENEALOGY; Name of loc., subdiv. CEMETERY RECORDS, CENSUS, NECROLOGY, REGISTERS OF BIRTHS.
 C67 300 cds. by subj. Bks., per. & pams. Freq. add.

VITAMINS
 Nj61 100 cds. by auth. & t. Bks., pams., per., lectures, reprints, rpts. Freq. add.

VOCAL MUSIC. *See* SONGS

VOCATIONS. *See also* BIOGRAPHY, VOCATIONAL; CIVIL SERVICE; FICTION, VOCATIONAL; List of Bibliographies, APPENDIX I
 C2 75 cds. by subj. Pams. Cur. add.
 C5 491 cds. by name of occup. Pams. Semi-yrly. add.
 C12 1316 cds. by auth. & subj. Bks., pams. & cat. Freq. add.
 C32-educ 1650 cds. by subj. Bks. & pams. Cur. add.
 C43-ref 2080 cds. by subj. Bks., pams., doc. & per. Freq. add.
 C49-j 1408 cds. by voc. Bks. Freq. add.
 C49-ref 2560 cds. by subj. Cur. add.
 C51 40p., tpd. shts. by voc. Bks. & leaflets. Infreq. add.
 C53 225 cds. by voc. Bks. & pams. Freq. add.
 Ct5 525 cds. by subj. Bks. & pams. Freq. add.
 D32-tech 400 cds. by subj. Bks. Freq. add.
 De1 800 cds. by subj. Bks., per. & pams. Occ. add.
 F2-r.a. 378 ent., tpd. shts. by voc. Bks. Yrly. add.
 G4-circ 1000 cds. by auth. Bks. & pams. Cur. add.
 I2 213 ent., tpd. shts. by subj. Occ. add.
 I13-r.a. 1075 cds. by voc. Bks., pams. & per. Freq. add.

I13-Wood. 5000 cds. by voc. Bks., pams. & per. Freq. add.
I18 3000 cds. by subj., t. & auth. Bks., per., pams. & newsp. Freq. add.
I21 2000 cds. by voc. Bks., pams. & per. Wkly. add.
I35 1600 cds. by subj. Bks., pams., per. & newsp. Cur. add.
I40 260p., tpd. shts. by voc. Bks. & pams. Occ. add.
I47 2000 cds. by subj. Bks., pams. & per. Freq. add.
I52 400 ent., tpd. shts. by voc. Bks., inc. biog. & fic. Yrly. add.
I53 100 cds. by voc. Pams. & bks. In proc.
I58 300 cds. by subj. Bks., pams. & per. Cur. add.
I62 900 cds. by subj. Bks., per. & pams. Freq. add.
I64 300 cds. by voc. Bks., per., pams. & monographs. Daily add.
I65-ref 300 cds. by voc. Bks. Freq. add.
I75 424 cds. by subj. Pams. Freq. add.
I79 1382 cds. by subj. Bks., pams. & per. Freq. add.
Ia18-ad 2000 ent., tpd. shts. by subj. Bks., per. & pams. Cur. add.
In33-ad 1463 cds. by subj. Bks. Cur. add.
M4-Kir. 1000 ent., tpd. shts. by voc. Bks., per. & pams. Freq. add.
M27-ref 1000 cds. by subj. Bks. Freq. add.
M28 400 cds. by voc. Pams. Freq. add.
Md2-bus 500 cds. by subj. Pams. Freq. add.
Me1 300 cds. by voc. Bks. Cur. add.
Mi6-circ 350 cds. by voc. Bks. & pams. Freq. add.
Mi13-ref Unest. cds. by voc. Bks., per., etc. Freq. add.
Mi17 337 cds. by voc. Bks., pams. & newsp. Freq. add.
Mi21-Cen. 500 ent., tpd. shts. by subj. Bks. Infreq. add.
Mi23 58 ent., tpd. shts. by subj. Bks. & pams. Freq. add.
Mn4 1150 cds. by voc. Bks., pams. & per. Freq. add.
Mn14-clip 420 cds. by subj. Newsp. & pams. Freq. add.

Mn14-Fran. 1700 cds. by voc. Bks. & pams. Freq. add.
Mn14-ref 2500 cds. by subj. Bks. & per. Cur. add.
Mo9 Unest. cds.
Mo15 773 cds. by subj. Bks. & pams.
N13 650 cds. by subj. Bks. Cur. add.
N22-r.a. 5000 cds. by subj. Bks., per. & pams. Cur. add.
N28-y.p. 2000 cds. by subj. Bks. & pams. Freq. add.
N35-Bronx 1000 cds. by voc. Bks. & pams. Freq. add.
N35-educ 100 cds. by subj. Bks. Cur. add.
N35-Morr. 1000 cds. by subj. Pams. Freq. add.
N46-educ 440 cds. by voc. Bks. & pams. Cur. add.
N53 300 ent., tpd. shts. by voc. Bks. & pams. Occ. add.
N60 1500 cds. by voc. Bks., pams. & per. Cur. add.
Nj5 325 cds. by voc. Bks., pams. & per. Freq. add.
Nj10 1000 cds. by subj. Bks., per & pams., etc. Freq. add.
Nj20 100 cds. by subj. Bks., per., & pams. Cur. add.
Nj64 240 cds. by voc. Bks., per. & pams. Mo. add.
Nj66 1100 cds. by subj. Bks. & pams. Freq. add.
Nj67-ref 2900 cds. by voc. Bks., per., pams., etc. Freq. add.
O1-r.a. 3960 cds. by subj. Bks. & pams. Cur. add.
O2 Unest. cds. by voc. & training course. Bks., per., pams, etc. Cur. add.
O5 Unest. cds. by subj. Bks.
O16-circ 600 cds. by subj. & auth. Bks. & pams. Cur. add.
O20-soc 2640 cds. by subj. Per. & newsp. Daily add.
O20-soc 10,560 cds. by voc. Bks. & pams. Cur. add.
O20-Ster. 585 ent., tpd. shts. by subj. Bks. & pams. No add.
O20-y.p. 4500 cds. by subj. Bks., per. & pams. Freq. add.
O26 2550 cds. by voc. Bks. & pams. Cur. add.
O29-hi. sch 400 cds. by subj. Bks., pams. & per. Cur. add.

O30 1900 cds. by subj. Bks. & per. Infreq. add.
O31 3400 cds. by auth. & subj. Bks., per., pams. & cat. Freq. add.
O37 600 cds. by subj. Bks., pams. & per. Cur. add.
O38 1125 cds. by subj. Bks. & pams. Cur. add.
O56-circ 2000 cds. by subj. Bks. Cur. add.
Or7-circ 500 cds. by voc. Pams. & per. Freq. add.
P12 95 cds. by subj. Bks., pams. & per. Infreq. add.
P18 300 cds. by voc. Bks. & pams. Cur. add.
P26 334 cds. by subj. Bks., pams. & per. Freq. add.
P39-Wyl. 511 cds. by subj. Bks., pams. & per. Cur. add.
P46 500 ent., tpd. shts. by voc. Bks. & pams. Freq. add.
P54-circ 560 cds. by subj. Bks., pams. & per. Freq. add.
Tx34 40 cds. by subj. Bks. Cur. add.
W20-McK. 1000 cds. by subj. Bks., per., pams. & newsp. Freq. add.
Wa10-par 1750 cds. by subj. Pams., bks. & per. Freq. add.
Wa14-circ 500 cds. by voc. Bks. No add.

VOCATIONS—SCHOOLS
N46-educ 50 cds. by name of course. Bks. Cur. add.

VOCATIONS—STORIES, JUVENILE
Ct2-j 200 ent., tpd. shts. by subj. Bks. Cur. add.

VOCATIONS—WOMEN
Me1 100 cds. by voc. Bks. Cur. add.

VOCATIONS, TECHNICAL
N8-tech 2640 cds. by subj. Bks. Freq. add.

VOICE OF THE NEGRO (per.). *In* NEGROES—PERIODICALS D6
D6 1904–1907. Cds. by auth., t. & subj. Infreq. add.

VOYAGES. *See* TRAVEL

WAGES
Nj52 1000 cds. by subj. Bks., per. & pams. Freq. add.

WAKEFIELD (MASS.)
M28 60 ent., tpd. shts. by class. Bks., per., pams. & newsp. Occ. add.

WALKER, DUGALD STEWART—DRAWINGS AND ENGRAVINGS
V7 102 cds., chron. Infreq. add.

WALKILL RIVER VALLEY (N.Y.)
N58 3650 ent., tpd. shts. by subj. Bk. indexed: William C. Hart, *Historic Walkill and Hudson river valleys.* In proc.

WALL STREET JOURNAL. *See also in* BUSINESS CONDITIONS P36-Lipp
Nj60-Pliny v. 66, 1915–date. Cds. by subj. Daily add.

WAR MEDICINE
N34a 1500 cds. by subj., chron. Per. Daily add.

WAR POSTERS. *See* POSTERS, WAR

WARREN CO. (KY.)—LAW. *See* LAW—KENTUCKY Ky2

WARREN CO. (KY.)—REGISTERS OF BIRTHS, ETC.
Ky2 126p., tpd. shts. by name, chron. Marriage register, 1797–1857. No add.
Ky2 111p., tpd. shts. by name. Marriage register, 1797–1857. Men's names. No add.

WARREN CO. (KY.)—REGISTER OF BIRTHS, ETC.
Ky2 112p., tpd. shts. by name. Marriage register, 1797–1857. Women's names. No add.
Ky2 112p., tpd. shts. by name chron. Marriage register, 1857–1917.

WARREN CO. (KY.)—WILLS
Ky2 6p., tpd. shts. by name. Will bk., 1821–1852. No add.
Ky2 47p., tpd. shts. by name. Will bk. "A," 1787–1814. No add.

WARS. *See also* Names of wars; U.S.—HISTORY, subdiv. names of wars
Mi13 1000 cds. by auth., t. & subj. Bks. David Gage Joyce war library. Freq. add.

WASHINGTON, GEORGE. *See also* List of Bibliographies, APPENDIX I
Ky2 92 cds. by auth. Bks. & per. Freq. add.
Mn11 Unest. ent., tpd. shts. by subj. Bks. & per. Freq. add.
P39-ref 2000 cds. by subj. Per. Per. indexed: *National historical magazine,* 1892–1931.

WASHINGTON (STATE)
Wa10-ref   1500 ent., tpd. shts. by subj. Bk. indexed: Herbert Hunt, *Washington, west of the Cascades.* No add.

WASHINGTON (STATE)—AUTHORS. See AUTHORS—WASHINGTON (STATE)

WASHINGTON (STATE)—CITIES AND TOWNS
Wa10-mun. ref   1000 cds. by subj. Newsp., pams., corr. & per. Occ. add.
Wa10-ref   4700 cds. by subj. Newsp., per. & bks. Freq. add.

WASHINGTON (STATE)—DIRECTORIES
Wa10-tech   630 cds. by subj. Doc. & rpts. Assoc. membership lists, radio stations, C.C.C. camps. Cur. add.

WASHINGTON (STATE)—DOCUMENTS
Wa13-educ   1500 cds. by subj., auth. & t. Cur. add.

WASHINGTON (STATE)—GEOLOGY. See GEOLOGY—WASHINGTON (STATE)

WASHINGTON (STATE)—HISTORY
Wa7   Unest. ent., tpd. shts. by subj. Bk. indexed: Lloyd Spencer and Lancaster Pollard, *A history of the state of Washington,* v. 1.
Wa14-ref   300 cds. by subj. Bks., per. & newsp. Tacoma & Wash. "firsts." Freq. add.

WASHINGTON (STATE)—INDIANS. See INDIANS—WASHINGTON (STATE)

WASHINGTON (STATE)—MINING AND METALLURGY. See MINING AND METALLURGY—NORTHWEST   Wa10-tech

WASHINGTON (STATE)—OFFICIALS AND EMPLOYEES
Wa7   3000 cds. by name. Legis. manuals, etc. Biennial add.

WASHINGTON (STATE)—SOCIETIES AND CLUBS
Wa10-ref   2400 cds. by name. Newsp. City, co. & state organiz. Freq. add.

WASHINGTON UNIVERSITY—PUBLICATIONS
Wa11-ref   6300 cds. by name. Bks. & per. Wash. & alumni authors. Cur. add.

WASHINGTON UNIVERSITY—PUBLICATIONS, FACULTY
Wa11-ref   2500 ent., tpd. shts. & cds. Fac. archives. Cur. add.

WASHINGTON EDUCATION JOURNAL
Wa10-par   v. 1, 1921–date. Cds. by subj. Cur. add.

WASHINGTON WEST OF THE CASCADES (bk.). *In* WASHINGTON (STATE)   Wa10-ref

WASHTENAW CO. (MICH.)—SOCIETIES AND CLUBS
Mi2   400 cds. by name. Ann Arbor & Washtenaw co. clubs. Freq. add.

WATCHES. See CLOCKS AND WATCHES

WATER
Nj61   50 cds. by auth. & t. Bks., per. & pams. Freq. add.

WATERWAYS
N8-tech   1500 cds. by subj. U.S. Eng. dept. pub. Freq. add.

WAUKEGAN (ILL.)—HISTORY
I76   500 cds. by subj. & name. Bks., pams. & newsp. Freq. add.

WAUKEGAN (ILL.)—SOCIETIES AND CLUBS
I76   160 cds. by name of organiz. Newsp. & programs. Yrly. add.

WAVERLEY COLLECTION OF RARE AND BEAUTIFUL MUSIC (bk.). *In* MUSIC   Nj15

WAYNESBORO (PA.)—HISTORY
P52   125 cds. by subj. Bks., pams., newsp. & pic. Freq. add.

WEATHER. See CLIMATOLOGY

WEDDING MUSIC. See MUSIC, WEDDING

WEDDINGS. See MARRIAGE CUSTOMS AND RITES

WELLESLEY COLLEGE—PUBLICATIONS
M30   2250 cds. by auth. Bks., pams., per. & newsp. Cur. add.

WERNER'S READINGS AND RECITATIONS (bk.). *In* READINGS AND RECITATIONS
C6-ref, In23-ref, Mo3-N.E., Mo3-Wash., Nb16, P4 (2)

WESLEYAN COLLEGE (GA.)—BIOGRAPHY
G17   1000 cds. by name. Coll. cat. since 1839 & bks. Fac. & trustees index. No add.

WEST—BIBLIOGRAPHY—IMPRINTS. See also List of Bibliographies, APPENDIX I
Me3   813 ent., tpd. shts., chron. Project of S.W. microfilm inc. early W. Amer. Occ. add.

WEST—CHARACTERS (IN LITERATURE)
C62-ref 500 cds. by name. Bks., newsp. & per. Occ. add.

WEST—HISTORY
C05-W. hist 23,350 cds. by subj. Bks., pams. Per. & newsp. Freq. add.

WEST—MAPS, HISTORICAL. *See* MAPS, HISTORICAL—WEST

WEST—PERIODICALS
Wa2 4000 cds. by subj., chron. Per. indexed: *Consumer's digest; Engineering and mining jl.; Pacific motor boat; Sunset; West coast lumberman.* Cur. add.

WEST—PICTURES. *See* PICTURES—WEST

WEST—PORTRAITS. *See* PORTRAITS—WEST

WEST COAST LUMBERMAN (per.) *In* WEST—PERIODICALS **Wa2**

WEST VIRGINIA—HISTORY
Wv2 Unest. cds. by subj. Bk. indexed: *West Virginia blue Book,* 1923–date. Freq. add.
Wv4-ref 1100 cds. by subj. Per. Freq. add.

WEST VIRGINIA BLUE BOOK. *In* WEST VIRGINIA—HISTORY **Wv2**

WEST VIRGINIA REVIEW
Wv1 v. 1. Cds. by auth., t. & subj. In proc.
Wv2 1924–date. Cds. by subj. Freq. add.

WESTCHESTER CO. (N.Y.)—BIOGRAPHY
N60 800 cds. by name. Newsp. Cur. add.

WESTCHESTER CO. (N.Y.)—HISTORY
N60 1000 cds. by subj. Bks., pams. & newsp. Per. indexed: *Westchester soc. hist. soc. Quarterly bulletin.* Westchester co. & White Plains. Freq. add.

WESTCHESTER CO. (N.Y.)—SOCIETIES AND CLUBS
N60 1200 cds. by name of organiz. Westchester co. & White Plains organiz. Daily add.

WESTCHESTER CO. HISTORICAL SOCIETY. QUARTERLY BULLETIN. *In* WESTCHESTER CO. (N.Y.)—HISTORY **N60**
N49 392 cds. by subj. Q. add.

WESTERN CITY (per.)
Or2 1938, 1939–date. Tpd. shts. & cds. Mo. add.

WESTERN PENNSYLVANIA ARCHITECTURAL SURVEY (per.)
P39-ref. art 2200 cds. by co. & subj. Arch. of 22 W. cos., inc. phot. No add.

WESTERN PENNSYLVANIA HISTORICAL MAGAZINE
P39-ref.-Pa. v. 1-19, 1918–1936. Cds. by auth., t. & subj. Cur. add.

WESTERN RESERVE UNIVERSITY—PUBLICATIONS, FACULTY
O25-ref 10,000 cds. by auth. Bks. & per. Yrly. add.

WESTERN SPY (newsp.). *In* GENEALOGY **O17**

WESTERN STORIES. *See also* NORTHERN STORIES **N44-ad**
K8-circ 526 ent., tpd. shts. by auth. Bks. W. & N. story index. Yrly. add.
Mi6-Red. 200 ent., tpd. shts. by auth. Bks. Mo. add.
Mi6-Rich. 250 ent., tpd. shts. by auth. Bks. W. & N.W. stories. Freq. add.
Nj21 380 ent., tpd. shts. by auth. Adventure in W. & N.W. Freq. add.
Nj58 248 cds. by auth. Freq. add.

WESTERN STORIES, JUVENILE
Nj19-j 50 ent., tpd. shts. by auth. J. fic., 4th grade up. Cur. add.

WESTERN WASHINGTON EXPERIMENT STATION BULLETIN
Wa14-ref 700 cds. by subj. Buls. to 1925. No add.

WESTMORELAND CO. (PA.)—PAMPHLETS
P15 60 ent., tpd. shts. by no. No add.

WESTWAYS (per.). *In* CALIFORNIA **C8-ref**
C6-ref 1934–date. Cds. by subj. Cur. add.
C32-per 1934–1938. Cds. by subj. No add.
C51 1922–date. Cds. by auth., subj. & t. Cur. add.
C52 1928–1933. Cds. by auth. & subj. No add.
C61-br 1929–1936. Cds. by subj. No add.
C63 1928–date. Cds. by auth., subj. & t. Cur. add.

WHEN THE WHIPPOORWILL (bk.). *In* SHORT STORIES **Tx12**

WHIPPANY (N.Y.)—REGISTERS OF BIRTHS, ETC.
Nj36 35p., tpd. shts. by name. Church members, marriages & baptisms. Pastorate of Rev. Jacob Green, & to settlement of Rev. Aaron Condit, 1746–1796. No add.

WHITE-HALL (ILL.) REGISTER AND REPUBLICAN (newsp.)
I78 1868–date. Cds. by names of people, bus. firms & events. Cur. add.

WHITE HOUSE CONFERENCE ON CHILD HEALTH (bk.). *In* CHILD STUDY **Ia14-med**

WHITE PLAINS (N.Y.)—HISTORY. *In* WESTCHESTER Co. (N.Y.)—HISTORY **N60**

WHITE PLAINS (N.Y.)—SOCIETIES AND CLUBS. *In* WESTCHESTER Co. (N.Y.)—SOCIETIES AND CLUBS **N60**

WHITE PLAINS (N.Y.) DAILY REPORTER (newsp.)
N60 600 cds. by subj. Daily add.

WHITMAN, WALT
Nj7-ad 41 ent., tpd. shts. by auth. Bks. Freq. add.
Nj7-Coop. 30 ent., tpd. shts. by auth. & type of work. Bks. Cur. add.
Nj7-Fair. 13 ent., tpd. shts. by subj. Bks. Infreq. add.

WHITTIER, JOHN GREENLEAF
M19 2000 cds. by subj., chron. Bks., per. & pams. Mat. by & about Whittier. Freq. add.

WHITTIER, JOHN GREENLEAF—SNOWBOUND
In12 5p., tpd. shts. by subj. Pams., bks., pic. & per. Background mat. No add.

WICHITA (KANS.)
K20 8350 cds. by subj. Newsp. In proc.

WICHITA (KANS.)—HISTORY
K20-ref 6200 cds. by subj. Newsp. Freq. add.

WIGGIN, KATE DOUGLAS. *In* AUTOGRAPHS **Me3**

WILCOX, ELLA WHEELER—WORKS
C32-lit 272p., tpd. shts., by 1st line & t. Bks. Occ. add.
I13-ref 1200 cds. by t. & 1st line. Bks. & per. Infreq. add.

WILCOX Co. (ALA.)—CENSUS
A1 700 cds. by name of head of family. 1820 Federal cens. No add.

WILD LIFE—CONSERVATION
G11 100 cds. by t. Bks., per. etc. Wildlife mgt. In freq. add.

WILDFLOWERS—PICTURES. *See* PICTURES—WILDFLOWERS

WILKES-BARRE (PA.)—AUTHORS. *See* AUTHORS—WILKES-BARRE (PA.)

WILKINSON, JAMES
Ky2 111 cds. by auth. Bks. & per. Freq. add.

WILLIAMSON Co. (ILL.)—CEMETERY RECORDS
I55 2000 cds. by subj. Oldest records from 1824. Freq. add.

WILLIAMSON Co. (ILL.)—EUROPEAN WAR, 1914–1918. *See* EUROPEAN WAR, 1914–1918—WILLIAMSON Co. (ILL.)

WILLIAMSON Co. (ILL.)—GENEALOGY. *See* GENEALOGY—WILLIAMSON Co. (ILL.)

WILLIAMSON Co. (ILL.)—HISTORY
I55 (1) 450 ent. by name. Centennial map, 1839–1939. No add.
I55 (2) 27p., tpd. shts. by subj. Bk. indexed: Milo Erwin, *History of Williamson co., Illinois.* No add.
I55 (3) 18p., tpd. shts. by subj. Bk. indexed: J. P. Wilcox, *Historical souvenir of Williamson co., Illinois.* No add.

WILLIAMSON Co. (ILL.)—REGISTERS OF BIRTHS, ETC.
I55 Several thousand ent., tpd. shts. by name. Court house records, 1839–1859. Marriage records of 1st 20 yrs. of co. In proc.
I55 Several thousand cds. by subj. First members of Christian church, from 1865. Occ. add.

WILLIAMSPORT (PA.)—HISTORY
P56 1500 cds. by subj. Pams., newsp., etc. Freq. add.

WILSON LIBRARY BULLETIN. *In* AUTHORS **C88, Ia20, M24, N4, O1-E, O7, O20-Euc. 100th, O60, P27a**; BIBLIOGRAPHIES **C14**; BIOGRAPHY **Mn14-Cam., Mn23-Mer., Nb2, O20-Coll., P36-ref, Wv2**; CHILDREN'S LITERATURE—BIOGRAPHY **Mo13-Cab.**

Wings (per.). *In* Authors N4, O60;
Biography C49-ref

Winnebago Indians. *See* Indians—Winnebago

Winnetka (Ill.)—History
I80   170 cds. by auth., t. & subj. Bks., newsp., pic., letters, etc. Cur. add.

Wisconsin
W3   410 cds. by subj. Bks. & pams. Freq. add.
W20-ad   2530 cds. by subj. Bks. & per. Occ. add.
W22-ad   1109 cds. by subj. Bks., pams. & per. Cur. add.

Wisconsin—Agriculture. *See* Agriculture—Wisconsin

Wisconsin—Biography
W10-ref   126,380 cds. by name. Bks., per. & newsp. Cur. add.

Wisconsin—Census
W10-ref   1,045,760 cds. by co. & per., chron. Cens., 1820–1870. No add.

Wisconsin—Documents
W13   5280 cds. by auth. Rpts., etc. Freq. add.
W13   7260 cds. by subj. Assembly & senate jls., 1848–1923. No add.

Wisconsin—History
W19   7920 cds. by auth., t. & subj. Per. indexed: *Wisconsin archaeologist: Wisconsin blue books, Wisconsin magazine, Wisconsin magazine of history, Fox river valley magazine; Wisconsin state historical society collections & proceedings, Green Bay historical bulletin.*

Wisconsin—Law. *See* Law—Wisconsin

Wisconsin—Legislation
W13   500 cds. by subj. Wisc. legis. Requests for Wisc. drafting service, 1927–date. Cur. add.
W13   500 cds. by subj. Wisc. legis. precedents; points of order in parliamentary proc. Biennial add.

Wisconsin Archaeologist (per.)
W11   1923–1932. Cds. by subj. No add.

Wisconsin Blue Books. *In* Wisconsin—History W19
W1   1923–1940. Cds. by subj. Yrly. add.
W20-Frank.   1917–1933. Cds. by subj. Infreq. add.

Wisconsin Magazine. *In* Wisconsin—History W19
W1   v. 4–9, 1926–1932. Cds. by subj. No add.
W9   v. 1–9, 1923–1932. Tpd. shts. by auth. & subj. No add.
W11   Cds. by subj. No add.
W23   v. 1–9, 1923–1932. Tpd. shts. by auth. & subj. No add.

Wisconsin Magazine of History. *See also in* Wisconsin—History W19
W11   v. 9, 1926–date. Cds. by subj. Q. add.

Wisconsin Memorial Day Annual
W19   1921–1935. Cds. by auth., t. & subj. No add.

Wisconsin State Historical Society Collections and Proceedings. *In* Wisconsin—History W19

Wit and Humor. *See* Humorous Stories

Wit and Humor of America (bk.)
T1-circ   450 cds. by t. No add.

Women
In31   100 ent. by subj. & name. Per. & newsp. Freq. add.
Wa14-ref   500 cds. by subj. Bks., pams. & per. Freq. add.

Women, Famous—Tennessee
T3-Mc.   100 cds. by name. Bks., per. & newsp. Occ. add.

Women, Pioneer
In35-gen   64 ent., tpd. shts. by name. Bk. indexed: Elizabeth Ellet, *Pioneer women of the west.* No add.

Wood
G11   50 cds. by t. Bks., per. & pams. Occ. add.

Wood Cuts. *See* Wood Engravings

Wood Engravings
P39-ref. art   275 cds. by art. Per. indexed: *Cornhill magazine*, 1860–1875, *Once a week*, 1859–1865. Cur. add.

Wood Preservation
Nj52   1000 cds. by subj. Bks., per. & pams. Freq. add.

Worcester (Mass.)
M32   600 cds. by subj. Newsp. Occ. add.

Worcester (Mass.)—Authors. *See* Authors—Worcester (Mass.)

WORCESTER (MASS.)—BIOGRAPHY
M32   605p., tpd. shts. by name. Bks. No add.

WORCESTER MAGAZINE
M32   1500 cds. by auth. & subj. No add.

WORKMEN'S COMPENSATION. See MEDICAL JURISPRUDENCE   Ia7

WORLD AFFAIRS BOOKS. In PAMPHLETS O59

WORLD WARS. See EUROPEAN WAR, 1914–1918; EUROPEAN WAR, 1939–1945

WORLD WIDE (per.). In CANADA—PERIODICALS   Ca13-per

WRITERS. See AUTHORS

WYOMING VALLEY (PA.)—HISTORY
P54-ref   65 cds. by name of per. Per. Cur. add.

YACHTS AND YACHTING—PHOTOGRAPHS
V5   162 cds. by subj. Freq. add.

YEARBOOKS. See also PERIODICALS   O20-bus
K9-ref   50 cds. by name. Infreq. add.

YORK CO. (PA.)—HISTORY
P57   100,000 ent., tpd. shts. by name of pers., place & subj. Hist. of York & Adams co. Occ. add.

YORK CO. (PA.)—REGISTERS OF BIRTHS, ETC.
P57   45,000 ent., tpd. shts. by surname for each church. Births, baptisms, marriages, burials, etc. Cur. add.
P57   8000 cds. by name. Newsp. Marriages & deaths, 1777–1850. Infreq. add.

YOUNG PEOPLE'S LITERATURE. See also FICTION   O1-W, O1-y.p.; FICTION, HISTORICAL   Ct5; List of Bibliographies, APPENDIX I
C18-r.a.   1200 cds. by subj. Bks.-fic. Cur. add.
C18-r.a.   1600 cds. by subj. Bks.-non-fic. Cur. add.
C32-ad   1320 cds. by subj. & auth. Fic. & non-fic. Freq. add.

C49-inf   2048 cds. by subj. Bks. Cur. add.
C49-j   1088 cds. by auth. Bks., intermediate. Cur. add.
Ca14   135 cds. by subj. Bks. Freq. add.
N28-y.p.   1500 cds. by subj. Bks., per. & pams. Freq. add.
N35-sch   1300 ent., tpd. shts. by auth. Per. indexed: *N.Y. public library bulletin* (Books for young people) supp. Yrly. add.
Nb14-r.a.   700 cds. by class. Bks. Freq. add.
Nj50-educ   1450 cds. by class. Bks. Freq. add.
O31   2087 cds. by auth. & subj. Bks. Freq. add.
O56-circ   3000 cds. by subj. Bks. Freq. add.
P54-circ   620 cds. by subj. Bks. Freq. add.

YOUNG PEOPLE'S LITERATURE—BOOK REVIEWS. See List of Bibliographies, APPENDIX I

YOUNG PEOPLE'S LITERATURE—FOREIGN LANGUAGES
Mi6-for   100 cds. by lang. & auth. Bks. Infreq. add.

YOUNGSTOWN (O.) VINDICATOR (newsp.)
O61-ref   1889–1940. Tpd. shts. by subj. In proc. Cur. add.

YOUTH
O20-S. Brook.   75 cds. by country. Per. Infreq. add.
O20-Un.   30 cds. by auth. & t. Bks. & pams. Cur. add.

YOUTH ORGANIZATIONS. See also CHICAGO—YOUTH ORGANIZATIONS
I13-Wood.   200 cds. by organiz. Freq. add.

ZOOLOGY
D14   300,000 cds. by auth., chron. by genera & species. Bks. & per. Parasitology. Cur. add.
Vt3   400 cds. by subj. Bks., per. & pams. U.S. govt. dept. rpts. Cur. add.

ZOOLOGY—PICTURES. See PICTURES—ZOOLOGY

APPENDIX I

List of Bibliographies

ABBREVIATIONS
I43-ref 200 cds. by auth. Bks. Abbrev. not in standard per. indexes nor in Granger. Freq. add.

ADULT EDUCATION
O16-circ 950 cds. by auth., t. & subj. Pams. Freq. add.

ADVENTURE STORIES
K8-circ 114 cds. by auth. Bks. Cur. add.
Mi6-Fenk. 40 cds. by auth. Fic. Cur. add.
I13-Hild. 5p., tpd. shts. by auth. Bks. Yrly. add.

AGRICULTURAL CHEMISTRY
Nj61 100 cds. by auth. & t. Bks., per., bul. Freq. add.

AGRICULTURE—PUERTO RICO
G11 10 cds. by t. Bks., per. & pams. Forestry & agric. in P.R. Infreq. add.

ALABAMA—OFFICIALS AND EMPLOYEES
A1 200,000 cds. by name. Appts. made by Gov. from 1818–1868. No add.

ALAMEDA (CALIF.)—AUTHORS. *See* AUTHORS—ALAMEDA (CALIF.)

ALAMEDA Co. (CALIF.)—DOCUMENTS
C43-ref 600 cds. by auth. Off. pub. of Oakland, Alameda co. & E. Bay mun. utilities district. Freq. add.

ALGAE
Nj61 20 cds. by auth. & t. Bks., per. & pams.

AMERICAN IMPRINTS
Ct8 100,000 cds. by auth. Early Amer. imprints (through 1876) in Conn. Occ. add.
N55 5600 cds. by auth. Bks. Early Amer. imprints in lib. Infreq. add.
Nj40 30,000 cds. by auth. Bks., per. & pams to 1876. Occ. add.

Nj58 16,900 cds. by auth., t. & subj. Bks. & per. Tyler lib. Freq. add.
Nj65 150 cds. by subj. Bks. Imprints before 1875. No add.
O17 3500 cds. by state, place & date. Occ. add.

AMERICAN LITERATURE
O2 Unest. ent., tpd. shts. by auth. Amer. lit., 1860–1888. In proc.
O2 225p., tpd. shts. by auth. Bks. Amer. lit., 1820–1860. Yrly. add.

ANIMAL STORIES
Nj21 85 ent., tpd. shts. by auth. Freq. add.

ANIMAL STORIES, JUVENILE
Mi6-Rich. 225 ent., tpd. shts. by auth. Freq. add.
Nj19-j 75 ent., tpd. shts. by auth. Cur. add.

ANIMALS
I72-j 75 cds. by auth. No add.
Mi6-Red. 200 ent., tpd. shts. by auth. Mo. add.
Wa8a 60 ent., tpd. shts. by class. Bks. Cur. add.

ARCHITECTURE
I11-Burn. (1) 400 cds. by class. Bks. on arch., lands. arch., city planning. Cur. add.
I11-Burn. (2) 125 cds. by auth. Bks. on arch. & lands. arch. in Amer. before 1895. Freq. add.
I11-Burn. (3) 200 cds. by class. Bks. Fontaine coll.: bks. used by Percier & Fontaine when they designed bldgs. for Napoleon. No add.
I11-Burn. (4) 600 cds. by class & date. Bks. on arch., lands. arch., city planning pub. before 1850. Cur. add.
N47-Mem. 131 cds. by date of pub. & auth. Arch. source bks., U.S. imprints to 1900 & for. rel. pub. in lib. Occ. add.

ARCHITECTURE—CHICAGO
I13-circ   18 ent., tpd. shts. by auth. Bks. Occ. add.

ARCHITECTURE, DOMESTIC
Tx5   Unest. ent., tpd. shts. by subj. Pams. & newsp. Small houses. Freq. add.

ARCHITECTURE, ENGLISH
C73-art   Unest. cds. by co., city & houses. Per., engravings, phot., reprod. English topography & arch. Cur. add.

ART
De1   Unest. ent., tpd. shts. by auth. & subj. Bks., per., pams., etc. Cur. add.
K20-ref   295p., tpd. shts. by country, art., subj. & t. Bks. & per. Modern art. No add.
M19   12,850 cds. by auth., subj. & t. Bks. & per. Freq. add.
N35-ref. art   18,000 cds. by auth. Art bks. in 10 art lib. in greater N.Y. city. Bks. Cur. add.
N35-Tre.   3960 cds. by class. Bks. Freq. add.
N35-Tre.   500 cds. by class. Bks. Art ref. bks. Freq. add.
Nj58   2100 cds. by auth., t. & subj. Bks. & per. Freq. add.
O23   Unest. cds. by auth. Bks. & per. Art & arch. Infreq. add.
Wa10-art   200 cds. by name of press & auth. Private press art bks. Cur. add.
Wa15   1787 cds. by auth., subj. & t. Bks. & pams. Art, archaeol. & rel. biog. Freq. add.

ART—BIBLIOGRAPHIES
N46-art   450 cds. by subj. & auth. Occ. add.

ART—CATALOGS
C73-art. ref   9240 cds. by owner. Christie & Sotheby sales of paintings, 1870–date. Cur. add.

ART—PHOTOGRAPHS
C73-art. ref   1500 cds. by art. & country. Braun coll. of phot. of paintings, sculp., arch., etc.

ART—SOUTH AMERICA
I5-ref   81 ent., tpd. shts. by auth. & art. Bks. & per. Occ. add.

ART, MEXICAN
Tx30   37 ent., tpd. shts. by auth. & t. Bks. & per. No add.

ART OBJECTS
N55   400 cds. by auth., t. & subj. Occ. add.
Nj46   Unest. cds. by subj. Occ. add.

ARTHUR, KING
I26   1586 ent., tpd. shts. Occ. add.

ARTISTS
T1-ref   800 ent., tpd. shts. by subj. Bks. Freq. add.

ATLANTA (GA.)—TRANSLATORS
G4-ref   250 cds. by subj. Pams., etc. Research workers & tr. Freq. add.

AUDIO-VISUAL AIDS
In12   350 ent., tpd. shts. by subj. Maps, charts, posters, pic., etc. Illus. mat. Freq. add.
Nj17   128 ent., tpd. shts. by subj. Bks. & per. Freq. add.

AUDUBON, JOHN JAMES
Ky2   46 cds. by auth. Bks. & per. Freq. add.
Ky8   31 cds. by auth. Bks. Freq. add.

AUTHORS—ALAMEDA (CALIF.)
C1   10 cds. by name. Freq. add.

AUTHORS—CHICAGO
I13-circ   43 ent., tpd. shts. by auth. Non-fic. Occ. add.
I13-circ   107 ent., tpd. shts. by auth. Fic. Occ. add.

AUTHORS—DELAWARE
De1   60 ent., tpd. shts. by auth. No add.

AUTHORS—MINNESOTA
Mn21-cat   1500 cds. by auth. Freq. add.

AUTHORS—NORTH DAKOTA
Nd3   33 cds. by auth. Bks., per. & pams. Cur. add.

AUTHORS, CATHOLIC
Nb14-r.a.   500 cds. by class. Bks. Freq. add.

AVIATION STORIES, JUVENILE
K14   22 cds. by auth. Bks. Infreq. add.
Tx3   39 ent., tpd. shts. by class. Bks. Freq. add.

BEREA (Ky.)
Ky1 400 cds. by auth. Bks., pams., per., leaflets, programs, etc. Freq. add.

BERGEN Co. (N.J.)—HISTORIC HOUSES
Nj21 32 ent., tpd. shts. by name of house. Hist. houses of Hackensack & Bergen co., N.J. Freq. add.

BERYLLIUM
Co9 100 ent., tpd. shts. by auth. Bks. & per. No add.

BIBLIOGRAPHIE EGYPTOLOGIQUE
M11-Egypt. Unest. cds. by auth., t. & subj. Egyptian bibl. since 1936. Cur. add.

BIBLIOGRAPHIES
Ca13-lib. sch 179 cds. by subj. Term projects of sch. Yrly. add.
I43-med 200 ent., tpd. shts. by subj. Per. Occ. add.
N59 50 ent. by subj. Infreq. add.
Or5-tech Unest. ent. by subj. Bks. & per. Freq. add.

BIBLIOGRAPHY—FIRST EDITIONS
N22-ref 500 cds. by auth. Bks. Infreq. add.
W2 158 cds. by auth. & t. Bks. Occ. add.

BIOGRAPHY
Ct15 140 cds. by auth. Bks. Autobiog. Freq. add.
I58 800 cds. by auth. Bks. & per. Freq. add.
Wv3 97 cds. by t. Bks.

BOOK RARITIES. *See also* AMERICAN IMPRINTS; BIBLIOGRAPHY—FIRST EDITIONS; BOOKS, PICTORIAL; INCUNABULA
Ca4 102 cds. by auth. Bks. & mss. Occ. add.
G16 200 cds. by auth. & t. Bks. pub. from 1740 to 1900. No add.
I26-rare 2500 cds. by auth. 16th cent. bks. Freq. add.
K10-cat 1000 cds. chron. by auth. Bks. pub. before 1830. Occ. add.
Me3 1525 cds. by subj. James Bowdoin coll.: bks. pub. prior to 1800. No add.
N8-ref 220 ent., tpd. shts. by t. Bks. & mss. Infreq. add.
N35-ref. res 211,000 cds. by place of imprint, chron. Amer. & for. imp. & unusual imprints, with emphasis on beginnings of print. Cur. add.

N45b 2050 cds. by class., chron. Bks. printed before 1801. Freq. add.
Nd3 Unest. cds. by date of bk. Bks., 1754–1894. No add.
O20-ref 1320 cds. by auth. & subj. Dealers' cat. & other sources of prices. Cur. add.
P54-ref 202 cds. by auth. Rare & out-of-print bks. in dealers' cat. Occ. add.

BOOK RARITIES—BOTANY
P36-bot 150 cds. by auth. Herbals, 1st ed., incunabula, pre-Linnean bks., out-of-print bks. Occ. add.

BOOK RARITIES—SCIENCE
I43-med 5000 cds. by auth. Amer. & for. bk. cat. Rare & old med. & sci. bks. Freq. add.

BOOK RARITIES, ENGLISH
I26 1100 ent., tpd. shts. by auth. English bks. & bks. print. in England before 1641, in lib.; supp. to record in Short t. cat. Infreq. add.

BOOK STORES
C44 25 cds. by name & loc. Book stores specializing in cook bks. Infreq. add.

BOOKS, FILMED
C32-fic 8580 cds. by mot. pic. t. No add.
I13-circ 575 cds. by mot. pic. t. Bks. Freq. add.
I13-Tild. 61 cds. by auth. Bks. Occ. add.
Ia12 170 ent., tpd. shts. by t. of bk. Bks. Infreq. add.
Ia18-ad 500 ent., tpd. shts. by auth. Bks. Occ. add.
Mn11 Unest. ent., tpd. shts. by name. Freq. add.
Mo7 150 cds. by auth. & t. Infreq. add.
Mo13-Soul. 210 cds. by auth. Freq. add.
N46-fic 300 cds. by mot. pic. t. Per. Semi-mo. add.
Nj31 150 cds. by mot. pic. t. & bk. Cur. add.
Nj58 220 cds. by mot. pic. t. Bks. Occ. add.
O20-Coll. 200 cds. by t. of bk. Bks. Occ. add.
O20-S. 350 cds. by mot. pic. t., bk. auth. & t. Bks. Freq. add.

BOOKS, ILLUSTRATED. *See* BOOKS, PICTORIAL

BOOKS, PICTORIAL
N35-ref. print   4500 cds. by name of country. Bks. Cur. add.

BOOKS, RARE. *See* BOOK RARITIES

BOOKS AND READING
M14   200 cds. by auth. & subj. Bks., pams. & per. Freq. add.

BOOKS AND READING—COLLEGES
Tx30   113 ent., tpd. shts. by subj. Bks., per. & pams. Pub. affairs for coll. students. No add.
Tx30   111 ent., tpd. shts. by subj. Bks. & per. List for coll. freshman. No add.

BOOKS AND READING—FOREIGN-BORN READING
Ct5   Unest. cds. Bks. in English. In proc.

BOOKS AND READING—HIGH SCHOOLS
G15a-j   1320 cds. by auth. Bks. Cur. add.
I41   92 ent., tpd. shts. by auth. Bks. Second-yr. English list. No add.
I41   327 ent., tpd. shts. by auth. & period. Bks. Novels for senior Eng. No add.
I79   110 ent., tpd. shts. by auth. Bks. Cur. add.
Ky8   375 ent., tpd. shts. by grade. Infreq. add.
Mi6-Mont.   320 cds. by subj. Bks. Freq. add.
N22-circ   150 cds. by auth. Bks. Infreq. add.
N35-Cath.   175 ent., tpd. shts. by t. Bks. Infreq. add.
N35-Cath.   200 cds. by t. Bks. Infreq. add.
O29-Elec.   250 cds. by class. Bks. Cur. add.

BOOKS AND READING—HOSPITAL READING
K11   Unest. cds. by auth. & t. Freq. add.
Mi31-H. Kief.   800 cds. by auth. Bks. Cur. add.

BOOKS AND READING—INSPIRATIONAL READING
I44   18 cds. by subj. Bks. Freq. add.

BOOKS AND READING—INTERNATIONAL MIND ALCOVE
Nb2   93 ent., tpd. shts. by auth. Infreq. add.

BOOKS AND READING—LENTEN READING
I44   47 ent., tpd. shts. by subj. Bks. Yrly. add.

BOOKS AND READING—MISSIONARY READING
O20-Coll.   250 cds. by t. World friendship bks. Infreq. add.

BOOKS AND READING—OUT-OF-PRINT BOOKS
Ct2-circ   698 cds. by auth. Freq. add.

BOOKS AND READING—OUT-OF-PRINT BOOKS, JUVENILE
Ct2-j   675 cds. by auth. Bks. Occ. add.

BOOKS AND READING—READABLE BOOKS
N22-r.a.   8000 cds. by subj. & auth. Bks. Cur. add.

BOOKS AND READING—READING COURSES
Or5-tech   Unest. ent. by subj. Bks. & per. Cur. add.

BOOKS AND READING—SIGHT-SAVING BOOKS
M24   50 ent., tpd. shts. by auth. Supp. to A.L.A. list, "Books for tired eyes." Infreq. add.
Mn23-St. Anth.   190 cds. by auth. Bks. Infreq. add.
O20-fic   3960 cds. by auth. Fic. in 12 point print or larger. Freq. add.
O56-circ   500 cds. by auth. & class. Bks. in 12 point type or larger. No add.

BOOKS AND READING—SIGHT-SAVING BOOKS, JUVENILE
Ct2-j   325 cds. by auth. Bks. in 16 pt., 18 pt., 36 pt. or larger type. Supp. to A.L.A. list, "Books for tired eyes." Cur. add.
Mi29-ext   75 ent., tpd. shts. by auth. Bks. Infreq. add.
Wa10-j   200 cds. by auth. Bks. Cur. add.

BOOKS AND READING—UNUSUAL SUBJECTS
F2-r.a.   15 ent., tpd. shts. by subj. Fic. & non-fic. Semi-yrly. add.

BOTANY—BOOK RARITIES. *See* BOOK RARITIES—BOTANY

BOTANY—UNION LISTS
D18   14,000 cds. by auth. Lib. in & outside of Wash., D.C. Infreq. add.

BOY SCOUTS—STORIES
  K14-j   30 cds. by auth. Bks. Infreq. add.
  Mi6-Rich.   28 ent., tpd. shts. by auth. J. fic. Freq. add.

BRAILLE
  M29   67 ent., tpd. shts. by subj. Bks. Reading lists of various types of lit. Freq. add.

CALIFORNIA
  C10   650 cds. by class. Bks. Travel, biog. & hist. Freq. add.

CALIFORNIA—FICTION. *See* FICTION—CALIFORNIA

CALIFORNIA—HISTORY
  C71-ref   195 ent., tpd. shts. by auth. Bks. Freq. add.

CALIFORNIA—NEWSPAPERS
  C73   1000 cds., chron. Newsp., 1846–1939. Occ. add.

CALIFORNIA—RUSSIANS. *See* RUSSIANS IN CALIFORNIA

CARMAN, BLISS—WORKS
  N45b   87 ent., tpd. shts. chron. Bks. & pams. Infreq. add.

CATALOGS, COLLEGE
  C52   315 cds. by off. name. Freq. add.
  I13-Wood.   250 cds. by name. Freq. add.
  I45   300 cds. by name. Freq. add.
  I71-ref   463 cds. by name. U.S., esp. Ill., inc. lib. sch. Freq. add.
  Mi13-ref.   600 cds. by name. Occ. add.
  M24   325 cds. by name. Cur. add.
  Mn14-tech   300 cds. by name & class. Tech. schools. Freq. add.
  N35-Wood.   250 cds. by name. Occ. add.
  Nj2   150 cds. by name. Infreq. add.
  Nj29   175 cds. by name. Freq. add.
  Nj70   186 cds. by name. Occ. add.
  O1-ref   500 cds. by name. Infreq. add.
  O11   500 cds. by name. Freq. add.
  Wa15   1200 cds. by name & dept. Freq. add.

CATHOLIC LITERATURE. *See also* AUTHORS, CATHOLIC
  C32-phil   800 cds. by class. Bks. Freq. add.

  C71-ref   160 ent., tpd. shts. by class. Bks. No add.
  Ky8   1400 ent., tpd. shts. by subj. Bks. & per. No add.
  M13-ref   500 cds. by auth. Bks. Freq. add.
  Mn11   Unest. ent., tpd. shts. by auth. Bks. No add.
  O20-fic   200 cds. by auth. Fic. & non-fic. Cur. add.
  O20-So.   123 ent., tpd. shts. by auth., t. & type of bk. Infreq. add.
  O37-Mad.   100 cds. by subj. Bks. Cur. add.

CATHOLIC LITERATURE, JUVENILE
  Ia4   1200 cds. by auth. Occ. add.
  Nj37-j   750 cds. & tpd. shts. by auth. & grade. Graded lists, grades 3-8. Occ. add.

CATHOLICS—PERIODICALS. *See* PERIODICALS—19TH CENTURY   D5

CEREALS, PREPARED
  C30   36 cds. by subj. & source. Bks., pams., etc. Occ. add.

CHARACTER SKETCHES
  I13-circ   10 cds. by auth. Bks. Occ. add.

CHEMISTRY. *See* TECHNOLOGY M4-sci (2)

CHESTERTON, GILBERT KEITH—WORKS
  Tx30   38 ent., tpd. shts. by auth. Bks. No add.

CHICAGO—ARCHITECTURE. *See* ARCHITECTURE—CHICAGO

CHICAGO—AUTHORS. *See* AUTHORS—CHICAGO

CHICAGO—BUSINESS
  I13-circ   28 ent., tpd. shts. by auth. Bks. Occ. add.

CHICAGO—DESCRIPTION & TRAVEL
  I13-circ   21 ent., tpd. shts. by auth. Bks. Occ. add.
  I13-circ   98 ent., tpd. shts. by auth. Bks. to read before visiting Chicago. Freq. add.

CHICAGO—INTELLECTUAL LIFE
  I13-circ   18 ent., tpd. shts. by auth. Bks. Occ. add.

CHICAGO—SOCIAL CONDITIONS
  I13-circ   20 ent., tpd. shts. by auth. Bks. Occ. add.

CHICAGO. UNIVERSITY — DISSERTATIONS, ACADEMIC
I15b-ref   13,200 cds. by dept. & auth. Masters & doc. theses. Cur. add.

CHICAGO—VOCATIONAL COUNSELING AGENCIES
I13-Wood.   15 cds. by name. Freq. add.

CHILD STUDY
C71-circ   200 ent., tpd. shts. by auth. Bks. & per. Child care, hygiene & sex educ. No add.
Mn24   39 ent., tpd. shts. by auth. & type of work. Bks. & pam. Child welfare to 1939. No add.
Mn24   51 ent., tpd. shts. by type of work. Bks., per. & pams. Child dependency & neglect. No add. since 1936. Infreq. add.
Nj39   200 ent., tpd. shts. by subj. Bks., per. & govt. doc. Child welfare. No add.

CHILDREN, HANDICAPPED
C30   22 ent. Pams. Infreq. add.

CHILDREN'S LITERATURE
C81-j   Unest. cds. by subj. & auth. Bks. 84 reading lists. Freq. add.
Ca1   300 cds. by auth. & t. Bks. Cur. add.
G4-circ   450 cds. by auth. Bks. Cur. add.
P5-j   500 ent., tpd. shts. by subj. & auth. Yrly. add.

CHILDREN'S LITERATURE—COUNTRY LIFE
Nj17   99 ent., tpd. shts. by subj. & loc. Bks. Occ. add.

CHILDREN'S LITERATURE—EDITIONS
Mn14-j   50 cds. by t. Bks. Infreq. add.
Mn23-sch   500 cds. by auth. Bks. Freq. add.

CHILDREN'S LITERATURE—GRADED BOOKS
N44-j   23p., tpd. shts. by auth. Bks. for 3d & 4th grades. Yrly. add.
N44-j   40p., tpd. shts. by auth. Bks. for 7th & 8th grades. Yrly. add.
Nj7-Coop.-j   224 ent., tpd. shts. by subj. Bks. for 4th, 5th & 6th grades. No add.
O20-Clark   1320 cds., tpd. shts. Bks. Yrly. add.

CHILDREN'S LITERATURE—HOLIDAYS
Mi6-Loth.   100 ent., tpd. shts. by class. Poetry, plays & stories. Cur. add.

CHILDREN'S LITERATURE—INEXPENSIVE BOOKS
C81-j   300 ent., tpd. shts. by auth. Bks. $1 or less. Infreq. add.

CHILDREN'S LITERATURE—MYSTERY AND DETECTIVE STORIES
Mi6-Rich.   60 ent., tpd. shts. by auth. Bks. Freq. add.

CHILDREN'S LITERATURE—OUT-OF-PRINT BOOKS. See BOOKS AND READING—OUT-OF-PRINT BOOKS, JUVENILE

CHILDREN'S LITERATURE—THANKSGIVING DAY
Nj71   38 ent., tpd. shts. by type & title. Stories, poetry & hist. Cur. add.

CHILDREN'S LITERATURE—TRAVEL
I72-j   200 cds. by name of country. Bks. for children 7–9, 10–14. No add.

CHILDREN'S LITERATURE, REGIONAL
Wv3   64 ent., tpd. shts. by state. Bks. A tour of the U.S. No add.

CHISHOLM (MINN.)—ACCIDENTS
Mn1   Unest. ent., chron. Newsp. Fatalities, 1914–1939. Yrly. add.

CHRISTMAS
C52   106 ent., tpd. shts. by class. Bks. Freq. add.
I2-Bra.   334 cds. by auth. & class. Bks., per. & pic. Infreq. add.
I13-circ (1)   48 ent., tpd. shts. by auth. Bks. Readings, recit. & programs. Freq. add.
I13-circ (2)   29 ent., tpd. shts. by auth. Bks. Hist. & legends. Bks. Freq. add.
M28   300 ent., tpd. shts. by subj. Yrly. add.
P6   100 ent., tpd. shts. by country. Bks. & per. Christmas in many lands. Yrly. add.

CHURCHES—LOS ANGELES. See LOS ANGELES—CHURCHES

CHURCHES—NEW BRUNSWICK (N.J.). See NEW BRUNSWICK (N.J.)—CHURCHES

CITIZENSHIP
Tx30   77 ent., tpd. shts. by auth. & t. Bks. & per. No add.

CIVIL SERVICE
P26   15 ent., tpd. shts. by auth. Bks. Progress of civil service. Infreq. add.

CLASSICAL LITERATURE
Nj7   306 cds. by auth. Bks. & pams. Latin & Greek bibl. Cur. add.

CLERGYMEN—LOS ANGELES. See LOS ANGELES—CHURCHES   C32-phil

CLEVELAND (O.)—ILLUSTRATORS. See ILLUSTRATORS—CLEVELAND (O.)

COLLEGE STUDENTS—RELIGION
Nb6   20 ent., tpd. shts. by t. Bks. & per. No add.

CONFEDERATE STATES OF AMERICA
Nc3   297 ent., tpd. shts. Infreq. add.

COOK BOOKS. See BOOK STORES   C44

COURSES OF STUDY
De1   350 ent., tpd. shts. by subj. Bks. Cur. add.
Nj17   107 ent., tpd. shts. by auth. Bks. & pams. Occ. add.

COURTS
D22   22 ent., tpd. shts. Extra-terr. cts. Infreq. add.

CRIME AND CRIMINALS
D22   73 ent., tpd. shts. by auth. Bks., surveys, per., etc. Housing & crime. Infreq. add.

CZECHOSLOVAKIA
N35-Web.   300 ent., tpd. shts. by class. Bks. Freq. add.

DAIRY PRODUCTS
C30   84 cds. by subj. & source. Bks., pams., per., etc. Freq. add.

DELAWARE—AUTHORS. See AUTHORS—DELAWARE

DEMOCRACY
Nj22   Unest. ent., tpd. shts. Bks. & per. No add.

DENTISTRY
O43   9 ent., tpd. shts. Pams. Orthodontia. Infreq. add.

DIARIES
O31   175 cds. by auth. Bks. Letters, diaries & jls. Occ. add.

DOG STORIES
Tx3   59 ent., tpd. shts. by class. Bks. Freq. add.

DOGS
Wa8a   60 ent., tpd. shts. by class. Bks. Cur. add.

EASTER
Mn14-ref   320 ent., tpd. shts. by auth. Bibl. Customs, poems, readings, sermons, stories & programs. Cur. add.

EDUCATION
Ct5   192 cds. by class. Bks. Cur. add.
De1   Unest. ent., tpd. shts. by auth. Bks., pams. & per. No add.
F2-r.a.   40 ent., tpd. shts. by subj. Bks. Indispensable bks. for a modern educ. Yrly. add.
Nj17   83 ent., tpd. shts. by auth. & subj. Bks. & per. Freq. add.
Nj42   10,450 cds. by t. & subj. Bks. Bd. of educ. lib. Freq. add.
O20-soc. educ   528 cds. by subj. Pams. Uncat. bibl. Freq. add.
T2   300 cds. by state. Bul., pams., etc. Infreq. add.

EDUCATION—PERIODICALS
N36   100 ent., tpd. shts. by t. Per. No add.

EDUCATION, SECONDARY
In12   5p. tpd. shts. by subj. Pams. & per. Coop. study of second. sch. standards.

EMINENT DOMAIN
D22   156 ent., tpd. shts. by auth. Bks., per., govt. doc., etc. Emergency powers of President to expropiate property in time of war. Infreq. add.

ENDOCRINOLOGY. See GLANDS, DUCTLESS

ENGINEERING
Nj48   475 ent., tpd. shts. by subj. Bks. Cur. add.
P32a   20,000 cds. by auth. Bks. & pams. Freq. add.

ENGLISH IMPRINTS
C73-ref   25,200 cds. by subj. Bks. Eng. bks., 1641–1700, 1701–1800. No add.
Nj40   500 cds. by auth. Bks. & pams. print. in England before 1701. Occ. add.

EPIC CENTURY (per.). *In* TEXAS   Tx7

ESPIONAGE. *See* SPIES

Etiquette
P26   33 ent., tpd. shts. by auth. Bks. & per. Infreq. add.

Europe—History
I51   68 ent., tpd. shts., chron. Bks. Modern European hist. in fic. & biog. Freq. add.
Nj16   195 ent., tpd. shts. by subj. Bks. Ancient & medieval European hist. Freq. add.
Nj66   145 ent., tpd. shts. by subj. Bks. Freq. add.

Europe—Literature
Tx30   60 ent., tpd. shts. by subj. Bks. Comparative European lit. hist. & crit. No add.

European War, 1914–1918—Fiction. See Fiction—European War, 1914–1918

Examinations, Comprehensive
P19   36 ent., tpd. shts. by auth. Bks. & per. No add.

Explorers
Tx3   18 ent., tpd. shts. by auth. Bks., etc. Explorers of 15th & 16th cent. Occ. add.

Feeble-Minded
Mn24   33 ent., tpd. shts. by auth. Bks., per. & pams. Extra-institutional care. No add.
Mn24   28 ent., tpd. shts. by auth. Bks., per. & pams. Concepts. No add.

Festivals
P12   15 cds. by auth. Bks. Festivals & pageants. Cur. add.

Feudalism
Nj22   36 ent., tpd. shts.

Fiction
T2   1000 cds. by auth. Bks. Freq. add.

Fiction—California
C43   16p., tpd. shts. by period, auth. & t. Cur. add.
C71-ref   17 ent., tpd. shts. by auth. Freq. add.

Fiction—Canada
Ca5-circ   166 ent., tpd. shts. by subj. Bks. No add.

Fiction—Editions
O20-fic   3960 cds. by auth. Cur. add.

Fiction—European War, 1914–1918
I46   13 cds. by auth. Bks. Infreq. add.

Fiction—Fall River (Mass.)
M18-ref   15 cds. by auth. Bks. Infreq. add.

Fiction—Family Life
Mi6-Fenk.   65 cds. by auth. Cur. add.

Fiction—Florida
F2-r.a.   45 ent., tpd. shts. by auth. Cur. add.

Fiction—Law
O20-Coll.   50 cds. by auth. Law & lawyers. Infreq. add.

Fiction—Medicine. See also Fiction—Physicians
Mi6-Rich.   42 ent., tpd. shts. by auth. Bks. on med. Freq. add.

Fiction—Michigan
Mi6-Rich.   17 ent., tpd. shts. by auth. Freq. add.

Fiction—Music
H3-art   90 cds. by auth. Cur. add.

Fiction—New York (State)
N1   200 ent., tpd. shts. by auth. Bks. Hist. fic. No add.

Fiction—North Carolina
Nc3   40 ent., tpd. shts. by auth. Bks. Cur. add.

Fiction—Novelettes
I41   85 ent., tpd. shts. by auth. Bks. No add.

Fiction—Orient
Nb14-N.   28 ent., tpd. shts. by auth. Occ. add.

Fiction—Physicians
I13-Hild.   3p., tpd. shts. by auth. Bks. Yrly. add.
Mi6-Fenk.   25 cds. by auth. Dr., nurse & hospital stories. Cur. add.
Nj37-circ   94 ent., tpd. shts. by auth. Bks. Dr. & nurses in fic. Freq. add.

Fiction—Translations
F2-r.a.   60 ent., tpd. shts. by country. Outstanding novels from every country. No add.

Fiction, Biographical
C75   31 cds. by auth. Bks. Freq. add.

FICTION, CATHOLIC
  N35-Cath.   150 cds. by auth. Bks. Infreq. add.

FICTION, DOMESTIC. *See* FICTION—FAMILY LIFE; FICTION, GENEALOGICAL

FICTION, FRENCH
  Nj7-Fair.   25 ent., tpd. shts. by subj. Bks. Infreq. add.

FICTION, GENEALOGICAL
  I13-Hild.   7p., tpd. shts. by auth. Bks. Yrly. add.
  Mi6-Rich.   76 ent., tpd. shts. by auth. Freq. add.

FICTION, JEWISH
  K8-circ   25 cds. by auth. Jew. stories. Cur. add.
  O20-MtP.   350 cds. by auth. Cur. add.

FICTION, PROLETARIAN
  Mi6-Rich.   73 ent., tpd. shts. by auth. Econ. & proletarian bks. Freq. add.

FICTION, PSEUDO-SCIENTIFIC
  O20-Coll.   25 cds. by auth. Infreq. add.

FICTION, PSYCHOLOGICAL
  I13-Hild.   5p., tpd. shts. by auth. Bks. Yrly. add.

FICTION, REPLACEMENT
  T9-lib   1700 cds. by auth. Infreq. add.

FICTION, ROMANTIC
  Mi6-Fenk. 100 cds. by auth. Cur. add.

FICTION, SOCIOLOGICAL
  F2-r.a.   8 ent., tpd. shts. by scope. Famous novels which have forced reforms & changed the trend of thot. No add.
  I13-Hild. 4p., tpd. shts. by auth. Bks. Soc. conditions & problems. Yrly. add.

FICTION, WESTERN
  Mi6-Camp. 200 ent., tpd. shts. by auth. Freq. add.

FILMED BOOKS. *See* BOOKS, FILMED

FIRST EDITIONS. *See* BIBLIOGRAPHY—FIRST EDITIONS

FLOODS
  N35-ref. sci   10,655 ent., tpd. shts. by state. Floods & storms in U.S. & terr. Occ. add.

FOOD FADS
  C30   15 cds. by subj. & source. Pams. Infreq. add.

FORDHAM UNIVERSITY—DISSERTATIONS, ACADEMIC
  N32a   9000 cds. by auth., t. & dept. Freq. add.

FOREIGN-BORN READING. *See* BOOKS AND READING—FOREIGN-BORN READING

FORESTS AND FORESTRY
  C9   3000 cds. by class. Bks. & per. Internatl. bibl. No add.
  G11   25 cds. by t. Per., pams., etc. Range mgt. Occ. add.
  K11   20 ent. Pams. Infreq. add.

FORESTS AND FORESTRY—PUERTO RICO. *See* AGRICULTURE—PUERTO RICO G11

FRONTIER AND PIONEER LIFE
  Mi6-Red.   70 ent., tpd. shts. by auth. Bks. Mo. add.

FRONTIER AND PIONEER LIFE—STORIES
  Wa8a   77 ent., tpd. shts. by class. Bks. Cur. add.

GALESBURG (ILL.)—BIOGRAPHY
  I45-ref   2950 cds. by name. Newsp. Freq. add.

GALVEZ, BERNARDO DE
  Tx17   10p., tpd. shts. by t. Bks., newsp., per. & mss. Freq. add.

GAMES. *See* RECREATION Mi11-circ-ref

GARDENS AND GARDENING
  Nj13   Unest. ent., tpd. shts. by class. No add.

GEOLOGY. *See* PRINCETON UNIVERSITY—DISSERTATIONS, ACADEMIC—GEOLOGY

GERMAN LANGUAGE
  Nj58   1500 cds. by auth. & t. Bks. Occ. add.

GERMAN LITERATURE
  I52   75 ent., tpd. shts. by subj. & lit. form. Bks. Background readings. Yrly. add.

GLANDS, DUCTLESS
  C30   50 ent. Bks., pams. & per. Occ. add.

GOVERNMENT DOCUMENTS
  De1   2000 cds. by t. Ser. doc. Daily add.

GOVERNMENT DOCUMENTS, STATE
U1 410 cds. by state & form. Freq. add.

GREAT BRITAIN—HISTORY—ELIZABETH
Ky15-circ 183 ent., tpd. shts. by subj. Bks.
P54-circ 60 cds. by auth. Bks. Infreq. add.

GUMS AND RESINS. See PLASTIC MATERIALS Nj3

HANDICAPPED CHILDREN. See CHILDREN, HANDICAPPED

HANDICRAFTS. See RECREATION Mi11-circ.-ref

HARBORS
Nb6 17 ent., tpd. shts. by auth. Bks. & pams. Infreq. add.

HAWAII
H4 5300 cds. by t. & auth. Bks., pams. & per. A bibl. by Ralph Hagedorn. Occ. add.

HAWAII—UNION LISTS
H4 7500 cds. by auth. Bks., ser. & pams. Hawaiiana. Occ. add.

HEALTH EDUCATION
P12 35 cds. by auth. Bks. Leadership in protective procedures. Cur. add.
P12 111 cds. by auth. Bks. Stud. teaching. Cur. add.

HELIOTHERAPY. See SUN BATHS

HISTORICAL MYSTERIES. See MYSTERIES, HISTORICAL

HISTORY, ANCIENT. See EUROPE—HISTORY Nj16

HISTORY, MEDIEVAL. See EUROPE—HISTORY Nj16

HISTORY, MODERN. See EUROPE—HISTORY I51

HISTORY, UNIVERSAL
Nj17 Unest. ent., tpd. shts. by subj. Bks. Supp. reading for world hist. Freq. add.

HOME ECONOMICS
C19 Unest. ent., tpd. shts. by subj. Bks. Yrly. add.
C71-circ 300 ent., tpd. shts. by class. Bks. Freq. add.
F2-r.a. 90 ent., tpd. shts. by class. Yrly. add.
Tx5 300 cds. by auth., subj. & t. Bks. Freq. add.

HOME LIBRARIES. See LIBRARIES, HOME

HORSES
Ky10 2500 cds. by auth., subj. & t. Bks., per. & pams. Keeneland lib. on race horses. Occ. add.
Tx3 35 ent., tpd. shts. by class. Bks. Freq. add.
Wa8a 31 ent., tpd. shts. by class. Bks. Cur. add.

HOSPITAL READING. See BOOKS AND READING—HOSPITAL READING

HOUSING. See also CRIME AND CRIMINALS D22
P39-Wyl. 56 ent., tpd. shts. by auth. Bks., per. & newsp. Cur. add.

HYGIENE
P12 158 cds. by auth. Bks. Personal hygiene. Cur. add.

ILLUSTRATORS
C73-rare 2600 ent., tpd. shts. by art. Imp. 19-20th cent. English & Amer. illus. In proc.

ILLUSTRATORS—CLEVELAND (O.)
O20-ref 7 cds. by name. Infreq. add.

INCUNABULA
C34-Hoose 40 cds., chron. Infreq. add.
Ct10 Unest. cds. by auth. 15th & 16th cent. bks. No add.

INDIANA
In12 22p., tpd. shts. by subj. Bks., per. & pams. Occ. add.

INDIANS
I13-Tild. 109 ent., tpd. shts. by auth. Bks. Occ. add.

INDIANS—STORIES
Tx3 61 ent., tpd. shts. by class. Bks. Freq. add.

INSPIRATIONAL READING. See BOOKS AND READING—INSPIRATIONAL READING

INTERIOR DECORATION
N50 242 cds. by class. Bks. Home furnishing & home planning.

INTERNATIONAL LAW AND RELATIONS
I13-Tild. 91 ent., tpd. shts. by auth. Bks. Cur. add.

INTERNATIONAL MIND ALCOVE. See BOOKS AND READING—INTERNATIONAL MIND ALCOVE

IOWA—PERIODICALS. *See* PERIODICALS
Ia12

IRELAND
P26   50 ent., tpd. shts. by subj. Bks., pams. & per. Ireland and the Irish. Infreq. add.

JAILS. *See* PRISONS

JEWS—FICTION. *See* FICTION, JEWISH

JEWS—PERIODICALS
O24   50p., tpd. shts. by auth. & subj. Yrly. add.

JOHN CRERAR LIBRARY, CHICAGO—REFERENCE LISTS
I43-ref   51 cds., chron. Cur. add.

JUVENILE DELINQUENCY
D22   105 ent., tpd. shts. by auth. Bks., per., pams. & rpts., 1936. Infreq. add.
D22   174 ent., tpd. shts. by auth. Bks., pams. & doc., 1937. Infreq. add.

LABOR AND LABORING CLASSES
D1   3500 cds. by auth., subj. & t. Bks., pams., per., newsp. & press releases. Freq. add.
Nj60-ind. rel   54,000 cds. by subj. & auth. Daily add.

LAFFITE, JEAN
Tx17   1320 cds. by t. Bks., per., newsp. & mss. Freq. add.

LANDSCAPE GARDENING. *See* ARCHITECTURE
I11-Burn. (1), (2), (4)

LANGUAGE AND LANGUAGES
I26-rare   13,699 ent., tpd. shts. by lang. Bks. & per. Linguistic lib. of late Prince Louis-Lucien Bonaparte. Freq. add.

LANTERN SLIDES
In12   38p., tpd. shts. by subj. Infreq. add.

LATIN LANGUAGE
C72   77 ent., tpd. shts. by auth. & class. Bks. Infreq. add.

LATIN LITERATURE
Ky5   123 ent., tpd. shts. by subj. Bks., per., etc. Freq. add.
N41   90 ent., tpd. shts. by auth. Bks. Freq. add.
N52   46 ent., tpd. shts. by auth. Bks. Infreq. add.

LAW
D22   77 ent., tpd. shts. by auth. Bks., per., etc. Construction of statutes. Infreq. add.
Nj44   2700 ent., tpd. shts. by auth., t. & subj. Bks. & pams. No add.

LAW—FICTION. *See* FICTION—LAW

LECTURE FOUNDATIONS
M14   Unest. cds. by lectureship. Bks., letters, etc.

LENTEN READING. *See* BOOKS AND READING —LENTEN READING

LIBRARIANS, CERTIFICATION OF
Tx30   117 ent., tpd. shts. by state. Per. No add.

LIBRARIES, HOME
Tx30   101 ent., tpd. shts. by auth. Bks. No add.
Tx30   25 ent., tpd. shts. by auth. Bks. for children of intermediate grades. No add.

LIBRARIES, SPECIAL
Nj39   40 ent., tpd. shts. by type. Bks. & pams. Manuals of instruction. Cur. add.

LIBRARY OF CONGRESS—BIBLIOGRAPHIES
I43-ref   400 cds. by subj. Freq. add.

LIBRARY SCHOOLS. *See* CATALOGS, COLLEGE
171-ref

LIBRARY SCIENCE
N55-lib. sch   63,025 cds. by auth., t. & subj. Bks. & per. Freq. add.
Tx30   86 ent., tpd. shts. by auth. & subj. Bks. & per. Larger units of lib. sci. No add.

LINCOLN, ABRAHAM
C73-Amer.   2640 cds. by auth. Bks. Occ. add.
Mn14-ref   230 ent., tpd. shts. by auth. Biog., plays, poetry & anecdotes. Occ. add.

LITERATURE
I41   540 ent., tpd. shts. by auth. Bks. Yrly. add.
N55-o.s.   100 ent. by auth. Edna Stowe Stewart mem. coll. of worthwhile bks. No add.
Nj27-j   1100 cds. by t. Parochial sch. course of study. Infreq. add.
Nj27-j   1900 cds. by t. Bks. Educ. dept. course of study. Infreq. add.

Nj27-sch 280 cds. by t. Bks. Course of study in lit. inc. art. No add.

Nj27-sch 2160 cds. by t. Bks. Course of study in lit. No add.

LONG, GENERAL JAMES
Tx17 Unest. ent., tpd. shts. by form. Bks., newsp. & per. Gen. James Long and Mrs. Jane H. Long. No add.

LONG, MRS. JANE H. *See* LONG, GENERAL JAMES **Tx17**

LOS ANGELES—CHURCHES
C32-phil 1550 cds. by denomination & name of church. Church dir., ministers & addresses. Cur. add.
C32-for 128 cds. by nationality. For. churches. Infreq. add.

LOS ANGELES—TRANSLATORS
C32-for 300 cds. by lang. Teachers & tr. of for. lang. Freq. add.

MCGILL UNIVERSITY—DISSERTATIONS, ACADEMIC
Ca13 1300 cds. by auth. Yrly. add.

MAINE
Me2 8300 cds. by auth. Bks. Occ. add.

MAINE—NEWSPAPERS
Me1 Unest. ent., tpd. shts. by t. Newsp. & holdings of lib. in state. Freq. add.

MAMARONECK (N.Y.)
N26 33 ent., tpd. shts. by auth. Bks., newsp., atlases & pams. Infreq. add.

MANUSCRIPTS
De1 Unest. cds. by auth. In proc.
M5 750 cds. by auth. Old letters, etc. Infreq. add.
Md4 4950 cds. by auth. Letters, diaries, wills, deeds, etc. Freq. add.

MAPS
Ca1 300 cds. by subj. Cur. add.
Ca10-ref 488 cds. by subj. Freq. add.
Mi24 64 cds. by subj. & symbol. Infreq. add.

MAPS, TOPOGRAPHIC
C73 30,360 cds. by state. Engravings, phot., reprod., & per. Amer. topography. Cur. add.

MARKET SURVEYS
O20-bus 8 cds. by auth. or organiz. In proc.

MARY, VIRGIN
Tx30 97 ent., tpd. shts. by subj. Bks. & per. No add.

MATERNITY WELFARE
C30 90 cds. by subj. & source. Bks., pams. & per. Freq. add.
Mn24 44 ent., tpd. shts., chron. Bks., pams. & per. Aid to dependent children, mothers' aid. No add.

MATHEMATICS
I79 183 ent., tpd. shts. by subj. Bks. Occ. add.
Nj17 265 ent., tpd. shts. by subj. Bks. & pams. Infreq. add.

MATHEMATICS—UNION LISTS
W12-Ext. 1000 cds. by auth. Bks. Union list of all bks. in city. Freq. add.

MAYA RESEARCH (per.). *In* MAYAS **L15**

MAYAS
L15 Unest. cds. by auth. Per. indexed: *Maya Research,* 1934–date. Cur. add.

MEDICAL ECONOMICS
C30 76 ent. Bks., pams. & newsp. Cost of med. care, health insurance, socialized med., etc. Freq. add.

MEDICINE
Nj65 150 ent., tpd. shts. by subj. Bks. Cur. add.
O14 2673 cds. by subj. Bks. & per. Freq. add.

MENKEN, ADAH ISAACS
Tx17 Unest. ent., tpd. shts. by t. Bks., newsp., & per. Cur. add.

MICHIGAN—FICTION. *See* FICTION—MICHIGAN

MIDDLE AGES—HISTORY. *See* EUROPE—HISTORY **Nj16**

MILK
C30 45 cds. by subj. & source. Bks., pams., per. & newsp. Occ. add.

MINNESOTA
Mn21-cat 8000 cds. by auth. Uncat. mat. Freq. add.

MINNESOTA—DOCUMENTS
Mn23-ref 43,470 cds. by class. Minn. & St. Paul doc. Daily add.

MISSIONARY READING. *See* BOOKS AND READING—MISSIONARY READING

MISSISSIPPI—NEWSPAPERS
Ms3   Unest. ent., tpd. shts. by town, newsp., chron. Freq. add.

MOLLUSKS
Nj60-Guy   110 ent., tpd. shts. by auth. Bks., per. & pams. No add.

MORMONS AND MORMONISM
C73-ref   230 ent., tpd. shts. by auth. Bks. Mormons & early Utah hist. No add.

MOTHER'S AID. *See* MATERNITY WELFARE

MUSIC—FICTION. *See* FICTION—MUSIC

MUSIC—THEORY
C73   Unest. ent. by comp. & ed., t., chron., first line. Mus. & bks. about mus., 1467–1800. Cur. add.

MUSICIANS
Nj17   115 ent., tpd. shts. by comp. Infreq. add.

MYSTERIES, HISTORICAL
F2-r.a.   15 ent., tpd. shts. by subj. Non-fic. Semi-yrly. add.

MYSTERY AND DETECTIVE STORIES
Mi6-Camp.   200 ent., tpd. shts. by auth. Bks. Freq. add.
Tx3   80 ent., tpd. shts. by class. Bks. Freq. add.
Wa8a   128 ent., tpd. shts. by class. Bks. Cur. add.

NATIONAL DEFENSE. *See* U.S.—DEFENSES

NATURAL RESOURCES
Nj24   80 ent., tpd. shts., No add.

NATURE
Tx5   200 cds. by auth. & t. Bks. Freq. add.

NAVAL SCIENCE
C73-Amer.   Unest. ent. tpd. shts. by auth. Bks. & mss. Marine life, navigation, merchant marine, naval engagements, inland waterways, nautical engravings, etc.
Md1   6000 ent., tpd. shts. by auth. Bks., per. pams. & govt. doc. Amer. & for. naval biog., gen. naval lit. No add.

NEBRASKA—HISTORY
Nb6   41 ent., tpd. shts. by auth. Bks. Freq. add.

NEGRO LITERATURE
Mi6-Sch.   107 cds. by auth. & class. Bks. Freq. add.

NEGROES
Nj34   200 cds. by auth. & subj. Bks. Freq. add.
Nj59   52 cds. by auth. Bks. Cur. add.

NEW BRUNSWICK (N.J.)—CHURCHES
Nj37-ref   Unest. ent., tpd. shts. by name. Churches & ministers. Occ. add.

NEW JERSEY
Nj7-ad   161 ent., tpd. shts. by auth. Bks. & pams. Freq. add.
Nj17   605 ent., tpd. shts. by subj. Bks., per. & pams. Freq. add.

NEW JERSEY—NEWSPAPERS
Nj40   1250 ent., chron. Cur. add.

NEW YORK (STATE)—FICTION. *See* FICTION—NEW YORK (STATE)

NEWBERRY MEDAL BOOKS
P40   31 ent. tpd. shts. by auth., t. & illus. Bks. No add.

NEWSPAPERS
C32-per   1620 cds., chron. by city. Newsp. Cur. add.
C73-ref   5800 cds. by country, state & city. Geog. list of newsp. Cur. add.
G16   200 cds. by name. Newsp. & per., 1823–1910. No add.
I26   3000 cds. by decade. Newsp., 1700–date. Freq. add.
I73-newsp   2300 cds. by t. & significant word in t. Gen. & class newsp. Cur. add.
Ky2   Unest. ent., tpd. shts. by t. Newsp. pub. before 1930. No add.
Ky2   200 cds. by city. Cur. add.
N45b   1843 cds., chron. & by name. Freq. add.
Nj40   3200 cds. by state & place. Freq. add.
Nj40   3200 cds. by t. Freq. add.

NORTH CAROLINA—FICTION. *See* FICTION—NORTH CAROLINA

NORTH CAROLINA—HISTORY
Nc1   58p., tpd. shts. by subj. & auth. Kemp Lummer battle scrapbks. on hist. & biog. Univ. of N.C., 1888–1894, 1893–1896.
Nc1   115p., tpd. shts. by subj. & auth. Stephen B. Weeks scrapbks., 10v. on hist. & biog. of N.C., 1888–1893.

NORTH DAKOTA—AUTHORS. *See* AUTHORS—NORTH DAKOTA

North Platte Valley (Nebr.)
Nb17 62 ent., tpd. shts. by auth. Bks. Infreq. add.

Northern Stories
Mi6-Red. 30 ent., tpd. shts. by auth. Mo. add.

Northwest
Wa8a 29 ent., tpd. shts. by class. Bks. Cur. add.

Novelettes. *See* Fiction—Novelettes

Nurses and Nursing
N30-t.c. Unest. ent., tpd. shts. & cds. by class. Bks. & pams. Adelaide Nutting hist. nursing coll. Freq. add.

Nurses in Fiction. *See* Fiction—Physicians **Nj37-circ**

Oakland (Calif.)—Documents. *See* Alameda Co. (Calif.)—Documents **C43-ref**

Open-Air Schools
C30 Unest. ent. Pams. & newsp. Infreq. add.

Orient—Fiction. *See* Fiction—Orient

Orthodontia. *See* Dentistry

Out-of-Print Books. *See* Books and Reading—Out-of-Print Books

Pageants. *See* Festivals **P12**

Peace
C7-circ 60 ent., tpd. shts. by auth. Bks. International peace. No add.

Periodicals. *See also* Newspapers **G16**
C34-per 128p., tpd. shts., chron. & by t. Cur. add.
C87 900 cds. by t. Infreq. add.
I26 2000 cds. by decade. Eng. & Amer. per., 1680–date. Freq. add.
Ia12 1200 cds. by t. Per. & Ia. pub. Cur. add.
In33-ad 175 cds. by subj. Cur. add.
K9-ref 350 cds. by t. Per. Freq. add.
K20-per 1950 cds. by subj. Cur. add.
Ky3 100 ent., tpd. shts. by t. Freq. add.
M6 Unest. cds. by t. Daily add.
M10 800 cds. Cur. add.
Me2-ref 125 cds. by subj. Cur. add.
Mn14-clip 1200 cds. by name. Per. not in Ayer. Infreq. add.
Mn14-tech 500 cds. by t. Tech. per. Cur. add.
Mn14-tech 225 cds. by subj. Cur. add.
Mn15-per 1200 cds., chron. Freq. add.
Ms1 135 cds. by t. Freq. add.
Ms2 150 cds. by t. Per. Cur. add.
N35-ref 3600 cds., chron. British & Amer. per., 1800–date. Cur. add.
N55-per 450 cds. Cur. add.
Nj50-circ 1100 cds. Cur. add.
O29-ref 1000 cds. by subj. Cur. add.
Sc3 200 ent., tpd. shts. & cds. by t. Cur. add.
Wa15 400 cds. by t. Indexed per. Infreq. add.

Periodicals—19th Century
D5 36 ent., tpd. shts., chron. Amer. per. chiefly Cath. 1812–1891. Infreq. add.
G18 75 cds. by t. Infreq. add.

Periodicals—Union Lists
Ct5 250 cds. by t. Per. in Greenwich, Old Greenwich, Port Chester, N.Y. & Rye, N.Y. lib. Infreq. add.
H4 9000 cds. by t. Per. in Honolulu libraries. Occ. add.
Ky15-ref 2800 cds. by t. Per. in Louisville libs. Occ. add.
M25 500 cds. by t. Per. in Va. libs. Occ. add.
N8-ref 19,800 cds. by t. Per. in Buffalo libs. Freq. add.
N10-ref 13,406 cds. by auth. & t. Per. in Buffalo libs. No add.

Periodicals, Early
Ia14-ser 1000 ent., tpd. shts., chron. Per., to 1800, 1800–1900. Cur. add.
Mn15-per 1200 cds., chron. Per. 1650–1850. Freq. add.
N45b 304 cds., chron. Per. to 1800, 1800–1900. Freq. add.
Nd3 17 ent., tpd. shts. by t. Old per. & newsp. No add.

Periodicals, School
In12 250 ent., tpd. shts. by t. Infreq. add.

Personnel Service in Education
Ia5 100 ent., tpd. shts. by form. Bks., pams. & per. Stud. guidance. Yrly. add.

PETROLEUM
  Co9   325 ent., tpd. shts. by phases of ind. Bks. & per.

PHOTOGRAPHS
  C73-rare   4000 cds. by subj. & person. In proc.

PHOTOGRAPHY IN CRIME DETECTION
  D22   235 ent., tpd. shts. by subj. Per., bks., etc. Infreq. add.

PHYSICAL EDUCATION AND TRAINING—ADMINISTRATION
  P12   47 cds. by auth. Bks. Cur. add.

PHYSICIANS—FICTION. See FICTION—PHYSICIANS

PHYSICS. See TECHNOLOGY   M4-sci (2)

PLANTATION LIFE
  Tx3   20 ent., tpd. shts. by auth. Bks. & ency. Occ. add.

PLASTIC MATERIALS
  Nj3   56 cds. by auth. Bks. & pams. Synthetic resins & plastics. Occ. add.

PLAYS
  N32a   1000 ent., tpd. shts. by auth. 18th & 19th cent. Eng. & Amer. plays. Infreq. add.

POLITICAL SCIENCE
  Ia12   50 ent., tpd. shts. by subj. Bks. Great game of politics. Freq. add.

PRINCETON UNIVERSITY—DISSERTATIONS, ACADEMIC—GEOLOGY
  Nj60-Guy.   90 ent., tpd. shts., chron. by auth. Ph.D. theses since 1913. Yrly. add.

PRINCETON UNIVERSITY—PUBLICATIONS, FACULTY—SCIENCE
  Nj60-Guy.   800 cds. by auth., chron. Geol. & biol. fac. pub. Freq. add.

PRISONS
  D22   46 ent. by auth. Bks., pams., rpts., etc. Jails. Infreq. add.
  D22   193 ent., tpd. shts. by auth. Bks. per., etc. Prisons. Infreq. add.

PROBATION
  D22   94 ent., tpd. shts. by auth. Bks., pams., etc. Infreq. add.

PSYCHOLOGY
  De1   Unest. ent., tpd. shts., & cds. by auth. Bks., pams. & per. Cur. add.

PUBLIC SANITATION. See SANITATION

PUERTO RICO—AGRICULTURE. See AGRICULTURE—PUERTO RICO

PUERTO RICO—FORESTS AND FORESTRY. See AGRICULTURE—PUERTO RICO   G11

PUNISHMENT—COLONIAL PERIOD
  Tx19   16 cds. by class. Bks. Freq. add.

RARE BOOKS. See BOOK RARITIES

READABLE BOOKS. See BOOKS AND READING—READABLE BOOKS

READERS AND PRIMERS
  K11   1800 cds. by auth. Freq. add.
  N43-j   350 cds. by class. Bks. Freq. add.

READINGS AND RECITATIONS. See CHRISTMAS   I13-circ (1)

RECONSTRUCTION. See U.S.—HISTORY—CIVIL WAR   W20-Horl.

RECORDS (IN BUSINESS AND INDUSTRY)
  Mn24   24 ent., tpd. shts. by auth. Bks., pams. & per. No add.

RECREATION
  Mi11-circ. ref   536 ent., tpd. shts. by auth. Inc. games & handicraft.

REFERENCE BOOKS
  D6-ref   667 cds. by class. Bks. & pams. Cur. add.

REFUGEES, BOOKS FOR. See BOOKS AND READING—FOREIGN-BORN

ROCHESTER UNIVERSITY—DISSERTATIONS, ACADEMIC
  N47   660 cds. by dept. Master & dr. theses. Yrly. add.

ROCHESTER UNIVERSITY—PUBLICATIONS
  N47   9240 cds. by auth. Bks. per., abstracts, bk. reviews, etc. Fac. & alumni pub., 1850–date. Yrly. add.

RUSSIANS IN CALIFORNIA
  C71-ref   Unest. ent., tpd. shts. by auth. Bks., per. & newsp. Infreq. add.

ST. PATRICK'S DAY
  I13-Tild.   15 ent., tpd. shts. by auth. Bks. Occ. add.

ST. PAUL (MINN.)—DOCUMENTS. See MINNESOTA—DOCUMENTS   Mn23-ref

SAMPLERS
N45b 172 cds. by country, chron. Amer. & European samplers 1705–1911. Infreq. add.

SANITATION
C30 Unest. cds. by subj. & source. Bks. & pams. Pub. sanitation. Occ. add.

SCHOOL HYGIENE
C30 Unest. cds. Bks., pams. & per. Stories, songs. Occ. add.

SCHOOL HYGIENE—CHILDREN'S PLAYS
C30 Unest. cds. Bks., pams., per. & newsp. Occ. add.
Mn14-clip 175 cds. Pams. & newsp. Infreq. add.

SCHOOL HYGIENE—GAMES
C30 Unest cds. Pams. & newsp. Occ. add.

SCHOOL LIBRARIES
In12 40p., tpd. shts. by class. Bks. & pams. Freq. add.

SCHOOL STORIES
Wa8a 60 ent., tpd. shts. by class. Bks. School & sports. Cur. add.

SCIENCE. *See also* TECHNOLOGY
C71-circ 400 ent., tpd. shts. by class. Bks. Freq. add.
Nj58 36,900 cds. by auth., t. & subj. Bks. & per. Freq. add.

SCIENCE—BOOK RARITIES. *See* BOOK RARITIES—SCIENCE

SEA STORIES
Tx3 70 ent., tpd. shts. by class. Bks. Freq. add.
Wa8a 107 ent., tpd. shts. by class. Bks. Cur. add.

SEATTLE (WASH.)—TRADE ASSOCIATIONS. *See* TRADE ASSOCIATIONS—WASHINGTON (STATE)

SEAWEEDS. *See* ALGAE

SELF IMPROVEMENT
Nj7-Coop. 23 ent., tpd. shts. by auth. Bks. No add.

SERIALS—UNION LISTS
H4 3573 cds. by auth. Ser. in Honolulu lib. Occ. add.

SERIALS, SCIENTIFIC—UNION LISTS
D19 9000 cds. by t. or name of issuing body. Ser. in lib. of Wash. Freq. add.

SEX INSTRUCTION. *See* CHILD STUDY C71-circ

SHORT STORIES
Wa8a 50 ent. by class. Bks. Cur. add.

SIGHT-SAVING BOOKS. *See* BOOKS AND READING—SIGHT-SAVING BOOKS

SOCIOLOGY
C72 85 ent., tpd. shts. by auth. & class. Bks. Problems of to-day. Cur. add.

SONGS
M3 750 ent., tpd. shts. by comp. Freq. add.

SOUTH AMERICA—ART. *See* ART—SOUTH AMERICA

SPANISH LITERATURE
Tx30 214 ent., tpd. shts. by type. Bks. & per. No add.

SPECIAL LIBRARIES. *See* LIBRARIES, SPECIAL

SPIES
F2-r.a. 20 ent., tpd. shts. by auth. Bks. Yrly. add.

SPORT STORIES. *See* SCHOOL STORIES Wa8a

SPORTS AND ATHLETIC GAMES
P12 37 cds. by auth. Bks. Gymnastic activities. Cur. add.

SPORTS FOR WOMEN
Tx30 36 ent., tpd. shts. by auth. Bks. No add.

STORMS. *See* FLOODS N35-ref. sci

STUART, BEN C.—WORKS
Tx17 968 cds. Newsp. art. by Stuart. No add.

STUDY, METHOD OF
In12 11p., tpd. shts. by auth. Bks., per. & pams. No add.

SUMMIT CO. (O.)
O28 Unest. cds. by name of township, city & village. Bks., pams., mss., newsp., maps & per. & pic. Freq. add.

SUMMIT CO. (O.)—NEWSPAPERS
O28 Unest. cds. by town, chron. Newsp. Occ. add.

SUN BATHS
C30 Unest. ent. Bks. & pams. Heliotherapy. Infreq. add.

TACOMA (WASH.)—TRADE ASSOCIATIONS.
See TRADE ASSOCIATIONS—WASHINGTON (STATE)

TECHNOLOGY
M4-sci (1)   3960 cds. by name. Bks., pams., sales cat., etc. Sci. & tech. bks., pub. before 1800. Occ. add.
M4-sci (2)   33,000 cds. by class, chron. Bks., per., pams. & pics. Tech., physics & chem. Cur. add.

TEETH
C30   48 ent. Bks., pams., newsp. & per. Occ. add.

TEXAS
Tx5   240 cds. by subj., auth. & t. Bks., newsp. & mss. Freq. add.
Tx7   Unest. cds. by subj. Per. indexed: *Texas weekly* & *Epic century*. Mo. add.
Tx15   1500 ent., tpd. shts. by auth., t. & subj. Bks.
Tx21-circ, ref, ord, hist & lib   4000 cds. by auth. Auction & dealers' cat. Cur. add.

TEXAS WEEKLY (per.). *In* TEXAS   **Tx7**

TEXTBOOKS
P26   36 ent., tpd. shts. by auth. Bks. Early sch. textbks. Infreq. add.

TOASTS
Mn14-ref   75 ent., tpd. shts. by type. Bks. Occ. add.

TRADE ASSOCIATIONS—WASHINGTON (STATE)
Wa10-tech   12 cds. by name. Letters. Seattle & Tacoma trade assoc. Infreq. add.

TRANSLATORS. *See* Names of loc., subdiv. TRANSLATORS, i.e. ATLANTA (GA.)—TRANSLATORS

TRAVEL
F2-r.a.   48 cds. by auth. Famous voyages around the world. Cur. add.
F2-r.a.   Unest. cds. by country. Hist. & travel ser. of every country in the world. Yrly. add.
Wv3   47 ent., tpd. shts. by countries. Bks.

TURGENEV, IVAN—WORKS
N45b   475 ent., tpd. shts. by auth. Turgenev coll. of French, English & German bks. No add.

TYPOGRAPHY
C73-rare   3500 ent., tpd. shts. by presses, printers or designers. Presses of modern (19th & 20th cent.) fine printing in lib. Cur. add.

U.S.—DEFENSES
N41   78 ent., tpd. shts. by class. Bks. & pams. Freq. add.
Nj9   27 cds. by subj. Bks. Cur. add.
Nj37   10 ent., tpd. shts, by t. Bks. No add.

U.S.—HISTORY—CIVIL WAR
W20-Horl.   70 ent., tpd. shts. by class. Bks. Civil war & reconstruction period. Freq. add.

U.S.—TERRITORIES
I13-Tild.   80 ent., tpd. shts. by class. Bks., pams. & per. & yrbks. Cur. add.

UNIVERSITIES AND COLLEGES—INSTITUTES
N47-ref   60 cds. by name of instit. Occ. add.

UTAH—HISTORY. *See* MORMONS AND MORMONISM   **C73-ref**

VERTEBRATES
Nj60-Guy.   460 cds. by auth. Bks. pub. in Eng. & German, 1880–1941. Occ. add.
Nj60-Guy.   600 cds. by country & state. Bks., per. & pams. Vert. (excl. birds) of N. Amer., Central Amer. & S. Amer. Freq. add.

VOCATIONS
I41   56 ent., tpd. shts. by auth. Bks. No add.
In12   152p., tpd. shts. by subj. Per. & pams. Freq. add.
W20-Horl.   250 ent., tpd. shts. by auth. Bks. Freq. add.

WASHINGTON, GEORGE
C73-Amer.   2640 cds. by auth. Bks. No add.
Mn14-ref   85 ent., tpd. shts. Poetry, plays & sermons. Occ. add.

WASHINGTON (STATE)—TRADE ASSOCIATIONS. *See* TRADE ASSOCIATIONS—WASHINGTON (STATE)

WEST—BIBLIOGRAPHY—IMPRINTS
Co4-W. hist   9855 cds. by auth. Bks. & pams. Freq. add.

WOMEN—RECREATION. *See* SPORTS FOR WOMEN

YOUNG PEOPLE'S LITERATURE
I4 550 cds. by auth. Freq. add.
N28-y.p. 1000 cds. by auth., subj. & t. Bks. Freq. add.
O31-Cal. 100 cds. by auth. Bks. Freq. add.

YOUNG PEOPLE'S LITERATURE—BOOK REVIEWS
O1-W 700 cds. by auth. Cur. add.

APPENDIX II

Author List of Books Indexed, in Whole or in Part, by Libraries

(For location in libraries, see under titles of books, in main alphabet.)

Abderhalden, Emil, ed. Handbuch der biologischen arbeitsmethoden. 2. aufl. Urban & Schwarzenberg, 1920–.
Allen, William B. A history of Kentucky. Bradley & Gilbert, 1872.
Appleton's annual cyclopedia. Appleton, 1861–1902.
Ashmun, Margaret. Modern short stories. Macmillan, 1914.
Atkinson, Joseph. History of Newark, New Jersey. W. B. Guild, 1878.
Bach, Johann Sebastian. Klavierwerke mit fingersatz und vortragszeichen . . . versehen von Carl Reinecke. 12v. Breitkopf, n.d.
Bacon, Mrs. Mary Schell Hoke (Dolores Marbourg, pseud.). Pictures that every child should know . . . Doubleday, 1908.
Baker, Joseph E., ed. Past and present of Alameda county, California. S. J. Clarke pub. co., 1914. 2v.
Beckwith, Hiram W. History of Vigo and Parke counties. H. H. Hill and N. Iddings, 1880.
Benedict, David. A general history of the Baptist denomination in America and other parts of the world. L. Colby & co., 1848.
Blanchard, Charles. Counties of Clay and Owen, Indiana. Historical and biographical. Chicago, F. A. Battey & co., 1884.
Blanchard, Leola Howard. Conquest of southwest Kansas. Wichita engraving press, 1931.
Brewster, Dorothy. A book of contemporary short stories. Macmillan, 1936.
Bridgman, William Charles. Basic songs for male voices. Acapella section. American book, 1936.
Brigham, Johnson. Des Moines, the pioneer of municipal progress and reform of the middle west, together with the history of Polk county, Iowa. S. J. Clarke pub. co., 1941.
Bromfield, Louis. It takes all kinds. Harper, 1938.
Brown, Leonard. Modern short stories. Harcourt Brace, 1937.
Brumbaugh, Martin G. A history of German Baptist brethren in Europe and America. Brethren pub. house, 1899.
Brunn, Heinrich von. Denkmäler grieschischer und römischer sculptur. F. Bruckmann, 1888–1900.
Brush, Katherine. This is on me. Farrar & Rinehart, 1940.
Bryant, Lorinda. Children's book of celebrated pictures. Century, 1922.
Burgess, Louis Alexander. Revolutionary soldiers of Virginia. Richmond press, inc., 1927. 2v.
Burgess, Louis Alexander. Virginia soldiers of 1776. Richmond press, inc., 1927. 2v.
Burton, Sir Richard Francis. Arabian nights entertainment.
Caldwell, Erskine. Jackpot. Duell, Sloan and Pearce, 1940.
Candler, Allen D. Colonial records of Georgia. Franklin-Turner co., pub. 26v.
Carpenter, Flora L. Stories pictures tell. Rand McNally, 1918. 8v.
Carr, Lucien. Missouri, a bone of contention. Houghton Mifflin, 1888.
Chronicles of America series, ed. by Allen Johnson. Yale university press, 1921. 50v.
Cist, Charles. Cist's Cincinnati miscellany. C. Clark, 1845–1846. 2v.

Claiborn, John F. H. Mississippi, as a province, territory and state. Power & Barksdale, 1880.
Classroom teacher. The classroom teacher, inc., 1927–1928. 12v.
Coe, Ida and A. J. Dillon. Story hour readers. American book co., n.d. 5v.
Coffman, Edward. The story of Russellville. The News-Democrat print., 1931.
Coward, Noel. To step aside. Doubleday, Doran, 1939.
Cox, James. Old and new St. Louis. St. Louis. The author, 1894.
Crane, Stephen. Twenty stories. Knopf, 1940.
Dandridge, Danske. Historic Sheperdstown. The Michie co., 1910.
Day, A. Grove. Coronado's quest. Univ. of Calif., 1940.
Dictionary of American biography. Scribner, 1928–1936. 20v.
Dubillet, Louise P. Some prominent Virginians. J. P. Bill & co., 1907. 4v.
Dunn, Jacob P. Greater Indianapolis. Lewis pub. co., 1910. 2v.
Dunn, Jacob P. Indiana and Indianans, a history of aboriginal and territorial Indiana and the century of statehood. Amer. hist. soc., 1919. 5v.
Durant, Samuel W. History of Allegheny county. L. H. Everts & co., 1876.
Duyckinck, Evert August. Portrait gallery of eminent men and women of Europe and America. Johnson, Fry & co., 1872–1874. 2v.
Edwards, Richard & M. Hopewell. Edward's great west. St. Louis, 1860.
Ellet, Elizabeth Fries Lummis. Pioneer women of the west. Scribner, 1854.
Ellis, James Fernando. Influence of environment on the settlement of Missouri. Webster pub. co., 1929.
Encyclopaedia Britannica. Ency. Britannica, co. 14th ed.
Encyclopedia of America biography. Amer. historical co., 1934–1941. n.s., v. 1-13.
Encyclopedia of Connecticut biography: genealogical memorial; representative citizens. Amer. historical soc., inc., 1917.
Edwin, Milo. History of Williamson county, Illinois. Herrin news, 1927.
Everybody's favorite series. Amsco music sales co., inc.
Ewen, David. Composers of to-day. Wilson, 1934. 2d ed.
Famous composers and their works. 3v., n.d.
Fante, John. Dago red. Viking press, 1940.
Faulkner, William. The unvanquished. Random house, 1938.
Fellowes, Edmund H. The English madrigal school. Stainer & Bell, 32v.
Fifty art songs. Schirmer, 1939.
Fifty-nine piano solos you like to play. Schirmer, n.d.
Fifty-six songs you like to sing. Schirmer, 1937.
Fifty-two sacred songs. Schirmer, 1939.
Force, Peter. American archives . . . Wash., 1837–1853. 9v.
French, Samuel & Thomas H. Lacy. Acting edition of plays. French, n.d. 146v.
Galsworthy, John. Quality and other stories. Scribner, 1927.
Garnett, Richard, ed. Universal anthology. Merrill & Baker, 1899–1902. 33v.
Garrett, Phineas. One hundred choice selections. Penn. pub. co., 1873–1920. 40v.
Georgian stories, with portraits of the authors. Putnam, 1926–1927.
Giafferri, Paul Louis de marquis. History of the feminine costume of the world . . . B. Westermann co. 20 pts. in 2v.
Goodspeed pub. co. History of Greene & Sullivan counties, Indiana. Goodspeed, 1884.
Goodspeed pub. co. History of Knox & Davies counties, Indiana. Goodspeed, 1886.
Goodspeed, firm, pubs., Chicago. History of Tennessee: Hamilton county. Goodspeed, 1887.
Goodspeed, firm, pubs., Chicago. History of Tennessee: Knox county. Goodspeed, 1887.
Goodspeed, firm, pubs., Chicago. History of Tennessee: middle Tennessee and west Tennessee. Goodspeed, 1887.
Goodspeed, firm, pubs., Chicago. History of Tennessee: twenty-five to thirty counties of east Tennessee. Goodspeed, 1887.
Gorin, Franklin. The times of long ago, Barren county, Kentucky. J. P. Morton & co., 1929.
Gould, Emerson W. Fifty years on the Mississippi. Nixon-Jones printing co., 1889.

Grayson, Charles. Stories for men, an anthology. Little Brown, 1936.
Grieg, Edvard H. Klavierwerke. Peters, 1893–1897. 4v.
Halley, William. The centennial yearbook of Alameda county, California. Oakland, The author, 1876.
Harris, David H., ed. Brief report of the meeting commemorating the early St. Louis movement . . . St. Louis, 1922.
Hart, William C., comp. Historic Walkill & Hudson river valleys, 1894–1923. Walkill valley Farmer's assoc., 1894–1904; Walkill valley pub. assoc., 1905–.
Harte, Francis Bret. Complete works. California ed. Houghton, 1929. 10v.
Harvard classics, ed. by Charles W. Elliot. Collier & son co., 1930. 30v.
Harvey, Oscar J. A history of Wilkes-Barre, Luzerne county, Pennsylvania. Raeder press, 1909.
Hastings, William Thomson & others. Short stories. Houghton, 1924.
Head, Idress. Historical and interesting places in St. Louis. St. Louis, The author, 1909.
Head, Idress. State of Missouri. Privately printed, n.d.
Hemingway, Ernest. The fifth column, and the first forty-nine stories. Scribner, 1938.
Heydrick, Benjamin A. Americans all; stories of American life of to-day. Harcourt Brace, 1920.
Highroads of history. Nelson, 13v.
Hinshaw, William Wade. Encyclopedia of American Quaker genealogy. Edwards bros., inc., 1936.
Historical memorial Presbyterian church, 1765–1895. Succasunna, N.J.
History of Allegheny county. L. H. Everts & co., 1876.
History of the Arkansas valley, Colorado. O. L. Baskin & co., 1881.
Horgan, Paul. Figures in a landscape. Harper, 1940.
Horne, Charles Francis, ed. The great events by famous historians. National alumni, 1926. 22v.
Horne, Charles Francis, ed. Great men and famous women. S. Hess, 1894. 4v.
Howe, Henry. Historical collections of Ohio, an encyclopedia of the state. H. Howe & son, 1890–1891. 3v. in 2.
Hubbard, Elbert. Little journeys to the homes of famous people. Putnam, 1924. 5v.
Hughes, James. A report of the causes determined by the late Supreme court for the District of Kentucky, 1785–1801. John Bradford, 1803.
Hunt, Herbert. Washington, west of the Cascades; historical and descriptive. Clark pub. co., 1917. 3v.
Hyde, William & Howard L. Conrad. Encyclopedia of the history of St. Louis . . . Southern history co., 1899. 4v.
Intercollegiate debates. Hinds, Noble & Eldredge, 1909–.
Isley, Bliss & W. M. Richards. Four centuries in Kansas. McCormich-Mathews, 1936.
Jahresberichte über die fortschritte der klassischen altertumwissenschaft, begründet von Conrad Bursian. S. Calvary & Co., 1879–1898; O. R. Reisland, 1879–.
Jamaica, N.Y. Records of the town of Jamaica, L.I., N.Y., v. 4–7, 1749–1897. Long Island historical soc., 1914.
Japan. Imperial Japanese commission to the Panama-Pacific international exposition. Japanese temples and their treasures. 1913. 3v.
Jefferson, Thomas. Notes on the state of Virginia. Hist. printing club, 1894.
Johnson, Lewis Franklin. The history of Franklin co., Kentucky. Roberts printing co., 1912.
Johnson, Lewis Franklin. History of the Frankfort cemetery. Roberts printing co., 1921.
Johnston, Rev. John C. Treasury of Scottish covenant. Andrew Elliot, 1887.
Jones, Paul A. Coronado and Quivíra. Lyons, pub. co., 1937.
Knapp, G. Prather. City worth seeing. Business men's league of St. Louis, 1916.
Kunitz, Stanley J. Authors to-day and yesterday. Wilson, 1933.
Kunitz, Stanley J. British authors of the nineteenth century. Wilson, 1936.
Kunitz, Stanley J. & Howard Haycraft. Junior book of authors. Wilson, 1934.
Kunitz, Stanley J. Living authors. Wilson, 1931.
Lake, D. L. & co. Atlas of Lawrence county, Indiana.

Latour, A. Lacarriere. Historical memoir of the war in West Africa and Louisiana in 1814–15. John Conrad & co., 1816.
Leary, Peter J. Newark, New Jersey, illustrated. Baker, 1893.
Lester, Katherine M. Great pictures and their stories. Mentzer, 1927.
Lindsley, John B. Military annals of Tennessee. J. M. Lindsley & co., 1886.
Lionberger, I. H. Annals of St. Louis and a brief account of its foundation & progress, 1764–1928. St. Louis, 1929.
List of Missouri's celebrities, as compiled and presented by the literature & reciprocity comm., 8th district Missouri federation of women's clubs, 1919–1921. 4p.
Littell, John. Family records, or genealogies of the first settlers of Passaic Valley and vicinity above Chatham. Feltville, N.J., David Felt & co., printer, 1851.
Lossing, Benson J. The American revolution and the War of 1812. N.Y. Book concern, 1875. 3v.
Lowther, Charles. Dodge City, Kansas. Dorrance, 1940.
Macclintock, Sander. Sainte Beuve's critical theory and practice after 1849. Univ. of Chicago, press, 1930.
McClure, Clarence Henry. History of Missouri. A. S. Barnes co., 1920.
Magill, John. Pioneer to the Kentucky immigrant. Univ. of Kentucky, 1942.
Mantle, Burns. Best plays of 1919–20—and the Yearbook of the drama in America. Dodd, Mead, 1920–date.
Marston, C. E. Geography of Missouri. (*In* Brigham, A. P. and C. T. McFarlane. Essentials of geography, v. 2. 1916.)
Masters in art; a series of illustrated monographs, v. 1-9, 1900–1908. Bates & Guild co.
Masters in music. Bates & Guild co., n.d. 6v.
Maugham, William Somerset. The mixture as before. Doubleday, Doran, 1940.
Merritt, Frank C. History of Alameda county, California. S. J. Clarke pub. co., 1928. 2v.
Methodist Episcopal church. Minutes of the annual conferences. N.Y. Meth. episcopal church, 1840.
Minnesota. Board of commissioners on publication of history of Minnesota. Minnesota in the Civil and Indian war, 1861–65. State of Minn., 1890–1893. 2v.
Mott, Frank Luther. Good stories. Macmillan, 1936.
Munsell's genealogical index-supplement. J. Munsell's sons, 1935.
New international yearbook. Funk & Wagnalls. VI, 1908–date.
Norton, Charles E., ed. Heart of Oak books. rev. ed. Heath, 1902–1903. 7v.
Oliver, Maude. First steps in the enjoyment of pictures. Holt, 1920.
Pageant of America; a pictorial history of U.S. Yale univ. press, 1925–1929. 15v.
Parker, Dorothy. Here lies. Viking press, 1939. Holt, 1920.
Peloubet's select notes on the International Sunday school lessons. Ryson press.
Pentz, William C. City of DuBois. Press of Gray printing co., 1932.
Perrin, William Henry. History of Bourbon, Scott, Harrison, and Nicholas counties, Kentucky. Baskin, 1882.
Perrin, William Henry, & G. C. Kniffin. Kentucky, a history of the state. F. A. Battey & co., 1886.
Perrin, William Henry. The pioneer press of Kentucky. J. P. Morton & co., 1888.
Peter, Robert. Fayette county. Baskin, 1882.
Petrequin, Harry J. St. Louis as it is today.
Petrequin, Harry J. Stories of old St. Genevieve. The Author, n.d.
Phelps, Edith May. Debaters' manual. Wilson, 1919–date.
Pittsburgh survey; findings: ed. by Paul Underwood Kellogg. (Russell Sage foundation pub.) Survey associates, 1909–1914. 6v.
Poffenbarger, Mrs. Livia Nye Simpson. Battle of Point Pleasant. State gazette, Point Pleasant, W. Va., 1909.
Pollard, Lancaster. Checklist of Washington authors. Seattle, 1940. Reprint Pacific Northwest Quarterly, vol. 31, no. 1.
Powell, Mary M. Public art in St. Louis, 1925. (Reprint from St. Louis public library *Monthly bulletin,* July–August, 1925.)

Prosch, Thomas Wickham. A chronological history of Seattle from 1850–1897. Mss. 1921.
Quisenberry, Anderson Chennault. Kentucky in the War of 1812. Ky. state hist. soc., 1915.
Racinet, A.C.A. Le costume historique. Firmin-Didot, 1888. 6v.
Railey, William Edward. Commissioned officers of the War of 1812. Ky. state hist. soc., n.d. mss.
Railey, William Edward. Roster of the Mexican War. mss.
Rawlings, Marjorie Kinnan. When the whippoorwill. Scribner, 1940.
Rayner, John A. The first century of Piqua, Ohio. Magee bros. pub. co., 1916.
Reference shelf . . . Wilson co., 1922/23–date.
Ridenour, George L. Early times in Meade county, Kentucky. Western recorder, 1929.
Rogers, Agnes. The American procession; American life since 1860 in photographs. Harper, 1933.
Saroyan, William. The trouble with tigers. Harcourt, Brace, 1938.
Saxon, Lyle. Father Mississippi. Appleton-Century, 1927.
Sayre, James Willis. Early waterfront days of Seattle. The Author, 1937.
Sayre, James Willis. This city of ours. Seattle school district no. 1, 1936.
Scarlatti, Domenico. Opere complete per clavicembalo, criticamente rivedute . . . da Alessandro Longo. Ricordi. 11v.
Scharf, John Tomas. History of St. Louis city and county. L. H. Everts & co., 1883.
Schramm, Wilbur L. The story workshop. Little Brown, 1938.
Schubert, Franz Peter. Lieder und gesänge. Breitkopf & Härtel, 1894–1895. 10v.
Schubert, Franz Peter. Pianoforte werke zu 2 händen. Breitkopf, n.d. 3v.
Schumann, Robert A. Klavierwerke; kritisch rev . . . von Hans Bischoff. Steingräber, n.d. 11v.
Schumann, Robert A. Lieder und gesänge für eine singstimme . . . hrsg. von Clara Schumann. Breitkopf, n.d. 4v.
Selby, Paul. Anecdotal Lincoln. Thompson & Thomas, 1900.
Shelley printing & publishing co. Saint Louis views. Shelley, 1935.
Shepard, Elihu H. The early history of St. Louis and Missouri. Southwestern bk. & pub. co., 1870.
Shepard, Martha. The first things of Toronto. mss. 1938.
Shōbi Shiryō. Materials for art study. 1913. 12v.
Sixty progressive piano pieces. Schirmer, n.d.
Skrainka, Philip. St. Louis, its history and ideals. Lambert-Deacon-Hull printing co., 1910.
Slaughter, Philip. A history of Bristol parish. Richmond, Va., B. B. Minor, 1846.
Smith, George Gilman, jr. History of Methodism in Georgia and Florida from 1785 to 1865, comp. by George H. Richter, jr. mss. 1932.
Smith, Joseph, jr. History of the Church of Jesus Christ of Latter-Day Saints. Deseret news, 1902. v. 7, 1932.
Smith, Zachariah F. History of Kentucky from its earliest discovery and settlement to the present date. Louisville, Ky. Courier-journal, 1886.
Snell, James P. History of Hunterdon and Somerset counties, New Jersey. Everts & Peck, 1881.
Snow, Marshall S. History of the development of Missouri and particularly of St. Louis. National press bureau, 1908. 2v.
Snowden's Sunday school lessons. Macmillan, 1921–date.
Society of arts and sciences, N.Y. O'Henry memorial award prize stories, 1923. Doubleday, 1924.
Spencer, Thomas Edwin. Story of old St. Louis. Pub. by authority of the Book committee of the St. Louis pageant drama assoc., 1914.
Spencer, Lloyd & Lancaster Pollard. A history of the state of Washington. 4v. American Historical Society, 1937.
Spofford, Ainsworth Rand, ed. Library of historic characters and famous events of all nations and all ages. J. B. Millet, 1900 12v.

Statesman's yearbook. Macmillan, 1864–date.
Steinbeck, John. The long valley. Viking press, 1938.
Stevens, Walter B. St. Louis, the fourth city. S. J. Clark pub. co., 1909.
Stryker, William S. Official register of the officers and men of New Jersey in the Revolutionary war. W. T. Nicholason & co., 1872.
Sullivan, Mark. Our times; the United States, 1900–1925. Scribner, 1932. 6v.
Tajima Shiichi, ed. Selected relics of Japanese art. 1899–1908. 20v.
Tajima Shiichi, ed. Toyo bijustsu taikwan (Masterpieces selected from the fine arts of the Far East.) 1908–1918. 15v.
Taylor, John. A history of ten Baptist churches. J. H. Holman, printer, 1823. 300p.
Turner picture studies, adapted to the several school grades. Turner co., 1908. v. 2–12.
University debater's annual. Wilson co., 1915–
Vasari society. Reproductions of drawings by old and modern masters. Oxford univ. press, 1906–1935. 25v.
Venturi, Adolfo. Storia dell'arte Italiana. V. Hoepli, 1901–   22v.
Viles, Jonas. History of Missouri for high schools. Macmillan, 1933.
W.P.A. Federal writers project. Kansas. Viking, 1939.
Walmsley, Harry R., ed. State of Missouri. Lewis printing co., 1932.
Waverley collection of rare and beautiful music. 4v.
Werner's readings and recitations. Werner & co., n.d. 58v.
West Virginia blue book. Jarrett pub. co., 1923–   .
Wharton, Edith. Ghosts. D. Appleton-Century, 1937.
White House conference on child health and protection, 1930. First series. D. Appleton-Century, 1932–1933.
Wier, Albert Ernest. Days of . . . Harcourt, 1934–1937. 8v.
Wier, Albert Ernest. Scribner radio music library. Scribner, 1931. 8v.
Wilcox, J. F., comp. & ed. Historical souvenir of Williamson county, Illinois. LeCrone press, Effingham, Ill., 1905.
Wilder, Marshall P. The wit and humor of America. Funk, 1911. 10v.
Willis, G. Lee. History of Shelby county, Kentucky. C. T. Dearing printing co., inc., 1929.
Wilson, Erasmus, ed. Standard history of Pittsburg, Pennsylvania. Goodspeed pub. co., 1898.
Wolfe, Thomas. From death to morning. Scribner, 1935.
Wood, Anthony. Athenae Oxonienses. 1813. 4v.
Wood, Clement & Gloria Goddard. Complete book of games. Halcyon House, 1937.
Wood, John W. Pasadena, California, historical and personal; a complete history of the organization of the Indiana colony. The Author, 1917.
Wood, Myron W., ed. & pub. History of Alameda county, California. M. W. Wood, 1883.
Wright, Robert M. Dodge City, cowboy capital. Wichita press, 1913.
Young, Perry. Mistick Krewe. Carnival press, 1931.